# PERU Staying the Course of Economic Success

EDITORS

Alejandro Santos and Alejandro Werner



INTERNATIONAL MONETARY FUND

Cover design: IMF Multimedia Services Division

**Cataloging-in-Publication Data**
**Joint Bank-Fund Library**

Peru : staying the course of economic success / editors Alejandro Santos and Alejandro Werner. – Washington, D.C. : International Monetary Fund, 2015.
pages ; cm
Includes bibliographical references.
ISBN: 978-1-51359-974-8

1. Peru – Economic conditions. 2. Fiscal policy – Peru. I. Santos, Alejandro. II. Werner, Alejandro M. III. International Monetary Fund.

HC227.P426 2015



Please send orders to:
International Monetary Fund, Publication Services
P.O. Box 92780, Washington, DC 20090, U.S.A.
Tel.: (202) 623-7430 Fax: (202) 623-7201
E-mail: publications@imf.org
Internet: www.elibrary.imf.org
www.imfbookstore.org

# Contents

# Foreword

*"Success depends on effort."*—Sophocles

This book is a timely look at a very important Latin American economic success story: Peru. When pondering the factors behind the country's recent economic achievements, many casual observers may think only of the strong uptick in the demand for commodities and, consequently, high commodity prices over the last decade. With this information in hand, they could easily conclude that Peru's economic success came without much exertion or its own unique challenges. That it was easily realized, with only minor difficulties. However, when I think of Peru and its accomplishments, I am reminded of the old adage by Sophocles that "success depends on effort."

Indeed, the narrative of Peru's economic transformation over the last three decades as contained in this book clearly demonstrates the validity of this well-worn proverb. The one constant that is woven throughout this volume is that the real story behind Peru's success is one of persistent and consistent effort—to structurally reform the economy and to construct and implement solid macroeconomic frameworks and policies. These were not easy labors, particularly given Peru's sociopolitical and economic struggles through the 1970s, 1980s, and 1990s. In this regard, I find this book to be a must read for anyone interested in understanding the real challenges in successfully transforming an emerging market economy, particularly one that depends so heavily on natural resources. In sum, I believe many lessons can be gleaned from this success story.

Finally, on a personal note, I fondly remember that Peru was the starting point of my first visit to Latin America as Managing Director of the IMF back in 2011. Since that inaugural trip, I have immensely enjoyed returning to Peru and the region in general. I, like many others, find Peru, and Latin America as a whole, to be a vibrant and dynamic region with a rich cultural heritage. I am delighted that the World Bank-IMF Annual Meetings are being held in Lima this year. I think you will all agree it is a great opportunity to showcase the country and the region, and to discuss its remaining challenges while highlighting its many successes.

*Christine Lagarde*
*Managing Director*
*International Monetary Fund*

# Abbreviations

| | |
|---|---|
| ARG | Argentina |
| BGR | Bulgaria |
| BOL | Bolivia |
| BRA | Brazil |
| CHL | Chile |
| COL | Colombia |
| CRI | Costa Rica |
| DOM | Dominican Republic |
| ECU | Ecuador |
| GTM | Guatemala |
| HTI | Haiti |
| HND | Honduras |
| MYS | Malaysia |
| MEX | Mexico |
| NIC | Nicaragua |
| PAN | Panama |
| PER | Peru |
| PRY | Paraguay |
| POL | Poland |
| ROU | Romania |
| SLV | El Salvador |
| THA | Thailand |
| TUR | Turkey |
| URY | Uruguay |
| VEN | Venezuela |
| ZAF | South Africa |

# About the Authors

**Adrian Armas**, a Peruvian national, is the Manager of the Department of Economic Studies at the Central Reserve Bank of Peru, where he developed his full professional career. Previously, he was the Head of the Monetary Sector of the Economic Studies Department (Central Reserve Bank of Peru). Mr. Armas actively participated in the implementation of the inflation targeting scheme in Peru and wrote various papers and articles on this topic published by the IMF, the European Central Bank, and the Bank for International Settlements. Mr. Armas studied Economics at Universidad del Pacífico in Peru and earned a master's degree in Economics from Boston University. He is currently a professor of Monetary Policy at Universidad del Pacífico.

**Laura Calderon**, a Peruvian national, is the principal advisor to the Minister of Economy and Finance of Peru. Before her current position, she was Deputy Minister of Economy and Finance. She has held several important positions in the public sector and international organizations including Superintendent of the Tax and Customs Authority of Peru, Technical Advisor on tax issues in the Fiscal Affairs Department of the IMF, Director of the Investment Promotion Agency of Peru, and Director of the National Institute of Intellectual Property. Ms. Calderon holds an MA and Licentiate in Economics from Pontificia Universidad Católica del Peru, as well as an MSc in Development Economics from Oxford University. Ms. Calderon has taught college- and graduate-level courses in economics at Pontificia Universidad Católica del Perú, Universidad del Pacífico, Universidad San Ignacio de Loyola, Universidad San Martin de Porres, and Universidad ESAN in Peru.

**Marco Camacho**, a national of Peru, is the General Director of the General Directorate of Public Income Policy at the Ministry of the Economy and Finance of Peru. Mr. Camacho holds a BA degree in Economics from Pontificia Universidad Católica in Peru, an MA in Economics from ILADES/Georgetown University (Santiago) in Chile, and has completed other graduate studies in Tax Administration and Public Finance Management. He also worked at the National Superintendence of Customs and Tax Administration as National Intendent of Tax Research and Planning and at the Metropolitan Municipality of Lima as Head of Municipal Tax Administration.

**Patricio M. Castro**, an Argentinean, holds a doctoral degree in engineering from the University of Buenos Aires in Argentina and a postgraduate degree from Stanford University. Mr. Castro worked in the private sector and in the Argentine central administration, where he held the position of Under-Secretary of the Public Function. He was a consultant to the World Bank and the Inter-American Development Bank prior to joining the Fiscal Affairs Department of the IMF as Technical Assistance Advisor with expertise in customs, social security, and tax administration. He retired from the IMF in 2014 as a Senior Economist in the Fiscal Affairs Department. During his career, he worked in tax and customs reform in many countries in Africa, Asia, and in most countries in Latin America. He has participated in numerous regional and international events and conferences on tax and customs issues, has published numerous papers on the subject, and is a contributor to the book *Changing Customs: Challenges and Strategies for the Reform of Customs Administration* (IMF 2003).

**Adrienne Cheasty**, from Ireland, is Deputy Director of the IMF's Western Hemisphere Department, where she has oversight of Peru, Ecuador, and Caribbean countries, program financing, and debt issues. She was previously Deputy Director of the IMF's Fiscal Affairs Department, responsible for fiscal policy design and country advice, with specific responsibility for Latin America. Earlier, she worked on numerous IMF-supported crisis programs in emerging markets and fragile states. Her research areas include measurement of the fiscal deficit, fiscal and financial issues, and natural resource management. She is a member of the World Economic Forum's Global Agenda Council on Fiscal Sustainability and has taught at Harvard University, Yale University, and Johns Hopkins University.

**Israel Fainboim**, a national of Colombia, holds an MA in Economics from the University of Pennsylvania. He is a Senior Economist in the Fiscal Affairs Department of the IMF. He has provided technical assistance on Public Financial Management to almost all Latin American countries and to China and Vietnam, and has been a consultant to the Inter-American Development Bank and the World Bank. He was a member of the Council on Fiscal Policy at the Ministry of Finance of Colombia, Secretary of Finance of Bogota, Research Associate at *Fedesarrollo*, and Professor of Public Finance at the Universidad de los Andes and La Pontificia Universidad Javeriana. He has published articles on treasury management, public investment, performance budgeting, public-private partnerships, and fiscal federalism, among other topics.

**Ricardo Fenochietto**, an Argentine national, is Senior Economist in the Tax Policy Division of the Fiscal Affairs Department at the IMF. Before joining the IMF, he was Professor of Public Finance at the Universidad Torcuato Di Tella in Argentina and a private consultant to multinational corporations. He has published extensively on taxation issues; his recent work focused on tax capacity, tax effort, and financial sector taxation. He is also peer reviewer for a number of public finance journals.

**Almudena Fernández Benito** holds bachelor's degrees in Law and in Economics and Business Administration from the Complutense University in Madrid, Spain, and is a Senior Controller and Certified Public Auditor for the Spanish government. She joined the IMF as Advisor on public financial management in the Fiscal Affairs Department. Before joining the IMF, she worked as Senior Advisor at the Budget Directorate in Spain.

**Mercedes García-Escribano** is Deputy Division Chief in the Expenditure Policy Division of the Fiscal Affairs Department at the IMF. Ms. García-Escribano holds a PhD in Economics from the University of Chicago. At the IMF, she has worked on the teams for Brazil, Peru, Colombia, Mexico, Austria, Spain, and Malta, and has published papers on fiscal (with emphasis on decentralization), financial sector, and labor market issues.

**Fei Han**, a Chinese national, is currently an Economist in the Monetary and Capital Markets Department at the IMF. His research interests focus primarily on macro-financial linkages, macroeconometric models, and financial interconnectedness and spillovers. Since joining the Monetary and Capital Markets Department, he has worked on banking analysis and stress testing for Asian and European countries, and market liquidity for the IMF's *Global Financial Stability Report*. His previous assignments at the IMF included country surveillance work on Latin American emerging markets in the Western Hemisphere Department, including Brazil, Peru, and Venezuela. He holds a PhD in Economics and an MA in Statistics from the University of California, Berkeley. He also holds an MA in International Finance and a BA in Finance from Peking University.

**César Liendo**, a Peruvian national, is the General Director of Macroeconomic Policy and Fiscal Decentralization at the Ministry of the Economy and Finance in Peru. He holds a BA in

Economics from Pontificia Universidad Católica del Perú and an MA in Economics from Universitat Pompeu Fabra in Barcelona, Spain. Before joining the Ministry of the Economy and Finance, Mr. Liendo worked for the Inter-American Development Bank, Scotiabank, and APOYO Consultoría. He also teaches at Universidad del Pacífico and Universidad San Ignacio de Loyola. He is in charge of the design of the Multiannual Macroeconomic Framework, which forms the basis for the public sector budget, as well as the analysis on developments, outlook, and risks to the Peruvian economy; fiscal revenues; and observance of fiscal rules, proposing fiscal measures if needed.

**Manuel Luy** is the Head of the Research Department at the Superintendency of Banking, Insurance and Private Pension Funds of Peru. Mr. Luy holds a BA in Economics from the Universidad del Pacífico in Peru. He has an MA in Development Economics from the University of Sussex in the United Kingdom and a master's degree in Finance from the Universidad del Pacífico. Mr. Luy has also worked as a consultant at the World Bank and the IMF, and lectures at the Universidad del Pacífico and in specialized programs at the Central Reserve Bank of Peru and the Superintendency of Banking, Insurance and Private Pension Funds.

**Giancarlo Marchesi** is the Director General for Private Investment Policy and Promotion at the Ministry of the Economy and Finance in Peru. Mr. Marchesi holds bachelor's and Licenciate degrees in Economics from the Universidad del Pacífico in Peru and a master's degree in Public Affairs from Princeton University. He has been a Manager in the Corporate Strategy Division and Deputy Manager in the Economic Studies and Investment Strategy Area at Banco de Crédito del Perú. Mr. Marchesi has also been a consultant for the World Bank's Independent Evaluation Group and the Ministry of the Economy and Finance's Directorate General of Economic and Social Affairs, as well as an independent consultant for Peruvian corporations in the fields of risk, corporate strategy, and mergers and acquisitions.

**Juan Alonso Peschiera**, a national of Peru, is an Economist in the Resident Representative Office of the IMF for Peru and Paraguay. Mr. Peschiera holds a BA in Economics from Pontificia Universidad Católica del Perú in Peru and an MSc in Finance from Universidad del Pacífico in Peru. Prior to joining the IMF, he worked at the Peruvian consultancy Macroconsult.

**Mario Pessoa**, a national of Brazil, holds a Master of Economics and Social Science degree from the University of Wales in the United Kingdom. He is Deputy Division Chief of the Public Financial Management Division II of the IMF's Fiscal Affairs Department. He has provided technical assistance on public financial management to countries in the Western Hemisphere, Africa, and Asia in treasury and debt management, medium-term fiscal frameworks, fiscal risks, and government accounting. Previously, he worked in Brazil at the National Treasury, Economic Policy Department, and Internal Control Office of the Ministry of Finance.

**Juan Pichihua**, a Peruvian national, is Director of the Directorate of Fiscal Decentralization Policy and Subnational Finances at the Ministry of the Economy and Finance. Mr. Pichihua holds a BA in Economics from the Universidad Nacional Agraria La Molina in Peru and an MA in Economics from ILADES/Georgetown University (Santiago) in Chile. He is a board member of the National Superintendence of Health Insurance in representation of the Ministry of the Economy and Finance and Principal Professor of Economics at the Universidad Nacional Agraria La Molina. He was General Director of Fiscal Decentralization and Social Affairs (Ministry of the Economy and Finance), Chief of Household Targeting System, and Consultant of Health Economics and Social Affairs.

**Javier Poggi** is the Chief Economist at the Superintendency of Banking, Insurance and Private Pension Funds of Peru. Mr. Poggi holds a BA in Economics from the Pontificia Universidad Católica del Perú. He has a Master of Science degree in both Economics and Banking, Finance and Investments from the University of Wisconsin-Madison. Currently, he presides over the Superintendency of Banking, Insurance and Private Pension Funds, special committee for the implementation of Basel II-III and Solvency II standards. He was a member of the Board of Directors of the Comisión Nacional Supervisora de Empresas y Valores (now, Superintendencia del Mercado de Valores). Prior to joining the Superintendency of Banking, Insurance and Private Pension Funds, he worked for the World Bank as an economic development consultant, covering a variety of issues.

**Zenón Quispe**, a national of Peru, is Advisor to the General Manager of the Central Reserve Bank of Peru. Mr. Quispe holds a BA in Economics from the Universidad Nacional San Cristobal de Huamanga in Peru, an MA in Political Economy from Boston University, and a PhD candidate in Economics from Oxford University. After working as Senior Economist in the External Sector Analysis Division, the Macroeconomic Analysis Division, and in the Macroeconomic Models Division, he has been the Head of the Monetary Program Section in the Monetary Policy Design Division of the Central Reserve Bank of Peru. Mr. Quispe is Professor of Monetary Theory and Policy at the Pontificia Universidad Católica del Perú and the Universidad de Piura in Peru. He also teaches Advanced Topics in Monetary Theory and Policy in the Summer Course in Economics of the Central Reserve Bank of Peru and in the Centro de Capacitación del Banco de Guatemala.

**Donita Rodriguez**, a national of Peru, is the Head of the Balance of Payments Statistics Division of the Central Reserve Bank of Peru. Miss Rodriguez holds a BA in Economics from Pontificia Universidad Católica del Perú and an MSc in Economics from the London School of Economics and Political Science in the United Kingdom. She also has been a Senior Analyst in the Macroeconomic Modeling Division and Junior Analyst in the Monetary Program Division of the Central Reserve Bank of Peru. She is a Lecturer in International Economics and International Finance—for undergraduate and graduate levels, respectively—at Pontificia Universidad Católica del Perú.

**Lucía Romero** is the Head of the Financial System Analysis Department at the Superintendency of Banking, Insurance and Private Pension Funds of Peru. Ms. Romero holds a BA in Economics from the Pontificia Universidad Católica del Perú and a master's degree in Economics from the Pontificia Universidade Catolica do Rio de Janeiro in Brazil. Prior to joining the Superintendency of Banking, Insurance and Private Pension Funds, she worked as an Assistant Professor in the Economics Department of the Pontificia Universidad Católica del Perú and as a researcher at the Instituto de Estudios Peruanos.

**Kevin Ross** is a Senior Economist in the IMF's Western Hemisphere Department. Prior to that, he was the IMF's Regional Representative for Peru and Paraguay. He has worked in the European Department on a number of advanced and transition economies. His research has mainly focused on monetary and exchange rate policies, banking sector competition, and investment.

**Renzo Rossini** is the General Manager of the Central Reserve Bank of Peru. In this capacity, he reports to the Governor and to the Board of the Central Reserve Bank of Peru, and is responsible for proposing changes to the monetary policy, the management of international reserves, and other aspects of the central bank. Prior to this, Mr. Rossini was the Manager of the Department of Economic Studies. His responsibilities included directing the collection of macroeconomic statistical data, the forecasting process, and the elaboration of monetary policy proposals. Mr. Rossini studied Economics at the Universidad del Pacífico in Peru and holds a master's degree in Economics from the London School of Economics. He is the author of several papers on monetary policy and is currently also a Professor of Economic Policy at the Universidad del Pacífico in Peru.

**Alejandro Santos**, a national of Mexico, is the IMF Senior Resident Representative for Peru and Paraguay. Mr. Santos holds a BA in Economics from Universidad Autónoma de Nuevo Leon in Mexico and a PhD in Economics from Yale University. He has been Advisor and Division Chief in the Western Hemisphere Department, as well as Mission Chief to many countries in the region. Mr. Santos has also been IMF Resident Representative in Russia and Bolivia. Prior to joining the Western Hemisphere Department, he worked in the European Department and the Policy Development and Review Department of the IMF, where he worked on many emerging market economies with IMF-supported programs (including Argentina, Brazil, Georgia, Korea, Indonesia, Russia, Turkey, Ukraine, and Uruguay).

**Alonso Segura** is the Minister of Economy and Finance of Peru, where he previously was Chief of Staff. He has been Chief Economist and Head of Strategy at Banco de Crédito del Perú, Peru's largest bank; Chief Economist at Banco Wiese Sudameris (now Scotiabank Peru); and Advisor to the Executive Director for the Southern Cone and Economist in the Fiscal Affairs Department at the IMF; among other positions. Mr. Segura has a BA in Economics from the Catholic University of Peru and holds a master's degree in Economics from the University of Pennsylvania, where he also pursued doctoral studies (PhD[ABD]). He holds international certificates in investments (Chartered Financial Analyst) and risk management (Financial Risk Manager). He has held teaching positions at the University of Pennsylvania, the Catholic University of Peru, and the Universidad del Pacífico in Peru. He is a Fulbright Scholar.

**Narda Sotomayor** is the Head of the Microfinance Analysis Department at the Superintendency of Banking, Insurance and Private Pension Funds of Peru. Ms. Sotomayor received her training as an Economist from the Pontificia Universidad Católica del Perú and holds a Master of Science degree in Agricultural Economics from The Ohio State University and a PhD from the University of Illinois at Urbana-Champaign. Before joining the Superintendency of Banking, Insurance and Private Pension Funds, she was a Research Fellow at the Center for Farm and Rural Business Finance of the University of Illinois at Urbana-Champaign and had worked as a consultant for diverse international organizations, including the World Bank, the U.S. Agency for International Development, and the Inter-American Development Bank. She has also worked as an Assistant Professor in the Economics Department of the Pontificia Universidad Católica del Perú.

**Melesse Tashu**, a national of Ethiopia, is an Economist in the Western Hemisphere Department of the IMF, where he covers Eastern Caribbean countries, Peru, and Ecuador. Mr. Tashu holds a BS in Statistics and an MS in Economics from Addis Ababa University, Ethiopia, and an MA in International Development from Harvard University. Before joining the IMF, Mr. Tashu worked for the National Bank of Ethiopia and World Vision International.

**Carolina Trivelli** currently serves as Project Manager for the Electronic Money Project of the Association of Banks in Peru. She has been Principal Researcher for the Institute of Peruvian Studies and Latin American Center for Rural Development. She is a former Minister of Development and Social Inclusion of Peru. She was Director General of the Institute of Peruvian Studies, President of the Consortium for Development of the Andean Ecoregion, and Board Member of the Network for the Development of Social Sciences in Peru and the Peruvian Society for Environmental Law. She is currently a Board Member of the Permanent Seminar on Agricultural Research, a member of the Board of Innova Schools, and a member of the Technical Advisory Committee on Measuring Poverty (Instituto Nacional de Estadística e Informática). She is currently President of the Board of Fundación Backus. Ms. Trivelli specializes in social policy issues, rural poverty, agricultural and rural finance, and rural development. She has taught at the Pontifical Catholic University of Peru and the University of the Pacific. She is currently a columnist for the newspaper *Perú 21*. Ms. Trivelli is an Economist; she holds an MSc in Agricultural Economics from Pennsylvania State University and a bachelor's degree in Social Science, majoring in Economics, from the Pontifical Catholic University of Peru.

**Alvaro Valencia** works as a consultant at the Directorate-General of Private Investment Policy and Promotion at the Ministry of the Economy and Finance in Lima, Peru. Mr. Valencia holds a BS in Economics from Universidad del Pacífico in Peru and a master's degree in Economics from Syracuse University in the United States. He has been Chief Executive Officer and President of American Power Corporation, a U.S.-based mining exploration company. Previously, Mr. Valencia has held several positions working for the equity research departments at CLSA Global Emerging Markets and BBVA Securities in New York and the Inter-American Development Bank. He has also worked as an investment banker specializing in corporate finance and mergers and acquisitions at the consulting company Macroconsult in Peru.

**Julio Velarde**, a Peruvian national, holds a BA in Economics from the Universidad del Pacifico in Peru, an MA in Economics from Brown University in the United States, and is a PhD candidate in Economics at Brown University. He has been the Governor of the Central Reserve Bank of Peru since 2006. He was also Chairman of the Latin American Reserve Fund, Member of the Board of Governors of the Central Reserve Bank of Peru, Dean of the Department of Economics at the Universidad del Pacífico, and Senior Full Professor in the Department of Economics also at Universidad del Pacífico. Mr. Velarde has been a member of the board of several commercial banks and nonfinancial corporations and advisor to international organizations. He is the author of several books and many articles on macroeconomics and economic policy.

**Mercedes Vera Martin**, a national of Spain, is Deputy Division Chief in the Middle East and Central Asia Department of the IMF. Ms. Vera Martin holds a dual bachelor's degree in Law and in Business Administration and Management from Universidad Pontificia Comillas in Spain, and a PhD in Economics from the London School of Economics. She has been IMF Mission Chief for Ecuador and Mauritania. Ms. Vera Martin has also worked in the Western Hemisphere Department, the Policy Development and Review Department, and the Monetary and Capital Markets Department during her career at the IMF has been engaged in a variety of issues across countries (including Argentina, Colombia, Dominican Republic, Haiti, Mexico, Peru, Romania, and Uzbekistan).

**Svetlana Vtyurina**, a national of Russia, is a Senior Economist in the Western Hemisphere Department of the IMF. She holds BA and MA degrees from the George Washington University in the United States. As an IMF economist, she covered emerging market economies and low-income countries in Central Asia, Africa, and Central and South America. Prior to that, she was an Advisor to the Executive Director for the Russian Federation at the IMF and a project consultant in the private sector.

**Alejandro Werner**, a Mexican citizen, is the Director of the Western Hemisphere Department of the IMF. Mr. Werner has had distinguished careers in the public and private sectors as well as in academia. Before joining the IMF, he served as Undersecretary of Finance and Public Credit of

Mexico; he was also Professor of Economics at the Instituto de Empresa in Spain, and Head of Corporate and Investment Banking at BBVA-Bancomer. Previously, he was Director of Economic Studies at the Bank of Mexico and Professor at Instituto Tecnológico Autónomo de México in Mexico. He has published widely. Mr. Werner was named Young Global Leader by the World Economic Forum in 2007. Mr. Werner received his PhD from the Massachusetts Institute of Technology.

**Yu Ching Wong**, a national of Singapore, is the IMF Resident Representative for Myanmar. Ms. Wong holds a BSocSci (Honors) in Economics from the National University of Singapore and a PhD in Economics from Keio University in Japan. Before taking up her position in Myanmar, she worked in the Western Hemisphere Department of the IMF as Desk Economist on Peru, Ecuador, and the Eastern Caribbean Currency Union; in the Finance Department, where she worked on concessional financing and debt relief; and at the IMF's Regional Office for Asia and the Pacific, on regional surveillance of emerging Asia. Prior to joining the IMF, Ms. Wong was Principal Economist working on China at the Japan Center for International Finance in Japan and Economist at Singapore's Ministry of Trade and Industry.

CHAPTER 1

# Overview

ALEJANDRO WERNER

Peru has been one of Latin America's main success stories for over a decade. Strengthened by solid macro policies and favorable external conditions, the country has enjoyed high growth and employment and low inflation amid gains in financial and social inclusion. Given that these achievements came on the heels of a turbulent economic past, it stands to reason that there are lessons to be learned from examining the policies and actions that contributed to these results. What challenges did the authorities confront in reforming the economy, particularly once Peru's growth momentum accelerated? What future challenges do the authorities foresee? This volume attempts to answer these questions, with chapters authored by notable Peruvian economists and IMF staff.

Part I sets the stage by providing a review of Peru's economic history over the last 30 years. Like many countries, Peru implemented misguided policies in response to the oil price shocks of the 1970s, resulting in a profound debt crisis in the 1980s. By 1989–90, the country was mired in hyperinflation, large internal and external imbalances, a multiple exchange rate system, rapid economic decline, and domestic terrorism. But fast-forward 25 years and a completely different picture emerges. In 2014, the Peruvian economy was considered one of the strongest performers in the region. In Chapter 2, Renzo Rossini and Alejandro Santos relate how this transformation was accomplished, describing how the authorities implemented their stabilization programs and reform agenda. The authorities' efforts turned the economy around and continue to bear fruit today. For example, during the commodity price boom and favorable external financial conditions over the past decade, Peru was able to successfully absorb a surge in investment flows without overheating or experiencing financial sector problems. Similarly, when the global financial crisis broke out, Peru had ample buffers and policy space to maneuver around the turbulence, and emerged unscathed. Since then, the economy has continued to grow despite weakening commodity prices.

The chapters in Part II report on the changes in Peru's macroeconomic policies. Chapter 3 on growth and Chapter 4 on investment highlight how the implementation of structural reforms, coupled with a favorable external environmental, drove the country's economic performance. In addition to describing the evolution of these structural reforms, Kevin Ross and Juan Alonso Peschiera explicitly measure the impact that terms-of-trade gains had on domestic incomes, which then spilled over into the rest of the economy. Using traditional growth accounting exercises, the authors also find that Peru enjoyed sizable gains in total factor productivity above the regional average. The next chapter, by Kevin Ross and Melesse Tashu, provides a detailed description of the policies and actions that fostered the investment boom, and how that boom has been closely aligned with developments in commodity prices and the mining sector. The authors' empirical results show that the increase in private investment was directly linked to macro stability, terms-of-trade gains, structural reforms, public investment, and global interest rates.

Improvements in fiscal policy and fiscal institutions played a critical role in Peru's transformation. In Chapter 5, Svetlana Vtyurina describes the policy decisions taken during a fiscal consolidation process that played out over the last 40 years as the high deficits of the 1970s and 1980s gradually evolved into the fiscal surpluses of more recent years. Interestingly, Peru has not recorded a primary deficit since 2003 and saw its debt ratio fall to around 20 percent of GDP in 2014.

Many observers have noted that the cornerstone of Peru's fiscal turnaround was the passing of a fiscal transparency law in 1999. As discussed by Cesar Liendo in Chapter 6, the law introduced a modern macro-fiscal framework and a fiscal rule, both of which have been gradually modified. These second-generation reforms have made the macro-fiscal framework simpler, more transparent, and more able to accommodate adjustments in the structure of the economy.

The discussion on fiscal rules is complemented by Svetlana Vtyurina's analysis in Chapter 7 of alternative fiscal stability frameworks for countries rich in natural resources. With pressing societal needs, there is a natural political desire to view resource revenues as permanent and to spend them immediately. The reality, however, suggests that these flows may be temporary and volatile, disrupting prudent budgetary planning. Thus, the permanent income hypothesis would imply that these revenues should only be used to smooth out consumption over generations, with current surplus funds invested in financial assets as savings. In this context, Vtyurina presents the choices confronting Peru and provides simulations under various approaches. She concludes that given Peru's long resource horizon, pressing infrastructure needs, and low public investment, a fiscal sustainability framework that efficiently invests these flows today in infrastructure would be optimal.

Reforms in tax policy and in public financial management have helped Peru achieve solid fiscal accounts. In Chapter 8, Ricardo Fenochietto, Laura Calderón, Marco Camacho, and Patricio Castro describe the Peruvian authorities' efforts to broaden the tax base, simplify tax rates, and reduce evasion and avoidance in an environment plagued by noncompliance and informality issues. Key components include the ongoing modernization of the tax collection agency (*Superintendencia Nacional de Administración Tributaria*) and mining taxation reform. Although much still needs to be done, these efforts have improved tax efficiency and overall revenue inflows. From the expenditure side, Chapter 9 on public financial management by Mario Pessoa, Israel Fainboim, and Almudena Fernández report on various improvements, including implementation of a medium-term budgeting and expenditure framework, results-based budgeting, state-of-the-art treasury and debt management, and improved information systems. Many of these reforms resulted from IMF technical assistance and an ongoing close technical dialogue between IMF staff and the Peruvian authorities.

Chapter 10, by Adrienne Cheasty and Juan Pichihua, reports on how fiscal decentralization has created its own challenges. Reallocating mineral revenues back to resource-producing regions has created a divide between the haves and have-nots in Peru's fragmented local regions. It has also made the regions important players in infrastructure investment and in education and health spending. However, local governments' pervasive problems with management capacity and the volatility of resource revenues continue to burden the country's overall budgeting system and complicate investment spending. In addition, under this decentralized system revenue flows toward mining communities, which may or may not be where the greatest social needs are. Both investment and social spending challenges are critical development issues for Peru that need to be addressed promptly.

A perennial question in emerging market countries centers on the most efficient way to fill infrastructure gaps. In Chapter 11, Giancarlo Marchesi and Alvaro Valencia review the Peruvian experience in addressing this crucial issue, stressing the country's heavy reliance on private sector involvement. The authorities initially focused on privatizations in the mid-1990s, given the nationalization of key industries in the 1970s and 1980s. These privatizations dramatically improved the efficiency of the economy and kick-started the growth renaissance in Peru. In the early 2000s, the focus shifted toward greater use of concessions and, by the end of the decade, more reliance on public-private partnerships. The current public-private partnership framework is considered to be well designed and efficient.

Three chapters on monetary policy provide a look at Peru's inflation-targeting framework. Two characteristics of the Peruvian economy—high dollarization and volatile credit cycles—have affected the formulation of the policy framework. As is well known, dollarization heightens the exposure of the real and financial sectors to exchange rate and liquidity shocks. Given its impact on balance sheets, dollarization also reduces the effectiveness of monetary policy. As a result, an economy can be prone to boom-bust credit cycles associated with volatile foreign currency credit flows. Dollarization also affects the transmission of monetary policy and increases the liquidity and solvency risks to the financial system. To address these risks, the Peruvian central bank (*Banco Central de Reserva del Perú* [BCRP]) has implemented a "hybrid" inflation-targeting framework that incorporates conventional monetary policy instruments with nonstandard policy tools (for example, sterilized foreign exchange interventions and frequent use of reserve requirements).

The BCRP policy framework has worked well. As documented by Adrián Armas, Alejandro Santos, and Melesse Tashu in Chapter 12, the inflation-targeting framework has helped reduce the level of inflation and anchored price expectations, while limiting exchange rate and foreign interest rate pass-through effects. Despite Peru's high rate of dollarization, the deviation of actual inflation outcomes from the midpoint of the BCRP's 1–3 percent target range has been small, comparing well with other LA6 countries.[1] Moreover, this stability has helped to gradually lower dollarization, with the rate declining from about 70 percent on introduction of the inflation-targeting framework in 2002, to under 40 percent today. Moreover, the functioning of the monetary policy transmission mechanism has improved, and shifting capital flows have not negatively affected financial stability.

Spillovers from the global financial crisis posed a major challenge to Peru's monetary policy. To combat the recessionary effects of the global slowdown, developed-country central banks implemented expansionary monetary policies that lowered interest rates to near zero and triggered quantitative easing policies. Within this context, Renzo Rossini, Adrián Armas, and Zenón Quispe in Chapter 13 describe how the BCRP confronted the spillover effects from these developed-country policies, which led to large capital inflows seeking higher yields. Their work offers a particularly close look at how the BCRP formulated a set of reserve requirements in response to shifts in credit and capital flows. In a similar vein, Chapter 14 by Renzo Rossini, Zenón Quispe, and Donita Rodríguez focuses on the BCRP's sterilized intervention policies, providing background information on their rationale and on their impact on financial markets.

Peru's financial sector performance has strengthened, along with financial supervision. In Chapter 15, Javier Poggi, Lucia Romero, Manuel Luy, and Narda Sotomayor provide a review of how the authorities used these good economic times to modernize and reinforce financial sector supervision and regulation. In Chapter 16, Mercedes García-Escribano investigates how macroeconomic stabilization and other policies have helped to gradually reduce dollarization.

Overall, Peru's financial sector regulation and supervision are considered to be among the best in the region. Chapter 17 by Kevin Ross and Juan Alonso Peschiera reveals how the profitability and cost-efficiency of the banking sector have improved since the banking crisis in the early 2000s. Although bank concentration and effective margins remain relatively high, the sector still appears to enjoy marked competition. In Chapter 18, Mercedes Vera-Martin describes Peru's set of macroprudential tools and policies and contrasts them with the regional experience.

The external sector contributions in this volume report on how trade liberalization and free trade agreements have transformed Peru's economy. The country opened its doors to international trade and financial flows in the early 1990s as part of the broader macroeconomic stabilization and structural reform agenda. Chapter 19 by Yu Ching Wong examines the evolution of Peru's trading boom and increase in foreign direct investment flows.

Chapters 20 and 21 on exchange rate movements by Melesse Tashu show that exchange rate smoothing through foreign exchange intervention has helped insulate Peru's real exchange rate from the effects of commodity price shocks, and that the exchange rate is broadly in line

[1]The LA6 are Brazil, Chile, Colombia, Mexico, Peru, and Uruguay.

with fundamentals. Nevertheless, continuing the policy of increasing flexibility would enhance the economy's ability to absorb external shocks and reduce the incentives to undertake unhedged risks.

Although the increase in openness described in Chapter 19 had enormous benefits for Peru, it also exposed the economy to the risks of external shocks. Chapter 22 by Fei Han empirically estimates the linkages between Peru's economy and two growth drivers—Chinese investment and U.S. monetary policy. These linkages are large and important in understanding how growth and investment will evolve.

Chapter 23 turns to social issues. Yu Ching Wong outlines how Peru has achieved reductions in poverty and inequality. Over the course of 10 years, the poverty rate in Peru declined by more than half: from 59 percent in 2004 to 23 percent in 2014. This means about half the population has moved into the middle class since the mid-2000s. Similarly, the extreme poverty rate fell to about 4 percent in 2014 from 20 percent in 2004. Income distribution has also improved, with the Gini coefficient declining from above 60 in 2002 to 44 by 2014. Although a large part of these improvements can be attributed to Peru's growth, the social and cash transfer programs undertaken by various government administrations also played a role. Despite these gains, Wong notes that social spending remains low in comparison to regional peers, and much more needs to be done in the areas of education, health, and gender inequality.

Part III presents three viewpoints on Peru's future challenges. The fiscal policy agenda will need to remain focused on strengthening institutions and frameworks. In Chapter 24, Alonso Segura, Peru's Minister of the Economy and Finance, outlines how the gradual evolution of Peru's frameworks and policies imparted a degree of stability and predictability to fiscal policy. Those frameworks and policies also helped create fiscal buffers that were useful in mitigating the negative effects of the global financial crisis and the current slowdown in metal prices. In the near term, the fiscal sustainability of many emerging marketing economies, including Peru, will again be tested by higher international interest rates, persistent depreciation pressures, lower permanent fiscal revenues, and lower potential growth. As in the past, Peru will need to diligently implement stable and sound fiscal policies that will promote the credibility necessary to attract foreign investment flows, lower financing costs for both the private and public sectors, and help sustain economic growth. In Minister Segura's view, the best way to create this virtuous circle is by strengthening the current macrofiscal framework in ways that optimize the functioning of fiscal policy. In particular, future reforms need to focus on tax policy, public expenditure management, and intergovernmental transfers.

Peru has significant space to increase permanent revenues and fortify the tax system, and Minister Segura indicates this could be accomplished mainly by widening the tax base by reducing informality. Measures could focus on reducing tax evasion and avoidance through the use of risk-based enforcement systems, tax and customs controls, and new information management systems. At lower levels of government, revenue-raising incentives could be provided to expand municipal taxation, particularly in the area of property taxation. Tax exemptions and excise taxation need to be harmonized, with tax regulations brought further in line with international best practices. If all of these measures were to be fully implemented, the overall equity, efficiency, and transparency of tax administration would improve, further contributing to a reduction of informality—and higher growth.

Much work needs to be done to improve the efficiency of public spending and intergovernmental transfers. Public expenditures need to be better prioritized through a thorough evaluation of prior outcomes and these results better communicated to the public. The rigidities and other biases in expenditure design that restrict timely countercyclical spending should be eliminated. In particular, Minister Segura floats the idea of establishing a separate fund or bank for public or public-private investment projects. This entity could lie outside of the budget and be swiftly activated in a countercyclical fashion. In addition, intergovernmental transfers from all financing sources need to be based on the predictability of public spending and on the capacity to absorb, measure, and evaluate the use of the transferred resources. Transfers based solely on the location of mining activity, and that do not take into account local authorities' ability to implement spending projects, have had a negative impact on public investment, development, and growth.

In Chapter 25, Julio Verlarde, the President of the BCRP, outlines a number of monetary policy challenges. He stresses that to implement an inflation-targeting regime in a highly dollarized economy, the BCRP needed to explicitly account for the financial cycle. Since real and financial cycles rarely coincide, and financial cycles tend to be longer in duration, the central bank had to lengthen the time horizon for monetary policy and adapt its nonconventional policy instruments. Looking ahead, it will be crucial to properly calibrate these policy instruments such that financial intermediaries internalize the financial risks, thus helping the financial system absorb shocks. If not implemented correctly, these instruments can be a source of inefficiencies that hinder capital market development.

The monetary policy framework will also need to be adjusted to developments in capital markets. As capital markets develop, it will become increasingly difficult for the BCRP to fully sterilize their interventions and control exchange rate movements. On the other hand, more developed financial markets are needed to hedge risky positions, blocking the source of shocks in the first place and eliminating the necessity of BCRP intervention. This predicament underscores the central bank's drive to dedollarize the economy with an array of reserve requirements. Then again, increased reliance on nonbank financing in Peru, such as bond issuance, weakens the effectiveness of reserve requirements and creates possible currency mismatches. It is also important to calibrate the monetary policy stance and the set of macroprudential measures with the microprudential regulations of financial system supervisors. This may not be an easy task.

The changing external environment will continue to affect monetary policy decisions. President Velarde notes that the gradual reversal of quantitative easing in the United States could imply a prolonged readjustment of dollar exchange rates. Thus, exchange rate pass-through effects could be nonlinear and asymmetric, with larger inflationary effects on depreciations than on appreciations. This is a problem because many countries in the region are already above or near their inflation targets. Given the importance of low inflation to central bank credibility, monetary transmission, and dedollarization efforts, the BCRP will need to continue to intervene to tame depreciations, with cyclical adjustments in reserve requirements to promote credit expansion. Finally, slower growth in China, the end of the commodity super-cycle, and investment bottlenecks indicate that potential growth will falter without structural reforms. Understanding the evolution of the Peruvian economy's potential output given this uncertainty will be crucial to the formulation of optimal policy.

The main social policy challenge going forward is to eradicate persistent pockets of poverty and social exclusion. Although Peru's social indicators have improved over the past decade in line with rapid economic growth and improvements in public policies, there are still high rates of poverty and malnutrition among the country's rural population, female-headed households, and native language speakers. As Carolina Trivelli notes in Chapter 26, the existence of these gaps in social inclusion was the catalyst behind the establishment of the Ministry of Social Development and Inclusion in 2011. Although prior attempts had been made to create a coordinated national strategy, most social programs and policies tended to be somewhat ad hoc and dispersed among various ministries and regions. Thus, the task confronting the Ministry of Social Development and Inclusion was to establish a clear road map of coordinated policy and program interaction among all levels of government to address these enduring gaps. The authorities' national strategy—"Inclusion for Growth" (*Incluir para Crecer*)—addresses that challenge by detailing an intergovernmental agenda that incorporates the country's five main social programs.

A concerted broad-based effort will be needed to continue to make progress above and beyond existing social inclusion gains. Trivelli stresses that authorities need to build wide-ranging public support for social inclusion programs by effectively communicating their importance for societal growth and development. Besides creating awareness of the issues, good communication will also help sustain and build budgetary financial support. Another issue is that, at present, not all citizens who qualify for social assistance are able to access it due to funding or logistical constraints. Finally, in implementing their national strategy, the authorities will need to continue to identify and track vulnerable populations, as well as develop and test new innovative programs against measurable benchmarks. Given the dispersion of rural locations, this will require that the Peruvian government establish an effective presence throughout Peru—something that has proven difficult in the past.

In conclusion, this volume presents a multifaceted look at Peru's economic accomplishments and future challenges. Each contribution, in its own way, explains how the country has been transformed into one of the better economic performers in Latin America, and examines what needs to be done to sustain future growth and development. The common thread throughout the volume—and its essential takeaway—is that structural reforms have provided good payoffs for Peru over the last 30 years. With the external environment now turning slightly less favorable than in the recent past, the authorities will need to revisit this lesson and redouble structural reform efforts as they confront the tasks ahead.

PART I

# Context

CHAPTER 2

# Peru's Recent Economic History: From Stagnation, Disarray, and Mismanagement to Growth, Stability, and Quality Policies

RENZO ROSSINI AND ALEJANDRO SANTOS

*Peru represents one of the best examples in Latin America of how a stabilization program and structural reform agenda should be implemented. Like most countries in the region, Peru suffered through the debt crisis of the 1980s, with its situation exacerbated by misguided policies. By 1989–90, the economy was mired in hyperinflation, external debt default, sharp economic decline, a large fiscal imbalance, an unsustainable public debt, a multiple exchange rate system, countless economic distortions, and domestic terrorism. The result was an unparalleled level of economic dislocation. The ambitious economic program of the mid-1990s addressed all of these problems and began a long process of structural reform that established the basis for achieving the highest growth rates in South America over the past two decades. The reform process included two macroeconomic milestones that cemented stability: the introduction of a Fiscal Responsibility Law in 1999 (modified in 2013) and the formal introduction of inflation targeting in 2002. The economy's growth path endured the Asian and Russian crises of 1997–98 and the global financial crisis of 2008–09. The adjustment and reform process was accompanied by a number of successful IMF arrangements and significant technical assistance.*

Despite the economic deceleration of 2014, economic growth in Peru over 2005–14 averaged 6.3 percent, the highest level in South America and the second highest in Latin America (after Panama, where the canal is being expanded) (Figure 2.1). This is not a small accomplishment, especially compared with the country's poor economic performance and relative stagnation during part of the 1970s and most of the 1980s. The rise of Peru as an economic star among emerging markets came as a surprise to many economic observers, analysts, and investment bankers, but not to economic historians. Peru had a long history of high growth in the post–World War II period, growing at 5 percent in the 1950s, 6 percent in the 1960s, and 5½ percent in the first half of the 1970s. By the mid-1970s, it is estimated that income per capita in Peru was broadly similar to that of Brazil, Chile, and Uruguay, and a third higher than Colombia (but still lower by about a quarter than Mexico). In that sense, Peru simply returned in the 1990s to a well-known growth path after 15 years of volatile stagnation in the second half of the 1970s and the 1980s.

The malaise of the economy came after the oil shocks of the 1970s and Peru's poor policy response (Table 2.1). Peru was not the only one; most advanced and emerging market economies at the time did not know how to respond to a large supply shock, and what is more, some may not even have been aware that their sluggish economic performance was due to that supply shock. This lack of awareness led to active demand management policies that in turn led to stagflation. Peru went through a cycle of expansionary policies and failed programs to address them (Pastor 2012). The United States suffered its own stagflation, experiencing double-digit inflation in the late 1970s, and then endured a painful disinflation process in the early 1980s that pushed interest

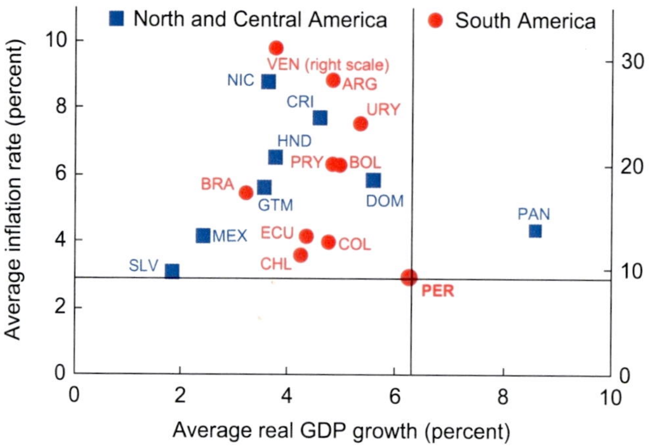


Source: IMF staff calculations.
Note: See page vii for a list of three-letter country codes used in this volume.

**Figure 2.1** Latin America: Real GDP Growth and Inflation, 2005–14 (*Percent*)

**TABLE 2.1**

## Peru: Economic Indicators, 1985–2014 (*Percent*)

| | Instability | The Great Stabilization | Poststabilization | Average |
|---|---|---|---|---|
| | 1985–90 | 1991–92 | 1993–2014 | 1985–2014 |
| | | (Annual Percentage Change) | | |
| Real GDP | –0.9 | 0.8 | 5.3 | 3.7 |
| Inflation (end of period) | 2,080 | 98.0 | 6.1 | 427.1 |
| Base Money | 1,358 | 79.2 | 19.1 | 290.8 |
| Real Exchange Rate (average)[1] | 18.6 | –1.9 | 0.2 | 3.8 |
| Terms of Trade (deterioration –) | –5.0 | –3.6 | 2.2 | 0.3 |
| | | (Percent of GDP) | | |
| Domestic Investment | 19.1 | 16.0 | 21.4 | 20.6 |
| National Savings | 14.0 | 11.0 | 18.3 | 17.0 |
| External Current Account | –5.1 | –5.0 | –3.1 | –3.6 |
| Gross International Reserves | 7.7 | 8.4 | 21.7 | 18.0 |
| Fiscal Balance[2] | –8.9 | –3.5 | –0.7 | –2.5 |
| Public Debt[2] | 71.3 | 67.6 | 40.1 | 48.2 |

Sources: Peruvian authorities; and IMF staff estimates.
[1]Effective, (–) = real depreciation.
[2]Nonfinancial public sector.

rates to record high levels. To complicate matters, Mexico, having enjoyed the oil shock as a producer, led the way in economic mismanagement in the region. Ultimately, unable to afford the higher interest payments, Mexico declared default on its external debt in August 1982. Peru suspended payments to commercial creditors seven months later in March 1983. Most countries in the region followed, as they suffered contagion from Mexico, and as banks became reluctant to renew credit lines in the region. This gave rise to the debt crisis in Latin America in the 1980s, which came to be known as the region's "lost decade."

The bad policies of the 1980s created the highest recorded inflation in Peru's history (over 7,600 percent in 1990) and its steepest economic decline (the economy contracted by about one-quarter between 1987 and 1990). It is estimated that the size of the economy by 1990 was similar to that in 1975. It took almost a decade to regain the peak (and overheated) level of GDP of 1987 (Ministry of the Economy and Finance 2003). The successful stabilization of the early 1990s stopped inflation, put public finances in order, reduced the debt burden, gave freedom and authority to the central bank to conduct monetary policy, implemented ambitious reforms, and set the foundation for sustained economic growth that continues to this day (Polastri 2007).

This chapter analyzes the economic performance of Peru and its policies from 1985–2014 by identifying six distinct periods (Table 2.2): (1) the instability of the second half of the 1980s, (2) the titanic stabilization of the early 1990s, (3) the sustained recovery during most of the 1990s, (4) the deepening reforms during most of the 2000s, (5) the global financial crisis of 2008–09, and (6) the postcrisis period of the last five years. During the entire period, Peru had almost uninterrupted IMF-supported (or monitored) programs and arrangements. These programs were some of the most successful operations in the IMF's history (Box 2.1).

## INSTABILITY AND MISMANAGEMENT (1985–90)

Desperate to find solutions to the country's macroeconomic problems, the Peruvian authorities undertook some of the most unique experiments in economic policy during the mid-1980s with disastrous results. By then, Peru was experiencing declining growth rates, debt service problems, and accelerating inflation fueled by large fiscal and quasi-fiscal deficits (Table 2.3). Government intervention in pricing, interest rates, credit allocation, and labor markets resulted in major distortions of relative prices and the deepening of the large informal economy. Inefficient import substitution was encouraged by means of quantitative import restrictions and high tariffs, and a generally overvalued exchange rate favored urban consumers, discouraged exports and agricultural production, and induced large-scale migration from rural to urban areas. In the late 1980s, this migration was given additional impetus by terrorist activities, which also affected production in mining, energy, and agriculture. Drug trafficking also became a problem. It is estimated that real GDP per capita declined by about 30 percent during the late 1980s.

Social indicators were no better. It is estimated that in the mid-1980s nearly 60 percent of the Peruvian population lived in poverty (that is, their basic human needs for food, shelter, education, and medical services were not met; World Bank 2015). That figure subsequently increased. Political violence claimed over 20,000 lives in the 1980s. Peru was then stricken by a cholera epidemic, largely as a result of the deterioration of social services and widespread lack of access to safe water supplies.

The administration that took office in mid-1985 attempted to address these problems by boosting domestic demand through credit expansion, tax reduction, increases in public sector employment, and government-mandated wage increases. At the same time, the administration sought to contain inflation through price and interest rate controls, subsidies, and delays in adjusting public sector prices, and attempted to protect the balance of payments through a complex multiple exchange rate system, higher tariffs, and quantitative restrictions on imports.[1] The hallmark government policy was to limit public sector external debt service payments to 10 percent of exports of goods and nonfactor services, and to service debt only to creditors expected to provide a positive net flow of resources to Peru.[2]

These policies generated a short-lived boom in 1986–87 that was followed by hyperinflation and a deep recession. The budget deficit rose sharply, domestic savings fell, and the external current account swung from approximate balance to a deficit of 7½ percent of GDP. By late 1987, financial disintermediation was accelerating, international reserves were depleted, and the public

[1]Other measures included fixing the exchange rate at a 12 percent lower (depreciated) level, a freeze on publicly administered prices after a mild increase, a lowering of the interest rate from 280 percent to 45 percent, a salary increase of 18 percent and a subsequent adjustment to increase real wages, conversion to local currency of foreign-currency-denominated bank certificates, and a private sector price freeze. See Velarde and Rodriguez (1992a).

[2]The limit did not cover short-term debt, payments in kind, debts to Latin American governments and regional organizations, or debts incurred after mid-1985. Peru did not allow the IMF to conduct Article IV Consultations in 1985 or 1986. Debt service payments to the IMF were suspended as of early 1986 (except for charges from the Special Drawing Rights Department), and in August 1986 Peru was declared ineligible to use the IMF's General Resources. Loan disbursements from the World Bank were suspended in May 1987. While Peru was initially able to avoid arrears to the IDB, loans were halted because of failure to meet agreed-upon conditions, and eventually Peru also ran arrears to the IDB.

**TABLE 2.2**

## Peru: Basic Institutional Information (1985–2014)

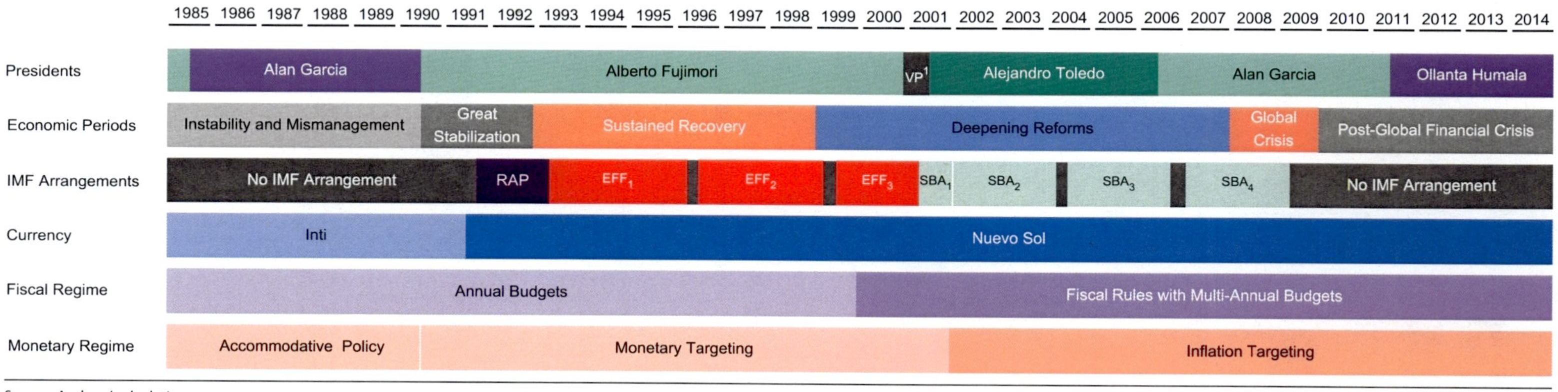


Source: Authors' calculations.

Note: EFF = Extended Fund Facility; RAP = Rights Accumulation Program; SBA = Stand-By Arrangement.

[1] After President Alberto Fujimorii was ousted by Congress in November 2000, Congress appointed Valentin Paniagua (VP) as Interim President for eight months.

## BOX 2.1. Peru: A Brief History of IMF Arrangements

Peru has a long history of IMF-supported programs. In 1954, Peru became the third country in the world to have a Stand-By Arrangement (SBA) with the IMF (after Belgium and Finland, both in 1952). The arrangement marked the first time a Latin American country used IMF funds.

Over the past 60 years, there have been a total of 24 IMF-supported or monitored programs in Peru. Of particular note, however, are the eight very successful IMF programs with Peru from 1991 to 2009. These included one IMF-monitored program under the Rights Accumulation Program (RAP) (1991–93); three Extended Fund Facilities (EFF) (1993–2001); and four SBAs (2001–09). Peru has no credit outstanding to the IMF, as the debt was fully repaid on time by 2007.

An unfortunate episode of protracted arrears to the IMF was resolved in the early 1990s. Following the Latin American debt crisis of the 1980s, Peru had trouble adjusting to additional external shocks and adopted an inadequate macroeconomic policy mix that precipitated a severe balance of payments crisis. By 1985, Peru was running arrears to the IMF, as the first administration of Alan Garcia (1985–90) unilaterally imposed a ceiling on external debt payments equivalent to 10 percent of foreign exchange earnings. These arrears were cleared in 1993, during the first administration of Alberto Fujimori (1990–95) following completion of the IMF-monitored RAP.

The IMF has supported the economic renaissance of Peru over the past two decades. The transformation of Peru's economy was accompanied by a sequence of virtually uninterrupted IMF programs, monitorings, and arrangements, along with a massive technical assistance program. The IMF arrangements were mostly precautionary: after clearing arrears to the IMF in 1993, Peru made only one purchase in 1997 associated with the debt and debt-service reduction operation with private creditors. Below is a brief description of IMF programs and arrangements in Peru since the 1990s.

- *Rights Accumulation Program.* This program (1991–93) supported the economic policies of the newly elected government of Albert Fujimori (1990–95), which included macroeconomic adjustment and structural reforms. The program met its main objectives of reducing inflation, creating conditions for sustained growth, gradually returning to external viability, and reestablishing relations with external creditors.[1]
- *Extended Fund Facilities.* These facilities (1993–2001) supported a strong stabilization effort as well as the first generation of reforms, including the Fiscal Responsibility Law (1999). During this eight-year period, the IMF approved three EFFs for a total amount of special drawing rights (SDR)[2] 1.7 billion. Under those arrangements, Peru made purchases totaling SDR 0.8 billion, and its outstanding credit peaked at SDR 0.75 billion (161 percent of quota) at end-1997 (Figure 2.1.1). No drawing was made in the last EFF (1999–2001).
- *Stand-By Arrangements.* These arrangements (2001–09) also favored economic stabilization and a continuation of structural reforms, including the introduction of inflation targeting (2002). During this eight-year period, the IMF approved four SBAs totaling SDR 0.84 billion, all of them precautionary, as no purchase was made.

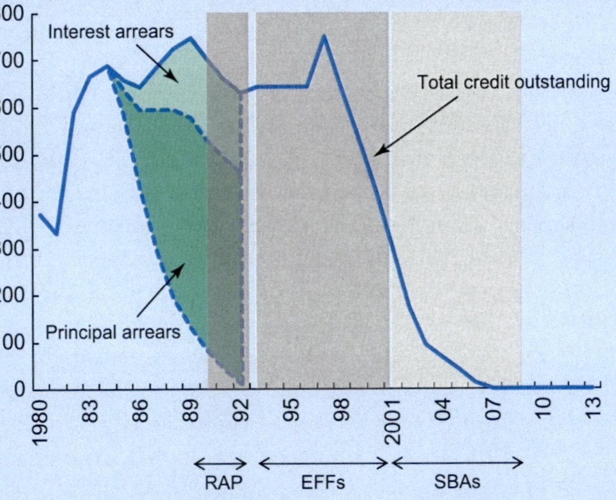


Sources: Boughton (2012); and IMF, *International Financial Statistics*.
Note: As of end-December 2013. Credit outstanding includes interest arrears. EFF = Extended Fund Facilities; RAP = Rights Accumulation Program; SBA = Stand-By Arrangement; SDR = special drawing rights.

**Figure 2.1.1** Peru: IMF Credit Outstanding, 1980–2013 (*Millions of SDRs*)

[1]During this RAP (1991–93), the authorities accumulated "rights" equivalent to the amount of IMF arrears, but no money was disbursed. Japan and the United States provided a bridge loan to Peru in March 1993 to settle its arrears to the IMF. Once the arrears were cleared, the amounts accumulated under the RAP were disbursed upon approval of the successor EFF (1993–96) and served to repay the bridge loan from Japan and the United States.

[2]Special drawing rights (SDR) are the unit of account for IMF transactions. SDR value is based on a basket of four international currencies (euro, Japanese yen, pound sterling, and U.S. dollar).

TABLE 2.3

Peru: Economic Indicators, 1985–90 (*Percent*)

| | 1985 | 1987 | 1990 | Average 1985–90 |
|---|---|---|---|---|
| | | (Annual Percentage Change) | | |
| Real GDP | 2.1 | 9.7 | –5.0 | –0.9 |
| Inflation (end of period) | 158.3 | 114.5 | 7,650 | 2,080 |
| Base Money | 227.8 | 153.7 | 5,094 | 1,370 |
| Real Exchange Rate (average)[1] | –18.0 | 37.8 | 41.0 | 18.6 |
| Terms of Trade (deterioration –) | –5.4 | –0.2 | –8.4 | –5.0 |
| | | (Percent of GDP) | | |
| Domestic Investment | 18.9 | 20.4 | 13.9 | 19.1 |
| National Savings | 18.4 | 12.8 | 8.9 | 14.0 |
| External Current Account | –0.5 | –7.5 | –5.0 | –5.1 |
| Gross International Reserves | 15.7 | 4.1 | 6.1 | 7.7 |
| Fiscal Balance[2] | –3.7 | –10.1 | –8.9 | –8.9 |
| Public Debt[2] | 79.8 | 60.6 | 69.0 | 71.3 |

Sources: Peruvian authorities; and IMF staff estimates.
[1]Effective, (–) = real depreciation.
[2]Nonfinancial public sector.

sector deficit was generating strong inflationary pressures that could no longer be repressed through price controls and subsidies. The fiscal difficulties were mainly attributable to the drop in central government revenues, which fell by almost one-half as a ratio of GDP (from 15 percent of GDP in 1985 to about 8 percent in 1989), reflecting the impact on excise tax collections of lags in adjusting public sector prices, reductions in tax rates, the erosion of tax revenues through inflation, and increasing tax evasion. This was only partly offset by cuts in expenditure, including public investment. In addition, a substantial quasi-fiscal deficit emerged as a result of the central bank's exchange rate losses and subsidized lending to the agricultural bank. By 1988, the deficit of the nonfinancial public sector, at almost 12 percent of GDP, was considerably larger than the money supply (M2) in local currency, a relationship that became even more adverse the following year as the process of financial disintermediation accelerated.

Measures taken in late 1988 and early 1989 temporarily reduced the fiscal deficit, but did not address the underlying structural problems. Economic activity continued to decline and inflationary pressures remained unabated. Real GDP fell by 20 percent in 1988–89 and prices rose 1,700 percent in 1988 and 2,800 percent in 1989. The recession and collapse of investment resulted in a decline in aggregate demand well in excess of the decline in GDP, reducing the external current account deficit and reconstructing international reserves. In the run-up to the April 1990 national elections, the authorities once more relaxed fiscal and monetary policies, permitted public enterprise prices to lag even further behind the general price level, and increased subsidies through the multiple exchange rate system. As a result, during the first half of 1990 consumer prices rose by 34 percent a month (an annual rate of over 3,000 percent) before accelerating to 63 percent in July, by which time the central bank's liquid international reserves once again were virtually exhausted. By mid-1990 more than two-thirds of Peru's US$22 billion external debt (about 75 percent of GDP) was in arrears, including about US$2.2 billion in arrears to the IMF, World Bank, and Inter-American Development Bank (IDB).

## THE GREAT STABILIZATION (1990–92)

In the early 1990s, the Peruvian economy faced a severe economic crisis characterized by hyperinflation and a sharp drop in output resulting from large fiscal imbalances, negative real interest rates, widespread wage and price controls and subsidies, and a highly distorted exchange rate system. In addition, the social environment had deteriorated due to increasing terrorism. Real

**TABLE 2.4**

**Peru: Economic Indicators, 1991–92 (*Percent*)**

| | Average 1985–90 | 1991 | 1992 | Average 1991–92 |
|---|---|---|---|---|
| | | (Annual Percentage Change) | | |
| Real GDP | –0.9 | 2.2 | –0.5 | 0.8 |
| Inflation (end of period) | 2,080.0 | 139.2 | 56.7 | 98.0 |
| Base Money | 1,357.7 | 96.2 | 62.1 | 79.2 |
| Real Exchange Rate (average)[1] | 18.6 | –7.6 | 3.8 | –1.9 |
| Terms of Trade (deterioration –) | –5.0 | –4.5 | –2.6 | -3.6 |
| | | (Percent of GDP) | | |
| Domestic Investment | 19.1 | 16.0 | 15.9 | 16.0 |
| National Savings | 14.0 | 11.4 | 10.6 | 11.0 |
| External Current Account | –5.1 | –4.5 | –5.4 | -5.0 |
| Gross International Reserves | 7.7 | 7.9 | 8.9 | 8.4 |
| Fiscal Balance[2] | –8.9 | –2.9 | –4.0 | -3.5 |
| Public Debt[2] | 71.3 | 68.9 | 66.3 | 67.6 |

Sources: Peruvian authorities; and IMF staff estimates.
[1]Effective, (–) = real depreciation.
[2]Nonfinancial public sector.

GDP in 1990 was 25 percent lower than three years before (30 percent in per capita terms) and similar to the level observed in 1975 (1965 in per capita terms).

The stabilization program that was implemented in the second half of 1990 and lasted through end-1992 drastically reformed the structure of the economy and created the basis for the solid and sustained growth in the two decades that followed (Table 2.4). The program was responsible for a number of achievements, including (1) sharply reducing the budget deficit through increases in the prices of government-provided services and by streamlining the tax system, strengthening tax administration, reducing the civil service, and liquidating some public development banks; (2) abolishing price controls, capital controls, and quantitative trade restrictions, unifying and floating the exchange rate, and liberalizing labor and financial markets; (3) opening up areas of economic activity previously reserved for the public sector (including the provision of public services) to private and foreign participation; and (4) strengthening the framework for the implementation of monetary policy and the institutional autonomy of the central bank (*Banco Central de Reserva del Perú* [BCRP]) and the superintendency of banks (*Superintendencia de Bancas, Seguro, y AFP* [SBS]); and (5) bolstering financial supervision and prudential regulation.

The government that took office in mid-1990 immediately implemented a program of macroeconomic and structural adjustment aimed at drastically reducing inflation and establishing conditions for sustained growth. The initial package of economic measures adopted in August 1990 focused mainly on eliminating the domestic financing requirements of the nonfinancial public sector, removing distortions, and opening the economy to foreign competition.[3] The measures included:

- *Price adjustments.* A 3,000 percent increase in fuel prices and an increase of about 1,000 percent in electricity, water, and telephone rates.
- *Tax exemptions.* Elimination of some exemptions to the value-added tax and reduction in its rate from 18 percent to 14 percent.

[3]The international community's reaction to the program was quite positive. Japan and the United States took the lead in organizing a donors' group that included nine European countries and Canada to provide financing. Separately, four Latin American countries (Chile, Colombia, Mexico, and Venezuela) offered short-term loans. In 1991, the Paris Club (a grouping of 17 nations) rescheduled maturities falling due in 1991–92 on official debt for US$4.6 billion under Houston terms (i.e., longer grace and repayment periods than in a traditional rescheduling).

- *New taxes.* Imposition of temporary taxes of 10 percent on exports and 1 percent each on net wealth and insured assets.
- *Foreign exchange market reform.* Unification of the exchange rate and allowing it to float.
- *Import tariffs and restrictions.* Abolition of virtually all quantitative import restrictions, abolition of some import tariff exonerations, and consolidation of the complex tariff system (with rates running to almost 120 percent) into three rates (15 percent, 25 percent, and 50 percent).
- *External payments.* Liberalization of restrictions on payments for current international transactions.
- *Financial liberalization.* Reduction in the marginal reserve requirements on banks' domestic currency liabilities from 80 percent to 40 percent, and increases in interest rate ceilings for domestic currency lending to nonbinding levels, thereby allowing interest rates to be determined by market forces.

As an integral part of the initial adjustment effort, the government created the Social Emergency Program to help offset the impact of the reduction of food subsidies and increased transportation costs on the most disadvantaged, as well as to improve basic health services. The program was a mechanism for coordinating and channeling public sector resources to the disadvantaged, primarily through existing nongovernmental organizations. It was initially expected that program expenditures would amount to 2 percent of GDP on an annual basis, financed by resources from the Treasury and from external donors, with food aid targeted at 7½ million people. In practice, however, the amount of available resources turned out to be less than expected. In 1991, the Social Emergency Program was replaced by the National System for Social Compensation and Development, which continued most of the initial program's activities.

After the initial stabilization measures, the authorities continued to pursue tight monetary and fiscal policies while broadening and deepening the structural changes in the Peruvian economy. In the area of prices and wages, discipline was maintained on public sector wages while prices and wages in the private sector were allowed to find their own level. Price controls were lifted and in August 1990 the government mandated a one-time cost-of-living bonus for all employees in the public and private sectors equivalent to 100 percent of their July 1990 wage, but with a floor equivalent to 200 percent of the minimum wage. It also announced that wages would be increased again once the magnitude of the initial price shock was clear, and a further 100 percent increase was decreed for all workers in the public sector in late August 1990, while the minimum wage was raised by 300 percent. In September 1990, the government announced that private sector wages would be determined freely, abolished wage indexation in public enterprises, and made wage increases subject to government approval. Subsequently, public sector salaries and the minimum wage were reduced significantly in real terms, while average real wages in the private sector increased. Public sector prices were raised again in December 1990 (fuel prices were raised by 50 percent and water and electricity tariffs by 30 percent). A policy of smaller and more frequent adjustments in these prices was instituted during the second quarter of 1991.

Incentives for voluntary retirement were offered in a bid to reduce public sector employment, resulting in a reduction of 50,000 employees, or about 8 percent of the civil service (excluding defense and police) in the first four months of 1991. The tax system was simplified in November 1990 by eliminating some exemptions to the income and value-added tax, and by abolishing a number of taxes with negligible yield. In March 1991, an initial list of 23 public enterprises was identified for privatization, and public sector monopolies for basic foods, fishmeal, gold, salt, advertising, and reinsurance were eliminated.

All in all, the largest fiscal adjustment in the recent history of Peru took place in 1990–91. During these two years, the primary balance of the nonfinancial public sector (NFPS) adjusted cumulatively by about 6 percent of GDP (from a primary deficit of 4 percent of GDP in 1989 to a primary surplus of 2 percent in 1991), whereas interest payments fell by about 2 percent of

GDP, leading to a reduction in the overall fiscal balance of the NFPS of some 8 percent of GDP (from a deficit of around 11 percent to 3 percent of GDP). This adjustment took place against a backdrop of deteriorating terms of trade of some 15 percent, which was a drag on tax collection. Remarkably, real GDP contracted by only 3 percent during this two-year period, and there were early signs of a recovery by late 1991 (Velarde and Rodriguez 1992b).

The central bank further reduced marginal reserve requirements on domestic currency liabilities in stages to 15 percent by February 1991. Interest rates on domestic currency deposits and loans continued to be freely determined in the market and interest rate ceilings on foreign currency loans were raised to nonbinding levels in 1991. The central bank's rediscount rate was linked to the average deposit rate in the banking system. To facilitate transactions and signal the change in the monetary regime, the central bank introduced a new currency, the nuevo sol, in July 1991 at the rate of 1 nuevo sol per 1,000,000 intis. To reduce the quasi-fiscal deficit, subsidized lending by the agriculture bank was eliminated in September 1990 and the bank was restricted to financing farms of 10 hectares or less and those in the jungle and mountain regions. To facilitate commercial bank lending to the agricultural sector, measures were taken to simplify the registry of land titles and reduce restrictions on the use of land for loan guarantees.

The 1987 law nationalizing the banking system, which could not be fully implemented, was repealed in December 1990. A new financial system law adopted in April 1991 included reorganization of the SBS, extension of the supervisory regulatory framework to include nonbank financial intermediaries, and development of a system of deposit insurance.

To reduce labor market rigidities, legislation was adopted in March 1991 to widen grounds and speed procedures for dismissal of workers under Peru's restrictive labor laws. The legislation established a system of semiannual payment of retirement contributions designed to eliminate the need for retroactive increases in contributions following a general salary increase.

The exchange rate system was further liberalized in October 1990 with the replacement of the system of export surrender certificates by a requirement of export surrender through the banking system, along with a broadening of the range of transactions that could be effected in the interbank market. In March 1991, all remaining restrictions on private sector current and capital transactions were eliminated (except for restrictions on the amortization of frozen working capital loans). The previously frozen foreign currency deposits in the banking system were freed and the opening of accounts abroad was authorized. Limitations on remittances of direct investment income and capital were removed, although foreign subsidiaries in the extractive sectors remained subject to contractual limitations. In April 1991, the export surrender requirement and the system of official registry of exchange transactions were eliminated. Taken together, these measures represented a major reform of the external payments regime.

In the area of international trade, following the elimination of quantitative restrictions and the initial tariff reduction of August 1990, the process of tariff reform was accelerated in March 1991. The maximum tariff was reduced to 25 percent, and most transactions were made subject to a 15 percent rate. In addition, a special tariff rate of 5 percent was introduced on imports of scrap iron by the then state steel company (Siderperu) and a variable surcharge was adopted for some 18 basic food imports to protect the agricultural sector. The temporary export tax was eliminated in March 1991 for all exporters other than large mining companies, and the system of temporary duty-free admission of imported inputs was extended to include all export industries. Subsidized pre-export credits (FENT) were eliminated, as was the granting of subsidies for nontraditional exports (CERTEX) for new operations.

From the outset of the program, the government announced its intention to normalize relations with the international financial community and began discussions with the IMF on an economic program that could serve as a framework for this process and for an appeal to external donors for balance of payments support. As further steps in this process, the government resumed debt service payments to the World Bank in October 1990 and the IDB in November 1990, although some payment delays reemerged after March 1991. By June 1991, arrears to the World Bank and the IDB were about US$90 million higher than they had been when payments were resumed.

In support of these policy efforts, the authorities requested in September 1991 that Peru's economic program (which went through end-1992) be presented to the IMF Executive Board for endorsement as an IMF-monitored Rights Accumulation Program (RAP) within the framework of the enhanced collaborative approach to overdue financial obligations to the IMF. Peru became the second country in the world (after Zambia) to embark on an RAP. The proposed access was special drawing rights (SDR)[4] 624 million, equivalent to the arrears Peru had with the IMF as of June 1991, with an initial amount of SDR 104 million being accumulated upon Executive Board endorsement of the program and the rest in five equal quarterly installments, upon the observance of the performance criteria and completion of the program reviews. The accumulated rights were to be available for purchase in connection with a subsequent upper credit tranche IMF arrangement that was to be submitted to the IMF board for approval following (1) satisfactory performance under the RAP, (2) settlement of overdue obligations to the IMF, and (3) appropriate assurances regarding the financing of the subsequent program supported by the IMF arrangement.

The RAP was designed to consolidate the progress already made in reducing inflation and advance the structural transformation of the economy. Specific objectives were to (1) reduce inflation to low single-digit monthly rates by end-1991 and to international levels by end-1992, (2) make progress toward a viable external payment position and reestablish relations with external creditors, and (3) increase economic growth to 2½–3 percent in 1991 and 3½ percent in 1992 (Figure 2.2). To achieve these objectives, the authorities were to continue to pursue tight monetary and fiscal policies (by sharply reducing the pace of expansion of the central bank's net domestic assets and adjusting the public accounts by 2 percent of GDP a year with almost no domestic financing), and to allow the exchange rate to be determined by market forces (but allowing the accumulation of some international reserves), while deepening the process of structural reform. Structural measures included further liberalization of labor and financial markets; relaxation of restrictions on private (domestic and foreign) participation in petroleum, mining, and other sectors; major reforms in the tax system and tax administration; a reduction in public employment and the establishment of a more progressive public sector salary structure; and the restructuring and in some cases privatization of public enterprises, including official banks.

Peru's successful completion of the RAP in December 1992 was key to the normalization of relations with the IMF and all other creditors. More importantly, the successful implementation of the 1990–92 economic program (supported by the RAP) set the stage for sustained growth and price stability in the following decades. While the RAP did not achieve all the ambitious objectives set out from the beginning, the program managed to reduce inflation by more than half in 1992, and it considerably strengthened Peru's external position, although the economy actually contracted. The program was considered to be quite successful and all performance criteria and indicative targets under the RAP for 1992 were attained (with the exception of the target of eliminating arrears to international organizations, which was actually achieved in the first quarter of 1993).

## SUSTAINED RECOVERY (1993–98)

The period from 1993–98 marked the resumption of sustained growth of the Peruvian economy, something that had not been seen since the 1960s and the first half of the 1970s. However, the period also included 1998, the only year of economic contraction in the poststabilization period, and a reminder of the vulnerabilities of the economy to external shocks. The strong economic performance was a reflection of positive external conditions, the closing of a negative output gap,

[4]Special drawing rights (SDR) are the unit of account for IMF transactions. SDR value is based on a basket of four international currencies (euro, Japanese yen, pound sterling, and U.S. dollar).

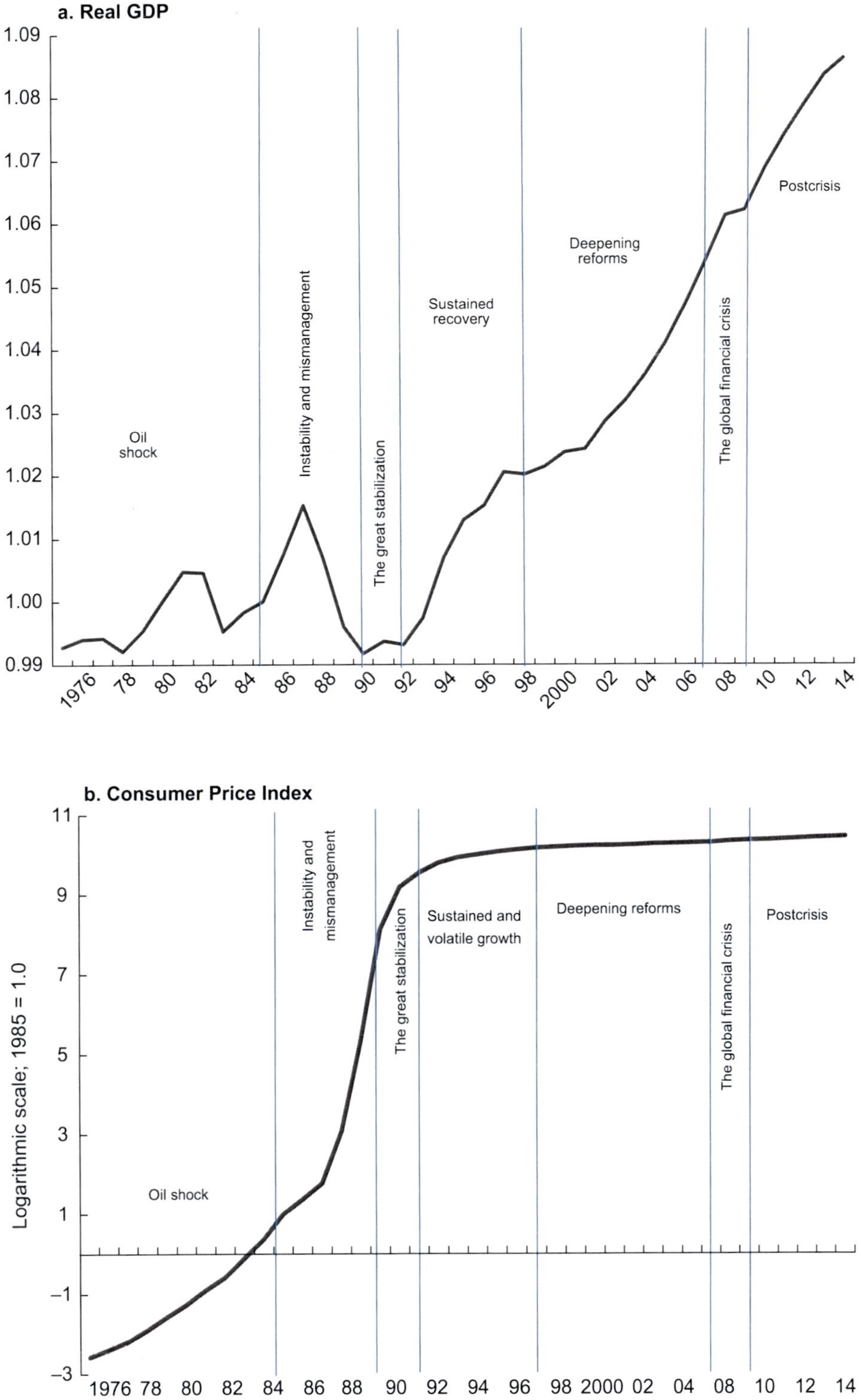


Source: Peruvian authorities.

**Figure 2.2** Peru: Real GDP and Consumer Price Index

and a strong record of policy implementation. Real GDP grew at an average rate of about 7 percent in 1993–97 (and contracted by half a percent in 1998), surpassing the level of real GDP of the previous peak in 1987. Economic policy aimed at promoting economic stability while implementing structural reforms that laid the foundation for high, sustainable growth and a reduction of vulnerabilities.

Peru cleared its arrears to the IMF in March 1993 with a bridge loan from Japan and the United States, which paved the way to lifting Peru's ineligibility for IMF resources (ending almost seven years of ineligibility). Following the successful completion of the RAP, the IMF Board approved the request for an Extended Fund Facility (EFF) covering March 1993–March 1996 for SDR 1,018 million. Upon approval of the EFF, Peru made the first drawing (or purchase, as the IMF calls it) in the amount of SDR 643 million (of which SDR 624 million corresponded to the rights accumulated under the RAP). The first drawing was mostly used to repay Japan and the United States for their bridge loans provided to clear the IMF arrears (Boughton 2012, Chapter 6).[5] Also in March 1993, Peru eliminated US$867 million in arrears to the World Bank following the successful completion of an accumulation procedure similar to that under the IMF. (Peru had cleared its arrears to the IDB in September 1991.)

The fiscal position was brought under control, with the combined public sector accounts reaching balance in 1997 (Table 2.5). Fiscal policy focused on adjustment and limiting domestic financing to the public sector. After several years of fiscal consolidation, the primary surplus of the NFPS reached over 2 percent of GDP in 1997. The public sector borrowing requirements were covered with privatization receipts, multilateral lending, and debt rescheduling (public and private creditors), with no need for borrowing in international capital markets.

The institutional framework for an independent monetary policy established by the Central Bank Charter (1992) was further enhanced by the Constitution of Peru (1993), which states that the BCRP is independent and carries out its duties to ensure monetary stability as its single aim.

Monetary policy was guided by controlling monetary aggregates to achieve preannounced inflation objectives (but not yet an inflation-targeting scheme), although inflationary expectations were entrenched due to lack of clarity on the nominal anchor (Velarde and Rodriguez 1994). A major challenge was the management of high private capital inflows, which produced rapid growth in credit to the private sector and appreciation pressures on the exchange rate. The central bank reacted by partially sterilizing the resulting reserve accumulation and increasing reserve requirements on dollar deposits to reduce credit expansion.

A number of structural fiscal reforms were implemented during this period:

- *Tax reform.* The tax system was revamped to simplify the income tax, broaden the basis of the value-added and excise taxes, and increase taxes on petroleum products. Tax revenue peaked at 14½ percent of GDP in 1996–97, up from 11 percent in 1990.
- *Pension system restructuring.* The pension system was reformed by putting in place a fully funded, defined-contribution private capitalization system of individual accounts. The government partially financed the transition to the private pension system with privatization receipts. However, the public pension system was maintained, with its preferential and general plans, and the constitutional reform needed to correct the large imbalances in the preferential system was delayed.
- *Public enterprise divesture.* Most public enterprises were transferred to the private sector, leading to substantial government receipts and investment flows.

[5]In addition to this EFF with the IMF, Peru had a second EFF in this period covering 1996–99 for SDR 300 million, including augmentation to finance the debt and debt service reduction operation. Both arrangements were concluded successfully, although the authorities decided to draw only about half of the resources available, preferring to treat the arrangements mostly as precautionary.

**TABLE 2.5**

**Peru: Economic Indicators, 1993–98 (*Percent*)**

| | Average 1991–92 | 1993 | 1996 | 1998 | Average 1993–98 |
|---|---|---|---|---|---|
| | | | (Annual Percentage Change) | | |
| Real GDP | 0.8 | 5.2 | 2.8 | –0.4 | 5.6 |
| Inflation (end of period) | 98.0 | 39.5 | 11.8 | 6.0 | 14.9 |
| Base Money | 79.2 | 33.6 | 9.2 | 5.5 | 25.4 |
| Private Credit | 190.6 | 74.0 | 48.2 | 21.0 | 46.8 |
| Real Exchange Rate (average)[1] | 5.0 | –10.3 | –0.4 | 0.2 | 0.2 |
| Terms of Trade (deterioration –) | –3.6 | –10.2 | –3.6 | –2.6 | 0.5 |
| | | | (Percent of GDP) | | |
| Output Gap[2] | –1.9 | –5.1 | 0.8 | 0.6 | 0.7 |
| Domestic Investment | 16.0 | 17.6 | 20.7 | 21.8 | 20.8 |
| National Savings | 11.0 | 10.4 | 13.9 | 15.7 | 14.0 |
| External Current Account | –5.0 | –7.2 | –6.8 | –6.1 | –6.9 |
| Gross International Reserves | 8.4 | 11.3 | 17.9 | 18.4 | 16.4 |
| Fiscal Balance[3] | –3.5 | –3.1 | –1.1 | –1.0 | –1.9 |
| Public Debt[3] | 67.6 | 71.0 | 53.9 | 44.8 | 54.9 |

Sources: Peruvian authorities; and IMF staff estimates
[1]Effective, (–) = real depreciation.
[2]Percent of potential.
[3]Nonfinancial public sector.

- *Financial system strengthening.* Important reforms of the financial system were also put in place. Institutional autonomy, prudential regulations, and the supervisory powers of the SBS were strengthened, and provisioning and capital requirements were raised. The process of closing official development (first-tier) banks was completed.

Reforms were also undertaken to impart flexibility in labor markets. Regulations on labor contracts, hiring practices, layoff clauses and related compensations, and collective bargaining were eased. Employment in Lima grew on average by 6½ percent a year during this period.

Peru finally normalized relations with all external creditors after difficult negotiations during this period:

- *Paris Club.* There were two additional reschedulings, the first in May 1993 covering maturities falling due in 1993–94 for US$1.9 billion on Houston terms, and the second in July 1996 covering maturities falling due in 1996–98 for US$6.7 billion, also on Houston terms. After these reschedulings, Peru graduated from Paris Club financing.
- *London Club.* A large debt and debt service reduction operation was conducted under the Brady initiative in March 1997. Peru offered four options in exchange for its defaulted loans (from March 1983): (1) a debt buyback at a deep discount, (2) a discount bond with a lower face value, (3) a par bond at below-market interest rates, and (4) a front-loaded interest reduction bond. Past due interest was exchanged for 20-year bonds (with 5-year grace periods). The upfront cost of the operation was US$1.4 billion, and it is estimated that it generated debt reduction of about one-half on a stock of US$10.6 billion in claims. There was overwhelming participation (over 99 percent).[6] Most creditors (about 78 percent) chose

[6]However, there were small holdouts. After the deal was announced, one creditor, Elliott Associates, bought about US$21 million in commercial claims on Peru in the secondary market, and did not participate in the Brady deal of 1997, instead filing a lawsuit in New York for recovery of the full value plus past due interest. Elliott Associates obtained a judgment against Peru in June 2000 for US$56 million and an attachment order against Peru's assets. It sought to attach the interest on Brady bonds and obtained a restraining order against Chase Manhattan Bank (the fiscal agent in charge

the frontloaded interest reduction bond, which had a 20-year maturity and 8 years of grace. IMF resources under the EFF (set-asides and augmentation) were used for this purpose; no IMF purchases were made after this operation. This was also graduation on rescheduling with commercial creditors.

- *Bilateral.* Peru repurchased the entire stock of its debt to the former Soviet Union (a non–Paris Club country) for about US$1.1 billion (inherited by Russia under the zero option, whereby Russia got all assets and liabilities of the Soviet Union) for about US$130 million.

Notwithstanding the economic progress achieved in many areas, Peru was reminded of its vulnerabilities in 1998. Two external shocks severely affected macroeconomic performance: (1) the withdrawal of foreign lines of credit worldwide in the wake of the Asian, Russian, and Long-Term Capital Management crisis of 1998; and (2) the El Niño weather phenomenon, which practically shut down the fishing industry and severely reduced agricultural output.[7] It is estimated that the cost of El Niño (including preventive measures and reconstruction) was close to 1 percent of GDP. As a result of these external and supply shocks, real GDP contracted by about half a percent in 1998.

The Russian crisis of 1998 highlighted financial dollarization as the main vulnerability of the Peruvian economy. As a result of the crisis, the domestic currency depreciated 13 percent in real terms, the balance sheet of nonbanking firms weakened and induced an increase of nonperforming loans in foreign currency from 5 to 10 percent, credit in foreign currency declined (with an annual decrease of –4 percent), and the number of banks declined from 26 to 14.

## DEEPENING REFORMS (1999–2007)

The period from 1999–2007 is associated with a transitory slowdown in growth, a swing in the fiscal accounts (deteriorating at the beginning and strengthening at the end), improvements in external conditions, and a widespread deepening of reforms (Table 2.6).[8] The economy grew on average at an annual rate of 4½ percent (compared to 5½ percent during the previous five years), while inflation was finally brought down to levels similar to those in advanced economies, averaging 2½ percent (compared to an average of almost 15 percent during the previous five years). The NFPS balance switched from a deficit of 3¼ percent of GDP in 1999 to a surplus of 3 percent in 2007. To put these developments in perspective, the swing in the fiscal accounts during this eight-year period is similar to the massive adjustment undertaken during the great stabilization of 1990–92, with the difference being that this improvement in the fiscal accounts was facilitated by a massive improvement in the terms of trade, which increased

of distributing the payments). Elliott Associates argued that the payment of interest to Brady bondholders violated a clause in its loan agreement that provided that the loan ranked equally with all other external debt (the *pari passu* clause). Facing this difficult trade-off, Peru decided to settle with Elliott Associates in order to avoid default on the Brady bond interest payments (IMF 2001). Argentina faced a similar situation in mid-2014 and took a different approach.

[7] El Niño is a weather disturbance that occurs every six or seven years and consists of rising ocean temperatures off the Pacific coast, which deprives the supply of plankton, resulting in lower availability of fish. Warmer temperatures also bring heavy rainfall and mudslides in the Andean and coastal regions, affecting agriculture and disrupting transportation. El Niño also affects the manufacturing sector involved in the processing of primary products.

[8] During the 1999–2007 period, Peru had one EFF and four Stand-By Arrangements (SBA) with the IMF, all of them precautionary (i.e., no money was used). The EFF was for SDR 383 million and covered the period 1999–2001. The first SBA was for SDR 128 million and covered 2001–02; the second was for SDR 255 million and covered 2002–04; the third was for SDR 287 million and covered 2004–06; and the fourth was for SDR 172 million and went beyond this period, covering 2007–09. The first SBA was requested by the Peruvian authorities during the interim government of President Valentin Paniagua to demonstrate continuity, despite the political turbulence associated with the resignation of President Alberto Fujimori.

TABLE 2.6

Peru: Economic Indicators, 1999–2007 (*Percent*)

| | Average 1993–98 | 1999 | 2003 | 2007 | Average 1999–2007 |
|---|---|---|---|---|---|
| | | | (Annual Percentage Change) | | |
| Real GDP | 5.6 | 1.5 | 4.2 | 8.5 | 4.6 |
| Inflation (end of period) | 14.9 | 3.7 | 2.5 | 3.9 | 2.4 |
| Interest Rate | 11.1 | 11.8 | 3.1 | 3.2 | 5.2 |
| Base Money | 25.4 | 17.0 | 10.1 | 28.2 | 15.5 |
| Private Credit | 46.8 | 6.7 | –4.5 | 33.3 | 5.0 |
| Real Exchange Rate (average)[1] | 0.2 | –8.3 | –2.6 | –0.8 | –1.6 |
| Terms of Trade (deterioration –) | 0.4 | –6.6 | 1.6 | 4.3 | 5.3 |
| | | | (Percent of GDP) | | |
| Output Gap[2] | 0.7 | –0.6 | –0.7 | 0.8 | –0.6 |
| Domestic Investment | 20.8 | 19.3 | 17.9 | 22.3 | 18.3 |
| National Savings | 14.0 | 16.4 | 16.4 | 23.8 | 17.7 |
| External Current Account | –6.9 | –2.8 | –1.6 | 1.5 | –0.6 |
| Gross International Reserves | 16.4 | 18.3 | 17.3 | 27.1 | 19.1 |
| Fiscal Balance[3] | –1.9 | –3.4 | –1.7 | 3.1 | –1.1 |
| Public Debt[3] | 54.9 | 51.1 | 48.7 | 29.9 | 43.7 |

Sources: Peruvian authorities; and IMF staff estimates.
[1]Effective, (–) = real depreciation.
[2]Percent of potential.
[3]Nonfinancial public sector.

metal-related taxation. The terms of trade improved a staggering 70 percent in this period as copper prices soared.

On the structural side, the 1999–2007 period is marked by two landmarks in macroeconomic management: (1) the introduction of fiscal rules (Ministry of the Economy and Finance, various years), and (2) the formal implementation of an inflation-targeting scheme. Both frameworks were very successful in containing fiscal imbalances, reducing public debt, and bringing inflation down to the lowest level in Latin America. In addition, Peru returned to international capital markets after an absence of almost three-quarters of a century.

The Fiscal Responsibility and Transparency Law, approved by Congress in December 1999, was perhaps the most important piece of legislation on the fiscal side in modern Peruvian history. It ensured fiscal sustainability and a rapid recline in public debt as a ratio of GDP and encouraged fiscal savings, improving the fiscal position and creating large fiscal space and buffers. The law set prudential fiscal rules, introduced a Fiscal Stabilization Fund (FSF), and promoted fiscal transparency. The rules were simple: (1) a deficit of the NFPS (excluding municipalities) was not to exceed 2 percent in 2000, 1½ percent in 2001, and 1 percent thereafter; (2) the growth of noninterest expenditures of the general government in real terms was capped at 2 percent per year; and (3) in an election year, noninterest expenditures in the first seven months of the year were not to exceed 60 percent of the annual budget and the deficit could not exceed 50 percent in the first six months. The rule could be suspended if a national emergency was declared.

The FSF was designed to smooth budgetary revenue over the business cycle. When current revenue as a percent of GDP exceeded the previous three-year average by more than 0.3 percent of GDP, the excess (over 0.3 percent of GDP) was to be saved in the FSF. Savings in the FSF were also supposed to include 75 percent of cash receipts from privatizations and 50 percent from concession projects. Initially, balances in the FSF were not supposed to exceed 3 percent of GDP.

Transparency was enhanced by requiring budget discussions to be based on a rolling three-year macroeconomic framework, including targets for the main fiscal aggregates (revenue, expenditure, deficit, public debt), the long-term path of debt service, and a statement by the finance minister on the objectives and guidelines of fiscal policy for the period. The central bank was expected to comment on the macroeconomic program, with its comments published along with the program. The finance minister was expected to present semiannual performance reports to Congress and an annual statement certifying ex post compliance with the law (and explanations in cases of deviations).

The Fiscal Responsibility and Transparency Law was modified several times (2003, 2007, and 2009). The Fiscal Management Responsibility Act was introduced in 2003 with the objective of achieving debt consolidation. Under this modification, the cap on real noninterest expenditures was increased to 3 percent per year (and later to 4 percent). It also increased the limit on the NFPS deficit to 2 percent in 2003 before reverting to 1 percent by 2005. In 2007, the definition of spending changed to central government consumption. These fiscal laws were eventually substituted by the new fiscal framework introduced in 2013.

The successful disinflation of the 1990s was conducted within a framework of monetary aggregate targeting. In practice, this took the form of controlling the net domestic assets of the central bank and achieving a net international reserve target. As disinflation unfolded in the 1990s, the behavior of monetary aggregates became more volatile and this measure was deemed unsuitable for communicating the stance of monetary policy (Rossini 2001). Against this backdrop, the central bank decided to formally adopt an inflation-targeting framework in January 2002 as the basis for conducting monetary policy (see Chapter 13). This was perhaps the most important monetary measure taken in the poststabilization period to cement stability and ensure low inflation rates. In July 2002, the central bank announced a medium-term inflation target of 2½ percent with a range of ±1 percentage point around the target.[9] An important milestone was the seminar organized in Lima by the BCRP and the IMF in 2001 to assess the conditions to adopt an inflation-targeting scheme for Peru.

Comprehensive inflation reports were to be issued initially three times a year (and then four times) to explain inflation performance, the considerations that guided monetary policy in the preceding months, and the central bank's inflation forecast. This forecast was to be based on a range of indicators (including market expectation surveys), inflation forecasting models, and other relevant factors such as the exchange rate, the fiscal policy stance, and aggregate demand conditions. The central bank changed from controlling monetary aggregates to controlling interest rates to achieve the inflation objective. The operational target for monetary policy was to be the policy interest rate, and the central bank continued intervening in the foreign exchange market. The inflation target was subsequently reduced from 2½ to 2 percent in February 2007 (with the same range of ±1 percentage point).

Inflation targeting turned out to be very successful and Peru became the country with the lowest inflation rate in Latin America over the next decade. However, implementation of the regime was not without problems. This was the first case of an inflation-targeting regime in the context of relatively large financial dollarization and starting with indicators of deflationary pressures (Armas, Ize, and Levy 2006). To make the nuevo sol competitive against the U.S. dollar in the eyes of depositors, the central bank decided to implement the inflation-targeting framework with a relatively low inflation target, the lowest to date in Latin America. The decision paid off: inflation was roughly on target and financial dollarization has gradually been reduced.

From the virtual financial autarky and default of the 1980s and the normalization of relations with creditors in the 1990s, Peru moved to having access to international capital markets in the 2000s. In February 2002, Peru issued a sovereign bond for the first time since 1928 (almost 70 years before). The transaction involved issuing a fixed-coupon, 10-year, global bond for US$1.42 billion, of which US$920 million was used to buy back existing Brady bonds (issued during the 1997 debt and debt service reduction operation) with a face value of US$1.2 billion. The strategic goal of the operation was to broaden the government's sources of financing, while extending the maturity profile of the public debt. At the time, the government relied on credits from official external sources (mainly multilaterals) and privatization receipts to finance the deficit, which were not a sustainable source of

[9] Later, starting in 2007, the inflation target was reduced to 2 percent with a range of ±1 percentage point around the target in order to align it to the median of inflation targets of other central banks.

financing because most state-owned enterprises had been sold by then, and Peru was expected to graduate from official lending.

In addition, the global bond provided a useful benchmark instrument for future bondholders and Peruvian firms. Until the global issue, Brady bonds were the only traded sovereign Peruvian debt, but they were difficult to price because of the complexities of the collaterals, and thus were poor benchmarks. The market of Brady bonds was known for pricing inefficiencies (again due to the collateral); Peru took advantage of this mispricing, and the exchange reduced the stock of public debt (about US$300 million) and generated a small saving in net present value terms. The exchange also provided some hedge against future interest rate hikes and increased somewhat the duration of Peru's debt. Access to international capital markets has been uninterrupted since, with successive improvements in the country's credit rating.

The government began a decentralization process in 2002. While the government recognized the risks associated with this policy, the objective was to promote a more responsive government structure to address local concerns. A sound legal framework was built for decentralization, including a plan for the distribution of government revenue and a timetable for the transfer of expenditure responsibilities, as well as the establishment of reporting requirements and fiscal rules for subnational governments.

A constitutional amendment that mandated political and fiscal decentralization was passed in 2002. The process was promoted by the general view that decentralization would help improve governance and public service delivery through enhanced accountability at subnational levels. Decentralization also aimed to ensure broader access to basic public services and reduce high poverty rates and regional income inequalities.

A key objective was to implement the decentralization process in a fiscally neutral manner. To that end, laws were enacted to guide the sequencing and procedures for the devolution of responsibilities, transfers of resources, and reporting provisions and fiscal rules for subnational governments. Five pieces of legislation were enacted for this purpose: (1) the Framework Decentralization Law of 2002, which mandated a clear, gradual, and fiscally neutral devolution of expenditures; (2) the Organic Law for Regional Governments of 2002, which detailed regional government expenditure responsibilities; (3) the Organic Law for Municipalities of 2003, which did the same for municipal expenditures; (4) the Accreditation System Law of 2004, which established a system to assess whether regional and local governments meet standards to qualify for the transfers; and (5) the Fiscal Decentralization Law of 2004, which established the sequence of transfers to regional governments and set fiscal rules and reporting provisions for subnational operations.

Other structural reforms were also deepened after 1999. Reform areas included privatization and economic concessions, sales and regulation of agricultural land, and efficiency of social protection programs. Reforms initially focused on ensuring a sustainable fiscal situation and more efficient provision of public services.

The authorities also announced plans during this period for comprehensive tax reform. The reform aimed at widening the tax base of the income and value-added taxes through the elimination of regional and sectoral exemptions, a rationalization of excise taxes, and improvements in tax administration. The tax reform was implemented in various stages, and by end-2003 the authorities had made progress in several areas. However, many sectoral and regional exemptions remained and a small tax on financial transactions was introduced.

Further efforts were also made to improve the finances of the pension system. These efforts concentrated on reducing the government subsidy in the preferential public pension plan, which the government subsidized at more than 90 percent. Contribution rates were raised substantially, pensions above a certain threshold became subject to income taxes, and future pensions were capped. This put pension benefits for contributors on an actuarial sound basis and generated some savings in net present value terms. However, a large gap remained for the preferential public pension plan.

## GLOBAL FINANCIAL CRISIS (2008–09)

Nothing on the horizon suggested that Peru's economy was about to endure the sharpest economic deceleration in the poststabilization period. Although there were signs of trouble in the world economy (especially in the United States), almost no one was predicting the worst global financial crisis since the Great Depression of the 1930s. In 2008, Peru was booming and the economy was growing by midyear beyond capacity at close to 11 percent. There were signs of overheating, with inflation running at almost 6 percent (partly due to higher food and fuel prices, and clearly above the inflation range), although the fiscal surplus was one of the highest in recorded history, reflecting high natural resource–related taxation and a strong economy, with public debt on a continuing downward path. Giving an even greater sense of security, Fitch and Standard & Poor's granted Peru investment grade in the first half of 2008 (the third country in the region to get such a grading after Chile and Mexico).[10]

However, the world changed in September 2008 with the collapse of the U.S. investment bank Lehman Brothers and the onset of the global financial crisis. Peruvian sovereign spreads immediately tripled to over 600 basis points, although they eased back to close to more normal levels by end-2009, while equity prices were still 60 percent lower than at end-2007. Following large foreign exchange purchases earlier in the year, the central bank intervened in the aftermath of the Lehman crisis by selling foreign exchange to limit market volatility and contain pressures on the nuevo sol, which had depreciated by about 6 percent against the U.S. dollar.

Fortunately, there was limited financial contagion from the global financial crisis thanks to a quick policy response. Fearing a credit crunch similar to that in the United States, and facing tight liquidity, reduced capital inflows, and a steepening of the government yield curve, the BCRP eased reserve requirements and placed repos and swaps in nuevos soles and U.S. dollars to provide additional liquidity. At the same time, the central bank signaled its intention to repurchase government fixed-income securities in the secondary market. Banks remained resilient, and a credit crunch was avoided, as the interbank market continued operating normally and credit channels were preserved. Large official reserves, which stood at $31 billion at end-2008, along with banks' limited reliance on external funding, helped to maintain stable liquidity conditions. However, dollarization rebounded (after declining markedly over the previous two years), reflecting concerns about the global financial crisis.

The authorities entered 2009 with the concern that a sharp and sudden deceleration in domestic private demand—which could be precipitated by a sharp fall in commodity prices, declining domestic confidence, or potential disruptions in the financial system—could compromise the "soft landing" they were trying to achieve following exceptionally high growth in 2008 and emerging signs of overheating. As a result of the continuing global financial crisis, Peru's growth declined substantially in 2009, with a few months in negative territory. The downturn was primarily linked to the collapse in global trade and uncertainty about global growth, temporarily amplified by a large inventory correction in Peru (Table 2.7).

The signs of a weak economy were evident. Inflation fell to near zero in the second half of 2009 (partly due to a decline in food and fuel prices). The external current account shifted from a deficit to a small surplus as the decline in exports was more than offset by the slowdown in import growth. Private investment fell by 30 percent in real terms but consumption proved more resilient thanks to sustained employment.

A timely policy response involving monetary easing and fiscal stimulus prevented a further deterioration of economic activity in 2009. In terms of monetary easing, the BCRP acted proactively to reduce the policy rate by 525 basis points in early 2009 to a historic low of 1¼ percent. Lending rates to the private sector also declined in line with the policy rate, fostering private investment. To provide a fiscal impulse, the authorities announced an anticrisis plan to shield the economy from

[10] By then, Peru had a precautionary SBA with the IMF for SDR 172 million covering the period 2007–09.

**TABLE 2.7**

**Peru: Economic Indicators, 2008–09 (*Percent*)**

| | Average 1999–2007 | 2008 | 2009 | Average 2008–09 |
|---|---|---|---|---|
| | (Annual Percentage Change) | | | |
| Real GDP | 4.6 | 9.1 | 1.0 | 5.1 |
| Inflation (end of period) | 2.4 | 6.7 | 0.2 | 3.4 |
| Policy Rate | 3.5 | 5.9 | 3.3 | 4.6 |
| Private Credit | 5.0 | 33.8 | 1.3 | 17.6 |
| Real Exchange Rate (average)[1] | –1.6 | 4.1 | 2.3 | 3.2 |
| Terms of Trade (deterioration –) | 5.3 | –10.9 | –2.4 | –6.8 |
| | (Percent of GDP) | | | |
| Output Gap[2] | –0.6 | 3.0 | –2.1 | 0.5 |
| Domestic Investment | 18.3 | 27.5 | 20.9 | 24.2 |
| National Savings | 17.7 | 23.1 | 20.4 | 21.7 |
| External Current Account | –0.6 | –4.3 | –0.5 | –2.4 |
| Gross International Reserves | 19.1 | 25.6 | 27.3 | 26.4 |
| Fiscal Balance[3] | –1.1 | 2.5 | –1.4 | 0.6 |
| Public Debt[3] | 43.7 | 26.9 | 27.2 | 27.0 |

Sources: Peruvian authorities; and IMF staff estimates.
[1]Effective, (–) = real depreciation.
[2]Percent of potential.
[3]Nonfinancial public sector.

the global crisis and improve investor confidence. The fiscal stimulus was largely financed with fiscal savings. It entailed a positive fiscal impulse of about 2½ percent of GDP in 2009 concentrated on higher public investment (1¼ percent of GDP) and support to the construction sector (¾ percent of GDP). This translated into an increase in real general government primary spending of 14 percent. The fiscal plan also included contingency measures, including guarantees (which in the end were not used) to support corporations, exporters, and smaller financial institutions.

The situation with the capital account normalized rapidly. A quick recovery of net foreign direct investment (FDI) flows and strong public sector flows compensated for portfolio outflows, partly driven by domestic pension funds. The public sector took advantage of improving global market conditions during 2009 and issued debt (US$2 billion) to prefinance operations and fully repay Paris Club debt. The nuevo sol recovered its pre-Lehman level against the U.S. dollar by end-2009, and started to appreciate in nominal and real effective terms. Appreciation pressures were associated with portfolio reallocation of domestic agents, including pension funds, and some foreign portfolio inflows. These pressures were intermittent, with temporary respites during episodes of heightened global volatility linked to sovereign risk developments in other regions prompting significant purchases by the central bank. As conditions stabilized, the central bank began to reverse some of the unconventional measures. After the second quarter of 2009, the central bank reduced the stock of foreign exchange swaps, repo operations, and foreign-exchanged indexed certificates of deposit.

Although Peru's economy contracted briefly during two quarters in 2009, growth resumed rapidly thanks to a skillful countercyclical policy response. All things considered, Peru came through this relatively large external shock relatively unscathed. The moral of the story is that it pays to have large buffers and significant policy space to react to unexpected shocks. When external credit markets were in distress, Peru had the resources and the macroeconomic room to implement a timely fiscal impulse and to loosen monetary policy.

## POSTCRISIS PERIOD (2010–14)

The effectiveness of the countercyclical response and the rapid economic recovery soon turned the policy debate from macroeconomic impulses to the optimal speed of stimulus withdrawal. Real GDP grew on average by 6¾ percent in the period 2010–13 (closing the negative output gap of

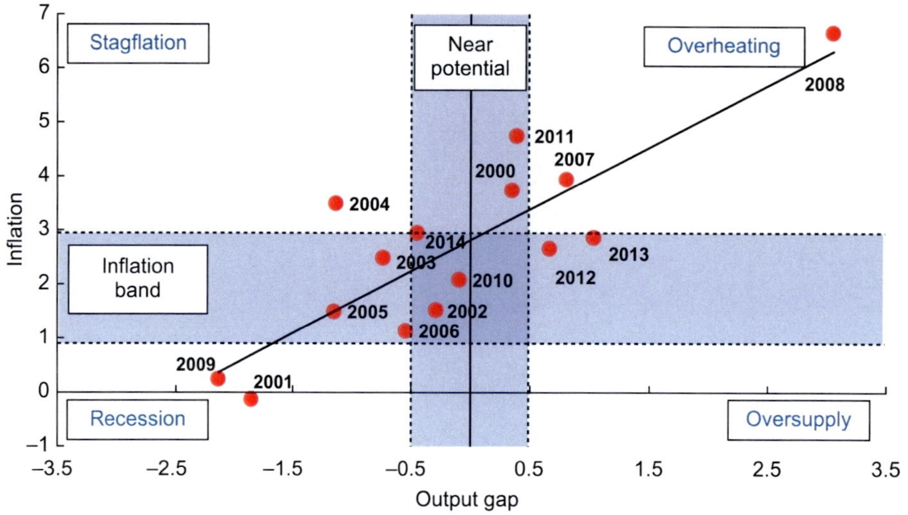


Source: IMF staff estimates.

**Figure 2.3** Peru: Inflation and Output Gap (*Percent*)

**TABLE 2.8**

Peru: Economic Indicators, 2010–14 (*Percent*)

| | Average 2008–09 | 2010 | 2012 | 2014 | Average 2010–14 |
|---|---|---|---|---|---|
| | | | (Annual Percentage Change) | | |
| Real GDP | 5.1 | 8.5 | 6.0 | 2.4 | 5.8 |
| Inflation (end of period) | 3.4 | 2.1 | 2.6 | 3.2 | 3.1 |
| Policy Rate | 4.6 | 2.1 | 4.3 | 3.8 | 3.7 |
| Private Credit | 17.6 | 14.3 | 12.4 | 13.4 | 16.3 |
| Real Exchange Rate (average)[1] | 3.2 | 2.5 | 7.8 | −2.0 | 1.2 |
| Terms of Trade (deterioration –) | −6.8 | 21.0 | −2.1 | −5.8 | 2.7 |
| | | | (Percent of GDP) | | |
| Output Gap[2] | 0.5 | −0.1 | 0.7 | −2.0 | 0.0 |
| Domestic Investment | 24.2 | 25.2 | 26.7 | 27.3 | 26.6 |
| National Savings | 21.7 | 22.8 | 23.5 | 22.3 | 23.2 |
| External Current Account | −2.4 | −2.4 | −3.3 | −5.2 | −3.4 |
| Gross International Reserves | 26.4 | 29.7 | 33.2 | 30.7 | 30.9 |
| Fiscal Balance[3] | 0.6 | −0.2 | 2.3 | −0.1 | 1.0 |
| Public Debt[3] | 27.0 | 24.3 | 20.4 | 19.7 | 21.2 |

Sources: Peruvian authorities; and IMF staff estimates.
[1]Effective, (–) = real depreciation.
[2]Percent of potential.
[3]Nonfinancial public sector.

2009), while core inflation—excluding food and fuel prices—remained under control (although headline inflation was temporarily outside the inflation range in 2011 and 2014 due to supply shocks) (Figure 2.3). However, the economy decelerated in 2014 as external conditions deteriorated, exports declined, and confidence eroded, leading to a contraction in private investment.

The signs of a recovery were clear by mid-2010 (Table 2.8). The economy was growing at almost 10 percent, driven by private domestic demand. For the year as a whole, real GDP expanded by 8½ percent. The inflation rate picked up to 2 percent (from almost zero the year before), whereas the current account deficit widened to some 2½ percent of GDP (from half a

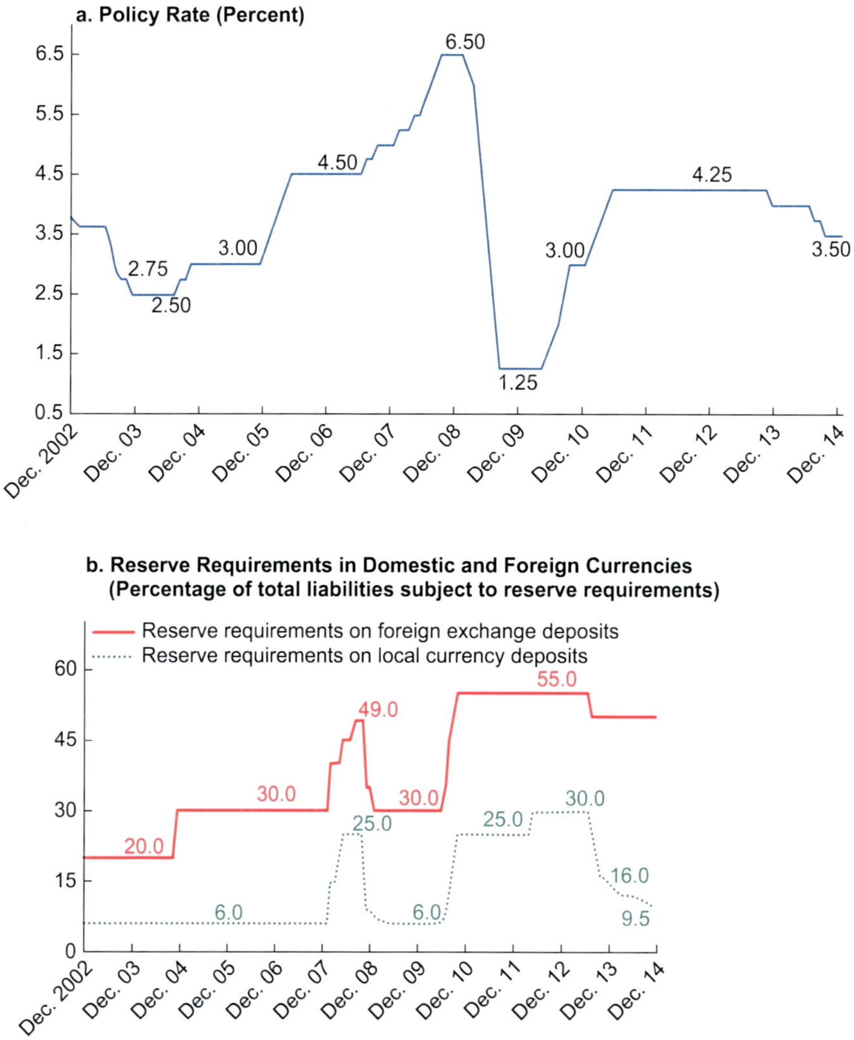


Source: IMF staff calculations.

**Figure 2.4** Peru: Policy Rate and Reserve Requirement

percent the year before). To prevent overheating risks, the authorities began the tightening cycle in 2010–11:

- *Monetary tightening.* The central bank was quick in tightening its stance; the policy rate was raised by 175 basis points in the second half of 2010 to 3 percent by year end (Figure 2.4a). The rate was further increased by 125 basis points in the first half of 2011 to 4¼ percent. Monetary policy was also tightened with restoration of a reserve requirement of 35 percent on short-term (less than two years) foreign credit lines (Figure 2.4b). Credit growth stayed at about 16 percent.

- *Fiscal consolidation.* The overall fiscal deficit fell from 1⅓ percent of GDP in 2009 to one-third of a percent in 2010, although its impact on demand was limited because real spending continued growing above potential and better terms of trade generated higher revenues. By 2011, the fiscal position strengthened further to a surplus of almost 2 percent of GDP as a result in part of expenditure restrictions imposed by the political process (presidential elections in April–June 2011) and the limited implementation of investment projects by the incoming administration in August 2011.

Subsequently, policies were geared toward modulating the business cycle while supporting growth. As policies were tightened after the stimulus, economic growth moderated. Real GDP grew 6½ percent in 2011 and about 6 percent in 2012–13.[11] The effective macroeconomic management of the global financial crisis and the proper withdrawal of the stimulus created a problem of its own, however, as Peru became an attractive destination for FDI and a magnet for capital inflows. By 2012, the financial account of the balance of payments recorded a surplus of over 10 percent of GDP (the largest in recorded history) and nonresident holdings of domestically issued public debt increased to over half of the total stock. In order to deter external financing, in May 2012 the authorities extended the 60 percent reserve requirement on foreign liabilities to those with maturity up to three years (from two years) and imposed a 20 percent reserve requirement on foreign liabilities with a maturity longer than three years.

Fearful that the inflows could be temporarily reverted, the central bank pursued a policy of foreign exchange intervention/sterilization while allowing some exchange rate flexibility as dictated by economic fundamentals. In the end, the central bank purchased about 6½ percent of GDP in foreign exchange in 2012 to prevent unsustainable credit expansion and undue appreciation of the currency while allowing the nuevo sol to strengthen by 8½ percent in real effective terms, according to the BCRP Annual Report. Foreign exchange intervention prevented large currency fluctuations, and indeed the nuevo sol remained the most stable currency among the financially integrated economies of Latin America (i.e., Brazil, Chile, Colombia, Mexico, Peru, Uruguay). International reserves reached over 30 percent of GDP in 2012.

To prevent a large monetary injection, the foreign exchange purchases had to be sterilized. The central bank controlled the liquidity generated by these purchases by placing its own securities with domestic financial institutions and relying heavily on reserve requirements policy in nuevos soles (increasing them by some 225 basis points) to supplement the sterilization efforts. It is estimated that these operations sterilized about 70 percent of the liquidity generated by the intervention. The remaining amount was absorbed by the fiscal surplus and the increase in the demand for money.

Fiscal policy played a key role in supporting monetary policy. The fiscal surplus increased from 2 percent of GDP in 2011 to 2⅓ percent of GDP in 2012. However, the fiscal effort was greater than suggested by the overall fiscal balance, as it is estimated that the structural fiscal position was strengthened by 1 percent of GDP in 2012. In any case, the higher fiscal surplus acted as a form of fiscal sterilization, as the public sector significantly increased its deposits at the central bank.

Despite a widening current account deficit, external stability risks were contained. The current account deficit widened from 2 percent of GDP in 2011 to about 3⅓ percent in 2012, mostly due to a deteriorating terms of trade, weak volume growth in mineral exports, and strong growth in import volume. It was more than financed by strong FDI flows.

The capital inflow problem came to an abrupt end following the announcement by the U.S. Federal Reserve in May 2013 of a potential "tapering" of its unconventional monetary policy. The news created confusion and uncertainty in the markets, and the magnitude of capital inflows declined significantly. The surplus of the financial account of the balance of payments dropped from over 10 percent of GDP in 2012 to about 5½ percent in 2013. The nuevo sol was under pressure and depreciated about 8½ percent against the U.S. dollar. For the first time in a long while, the BCRP intervened by selling foreign exchange.

[11] GDP data were revised and calculated under a new base (2007). The data were released in 2014. Under the old base (1994), real GDP growth declined to about 5 percent in 2013.

The external position deteriorated in 2013 mostly due to weak export performance and higher interest rates abroad, leading to a current account deficit of 4½ percent of GDP. However, the current account deficit continued to be easily financed despite lower private capital inflows. While demand for external financing fell following the U.S. announcement in May 2013, international bond issuance by Peruvian firms already had reached historic highs above US$6.5 billion in 2013.

Under the old GDP statistics (base year 1994), there were some signs of a slowing in the economy in the second half of 2013. The concern was strong enough for the public sector to reduce its fiscal surplus from 2⅓ percent of GDP in 2012 to merely three-quarters of a percent in 2013. Primary spending was increased to achieve social goals and cover higher wages following a civil service reform, and mining-related revenues fell due to weak metal prices. After having kept the policy rate unchanged for 2½ years, the central bank reduced its rate by a quarter of a percentage point to 4 percent in November 2013, citing slower domestic and global growth and declining inflationary expectations. Concerns over an economic slowdown turned out to be unfounded, however. The revised GDP statistics showed robust growth in the second half of 2013, with the economy growing at 5¾ percent for the year as a whole.

Important reforms were also introduced in 2013. These included a far-reaching civil service reform that standardized workplace regulations and salary scales, increased training for staff, and instituted performance evaluations. A private pension system reform was directed toward generating greater public access and lower fees. The fiscal framework was revamped by Congress in October 2013 to introduce structural fiscal rules. The new framework aimed to (1) introduce a countercyclical component to budget formulation, (2) strengthen accountability by establishing a fiscal council, and (3) better delineate the relationship and fiscal practices between the national and subnational governments. The law became binding for the 2015 budget.

In the first half of 2014, Peru's economy experienced its sharpest deceleration since the global financial crisis of 2008–09. Real GDP grew 2.5 percent in 2014. Key factors in the deceleration were lower exports and lower private investment given uncertainties about external conditions in a world economy with mediocre growth. Current and capital outlays by regional governments were also down, reflecting lower natural resource income and regional corruption scandals. Supply factors related to extraction problems in a few large mines, and a crackdown on illegal gold mining, also contributed to the poor economic performance.

This generated a quick policy response. The central bank relaxed monetary conditions by reducing reserve requirements and reducing its policy rate by a quarter of a point in July and then by another quarter point in August 2014 to 3½ percent. In June–July, the government announced a number of measures, amounting to some 1 percent of GDP, to support aggregate demand and increase potential output. The measures involved additional capital and social spending, a write-down of unpaid interest on old tax obligations, and a one-time small wage bonus to all public employees to support private consumption.

## CONCLUSIONS

Peru's strong economic performance over the past two decades can be attributed to solid macroeconomic stabilization and strong economic fundamentals. These achievements were consolidated during the great stabilization of the early 1990s and the period of continuous structural reforms in the late 1990s and early 2000s. A quick look at the output gap over the past three decades shows that the business cycle was tamed and Peru achieved its aim of high growth and low inflation after the great stabilization of 1990–92 (Figure 2.5).

While the magnitude of the adjustment achieved during the great stabilization period of the early 1990s was large, the actual size of the primary fiscal balance consistent with stabilization and growth was not that large. The primary balance adjusted by some 6 percent of

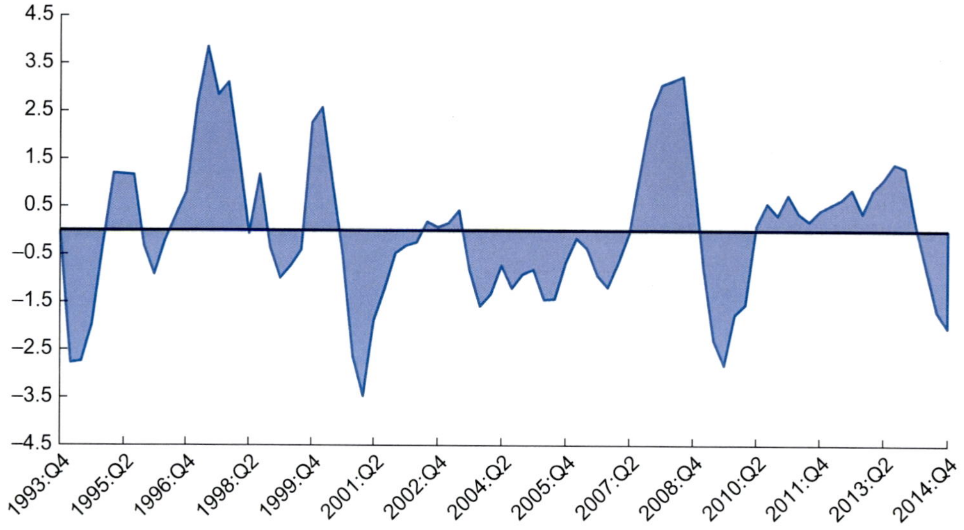


Source: Central Reserve Bank of Peru.
Note: Estimated using the Hodrick-Prescott filter.

**Figure 2.5** Peru: Output Gap (*Percent of potential output*)

GDP when it moved from a deficit of about 4 percent of GDP in 1989 to a surplus of about 2 percent of GDP in 1991, which is an average adjustment of 3 percent per year. However, the average level of the primary balance for the rest of the 1990s and the 2000s was close to 1½ percent of GDP, which in itself is not a particularly large surplus, but was enough to secure long-lasting stabilization.

The importance of effective macroeconomic management can never be overemphasized. The volatile stagnation of the period from 1975–90 was a major setback for Peru's economic aspirations. With the experience of the economy having grown at about 5½ from 1950–75, and at 5¼ percent from 1993–2014, the question is, what would be the level of per capita income today if the volatile stagnation of 1975–90 had never taken place? The answer is that Peru's economy would be more than 2½ times bigger than it is today (assuming the economy had grown at the constant rate of 5½ percent since 1975). This translates into income per capita (in purchasing power terms) of about US$32,000, which is similar to the level of income per capita of Italy, Spain, Korea, or New Zealand.

Although macroeconomic performance over the past two decades has been stellar and prospects look very good, much remains to be done in Peru. Using the United States as a comparative benchmark, income per capita in Peru declined from almost 30 percent in the mid-1970s to 14 percent in the early 1990s, and it is currently at about 22 percent (Figure 2.6). In the mid-1970s, Peru had a level of income per capita similar to the average of the region. But today it has fallen behind: its income level per capita is similar only to that of Colombia and is 20 percent lower than that of Brazil, 30 percent lower than Mexico, 40 percent lower than Uruguay, and 50 percent lower than Chile. Achieving the level of income of resource-rich advanced economies like Australia or Canada would require that Peru grow at a sustained rate of 5½ percent for a quarter of a century.

The lesson, then, is simple and clear. To achieve a more advanced stage of development, Peru needs to preserve macroeconomic stability and deepen its structural reforms to secure and sustain high levels of growth in the years ahead.

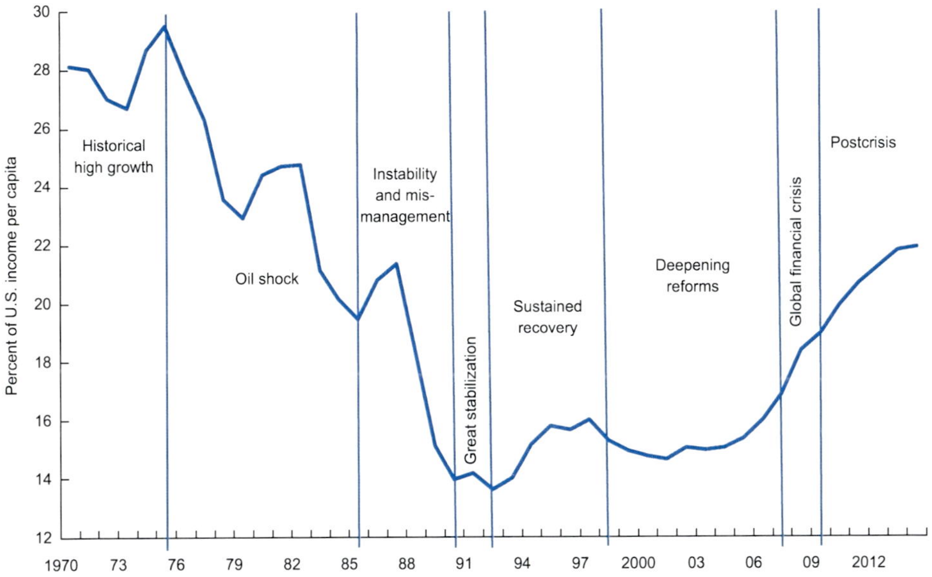


Source: IMF, World Economic Outlook Database.

**Figure 2.6** Peru: Income per Capita (*Percent of U.S. income per capita*)

## REFERENCES

Armas, A., A. Ize, and E. Levy. 2006. *Financial Dollarization: The Policy Agenda.* Washington: International Monetary Fund.

Boughton, James. 2012. *Tearing Down Walls: The International Monetary Fund 1990-1999.* Washington: International Monetary Fund. https://www.imf.org/external/pubs/ft/history/2012/

International Monetary Fund. 2001. Involving the Private Sector in the Resolution of Financial Crisis. Paper prepared by the Policy Development and Review and Legal Departments. January 11.

Ministry of the Economy and Finance. Various years. *Marco Macroeconómico Multianual.* Lima.

———. 2003. *Deuda Pública 1970-2002: Experiencia Histórica y Perspectiva.* Lima.

Pastor, Gonzalo. 2012. *Perú: Políticas Monetarias y Cambiaria, 1930-1980.* Lima: Central Bank of Peru.

Polastri, Rossana. 2007. Macroeconomic Framework for Sustainable Growth. In *An Opportunity for a Different Peru,* edited by Marcelo Giugale, et al. Washington: World Bank.

Rossini, Renzo. 2001. Aspectos de la adopción de un régimen de metas de inflación en el Perú. Economic Study No. 7, Central Bank of Peru.

Velarde, Julio, and Martha Rodriguez. 1992a. *De la Desinflación a la Hiperinflación en Perú: 1985-90.* Lima: Universidad del Pacifico.

———. 1992b. *El Programa Económico de Agosto de 1990; Evaluación del Primer Año.* Lima: Universidad del Pacifico.

———. 1994. *El Programa de Estabilización Peruano; Evaluación del Periodo 1991-1993.* Lima: Universidad del Pacifico.

World Bank. 2015. *Poverty Headcount Ratio.* Washington, DC: World Bank Development Research Group Databank.

PART II

# The Successful Economic Story of Peru

# CHAPTER 3

# Explaining the Peruvian Growth Miracle

KEVIN ROSS AND JUAN ALONSO PESCHIERA

*Peru had one of the best growth records in Latin America from 1993 to 2013. On a per capita basis, growth averaged about 4 percent a year during the period, well above the Latin American average of 1¾ percent. This exemplary result came on the heels of a "lost decade and half" (1975–92), during which GDP per capita actually fell. Thus, after credible stabilization policies took hold, a natural rebound or cyclical convergence may explain part of the economy's expansion. However, a bigger reason for Peru's growth was the implementation of structural reforms that improved economic efficiency and productivity. These improvements allowed Peru to fully take advantage of the favorable external financing conditions and positive terms-of-trade shocks of the last decade.*

The aim of this chapter is to better understand the main forces behind Peru's strong growth performance. The chapter first presents some stylized facts about Peruvian growth dynamics in a historical context, and then highlights developments in structural reforms and terms-of-trade gains. The chapter then examines the sources of growth through a simple growth accounting exercise and compares Peru with other countries in the region. Finally, a vector error correction model is used to ascertain which variables have best determined long-term GDP per capita growth.

The results indicate that an increase in total factor productivity (TFP) accounted for most of the uptick in Peru's pace of growth. After declining in the 1980s and part of the 1990s, TFP growth reached annual average rates of about 2½ percent—one of the highest levels in the region. While part of this could be attributed to cyclical forces, given the residual nature of TFP, it coincides with a marked acceleration in structural reforms. Labor and capital accumulation, reflecting higher formal employment and favorable external financial conditions and investment, also played important roles.

Decomposition of the growth of the GDP and gross domestic income (GDI) demonstrates the importance of accounting for the income impact of terms-of-trade shocks. Overall, these added income effects spill over to the rest of the economy as higher expenditures, and imply that the economy was doing much better than the recorded real GDP growth figures. Also, these effects turn negative when the terms of trade reverse. Finally, long-run cointegration equations confirm the view that macroeconomic stabilization, strong external conditions, and structural reforms determine long-run per capita GDP. These results are broadly in line with the literature on growth in Latin America.

## STYLIZED FACTS

Prior to 1975, output per capita in Peru followed a relatively steady upward trend.[1] However, in the late 1960s, state intervention in the economy was expanded through greater use of import substitution and the nationalization of key natural resource sectors. Increased public spending and continued access to external finance resulted in an unsustainable buildup of external debt, and much slower growth by the mid-1970s.

[1] Real GDP per capita grew by about 2.7 percent from 1900–75 (Maddison Project 2013).

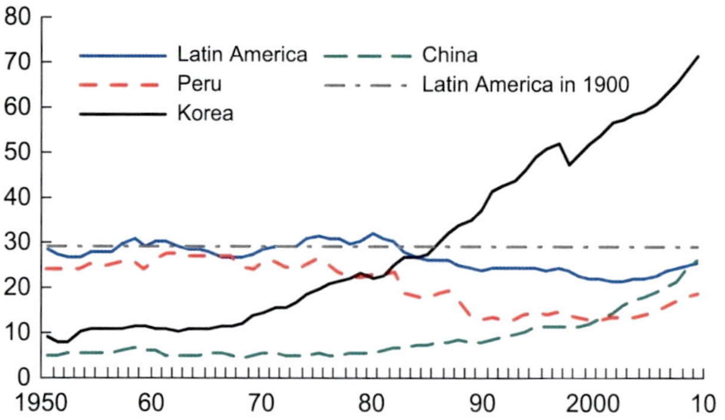


Sources: Maddison Project (2013).

**Figure 3.1** GDP per Capita Relative to that in the United States, 1950–2010

In the 1980s, the economy suffered through boom-bust cycles, hyperinflation, and negative growth (Figure 3.1). Persistent negative terms-of-trade shocks, policy missteps, and a sharp fall-off in exports led to two major output collapses, one at the beginning and the other at the end of the decade. At the same time, annual inflation averaged over 1,000 percent from 1980–91 as stabilization policies failed, price and quantity controls were installed, and tariffs rose. As a result, average real GDP per capita growth actually contracted by 1¾ percent in Peru during 1980–92, while it was basically flat in the rest of Latin America.

Since the early 1990s, however, Peru's GDP per capita growth has surpassed global and regional averages. A new growth dynamic was initiated at the start of the decade through implementation of deep-seated structural reforms, the opening of the economy to trade and investment, and the installation of well-designed stabilization policies. Growth rebounded over 1993–97 as the fall in the terms of trade abated, but was derailed by spillover effects from regional currency crises at the end of the decade. With sound macro and investment frameworks fully in place, the country was well positioned to take advantage of the commodity boom that began around 2003. Average real GDP per capita growth was 2 percent from 1992–2003 and then accelerated to 5¼ percent on average during 2004–13. However, as seen in Figure 3.1, it took over 30 years for GDP per capita to return to its 1975 level.

From the demand side, consumption and investment have been the main contributors to growth, especially after the onset of the commodity price boom in the early 2000s. Of the 6.4 percent average GDP growth rate from 2004–13, consumption and investment contributed 4.4 percentage points and 3 percentage points, respectively. Reflecting a strong surge in imports, the contribution of net exports was approximately –1 percent. From a structural perspective, the supply side of the economy also became much more reliant on services and construction.

Strong growth outcomes have led to a significant reduction in poverty and a burgeoning middle class in Peru. After remaining stubbornly high during the economic crisis of the late 1980s and early 1990s, poverty and inequality metrics started to improve around 2004–05. The poverty rate declined by more than half from around 59 percent in 2004 to 24 percent in 2013. This means that some 9 million people (about a third of the population) moved into an expanding middle class over those 10 years. Similarly, the extreme poverty rate fell to under 5 percent in 2013 from 25 percent in 2002. The distribution of growth also improved, with Peru's Gini coefficient declining from 54 in 2002 to 45 in 2013. Nevertheless, the data continue to show a sharp distinction between urban and rural areas. The poverty rate is over 53 percent in rural areas and only around 15 percent in urban settings.

It is interesting to note that prior to the commodity price surge, many observers lamented Peru's slow advances in growth and employment and limited reduction in poverty. Carranza,

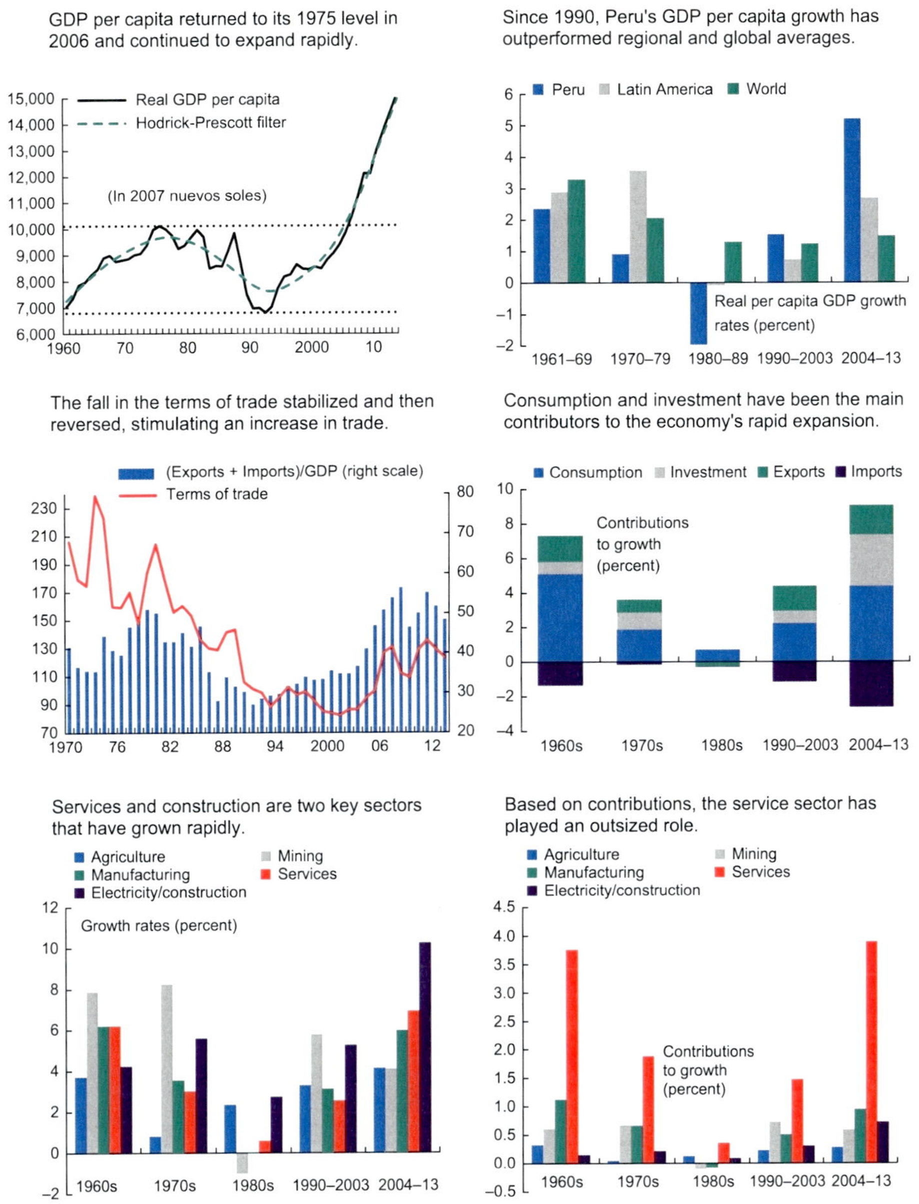


Sources: Central Reserve Bank of Peru; Peru National Statistics Institute; and IMF staff calculations.

**Figure 3.2** Economic Growth in Peru

Fernandez-Baca, and Morón (2005) found that deterioration in democratic institutions in the 1990s offset the positive growth effects of the strong fiscal and monetary frameworks and policies that were being implemented. Hausmann and Klinger (2008) stressed that a lack of export diversification was a key factor that constrained growth. Polastri (2007) counseled against populist demand stimulus measures and argued that determined structural reforms would gradually bear fruit, whereas Loayza, Fajnzylber, and Calderón (2005) argued that the 2½ to 3 percentage points added to growth by structural reforms and stabilization programs of the 1990s were less than initially expected.

Convergence toward industrial-country GDP per capita levels has remained slow (Figure 3.2). Based on 1990 international dollar Gheary-Khamis purchasing power parity units, Peru and the rest of Latin American hovered at around 30 percent of U.S. levels until the 1980s debt crisis, at which time the gap widened. While some closing of the gap took place in the most recent decade, there is a substantial amount of convergence space available.

## STRUCTURAL REFORMS

Peru has made great strides in implementing structural reforms over the last 25 years. These include policy measures that have improved the efficient allocation of resources and generally resulted in a more open and competitive economy. The reforms have improved the functioning of the economy, and they set the stage for the country's investment boom since the early 2000s.

Quantifying these structural improvements is generally difficult. Lora (2012), however, has constructed a Structural Reform Index (SRI) that measures improvements in trade, financial, tax, privatization, and labor policies. The total structural reform index (standardized from 0 to 1) is a simple average of subindices in these five policy areas (Figure 3.3). Lora's SRI ends in 2010, so we have extended the SRI forward for 2011–13 using similar subindices from the World Economic Forum's Global Competitiveness Index database. The database has also been extended backward from 1985 to 1970 using data from Morley, Machado, and Pettinato (1999).

In general, the SRI does a good job of approximating overall trends in economic liberalization. Between the mid-1980s and late 1990s there was a significant improvement in structural policies in Latin America, motivated in part by the desire to move away from state intervention and domestic market protectionism. However, first-generation reform efforts diminished after the Asian and Russian crises in the late 1990s, reflecting a lack of second-generation reforms.

Overall, the index reveals that, by far, Chile has been the regional leader in structural market policy reforms. Still, it is interesting to note that Peru, which had been at the bottom of the relative ranking in the mid-1980s, is now also a regional leader, ahead of Brazil, Argentina, Colombia, and Mexico. It has cut in half its original gap with Chile (from 0.22 to 0.11), increasing its overall reform index from 0.28 in 1985 to 0.69 in 2009. However, over 2010–13, Peru lost momentum and stagnated at around 0.66 under the extensions to the data used in this study. This is mostly due to weaker Global Competitiveness Index evaluations of tax incentives to work and invest, and in overall labor market efficiency.

Descriptions of the five policy areas covered by the SRI and of the index as it relates to Peru are as follows (Figure 3.3):

- The *financial reform index* is a composite based on the use of reserve requirements, financial transaction taxes, interest rate liberalization, and the quality of bank supervision. In Peru, improvements in the 1990s started with interest rate liberalizations and steady gains in bank supervision. In 1998, reserve requirements were cut, but starting in 2004 they were adjusted much more frequently given their use in the central bank's monetary policy framework.
- The *trade reform index* focuses on average tariff rates. Peru made significant reductions in external tariffs in 1990, 1992, 1997, 2004, and 2008 as a result of various free trade agreements. Prior to 1990, average tariffs were about 66 percent. By 1991, average tariffs dropped to 17 percent—an 80 percent reduction—and continued to decline to about 10 percent by the mid-2000s. In 2013, average trade tariffs stood at less than 6 percent.
- The *privatizations index* is a simple average of total private sector participation in infrastructure projects as a proportion of GDP. While private sector participation in Peru started relatively late in comparison with other countries, it has quickly outpaced outcomes in Mexico, Colombia, and Brazil.
- The *labor market index* is a simple average of subindices that cover hiring and firing costs, flexibility of hiring and hourly work rules, minimum wages, and the degree of social security

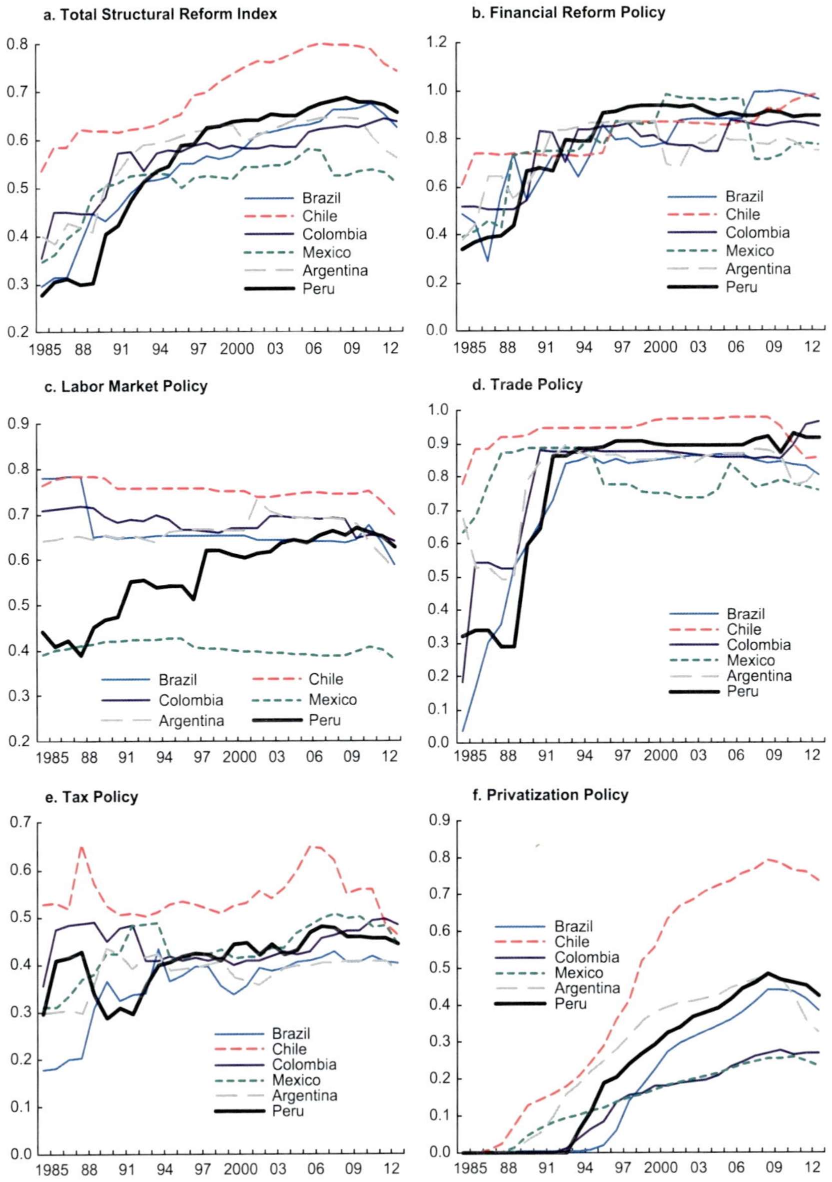


Source: Lora (2012).
Note: The 2010–13 data has been extended by IMF staff.

**Figure 3.3** Peru: Structural Reform Indices

taxation and other labor costs. Since 1988, Peru has made steady improvement in labor market structural reforms, particularly with adjustments in firing costs in 1992 and labor contracting legislation in 1998. Nevertheless, Peru's labor market policy reform index still lags Chile, Argentina, and Colombia.

- The *tax policy reform index* is comprised of four subindices that cover income and corporate tax rates and their productivity, as well as the basic value-added tax rate and its productivity. The index for Peru deteriorated in the early 1990s due mostly to low collection and has steadily improved in line with greater collection efforts. Peru now stands above Brazil, Argentina, and Colombia.

## THE IMPORTANCE OF TRADING GAINS GIVEN TERMS-OF-TRADE SHOCKS

Many authors have stressed that external factors—especially terms-of-trade shocks—play a large role in driving economic growth in commodity-exporting countries in South America.[2] For example, a protracted increase in commodity prices should raise profit margins on commodity-related projects, leading to more investment in these and related sectors like transportation, infrastructure, and services. In a similar vein, asset and collateral values would also expand, leading to further capital inflows and affecting credit dynamics. As a result, aggregate real incomes in the economy would be augmented, boosting consumption.

Kohli (2004, 2006, and 2007) has pointed out that differences between GDP and GDI growth rates can be substantial in countries that experience large terms-of-trade movements. As he notes, an improvement in the terms of trade is generally considered as enhancing income and welfare, and is similar to technical progress in that the country gets more for less. In national income accounting, however, a terms-of-trade change is treated as a price phenomenon rather than a real development. Thus, an increase in export prices or a drop in import prices will raise both the GDP deflator and nominal GDP by similar amounts, leaving real GDP basically unchanged even though real income and real value added have increased.

Kohli focused on a variety of countries and showed that trading gains and losses that result from changes in the terms of trade and in the real exchange rate (the price of tradables relative to nontradables) can drive a significant wedge between GDP and GDI. Analyzing this gap allows for fully understanding the real changes in purchasing power and income—which is critical to understanding an expenditure channel that could be driving growth in the economy and for crafting well-designed policy responses. For example, Adler and Magud (2013) focus on these income windfalls in Latin America and their impact on investment and savings behavior.

Following Kohli (2006), let $V_{Y,t}$ be the growth factor of nominal GDP;[3] $P_{N,t}$ be the growth factor of the price deflator of domestic GDP components (consumption, investment, and government spending aggregated into a nontraded good); and $P_{Y,t}$ be the growth factor of the traditional GDP price deflator, which includes all components of aggregate demand.

The index of real GDP ($Q_{Y,t}$) can be defined as:

$$Q_{Y,t} \equiv \frac{V_{Y,t}}{P_{Yt}}, \tag{3.1}$$

and the index of real GDI ($Q_{Z,t}$) can be defined as:

$$Q_{Z,t} \equiv \frac{V_{Y,t}}{P_{Nt}}. \tag{3.2}$$

Obviously, the difference between the two is based on the different price deflators, with the GDP deflator including traded goods. Thus, the ratio of real GDI to real GDP can be set equal to the "trading gains factor" ($T_t$), which is also equal to the ratio of the two price indexes used to deflate nominal GDP:

$$T_t \equiv \frac{Q_{Z,t}}{Q_{Y,t}} \equiv \frac{P_{Y,t}}{P_{N,t}}. \tag{3.3}$$

[2]For Latin America, see Izquierdo, Romero, and Talvi (2007), Österholm and Zettelmeyer (2008), and Céspedes and Velasco (2011). For Peru, see Hausmann and Klinger (2008) and Mendoza (2013).

[3]A growth factor is 1 plus the growth rate in decimal form. For instance, if growth is 3 percent, then the growth factor is 1.03.

If we define the price of traded goods ($P_{T,t}$) as the geometric mean of export ($P_{X,t}$) and import price indexes ($P_{M,t}$), the real exchange rate ($S_t$) can be determined as the price of traded goods in terms of nontraded goods,

$$S_t \equiv \frac{P_{T,t}}{P_{Nt}}, \tag{3.4}$$

and the "terms-of-trade" ($H_t$) as,

$$H_t \equiv \frac{P_{X,t}}{P_{M,t}}. \tag{3.5}$$

Taken together, it can be shown that the total trading gain is the product of the real exchange rate and the terms-of-trade effect:[4]

$$T_t = H_t \cdot S_t. \tag{3.6}$$

Finally, real GDI can be decomposed in the following manner:

$$Q_{Z,t} = Q_{Y,t} \cdot H_t \cdot S_t. \tag{3.7}$$

Table 3.1 presents the estimates for real GDP, real GDI, total trading gains, and the terms-of-trade and exchange rate effects for 2004–13 as well for the 1993–2003 and 2004–13 subperiods. Cumulative growth factors for four more subperiods are also reported.

The results indicate that, on average, trading gains were nonexistent during 1993–2003 such that the average real GDP growth factor was larger than the GDI factor. However, during the most recent decade (2004–13), trading gains averaged 1.3 percent per year, with 1 percentage point coming from the terms-of-trade effect and 0.3 percent from the real exchange rate variable.

Overall, trading gains show a significant amount of volatility, suggesting that a myopic look at real GDP figures could be very misleading. For example, trading gains were as high as 6.5 percent in 2006 and as low as –3 percent in 2008. Thus, in 2006 real incomes actually grew by 14.6 percent, with the terms of trade adding 5.2 percentage points and exchange rate movements 1.3 percent. In 2008, real GDP was 9.1 percent, but real incomes actually grew closer to 6 percent. Moreover, while real GDP grew by a healthy 5.8 percent in 2013, incomes rose by a much smaller 4.5 percent.

A closer look at subperiods indicates that trading gains were positive for four consecutive years from 2004–07, then turned negative during the height of the financial crisis in 2008–09. These gains bounced back strongly in 2010–11 before again becoming negative during 2012–13. Most of these shifts were due to terms-of-trade effects.

From 2003 to 2007, real GDP increased by a cumulative 30.2 percent, whereas real incomes actually increased by 45.9 percent. The 12.1 percent cumulative trading gain over these four years can be decomposed into a 9.5 percent terms-of-trade effect and 2.4 percent real exchange rate effect. Similar substantial differences are reported in other subperiods as well, further strengthening the case for looking at the impact that terms-of-trade changes are having on real incomes and real purchasing power.

[4] In the calculation, each period terms-of-trade effect is weighted by the sum of the two-year average export and import shares, while each period real exchange rate effect is weighted by the difference between these export and import shares. See Kohli (2006) for details.

**TABLE 3.1**

**Peru: Real GDP, Real GDI, and Trading Gains**

| Year | Real GDI | Real GDP | Trading Gains | Terms-of-Trade Effect | Exchange Rate Effect |
|---|---|---|---|---|---|
| | | | (Average Annual Growth Factors) | | |
| 1993 | 1.024 | 1.052 | 0.973 | 0.992 | 0.981 |
| 1994 | 1.125 | 1.123 | 1.001 | 1.014 | 0.988 |
| 1995 | 1.071 | 1.074 | 0.997 | 1.007 | 0.990 |
| 1996 | 1.017 | 1.028 | 0.989 | 0.995 | 0.994 |
| 1997 | 1.066 | 1.065 | 1.001 | 1.007 | 0.995 |
| 1998 | 0.981 | 0.996 | 0.984 | 0.983 | 1.001 |
| 1999 | 1.002 | 1.015 | 0.987 | 0.993 | 0.995 |
| 2000 | 1.024 | 1.027 | 0.997 | 0.999 | 0.998 |
| 2001 | 1.001 | 1.006 | 0.995 | 0.995 | 1.001 |
| 2002 | 1.057 | 1.055 | 1.003 | 1.003 | 1.000 |
| 2003 | 1.049 | 1.042 | 1.008 | 1.008 | 1.000 |
| 2004 | 1.075 | 1.050 | 1.024 | 1.022 | 1.002 |
| 2005 | 1.080 | 1.063 | 1.016 | 1.010 | 1.006 |
| 2006 | 1.146 | 1.075 | 1.065 | 1.052 | 1.013 |
| 2007 | 1.098 | 1.085 | 1.012 | 1.008 | 1.003 |
| 2008 | 1.059 | 1.091 | 0.970 | 0.971 | 0.999 |
| 2009 | 1.005 | 1.010 | 0.994 | 0.996 | 0.999 |
| 2010 | 1.135 | 1.085 | 1.047 | 1.042 | 1.004 |
| 2011 | 1.087 | 1.065 | 1.021 | 1.018 | 1.004 |
| 2012 | 1.052 | 1.060 | 0.993 | 0.995 | 0.998 |
| 2013 | 1.045 | 1.058 | 0.988 | 0.988 | 1.000 |
| 1993–2003[1] | 1.037 | 1.043 | 0.994 | 1.000 | 0.995 |
| 2004–13[1] | 1.077 | 1.064 | 1.013 | 1.010 | 1.003 |
| | | | (Cumulative Growth Factors) | | |
| 2004–07[2] | 1.459 | 1.302 | 1.121 | 1.095 | 1.024 |
| 2008–09[2] | 1.064 | 1.103 | 0.965 | 0.967 | 0.998 |
| 2010–11[2] | 1.234 | 1.154 | 1.069 | 1.061 | 1.008 |
| 2012–13[2] | 1.099 | 1.121 | 0.981 | 0.982 | 0.998 |

Sources: Peru National Statistics Institute; and IMF staff estimates.
Note: GDI = gross domestic income.
[1]Geometric means.
[2]Product of yearly growth factors.

## GROWTH ACCOUNTING

To better understand the sources of growth in Peru and in the region, a simple accounting framework is used to decompose output growth into the contributions from accumulation of capital and (quality-adjusted) labor, and changes in TFP.

The following standard Cobb-Douglas production function is assumed:

$$Y_t = A_t K_t^{\alpha} \left(L_t h_t\right)^{(1-\alpha)}, \tag{3.8}$$

where $Y_t$ represents domestic output in period $t$, $K_t$ the physical capital stock, $L_t$ the employed labor force, $h_t$ human capital per worker, and $A_t$ TFP. The assumptions for $\alpha$, the capital share of output, are based on Loayza, Fajnzylber, and Calderón (2005) (i.e., $\alpha = 0.4$).

Annual data for most variables are taken from Penn World Table Version 8.0 (Heston, Summers, and Aten 2012) for the period 1980–2011 and from other sources (mainly individual-country national statistical offices and the IMF's World Economic Outlook database) for 2012–13 data.

Using equation (3.9), GDP growth can be decomposed as follows (denoting by $x$ the growth rate of a variable $x$):

$$\hat{Y} = \hat{A} = \alpha\hat{K} + (1-\alpha)\hat{L} + (1-\alpha)\hat{h}, \tag{3.9}$$

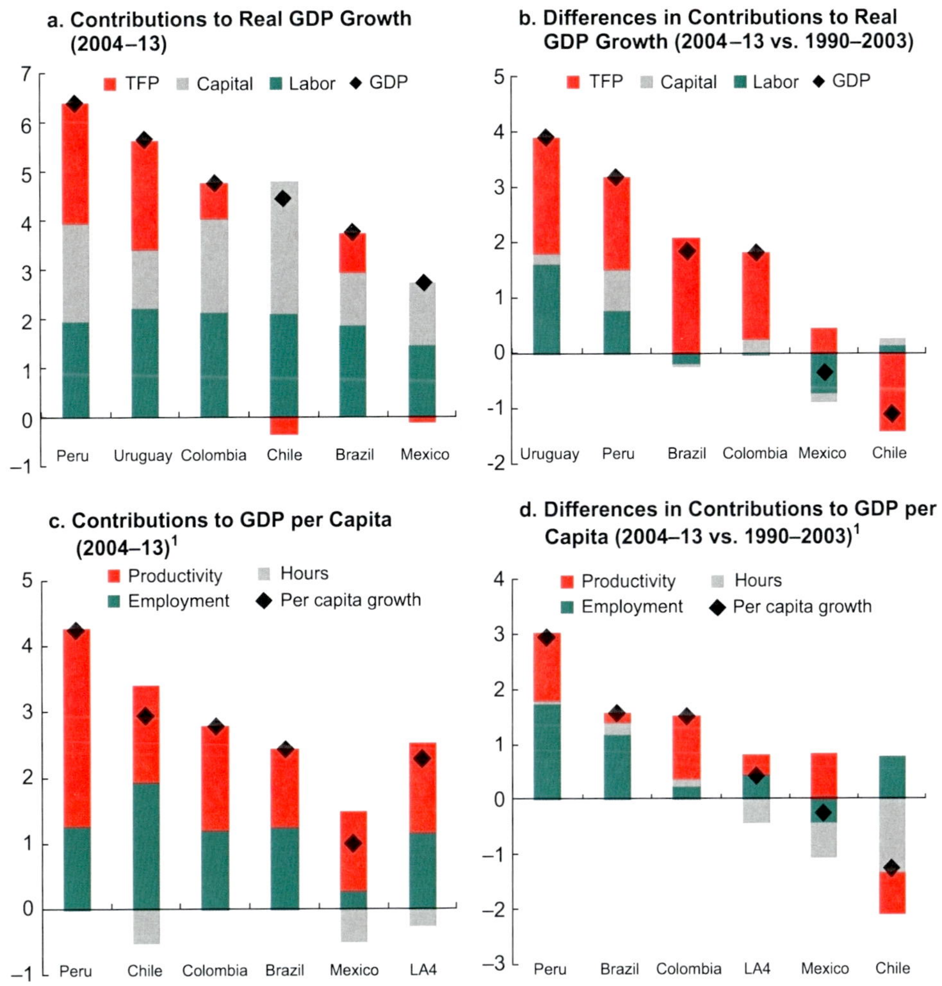


Sources: Penn World Tables; PWT 8.0; national statisical offices; and IMF staff estimates.

Note: TFP = total factor productivity.

[1]LA4 average includes Brazil, Chile, Colombia, and Mexico. Uruguay data was incomplete and therefore was excluded.

**Figure 3.4** Growth Accounting Exercise (*Percent*)

where changes in GDP are explained by changes in factor accumulation (quality-adjusted labor and capital) and TFP.

Changes in TFP measure how efficiently factors of production are used in the production process. The changes capture technological improvements as well as the efficiency in allocating inputs. As usual in growth accounting exercises, it is important to note that the estimated TFP results should be interpreted with care. By definition, the TFP estimate is a residual—the difference between output growth and growth in the quantity and quality of inputs. Thus, any measurement errors in the accumulated labor and capital series will be automatically captured by TFP. For instance, changes in the quality of the capital and labor stocks that we fail to account for, or changes in capital utilization, would be reflected in TFP.

Figure 3.4 and Table 3.2 present the results from the growth accounting exercise. While other previous periods are reported for comparative purposes, the focus is on the most recent decade (2004–13) and how it differs from the 1990–2003 period. The exercise results in the following findings:

- Peru stands out for having both the highest average real GDP and real per capita growth rate during the most recent decade (2004–13). Growth averaged 6.4 percent, about

**TABLE 3.2**

## Growth Accounting (*Percent*)

| | Average GDP Growth | Contributions | | | Growth Rates | | | | |
|---|---|---|---|---|---|---|---|---|---|
| | | Labor | Capital | TFP | Per Capita GDP | Employment/ Population | Labor Utilization | Labor Productivity | Capital Deepening |
| **Peru** | | | | | | | | | |
| 1970–79 | 3.5 | 2.6 | 1.8 | −1.0 | 0.6 | -0.1 | -0.3 | 1.0 | 0.8 |
| 1980–89 | 0.4 | 2.9 | 1.2 | −3.8 | −1.8 | 1.4 | -0.3 | -2.8 | -0.6 |
| 1990–2003 | 3.2 | 1.2 | 1.3 | 0.8 | 1.3 | -0.5 | -0.1 | 1.8 | 1.3 |
| 2004–13 | 6.4 | 2.0 | 2.0 | 2.4 | 4.2 | 1.3 | 0.0 | 3.0 | 0.9 |
| **Brazil** | | | | | | | | | |
| 1970–79 | 8.5 | 2.6 | 3.4 | 2.5 | 4.8 | 1.3 | -0.6 | 4.1 | 2.2 |
| 1980–89 | 3.0 | 2.8 | 1.9 | −1.7 | 0.7 | 0.6 | -0.6 | 0.7 | 0.3 |
| 1990–2003 | 1.9 | 2.1 | 1.1 | −1.3 | 0.9 | 0.1 | -0.2 | 1.0 | 0.7 |
| 2004–13 | 3.8 | 1.9 | 1.1 | 0.8 | 2.4 | 1.3 | 0.0 | 1.2 | 0.1 |
| **Chile** | | | | | | | | | |
| 1970–79 | 2.5 | 1.3 | 1.7 | −0.5 | 0.3 | −0.4 | −0.1 | 0.9 | 1.2 |
| 1980–89 | 4.4 | 2.6 | 1.1 | 0.7 | 3.1 | 1.4 | 0.1 | 1.5 | -0.5 |
| 1990–2003 | 5.6 | 2.0 | 2.6 | 1.0 | 4.2 | 1.1 | 0.8 | 2.2 | 1.9 |
| 2004–13 | 4.4 | 2.1 | 2.7 | −0.4 | 2.9 | 1.9 | −0.5 | 1.5 | 1.7 |
| **Colombia** | | | | | | | | | |
| 1970–79 | 5.8 | 3.0 | 1.9 | 1.0 | 2.8 | 1.4 | −0.4 | 1.9 | 0.1 |
| 1980–89 | 3.4 | 2.3 | 1.8 | −0.6 | 1.7 | 0.5 | −0.5 | 1.7 | 0.9 |
| 1990–2003 | 2.9 | 2.2 | 1.6 | −0.9 | 1.3 | 1.0 | −0.1 | 0.4 | 0.8 |
| 2004–13 | 4.8 | 2.2 | 1.9 | 0.7 | 2.8 | 1.2 | 0.0 | 1.6 | 0.9 |
| **Mexico** | | | | | | | | | |
| 1970–79 | 6.4 | 3.9 | 2.5 | 0.0 | 3.2 | 2.0 | −0.1 | 1.3 | 0.2 |
| 1980–89 | 2.3 | 3.1 | 1.5 | −2.3 | 0.6 | 1.5 | 0.0 | −0.8 | 0.0 |
| 1990–2003 | 3.0 | 2.2 | 1.4 | −0.6 | 1.2 | 0.7 | 0.2 | 0.4 | 0.5 |
| 2004–13 | 2.6 | 1.5 | 1.3 | −0.1 | 1.0 | 0.3 | −0.5 | 1.2 | 0.6 |
| **Uruguay** | | | | | | | | | |
| 1970–79 | 2.7 | 1.0 | 1.5 | 0.2 | 1.6 | 0.1 | ... | ... | 0.0 |
| 1980–89 | 0.7 | 1.8 | 1.0 | −2.1 | 0.7 | 1.5 | ... | ... | 0.0 |
| 1990–2003 | 1.7 | 0.6 | 1.0 | 0.1 | 1.8 | 0.0 | ... | ... | 0.0 |
| 2004–13 | 5.6 | 2.2 | 1.2 | 2.2 | 0.0 | 0.0 | 0.0 | 0.0 | 0.0 |

Sources: Central Reserve Bank of Peru; Penn World Table 8.0 (Heston, Summers, and Aten 2012); and IMF staff estimates.
Note: TFP = total factor productivity.

2 percentage points higher than the rest of the LA6 average.[5] Per capita growth was 4.2 percent, which was also 2 percentage points above the regional average.

- For all countries, capital and labor accumulation together represented the main growth contributor. For above-average growth countries like Peru, Uruguay, and Colombia, TFP made important contributions to growth as well. In the case of Peru, TFP was the main individual contributor—2.4 versus 2 percentage points for both individual capital and labor inputs.
- The recent acceleration in growth in Peru and the region is mostly due to a surge in TFP. The contribution of TFP in 1993–2003 was low or negative throughout the region. However, as of 2004, TFP increased sharply, explaining over 1 percentage points of the higher growth since 2004 as compared to 1993–2003. Peru experienced a turnaround of about 1.6 percentage points, with the TFP contribution moving from 0.8 to 2.4 percentage points. Peru also saw around three-quarters of a percentage point increase in labor and in capital contributions.

[5]The LA6 are Brazil, Chile, Colombia, Mexico, Peru, and Uruguay.

- Peru's high GDP per capita growth can be linked to strong labor productivity growth. Employment ratios improved as well, but the average number of hours worked remained constant. Compared to 1993–2003, about 1¾ percentage points of the 3 percentage point improvement in Peru's growth per capita can be attributed to greater employment ratios, with the rest linked to productivity.
- The contribution of capital deepening to labor productivity, while substantial, was actually lower during 2004–13 relative to 1993–2003. In the case of Peru, capital deepening contributed some 30 percent of labor productivity growth during 2004–13 versus 70 percent in 1993–2003. This is because the capital-per-worker ratio grew by only 2.2 percent, about 1 percentage point lower than 1993–2003.

## DETERMINANTS OF GROWTH IN PERU

This section evaluates the fundamental determinants of GDP per capita in Peru through the use of well-established cointegration techniques. The set of explanatory variables generally considered to have a long-run relationship with real per capita output encompasses broad-based developments in external conditions, domestic macroeconomic stabilization, structural reforms, and other institutional features. However, within these subgroupings a variety of proxy variables or growth covariates have been proposed and evaluated in past empirical studies (Chang, Kaltani, and Loayza 2005; Loayza, Fajnzylber, and Calderon 2005; Jenker 2006; Swiston and Barrot 2011; and Zettelmeyer 2006). Given data availability and the focus on a single country, we use the most common set of explanatory variables usually seen in other empirical studies.

Specifically, the following simple vector error correction (VEC) model is evaluated in order to examine the long-term determinants of real GDP per capita (*g*) in Peru:

$$\begin{aligned} g_t &= \alpha + \beta_1 gla_t + \beta_2 tot_t + \beta_3 cpi_t + \beta_4 sri_t \\ &\quad + \beta_5 cl_t + \beta_6 edu_t + \beta_7 infra_t + \varepsilon_t . \end{aligned} \tag{3.10}$$

The variable *gla* is real GDP growth in Latin America, while *tot* denotes terms-of-trade growth—both standard proxies for external sector developments. Domestic stabilization is represented by the consumer price index in Peru (*cpi*), while *sri* reflects the Lora structural reform index described earlier in this chapter. The variables representing civil liberties (*cl*), education (*edu*), and public infrastructure (*infra*) capture important complementary policies. We focus first on a base model that includes stabilization, external conditions, and structural reforms.

As a supplement to the growth accounting exercise that examined capital and labor contributions, we also use an investment-to-GDP ratio (*inv*) instead of Latin American real GDP in some VEC estimations. Given the boom in investment and its link to foreign direct investment and commodity price developments, this can also be considered to reflect external conditions. The data used in the model are annual and run from 1970 to 2013. Standard stationarity tests indicate all of the variables have unit roots, indicating their suitability for inclusion in the VEC model. A more detailed description with sources can be found in Annex 3.1.

In what follows, standard trace and max eigenvalue tests are used to determine the presence of cointegration among the variables. One estimation challenge is the direction of causality among the variables. By definition, cointegration is a search for common stochastic or deterministic trends among the variables. A finding of cointegration indicates that the variables are jointly determined, implying a degree of endogeneity. Thus, we undertake Toda-Yamamoto (T-Y) tests on the direction of causality in cointegrated systems for each of the explanatory variables. A second estimation challenge is how to account for convergence forces. The cyclical convergence

**TABLE 3.3**

**Long-Term Determinants of Real GDP Per Capita in Peru**

| | (1) | (2) | Causality *P*-values[1] (*Y* => *X*) | (*X* => *Y*) |
|---|---|---|---|---|
| Investment-to-GDP Ratio | 0.31 (1.74)[c] | | 0.440 | 0.072 |
| Latin America GDP | | 0.64 (12.73)[a] | 0.733 | 0.001 |
| Inflation | −0.04 (2.80)[a] | −0.02 (3.68)[a] | 0.902 | 0.043 |
| Structural Reform Index | 1.17 (7.51)[a] | 0.99 (8.88)[a] | 0.671 | 0.010 |
| Terms of Trade | 0.80 (3.00)[a] | 0.63 (7.26)[a] | 0.988 | 0.007 |

Source: IMF staff estimates.

Note: The table reports the long-term cointegration equation for real GDP per capita. The *t*-statistics are in parentheses, with superscripts *a*, *b*, and *c* indicating significance at the 1 percent, 5 percent, and 10 percent levels.

[1]Based on Toda-Yamamoto causality tests. The first column is based on the null of GDP per capita causing the explanatory variable. The second is based on the null of the explanatory variable causing GDP per capita.

to equilibrium is represented by the presence of a negative and significant error correction term that is included in the short-run dynamics.

Table 3.3 presents the results from the long-run cointegrated equations. All variables in the base estimation have the right sign and are statistically significant. A 1 percentage point increase in Latin American GDP or investment-to-GDP ratios result in 0.6 percent and 0.3 percent increases in Peru's GDP per capita, respectively. A similar improvement in the terms of trade or structural reforms increases GDP per capita by about ¾ percent and 1 percent, respectively. As expected, a rise in the price level has a negative impact on GDP per capita, with a 1 percent consumer price index increase translating into a 0.02 to 0.04 decline in output per capita. All of these variables passed the T-Y causality tests.

Attempts to find cointegration relationships with the other complementary institutional variables (civil liberties, education, and infrastructure) failed. The use of these integrated variables added unit roots to the system or resulted in insignificant error correction terms. All three are highly correlated with the structural reform index, which made it difficult to find consistent estimates. The models were also estimated in log-first differences with similar results. Obviously these variables should play a role in long-term GDP per capita growth in Peru. However, the data proxies available to reflect these characteristics are relatively limited.

## CONCLUSIONS

This chapter has reviewed a number of factors that drove Peru's impressive growth performance over the last two decades. The steep contraction and socioeconomic turbulence during the 1980s created a consensus to implement deep-rooted structural reforms and a solid macroeconomic stabilization plan. It also was the impetus to gradually modernize macroeconomic and investment frameworks, which stabilized the economy and fostered domestic and foreign investment. These reforms were broad-based, affecting financial, trade, tax, and labor market sectors and institutions. They strengthened the competitiveness of the economy and, by our structural reform metric, moved Peru ahead of many of the main regional players. When the commodity price boom took place, Peru was more than ready to absorb a substantial surge in investment flows. Given their terms-of-trade source, these positive shocks also had sizable income effects that affected the whole economy and further raised activity and domestic investment expectations.

Taken together, this virtuous circle of events also led to a rise in employment, capital accumulation, and labor productivity.

Against this backdrop, Peru's track record of sustained growth can provide a number of lessons and recommendations going forward. First and foremost, continued care and attention needs to be directed toward the institutions and frameworks that nurture and support Peru's economy. These are the fundamental building blocks of sustained growth. Next, long-awaited second-generation reforms critical to the growth process need to be discussed, designed, and implemented. Many of these reforms are well known, and standard metrics are available to measure their progress. For example, excessive nonwage compensation costs have created rigid labor markets and contributed to increased informality in Peru. High transaction costs and low financial education levels have also led to limited financial inclusion and muted financial deepening. These problems, coupled with persistent and burdensome bureaucratic procedures and large infrastructure gaps, have kept firm sizes small, limiting productivity gains and the integration of these firms into global trading networks. As in the past, it may take a while to see the growth effects, but they do materialize over time—especially in the presence of favorable external conditions. It is encouraging to see that the Peruvian authorities are now taking steps to address these structural reform areas.

## ANNEX 3.1. DATA AND SOURCES

*GDP per capita growth for Peru (g):* Log of real GDP per capita. Source: Central Reserve Bank of Peru (*Banco Central de Reserva del Perú*).

*GDP for Latin America (gla):* Log of real GDP in Latin America. Source: World Bank, World Development Indicators.

*Inflation (inf):* Log of 1 plus the consumer price index for Peru. Source: Central Reserve Bank of Peru (*Banco Central de Reserva del Perú*).

*Terms-of-trade growth (tot):* Log of terms of trade for Peru. Source: World Bank, World Development Indicators.

*Structural reform index (sri):* Log of the composite SRI. SRI is constructed by using the Morley, Machado, and Pettinato (1999) index to extend Lora's (2012) index back from 1985 to 1970. The index is extended forward (2010–13) using the related subindices from the World Economic Forum's Global Competitive Index database.

*Civil liberties index (cl):* Log of index for civil liberties ranking freedom from 1 to 7, with 1 being the highest level of freedom. Source: Freedom House.

*Infrastructure (infra):* Log of the number of telephone lines per 1,000 inhabitants. Source: World Bank, World Development Indicators.

*Education (edu):* Log of index of human capital per person, based on years of schooling and returns to education. Source: Penn World Table 8.0 (Heston, Summers, and Aten 2012).

*Investment ratio (inv):* Log of total-investment-to-GDP ratio for Peru. Source: Central Reserve Bank of Peru (*Banco Central de Reserva del Perú*).

## REFERENCES

Adler, G., and N. Magud. 2013. "Four Decades of Terms-of-Trade Booms: Savings-Investment Patterns and a New Metric of Income Windfall." Working Paper No. 13/103, International Monetary Fund, Washington, DC.

Carranza, E., J. Fernandez-Baca, and E. Moron. 2005. "Peru: Markets, Government and the Sources of Growth." In *Sources of Growth in Latin America: What Is Missing?* Washington, DC: Inter-American Development Bank.

Céspedes, L. F., and A. Velasco. 2011. "Was This Time Different? Fiscal Policy in Commodity Republics." BIS Working Paper 365, Bank for International Settlements, Basel.

Chang, R., L. Kaltani, and N. Loayza. 2009. "Openness Can Be Good for Growth: The Role of Policy Complementarities." *Journal of Development Economics* 90 (1): 33–49.

Hausmann, R., and B. Klinger. 2008. "Growth Diagnostics in Peru." Center for International Development Working Paper No. 181, Harvard University, Cambridge, Massachusetts.

Heston, A., R. Summers, and B. Aten. 2012. Penn World Table Version 8.0. Center for International Comparisons of Production, Income and Prices at the University of Pennsylvania.

Izquierdo, A., R. Romero, and E. Talvi. 2007. "Booms and Busts in Latin America: The Role of External Factors." IDB Research Department Working Paper No. 631. Inter-American Development Bank, Washington, DC.

Jenker, E. 2006. "Growth and Reform in Peru Post-1990: A Success Story?" Peru Selected Issue Country Report 07/53, International Monetary Fund, Washington, DC. http://www.imf.org/external/pubs/ft/scr/2007/cr0753.pdf.

Kohli, U. 2004. "Real GDP, Real Domestic Income, and Terms-of-Trade Changes." *Journal of International Economics* 62: 83–106.

———. 2006. "Real GDP, Real GDI, and Trading Gains: Canada, 1981-2005." *International Productivity Monitor* 13 (Fall): 46–56.

———. 2007. "Terms-of-Trade Changes, Real GDP, and Real Value Added in the Open Economy: Reassessing Hong's Growth Performance." *Asia-Pacific Journal of Accounting and Economics* 14: 87–109.

Loayza, N., P. Fajnzylber, and C. Calderón. 2005. *Economic Growth in Latin America and the Caribbean: Stylized Facts, Explanations, and Forecasts.* Washington, DC: World Bank.

Lora, E. 2012. "Structural Reforms in Latin America: What Has Been Reformed and How to Measure It" (updated version). IDB Working Paper Series No. 346, Inter-American Development Bank, Washington, DC.

Maddison Project. 2013. http://www.ggdc.net/maddison/maddison-project/home.htm

Mendoza, W. 2013. "Contexto internacional y desempeño macroeconómico en America Latina y el Perú: 1980-2012." Economics Department Working Paper 351, Lima.

Morley, S. A., R. Machado, and S. Pettinato. 1999. "Indexes of Structural Reform in Latin America." ECLAC Series on Economic Reforms 12. Economic Commission on Latin America and the Caribbean Economic Development Division, Santiago.

Österholm, P., and J. Zettelmeyer. 2008. "The Effect of External Conditions on Growth in Latin America." *IMF Staff Papers* 55 (4): 595–623.

Polastri, R. 2007. "Macroeconomic Framework for Sustainable Growth." In *An Opportunity for a Different Peru,* edited by Marcelo Guigale, Vicente Fretes-Cibils, and John Newman. Washington, DC: World Bank.

Swiston, A., and L. Barrot, 2011. "The Role of Structural Reforms in Raising Economic Growth in Central America." Working Paper 11/248, International Monetary Fund, Washington, DC.

Zettelmeyer, J. 2006. "Growth and Reforms in Latin America: A Survey of Facts and Arguments" IMF Working Paper 06/210, International Monetary Fund, Washington, DC.

CHAPTER 4

# Investment Dynamics in Peru

KEVIN ROSS AND MELESSE TASHU

*Over the period from 2004–13, investment spending contributed close to half of Peru's annual average real GDP growth of 6.4 percent—a much larger contribution than in previous periods. A series of structural reforms in the 1990s, increased political stability, and the implementation of a solid macroeconomic framework in the early 2000s set the stage for this investment boom, allowing the country to take advantage of a sharp and prolonged improvement in its terms of trade and historically low global interest rates. Actions were also taken to strengthen public investment implementation, particularly at the local and regional levels, and to enhance the overall investment climate. Now that commodity prices have softened and interest rates are beginning to reverse, it will be crucial to implement initiatives that address the next generation of structural reforms in order to sustain economic growth.*

Investment is a major component of aggregate demand for goods and services in an economy. An increase in investment expenditures directly affects the demand for the various factors of production and causes an acceleration in output. At the same time, given basic consumption-smoothing behavior, changes in investment spending are also associated with more output volatility. If well placed, investments in infrastructure, technology, machinery and equipment, and human capital can increase an economy's productivity and long-term growth potential. In this context, many developing countries have focused on fostering and attracting both domestic and foreign investments in order to improve economic growth.

In Peru, robust investment growth has been one of the main driving forces behind the country's recent economic success. The economy contracted in the 1980s, due mostly to a marked decline in investment. In the 1990s, growth averaged 4 percent, with investment contributing 1 percentage point. In the 2000s, the economy expanded by 5½ percent per year with investment adding slightly over 2 percentage points. However, looking at the decade from 2004–13, real GDP growth averaged 6.4 percent, with investment supplying a full 3 percentage points—a contribution that is close to half of total growth.

Four fundamental factors have underpinned this surge in Peruvian investment:

- *Implementation of structural reforms—particularly in the 1990s.* Between the mid-1980s and late 1990s there was a sizable improvement in structural policies in Peru and in Latin America in general, motivated in particular by the desire to move away from state intervention and the protection of domestic markets. According to the Inter-American Development Bank's Structural Reform Index, Peru has made substantial improvements in the areas of trade, financial, tax, privatization, and labor policies. While Chile remains the regional leader in structural reforms, Peru moved from last place in 1985 to second place in 2010 among the six financially open Latin American (LA6) economies.[1]
- *Improved political stability.* After a period of economic and political turmoil in the 1980s and 1990s, Peru implemented a new market-friendly constitution in 1993 and defeated an ongoing terrorism threat. Around the turn of the new century, the country entered an era of relative stability and reemerged as a stronger and more stable democracy.

[1] LA6 comprises Brazil, Chile, Colombia, Mexico, Peru, and Uruguay.

- *A solid macroeconomic framework and reduced policy uncertainty.* Fiscal policy in Peru is governed by a modern fiscal transparency and responsibility law, with a set of fiscal rules that has been gradually improved. At the same time, the central bank has skillfully implemented an inflation-targeting monetary policy framework. The results have been dramatic, with low inflation amidst strong growth, fiscal surpluses, low debt, and declining real and nominal interest rates. Investment surveys and rating agencies have all noted the improvement in macro policies and the investment environment, leading to successive credit rating upgrades to the second-best investment grade rating in the region after Chile.
- *Very favorable external conditions, with significant increases in commodity prices and a sustained fall in real world interest rates.* As noted in Adler and Magud (2013), Latin America has benefited from a commodity price boom in the last decade that has been more persistent than previous booms and associated with much higher income gains. For example, Peru has enjoyed a cumulative income windfall of around 85 percent of GDP since 2003, with a larger share of this windfall allocated to domestic investment than in previous episodes. The sustained fall in real world interest rates,[2] combined with Peru's improved credit rating, have also allowed Peruvian firms to gain better access to cheap external financing.

However, these last two external factors—strong export commodity price gains and favorable international financing conditions—have already started to reverse. Going forward, this adverse development will affect expectations and investment in Peru, which the authorities will need to counterbalance via further structural reform measures. Well aware of these developments, the current Peruvian administration is implementing a number of measures that should help to streamline and speed up the investment process.

The objective of this chapter is to describe recent investment dynamics in Peru and empirically assess the relationship between private investment and its fundamentals. The next section describes the status of the country's current investment framework. The chapter then provides some stylized facts about Peruvian investment dynamics in recent decades, before moving to the empirical analysis. The chapter concludes with a look at policy implications.

## THE INVESTMENT FRAMEWORK

The Peruvian government has actively sought to attract foreign investment and foster domestic investment. The country has created a solid foreign investment and investment promotion legal framework, with the 1993 constitution guaranteeing equal treatment for foreign and domestic investors. Peru is an adherent to the Organisation for Economic Co-operation and Development's Declaration and Decisions International Investment and Multinational Enterprises (Organisation for Economic Co-operation and Development 2011a) and follows the Organisation for Economic Co-operation and Development's *Guidelines for Multinational Enterprises* (Organisation for Economic Co-operation and Development 2011b).[3] The country has implemented various trade promotion and tax stability agreements, and improved its dispute arbitration regulations. Its rankings on the World Bank's Doing Business Indicators and other investor protection–related rankings are high for the region, and rating agencies have complimented its favorable investment climate. Moreover, Peru has decentralized government functions, stressing infrastructure investments at the national, regional, and local levels. In addition to needed reforms to its investment process, as outlined in Box 4.1, Peru has reinforced its public investment spending along three lines:

1. *Investment promotion:* The government created a private investment promotion agency (*Pro-Inversion*) in 2002. The agency is a public institution under the Ministry of the

[2]The 10-year U.S. Treasury real interest rate fell from about 5½ percent on average during the 1980s to about 1½ percent on average during the 2004–13 period.

[3]The guidelines require equal treatment of foreign and domestic investors and set standards for responsible business conduct. Peru also participates with other emerging market countries in the work of the Organisation for Economic Co-operation and Development Investment Committee.

**BOX 4.1. Peru: Initiatives to Speed Up Investment**

Peru launched various investment incentive packages in 2013–14 to facilitate public and private investment, especially in energy, mining, and infrastructure, and to reduce the red tape involved in the investment process.

**Administrative Enhancements**

- *Specialized monitoring unit for investments.* The new unit will aim to remove bureaucratic obstacles to the most important infrastructure, mining, and energy projects.
- *Measures to facilitate the investment.* Increased powers for the competition authority to penalize public entities and officials that generate bureaucratic obstacles, while at the same time providing incentives for speeding up projects as part of the program to modernize municipalities.
- *Actions to promote the development of small and medium-sized enterprises (SMEs).* Promoting the use of negotiable bills to increase the liquidity of SMEs and to make government payments more predictable.

**Tax-related Incentives**

- *Administrative directives to boost competitiveness.* Provide tax credits for research and training, and reduce the time required to process value-added tax refunds.
- *Tax liability reductions for investments in public goods.* Expand the "Works for Taxes" Program (*Obras por Impuestos*) to include all public investment classifications, maintenance, and preinvestment studies. All projects will be approved a priori in the national investment plan (*Sistema Nacional de Inversión Pública*).

**New Legislation**

- *Certification of the nonexistence of archeological objects.* Certification of nonarcheological items, which allows for construction to begin, will be reduced to 20 days. If the government fails to respond within that period, the request will be automatically approved.
- *Expropriations.* Reduce the time needed to process imminent domain expropriations by allowing them to proceed without payments being finalized. Infrastructure projects can now be fast-tracked.
- *Environmental impact studies (EIS).* One-stop shop for EIS, with new streamlined regulations and a faster EIS approval process.
- *Public procurement:* Standardized requirements for public procurement with more direct contracting between public sector entities and suppliers.
- *Stock market.* New legislation reduces the requirements and costs for accessing finance through the capital market for SMEs.

Economy and Finance and is responsible for promoting private investment in public infrastructure and public services, based on national initiatives. *Pro-Inversion* has handled privatizations of state-owned assets and concessions of major infrastructure projects. Major concession areas include ports, power generation, electrical transmission lines, oil and gas distribution, and telecommunications.

2. *Public-private partnerships (PPPs):* Peru's 1996 Public Works Concession Law forms the basis of a well-developed PPP framework.[4] Recent reforms streamlined regulations on cofinancing and private sector involvement, and created a list of priority PPP investment projects for ports, water and transport, and regional airports. The projects are vetted through a national selection process for public investment (*Sistema Nacional de Inversión Pública*). Some $14 billion in PPP concessions were awarded during 2011–14.
3. *Public works in lieu of taxes:* The "Works for Taxes Program" (*Obras por Impuestos)* allows private companies to fund and implement public projects chosen by regional and local governments, and to deduct the total amount of investment from their future income tax obligations. In turn, the regional and local governments provide up-front funding from their royalties and customs revenues. Since 2008, the year in which the program was enacted, private companies have built a number of basic public infrastructure works such as schools, hospitals, water and sewage facilities, and transport infrastructure.

[4]The Economist Intelligence Unit's 2012 Infrascope Report rates Peru's institutional and regulatory PPP framework as the best in the region. The report rates overall PPP frameworks based on (1) institutions, (2) regulations, (3) the investor climate, (4) operational maturity, (5) financial facilities, and (6) subnational programs.

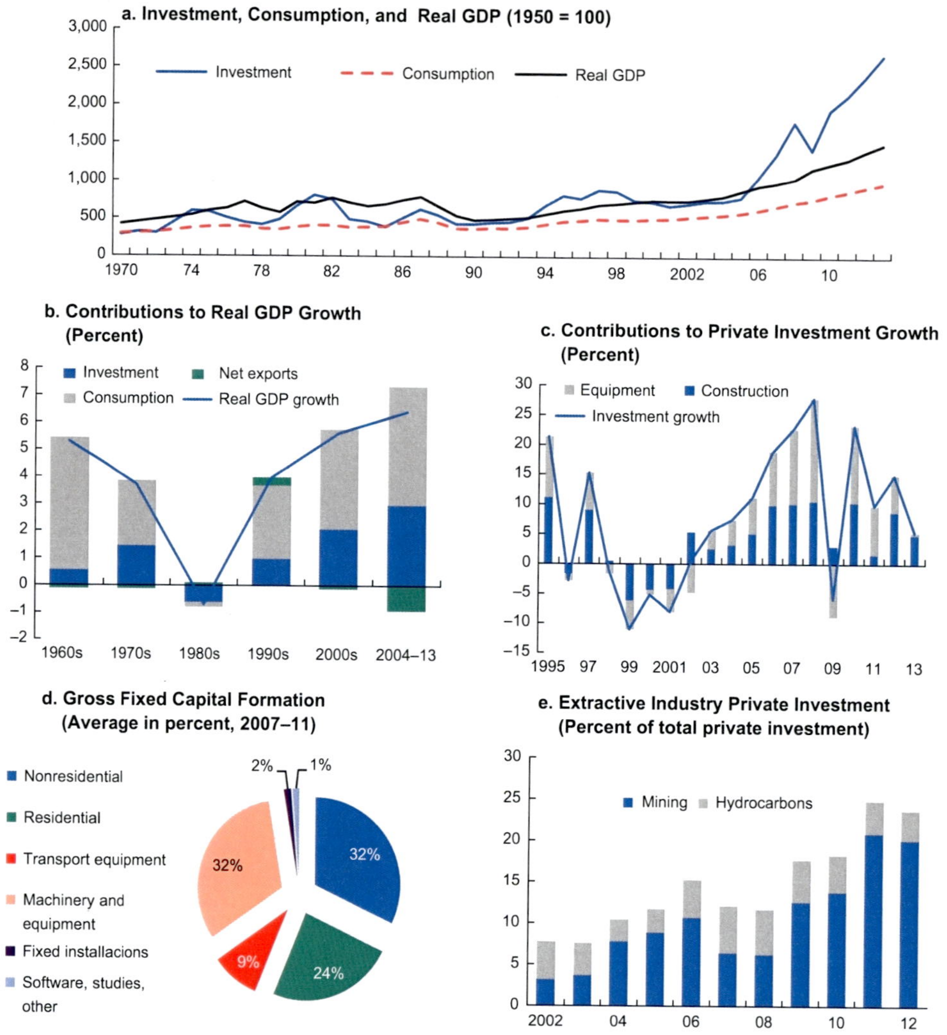


Sources: Central Bank of Peru; Ministry of Energy and Mining; National Statistics Institute; IMF, World Economic Outlook database; and IMF staff estimates.

**Figure 4.1** Peru: Investment Dynamics

## PERUVIAN INVESTMENT: STYLIZED FACTS

This sections looks at the characteristics of private and public investments in the country, as well as foreign direct investment (FDI) and savings and investment.

### Private Investment

Private investment growth was volatile during the 1970s and early 1980s. After declining throughout the first administration of President Alan Garcia, private investment gradually rebounded with the implementation of fundamental reforms during the first half of the 1990s, before moderating again by the end of the 1990s as external shocks lowered capital inflows. Investment has swelled rapidly since 2004, far outpacing a relatively healthy rise in consumption. Some of the key developments regarding private investment are described below.

- The need of the Peruvian *mining industry* for capital equipment has helped drive the investment boom (Figure 4.1).

- *Equipment* and *construction* investment were key drivers of private investment over the last decade. Total private investment growth averaged about 15½ percent during 2003–08, with equipment investment contributing about 8¾ percentage points and construction contributing about 7 percentage points during this period. After a sharp drop during the height of the global financial crisis in 2009, private investment growth rebounded, averaging 13¼ percent in 2010–13. Equipment investment contributed the lion's share, particularly in 2010–11.
- Most *construction investment* has been nonresidential investment. Nonresidential and residential investment as a percentage of total investment averaged 32 and 24 percent, respectively, during 2007–11 (the most recent period with detailed breakdowns). Nonresidential investment growth contributed 7½ percentage points to the 11 percent growth in construction investment during this period. Machinery and equipment (which included exploration and research) averaged 32 percent of total investment, while transport equipment accounted for 9 percent. Other installations and software made up the remaining 3 percent.
- *Investment in the minerals sector* has been booming. Investment in the sector grew at an annual rate of 32 percent in real terms during 2003–12. As a share of total private investment, investment in the minerals sector increased from 3 percent to over 20 percent during that period. Mineral commodity investments are concentrated in copper (68 percent), gold (13 percent), iron ore (13 percent), copper-zinc (4 percent), and other poly-metallic minerals (6 percent). About 70 percent of all FDI goes into the extractive industry sector. Peru, on par with Chile, was the fifth largest global destination for exploration of nonferrous metals, behind Canada, Australia, the United States, and Mexico. A number of copper mines set to come on stream between 2015 and 2022 are expected to significantly expand copper production.

## Public Investment

Public investment spending has increased in line with private investment, reflecting investment promotion initiatives and the need to fill large infrastructure gaps (Figure 4.2). Some of the key developments regarding public investment are described below.

- As a percent of GDP, *public investment spending* increased from about 3 percent in the early 2000s to about 5¾ percent in 2013. In the same period, private investment jumped from 14¼ percent to 19¼ percent of GDP. Over the past decade, public investment contributed 2¾ percentage points (21 percent) to the average annual growth in total real fixed capital investment of 12¾ percent.
- Local government spending has been a major factor in the rise in public investment. Local investment spending tripled, increasing from less than 1 percent of GDP in 2007 to 2½ percent of GDP by 2013. Taken together, national and regional fixed investment spending increased from about 1½ to 3 percent of GDP. To some extent, these results are a reflection of the decentralization process and the government's efforts to bring investment projects to the local and municipal levels.
- *Implementation of planned public investment spending has improved.* The increase in metal prices, and thus royalty and "canon" revenues, has relaxed financial resource constraints at the national level and at lower levels of government in specific mining regions. At the same time, the decentralization process has created a number of new jurisdictions with relatively inexperienced capital spending administrative units. Deep and frequent employee turnover after elections, coupled with human resource limitations, led to capital spending shortfalls in the past, but the public sector is getting much better at implementing capital spending

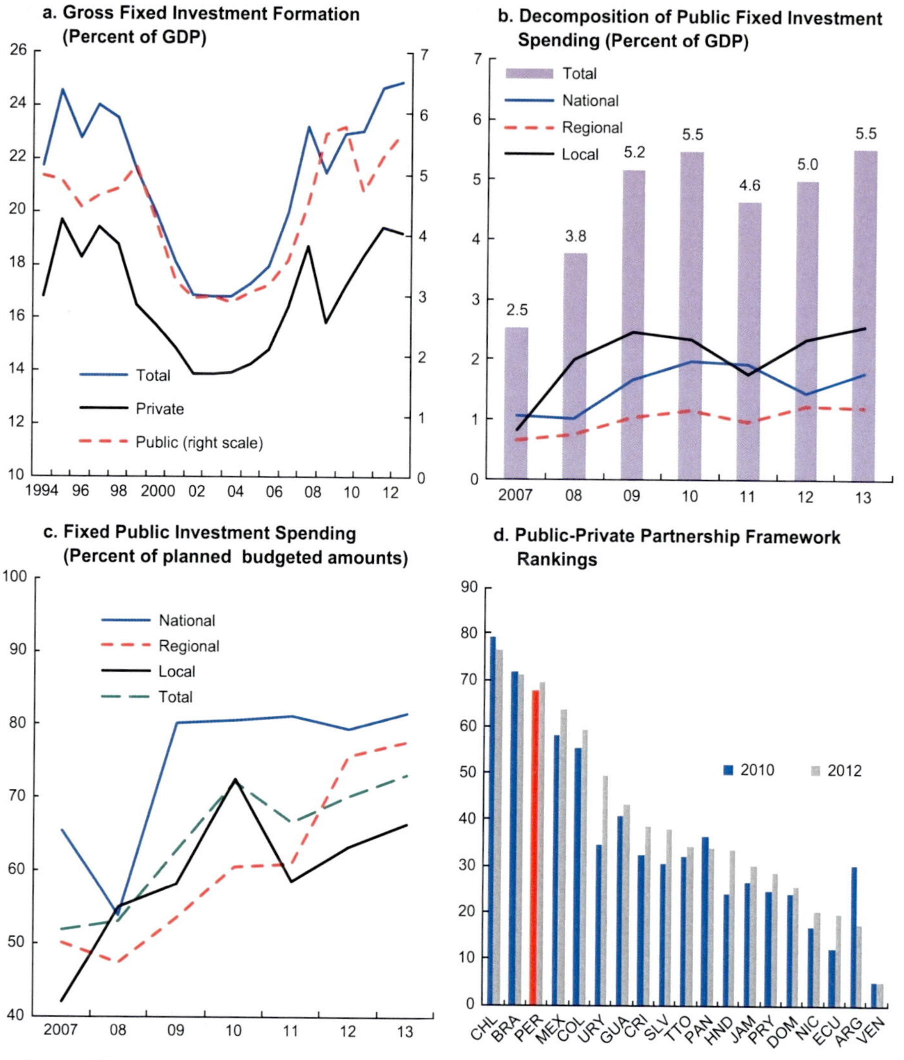


Sources: 2012 Infrascope Report; Economist Intelligence Unit; National Statistics Institute; and IMF staff estimates.
Note: See page vii for a list of three-letter country codes used in this volume.

**Figure 4.2** Peru: Public Investment Dynamics

budgets. Overall, fixed public investment spending is now about 73 percent of budgeted amounts—up 20 percentage points from 2007.

- *Infrastructure gaps remain large.* According to the World Economic Forum's measure of infrastructure quality, Peru is ranked 105th out of 144 countries. The Peruvian National Infrastructure Investment Association (*Asociación para el Fomento de la Infraestructura Nacional* 2012) has estimated the national infrastructure gap at some $88 billion for 2012–21 (a third of projected GDP). Deficit areas include energy, telecommunications, transport, health, and education. Clearly, improved infrastructure would have a positive effect on productivity, investment, and growth. Rozas (2008) notes that improving infrastructure services and making them more widely available increases factor productivity and lowers production costs. The increased profitability encourages investment and increases potential GDP growth.

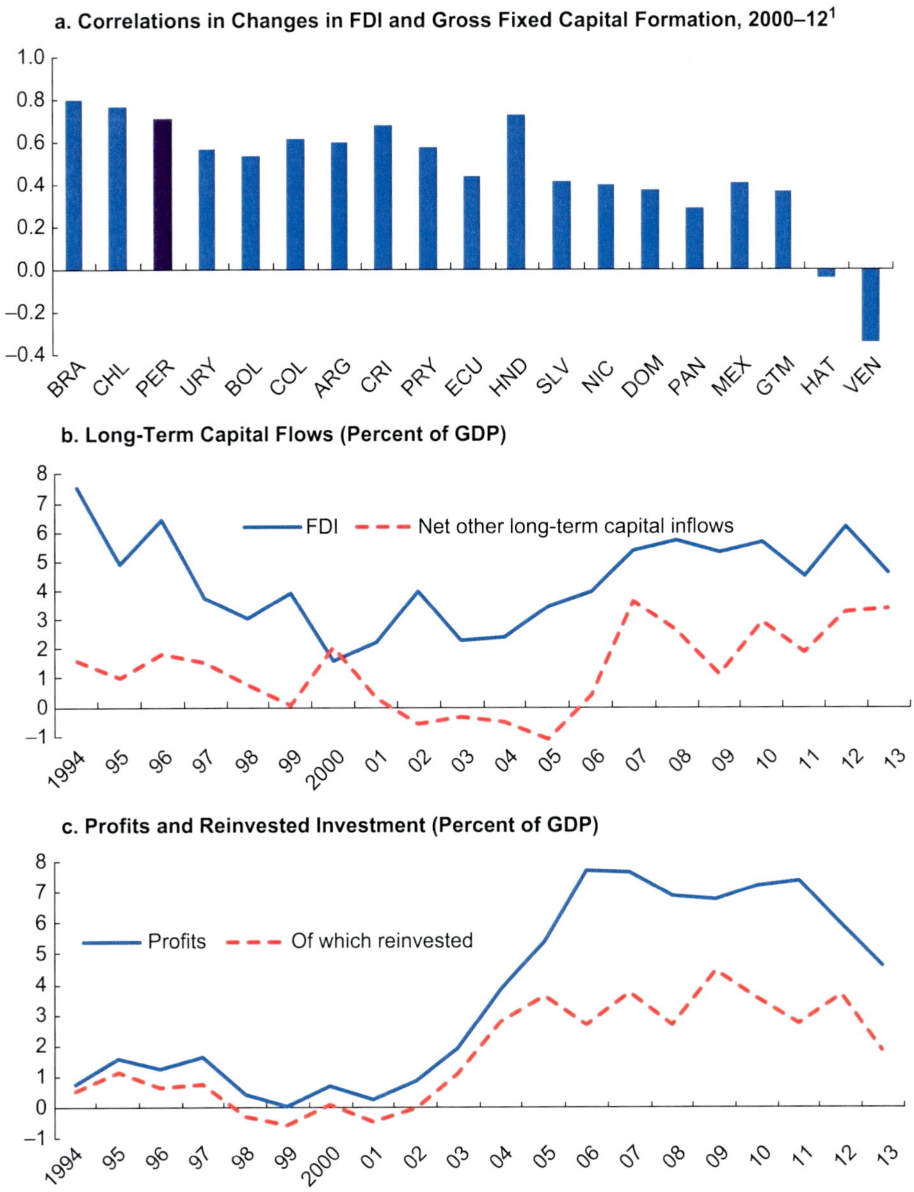


Sources: Central Bank of Peru; Economic Commission on Latin America and the Caribbean; and IMF World Economic Outlook database.
Note: See page vii for a list of three-letter country codes used in this volume. FDI = foreign direct investment.
[1]See Economic Commission on Latin America and the Caribbean (2013).

**Figure 4.3** Peru: Long-Term Capital Flows, Profits and Reinvestment Rates, and Foreign Direct Investment–Investment Correlations

## Foreign Direct Investment

The relationship between FDI and the reinvestment of profits plays a key role in investment dynamics (Figure 4.3). Some of the key developments regarding FDI are described below.

- In general, *the ratio of FDI to total investment* stands at about 20 percent for advanced economies, and can be higher in countries more dependent on natural resources. Investment and FDI tend to respond to similar driving factors. Thus, the correlation coefficient between changes in FDI and gross capital formation is high, especially in commodity exporters. Countries like Peru and Chile receive a significant amount of FDI investment related to natural resource extraction, which has led to marked increases in mining investment, and spillover investment to the rest of the economy.

- *Long-term capital flows in Peru have rebounded in recent years as profits expanded.* Long-term capital inflows as a percent of GDP declined steadily from 8–9 percent to about 2 percent during 1994 to 2004, before rising back to 8–9 percent of GDP in 2006–13. FDI accounted for most of the long-term inflows, but since 2005 the long-term portfolio and long-term loans have also played an important role. A substantial amount of FDI inflows emanate from profits that have been generated from current FDI stocks. Relatively low profits from FDI stocks from 1994 to 2003 (averaging about 1 percent of GDP) were reversed in 2004–13 when profits expanded (averaging 6¼ percent of GDP). The amount reinvested was 3¼ percent of GDP, or about half of the amount generated.[5]

### Savings and Investment

Savings and investment gaps have worsened (Figure 4.4). In 2006, Peru had a current account surplus of 3¼ percent of GDP while the rest of the LA6 had an average surplus of about ¾ percent of GDP. Since then, current account positions have worsened, as savings dynamics have not fully covered the upward trends in investment spending. Unlike the rest of the LA6, the Peruvian public sector is a net saver, while the private sector has increasingly gone into deficit. Thus, the private sector savings–investment gap has widened substantially, mostly due to expanding investment as private sector savings remained relatively unchanged. This shows the importance of encouraging private sector savings through capital market and pension system reforms.

## EMPIRICAL ANALYSIS

### The Modeling Framework

Most empirical studies on aggregate investment are based on a version of the neoclassical flexible-accelerator theory of capital, which shows that the desired level of capital is positively related to the level of expected output and negatively related to the expected user cost of capital (Jorgenson 1963). For developing countries, the models are often applied with modifications, since key assumptions such as perfect financial markets and little or no government investment are not applicable in developing economies (Greene and Villanueva 1991).

One important modification is the role of uncertainty. Bernanke (1983) and Pindyck (1991) argue that investment is sensitive to uncertainty because expenditures on fixed capital are economically irreversible in the sense that they are mostly sunk costs that cannot be recovered. Since new information relevant for assessing the returns on long-term projects arrives over time, an uncertain environment increases the incentives for waiting and hence reduces investment. Le (2004) incorporates the role of uncertainty into an investment model based on the optimal condition for a representative agent maximizing his or her expected utility. In this model, the optimal level of investment depends positively on the expected value of the return and negatively on the variance (uncertainty) of the return on domestic investment.

For our empirical purposes, the modified neoclassical flexible-accelerator model is specified as:

$$y_t = \alpha + X_t\beta + \varepsilon_t,$$

[5] Reinvestment rates tend to be relatively high in extractive-industry countries given their sizable capital import requirements and high profitability. During 2004–13, reinvestment rates were about 25 percent for Mexico and Colombia, and close to 60 percent for Chile.

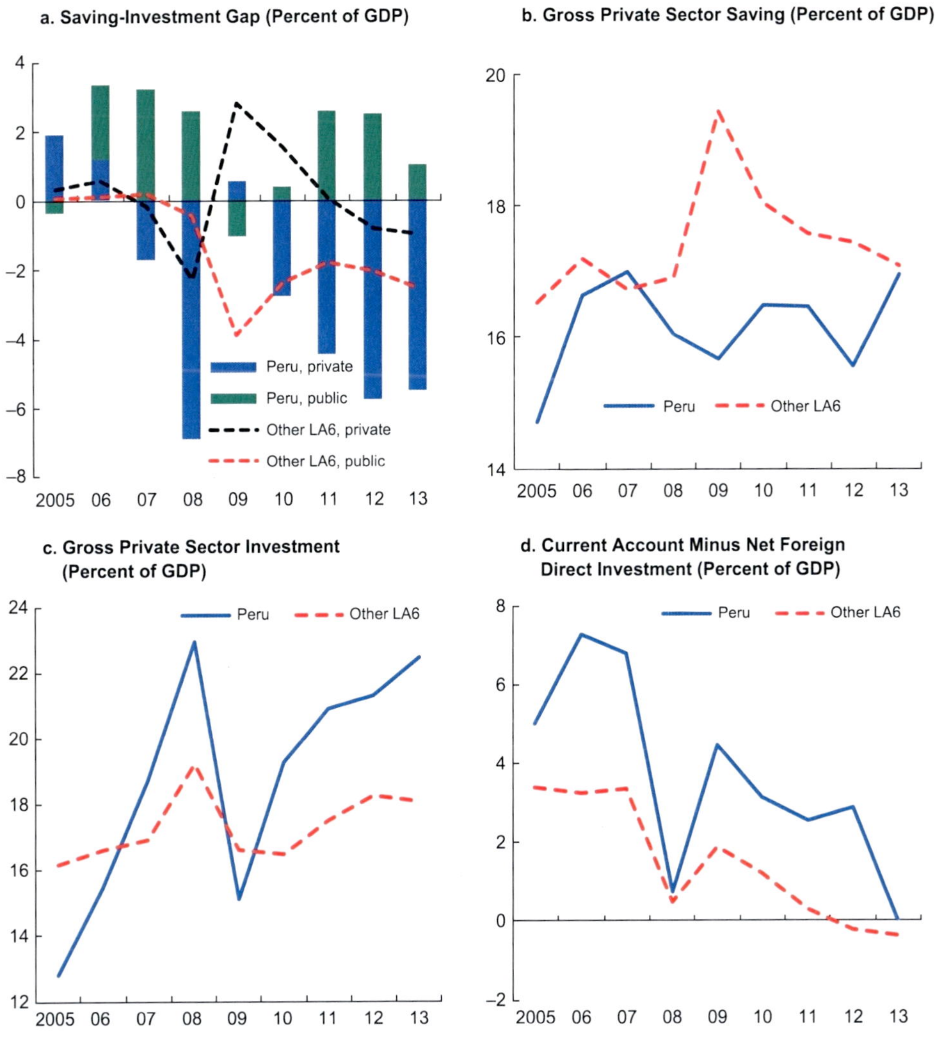


Sources: IMF, World Economic Outlook database; and IMF staff estimates.
Note: The LA6 are Brazil, Chile, Colombia, Mexico, Peru, and Uruguay.

**Figure 4.4** Peru and LA6, Savings and Investment Balances

where, $y_t$ is the log of private investment to GDP ratio; $X_t$ represents logs of a set of variables that affect investment through their effects on the expected rate of return, the variance of the return, and the user cost of capital; $\varepsilon_t$ is the stochastic error term; $\alpha$ is the constant term; $\beta$ are the elasticities to be estimated; and $t$ refers to time indices.

## *Factors Affecting the Expected Rate of Return*

GDP or growth of GDP is often used as a key determinant of expected rate of return in empirical studies.[6] The problem with this practice is that both output and investment are simultaneously determined. As a result, there is an endogeneity problem. Most studies attempt to address this problem by using lagged GDP/growth of GDP instead of contemporaneous levels. Nevertheless,

[6]See Greene and Villanueva (1991), Le (2004), Jongwanich and Kohpainboon (2008), and Ang (2010).

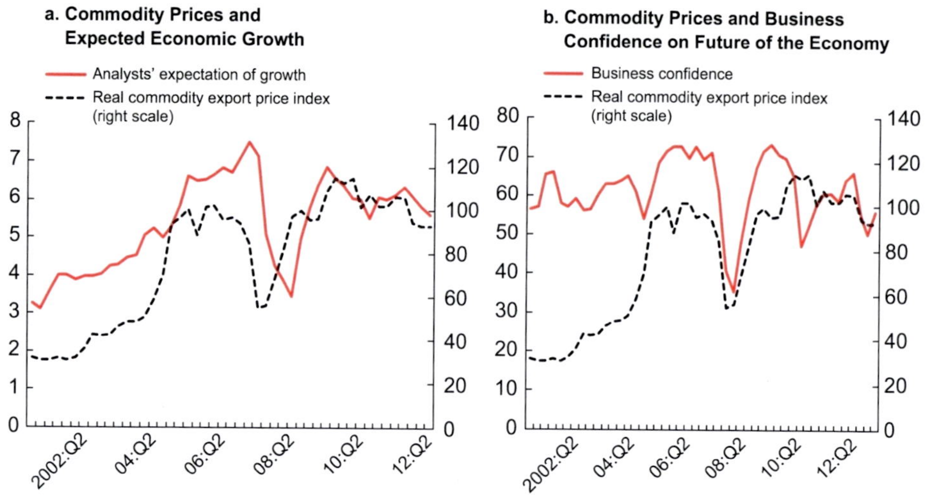


Sources: Haver Analytics, IMF, International Financial Statistics database and World Economic Outlook database; and IMF staff calculations.

**Figure 4.5** Peru: Commodity Prices and Expected Economic Activity

investment decisions are made based on the expected rate of returns, and past levels of output may not be a good indicator of expected output, in particular in developing economies.

To address the simultaneity problem in the investment-output relationship, we specify private investment as a function of underlying exogenous factors that determine expected output and investment, including real prices of major export commodities, structural reforms, and government investment in infrastructure and human capital. Since expected economic output is mostly driven by these factors, excluding output from the regression will not lead to omission bias in the econometric estimation.

In commodity-dependent economies, in particular, the real prices of major export commodities are key determinants of output and the expected return on investment, not only in the commodity sector, but also in the rest of the economy through their effect on income and the current account, the budget, and the profitability of sectors that are correlated with the commodity sector (Cardoso 1993). As shown in Figure 4.5, there is a high correlation between the real commodity export price index and expected growth of the Peruvian economy.

Structural reforms such as trade and financial openness, labor market reforms, and privatization can also affect the expected rate of return on investment by improving the productivity and efficiency of private investment. Similarly, government investment in complementary goods and services such as infrastructure, human capital, and improving the efficiency of public services can enhance the productivity of the private sector and encourage private investment.[7]

## *Factors Affecting the Variance of Return*

Empirical studies show that macroeconomic volatility, resulting from policy and external shocks, and political instability are major sources of uncertainty in developing economies and have a significant negative impact on private investment.[8] A number of variables, including real exchange rate volatility, inflation volatility, output volatility, terms-of-trade volatility, and external debt burden, are often used as indictors of macroeconomic uncertainty. For the sake of parsimony, however, we rely on real exchange rate volatility, which could reflect the uncertainty

[7]If involved directly in the productive sector of the economy, government investment may also affect private investment negatively by competing for limited physical and financial resources (Greene and Villanueva 1991).

[8]See Greene and Villanueva (1991), Le (2004), Jongwanich and Kohpainboon (2008), and Ang (2010).

resulting from both macroeconomic policy and external shocks. A measure of political risk is also included to control for the role of political uncertainty.

### *Factors Affecting the User Cost of Capital*

For financially open economies, the world interest rate is a key determinant of the user cost of capital. An increase in the world real interest rate leads to an increase in the user cost of capital and is expected to have a negative impact on private investment in financially open developing economies. World interest rates can also be a proxy for availability of external finance (capital flows), as lower world interest rates could push capital to emerging economies as international investors search for better yields.

## Data and Sources

Data on private investment and government investment as a percent of GDP are obtained from Peru's central bank (*Banco Central de Reserva del Perú*).

The *structural reform index*, which is obtained from Lora (2012), measures improvements in trade, financial, tax, privatization, and labor policies. The total structural reform index (standardized from 0 to 1) is a simple average of subindices in these five policy areas. We extended Lora's data from 2010–13 using similar indicators from the World Economic Forum's Global Competitiveness Index database. The rest of the variables are constructed as described below.

The *real commodity export price index* is constructed as the weighted average world price indices of copper, gold, lead, and zinc (Peru's major export metals), deflated by the manufacturing export unit value index of advanced economies.

*Real exchange rate volatility* is measured by the variance of a generalized autoregressive conditional heteroskedasticity process of order 1 [GARCH(1,1)] specification. More specifically, real exchange rate volatility is constructed as described here. First, the log of the real effective exchange rate is specified as an AR (1) process on monthly data for the period 1980–2013. Second, the estimated variance of the error term from this model is specified as a function of its first lag and the first lag of the square of the error term. The predicted value from the dependent variable (the variance of the error term), expressed in percent, is taken as a measure of real exchange rate volatility. The quarterly figures are obtained by averaging corresponding monthly data. The GARCH-based variance is considered a better measure of uncertainty than alternative measures such as the sample standard deviation because it specifically reflects the unpredictable innovations in a variable instead of simply showing the overall variability from past outcomes.

*Political uncertainty* is determined using the political risk rating indicator of the Political Risk Service Group (PRSG). The political risk rating is a means of assessing the political stability of a country on a comparable basis with other countries by assessing risk points for each of the component factors of government stability, socioeconomic conditions, investment profile, internal conflict, external conflict, corruption, military in politics, religious tensions, law and order, ethnic tensions, democratic accountability, and bureaucracy quality. The ratings range from a high of 100 (least risk) to a low of 0 (highest risk). The political uncertainty variable used in this study is the reverse of PRSG's risk rating, calculated as 100-PRSG's risk rating, so that higher values reflect higher political risk/uncertainty.

The *real world interest rate*, which is the real interest rate on U.S. Treasury 10-year bonds, is calculated as the difference between the nominal interest rate and the Cleveland Federal Reserve's 10-year expected U.S. inflation rate. The data source is Haver Analytics.

## Graphical Analysis

As shown in Figure 4.6, private investment is positively correlated with the structural reform index, the real commodity export price index, and government investment. It is negatively correlated with real effective exchange rate volatility, political uncertainty, and the U.S. real

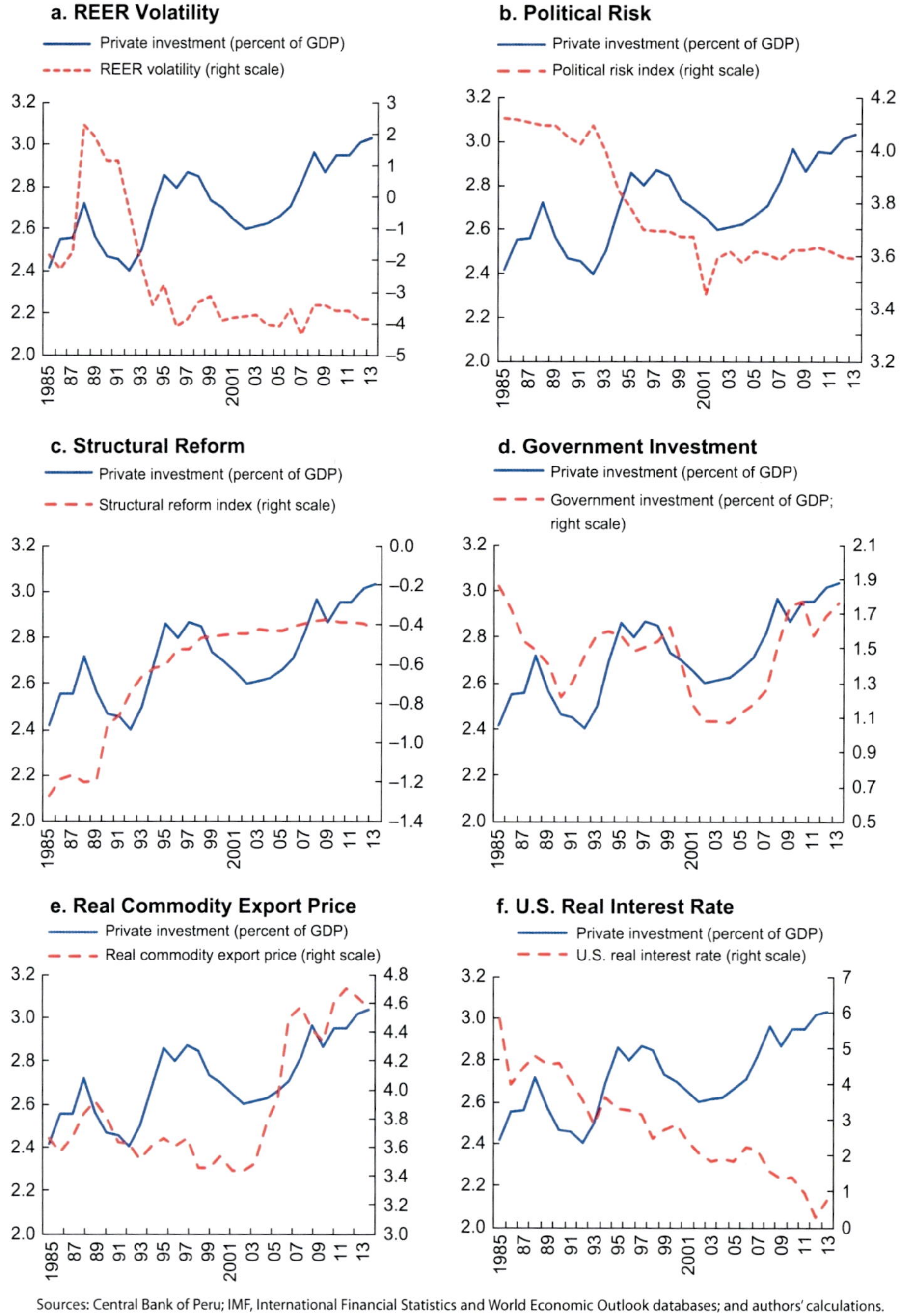


Sources: Central Bank of Peru; IMF, International Financial Statistics and World Economic Outlook databases; and authors' calculations.
Note: All variables, except the U.S. real interest rate, are expressed in natural logarithm form. REER = real effective exchange rate.

**Figure 4.6** Peru: Potential Determinants of Private Investment

interest rate. There is also graphical evidence that domestic factors in Peru such as structural reforms and improvements in macroeconomic and political uncertainty were the main drivers for the initial increase in private investment in the 1990s. These gains seem to have subsided in the 2000s, when improvements in external factors, in particular commodity price increases, seem to have been the main drivers of private investment.

**TABLE 4.1**

**Long-Term Determinants of Private Investment in Peru**

| | (1) | (2) | (3) | (4) |
|---|---|---|---|---|
| Real Export Commodity Price Index | 0.481 | 0.448 | 0.394 | 0.444 |
| | *(6.306)**** | *(4.279)**** | *(5.065)**** | *(4.712)**** |
| REER Volatility | 0.055 | −0.007 | 0.065 | 0.004 |
| | *(4.434)**** | *(−0.378)* | *(4.504)**** | *(0.264)* |
| Structural Reform Index | 0.320 | 0.667 | ... | 0.133 |
| | *(2.347)*** | *(3.178)**** | ... | *(0.769)* |
| U.S. Real Interest Rate | −0.189 | −0.250 | −0.151 | −0.158 |
| | *(−6.137)**** | *(−6.115)**** | *(−4.210)**** | *(−4.440)**** |
| Political Uncertainty | −1.683 | ... | −1.935 | −1.103 |
| | *(−7.606)**** | ... | *(−7.507)**** | *(−4.335)**** |
| Government Investment | 0.464 | 0.215 | 0.494 | 0.169 |
| | *(8.574)**** | *(2.496)*** | *(8.011)**** | *(3.724)**** |

Note: All variables except the U.S. real interest rate are expressed in natural logarithm form. Constant terms, trends, and seasonal dummies are included in all specifications, but the results are not reported. Lag length for the error correction model specifications is 2. Numbers in parenthesis are *t*-values. *, **, and *** indicate significance at the 10 percent, 5 percent, and 1 percent levels, respectively. REER = real effective exchange rate.
(1) Baseline regression estimated by the error correction model method.
(2) Baseline regression without the political risk indicator.
(3) Baseline regression without the structural reform index.
(4) Results estimated by the fully modified ordinary least squares method.

## Estimation Methods and Results

The sample covers quarterly data from 1984–2013 based on data availability for all of the main variables. Unit root test results show that all of the variables have unit root. As a result, the baseline results are obtained by estimating an error correction model. Since the structural reform index is available only at the annual level, it is assumed that all quarters of a year have similar values.[9]

The estimation results are shown in Table 4.1.[10] The baseline results, column (1), are estimated using the error correction model. With the exception of real exchange rate volatility, which becomes statistically significant with an unexpected positive sign, all of the explanatory variables have statistically significant coefficients with expected signs.[11] The unexpected sign on the coefficient of real exchange rate volatility appears to be due to the high colinearity between political uncertainty and real exchange rate volatility, with a correlation coefficient of about 0.8. When the political risk indicator is dropped from the model [column (2)], the sign of the real exchange rate volatility coefficient becomes negative but statistically insignificant.

According to the baseline results, a 10 percent increase in the terms of trade, the structural reform index, or the government-investment-to-GDP ratio could lead to an increase of 4.8 percent, 3¼ percent, or 4½ percent, respectively, in the private-investment-to-GDP ratio. On the other hand, a 10 percent increase in the political risk index could lead to a 16¾ percent drop in the private-investment-to-GDP ratio. Similarly, a percentage point (100 basis point) increase in the U.S. real interest rate would lead to a ¼ percent decline in the private-investment-to-GDP ratio.

The baseline regression is re-estimated without the structural reform index to see if the results are affected by our ad hoc assignment of quarterly values in this variable. As shown in column (3) of Table 4.1, the results of the remaining variables are not sensitive to the exclusion of the

[9] Although this is an arbitrary assumption, it may not affect the analysis significantly, since the structural reform index is a slow-changing variable, except during the early 1990s, when it jumped significantly following the constitutional reform.

[10] Johansen cointegration tests (both the Trace and Maximum Eigenvalue cointegration tests) show evidence of a statistically significant cointegration vector between private investment and the dependent variables.

[11] Constant terms, trend, and seasonality dummies are included as exogenous variables in the cointegration specification.

**TABLE 4.2**

## Granger Causality Test Results

| Null Hypothesis | *P*-values for Lag Length 1 | 2 |
|---|---|---|
| Commodity price does not Granger cause private investment | 0.0023 | 0.0657 |
| Private investment does not Granger cause terms of trade | *0.7632* | *0.7771* |
| REER volatility does not Granger cause private investment | 0.0020 | 0.0223 |
| Private investment does not Granger cause REER volatility | *0.3555* | *0.2128* |
| Structural reform does not Granger cause private investment | 0.0021 | 0.0449 |
| Private investment does not Granger cause structural reform | *0.7791* | *0.8562* |
| US real interest rate does not Granger cause private investment | 0.0021 | 0.0629 |
| Private investment does not Granger cause U.S. real interest rate | *0.4654* | *0.2099* |
| Political uncertainty does not Granger cause private investment | 0.0020 | 0.0998 |
| Private investment does not Granger cause political uncertainty | *0.9523* | *0.4276* |
| Government investment does not Granger cause private investment | 0.0582 | 0.0001 |
| Private investment does not Granger cause government investment | *0.2025* | *0.1221* |

Note: Based on quarterly data from Peru. All variables except the U.S. real interest rate are expressed in natural logarithm form. REER = real effective exchange rate.

structural reform index. Finally, column (4) shows the cointegration relationship re-estimated using the fully modified ordinary least squares method to test the robustness of the baseline results to changes in specification/methodology. With the exception of the structural reform index, which becomes statistically insignificant, the rest of the results remain broadly unchanged.

### Is There Evidence of Reverse Causality Problems?

The interpretation of the above regression results as causal effects of the explanatory variables on private investment was based on the assumption that causality runs from the explanatory variables to private investment, but not in the reverse direction. The assumption was made in part because most of the variables are exogenous by choice. Granger causality tests are conducted to test the validity of this assumption. The results confirm that causality indeed runs from the explanatory variables to private investment, but not in the reverse direction, as the null hypothesis that "*X* does not Granger cause private investment" is rejected for all explanatory variables *X*, whereas the reverse null hypothesis could not be rejected at conventional levels of significance (Table 4.2).

## CONCLUSIONS

This chapter has investigated the dynamics and determinants of private investment in Peru using both descriptive and empirical analyses. The results show that external factors (commodity prices and U.S. real interest rate), political stability, and structural reforms are key factors driving private investment in Peru. There is also strong statistical evidence that public investment is complementary to private investment.

The commodity price boom and the cheap external financing that have underpinned vigorous private investment growth in the past decade have receded. Commodity prices have been falling since 2012, and the costs of external financing increased following the Federal Reserve's announcement of tapering unconventional monetary policy in May 2013. As a result, growth of private investment has slowed in Peru. For instance, the private-investment-to-GDP ratio in Peru declined from about 21½ percent in the first quarter of 2013, when it was at its peak, to about 20 percent toward the end of 2014. Commodity prices are expected to fall further in the medium term due to the expected moderation and rebalancing of growth in China, and global interest rates are expected to rise due to anticipated monetary policy tightening in the United States.

Looking ahead, given the unfavorable external conditions, policymakers in Peru need to redouble structural reform efforts to support the growth of private investment. On the domestic front, maintaining macroeconomic and political stability and rebooting structural reform measures are keys to enhancing private investment in the region. Compared to the 1980s and 1990s, macroeconomic and political institutions are now much more developed. Consequently, the room for further improvement in this area is somewhat narrower and the marginal contribution to private investment growth will most likely be smaller. Nonetheless, reversals of this progress could derail confidence and private investment, and need to be avoided at all cost.

This leaves second-round structural reforms and public investment in complementary goods and services as the main policy tools for jumpstarting private investment in Peru. In this regard, the country's recent efforts to reduce red tape and the overly complicated system of permits are most welcome.

## REFERENCES

Adler, Gustavo, and Nicolas E. Magud. 2013. "Four Decades of Terms-of-Trade Booms: Saving-Investment Patterns and a New Metric of Income Windfall." Working Paper 13/103, International Monetary Fund, Washington, DC.

Ang, James B. 2010. "Determinants of Private Investment in Malaysia: What Causes the Post Crisis Slumps?" *Contemporary Economic Policy* 28 (3): 378–91.

Asociación para el Fomento de la Infraestructura Nacional. 2012. "Por un Perú Integrado: Plan Nacional de Infraestructura 2012–2021." Asociación para el Fomento de la Infraestructura Nacional, Lima.

Bernanke, Ben S. 1983. "Irreversibility, Uncertainty, and Cyclical Investment." *The Quarterly Journal of Economics* 98 (1): 85–106.

Cardoso, Eliana. 1993. "Private Investment in Latin America." *Economic Development and Cultural Change* 41 (4): 833–48.

Economic Commission on Latin America and the Caribbean. 2013. "FDI in Latin America and the Caribbean." Economic Commission on Latin America and the Caribbean Briefing Paper, Santiago.

Greene, Joshua, and Delano Villanueva. 1991. "Private Investment in Developing Countries." *IMF Staff Papers* 38 (1): 33–58.

Jongwanich, Juthathip, and Arhchanun Kohpaiboon. 2008. "Private Investment: Trends and Determinants in Thailand." *World Development* 36 (10): 1709–724.

Jorgenson, Dale W. 1963. "Capital Theory and Investment Behavior." *American Economic Review* 53 (2): 247–59.

Le, Quan V. 2004. "Political and Economic Determinants of Private Investment." *Journal of International Development* 16: 589–604.

Lora, Eduardo. 2012. "Structural Reform in Latin America: What Has Been Reformed and How Can It Be Quantified" (updated version). IDB Working Paper IDB-WP-346, Inter-American Development Bank, Washington, DC.

Organisation for Economic Co-operation and Development. 2011a. "Declaration and Decisions International Investment and Multinational Enterprises." Organisation for Economic Co-operation and Development, Paris, 25 May. http://www.oecd.org/daf/inv/investment-policy/oecddeclarationanddecisions.htm

———. 2011b. "International Investment and Multinational Enterprises." Organisation for Economic Co-operation and Development Publishing, 25 May. http://dx.doi.org/10.1787/9789264115415-en

Pindyck, Robert S. 1991. "Irreversibility, Uncertainty, and Investment." *Journal of Economic Literature* 29 (3): 1110–148.

Rozas, P. 2008. "Problemas y desafíos en el financiamiento de la infraestructura en América Latina." CEPAL Review No. 101 (August), Economic Commission on Latin America and the Caribbean, Santiago.

## CHAPTER 5

# The Role of Fiscal Policies in Peru's Transformation

SVETLANA VTYURINA

*The average nonfinancial public sector fiscal deficit in Peru increased to an astounding 8.5 percent of GDP in the 1980s, when periods of fiscal expansion were intertwined with short-lived and half-hearted attempts at fiscal adjustments. By 1990, rampant hyperinflation and massive economic dislocation left few options but to address severe macroeconomic imbalances through tough adjustment policies. Austerity and deep structural and institutional reforms paid off, as the fiscal deficit moderated to an average of 3 percent of GDP in the 1990s, turned into a balance in the early 2000s, and became a fiscal surplus from 2000–14. The painful memories of the late 1980s, and the lessons learned from the implementation of appropriate policies, have since guided the conduct of macroeconomic policies and institutional reforms. This has enabled Peru to attain exceptional growth rates and solidify its place as one of the most crisis-resilient emerging market countries in the world, accumulating significant fiscal and monetary buffers and boasting a stable economic and business environment. Going forward, Peru is well placed to deal with both external and domestic challenges in the conduct of fiscal policy.*

Peru's fiscal policy management challenges revolve around three pillars: (1) tax collection and policy management, (2) prioritization and execution of expenditures, and (3) debt administration (which accounts for the budget constraint due to financing considerations). Fiscal policy affects the overall economy through the influence of taxation and spending on inflation and aggregate demand and employment, as well as on incomes and the standard of living, which is affected by the management of infrastructure and social spending (Santa Maria, Saavedra, and Burga 2009).

This chapter reviews the efforts of six administrations in managing Peru's fiscal policy around the aforementioned pillars over a period of more than 30 years. It highlights the effects of reforms in the 1990s and 2000s on the course of fiscal policy going forward, and concludes by weighing in on future challenges to fiscal policy management.

## THE TURBULENT 1980s

### Difficult External Conditions and Expansion of the State

The second administration of President Fernando Belaúnde (1980–85) inherited challenging economic conditions, including inflation at 60 percent. In late July 1980, the government announced an ambitious program to increase growth by eliminating distortions, imposing fiscal discipline to suppress inflation, and taking steps to preserve a viable external position.[1] However, when the price of metals dropped in 1981, the government reduced the export tax and exempted mining companies from the tax altogether in order to support the export sector. There was an offsetting increase in other taxes and a modification of scales, rates, and deductions, all of which

[1] For a detailed account of fiscal policy in this period see Arias, Cuba, and Salazar (1997); Pastor and Wise (1991); and Melgarejo and Mendoza (2008).

TABLE 5.1

Tax Revenue Composition, 1970–2013 (*Percent of GDP*)

| | 1970–79 | 1980–85 | 1985–89 | 1990–99 | 2000–09 | 2010–13 |
|---|---|---|---|---|---|---|
| **Total** | **14.2** | **15.1** | **11.7** | **13.2** | **14.3** | **16.1** |
| Income Tax | 3.8 | 3.2 | 2.3 | 2.5 | 4.7 | 6.8 |
| Capital Tax | 0.7 | 0.6 | 0.5 | 0.3 | 0.0 | – |
| Export Tax | 0.9 | 0.9 | 0.2 | 0.0 | – | – |
| Import Tax | 2.7 | 3.2 | 2.3 | 1.6 | 1.1 | 0.3 |
| General Sales Tax (IGV) | 4.1 | 4.4 | 2.4 | 5.4 | 7.4 | 8.6 |
| Domestic | 3.0 | 2.6 | 1.5 | 3.1 | 4.2 | 4.8 |
| Imports | 1.1 | 1.8 | 0.9 | 2.3 | 3.2 | 3.8 |
| Selective Consumption Tax (ISC) | 1.6 | 3.2 | 4.2 | 2.8 | 1.7 | 1.0 |
| Fuels | 0.7 | 2.2 | 2.5 | 1.7 | 1.1 | 0.5 |
| Other Revenue | 0.9 | 1.0 | 1.7 | 1.1 | 0.6 | 0.5 |
| Other Revenue | 0.8 | 0.8 | 0.8 | 1.2 | 1.1 | 1.3 |

Source: Central Reserve Bank of Peru.

prevented an immediate decline in the tax-to-GDP ratio, but with limited success. The changes further complicated an already cumbersome and complex tax system. Taxes as a percentage of GDP declined from an exceptionally high level of 18.6 percent in 1980 to 12.2 percent of GDP by end-1983, although they held up, on average, for the first half of the decade (Table 5.1).

Despite the initial efforts to maintain fiscal discipline, the government saw a need for a sizable public investment program, as well as an increase in real outlays for public health and education employees, following a period of cutbacks in social services. In particular, to retain qualified personnel, the real remuneration of skilled civil servants was raised and large general wage adjustments were later granted on a quarterly basis to public sector employees and nonunionized private sector workers. To a large extent, these general increases neutralized the impact of corrective price adjustments for a number of basic food items and contributed to the continuation of inflation.

The government's investment program was very ambitious, calling for public investment equivalent to around 10 percent of GDP in communications, irrigation, roads, and defense (to fight drug trafficking and terrorism), all with the aim of supporting private activity. Investment (including investment by state-owned enterprises) did pick up, increasing from 7 percent of GDP in the previous decade to 10 percent by 1982–83. However, these efforts were weighed down by weak administrative capacity to sustain the execution of projects, and investment dropped back to 7.4 percent of GDP by end-1985.

In view of these large outlays, the administration recognized that strict control over the rest of the current spending categories was essential to improve the allocation of public sector resources. To this end, the authorities adopted a number of measures, including (1) conducting a major overhaul of the mechanisms of budgeting, cash management, and follow-up on government programs at the central government level; (2) having all of the major state-owned enterprises (SOEs) operate under a new law aimed at improving their operational efficiency;[2] and (3) improving and centralizing a system of approval and accounting for all public sector internal and external indebtedness. As a result, nonfinancial current public spending declined from 13.7 percent of GDP in 1980 to 12.5 percent in 1984 (Figure 5.1). But total public sector spending still averaged 27 percent of GDP for the first half of that decade, up from an average of 22 percent in the 1970s. The deficit reached an all-time high of 11.6 percent of GDP in 1983, driven by both primary and interest spending, but came down to 7.9 percent by end-1984.

Expansionary fiscal policies and higher costs of external borrowing put pressure on financing. The government tried first to attract financing from the banking system (while limiting private sector credit, presumably to contain inflation), then by using social security funds, and finally via

[2]From 1970 to 1977, the number of SOEs increased from 15 to 174 (Arias, Cuba, and Salazar 1997).

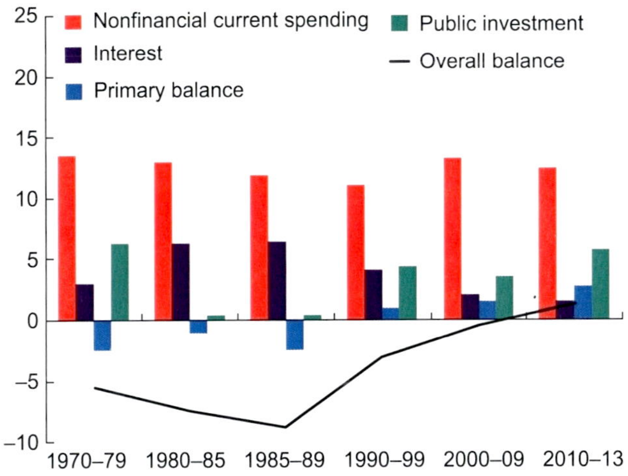


Sources: Central Reserve Bank of Peru; and Ministry of the Economy and Finance.

**Figure 5.1** Fiscal Expenditures and Balances, 1970–2013 (*Simple averages, in percent of GDP*)

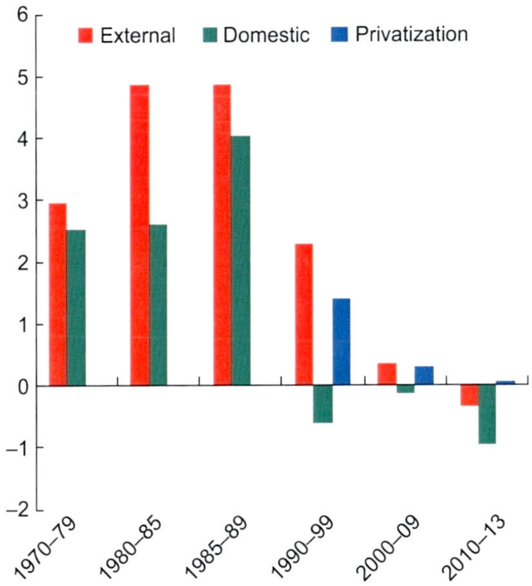


Sources: Central Reserve Bank or Peru; and Ministry of the Economy and Finance.

**Figure 5.2** Financing of Nonfinancial Public Sector Balances, 1970–2013

monetary emission from the central bank. This contributed to the inflationary pressures in the second half of the 1980s and to huge increases in the value of external indebtedness because of the devaluation of the currency (Figure 5.2). The ratio of public external debt to GDP more than doubled from 14 percent of GDP in 1979 to about 30 percent in 1985. The heavy reliance on debt resulted in an unsustainable trajectory of rising interest payments, doubling from 13 percent of total expenditure in 1970s to 25 percent in 1980. While the primary fiscal deficit came down from 4.9 percent of GDP in 1983 to 0.7 percent by the end of 1984, inflation reached 110 percent by end-1984.

## Worsening Conditions

The first administration of President Alan Garcia (1985–90) adopted a number of policies that simultaneously attempted to reduce inflation while boosting growth (through higher real wages and transfers and lower taxes), with less than satisfactory results.[3]

An income policy was implemented that raised real wages in order to improve the distribution of income by granting proportionally higher wages to poorer segments of the population. The minimum wage was unified across sectors and regions and increased by about 50 percent in real terms. In addition, the government mandated general wage increases for nonunionized employees in the private sector and for public sector employees. Public wages and transfers increased by 2 percentage points of GDP, constituting 80 percent of nonfinancial expenditures. Private sector real wages and salaries, including surcharges for overtime work, increased by 22 percent and 30 percent, respectively, in 1986.

On the revenue side, some tax rates were reduced and several taxes were eliminated. The reform of the income and net worth taxes helped simplify the system by eliminating a number of exemptions and other tax incentives. It also redistributed the tax burden by making the system more progressive and by granting preferential treatment to the agricultural and fishing sectors. However, tax revenues fell rapidly (see Table 5.1).

Capital spending, however, declined as a result of implementation capacity, financing problems, and uncertainties, with public investment falling to 4 percent of GDP by the end of the decade. This was especially evident at the level of SOEs, as their spending was halved by the end of the decade. The interest paid on debt remained at about 6 percent of GDP, constituting between 50 percent and 70 percent of the total deficit. Due to external financing constraints, the deficits became increasingly financed by the central bank by printing money, which fueled inflation, and by increasing arrears to creditors, suppliers, and workers. At the same time, the administration tried to tackle inflation by directly controlling costs, while public tariffs were left intact and some prices for public services were reduced without adjustments of the input costs for the service companies. This led to the erosion of their profits, creating the need for subsequent subsidies from the government.

By late 1987, the government was making tax and public sector price adjustments with increasing frequency. However, these measures were not integrated into a comprehensive strategy and were inadequate to reduce the fiscal and quasi-fiscal deficit on a permanent basis. This was because the changes in public sector prices were offset by increases in costs resulting from the government's attempts to maintain the level of real wages through backward indexation. At the same time, other revenues declined in real terms owing to collection lags and lower imports.

In an effort to halt economic deterioration, the administration took additional measures in September 1988, including a 300 percent increase in petroleum prices, hikes of 100–250 percent in subsidized food prices, an increase in the value-added tax and capital tax rates and a temporary export tax, a tax on balances in checking accounts, and a one-time tax of 2.5 percent of enterprises' revenues. At the same time, most wages were raised by 50–100 percent and the minimum wage by 150 percent. By end-1988, the fiscal deficit reached 10 percent of GDP. Despite tariff adjustments for SOEs, their costs grew at a higher rate resulting in a record high deficit of 5.1 percent of GDP. Dry of financing, the government forced the private sector to lend to the government through compulsory purchases of government bonds in the amount of 30 percent of their gross earnings (this program provoked very negative reactions from the private sector and was soon canceled).

By the end of the 1980s, the tax burden dropped by 7 percentage points of GDP, and total public and private external debt, including interest arrears and imputed interest on arrears, was estimated at US$19.3 billion, equivalent to 104 percent of GDP. Some two-thirds of the debt was in arrears.

[3]In a unilateral decision, the government announced a limit on the service of foreign debt to 10 percent of export receipts, although through 1987 it selectively honored obligations that would generate trade and development financing.

**TABLE 5.2**

| Selected Tax Measures during the Adjustment |
|---|
| Reduced the number of taxes from 68 to 4 (general sales tax, selective consumption tax, income tax, and tariffs) |
| Extended IGV tax to hydrocarbons and certain services |
| Suspended 41 benefits and exemptions of general sales tax and selective consumption tax |
| Increased IGV from 12 to 14 percent, then to 16 and 18 percent (later reversed) |
| Reduced income tax rate from 35 to 30 percent for companies and repealed many exemptions |
| Widened the base for ISC to include financial institutions |
| Applied a temporary tax on interest on foreign currency accounts |
| Created additional taxes such as capital contribution and tax on secured property |
| Reduced the dispersion in tariff rates and eliminated several customs taxes |
| Decreased the income tax rate for individuals and reduced the maximum rate for large earners to 60 percent |

Source: Author's compilation.

## RECOVERY AND STABILIZATION IN THE 1990s AND 2000s

### Peruvian "Shock Therapy"

On August 8, 1990, the first administration of President Alberto Fujimori (1990–95) announced a series of measures that included a 3,000 percent increase in gasoline prices (in an attempt to raise government revenues), sharp upward adjustments in food and public sector prices, and a large devaluation.[4] A 90-day emergency program also included lifting of capital controls, strict monetary policy, and daily cash management of the Treasury.

While the "Fuji-shock" was well received by the international community, there was still nearly US$2 billion in arrears to multilateral institutions and official lenders, and this impeded any quick return of official capital. The government started settling arrears with the IMF through a Rights Accumulation Program, negotiated the resumption of funding with the World Bank and Inter-American Development Bank, and was able to obtain loans in 1992.[5] Drastic changes to the tax system by 1993 included the introduction of the minimum income tax. Equally importantly, in 1991, the tax agency (*Superintendencia Nacional de Administración Tributaria*) started a comprehensive structural reform that included changing its legal structure. Not least due to these reforms, tax collections increased by 4 percentage points by 1994 to 13.5 percent of GDP (Tables 5.1 and 5.2).[6]

The government also implemented expenditure control mechanisms by establishing a cash management committee with participation of the Treasury, the Central Reserve Bank of Peru (*Banco Central de Reserva del Perú*), and Banco de la Nation (which until then had operated as the fiscal agent of the government). Current expenditure of the central government was curtailed through implementation of a voluntary employee retirement program, which was later supplemented with mandatory employment reductions. During 1991, nearly 50,000 employees were laid off or left via the voluntary retirement program, leaving the number of central government employees at around 800,000. This program ended in January 1992 and was then adopted by public enterprises. Moreover, backward-looking indexation of salaries was abolished. The deficits began to be financed with privatization receipts (Box 5.1).

Given these changes, lending from international financial institutions resumed in 1993. Peru was also able to negotiate extraordinary terms for the rescheduling of payments and arrears to the bilateral creditors of the Paris Club.[7] In addition, the country was able to repurchase a third of its debt to commercial creditors in the secondary market. From then on, the government aimed

[4] For a detailed account of the 1990 program, see Abusada, Morón, and Valderrama (2000); and Portocarrero and others (2006).
[5] See Chapter 2 for more details on relations with the IMF during this period; see also Remmer (1986) and McNelis (1987).
[6] See Chapter 8 on tax policies.
[7] See Chapter 2 on the Paris Club restructuring.

**BOX 5.1. Peru's Privatization Program**

The Peruvian government developed a major program in 1991 to divest all of its holdings in 180 public enterprises. The existing legal framework was modified on September 9, 1991, to accommodate four different potential approaches to privatization—direct sale, minority offers of stakes to national or foreign investors, participation agreements, service agreements and the like, and termination of activities and operations—and establish the corresponding new procedures.

A high-level commission for privatization was created (COPKI) with the authority to centralize and implement the privatization program. In addition, legislation was introduced during the second half of 1991 requiring the management of a number of public enterprises (Aeroperu, Ecasa, Enapu, Enatru, Enfersa, Fertisa) to drastically reduce operating costs and employment, and to develop a strategic plan for the company.

From 1992 to 2007, privatizations amounted to 16.7 percent of GDP, on a cumulative basis, with 80 percent of divestitures carried out during the terms of President Alberto Fujimori.

to consolidate the gains made since August 1990 in stabilizing the economy by broadening the scope of structural reforms. The reforms in the fiscal area, among others, envisaged opening the social security system to private participation and reforming public enterprises and official banks.

Tighter expenditure control, a rebound in tax collections, and a reduction in the interest rate bill led to the first primary surplus in 1990, and an overall budgetary surplus emerged by 1997. By 2001, the share of interest payments of total expenditure had been reduced to 12 percent.

However, in the late 1990s, fiscal difficulties originating from adverse external developments prompted the passage of expansionary domestic policies. In the first half of 1998, the El Niño weather pattern had a significant impact on the fishing industry and fish exports, subsequently reducing fiscal revenues. Financial contagion hit the Peruvian economy in mid-1998 as foreign banks drastically curtailed the availability of credit lines to Peruvian banks in the wake of the Russian crisis. As a result, the economy entered into recession. Declining economic activity led to lower tax revenue, just when the tax rate on rice and the solidarity tax rate were reduced and the tax on net assets eliminated. Current noninterest expenditures (e.g., education and pensions) were increased by 1 percentage point of GDP by end-2000 as the business cycle coincided with the political cycle in the run-up to the 2000 presidential elections. As a result, the fiscal position deteriorated into an overall fiscal deficit of 3.2 percent of GDP in both 1999 and 2000.

To reassure the public about the temporary nature of the fiscal relaxation and to avoid the recurrence of such policies, the government introduced the Law on Fiscal Prudence and Transparency (LPTF) in 1999, which limited deficits and growth of expenditures during pre-election years, set a debt target, and introduced a Fiscal Stabilization Fund.[8] While the stock of total public debt substantially decreased, it was still at about 45 percent of GDP at the end of 2001, with external debt representing around 70 percent of total public debt. Most of that debt was long-term, but its service costs were still high, and vulnerabilities included foreign-currency risk exposure and rollover risks that made debt dependent on changes in foreign investor confidence.

## Maintaining Stability

Despite the setbacks of the late 1990s, Peru entered the twenty-first century with stronger economic fundamentals than in any of the three previous decades.[9] Nonetheless, significant constraints remained, including limited policy credibility following a long history of political instability, the lack of a governmental track record in complying with new fiscal rules, and policy uncertainty due to continuous changes in the tax regime and regulations that affected prospects for attracting

[8] See Chapter 6 on the history of fiscal rules.

[9] For more details see Castro and Yamada (2010).

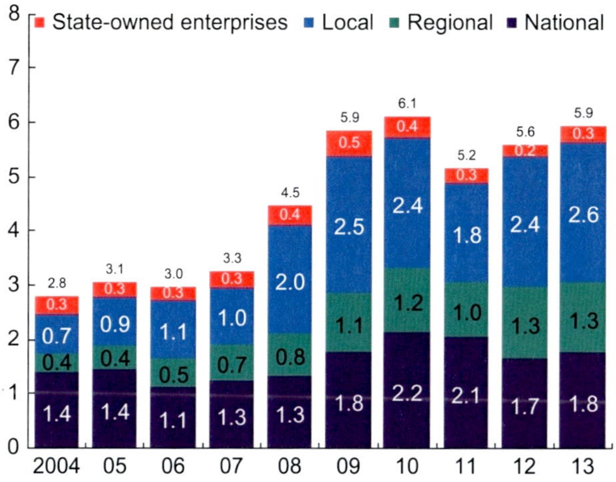


Sources: Central Reserve Bank of Peru; the Financial Management Information System (SIAF) of the Ministry of the Economy and Finance; and other government agencies.

**Figure 5.3** Nonfinancial Public Sector Investment (*Percent of GDP*)

foreign investment. There was also little domestic consensus about further pension reform, privatization plans, or an inefficient judicial system and weak local government institutions.

To increase the falling tax revenue resulting from the external crises, the administration of President Alejandro Toledo (2001–06) introduced another set of tax measures, and *Superintendencia Nacional de Administración Tributaria* implemented a number of structural measures. The subsequent rebound in economic activity, improved tax collection and administration, and positive terms of trade developments led to a 1 percentage point increase in the tax-to-GDP ratio to 14.4 percent by 2005 (see Table 5.1). On the public spending side, reforms focused on improving the efficiency of expenditure and on optimizing the use of public resources. This included establishment of the National Public Investment System (*Sistema Nacional de Inversión Pública* [SNIP]) to identify investment projects in both social and economic areas.

Strong tax collection allowed for increases in the level of current spending, and, in particular, salaries and pensions, which by 2003 constituted over 70 percent of expenses in this category. However, the goal of continuing fiscal consolidation led to a reduction in capital spending to levels not seen since the 1970s, reaching 3 percent of GDP by end-2004. Austerity was not the only reason for such a reduction—it also reflected problems with expenditure execution at all levels of government, with rates of execution at the regional level at only 55 percent of total allocated spending. This was in part a result of the incipient decentralization process that started in 2003–04, by which resources and fiscal responsibilities were transferred to regional and local governments.[10] By 2010, however, capital spending doubled to about 6.1 percent of GDP, with more than 40 percent of it being spent locally (Figure 5.3).

All in all, primary surpluses, which had evaporated in the previous four years, reappeared again in 2003 and have continued since then. The overall surplus reappeared in 2006 (after the one-off observation in 1997) and was only reversed during the 2008–09 global financial crisis. Much of the improvement in the overall balance over the two decades was due to the reduction in interest rate payments, which decreased from a record level of almost 9 percent of GDP to less than 1.5 percent between 1990 and 2009 (Figure 5.4). Debt levels and their cost were drastically reduced (Box 5.2).

High metal prices, fiscal surpluses, prudent fiscal management, and the inability of regional governments to spend transfers led to an accumulation of large savings. The resources of the

[10] See Chapter 10 on fiscal decentralization and its challenges.

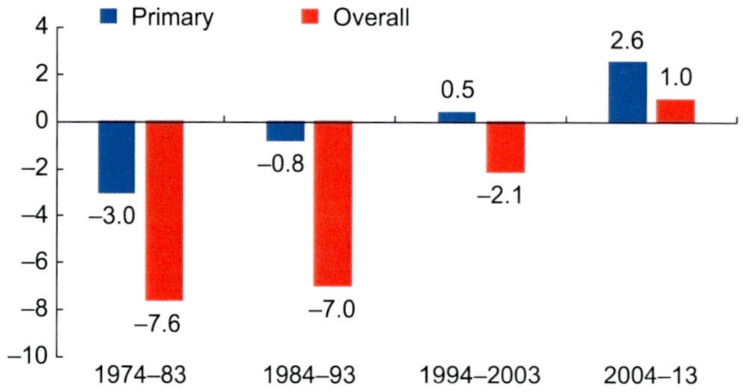


Sources: Central Reserve Bank of Peru: and Ministry of the Economy and Finance.

**Figure 5.4** Nonfinancial Public Sector Balances (*Percent of GDP*)

## BOX 5.2. Successes in Debt Management

Strong economic performance enabled Peru to return to the capital markets in 2002 after 70 years of absence. Peru issued a US$500 million, 10-year bond in that year, combined with a retirement of Brady bonds amounting to US$930 million. This lowered the country's debt servicing costs, albeit at the expense of a shorter maturity. Equally important, the government took a series of steps to optimize debt management policy.

In 2003, the Market Makers Program was implemented to develop an internal public debt market and deepen the financial markets. Implementation of this program resulted in greater liquidity of sovereign bonds and establishment of a sovereign yield curve that serves as a reference for private sector bond issues in local currency.

At the end of 2009, the public sector took advantage of improving global market conditions and issued debt (US$2 billion) for prefinancing operations and for full repayment of Peru's Paris Club debt.

To improve public debt management and optimize the related administrative and legal procedures, the government strengthened the National Public Debt Directorate (currently the General Directorate of Debt and the Public Treasury) and improved the regulatory framework. Debt declined from 50 percent to 20 percent of GDP over the 10-year period from 2003 to 2013 (Figure 5.2.1).

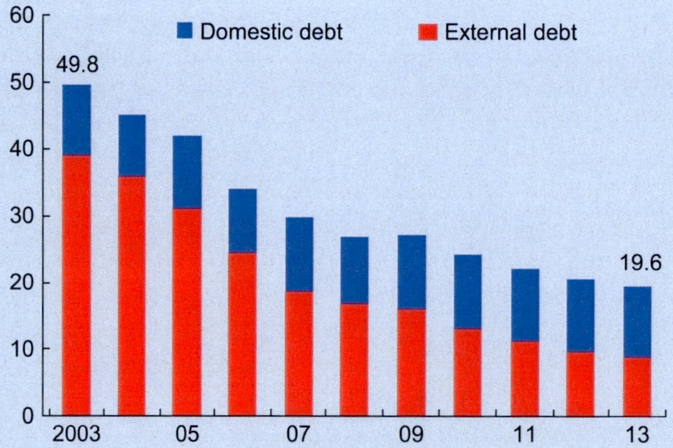


Sources: Central Reserve Bank of Peru; and Ministry of the Economy and Finance.

**Figure 5.2.1** Public Debt (*Percent of GDP*)

**BOX 5.2 (*Continued*)**

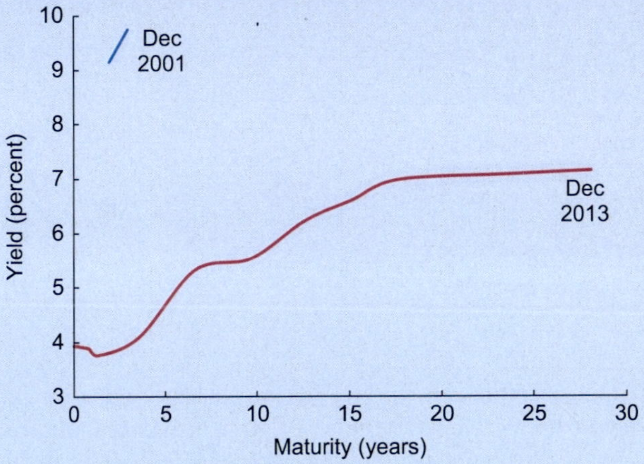


Sources: Central Reserve Bank of Peru; and Ministry of the Economy and Finance.

**Figure 5.2.2** Sovereign Yield Curve, 2001–2013 (*Percent*)

Peru received an investment-grade rating from the main rating agencies in 2008–09. Fitch Ratings granted investment-grade to Peruvian instruments in April 2008, followed by Standard & Poor's in July of the same year, and Moody's Investors Service in December 2009. Awarding of the investment-grade rating allowed Peru to access new sources of financing at lower interest rates. This had positive repercussions for the entire economy and promoted higher investments and sustainable growth, resulting in a lower yield and the extension of the maturity of sovereign bonds (Figure 5.2.2).

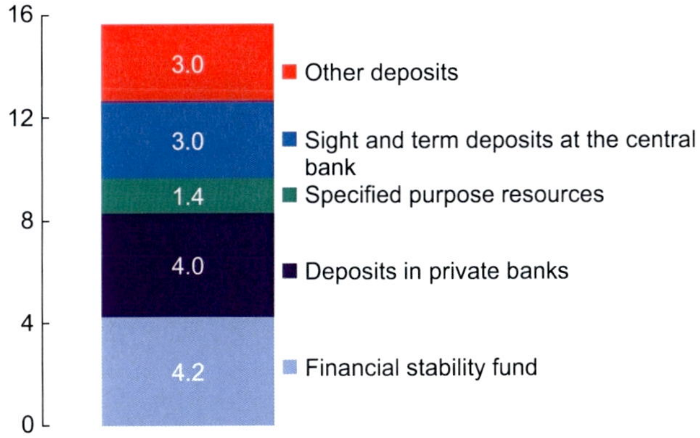


Source: Ministry of the Economy and Finance.

**Figure 5.5** Public Sector Deposits (*Percent of GDP*)

Financial Stability Fund increased significantly to close to 4 percent of GDP. In 2000, savings totaled US$100 million; by 2013, they had risen to US$8.6 billion (Figure 5.5).

The government also implemented a number of other important institutional changes that are described below.

- Major changes were introduced to the pension system. Inequitable schemes that constituted a significant risk for fiscal sustainability were eliminated, as they had very low beneficiary contributions that were not commensurate with the benefits received at retirement.

**TABLE 5.3**

**Peru's Anticrisis Fiscal Measures**

| | Billions of Nuevos Soles |
|---|---|
| Support to Construction Sector | 3,120 |
| Access to Drinking Water | 200 |
| Support to SMEs and Export Sector | 1,360 |
| Public Investment | 5,002 |
| Investment Continuity Initiative | 1,500 |
| Key New or Accelerated Projects (68) | 1,008 |
| Fund for Regional and Local Public Investment | 2,294 |
| Other | 200 |
| Social Programs and Targeted Support to Workers | 550 |

Source: Ministry of the Economy and Finance.
Note: SMEs = small and medium-sized enterprises.

Moreover, in some instances, the pension received by the beneficiary was equal to the last salary received, which required a lower number of years of service and did not include a minimum retirement age. It is estimated that the elimination of these regimes as part of the pension reform generated fiscal savings of more than US$5 billion in present value terms.

- Access to public information, especially information related to the fiscal accounts, was improved. The Transparency and Access to Public Information Law enacted in 2002 sought to create greater transparency in the management of public finances by establishing mechanisms to access fiscal information and requiring the Ministry of the Economy and Finance to publish information such as fiscal statistics, institutional reports on fiscal policies, and the multiannual macrofiscal framework (and the extent to which it is consistent with the annual budget).
- Performance-based budgeting was introduced in 2007 and a road map was established for its gradual implementation in all government entities across all levels of government. Performance-based budgeting constituted a new approach to preparing the public budget in that spending programs to be financed with public resources were designed, executed, and assessed on the basis of their effect on the population, particularly the most vulnerable segments. This approach has had significant success, particularly with the Nutrition Program to reduce chronic malnutrition among children under the age of five and the Neonatal Health Program to reduce maternal and neonatal mortality.

Following exceptionally high growth of 9.8 percent in 2008, activity in Peru decelerated sharply in 2009 due to the global crisis. Peru's strong policy framework and proactive response were key to limiting the impact of the crisis by avoiding a credit crunch, supporting economic activity, and sustaining employment. In mid-2009, the government announced the Plan for Sustaining Economic Growth, Employment, and Poverty Alleviation in a Global Crisis, which presented a set of fiscal measures equivalent to nearly 3 percent of GDP that could be ready for implementation if conditions warranted (Table 5.3). The substantial fiscal stimulus—mainly for infrastructure and maintenance projects and largely self-financed with fiscal financial assets—aimed to sustain domestic demand, boost business confidence, and sustain employment. The fiscal plan also included contingency measures, including guarantees to support corporations, exporters, and smaller financial institutions, which in the end were not needed. The government also lined up access to contingent credit lines from official creditors of up to $9.2 billion.

Real activity gained traction in the second half of 2009, not least supported by acceleration in execution of the fiscal stimulus. Subsequently, once there were clear signals of a robust and sustained recovery of private expenditure, the fiscal stimulus began to be withdrawn in 2010. Subsequently, measures were taken to reduce the rate of growth of public spending and comply

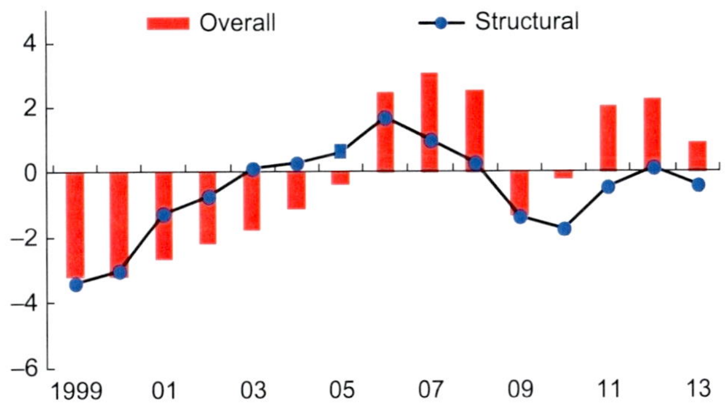


Sources: Central Reserve Bank of Peru; and Ministry of the Economy and Finance.

**Figure 5.6** Overall and Structural Balances of the Nonfinancial Public Sector (*Percent of GDP*)

with the fiscal rules for the national government, especially for goods and services, investment projects, and restrictions on the use of the Contingency Reserve, among other rules.[11]

In the end, the economy emerged practically unscathed from the 2008–09 global crisis. At that time, the authorities intended to carefully manage fiscal spending, gradually lower the fiscal deficit, and return in 2011 to the 1 percent of GDP deficit limit established by the Fiscal Responsibility and Transparency Law. This followed a 2.5 percent surplus in 2008 and a 1.4 percent deficit in 2009 (Figure 5.6). This was intended to help preserve fiscal cushions, which had proved very important during the crisis, and prepare for the risk of a possible relapse in global growth.

Simultaneously, the government undertook several initiatives to improve the quality and efficiency of public spending, including by fostering capacity building at the subnational level. There were also efforts to assess the potential medium-term implications of contingent fiscal liabilities, including those derived from public-private partnerships (PPP) and remaining public sector pension schemes. The authorities intended to pay special attention to maintaining appropriate risk sharing between the public and private sector in PPP initiatives. They also continued efforts to strengthen the financial management information system (SIAF), as well as administration of the single treasury account. Some of these reforms were adopted in the context of IMF-supported programs over 2001–09, and most have been completed (Annex 5.1).

## SOLIDIFYING SUCCESS AND RESILIENCE TO CRISES

The administration of Ollanta Humala (2011–16) inherited a country that was one of the top performers among the world's emerging market economies. Real GDP expanded rapidly and grew 8¾ percent in 2010, one of the highest rates in the region and the world, driven by private domestic demand. In 2011, following some early overheating signs, the government continued to exit from the 2009 fiscal stimulus, although more by accident than design. The overall deficit fell from 1.3 percent of GDP in 2009 to 0.2 percent in 2010 and then turned into a sizable surplus in 2011. Capital expenditures were weak in 2011 due to low implementation of

[11]The main measures included (1) a reduction in the growth of expenditures on goods and services for 2010 to less than 3 percent of the nominal value executed in fiscal year 2009, (2) a reduction to no more than 25 percent of the total amount of the budget allocated for public investment projects not yet implemented, (3) a maximum threshold on transfers of resources from the Contingency Reserve of 75 percent of the amount authorized in the Budget Law, (4) the suspension of new borrowing operations, and (5) the suspension of processing of additional requests for resources via supplementary appropriations against ordinary resources until December 31, 2010.

investment projects at the subnational level (related to the political cycle). Underexecution of public investment projects was so low that it prompted the authorities to adopt measures to foster capital execution (still within the 2011 budget limits). Tax collections improved by 1 percent of GDP a year in 2010 and 2011, helped by strong economic activity, positive terms of trade, and the revised framework for mining taxation in late 2011. However, several measures in 2011 eroded the tax base, including a reduction in the value-added tax rate (by 1 percentage point), the financial transaction tax, and import duties. Despite these measures, tax collection reached about 16 percent of GDP in 2011, but was still low by international standards.

The revenue overperformance and the low expenditure execution led to a surplus of about 2 percent of GDP in 2011 compared with a fiscal deficit of 1 percent included in the 2011 budget. The stronger-than-expected fiscal position of 2011 proved useful in reducing overheating concerns and rebuilding fiscal buffers. The fiscal stance in 2012 was also tighter than envisaged in the original budget, reaching 2.3 percent of GDP in 2012 (versus a budgeted 1 percent surplus), again due to higher-than-forecast revenues and lower budget implementation despite efforts to accelerate public sector investment.

In April 2012, the authorities modified the current expenditure limit under the LPTF, mainly by excluding infrastructure maintenance from the expenditure cap (to align it with public investment), and by excluding current expenditures associated with some social programs and equipment for military and police forces due to higher social and security needs. In addition, a temporary target for the structural fiscal balance was introduced that required an annual adjustment of at least ¼ percent of GDP to maintain a fiscal path consistent with reaching zero structural balance over the medium term. However, the structural balance objective was achieved ahead of schedule by end-2012 due to the stronger-than-expected fiscal outcome, and the proposed fiscal adjustment was no longer binding for 2013, as the fiscal accounts had already reached a small structural surplus.

The government approved important (second-generation) fiscal reforms with a view to streamline government procedures and make public services more efficient. Public service reform was approved in 2013, while public procurement regulations and engagement with the private sector on public infrastructure projects was improved with the aim of attracting greater interest (Annex 5.2). The LPTF was also revamped, including through the introduction of the structural balance target.

Fiscal policy became more supportive of the economy in 2013 and 2014 given the challenging external environment. The fiscal surplus was reduced to around 1 percent of GDP in 2013 and toward a balance in 2014 as a result of (1) budgeted allowances to achieve social inclusion goals and higher wages following the civil service reform, as well as extra bonuses to public sector workers; (2) efforts to increase capital spending; and (3) falling mining-related revenues as metal prices weakened. Starting in mid-2014, the authorities proposed a series of stimulative fiscal packages to reinvigorate growth and investment, including through cuts in corporate income tax rates (Box 5.3).

## THE OUTSTANDING AGENDA

Peru constitutes a true success story in putting its fiscal house in order, which took more than two decades of continuous implementation of sound economic policies. As a result, Peru emerged as one of the regional leaders in fiscal prudence (Figure 5.7). However, it is important to recognize that several challenges remain in the fiscal area.

The fiscal framework approved in 2014 will have to be fully embedded into the budget process, including by strengthening medium-term public financial management and planning. Over the medium term, it is important to maintain the relative size of the fiscal buffers (as the economy grows) through the accumulation of small fiscal structural surpluses, which would also address contingent liabilities and natural disaster risks, which are high in Peru. In this regard, the

## BOX 5.3. Steps in 2014–15 to Stimulate Growth and Investment[1]

Measures to stimulate growth and investment amounting to around 2 percent of GDP were announced in the second half of 2014 when it became clear that the economy was softening rapidly. About ¼ percent of GDP was spent in 2014, while some expenditure items were reprioritized to ensure stimulus though spending, with the rest of the measures planned for 2015 (including support for public-private partnerships and reprioritization of capital spending). Direct capital allocations could amount to slightly less than ½ percent of GDP. Some of the measures, however, require congressional approval.

On the revenue side, the approximate impact of tax measures is estimated by the authorities at 1¼ percent of GDP in 2015, mostly due to the decrease in income tax rates. The corporate tax rate will decline from 30 percent to 26 percent over the next four years, while the dividend tax will increase for payments to nonresidents. Personal income tax was reduced for the lowest income segment from 15 percent to 8 percent. A gradual elimination of value-added tax withholding schemes, which were deemed to be negatively affecting the liquidity of small firms, and a gradual reduction of the drawback mechanism, were also adopted. On the expenditure side, measures are estimated at about 1 percent of GDP for 2015. They include increases in capital and current spending, repayment of debt in arrears, and social assistance allocations.

On the regulatory side, speeding up investment is mostly targeted at streamlining requirements for both public and private investment by (1) reducing the maximum time for registration, amendments, and registration renewals required of large-scale investment projects by approximately 25 percent; (2) implementing changes in the approval of archeological certificates that are expected to reduce discretion and add predictability to investments; (3) extending a tax benefit and the accelerated depreciation benefit for hydroelectricity generation until December 31, 2025, with a targeting investment totaling almost US$3 billion; (4) increasing the depreciation rate from 5 to 20 to spur construction of housing; and (5) increasing the percentage of mining revenues (canon) that may be used to finance maintenance of infrastructure from 20 percent to 40 percent. Additional measures include:

- Expedited expropriation of properties required for infrastructure projects.
- Greater funding and subsidies to encourage productivity growth in the small businesses sector.
- More direct contracting between the public sector and suppliers, and contracting between the Peruvian government and foreign governments in all sectors, not just defense.
- Standardized requirements for public procurement and prevention of price fixing among public sector suppliers.

[1]This box is based on information from the Ministry of the Economy and Finance. More detail can be found in the Multi-Annual Macroeconomic Framework publication (April 2015) at http://www.mef.gob.pe/.

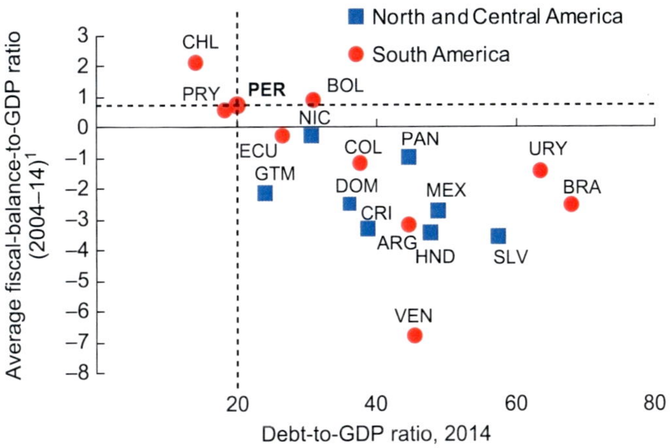


Source: IMF, World Economic Outlook database.
Note: See page vii for a list of three-letter country codes used in this volume.
[1]General government.

**Figure 5.7** Fiscal-Balance-to-GDP and Debt-to-GDP Ratios, Selected Latin American Countries structural target should take into account the desired level of financial balances and the public investment path. Further scaling up of public investment over the medium term is needed, but it should be in line with enhancements in public financial management capacity and the legal framework at the subnational as well as the national level in order to ensure high rates of return for investment projects.

With tax revenue under pressure from the fall in revenue from metals and the implementation of recent tax measures, achieving ambitious tax targets will require more resolute efforts. Despite progress in this area, additional efforts are needed to reduce the high level of informality and tax evasion, and to decrease exemptions that amount to about 2 percent of GDP. The provision in the new fiscal law to publish data on exemptions and contingent liabilities, along with budget documentation, will increase transparency and accountability.

As commodity prices increased in the past, and as part of the decentralization strategy, royalty distribution ("canon" schemes) generated significant amounts of revenues in places where extractive industry activities took place. This has resulted in a marked imbalance—particularly in relation to where rural poverty exists—and prompted fiscal authorities to rethink how these revenues should be distributed to achieve development goals, while bearing in mind that extractive industry locations bear much of the environmental costs of these activities. Thus a rapid and complete shift of revenues across regions may unnecessarily create social tensions. Also, the drop in metal prices in 2014–15, which could be seen as a permanent development over the medium term, calls for careful management and planning of existing resources.

Raising more resources to increase social expenditure and further enhance the efficiency of social spending through better-targeted social programs is necessary to achieve more socially inclusive growth.[12] In this context, the government has prioritized its social programs through the household targeting system so as to place greater focus on the 800 poorest districts. Increasing the efficiency of public investments would also reduce the regional gaps in physical and human capital and bring about greater redistribution over the medium term.

## ANNEX 5.1. SELECTED STRUCTURAL PERFORMANCE CRITERIA AND BENCHMARKS UNDER IMF STAND-BY ARRANGEMENTS 2003–09

- Submit to Congress legislation to eliminate the special wage tax (IES).
- Complete a census of government employees and pensioners.
- Develop a satisfactory action plan for reforming the pension regimes for the police and military.
- Grant concessions or enter into PPPs for the construction and maintenance of at least two major roads.
- Introduce in Congress a constitutional amendment and, once approved, introduce draft laws to allow for a comprehensive reform of *Cedula Viva* (a public pension system).
- Implement a satisfactory law providing objective criteria for certifying that regional governments have the administrative capacity to take on devolved expenditure.
- Grant concessions or enter into PPPs for the construction and maintenance of the portion of the Pan-American Highway from Pucusana to Ica, and for a large regional integration highway in the north of Peru.
- Have the Ministry of the Economy and Finance establish a reporting system of public liabilities associated with PPPs and concessions, and issue a norm requiring the annual

[12] See Chapter 26 for advances in the social area.

publication of such liabilities in the Multiyear Macroeconomic Framework beginning in 2006.

- Unify the central government budget formulation system and the integrated Financial Management System (SIAF).
- Issue the implementing regulations of the Fiscal Decentralization Law that support prudent budget decisions and management of the regional and local governments.
- Complete plans for implementing a Treasury Single Account and update the budget classification system to international standards.
- Start implementing a law on public indebtedness.
- Prepare an action plan to introduce a permanent framework for PPPs.
- Establish a unit at the Ministry of the Economy and Finance to monitor the operations of subnational governments and assess their performance with respect to fiscal rules.
- Clarify the tax treatment of financial derivatives and securitized transactions.
- Prepare the 2008 budget according to the modernized budget classification system and incorporate into the charts of accounts.
- Submit to Congress an amendment to the National Investment System (SNIP) Law to allow for outsourcing the studies required for the formulation and approval of investment projects.

## ANNEX 5.2. PROMOTION OF PRIVATE AND PUBLIC INVESTMENT INITIATIVES TO SUPPORT INFRASTRUCTURE DEVELOPMENT AND PROVISION OF PUBLIC SERVICES IN 2013–14[13]

Despite the progress made in recent years to Peru's public service infrastructure, there remains a growing infrastructure gap of about US$88 billion (44 percent of GDP in 2013).[14] To address this gap, the government made a series of regulatory changes in 2013–14 to the institutional and legal framework for investments involving PPPs. It also cofinanced a private initiative and the Public Works in Lieu of Taxes Program (*Obras por Impuestos*) in order to promote private sector participation in public infrastructure development.

### Public-Private Partnerships

In March 2014, amendments to the PPP law were enacted to improve the PPP process, including by enhancing the formulation and design of projects and the budgetary handling of the various commitments involved in such projects.

For the project formulation phase, the Ministry of the Economy and Finance and the public promotion agency PROINVERSIÓN can now provide assistance to nonfinancial public sector entities to identify PPP projects and expand their promotion at all levels of government.[15] In addition, a national PPP registry was created to make the project prioritization and formulation phase more predictable. The scope of the sectors in which PPP projects may be formulated was

[13]The source for this annex is Peru's Ministry of the Economy and Finance.

[14]As estimated by the 2012–21 National Infrastructure Plan (Association for the Promotion of National Infrastructure 2012).

[15]In 2013, PROINVERSIÓN awarded 11 projects under the PPP approach for an investment amount of close to US$5 billion, a record high.

expanded to include applied research, technological innovation, and services related to infrastructure and public services.[16]

As for the project design phase, the law prohibits government entities from taking actions or issuing provisions that constitute bureaucratic hurdles to obtaining permits, licenses, or authorizations for the development of PPPs. As well, some procedures were eased to shorten the time for the promotion process as well as for the solicitation of opinions, approval of studies, etc.

Finally, the law established mechanisms to strengthen the relationship between the multiyear budget process and the PPP investment promotion processes. In this way, a cofinanced PPP private investment promotion process cannot be carried out without the corresponding budget being available. As well, the multiyear assignment of budget ceilings will have to take into account the commitments undertaken in projects already awarded or about to be awarded.

## Cofinanced Private Initiatives

A cofinanced private initiative is a PPP in which the project is proposed by the private sector from the formulation or design stage. These initiatives may be self-sustaining (if the flow of projected revenue is sufficient to cover the investment and operating and maintenance expenditures), or cofinanced in the event that expenditures will be higher than revenues and a government contribution will be required to cover the gap. Recent provisions aim to regulate the treatment of cofinanced initiatives so as to give priority to projects intended to cover the infrastructure and public service deficit.

## Public Works in Lieu of Taxes Program (*Obras por Impuestos*)

The *Obras por Impuestos* program allows a private company, either individually or in a consortium, to finance and execute public projects selected by regional and local governments and then recover the total amount of the investment against its category of income taxes. The regional and local governments in turn cover the interest-free financing from their *canon* (resource revenue transfers), *sobrecanon* (other transfers), royalties, customs revenue, and investment resources for up to 10 years following the completion of the works. Under this scheme, regional and local governments simplify their procedures and therefore accelerate the execution of works. In 2013, investments totaling 405 million nuevos soles were made under this program.

In 2014, new regulations were approved to make the OXI Program more efficient and attractive during both formulation and execution phases. For the project formulation phase, the scope of application of the program was expanded in terms of its institutional coverage and the types of public interventions:

- Institutional coverage. Public universities receiving canon resources and royalties were incorporated into the program, allowing them to develop projects under it. The use of funds such as FONIPREL and FONIE was authorized to finance the development of projects under regional and local governments that do not receive canon resources or other specific resources.
- Coverage of types of public interventions. The OXI Program was expanded to any public investment project that is declared viable within the framework of the SNIP (previously applied primarily to infrastructure projects). Project maintenance can be included to contribute to project sustainability. Projects can also be carried out in combination with PPPs for the operation and maintenance phases.

[16] For example, transportation, electricity, sanitation, health, education, hydrocarbons, tourism, corrections services, and other sectors.

- The law also proposes more flexibility in the timing of the selection process. In the event of only one bidder, a direct award will be made, while the selection of the supervisor will be done at the same time using procedures similar to those for private companies.

During the execution phase, improvements were also made to the regional and local Public Investment Certificates (CIPRL).[17] Private companies can now use the CIPRLs against their income tax payments. In addition, it will be possible for the limits on the issuance of CIPRLs (that is, the execution of projects by this means) to be updated annually and to be revolving.

## REFERENCES

Abusada, Du Bois, Eduardo Morón, and José Valderrama. 2000. "La reforma incompleta: rescatando los noventa." Centro de Investigación de la Universidad del Pacífico, Instituto Peruano de Economía, Lima.

Arias, Luis, Elmer Cuba, and Raúl Salazar. 1997. "La Sostenibilidad de la Política Fiscal en Peru: 1970–1996." IDB Network of Centers for Development Working Paper R-316, Inter-American Development Bank, Washington, DC.

Asociación para el Fomento de la Infraestructura Nacional. 2012. "Por un Perú Integrado: Plan Nacional de Infraestructura 2012–2021." Asociación para el Fomento de la Infraestructura Nacional, Lima.

Castro, Juan Francisco, and Gustavo Yamada. 2010. "La economía peruana en la última década: Mejor desempeño y mayor resiliencia a las crisis." Paper prepared for the International Conference on Economic Policies in Latin America, Universidad del Pacifico, Centro de Investigaciones.

McNelis, Paul D. 1987. "Stabilization, Debt and IMF Intervention: Development Trade-offs in Ecuador and Peru." *Trócaire Development Review.* http://www.trocaire.org/resources/policyandadvocacy/trocaire-development-review-1987.

Melgarejo, Karl, and Waldo Mendoza. 2008. "La Efectividad de la Política Fiscal en el Peru, 1980-2006." Working Paper 262, Pontificia Universidad Católica del Peru. http://www.pucp.edu.pe/departamento/economia/images/documentos/DDD262.pdf.

Pastor, Jr., Manual, and Carol Wise. 1991. "Peruvian Economic Policy in the 1980s: From Orthodoxy to the Heterodoxy and Back." Working Paper No. 161, Kellogg Institute for International Studies, Notre Dame, Indiana.

Portocarrero Maisch, Javier (editor), Enrique Cornejo, Javier Cuba, Félix Jiménez, Javier Kapsoli, Waldo Mendoza, Eduardo Morón, Jean-Paul Rabanal, and José Valderrama. 2006. "Desafíos de la Política Fiscal en el Perú." Consorcio de Investigación Económica y Social, Lima. http://www.mef.gob.pe/contenidos/pol_econ/documentos/Desafios_politica_fiscal.pdf.

Remmer, Karen L. 1986. "The Politics of Economic Stabilization: IMF Standby Programs in Latin America, 1954–1984." *Comparative Politics* 19 (1): 1–24.

Santa Maria, Hugo, José Carlos Saavedra, and Lucero Burga. 2009. "Historia de la Política Fiscal en el Peru 1980–2009." http://www.ifaperu.org/uploads/articles/274_08_ct29_hsm.

[17] Certificates issued by the Ministry of the Economy and Finance to the private company that financed a works project from its income tax.

CHAPTER 6

# Evolution of Fiscal Rules in Peru

CESAR LIENDO

*Given the history of fiscal mismanagement in Latin America in the 1970s and 1980s, several countries in the region started experimenting with greater institutionalization of fiscal policy in the late 1990s and early 2000s. Examples included Colombia (1997), Peru (1999), Chile (2000), Brazil (2001), and Mexico (2003). In Peru, the macrofiscal framework introduced by the Law on Fiscal Prudence and Transparency (LPTF) was indeed critical to the country's economic recovery, but it is also important to note that the structure of the economy changed after enactment of the law, and that limitations in its design led to frequent modifications to the rules. The second-generation reform of the rules in 2014 aimed to make the LPTF rules permanent, but included well-defined exit clauses that are more transparent and simpler. To enhance their effectiveness, rules were supported by appropriate enforcement mechanisms, including provisions to correct past deviations. Finally, the new macrofiscal framework incorporating the second-generation reforms was designed to accommodate adjustments to potential structural changes affecting the Peruvian economy over the medium term. This greater flexibility is counterbalanced by the introduction of a Fiscal Council that will act as an auditor of fiscal policy. Significant changes to the operation of the budget of the public sector are still required for implementation of the new macrofiscal framework.*

## THE ORIGINAL FRAMEWORK

Peru's macrofiscal framework was institutionalized in 1999 with the enactment of the LPTF.[1] The main objective of this law was to establish a commitment toward fiscal balance over the business cycle, with fiscal surpluses built up during favorable periods and only moderate, nonrecurring fiscal deficits allowed during periods of lower growth. The law also included macrofiscal rules at the national level directed toward reducing discretion and improving the institutionalization of fiscal policy.[2,3] Exit clauses or exception rules were added to allow for more flexible fiscal management during national emergencies or international crises that seriously affected the national economy (for which a request from the Executive Branch to Congress would be required) or when there was sufficient evidence of a decline in real GDP supported by a report by the Ministry of the Economy and Finance (MEF) to Congress. Finally, a countercyclical instrument called the Fiscal Stabilization Fund was established.

The LPTF also included a proposal to prepare the public budget in two stages. The first stage consists of the approval by the Council of Ministers of the Multiyear Macroeconomic Framework (MMM), a document that contains fiscal policy guidelines and establishes overall spending and borrowing limits that are consistent with the fiscal rules and the country's macroeconomic

[1]The LPTF was enacted in December 1999 as Law No. 27245.

[2]The nonfinancial expenditure rule was applied to general government, limiting its growth to the annual average inflation rate plus 2 percentage points, while the deficit rule covered the consolidated public sector, whose fiscal deficit could not exceed 1 percent of GDP. It should be noted that the latter rule was subject to amendments or waivers in the early years, reflecting a gradual convergence toward the numerical limit.

[3]See also Supreme Decree No. 151-2004-EF (LRTF Regulation), Supreme Decree No. 066-2009-EF (Single Codified Text of the LRTF), and Supreme Decree No. 073-2009-EF (Annex of Definitions).

**TABLE 6.1**

**Conditions Set Out in the Fiscal Responsibility and Transparency Law for the Use of Fiscal Stabilization Fund Resources**

| Conditions to Be Met | Maximum Amount Allowed |
|---|---|
| • Decline in current revenues from ordinary sources exceeding 0.3 percent of GDP in comparison to the average over the previous three years | • Amount equivalent to the decline in revenues exceeding 0.3 percent of GDP and up to 40 percent of the resources of the Fiscal Stabilization Fund |
| • In national emergencies or international crises that can seriously affect the national economy or when there is sufficient evidence that GDP is declining in real terms<br>• The Fiscal Responsibility and Transparency Law (LRTF) regulation indicates that an emergency situation is considered to exist when real GDP growth is negative for three consecutive quarters or when there is a significant increase in international interest rates that raise annual interest payments to more than 0.4 percent of GDP<br>• The law indicates that "national emergency" should be understood to be the existence of a serious risk to the country's economic viability | • No limit established |
| • In the event the cumulative resources of the Fiscal Stabilization Fund exceed 4 percent of GDP | • Amount equivalent to the surplus accumulation above 4 percent of GDP is to be used only to reduce the public debt |

context. In the second stage, the annual budget is approved, breaking down expenditure by category for each *pliego* (budgetary entity receiving an appropriation), reflecting the government's priorities while respecting the fiscal rules reflected in the MMM limits. The LPTF also includes several rules on the control and monitoring of fiscal accounts as well as a process of reporting compliance with the fiscal rules to Congress.

In 2003, the LPTF was amended and renamed the Fiscal Responsibility and Transparency Law (LRTF).[4] The main amendments involved a change in the coverage of the national fiscal rules and improvements to the definition of the exception rules and the resources forming part of the Fiscal Stabilization Fund (Table 6.1), along with the introduction of fiscal rules for the regional and local governments in the context of the expansion of the fiscal decentralization process and tax efforts.[5,6]

The main objectives of this macrofiscal framework were to:

- Strengthen a multiyear vision with the three-year macrofiscal framework (the MMM), which sets out the government's medium-term vision for its fiscal policy, taking into account the projected macroeconomic context.
- Formalize the countercyclical role of fiscal policy with the creation of the Fiscal Stabilization Fund, which allows public resources to be saved in "good" years for use in "bad" years by means of a temporary expansion of public spending. It should be noted that specific clauses were established to govern the use of the resources of the Fiscal Stabilization Fund.
- Enhance the transparency of fiscal management by including a Declaration of Fiscal Policy Principles that provides an ex ante explanation of the guidelines and medium-term objectives of the fiscal policy to be implemented. This document is accompanied by monitoring and tracking reports and an ex post Fiscal Accountability Declaration to verify

[4] Law No. 27958, enacted in May 2003.

[5] With regard to the fiscal decentralization process, it should be noted that the first direct election of regional authorities took place in 2002, with their terms of office beginning in 2003 for a period of four years. See Chapter 10 for a more detailed description of the process.

[6] See Chapter 8 on tax reforms.

compliance with the fiscal rules as well as the amount by which the macrofiscal targets set out in the MMM have been missed, thus promoting accountability.[7] If there are significant deviations between the MMM projections and the actual outcomes, the differences must be justified and corrective measures adopted. Finally, the approval of the MMM (by the Council of Ministers) is subject to the technical opinion of the central bank (*Banco Central de Reserva del Perú*) to ensure compatibility with the bank's forecasts for the balance of payments, net international reserves, and monetary policy.

- Improve budget programming procedures. The focus of the two stages mentioned above is complemented ex post by the quarterly updating of estimated fiscal revenues for the year (and, therefore, the implied spending limits).

Two fiscal rules were also introduced:[8]

- *A limit on the fiscal deficit of the nonfinancial public sector of 1 percent of GDP.* In the event there is sufficient evidence that real GDP has been declining for three consecutive quarters or in case of a national emergency (and subject to a prior report by the MEF to Congress), compliance with this macrofiscal rule will not be mandatory and the deficit may rise to a maximum of 2.5 percent of GDP. This exception may be maintained for up to three years, with subsequent annual reductions of 0.5 percent of GDP per year.
- *A ceiling on the annual increase in current expenditure by the central government of 4 percent in real terms.* Current expenditure is understood to be the sum of remuneration, goods and services, and pensions. It should be noted that this rule in particular was amended on a number of occasions, resulting in a reduction in the coverage of the levels of government and the coverage of expenditures subject to the rule, with a view to promoting public investment. Initially, the rule was designed for the general government and covered all nonfinancial expenditure. The numerical limit was raised from an initial 2 percent to 3 percent in real terms in 2004 and to 4 percent in real terms in 2008, reflecting the estimate of the potential growth of the Peruvian economy. The differentiated treatment in the fiscal rule between public investment and current expenditure resulted in a growth rate for the stock of public capital that was out of line with expenditure on maintenance and equipment of that stock, thus limiting the impact of public investment on social welfare. It should be noted that this distortion in the treatment of public investment and current expenditure created perverse incentives to amend the rules. In 2012, expenditure on infrastructure maintenance, goods and services for social programs in the context of performance-based budgeting, and equipment for public order and security were excluded from the coverage of the current expenditure rule. Subsequently, in 2013 and 2014, only the fiscal deficit rule remained in effect.

While the macrofiscal framework introduced by the LRTF was key to consolidate sustainability, the structural characteristics of the Peruvian economy have changed since enactment of the law in 1999, creating several issues with the current framework:

- *Different stages of fiscal stabilization.* At the beginning of the 2000s, fiscal stabilization was in the early stages, with public debt standing at close to 50 percent of GDP and virtually no public financial assets, whereas currently public finances are in a consolidation phase, with public debt amounting to approximately 20 percent of GDP.

[7] According to Article 13 of the Single Codified Text of the LRTF, on May 31 of every year the MEF must submit to Congress and publish a Fiscal Accountability Declaration for the previous year, analyzing revenues, expenditures, the fiscal balance, and its financing, as well as other macroeconomic indicators, making comparisons with the projections in the MMM for the previous year. Compliance with the macrofiscal rules is also assessed.

[8] A borrowing rule was also established, which in essence must always be complied with, and rules for election years were introduced to distribute spending responsibilities between the incoming and outgoing administrations in years in which the national government changes (that is, late July of each election year).

- *The high profile of public investment in the medium-term economic growth process.* At the beginning of the last decade, the ratio of public investment to GDP was only 2.8 percent of GDP, while currently it stands at almost 6 percent of GDP, above the level in other countries in the region such as Uruguay and Colombia (4 percent of GDP), Chile (3 percent), and Brazil (2 percent).
- *Higher levels of expenditure by regional and local governments.* Currently, the investment by these levels of government (regional and local) represents 67 percent of total public investment. The macrofiscal framework has been designed for these levels of government, but, as noted in the 2013 report of the Commission to Strengthen the Macrofiscal Framework, flaws in design, transparency, recording and monitoring, and compliance persist and require correction.[9]
- *Implementation of this framework has not resulted in the reduction or elimination of the procyclical bias of fiscal policy.* A fiscal deficit rule (which is procyclical by definition), together with an expenditure rule whose coverage is limited to current expenditure, will not ensure an acyclical or countercyclical fiscal policy response. Regional and local governments were the main determinants of the procyclical pattern of public expenditure. An important source of this expansionary behavior by the regional and local governments resulted from the use of strong balance sheet positions (which are not under the control of the fiscal authority) and the system of transfers to regional and local governments, which is not dependent on a structural or medium-term price.[10] The growth of nonfinancial expenditure by the national government was close to the potential growth of the economy, whereas the growth of such expenditure in the case of the regional and local governments was much higher, amplifying the expansionary economic cycle (Table 6.2).
- *Greater importance of the natural resource sectors in public finances.* At the beginning of the 2000s, fiscal revenues from the natural resource sectors were equivalent to 2.4 percent of total general government revenues, whereas this share increased to 12.4 percent in 2014.[11] In addition, the volatility of fiscal revenues from the natural resource sectors during the same period (measured by the coefficient of variation) was more than double that of other fiscal revenues. The report of the Commission to Strengthen the Macrofiscal Framework noted in this regard that the rules should be redefined in the context of high fiscal dependency on resources from commodity exports, the prices of which are very volatile and are subject to a high degree of uncertainty, which reinforces the importance of avoiding a procyclical fiscal position, with rules providing ample coverage of expenditure and promoting savings in periods of high prices for commodities and, at the same time, strengthening the capacity to confront crises with sufficient resources in the circumstances that require countercyclical policies. Although in the coming years metal prices are expected to be lower than those recorded in previous years, a series of mining projects are expected to start operations, doubling copper output by 2017.
- *Greater openness to trade, which may reduce the effectiveness of fiscal policy (especially if expenditures are on imported goods).* The degree of openness to trade, measured as the ratio of exports plus imports to GDP, was 34 percent at the beginning of the last decade and currently stands at 50 percent.

[9]The Commission to Strengthen the Macrofiscal Framework was created by law No. 29854.

[10]The balance sheet positions of the regional and local governments are accumulated unused resources from previous fiscal years, of which the main source of financing is the payment of the canon (50 percent of the income tax for the previous year) and royalties from the extractive sectors such as mining and gas. At end-2013, the balance sheet positions of the regional or local governments were equivalent to S/. 7.4 billion (1.4 percent of GDP).

[11]Revenues from the mining and hydrocarbons sectors includes the Category 3 Income Tax, adjustments, royalties, the Special Mining Tax, Special Mining Contribution, and the *Remanente de utilidades mineras.*

**TABLE 6.2**

**Peru: Nonfinancial Expenditure by the General Government** *(Percent change in real terms)*

| | 2007 | 2008 |
|---|---|---|
| General Government | 7.6 | 12.6 |
| National Government | 5.3 | 6 |
| Regional Government[1] | 14.4 | 5.2 |
| Local Government[1] | 8.3 | 47.8 |

Source: Ministry of the Economy and Finance.
[1]Subnational governments represent about 40 percent of total general government spending.

- *A significant level of explicit contingent liabilities, which would increase the amount of public debt significantly.* In recent years, the number and amount of contingent liabilities have risen substantially and this unfavorable trend could continue in the future.[12] According to the 2012–14 MMM published in May 2011, explicit contingent liabilities totaled 7.4 percent of GDP in 2010. The main liabilities are legal actions (3.4 percent of GDP), especially labor or civil suits, and nonfinancial guarantees set out in concession contracts (2.1 percent of GDP), such as the minimum annual guaranteed revenues or investment returns, among others.

The macrofiscal framework set out in the LRTF has not been sufficiently flexible to adapt to the economic and institutional changes mentioned above. This has resulted in continuous amendments to the LRTF over the past decade, affecting its predictability, simplicity, and transparency (Annex 6.1).[13]

## SECOND-GENERATION INSTITUTIONAL FRAMEWORK

The Commission to Strengthen the Macrofiscal Framework was created to strengthen Peru's fiscal management by assessing and developing a proposal to improve the existing macrofiscal framework, especially in terms of the accountability and transparency mechanisms and fiscal rules. The commission was made up of representatives of the MEF and the central bank, along with four independent professionals who are experts in fiscal matters. This commission was given the mandate to prepare a document setting out proposals for strengthening Peru's macrofiscal framework in the coming years, with cooperation in the technical areas from the MEF and the central bank. The commission also received comments and suggestions from international organizations.

In accordance with the recommendations of the commission, the MEF prepared a regulatory proposal for the macrofiscal framework that makes it more comprehensive, transparent, and flexible; removes the volatility of public revenues affected by commodity prices; strengthens the automatic stabilizers in the economy; uses countercyclical fiscal policy for significant economic downturns and not for purposes of fine-tuning; establishes the responsibilities of each competent authority (national, regional, and local governments) in terms of the coverage of public expenditure; simplifies the rules for the regional and local governments; strengthens accountability; and creates greater institutionalization. The Law to Strengthen Fiscal Responsibility and Transparency

[12]Explicit contingencies are defined as liabilities formalized in a legal instrument. Also included are liabilities in the form of Certificates in Recognition of the Right to Annual Payments for Works issued by the licensor certifying and accrediting its direct, general, unconditional, and irrevocable obligation to pay.

[13]The fiscal rule in effect for 2013 establishes that the fiscal balance of the nonfinancial public sector cannot be negative. The subnational rules are based on the provisions of Emergency Decree No. 108-2009 published on November 9, 2009.

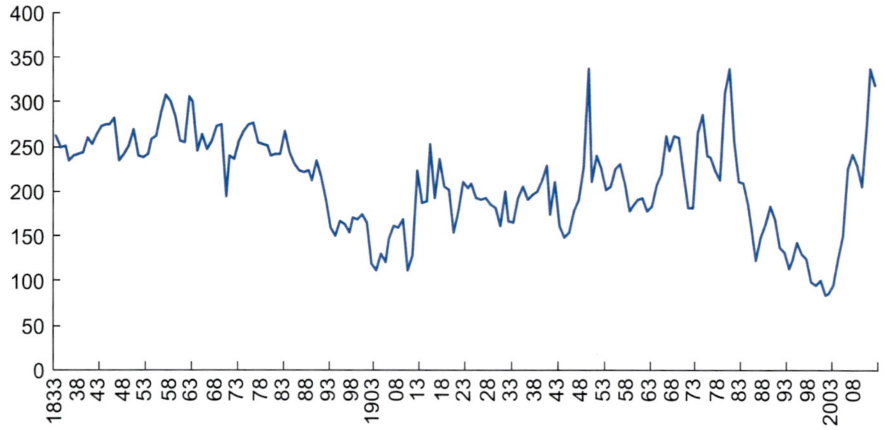


Source: Ministry of the Economy and Finance.

**Figure 6.1** Peru: Index of Prices of Exported Metals, 1833–2012 (*In real terms, seasonally adjusted*)

(Law No. 30099), incorporating the commission's recommendations, was approved on October 31, 2013, and entered into effect with the budget for 2015.

The new macrofiscal framework constitutes a step forward in the process of institutional change that began early in the 2000s with the LRTF. In this context, the macrofiscal framework proposed the following objectives to be achieved under a more flexible and predictable system that, in turn, strengthens the commitment to fiscal accountability:

- *Create greater predictability of public spending by delinking it from the most volatile source of public revenues, that is, revenues from the natural resource sectors (Annex 6.2).* Public expenditure should not be volatile, since this leads to efficiency and management capacity costs at the level of sectoral policies. Public spending should therefore be isolated from the high volatility of revenues from Peru's main export commodities. Historically, the behavior of commodity prices has been volatile, erratic, and difficult to predict. In addition to significant short-term price fluctuations, commodity price cycles can be very long. According to the report of the Technical Commission for the Improvement of the Macrofiscal Framework (2013), the average duration of export price cycles is approximately 36 years (Figure 6.1).
- *Ensure fiscal solvency by maintaining a low level of public debt,* which makes it possible to deal with negative shocks such as severe natural disasters, contingencies, international financial crises, etc.
- *Smooth out the business cycle by using timely countercyclical measures only in contexts in which the economy deviates significantly from its medium-term trend.* Fiscal policy in Peru has limitations in serving as an instrument of adjustment because (1) fiscal policy operates with a significant lag; (2) it is not possible to fully control the entire fiscal stimulus (expenditures of regional and local governments financed from the canon, compensation funds, and tax revenues of the local governments); (3) the current system of transfers is procyclical and finances a significant percentage of expenditure, especially public investment; (4) there is uncertainty regarding the size of the fiscal multipliers; and (5) there is ex ante uncertainty regarding the origin of the shock (supply or demand). Difficulties in controlling these factors would mean that fiscal policy ultimately could add greater volatility to GDP in the short term if not properly calibrated.

- *Simplify the fiscal rules of regional and local governments.* The main issues to be confronted here result from the heterogeneity of these governments' public finances, the low level of compliance with the fiscal rules, and the scarcity of corrective measures owing to a lack of effective and timely information, monitoring, and guidance mechanisms, as well as a lack of incentives.
- *Improve the institutional framework of the Fiscal Stabilization Fund* by providing it with a Technical Secretariat whose functions include the proposal of investment guidelines to the Fiscal Stabilization Fund board to improve investment returns.
- *Strengthen fiscal institutionalization by creating a Fiscal Council.* The new macrofiscal framework abandons the previous rigid system of fiscal rules; however, this greater discretion should be "restricted" in the sense of having an autonomous entity that "audits" or validates.

The new macrofiscal rule applies to the nonfinancial expenditure of the national government that is supported in a fiscal year prior to cyclical adjustment to the balances of the nonfinancial public sector. This fiscal rule seeks to limit the fiscal aggregate that is under the control of the national government and, at the same time, make it more comprehensive than the previous expenditure rule. Thus, the nonfinancial expenditure rule for the national government includes all nonfinancial expenditures; transfers to nonfinancial public sector entities, with the exception of resources from the canon, the *sobrecanon* (other transfers), and royalties; the Municipal Compensation Fund (FONCOMUN); the Camisea Socioeconomic Development Fund (FOCAM); and participation in customs revenues (the case of regional and local governments). Based on figures for 2013, the new expenditure rule covers 81.5 percent of nonfinancial expenditure of general government, while the previous expenditure rule covered only 46.1 percent.[14]

A cyclical adjustment seeks to delink public finances from their temporary component, that is, the portion affected by cyclical changes in real GDP and changes in commodity prices that significantly influence the design of budgetary expenditure limits. The incorporation of cyclical adjustment indicators in the documents guiding fiscal policy in Peru is a recent development. Starting in 2006, the MEF incorporated indicators for the structural fiscal balance of the nonfinancial public sector in the MMM. In 2012, the MEF authorized the institutionalization of this type of fiscal indicator as a tool for analyzing fiscal policy and published a working paper detailing the methodology used.

Thus, with the approval of Law No. 30099, the methodology for calculating the structural fiscal balance had legal support. It now forms an important part of the budgetary planning process and the determination of the fiscal rules. Also, to increase the required transparency of all fiscal rules, the Second Additional Transitional Provision of Law No. 30099 called for the creation of a Technical Working Group of independent experts to prepare the methodology for the structural accounts of the nonfinancial public sector.

An important feature of the proposed methodology of the Technical Working Group was simplicity, so that the methodology would be more transparent and could be reproduced by external agents. A simple methodology—at least during the initial phase of implementation of the fiscal rule that will guide the country's budgetary process—will facilitate communication and understanding of the concepts and general guidelines of the new fiscal rule. It should be noted that various commodity-exporting countries such as Chile, Colombia, Norway, Canada, and Australia currently incorporate structural balance exercises in their macrofiscal frameworks.

A component of this macrofiscal framework is the announcement of an ex ante structural guideline, which will have a binding effect for formulation of the budget. To determine the expenditure rules that will have that binding effect, it will be necessary for the incoming government,

[14]The Technical Working Group was created by Ministerial Resolution No. 373-2013-EF/10 to provide technical recommendations on the methodology of calculating the structural balances, and its report was published on December 24, 2013.

during the first 90 days of its term, to define and announce in a Macrofiscal Policy Declaration its fiscal policy objectives for its governing period and the impact of those objectives on the structural economic balance of the nonfinancial public sector (the ex ante structural guideline). It should be noted that this structural guideline is binding for the preparation of the public budgets. However, the ex post assessment focuses on the expenditure threshold that is derived from the ex ante structural guideline. The current rule thus differs from the Chilean case, in which the fiscal aggregate used for the fiscal rule is the structural fiscal balance. The reason for this is that, given thc level of development of the Peruvian economy, there is still room to implement reforms that permanently affect fiscal revenues. This could generate some instability in the tax base (structural), making ex post compliance with a rule on the structural fiscal balance difficult.

The determination of the ex ante structural guideline has a limit of −1 percent of GDP, which is justified by the following factors:

- In a stress scenario in which economic growth is lower and financial costs for the sovereign debt are higher than that recorded in the previous decade, a structural deficit of 1 percent of GDP is consistent with a downward trend in the public debt-to-GDP ratio, maintaining the macroeconomic credibility of the country on the international financial markets.
- Bearing in mind the current levels of Peru's public debt (low by international standards), and with a view to identifying a debt level that would jeopardize fiscal sustainability and thus require the use of corrective measures, an analysis was made of the medium-term trends in variables that are decisive for fiscal sustainability. These included GDP growth, the cost of financing of the sovereign debt, exchange rate depreciation, and other factors.[15,16] Assuming GDP growth of 4 percent (similar to the 1951–2011 average and below the average growth of 6.4 percent during the past decade), a cost of financing the sovereign debt of 10 percent (double that recorded in the past decade), exchange rate depreciation of 6 percent (exchange rate depreciation during the period 1995–2012 was 1.2 percent), and a primary balance for the nonfinancial public sector of between 1 and 1.5 percent of GDP (the 1990–2012 historical average was 1.4 percent), the debt would fluctuate around 30 percent of GDP. In other words, even stress assumptions in comparison with the historical behavior of the Peruvian economy show that public debt increases only to 30 percent from current levels.
- Important infrastructure and social gaps need to be closed. With the definition of an ex ante structural guideline of −1 percent of GDP, it becomes clear that transitional fiscal revenues would be invested to close the significant existing infrastructure and social gaps, with a high level of economic and social return.

The multiyear projection of nonfinancial expenditure levels of the general government can be calculated by combining this ex ante guideline for the structural fiscal balance of the nonfinancial public sector with the multiyear projection of structural revenues of general government, the primary balance for nonfinancial public enterprises, and the payment of interest. The following key equation is used:

$$GNFGG_t = IEstructurales_t + IK_t + RPEmpresas_t - Intereses_t - Guía\ Estructural_t,$$

where $GNFGG_t$ is the nonfinancial expenditure of general government, which is the sum of structural revenues of general government, capital revenues and the primary balance of the public

[15] A standard fiscal sustainability exercise was carried out on the basis of the work of Buiter (1985) and Blanchard (1990).

[16] We define real interest rates on the domestic and external debt expressed in domestic currency as $r_t^d = \frac{(1+i_t^d)}{(1+\pi_t)} - 1$ and $r_t^E = \frac{(1+i_t^*)(1+e_t)}{(1+\pi_t)} - 1$, obtaining an average interest weighted by the composition of the public debt.

enterprises (*IEstructurales*$_t$, $IK_t$ and *RPEmpresas*$_t$, respectively), minus debt service interest (*Intereses*$_t$), and an ex ante guideline established for the entire period of the respective government.

For its part, the expenditure rule of the regional and local governments establishes that growth of projected nonfinancial expenditure will be based on the average growth of annual own revenues over the previous four years.

Taking into account that general government includes the national, regional, and local governments, the national government's nonfinancial expenditure rule is determined as the difference between the nonfinancial expenditure of general government (defined in the cyclical adjustment exercise) and the nonfinancial expenditure of the regional and local governments (defined by their own fiscal rules) for a period of three years. This could be revised annually during preparation of the budget, as long as there are no changes or amendments to the Macrofiscal Policy Declaration or the methodology for calculating the structural accounts.

This new definition of the expenditure rules responds to a clearer and more transparent delimitation of the responsibilities of the various levels of government, in a context of significant fiscal decentralization. It should be noted that the national government's expenditure rule includes both current and capital expenditure, with a view to strengthening consistency between the expansion of the stock of public capital and expenditure on the maintenance and equipment of that stock. In this regard, the Commission to Strengthen the Macrofiscal Framework reports that the distinction between "public investment" and "current expenditure" of the public sector is weak and partially fictitious because some public investments do not generate a substantive social return, while many components of current expenditure, such as the maintenance of public infrastructure and expenditure on health and education, can have a higher level of return. Below is the description of the main components of the rules:

- Expenditure rules—The fiscal rule on national government nonfinancial expenditure provides some flexibility in the determination of expenditure limits, and these limits can thus be amended under very specific circumstances, with prior detailed substantiation. These circumstances include a countercyclical response in the event of a significant deviation of GDP from its level of 2 percent of potential or medium-term GDP up to an amount equivalent to 25 percent of the estimated deviation of GDP or ½ percent of GDP. The establishment of a limit on the countercyclical response seeks to partially moderate or cushion the impact. In the case of a major deviation of GDP from its potential or medium-term level, the exception clause could be activated, which allows for the amendment of the ex ante structural guideline, and a larger countercyclical response could thus be implemented. The establishment of a threshold of 2 percent of potential GDP for implementing countercyclical measures responds to the objective of reserving fiscal policy for low-probability but high-impact events. Thus, in accordance with this threshold, countercyclical fiscal measures could have been applied in 2001, 2008, and 2009 to reduce the volatility of the economic cycle (Figure 6.2).
- Limits on unspent balances—Underexecution of authorized expenditure in the previous year cannot exceed 0.2 percent of GDP. This limit is consistent with the average amount of continued investments over the past seven years (0.25 percent of GDP). To the extent that authorized expenditure is a reflection of permanent fiscal revenues, this expenditure must be allowed to be executed over a multiyear period; the limit of 0.2 percent of GDP is intended to give predictability to the budget planning process.
- Increases in spending due to tax regime changes—Expenditure can be increased if there are permanent changes stemming from tax measures that generate permanent changes in fiscal revenues of at least 0.3 percent of GDP. The accuracy of the estimate of the impact of these tax changes is corroborated by the Fiscal Council, with a view to giving greater transparency to fiscal management.

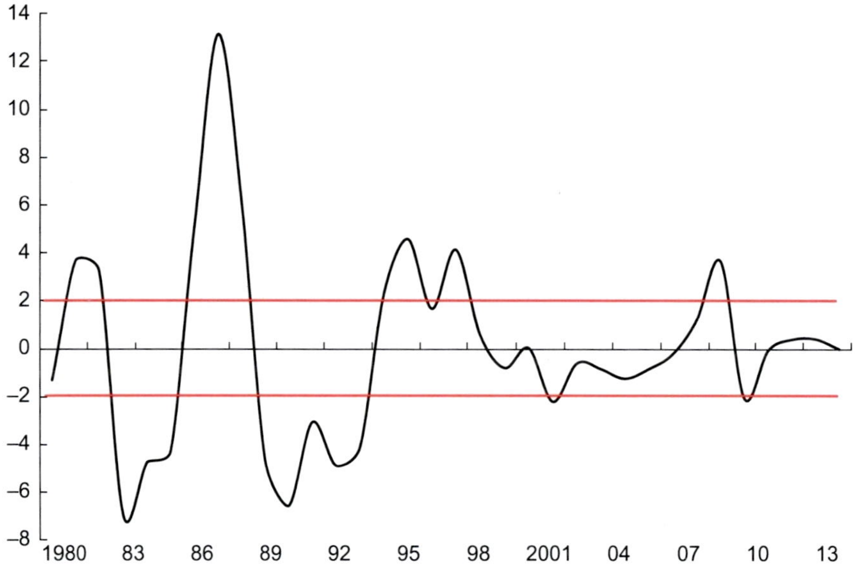


Sources: Central Reserve Bank of Peru; and Ministry of the Economy and Finance.

**Figure 6.2** Peru: Output Gap (*Percent of potential GDP*)

Compliance with the fiscal rules must go hand-in-hand with corrective measures in the case of deviations. This strengthens the commitment of the macrofiscal framework to responsible fiscal management. The new macrofiscal framework considers two types of corrective measures.

- The first corrective measure proposes the creation of an account to offset and correct deviations (called the notional account in the economic literature). In other words, in the event that accrued expenditure by the national government exceeds the limits established by the fiscal rule in a particular year, the deviation will be recorded in this notional account. If the cumulative balance in this account is less than ½ percent of GDP, the nonfinancial expenditure limit for the national budget will be reduced at least proportionately in the following two years, as long as a negative GDP gap greater than 2 percent of potential GDP is not projected. In the event that the cumulative balance recorded in the notional account is higher than or equal to ½ percent of GDP, the reduction in the nonfinancial expenditure limit of the national government is immediate. In this way, the account to offset and correct deviations applies automatic sanctions in the event of noncompliance with the fiscal rules. Likewise, to minimize the perverse incentive of postponing and thus passing on the correction to future governments, it was established that the balance of the notional account should not be greater than 0.3 percent of GDP at the end of a government's term.
- The second corrective measure of the macrofiscal framework, in line with the objective of ensuring fiscal sustainability, proposes that if it is verified or predicted that the public sector's public debt will be higher than 30 percent of GDP in the following three years, the Macrofiscal Policy Declaration and the ex ante structural guideline of the nonfinancial public sector will be amended, incorporating appropriate measures to restrict expenditure or increase revenues, so as to return to a level of debt lower than this threshold within a period of no more than seven years. It should also be noted that an expenditure rule was established for human resources (the payroll rule), limiting expenditure to the threshold established by applying the growth rate for potential GDP in nominal terms to the estimated limit of nonfinancial expenditure on personnel and pensions in the previous year.

To determine the nominal limit of this expenditure, the midpoint of the target inflation range established by the *Banco Central de Reserva del Perú* will be used.

The proposed macrofiscal framework seeks to be more flexible than the previous framework and is based on an ex ante cyclical adjustment exercise. To that end, it is necessary to improve the transparency of fiscal management through the creation of a Fiscal Council. The purpose of this council is to provide independent technical analyses of macrofiscal policy by issuing nonbinding opinions on the following issues: (1) the amendment of and compliance with the fiscal rules, (2) the fiscal projections contained in the MMM, (3) short- and medium-term fiscal developments, and (4) the methodology for the calculation of the structural accounts and potential GDP. The reports issued by this Fiscal Council, which will be made up of at least three independent professionals with broad experience in fiscal matters, should be published and made available to the general public.

In summary, the new macrofiscal framework has been designed to allow for adjustments to potential structural changes affecting the Peruvian economy over the medium term. This greater discretion is "restricted" in the sense that it is accompanied by a Fiscal Council that will act as ex ante and ex post auditor of fiscal policy. A lengthy pending agenda remains and, for purposes of implementation of the new macrofiscal framework, significant changes are needed in the operation of the public sector budget.

## ANNEX 6.1. CHANGES, SUSPENSIONS, AND EXCEPTIONS TO FISCAL RULES

| Year | Expenditure Rule | Deficit Rule |
|---|---|---|
| 2000 | | The maximum fiscal deficit may not exceed 2 percent of GDP in 2000.[1] |
| 2001 | | Application of the numerical deficit rule was suspended in 2001. |
| 2002 | | Application of the numerical deficit rule was suspended in 2002. |
| 2003 | Application of the fiscal expenditure rule was waived. | The maximum fiscal deficit may not exceed 2 percent of GDP.[2] |
| 2004 | • The limit on nonfinancial expenditure by the general government was amended from 2 percent to a real level of 3 percent.<br>• Seven fiscal rules were introduced for regional and local governments. | The maximum fiscal deficit may not be more than 1.5 percent of GDP.[3] |
| 2005 | Application of the fiscal expenditure rule was waived. | |
| 2006 | Application of the fiscal expenditure rule was waived. | |
| 2007 | • Institutional coverage was amended from the general government to the central government and coverage of nonfinancial expenditure to current expenditure (remuneration and goods and services).<br>• Starting in 2007, use of the central bank target (2 percent) rather than the GDP deflator for the calculation of real growth of expenditure. | |
| 2008 | • The definition of current expenditure was expanded (remuneration, goods and services, and pensions) and the limit on current expenditure was amended from 3 to 4 percent. | |
| 2009 | In 2009, application of the fiscal expenditure rule was suspended owing to implementation of the Fiscal Stimulus Plan, and temporary limits were established (10 percent for 2009 and 8 percent for 2010). | Application of the fiscal deficit rule was suspended owing to implementation of the Fiscal Stimulus Plan, and a new limit of 2 percent of GDP was established. |
| 2010 | In 2010, the fiscal rules of the regional and local governments were amended and reduced (from seven fiscal rules to five).[4] | Application of the fiscal deficit rule was suspended owing to implementation of the Fiscal Stimulus Plan, and a new limit of 2 percent of GDP was established. |

*(continued)*

## ANNEX 6.1. (*continued*)

| Year | Expenditure Rule | Deficit Rule |
|---|---|---|
| 2011 | The rise in the average annual consumer price index for Metropolitan Lima rather than the central bank target was used to calculate real growth of current expenditure. | |
| 2012 | • Expenditure on maintenance of infrastructure, goods and services of social programs covered by the performance-based budgeting scheme, and equipment intended for public order and security were excluded from current expenditure.<br>• The rise in the average annual consumer price index for Metropolitan Lima rather than the central bank target was used to calculate real growth of current expenditure. | |
| 2013 | Application of the fiscal expenditure rule was waived. | The nonfinancial public sector balance for 2013 could not show a deficit.[5] A surplus of 0.9 percent of GDP was recorded. |

Source: Ministry of the Economy and Finance legal rules.

[1]The Single Additional Transitional Provision of the Law on Fiscal Prudence and Transparency (Law No. 27245) indicated that the maximum fiscal deficit may not exceed 2 percent of GDP for 2000 or 1.5 percent of GDP for 2001.

[2]The Second Additional Transitional Provision of the Fiscal Responsibility and Transparency Law (LRTF) (Law No. 27958, which amended Law No. 27245) indicated that the maximum fiscal deficits of the nonfinancial public sector for 2003 and 2004 may not exceed 2 percent and 1.5 percent of GDP, respectively. The transition period for the fiscal deficit ended in 2004. Starting in 2005, the fiscal deficit rule was governed by the limits established in Article 4(1)(b) of the LRTF (1 percent of GDP).

[3]Article 4(2)(d) and (e) and Article 5-A of the Single Codified Text of Law No. 27245 introduced seven fiscal rules for regional and local governments, which were in effect starting in 2009.

[4]Emergency Decree No. 108-2009 suspended application of the fiscal rules for regional and local governments set out in the Law on Fiscal Responsibility and Transparency for 2009 and 2010 and established fiscal rules for these years (five rules). The effect of this provision was extended to the following years by the 2011 and 2012 Budget Laws.

[5]The Sixth Additional Final Provision of Law No. 29952, the Law on the Financial Equilibrium of the Budget of the Public Sector for 2013. According to the same provision, this rule was applied in replacement of the provisions of Article 4(1)(a) and (b) of the Single Codified Text of the Law on Fiscal Responsibility and Transparency.

## ANNEX 6.2. FUEL STABILIZATION FUND

The Fuel Price Stabilization Fund (FEPC) was created to prevent volatility in the prices of crude oil and its derivatives on the international market from affecting domestic prices and end-users in Peru. The empirical evidence and international experience with petroleum-based fuel price stabilization policies in emerging net-importing countries shows that a mechanism such as the FEPC should (1) reduce the volatility of domestic prices of petroleum-based fuels, (2) mitigate the impact of supply shocks on the local economy, (3) minimize fiscal costs so as not to affect fiscal sustainability, (4) direct benefits to the most vulnerable segments of the population, and (5) avoid distortions in relative prices (Appendix Figure 6.2.1) (Arze del Granado, Coady, and Gillingham 2010; Bacon and Kojima 2008; Coady and others 2012; Hamilton 2005; International Energy Agency and others 2010; IMF 2008; Jiménez-Rodríguez and Sánchez 2004; and Kojima 2009).

The FEPC establishes a band or range of prices based on the reference prices for each fuel published each week by the state energy and mining investment regulator (OSINERGMIN). Thus, when the reference price for a particular fuel is above a particular maximum threshold (or ceiling), the domestic price will not increase; and when the reference price is below a minimum level (or floor), refineries will maintain their domestic prices to recover the foregone amounts at the higher prices. In this way, when prices are above the maximum level (ceiling), refineries will absorb the costs and this will be offset by the recovery of the foregone amount when prices are below the minimum level (floor). The assets of the FEPC consist of the contributions and discounts offered by the refineries on the prices of their products, depending on whether the reference prices for fuel are above or below the price stabilization bands.

On the basis of international practices, the MEF has been reforming the operations of the FEPC to reduce the level of discretion in its operations, achieve greater transparency, and reduce

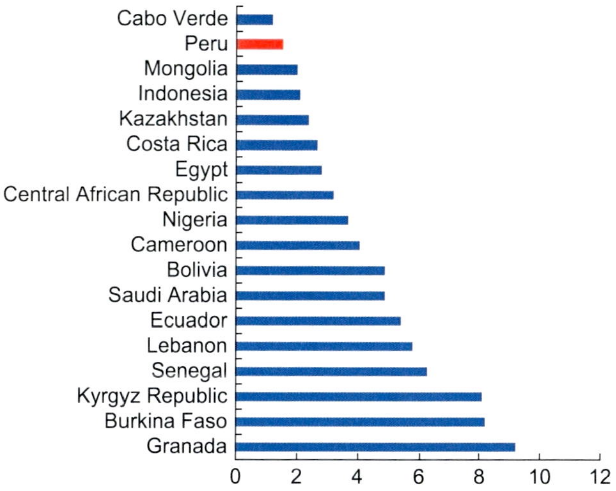


Source: IMF staff calculations.

**Appendix Figure 6.2.1** Peru: Fiscal Cost of Oil Price Stabilization Mechanisms, Selected Countries (*Percent of GDP, 2013*)

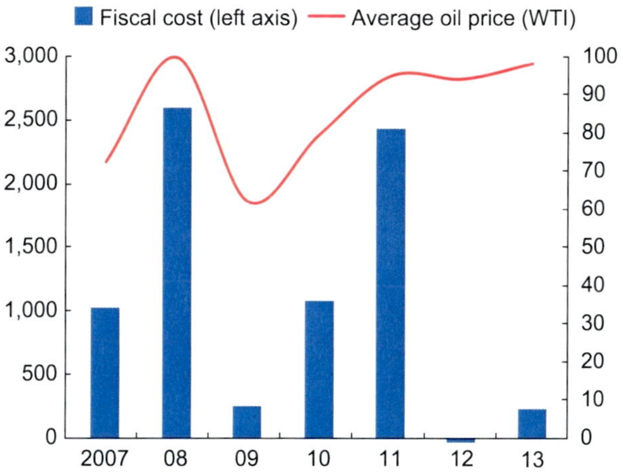


Sources: Ministry of Energy and Mining; Ministry of the Economy and Finance; OSINERGMIN.

**Appendix Figure 6.2.2** Peru: Fiscal Cost of Fuel Price Stabilization Fund (*Millions of nuevos soles and U.S. dollars per barrel*)

the fiscal cost. Examples of these reforms include establishment of periodic rules to update prices, an increase in the periodic variations in the price bands, exclusion of specific segments that do not represent vulnerable segments of the population, and exclusion of fuels such as high-octane gasoline and gasohol. These measures have helped reduce the fiscal cost significantly, making Peru one of the countries with the lowest fiscal cost associated with fuel price stabilization mechanisms (Appendix Figure 6.2.2). The reforms undertaken to improve the operation of the FEPC reduced its total fiscal cost from about 0.7 percent of GDP in 2011 to 0.04 percent by 2013.

## REFERENCES

Arze del Granado, J., D. Coady, and R. Gillingham. 2010. "The Unequal Benefits of Fuel Subsidies: A Review of Evidence for Developing Economies." Working Paper 10/202, International Monetary Fund, Washington, DC.

Bacon, R., and M. Kojima. 2008. "Coping with Oil Price Volatility." World Bank Energy Sector Management Assistance Program Working Paper, August, World Bank, Washington, DC.

Blanchard, O. 1990. "Suggestions for a New Set of Fiscal Indicators." OECD Working Paper No. 79, Organisation for Economic Co-operation and Development, Paris.

Buiter, W. 1985. "A Guide to Public Sector Debt and Deficits." *Economic Policy: A European Forum* 1 (November): 13–79.

Coady, D., J. Arze del Granado, L. Eyraud, H. Jin, V. Thakoor, A. Tuladhar, and L. Nemeth. 2012. "Automatic Fuel Pricing Mechanisms with Price Smoothing: Design, Implementation, and Fiscal Implications." IMF Technical Note and Manual, December, International Monetary Fund, Washington, DC.

Hamilton, J. 2005. "Oil and the Macroeconomy." In *The New Palgrave Dictionary of Economics,* edited by Steven N. Durlauf and Lawrence E. Blume. New York: Palgrave-Macmillan.

International Energy Agency, Organization of Petroleum Exporting Countries, Organisation for Economic Co-operation and Development, and the World Bank. 2010. "Analysis of the Scope of Energy Subsidies and Suggestions for the G-20 Initiative." Paper prepared for the G-20 meeting, Toronto, June.

International Monetary Fund. 2008. "Food and Fuel Prices—Recent Developments, Macroeconomic Impact, and Policy Responses." Prepared by the Fiscal Affairs, Policy Development and Review, and Research Departments. June 30. http://www.imf.org/external/np/pp/eng/2008/063008.pdf.

Jiménez-Rodríguez, R., and M. Sánchez. 2004. "Oil Price Shocks and Real GDP Growth Empirical Evidence for some OECD Countries." ECB Working Paper No. 362, European Central Bank, Frankfurt.

Kojima, M. 2009. "Governments Response to Oil Price Volatility: Experiences of 49 Developing Economies." Extractive Industries for Development Series No. 10. World Bank, Washington, DC.

Technical Commission for the Improvement of the Macrofiscal Framework (*Comisión Técnica para el Perfeccionamiento del Marco Macrofiscal*). 2013. "Marco Macrofiscal del Perú, propuestas para fortalecerlo." Research Document of the Ministry of Economy and Finance of Peru. July.

CHAPTER 7

# Fiscal Framework Alternatives for a Resource-Rich Country

SVETLANA VTYURINA

*Many resource-rich developing countries have to reconcile high development and infrastructure needs with low per capita incomes, scarcity of domestic capital, and limited access to international capital markets. They face the challenge of transforming resource wealth into other assets that support sustained development, while also maintaining mechanisms to avoid the boom-bust cycles that stem from volatility in natural resource revenues. Given these challenges, common advice based on traditional consumption-savings/investment theories has been difficult to assimilate and justify at the individual country level. Conscious of this experience, the IMF has recently developed a macrofiscal framework that presents new policy analysis tools for resource-rich developing countries that could help them target multiple objectives of development and saving.*

In Peru, growth has been at historic highs over the past decade, but the country still has a significant infrastructure gap, and a quarter of its population still lives in poverty.[1] Like other resource-rich developing countries, Peru has been confronted with the problem of finding an optimal solution to raise income per capita through sustainable growth and investment, while safeguarding macro stability against the price volatility and exhaustibility of its natural wealth. Although Peru depends much less on resource revenues than many oil-producing countries, the linkages to the fiscal accounts and the real economy are significant enough to warrant the design of a fiscal anchor to help the country deal with the challenges posed to fiscal management by the "resource curse."[2] A fiscal framework along the lines recently approved by the authorities, anchored by suitable fiscal rules and a strong institutional setup, should help Peru attain these multiple objectives.

## ANALYTICAL CONSIDERATIONS FOR RESOURCE MANAGEMENT

Virtually all natural resource–rich countries are faced with two main issues relating to the proper use and the price volatility of resource wealth: (1) how much of resource revenues should they consume and invest and how should they save the remainder, and (2) how to cope with the uncertainty and price volatility of resources, which affect exports, revenues, and nonresource GDP growth.[3] As mentioned earlier, for resource-rich developing countries, determining how to use resource revenues is complicated by greater pressure to spend, as their development needs are sizable. However, it is important to consider the length of the extraction horizon. If the horizon is relatively long, then in the short- to medium-term identifying policies to cope with price uncertainty takes precedence over the issue of exhaustibility. Uncertainty, in turn, relates to the

[1]Some analysts estimated Peru's infrastructure gap in 2012 to be around 44 percent of GDP, or about $88 billion.
[2]The term "resource curse" was coined by Richard M. Auty (1993) to describe the phenomenon that many resource-rich developing countries often develop more slowly than countries with fewer natural resources.
[3]This section draws on IMF (2012a, 2012b, 2013b).

size of reserves, extraction potential in a given period, average prices, and the likely volatility of the reserves in the short term.

While estimating reserves and production levels is certainly difficult, a much greater challenge is how to deal with commodity price fluctuations. Given the ever-changing global environment, it has proven extremely difficult to forecast prices with a reasonable degree of confidence, even over the medium term. Large swings in prices also complicate the task of policymakers who want to assess whether a shock is permanent (warranting adjustment) or temporary (warranting smoothing). In addition, production might be disrupted by technical difficulties, accidents, strikes, social and political unrest, and cross-border disputes. Production forecasts may prove too optimistic because of delays in investment or for economic reasons (e.g., a drop in international demand or substitution with other commodities).

Volatility and uncertainty call for a holistic approach to natural resource management. Many countries deal with the unforeseen swings in resource envelopes by building up a liquidity fund to smooth consumption spending. Saving for precautionary (prudential) reasons is conceptually different from other motives, such as saving for future generations or temporarily parking revenue to minimize absorptive-capacity disruptions. Additional savings can be used to pay down debt, ramp up domestic investment spending, or invest in external financial assets (e.g., when absorptive capacity constraints make it impossible to invest faster).

## ROLE OF NATURAL RESOURCES IN PERU

Peru is rich in various natural resources. In recent years, Peru occupied a leading position in the global production of the following mineral commodities: copper (third after Chile); silver (second after Mexico); tin (third after China and Indonesia); zinc (third after China and Australia); lead (fourth after China, Australia, and the United States); molybdenum (fourth after China, the United States, and Chile); and gold (sixth after China, Australia, the United States, Russia, and South Africa).[4] In Latin America, Peru was first in the production of gold, lead, tin, and zinc, and second in the production of cadmium, copper, mercury, molybdenum, phosphate rock, selenium, and silver.

Peru also has large actual and potential reserves, including of natural gas (Table 7.1). In 2012, Peruvian mining production amounted to $27 billion, equivalent to about 4 percent of global mining production, placing the country in seventh place among the world's largest mining producers. Peru's economy is relatively dependent on extraction and export of natural resources. In 2013, Peru's resource GDP constituted about 12 percent of nominal domestic product, compared to about 6 percent in 2002 (2007 base year; see Table 7.2). In real terms, however, this share actually decreased from over 15 percent of GDP in 2002 to about 12 percent in 2013 due to changes in the terms of trade. After growing at an average of 7 percent in the first half of the 2000s in real terms, the sector's growth rate in 2013 slowed to almost the same rate of a decade earlier of about 3.5 percent. Exports (which broadly follow production) accounted for 11.5 percent of GDP in 2013, growing 5 percentage points in dollar terms over the past decade.

Investment in the minerals and petroleum sector in Peru has been growing at an impressive rate. This has been due to increased world demand (not least from China) and low extraction costs, but also due to the country's macroeconomic stability, a good investment climate, and increasing engagement of operating companies with local communities. The stability of the Peruvian judicial framework has also helped encourage investment in this sector. Foreign direct investment—of which 70 percent goes to the extractive sector—tripled over the past decade to

[4] Data for 2013 were not fully available. Ranking may vary by ±1. Chile produces 5.7 million tons of copper, followed by China at 1.65 million tons and Peru at 1.3 million tons.

TABLE 7.1

| Peru: Mineral Reserves, 2011 *(Thousand metric tons unless otherwise specified)* | | |
|---|---|---|
| **Commodity** | | **Reserves** |
| Coal, All Types | | 1,100,000 |
| Copper | | 90,000 |
| Gold | Metric tons | 2,762 |
| Iron Ore | | 10,853 |
| Lead | | 9,106 |
| Molybdenum | | 450 |
| Natural Gas | Billion cubic meters | 823 |
| Natural Gas Liquids | Million barrels | 1,550 |
| Petroleum Crude | Million barrels | 3,055 |
| Phosphate Rock | | 820 |
| Salt | | 100,000 |
| Silver | Metric tons | 120,000 |
| Sulfur | | 150,000 |
| Tin | | 160 |
| Uranium | | 100 |
| Zinc | | 25,137 |

Source: Ministry of Energy and Mines of Peru (2012).

TABLE 7.2

| Resource Dependency | |
|---|---|
| | 2013 |
| **Real Sector** | |
| Mineral Value Added as Percent of Nominal GDP[1] | 11.7 |
| Mineral Value Added Percent of Real GDP[1] | 12.1 |
| **Fiscal Accounts** | |
| Resource Revenue as Percent of Nominal GDP | 2.8 |
| Resource Revenue as Percent of Total Fiscal Revenue | 12.5 |
| Excluding Metal Minerals | 5.0 |
| Excluding Hydrocarbons | 7.5 |
| Resource Revenue from Taxes as Percent of Total Tax Revenue | 14.1 |
| Metal Minerals Revenue as Percent of Total Resource Revenue | 40.0 |
| Hydrocarbons Revenue as Percent of Total Resource Revenue | 60.0 |
| Metal Minerals Revenue of Percent of Exports Value of Metals | 9.6 |
| Hydrocarbons Revenue as Percent of Exports Value of Hydrocarbons | 63.9 |
| **External Sector** | |
| Resource Exports as Percent of GDP | 14.1 |
| Resource Exports as Percent of Total Exports of Goods | 67.5 |
| Excluding Metal Minerals | 55.1 |
| Excluding Hydrocarbons | 12.3 |

Sources: Central Reserve Bank of Peru; Ministry of Economy and Finance; Peru's statistical agency; and IMF staff calculations.
[1]2007 base year. Minerals and hydrocarbons.

some 6 percent of GDP in 2013. Investment in the minerals and hydrocarbon industries was about $9.7 billion and $1.7 billion in 2013, respectively, together resulting in a sevenfold increase since 2001 (see Figure 7.2). In 2012, Peru was fifth among global destinations for exploration of nonferrous metals, behind Canada, Australia, the United States, and Mexico, and at par with Chile (Metals Economics Group 2013).

According to the Ministry of Energy and Mines, the estimated mining investment portfolio is comprised of 52 major projects, including those in the design and approval process, amounting to some $61 billion (Table 7.3). Most of the projects are located in Apurimac (20 percent of

**TABLE 7.3**

**Investment in Minerals Industry**

| Local Company | Name of the Project | Mineral | US$ Million |
|---|---|---|---|
| **Expansion Stage** | | | |
| SPCC | Fundición | Copper | n/a |
| SPCC | Toquepala | Copper | 1,050 |
| SPCC | Refinería de Ilo | Copper | n/a |
| Compania Minera Miski Mayo S.R.L. | Bayovar | Phosphates | 520 |
| Shougang Hierro Peru S.A.A. | Marcona | Iron | 1,500 |
| Sociedad Minera Cerro Verde S.A.A. | Cerro Verde | Copper | 4,600 |
| Sociedad Minera El Brocal S.A.A. | Colquijirca | Polymetallics | 432 |
| Minera Chinalco Perú S.A. | Toromocho[1] | Copper | 1,320 |
| **Construction Stage** | | | |
| Anabi S.A.C. | Anama | Gold | 40 |
| Anglo American Quellaveco S.A. | Quellaveco | Copper | 3,300 |
| Bear Creek MiNING COMPANY | Corani | Silver | 750 |
| Fosfatos del Pacifico S.A. | Fosfatos | Phosphates | 500 |
| Invicta Mining Corp S.A.C. | Invicta | Polymetallics | 93 |
| Minera Kurikullu USA | Ollachea | Gold | 170 |
| Minera Ares S.A.C. | Crespo | Gold, silver | 110 |
| Minera Chinalco Perú S.A. | Toromocho | Copper | 3,500 |
| Minera Shouxin Perú S.A. | Explotacion de relaves | Copper, iron, zinc | 239 |
| Minera Yanacocha S.R.L. | Minas Conga | Copper, gold | 4,800 |
| Minera Sulliden Shahuindo S.A.C. | Shahuindo | Gold | 208 |
| Hudbay Minerals Inc. | Constancia | Copper | 1,546 |
| Xstrata Las Bambas S.A. | Las Bambas | Copper | 5,200 |
| Minera Suyamarca S.A.C. | Inmaculada | Gold, silver | 370 |
| Reliant Ventures S.A.C. | San Luis | Gold, silver | n/a |
| **Total Ongoing** | | | **30,248** |
| **With Submitted Environmental Studies and in Exploration (29 projects)** | | | **31,031** |
| **TOTAL** | | | **61,279** |

Source: Ministry of Energy and Mines (2013).
[1]Completed but production has not started (as of June 2014).

total), Arequipa (16 percent), and Cajamarca (15 percent) (Figure 7.1). More than 45 percent of projects are already in the exploration stage, 15 percent are being expanded, and environmental studies have been approved for 36 percent of the total. Production of the country's flagship mineral—copper—is expected to double over the next several years with the coming on stream of four large mines (Toromocho,[5] Las Bambas, Constancia, and Cerro Verde). According to the Hydrocarbons Committee, the portfolio of projects in the hydrocarbon sector amounted to more than $10 billion in 2013.[6]

The leading countries investing in Peru's mining sector are China ($13.8 billion), the United States ($10.1 billion), and Canada ($8.9 billion). The cumulative level of mineral commodity investments are $38.9 billion in copper, $6.9 billion in gold, $7 billion in iron ore, $1.8 billion in phosphates, and $3.6 billion in polymetallic minerals, including around $1 billion in silver (Ministry of Energy and Mines 2013).

Resource revenue is an important source of revenue for Peru's budget (Figure 7.2, Table 7.2). The significance of resource revenue is further underscored by the revenue-sharing agreements established by law between the central government and resource-producing regions (in particular, under what is known as the mining royalties canon or *canon minero*). These regions, in turn, are required to spend funds on infrastructure and education projects.

[5]The Toromocho project reached the construction stage in December 2013 but production was postponed due to a discovery of a lower-grade copper.

[6]Major projects include the southern gas pipeline, the liquefied petroleum gas pipeline between Pisco and Lima, and the petrochemical and oil tender.

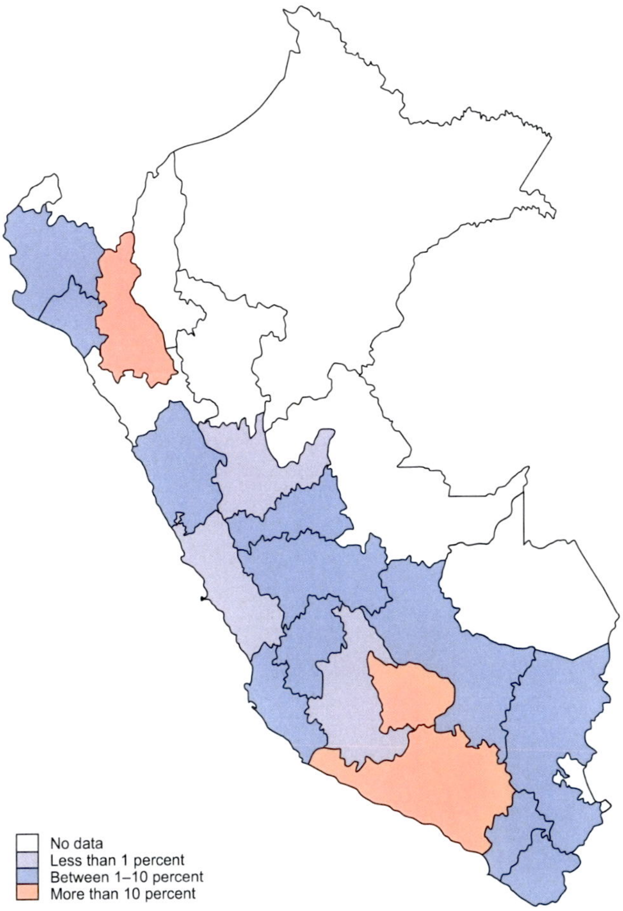


Source: Ministry of Energy and Mines.

**Figure 7.1** Peru: Share of the Portfolio in Mining Projects, 2013

Managing Peru's mineral wealth is complex because of decentralization arrangements giving regional and local governments a claim on mining revenues. Subnational governments' own-revenues are relatively low, with their main source of income being transfers from general government natural resource revenues. Subnational governments receive 50 percent of the canon. All royalties paid by mining companies are transferred to the region where exploration takes place. Hydrocarbon exploration companies also pay royalties, half of which are transferred to subnational governments. Transfers from mining revenue can be used only for capital spending, which is usually underexecuted and results in subnational governments' accumulating financial assets despite running overall deficits (IMF 2013a).

Based on recommendations of tax experts, mining taxation reform approved in September 2011 aimed to increase the progressivity of the tax system, while preserving the competitiveness of the sector (Otto 2002). The new reforms included (1) new royalties based on operating profits of 1 percent to 12 percent to replace the sales-based royalties for companies with no stability contracts with the government;[7] (2) a new special mining tax (IEM) that goes to the central government and is levied on a sliding scale between 2 percent and 8.4 percent of operating margins (ratio of operating profit divided by net sales), applicable to companies with no tax stability contracts;

[7]Tax stability contracts were offered to mining companies to ensure a stable legal, tax, and administrative environment to attract multinational companies in the mid-1990s.

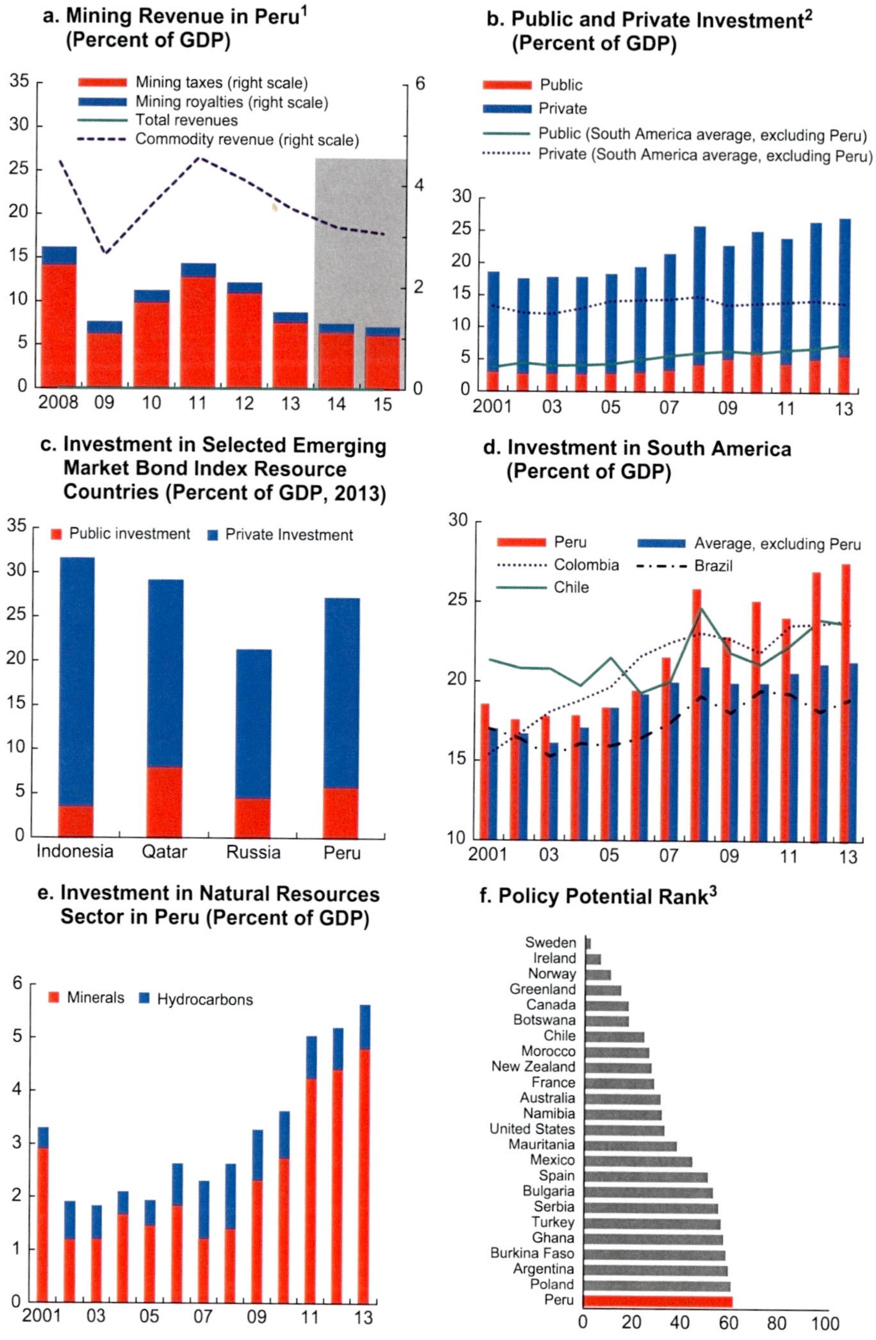


Sources: Fraser Institute; IMF, World Economic Outlook database; Ministry of the Economy and Finance; Ministry of Energy and Mines; and IMF staff estimates.

[1]Net of restitutions.

[2]National Accounts data.

[3]1 = greatest potential; ranking for 2013/2012; shows countries ranked above Peru only.

**Figure 7.2** Mining and Revenue Investment

**TABLE 7.4**

**Doing Business in Selected Latin American Countries**

| | Ranking (2014) | | | | | |
|---|---|---|---|---|---|---|
| | Brazil | Chile[1] | Colombia | Mexico | Peru | Uruguay |
| Ease of Doing Business | 116 | 37 | 43 | 53 | 42 | 88 |
| Starting a Business | 123 | 32 | 79 | 48 | 63 | 43 |
| Dealing with Construction Permits | 130 | 84 | 24 | 40 | 117 | 154 |
| Getting Electricity | 14 | 40 | 101 | 133 | 79 | 23 |
| Registering Property | 107 | 55 | 53 | 150 | 22 | 167 |
| Getting Credit | 109 | 53 | 73 | 42 | 28 | 73 |
| Protecting Investors | 80 | 32 | 6 | 68 | 16 | 98 |
| Paying Taxes | 159 | 36 | 104 | 118 | 73 | 146 |
| Trading Across Borders | 124 | 48 | 94 | 59 | 55 | 90 |
| Enforcing Contracts | 121 | 70 | 155 | 71 | 105 | 105 |
| Resolving Insolvency | 135 | 98 | 25 | 26 | 110 | 51 |

Source: World Bank, Doing Business Indicators (2014).
[1]2013.

and (3) a special (voluntary) levy (GEM) of 4 percent to 13 percent of profits on the extraction of mineral resources, targeting companies holding stability contracts. The reform was well received by the investor community. At the time, revenues were expected to increase by about 0.5 percent of GDP on an annual basis, but the sharp drop in metal prices and demand since then has lowered the effective tax rate.

Future growth of the extractive industry will depend on further improving the investment climate. In the volatile global environment that affects commodity prices, special attention is being placed on cultivating domestic investment conditions that safeguard previous commitments and generate new investment. Political stability, a reasonable tax regime, and adherence to best business practices have been identified as key elements to maintaining investor interest. According to the World Bank's Doing Business Indicators, Peru's relative strength lies in protecting investors, ease of getting credit, and registering property (Table 7.4). While Peru compares relatively well with other countries in the region, there is a need for additional measures to enhance competitiveness in such subcategories as enforcing contracts, resolving insolvency, dealing with construction permits, ease of paying taxes, and obtaining electricity.

Peru dropped four spots in the 2014–15 global competitiveness rankings published by the World Economic Forum, with a ranking of 65th out of 143 economies. Peru's relatively low rankings in the functioning of institutions (118th), progress in improving education (134th), and technological adoption (92nd) explain the decline and support the notion of a certain exhaustion of the sources of Peru's competitiveness gains of past years. Among these gains are a very strong macroeconomic performance (21st) and high levels of efficiency in its goods (53rd), financial markets (40th), and labor markets (51st), despite rigidity in hiring and firing practices (130th). The rankings suggest that Peru needs to strengthen its public institutions (ranked 127th) by increasing government efficiency (116th), fighting corruption (103rd), and improving infrastructure (88th), while also building its capacity to diversify its economy by raising the quality of education (134th), boosting technology adoption (92nd), and raising innovation capacity (117th).

In relation to the mining industry in particular, the Fraser Institute's annual informal mining survey assesses the perceptions of 742 mining company executives in 96 jurisdictions (including subnational levels) with regard to various areas of optimal and suboptimal public policies that might affect the hospitality of a jurisdiction to mining investment (Figure 7.2, panel f; Green and Jackson 2015).[8] The survey's Policy Potential Index is based on answers to survey policy questions, including

[8]The survey was first conducted in 1997 (Peru was added to the sample in 1999).

on such issues as uncertainty concerning the administration, interpretation, and enforcement of existing regulations, environmental regulations, regulatory duplication and inconsistencies, taxation, uncertainty concerning disputed land claims and protected areas, infrastructure, socioeconomic agreements, political stability, labor issues, the geological database, and security. With respect to the region, Chile is the top-ranked jurisdiction in the Policy Potential Index, followed by Mexico, Argentina, and Peru. In its Mineral Potential Index, which mostly concentrates on geological reserves, Peru ranks fifth after Chile, Guyana, Mexico, and Argentina. Managers' comments for the region showed concern about resource nationalism and mining opposition in some areas, while policies to formalize informal miners (Peru) and redistribute mining royalties to the local level were positively received by some companies. About 15 percent of respondents saw a need to improve Peru's conditions for mining. While the taxation regime, infrastructure, and fairness of the legal process were viewed positively, socioeconomic agreements/community development conditions, labor regulations, and security were seen as issues that deter investment.

The preoccupation with social instability, in particular, is driven by the fact that social conflicts in Peru have increased by 300 percent during the last five years, with 149 recent disputes involving extractive industries. While mining regions within Peru have benefited from an established transfer mechanism, local and regional governments have a limited capacity to manage such windfall revenue, and governance challenges appear to be limiting the benefits from mining at the regional and local levels. Much of the funding remains unspent, contributing to anti-mining protests and depriving poor communities of necessary infrastructure such as water treatment facilities, roads, education, and healthcare. The absence of government services may have created unrealistic demands—and dependency—on the mining companies.

The authorities are well aware of these challenging issues and have been working with local governments and investors on finding best-suited solutions to accommodate local development and infrastructure needs and benefit from Peru's vast natural wealth.[9] In 2013, the government announced reforms aimed at reducing excessive paperwork and facilitating faster granting of permits. In June 2014, the government took additional steps to invigorate the investment climate by introducing changes to the tax stability regime applicable to mining companies,[10] expedite the approval of environmental impact studies required for investments in extractive industries, and streamline environmental regulations. It also increased penalties for environmental infractions and the powers of the Specialized Unit on Investment Monitoring of the Ministry of the Economy and Finance.[11] However, due to limitations in capacity implementation, these reforms will likely need time to have an impact.

## FISCAL FRAMEWORK IN PERU

The Law on Fiscal Prudence and Transparency (LPTF) was approved in December 1999. It included several numerical rules, including a zero fiscal deficit in general (over the cycle), an increase of nonfinancial general government spending below 2 percent in real terms, and expenditure ceilings on nonfinancial expenditure below 60 percent in the first seven months of the electoral year (see Chapter 6 on fiscal rules). These rules had two exceptions allowing for a fiscal

[9]The mining law (*Canon Minero*) includes a nonbinding consultation clause (*Consulta Previa*) that requires investors to meet with the local community to discuss the future project and identify solutions to any issues (environmental, social, etc.) that may arise from its implementation.

[10]Some provisions with respect to stability contracts were deemed outdated and were amended in July 2014 under the law establishing new tax measures, simplifying procedures and permits, and promoting the pick-up of investment. The floors on investment and production under the stability contracts were increased to reflect the size of current investments; for projects above $500 million, tax rates will be set for a 15-year period. The law also allows the companies to expand ongoing projects under the stability contract without restarting the application process.

[11]Public entities will have 45 days to evaluate environmental impact studies. A maximum penalty to be imposed during the next three years for environmental infractions will be 50 percent of the corresponding amount set in existing legislation.

deficit below 2 percent of GDP: one for emergency situations and another for recessions. Transparency of the fiscal process has also improved by periodically publishing information on the Economic Transparency Portal (*Portal de Transparencia Económica*), presenting a multiyear budgeting framework, mandating a pre-election fiscal report together with an annual review of contingent fiscal risks and tax expenditure to be published in the annual budget, and preparing a quarterly report on budget expansions and their implications for the macroeconomic framework. In early 2003, the LPTF was amended to (1) allow a more realistic adjustment period for the medium-term fiscal target following a recession, (2) require automatic adjustments in fiscal policy when it is off-track in nonrecessionary years, and (3) extend rules of fiscal discipline to all levels of government.

The Fiscal Stabilization Fund (FSF) was approved together with the LPTF and created with 75 percent of privatization proceeds and 50 percent of concessions. Its resources were to be mainly dedicated to poverty alleviation programs, and activated when current revenue was at least 0.3 percent of GDP below its average in the last three years. The FSF was to accumulate 10 percent of privatization proceeds and 10 percent of concessional fees, use a portion of a fiscal surplus of the previous year, and be capped at 4 percent of GDP.

This fiscal regime served the country relatively well. By limiting real current spending at a rate lower than the growth of the economy, it was highly successful in reducing Peru's debt from 44 percent to 20 percent of GDP from 2004 to 2013, and the public sector now boasts financial assets of some 15 percent of GDP. However, the LPTF fell short of providing an adequate fiscal anchor and a framework to deal with commodity-related challenges, did not prevent procyclicality, and was not applied consistently in its coverage (IMF 2010, 2012c). Fiscal policy was procyclical in 2008 due to increased spending beyond the limits imposed by the LPTF, as well as in 2010, despite the rapid recovery of output following the 2009 global financial crisis. Moreover, the LPTF allowed for discretional changes in tax rates, as in 2011, when the authorities reduced several tax rates, which was procyclical. Expenditure caps were changed several times, including through the use of deflators and targets for real growth rates and transactional coverage used to set the cap (i.e., from current to consumption expenditures). Moreover, the institutional coverage of the rule was not applied consistently across subsectors because expenditure caps applied only to the central government, while the overall deficit limit covered the nonfinancial public sector. The use of exceptional clauses proved to be challenging, and there was no direct mechanism for saving high-cycle commodity revenues, despite the existence of the FSF. Finally, subnational governments were constrained by a different set of rules.

To address the aforementioned shortcomings, the LPTF was amended in October 2013 to be applied to the 2015 budget.[12] The revised framework, among other things, outlines a stronger regulatory structure though a more comprehensive spending rule, creates an independent body to contribute to the technical analysis of fiscal and macro policy, and introduces corrective actions in cases of breaches in the fiscal rule. Some detailed provisions include the following:

- *Structural fiscal objective.* After general elections, the new administration within 90 days of taking office has to present a declaration of the macrofiscal policy for the period of the presidential mandate, with a numerical structural fiscal objective for the presidential period that should not exceed a deficit of 1 percent of GDP.[13,14]

[12]The design of the new fiscal framework followed the recommendations of the commission of experts appointed in 2012, and involved the participation of the central bank, technical assistance from the IMF, and input from independent experts to provide more transparency and commitment to the process.

[13]The structural fiscal balance corrects for the business cycle (which affects nonmining revenues) and deviations of metal prices from a long-term price (which affects mining-related revenues).

[14]An official methodology to calculate the structural fiscal target, based on the nonbinding opinion of an expert committee, was adopted in 2014. Under this methodology, noncommodity-related revenues are adjusted by the nonprimary GDP output gap. Direct taxes and royalties levied on the mining and hydrocarbon sectors (i.e., natural resource revenue) are

- *Budgetary implications.* The limit of nonfinancial public spending has to be aligned to the structural fiscal objective as well as the assumptions on revenues consistent with the business cycle and commodity prices. The limit can be altered if spending in the previous year was less than budgeted. In that case, the amount of the subsequent year's spending can be adjusted upward by no more than 0.2 percent of GDP.
- *Countercyclical policy.* If there is a positive or negative output gap of at least 2 percent of potential GDP, the spending limit should be adjusted through transitory countercyclical measures that together cannot exceed 0.5 percent of GDP.
- *Fiscal revenues.* If measures are adopted to generate a permanent increase in fiscal revenues of at least 0.3 percent of GDP, the spending limit can be adjusted by the same amount.
- *Regional and local governments.* The level of debt cannot be more than 100 percent of the average total current revenues of the past four years, and the annual growth of nonfinancial expenditure cannot be more than the moving average growth of annual revenues over the past four years. The governments can only borrow under the state guarantee and only for capital projects.
- *Corrective measures.* In case of deviations from the spending limit, corrective measures are to be taken within two years if overspending is below ½ percent of GDP, and immediately if it is above this threshold, with an exception for those years when there is a negative output gap of more than 2 percent of potential GDP.

## ALTERNATIVE FISCAL BALANCE TARGETS AND SUSTAINABLE INVESTMENT APPROACH

### Simulating Alternative Fiscal Rules Based on the Permanent Income Hypothesis

While Peru's new fiscal framework establishes an important structural anchor, targeting a nonresource primary balance could be an alternative that would also help generate a certain level of savings. Above the line, the overall fiscal balance can be decomposed into resource revenues, nonresource revenues, primary expenditure, income from financial assets, and interest payments on the stock of liabilities. The overall fiscal balance is also equal to the change in the net financial assets. Below the line, the nonresource primary balance is defined as the difference between nonresource revenues minus primary expenditure. Resource-rich countries often run overall fiscal surpluses, which can facilitate the accumulation of substantial financial assets over time, but the nonresource primary balance is often in deficit. In this exercise, the nonresource primary balance is anchored around the expenditure envelope that could be maintained over the long term and is consistent with the stabilization of net resource wealth. Over long horizons, the net present value (NPV) of future resource revenues should be equal to the NPV of future nonresource primary balances. Over a shorter horizon, a stable level of net wealth should be maintained. Simulations can help analyze and visualize the trade-offs associated with alternative permanent income hypothesis (PIH)-based

---

instead assumed to depend on a Peru-specific export price index that reflects the country's commodity-related export basket (no cyclical adjustment is made to expenditures, capital revenue, or the balance of state-owned enterprises). To calculate the price gap between current and structural prices (to be used to compute structural resource revenue), the methodology assumes a 30-year price cycle according to which current market prices would steadily decline over the next 20 years, converging to pre-2002 levels by 2033. Then, structural prices are derived using an HP filter over the 1980–2033 price series, and the price gap is obtained as a difference. The methodology can be revised every three years and is to be assessed by the fiscal council. It can be accessed at http://www.mef.gob.pe/contenidos/archivos/descarga/informe_metodologia_estructural.pdf.

approaches.[15] A comparison of the primary balance path under the three approaches (which are more or less accommodative to public investment) gives policymakers a better understanding of the trade-offs implied when deciding to invest or save. The framework provides estimates for long-term paths of nonresource primary balance and financial savings under different scenarios.

*The PIH-based rule*

- *Intertemporal budget constraint.* To be sustained for an infinitely long period, the annual level of the primary balance should be equal to the return on net wealth, adjusting for inflation.
- *Inadequacy.* However, the PIH-based rule might be inadequate for resource-rich developing countries, as some tilting of consumption paths toward relatively poorer current generations may be welfare-improving.

*The modified PIH (MPIH)-based rule*

- *Scaling up.* This approach accommodates the scaling up of public investment.
- *Frontloading.* This assumes that the government frontloads investment spending above the baseline forecasts until the last year of investment frontloading, year *F*. The additional frontloaded capital spending could be financed by "saving" less natural resource revenue during the scaling-up period.
- *Possible policy failure.* The approach is based on two additional assumptions: (1) the frontloading investment may not have a growth impact; and (2) over the long run (year *T*), the level of financial wealth from this frontloaded investment scenario has to be equal to the level from the usual PIH fiscal framework, requiring some future adjustment.
- *Future adjustment.* These two assumptions together imply that the frontloaded investment has to be fully compensated for by a fiscal adjustment in the medium term (spread over $T - F$ years). Hence, the level of financial wealth after year *T* would be the same for the two alternative fiscal paths.
- *Outlines worst case scenario.* The MPIH approach provides a measure of possible future fiscal adjustment needs if the scaling up of investment does not have an impact on growth. It therefore provides a future fiscal adjustment path in a worst-case scenario where higher public investment has no impact on growth and hence provides a measure of the potential implications for future fiscal adjustment.

*The fiscal stability framework–based rule*

- *Tolerates lower savings.* This approach stabilizes net wealth at lower levels than the PIH or the MPIH. Higher investment is assumed to have a positive impact on growth, which generates higher nonresource revenue, but also increases operation and maintenance outlays.
- *Asset substitution strategy.* The intuition behind this framework is that instead of accumulating higher financial savings, the country has accumulated higher physical assets that also provide a fiscal and social return.

Several key assumptions underpin the simulations in the case of Peru: (1) hydrocarbon reserves last until 2050 at 2013 production rates, (2) other commodities have various production horizons ranging between 5 and 50 years, (3) the nonresource sector grows at a constant growth rate of 4 percent in real terms per year, (4) the hydrocarbon and mineral revenue share accruing to the government remains constant, and (5) inflation is at 2 percent per year, while the average real rate of return on financial assets is 1 percentage point above the nonresource growth rate. The simulations compute fiscal sustainability benchmarks and enable a comparison of the paths for

[15]The simulations were generated with a model developed by the IMF's Fiscal Affairs Department (IMF 2012b).

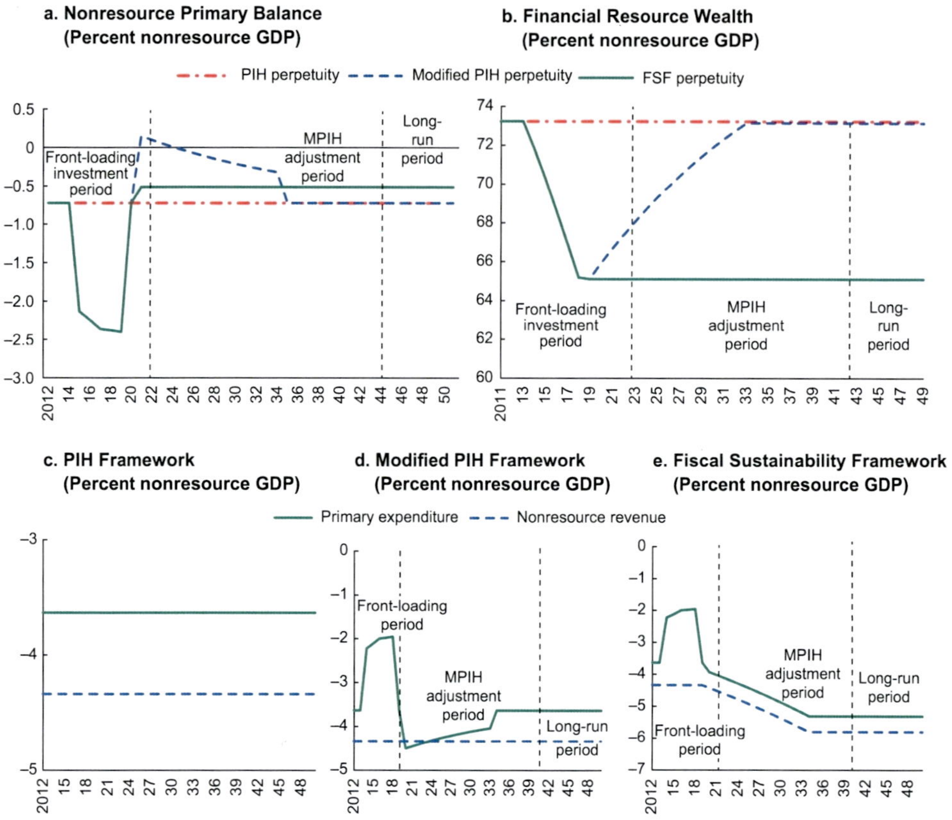


Source: IMF staff calculations.

Note: FSF = fiscal sustainability framework; PIH = permanent income hypothesis; MPIH = modified permanent income hypothesis.

**Figure 7.3** Fiscal Sustainability Frameworks

the nonresource primary deficit, financial wealth, primary expenditure, and nonresource revenue for three alternative PIH-based rules (Figure 7.3):

- *The traditional PIH rule*, where the nonresource primary balance remains constant over time and is financed with the rate of return on the NPV of projected resource revenues. In this case, the PIH sustainability benchmark is equal to about −7 percent of nonresource GDP.
- *The modified PIH rule,* which allows for an increase in the nonresource primary balance above the PIH sustainability benchmark by about 1 percentage points of nonresource GDP per year on average during 2013–19 (if investment increases 20 percent a year). The simulation provides an estimate of the intertemporal trade-off between an increase in spending in the short term and future fiscal adjustment needs, given that the additional investment is not expected to generate higher growth. As shown in Figure 7.3, the frontloaded investment would need to be offset with a consolidation effort of about 0.2 percent of nonresource GDP per year on average, smoothed over 18 years, in order to return to the PIH benchmark of about −1 percent by 2036.
- *The fiscal sustainability framework,* which incorporates the positive impact of higher public investment on growth and nonresource revenues, and generates a fiscally sustainable path that is consistent with a lower level of financial wealth. Under this approach, fiscal spending can still be stabilized at a higher level because part of the resource wealth has been transformed into physical assets, and higher growth will have "fiscal returns" through larger nonresource revenues and notwithstanding lower financial wealth relative to the PIH and MPIH approaches.

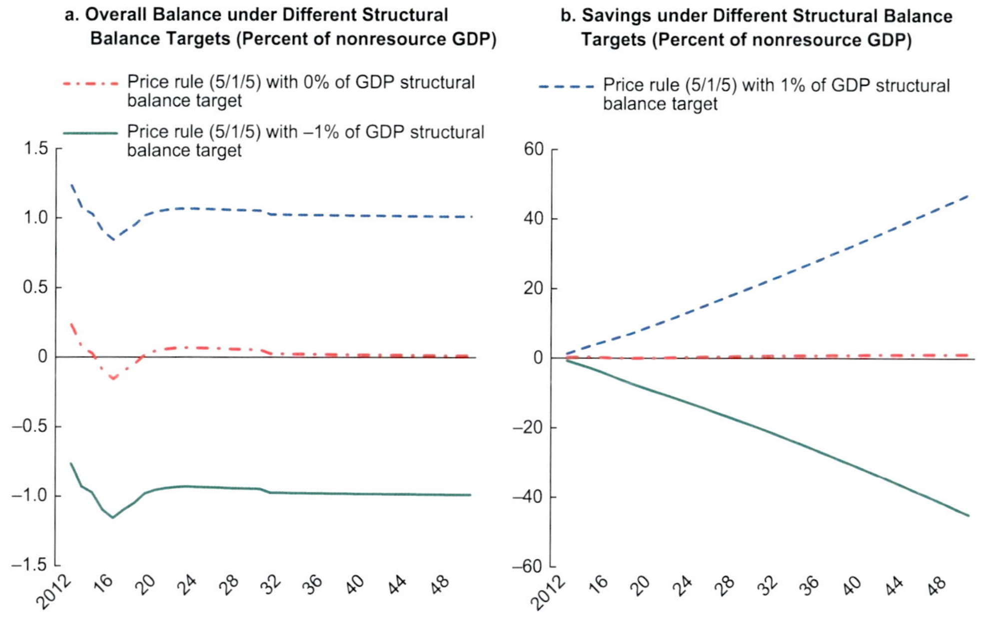


Source: IMF staff calculations.

Note: The 5/1/5 rule uses five years of past prices for copper, the current year price, and a five-year projection for the calculation.

**Figure 7.4** Projected Outcomes with the Different Structural Primary Balance Targets with Price Rules 5/1/5

## Structural Primary Balance-Based Sustainability Framework

As discussed above, the choice of fiscal targets should also depend on the duration of the resource reserve horizons. For resource-rich developing countries with short reserve horizons, exhaustibility is the main concern, and the key fiscal indicator to assess the fiscal stance should be the nonresource primary balance—in some variant of the framework described above. However, excluding resource revenues from fiscal targets (as the nonresource primary balance rule suggests) is less relevant to countries with relatively long horizons (Peru) and to countries that derive an increasingly large part of their revenue from natural resources. In this case, a structural primary balance is a more relevant target that complements the nonresource primary balance indicator.

To address cyclicality and sustainability issues, targeting a structural primary balance with some sort of price smoothing and/or expenditure growth rules would be appropriate.[16] While a price-based smoothing rule does not offer a direct link to sustainability benchmarks, it can help support solvency through prudent forecasting of structural revenues by deliberately under-projecting the sustainable resource price.[17] On the other hand, an expenditure growth rule can help to limit procyclicality and help guide the scaling up of public investment. Figure 7.4 presents the results for overall balances and savings when targeting a structural primary balance of between −1 percent and 1 percent of GDP under a 5/1/5 rule.[18]

[16]See IMF (2010, 2012c) on considerations for structural rules options.

[17]The IMF's Fiscal Affairs Department model also facilitates the simulations of alternative price-based fiscal rules. This would not be a straightforward exercise to apply in Peru, as it depends on several commodity prices, different production capacities, and resource horizons. If considered, however, results may point to the trade-offs of alternative price-based rules in terms of smoothing out volatility and generating different levels of financial assets. For a given price formula, higher/lower structural targets would be associated with an increase/decrease in the level of financial savings over time. The Fiscal Affairs Department model is not yet set up to accommodate multiple commodities (which is the case in Peru). For scenarios that take into account different production horizons and reserves to calculate the government's intake from the resource revenue, outcomes were normalized by a constant relative price of copper to project an overall metals production level.

[18]The 5/1/5 rule uses five years of past prices, the current year price, and a five-year projection for the calculation.

## Alternatives for Peru

In Peru, considerations for savings need to be balanced against expenditure needs that could boost potential economic growth. As mentioned, Peru has pressing social needs (with high levels of poverty in rural areas) and ranks relatively low in education and human capital. There are also large public infrastructure investment needs that could enhance economic growth in the future. While Peru compares favorably with its South American neighbors in terms of its overall ratio of investment to GDP, with private investment averaging 22 percent of GDP against 19 percent for the rest of South America, it does not come out as well when it comes to public sector investment, which averages less than 4 percent against more than 5 percent for the region, although efforts have been made in the past few years to raise the average (see Figure 7.2). Besides other fiscal pressures and priorities, this relatively low spending on public investment could also be explained by short- and medium-term capacity constraints that have hampered its effectiveness and execution.[19] Therefore, Peru is, perhaps, best placed to take a gradual approach to increasing investment spending (PIH) and save more of its resource revenues in financial assets, even if only temporarily, while investment capacity is built domestically. Sustainable—or gradual—investing will also continue to mitigate Dutch disease and reduce the costs of absorptive capacity constraints.

However, the need to close the infrastructure gap may require an alternative fiscal framework. The PIH, or even the MPIH, could be seen as too constraining for Peru's circumstances, since public investment is not very high by emerging market standards. Peru could thus consider applying the fiscal sustainability framework with a fast scale up of investment spending. This would be consistent with recent IMF guidance for resource-rich developing countries with relatively longer reserve horizons, which puts less emphasis on the issue of the exhaustibility of resources for medium-term planning. Introducing a fiscal sustainability framework, however, would require expedient improvements in capacity constraints and a good public understanding of the rule to generate better support for its credibility and enforcement. Furthermore, to ensure quality and continuity of investment, there is merit to first developing a long-term national infrastructure plan.

Taking the above considerations into account, it would seem most appropriate to target a structural primary balance supported by price rules. Simulations show that with a structural primary balance rule of −1 percent of GDP, the cumulative financial saving would be negative, whereas with a zero structural primary balance target the cumulative saving would be nil by 2040, around the time when copper reserves are projected to be exhausted (see Figure 7.4). A target of a structural primary balance of 1 percent of GDP seems more reasonable and would generate a cumulative financial saving of over 40 percent of nonresource GDP over the same period at the overall nonfinancial public sector balance. Over the past decade, Peru has averaged an overall nonfinancial public sector surplus of almost 1 percent of nonresource GDP and 1.8 percent in structural primary balance to GDP (Figure 7.5). Peru's new fiscal framework gives an opportunity to implicitly target a structural balance in the medium term, and the authorities would be well advised to aim for structural primary surpluses between ½ percent and 1 percent of GDP to successfully pursue multipronged objectives of sustainability, continuing to accumulate buffers and savings, and persevering with the investment and development agenda.

[19] Capital spending execution has averaged about 85 percent of the budgeted amounts over the past several years.

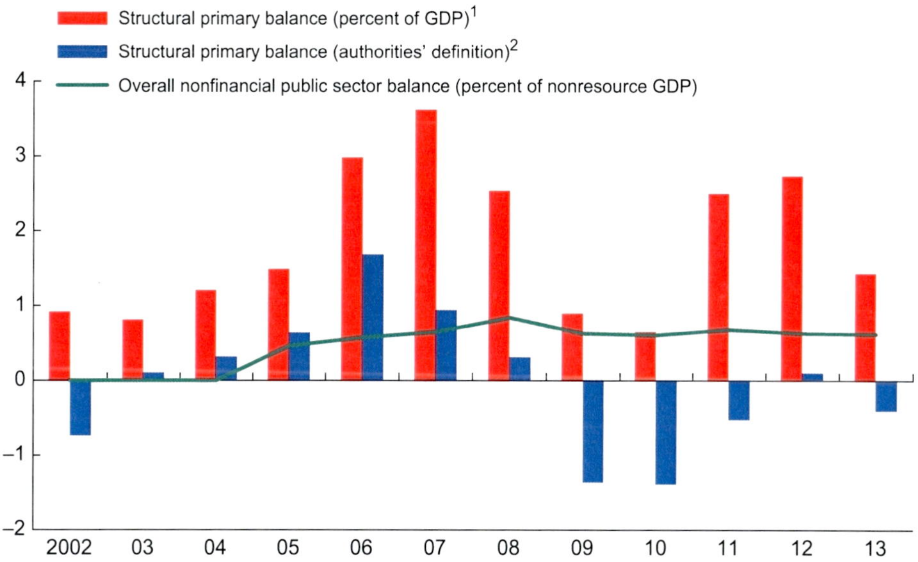


Sources: Ministry of Economy and Finance; and IMF staff calculations.

[1]Adjusted for economic cycle and commodity prices. Uses as equilibrium commodity prices a moving average estimate that takes five years of historical prices and three years of forward prices according to the IMF's World Economic Outlook database.

[2]Uses methodology approved in Ministerial Resolution N037-2014-EF/15 at www.mef.gobpe/contenidos/archivos-descarga/infrome_metodologia_estructural.pdf.

**Figure 7.5** Fiscal Balances

# REFERENCES

Auty, Richard. 1993. *Sustaining Development in Mineral Economies: The Resource Curse Thesis.* New York: Rutledge.

Green, Kenneth P., and Taylor Jackson. 2015. "Survey of Mining Companies 2014." Fraser Institute. February 28. http://www.fraserinstitute.org/research-news/display.aspx?id=22259.

International Monetary Fund. 2010. "Performance of Alternative Fiscal Rules: An Application to Peru." Country Report No. 10/99, International Monetary Fund, Washington, DC.

———. 2012a. "Fiscal Regimes for Extractive Industries: Design and Implementation." Policy Paper, International Monetary Fund, Washington, DC.

———. 2012b. "Macroeconomic Policy Frameworks for Resource-Rich Developing Countries—Analytical Frameworks and Applications." Policy Paper, International Monetary Fund, Washington, DC.

———. 2012c. "Towards a Structural Fiscal Framework." Country Report No. 12/27, International Monetary Fund, Washington, DC.

———. 2013a. "Fiscal Objectives: Lower Debt or Higher Savings." Country Report No. 13/46, International Monetary Fund, Washington, DC.

———. 2013b. "Revamping the Fiscal Framework in Azerbaijan." Country Report No. 13/165, International Monetary Fund, Washington, DC.

Metals Economics Group. 2013. "2013 Worldwide Exploration Trends." http://www.commodities-now.com/reports/metals-and-mining/14014-worldwide-exploration-trends-2013.html.

Ministry of Energy and Mines. 2012. *Anuario de la Minería del Perú.* Lima.

———. 2013. "Libro Anual de Reservas de Hidrocarburos." Ministry of Energy and Mines of Peru, Lima.

Otto, James M. 2002. "Position of the Peruvian Taxation System as Compared to Mining Taxation Systems in Other Nations." Ministry of the Economy and Finance of Peru, Lima.

World Bank. 2014. Doing Business Indicators. Washington: World Bank.

CHAPTER 8

# The Tax System and Administration as Pillars for Solid Fiscal Accounts

RICARDO FENOCHIETTO, LAURA CALDERÓN, MARCO CAMACHO, AND PATRICIO CASTRO

*There have been many reforms of the Peruvian tax system and administration over the past four decades, although major challenges remain. The tax system has been beset with serious problems during the period, including lack of stability in tax laws and regulations, widespread informality and tax noncompliance, and a proliferation of exemptions. To some extent these continue to impede efficiency today, although significant steps have been taken to modernize the tax system in line with international trends. While tax pressure in Peru is relatively low, it is not because of low tax rates, which compare well with other countries, but rather as a result of the problems identified above. A specific concern that still needs to be addressed is that Peru's dependence on taxes from natural resources makes it vulnerable to price fluctuations. Further improving equity and eliminating distortions are also important priorities going forward. Progressive reform of the tax administration in the 1990s and 2000s transformed the system into a high-quality and reasonably efficient administration that saw tax collection improve on average by 4 percent of GDP over the period. Nonetheless, the tax administration still needs to tackle some challenges that could help support Peruvian tax policy reforms.*[1]

Today Peru has a modern tax system that follows international practices and a relatively efficient tax administration that boasts highly qualified staff, operates under strategic management principles, and widely applies information technology (IT) in its services. Although tax and nontax revenues have increased only marginally since the 1970s (Table 8.1), significant changes in both tax policy and administration have transformed the tax system.[2] The transition from a regime plagued with exemptions, small taxes, fees (most with cascading effects), and very high customs duties to a system of reasonably high-quality and efficient tax administration was not easy and took several decades. That said, the current tax system is not without weaknesses and the authorities continue to take important steps to further improve its quality.

## THE EVOLUTION OF THE TAX SYSTEM

### The 1980s

Peru's tax system during the 1980s was characterized by a large number of taxes with multiple rates, and continuous changes to the system. The value-added tax (VAT) had up to eight rates that varied between 6 percent and 18 percent. The global income tax system, which had

The authors are grateful to Enrique Rojas, John Norregaard, Svetlana Vtyurina, and Eduardo Sotelo for their comments and suggestions during the drafting of this chapter.

[1] This chapter uses the term "tax administration" to refer to both customs and domestic tax administration.

[2] This chapter includes the analysis of nontax collection also because it primarily consists of royalties and other revenue from the mining sector, which in some ways could be a replacement or substitute for the corporate income tax. On the other hand, the chapter does not include subnational government revenue due to the lack of data for most of the period (subnational government revenues have not been significant—in 2013 they accounted for only 0.47 percent of GDP).

**TABLE 8.1**

**Peru: Annual Average Tax Revenue by Decade, Excluding Social Security**
*(Percent of GDP)*

| | 1971–80 | 1981–90 | 1991–2000 | 2001–10 | 2011–14 |
|---|---|---|---|---|---|
| **Total** | **14.6** | **12.6** | **13.4** | **14.5** | **16.4** |
| Income[1] | 3.9 | 2.3 | 2.7 | 5.1 | 7.0 |
| Individuals | | | 1.3 | 1.7 | 2.5 |
| Corporations | | | 1.9 | 3.4 | 4.6 |
| Property | 0.7 | 0.6 | 0.2 | 0.0 | 0.0 |
| Export | 1.1 | 0.3 | 0.0 | 0.0 | 0.0 |
| Import | 2.7 | 2.5 | 1.7 | 1.0 | 0.3 |
| Value-added Tax | 4.3 | 3.2 | 5.8 | 7.5 | 8.7 |
| Excise | 1.7 | 3.7 | 2.6 | 1.6 | 1.0 |
| Other | 0.8 | 0.9 | 1.1 | 1.1 | 1.4 |
| Tax Refunds | –0.6 | –1.0 | –0.7 | –1.7 | –2.1 |

Source: IMF staff estimates.
[1]Data for personal and corporate income taxes are available since 1994.

replaced a schedular tax system in 1968, was modified several times during the decade.[3] The personal income tax (PIT) went from having 24 rates to having "only" nine in 1989, while the number of corporate income tax (CIT) rates went from four to one (35 percent). The number of deductions in both the PIT and the CIT increased significantly, eroding the tax base and complicating tax administration.

In 1982, an important milestone in tax policy was the creation of the general sales tax (GST), a type of VAT that replaced the previous consumption and production taxes.[4] The GST was complemented with excise taxes,[5] and the first simplified scheme for small taxpayers. Several tax exemptions were created for certain goods as well as for transactions in border areas and departments in the Amazon. Most of them remain in force today.

Excise taxes were established primarily for revenue purposes and imposed on fuel and luxury goods. They were central instruments of tax policy and used to compensate for the reduction of public resources due to fluctuating commodity prices and the effects of natural disasters related to ocean warming (the El Niño phenomenon). For most of the 1980s, these taxes were the most important in terms of revenue, generating on average 29 percent of the total.

While tax policies changed substantially, there were no major improvements in tax administration operations or regulations. Repeated reorganizations were carried out with the support of international organizations, but the results always fell short of initial goals. The National Superintendency of Tax Administration (*Superintendencia Nacional de Administración Tributaria* [SUNAT]) was created in 1989, but a fundamental reform of the tax administration was not carried out until the early 1990s.

In this context, total tax revenues reached on average only 12.6 percent of GDP (see Table 8.1). Income taxes (PIT and CIT) reached levels of slightly over 2 percent of GDP, the GST 3 percent, and excise taxes 3.7 percent. In sum, the decade closed with a weak tax system plagued with exemptions and multiple rates that did not reflect any long-term vision.

[3]A global income tax is one levied (typically at progressive rates) on the sum of the taxpayer's income from all sources; this is in contrast to a schedular tax system, under which different types of income (wages, interest, etc.) are taxed separately.

[4]The abbreviation VAT is used to refer to value-added taxes in general, and the abbreviation GST refers to the Peruvian value-added tax (*Impuesto General a las Ventas*).

[5]The creation of the excise taxes, which were mainly applied to sumptuary goods, had revenue purposes. During this decade, these taxes were the most important and constituted on average 29 percent of total revenue.

## The 1990s

The beginning of the 1990s in Peru was marked by hyperinflation, sharp recession, isolation of the economy from the international financial system, and terrorism. With the fiscal deficit reaching record levels, not least due to tax revenues approaching their lowest mark of 8.4 percent of GDP in 1989, the Peruvian government embarked on a consolidation path.[6]

A set of legislative decrees introduced important tax policy reforms that incorporated the principles of efficiency and equity, and eliminated more than 60 small taxes and fees and 40 exemptions. The tax system was based on four pillars: the GST, the CIT and PIT, excise taxes, and customs duties. A simplified scheme (*Regimen Unico Simplificado*, RUS) was also introduced for small taxpayers. In 1989, SUNAT (domestic taxes) and SUNAD (customs, *Superintendencia Nacional de Aduanas*) became autonomous institutions. To a large extent, as a result of these changes, revenue increased from 8.4 percent of GDP in 1989 to 13.2 percent in 1999.

On the administration side, the comprehensive modernization of SUNAT in 1991 was one of the most important changes of the decade. A number of significant improvements to the institution included hiring and training new and qualified staff, increasing salaries in line with new staff responsibilities, acquiring new buildings, creating a large taxpayer unit, and upgrading technology. In addition, an invoice system was put in place, among other measures taken to improve tax compliance. In 1994, a short-term revenue improvement plan, developed jointly by SUNAT and the IMF Fiscal Affairs Department, was successfully completed, and subsequently contributed to the increases in tax revenue described above.

Despite these improvements, there was still room to make SUNAT and collection more efficient. Noncompliance was still higher than regional averages. In 1992, for example, Peru had a broad-based GST with a rate of 18 percent that yielded only 2.4 percent of GDP.[7] This level of performance was low by international standards and reflected a high level of evasion in all sectors of the economy, especially among large taxpayers. SUNAT had to implement audit and control programs to cover all sectors and taxpayers, as the collection control system of tax returns and payments for large taxpayers had been extended to SUNAT's regional departments. Coverage of small and medium-sized taxpayers was still weak.

The significant improvements in tax policy and administration during the 1990s eventually contributed to raising total revenue to 13.4 percent of GDP on average over the decade (see Table 8.1) and to a peak of 14.7 percent in 1997. This helped restore the country's public sector accounts to balance. However, in the late 1990s Peru's economy weakened, mainly as a result of adverse external shocks (a liquidity squeeze stemming from the international financial crisis) that reduced the terms of trade, the negative effects of the El Niño weather phenomenon, domestic political turmoil, and slow progress in structural reforms. In particular, consensus had not yet been achieved on the need to eliminate important regional and sectoral exemptions from both the income tax and the GST.

To get immediate and short-term gains in revenue, the government began to introduce several moratoriums (amnesties and fractional amnesties known as *fraccionamientos*) in 1996 and 1997 that contributed to decelerating revenue growth in the final years of the decade.[8] In order to stimulate the slow-growing economy, the government continued granting more benefits and relief that kept eroding the tax base. The tax administration was also weakened due to the granting of new amnesties. As a result, and despite the positive effect of certain tax administration measures, revenues began to weaken again, declining to 12.8 percent by 2001.

---

[6]See Chapter 5 on fiscal policies.

[7]During the later years of the 1990s, the GST base was broadened by way of eliminating several exemptions (some of them products of the agricultural sector) that were subsequently reimposed at the end of the decade.

[8]SUNAT had to divert resources to administer tax relief and moratoriums that could have been used for audits and other essential functions. In addition, the tax relief and moratoriums probably affected taxpayer behavior by prompting them to expect new tax relief in the future.

## The New Millennium

Following the road taken in the late 1990s, and departing from international best practices, the government approved four general tax amnesties in 2002 (including the *fraccionamientos*). The number of amnesties approved signaled to taxpayers that these were not one-off events. The amnesties covered tax obligations under previous amnesties and under litigation as well. It was clear that the number of tax amnesties and the benefits they included would undermine compliance.

Contrary to expectations, the amnesties did not generate enough revenue, and collection fell in 2002. To offset the reduction in revenue, the government introduced a comprehensive reform in 2002 that included tax policy and administration measures to strengthen collection and control. The reforms yielded an increase in collection of 0.8 percent of GDP. The administrative measures mainly involved an audit plan for large taxpayers, the unification of SUNAT and SUNAD (with their own budgets, retaining 2 percent of collections), the introduction of a withholding system for the GST, and intensification of the control of tax collection and GST refunds.

The tax policy measures aimed to increase tax bases and improve the neutrality of the tax system. Main measures included elimination of a few GST exemptions (on fertilizers and for specific regions of the country, with a portion of the increased revenue to be allocated to poverty relief programs in these same regions), an increase of the top marginal PIT rate from 27 percent to 30 percent and of the excise on kerosene, and introduction of an advance payment scheme for the minimum CIT. To increase the transparency of the tax system, the reform also provided for inclusion of tax expenditures in the budget starting in 2003.

To further support collection, the government introduced the controversial banking transaction tax at a rate of 0.15 percent and the temporary tax on net assets (minimum CIT) at a rate of 0.6 percent, to take effect in 2004. It is worth mentioning that the banking transaction tax rate was progressively reduced to 0.05 percent by 2010 and to 0.005 percent in 2011. It thus became more important as a source of information than as a collection tool. The reform also redefined the concept of excise taxes: as of 2004, excise taxes began to be set taking into account negative externalities and not only for revenue purposes as in preceding years.

Revenue began to recover starting in 2005, reaching 14.4 percent of GDP. Significant gains were also achieved in CIT collection that year due to high mineral prices. The extension of the coverage of GST withholding schemes also contributed to the GST's good revenue performance. In the mid-2000s, further changes in tax policy were undertaken, including (1) the reduction of specific excise tax rates on petroleum products (diesel, particularly) to mitigate the impact of higher world oil prices on the economy (June 2004), and (2) the introduction of a royalty on the gross income of mining companies (June 2005). In 2011, the government began to work in close cooperation with Congress on a proposal to change the base of royalties from gross sales to a proxy of profits (with less adverse effects on investment).

As a consequence, collection increased to 16.4 percent of GDP in 2007. However, the global financial crisis in 2008 negatively affected economic growth and thus Peru's revenue performance, with the tax-to-GDP ratio falling to 14.4 percent of GDP by end-2009 (Annex 8.1). Other factors also contributed to this decline. For example, tax revenue was affected by the elimination of custom duties associated with the free trade agreement with the United States.[9] Starting in 2010, the income tax base was broadened: a dual tax system was introduced aimed at taxing

[9]The Andean Trade Promotion and Drug Eradication Act, in place from 2002 to 2005, had been a scheme of trade preferences extended by the United States to Peru and other countries of the region. In contrast, the Peruvian free trade agreement with the United States was a permanent framework that provided a more secure environment for trade and investment decisions. The agreement has a broader scope than that of the Andean Trade Promotion and Drug Eradication Act, including reciprocal commitments on trade in goods and services, investment, labor legislation, and intellectual property rights. The free trade agreement was ratified by the Peruvian Congress in June 2006. With the ratification of the agreement, Peru immediately eliminated tariffs on around 80 percent of its imports from the United States; tariffs on sensitive products were eliminated gradually over 5, 7, and 10 years.

interest and capital gains at a rate of 6.25 percent (dividends were already taxed), and the tax benefits for refurbishing used cars provided via CETICOS (*Centro de Exportación, Transformación, Industria, Comercialización y Servicios*) expired and were not extended.

The Peruvian government also embarked on a fiscal decentralization process during the 2000s.[10] Once the 2004 Fiscal Decentralization Law was approved, regions pressed to speed up the transfer of functions to subnational governments. As a result, by the end of 2007, the central government transferred 185 functions to regional governments. By 2009, Peru had a growing and dynamic mining sector and mining regions were slated to receive greater income from the revenues generated by mining.[11] Private mining companies agreed to make voluntary contributions to social and infrastructure spending in regions in which they operated. However, revenue from the mining sector did not exceed 0.1 percent of GDP and the general perception was that the maximum contribution was far from being reached. To address this, the authorities introduced a more progressive mechanism in 2011 (Annex 8.2).

Perhaps the most relevant event during this period, at least on the administrative side, was the merger of the tax and customs administrations into a single agency in 2003. The trend to establish a single revenue agency started with the creation of such an agency in Spain in 1992.[12] This was soon followed in Latin America by Mexico (1995), Argentina (1997), Guatemala (1997), and Colombia (1998). Thus, when Peru undertook this merger it was adhering to a rather successful model in the region. However, the design of the law diverged from regional models. In Peru the merger was conceived as "absorption" (the law called it a *fusión por absorción*) of customs by the tax administration, rather than a merger of roughly equal agencies. This created a number of organizational problems for SUNAT, not least of which was that customs staff felt that they had lost relevance and importance in the new organization, and resources and IT systems were not distributed evenly.[13]

The authorities sought to deal with the challenges created by the merger. With the help of IMF technical assistance, a number of measures were identified as part of SUNAT's modernization strategy to improve taxpayer services and trade facilitation, enhance control of taxpayer compliance, and increase revenue collection. A comprehensive Compliance Improvement Program (CIP) was established and put in place measures to strengthen audit, collection, and enforcement strategies to better address compliance risks. The establishment of the CIP in 2012 and the implementation of these measures have signaled a period of profound change for SUNAT. This has included a comprehensive redesign of its organizational structure to better balance integration of the two lines of business, a new career system for SUNAT staff, and a new coordinated border management strategy. Other parts of the reform strategy included updating the strategic plan to incorporate new reform priorities, developing a corporate IT strategic plan aimed at integrating the disparate IT platforms for domestic taxes and customs systems, and strengthening communications to enhance ownership across SUNAT.

The measures put in place have succeeded in strengthening tax revenue. During the first decade of the 2000s, the tax revenue-to-GDP ratio averaged 14.5 percent, while from 2011–14 this average rose to 16.5 percent (see Table 8.1) Excise tax yields have fallen as income tax revenue has risen. Excise taxes dropped from 1.9 percent in 2000 to 1 percent in 2013, while income taxes rose from 2.9 percent to 6.7 percent over the same period.

---

[10] See Chapter 10 on fiscal decentralization.

[11] In 2010, Peru was the second largest global producer of copper and the sixth largest producer of gold. Peru fell to third place in copper production in 2013 due to China's increase in production.

[12] Brazil's *Receita Federal* had been united since the late 1970s, but it was seen as an exceptional case.

[13] The resulting organization was unbalanced and struggled for a while with the fact that there were two different career systems with different salary scales and rules for the two lines of business, as well as different sets of procedures for functions that could have benefited from common strategies—such as revenue collection, risk management, and arrears collections. Although several analysts pointed to these imbalances and recommended a number of measures to mitigate the risks thus created, it was not until 2011 that the structural problems originated in the merger began to be addressed. Even now, however, existing operational systems for domestic taxes and customs duties are not integrated.

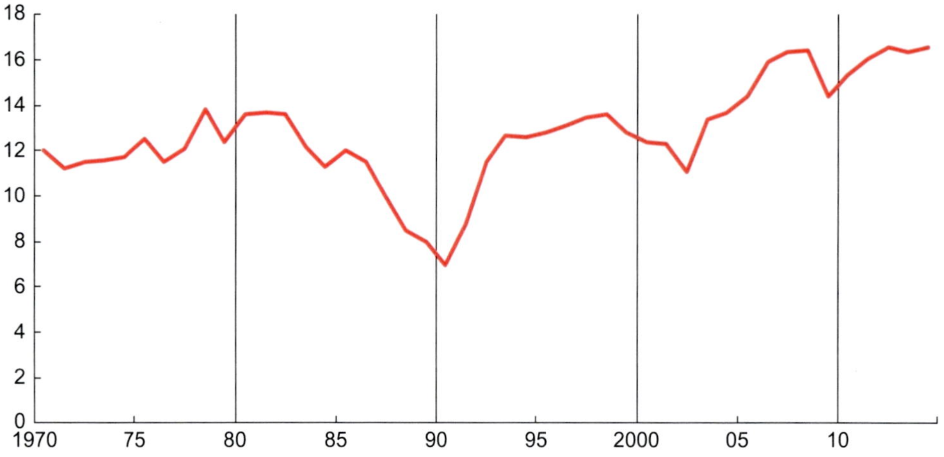


Source: IMF staff with data from the Ministry of the Economy and Finance.

**Figure 8.1** Peru: Central Government Tax Revenue (*Percent of GDP*)

# THE CURRENT TAX SYSTEM

## Tax Policy

The current Peruvian tax system is made up of four main taxes (the GST, PIT and CIT, excise tax, and import tax) and some low-yield taxes. Peruvian tax rates are around the average in other Latin American countries and the taxes are in line with principles of revenue adequacy, efficiency, and equity. Currently, these rates are being lowered in order to accomplish important macroeconomic objectives.

Central government tax revenue increased from 12 percent of GDP in 1970 to 16.6 percent in 2014 (Figure 8.1). This reflected the impact of economic growth, as well as sound tax policy and administrative measures, such as the reduction of noncompliance, the broadening of tax bases, and the development of a fiscal regime for the mining sector. During this period, inefficient taxes were eliminated and revenue was concentrated in the GST (its collection more than doubled) and income taxes. GST noncompliance was reduced from 46.3 percent of potential revenue in 2001 to 29 percent in 2012. SUNAT maintains reasonable levels of efficacy and efficiency. Nevertheless, evasion remains high considering Peru's level of development and when compared to similar countries in Latin America.

The composition of central government tax revenue has also changed (Figure 8.2). The share of the GST and taxes on income increased from 46 to 78 percent of total revenue, while trade taxes declined from almost 22 percent to less than 3 percent. The elimination of the tax on companies' assets and the assignment of the property tax to local governments explain the reduction of wealth tax revenues. The elimination of export taxes and trade liberalization explains the reduction of trade taxes. More than 70 "small" taxes with very low levels of revenue were eliminated.

The GST is the main source of tax revenue, followed by taxes on income. In 2014, the GST accounted for 6.8 percent of GDP (net of refunds), or 36.5 percent of total revenues, while the CIT yielded 21.6 percent of total revenue and the PIT 15.4 percent. Taking into account the inexistence of turnover taxes and the low level of revenue from customs duties (0.03 percent of GDP) and the banking transaction tax (BTT), Peru today has a relatively efficient tax system.[14] The GST has a relatively wide base and only one rate of 18 percent (of which 2 percentage points are allocated to the Regional Promotion Fund). Its productivity and efficiency have increased significantly, while GST noncompliance has been significantly reduced (Figure 8.3 and Box 8.1).

[14]The banking transaction tax rate has been reduced to only 0.05 percent, with its main objective to inform SUNAT of bank transactions.

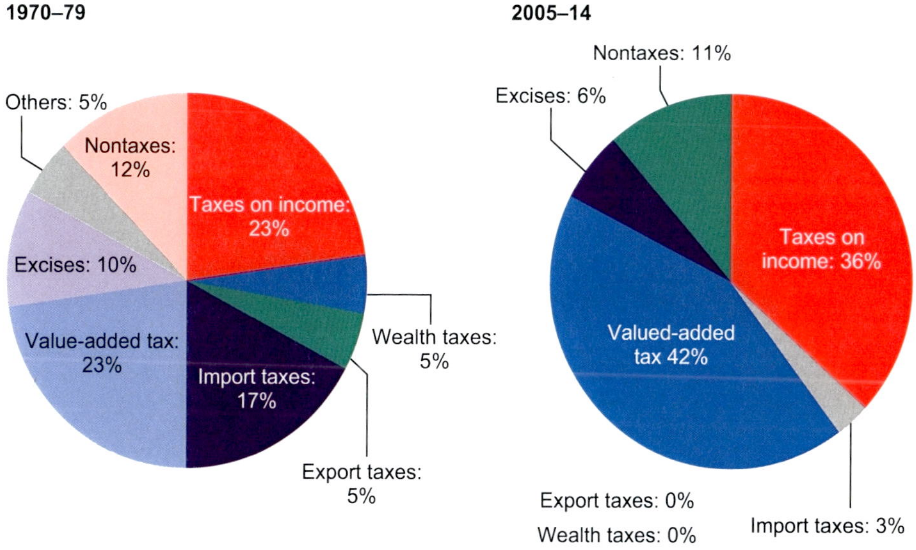


Source: IMF staff with data from the Ministry of the Economy and Finance and the National Superintendency of Tax Administration (SUNAT).

**Figure 8.2** Peru: Composition of Central Government Tax Revenues, 1970–79 and 2014–15 (*Percent*)

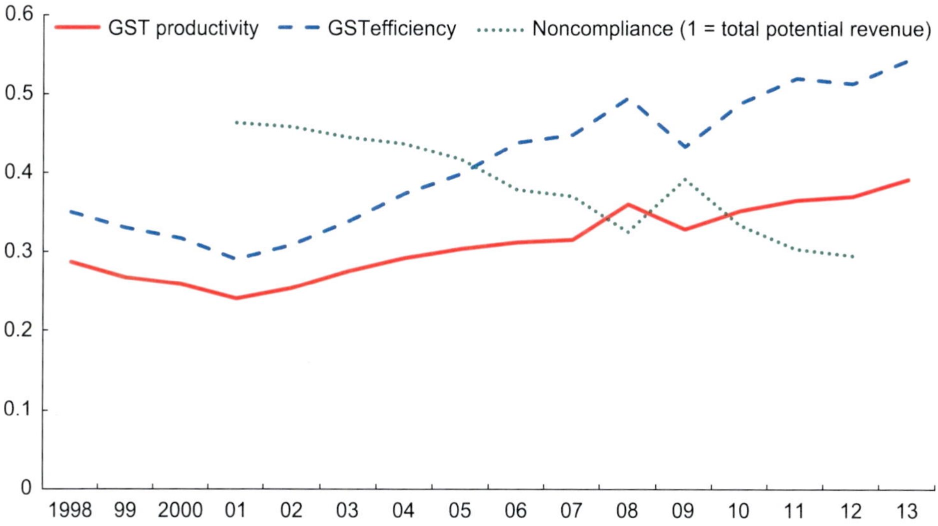


Source: Ministry of the Economy and Finance; National Superintendency of Tax Administration (SUNAT); and IMF staff estimates.
Note: GST = general sales tax.

**Figure 8.3** Peru: Value-Added Tax Productivity, Efficiency, and Gap

The design of both the PIT and CIT in Peru is solidly in accordance with general principles of taxation. Due to improvements in control, the elimination of some exemptions, the introduction of the minimum CIT on net wealth, and economic growth, income tax revenue increased significantly over the past decade (from 4.5 percent in 2005 to 7 percent in 2014; see Annex 8.1). Both CIT and PIT rates are near the average of the region, thus avoiding any distortion of competition (Table 8.2). Peru's standard CIT rate in 2014 (30 percent) was somewhat higher than the regional average (27.3 percent), as was the top PIT rate (30 percent in Peru and 27.5 percent

**BOX 8.1. The Value-Added Tax C-Efficiency Ratio**

A common measure of value-added tax (VAT) performance is the ratio of its revenue to consumption (GDP) divided by the VAT rate. This measure is commonly referred to as the C-efficiency ratio (VAT productivity when the GDP is used instead of consumption). It represents the percentage of consumption (GDP) that each percentage point of the VAT rate collects (e.g., the C-efficiency ratio for the Peruvian general sales tax was 51.4 percent in 2012). The ratio is a useful tool for analyzing the performance of the VAT within a country over a given period of time. A low ratio indicates erosion of the base (either through zero-rating or exemptions) and/or noncompliance. The C-coefficient has to be used with care in cross-country comparisons because methodologies to estimate it usually differ.

The main practical advantage of the VAT C-coefficient is that the data requirement for estimating it is relatively modest. And it can provide a rapid first assessment and expression of the potential revenue gain from increasing the VAT rate. There are, however, both conceptual and practical (measurement) issues to be considered in using the VAT C-efficiency ratio. From the conceptual point of view, there is no deep welfare basis for the use of C-efficiency in assessing the VAT. An increase in the C-efficiency ratio does not necessarily imply a better scenario; it can be increased, for example, by delaying VAT refunds to exporters, or by introducing exemptions for intermediate goods (cascading). In welfare terms, therefore, not much can be read into changes in C-efficiency.

From the measurement side, there are a number of issues. The definitions of revenue (the numerator) and consumption (the denominator) are usually not uniform, which affects the comparison between countries in particular. One issue, for instance, is the need to exclude revenue from purchases of nonresidents (the VAT is a tax on domestic consumption). However, not all countries exclude VAT revenue from nonresidents in calculating the VAT revenue used in C-coefficient estimates. Although in many cases the implications can be small, they are not necessarily small in others. That is why countries with a high level of re-export trade (sales to people who cross the border from neighboring countries to make purchases), or small economies with a high component of tourism, usually present high VAT C-efficiency.

Other issues arise when measuring the consumption base. Consumption from the national accounts usually used to measure the VAT C-coefficient (sometimes with adjustments) can differ significantly from the aggregate of consumption subject to the VAT. The value of owner-occupied housing services, for instance, is generally included in national account measures of consumption as an imputed rental value, while no country includes it in the VAT base because it is not feasible in practice. Another issue, and perhaps the most quantitatively significant problem, is the treatment of the public sector and nonprofit organizations. For instance, most public services cannot be expressed in market prices (e.g., basic education, health, or national defense). The national accounts' approach to such items is to treat them as consumption by the government, not households, and to proxy their value by their cost of production, adding the cost of goods and services purchased and the labor and capital costs incurred.

in the region).[15] The PIT exemption threshold is equivalent to 79 percent of GDP per capita (adjusted by purchasing power parity, in constant 2011 U.S. dollars). Although this exemption eliminates a significant share of the population from the PIT, it is in line with the region and appropriate for a developing country. Similarly, the threshold at which the top marginal rate is applied (6.4 times) is somewhat above the regional average (5.2 times).

The central government tax system also includes excises, customs duties, the banking transaction tax, and the RUS. Excise revenue decreased from 2.2 percent of GDP in 2003 to 1 percent in 2013 mainly because of the reduction of taxation on oil and derivatives to mitigate the increase in prices of these goods. The level of revenue reached by the RUS is also not significant, but the tax has contributed to simplifying the tax system (both for the private sector and SUNAT).

Taxes on property are the main source of tax revenue at the local level, representing 0.33 percent of GDP in 2012 (and 70 percent of total revenue). Two taxes are applied on property: one on the holding of immovable property (rates vary between 0.2 and 1 percent) and another (*Alcabala*) on the transaction of immovable property (at a rate of 3 percent).[16] While the

[15] As described later in this chapter, the Peruvian government plans to reduce the CIT rate to 26 percent in 2019.

[16] In 2012, revenue from holding immovable property was only 0.18 percent of GDP and revenue from transactions of immovable property was only 0.15 percent.

**TABLE 8.2**

## Value-Added Tax, Corporate Income Tax, Personal Income Tax, and Dividend Rates, Selected Countries, 2013

| Country | Bracket of Top PIT (multiple of GDP/capita PPP) | Top PIT Rate | Bracket of Top PIT US$ | Minimum PIT Rate | Standard CIT Rate | GDP per Capita, Constant 2011 US dollars PPP | PIT Exemption to PPP | PIT Exemption in US$ | Rate for Dividends (percent) | | VAT Standard Rate |
|---|---|---|---|---|---|---|---|---|---|---|---|
| | | | | | | | | | Residents | Nonresidents | |
| Argentina | | 35.0 | 14,101 | 9.0 | 35.0 | | | 10,600 | 10.0 | 10.0 | 21.0 |
| Brazil | 1.9 | 27.5 | 27,138 | 7.5 | 34.0 | 14,555 | 1.00 | 14,589 | 0.0 | 0.0 | |
| Chile | 5.7 | 40.0 | 123,549 | 4.0 | 20.0 | 21,714 | 0.51 | 11,119 | Progressive rates[1] | 35 - CIT | 19.0 |
| Colombia | 4.9 | 33.0 | 58,940 | 19.0 | 34.0 | 11,977 | 1.51 | 18,062 | 0.0 | 0.0 | 19.0 |
| Costa Rica | 2.3 | 25.0 | 30,899 | 10.0 | 30.0 | 13,431 | 0.46 | 6,190 | 15.0 | 15.0 | 13.0 |
| Dominican Republic[2] | 1.7 | 25.0 | 18,839 | 15.0 | 28.0 | 11,323 | 0.80 | 9,064 | 10.0 | 10.0 | 18.0 |
| Ecuador | 10.5 | 35.0 | 106,200 | 5.0 | 22.0 | 10,135 | 1.03 | 10,410 | Progressive rates[1] | 0.0 | 12.0 |
| El Salvador[3] | 3.0 | 30.0 | 22,875 | 10.0 | 30.0 | 7,515 | 0.75 | 5,664 | 5.0 | 5.0 | 13.0 |
| Guatemala[4] | 1.7 | 7.0 | 11,819 | 5.0 | 28.0 | 7,063 | 0.89 | 6,303 | 5.0 | 5.0 | 12.0 |
| Honduras[5] | 5.3 | 25.0 | 23,552 | 15.0 | 29.0 | 4,445 | 1.17 | 5,181 | 10.0 | 10.0 | 15.0 |
| Mexico | 13.5 | 35.0 | 220,588 | 1.9 | 30.0 | 16,291 | 0.41 | 6,618 | 10.0 | 10.0 | 16.0 |
| Nicaragua | 4.3 | 30.0 | 18,918 | 15.0 | 30.0 | 4,425 | 0.85 | 3,784 | 5.0 | 5.0 | 15.0 |
| Panama | 2.7 | 25.0 | 50,000 | 15.0 | 25.0 | 18,793 | 0.59 | 11,000 | 10.0 | 10.0 | 7.0 |
| Paraguay | 6.3 | 10.0 | 48,979 | 8.0 | 10.0 | 7,787 | 0.42 | 3,265 | General rates[6] | 15.0 | 10.0 |
| **Peru**[7] | **6.4** | **30.0** | **72,951** | **15.0** | **30.0** | **11,400** | **0.79** | **9,057** | **4.1** | **4.1** | **18.0** |
| Uruguay | 9.0 | 30.0 | 171,245 | 10.0 | 25.0 | 18,966 | 0.52 | 9,826 | 7; 12 | 7.0 | 22.0 |
| Simple Average without Peru | 5.2 | 27.5 | 63,176 | 10.0 | 27.3 | 12,030 | 0.78 | 8,778 | | | 15.1 |

Source: IMF staff based on data from the International Bureau of Fiscal Documentation and country authorities.
Note: CIT = corporate income tax; PIT = personal income tax; PPP = purchasing power parity; VAT = value-added tax.
[1]The CIT is granted as tax credit.
[2]The VAT rate is reduced to 16 percent starting 2015.
[3]The CIT rate is reduced to 25 percent for companies whose taxable income does not exceed US$150,000.
[4]Starting in 2015, the CIT rate is reduced to 25 percent.
[5]The CIT rate is 25 percent; during 2014 there is a surtax of 4 percent (temporally solidarity contribution).
[6]Only 50 percent of the dividends received.
[7]The CIT rate was gradually reduced to 26 percent and the minimum PIT rate to 8 percent as of 2015.

### BOX 8.2. Taxation and Growth

Under the neoclassical growth model, the level and structure of taxes have no effect on the long-term rate of growth, but only on the level of national income. However, more recent models of endogenous growth and empirical studies anticipate a potential effect of taxation on a country's rate of economic growth. Research based on Organisation for Economic Co-operation and Development countries suggests a "tax and growth" ranking in which property taxes are the least harmful taxes for growth over the long run, followed by consumption taxes, personal income taxes (PIT), and corporate income taxes (CIT) (Arnold 2008). An IMF study covering 69 countries from 1970–2009 reported similar results: increasing income taxes while reducing consumption and property taxes is associated with slower growth over the long run (Acosta-Ormaechea and Yoo 2012); however, the adverse growth effect of the PIT is not found for developing countries with PIT revenue ratios as low as in Peru.

After the property tax, the VAT appears to be the least damaging of the major taxes in terms of growth. In contrast, theoretical and empirical studies show that the PIT has adverse effects for growth: it negatively affects labor supply and savings more than other taxes, and thereby growth. When the top marginal rate is very high, there may be gains in labor supply by reducing the progressivity of the PIT schedule. This implies a potential trade-off between growth-enhancing tax policies and distributional effects. The result that the PIT is worse for growth than the VAT should be further examined by studies that explore the respective effects of the two taxes on inequality. The challenge of a tax system is to strike an acceptable balance between opposing objectives while preserving the sustainability of public finances—which itself is a fundamental building block of a competitive economy.

Like the PIT, the CIT has been associated with lower growth because taxes on corporate profits affect private investment. Reflecting this, an increase in consumption taxes accompanied by a reduction in income taxes would have a positive and significant effect on long-term growth. However, it is also noteworthy that the CIT affects both the normal return to capital and economic rents (such as those from minerals and petroleum). While the CIT on normal returns may be very distortive, it is not distortionary in terms of economic rents.

The design of the CIT is also related to growth, and not only in terms of its revenue-generating potential. Policymakers should also address the number and size of exemptions. Governments across the region (Peru is no exception) have used and continue to use tax incentives (e.g., for activities or geographic areas) to attract investment. However, the effects of these initiatives have been ambiguous. Moreover, tax incentives have complicated tax administrations and eroded CIT bases, putting the sustainability of public finances and the long-term rate of economic growth at risk.

virtues of immovable property taxes are very clear (relatively low efficiency costs, a benign impact on growth—see Box 8.2—and a high score in terms of fairness), taxes on sales can have very negative effects, especially in Peru where these rates are high (encouraging informal transactions in cash to partially avoid the tax).

The simplified RUS regime covered 56 percent of taxpayers in 2013 (without including employees), but generated less than 0.17 percent of total tax revenue. The CIP and SUNAT's corporate IT strategy are expected to improve the performance of this regime, but further development is needed to make it administratively more efficient and less distorted.

Fiscal revenue from mining remains significant. For example, between 1999 and 2013, while tax and nontax revenues in nominal terms quadrupled, revenues from the mining sector increased more than seven times. The government has introduced an efficient tax reform to the mining sector that moves toward a progressive regime. In 2013, revenue from the mining sector accounted for about 1.1 percent of GDP (a decline from the all-time high of about 3.7 percent in 2007). While tax revenue from the sector in 2007 represented 16 percent of general government revenues, its share was reduced to 5 percent by 2013, reflecting improved collection of other taxes and a reduction in the prices of metals (Annex 8.2).

During 2012 and 2013, a series of tax policy measures was introduced to improve tax collection, strengthening the administration's capacity to control tax evasion and avoidance. Among these measures were modifications to the GST, PIT and CIT, the Tax Code, and the General Customs Law (all of which had a direct impact on tax collection). A new general antiavoidance law was also passed, with some additional amendments and improvements to specific antiavoidance regulations.

Last but not least, in 2014 a set of tax policy measures was approved to strengthen the competitiveness of the Peruvian economy, of which the most significant were:

- A rationalization of PIT rates, with the lowest rate set at 8 percent (slightly more than half the previous lowest rate of 15 percent) and the highest remaining at 30 percent.
- Reduction of the nominal CIT rate from 30 to 28 percent in 2015 and 2016, to 27 percent in 2017 and 2018, and to 26 percent in 2019.
- The introduction of tax credits in the CIT to enhance labor productivity.
- The simplification of VAT withholding schemes:[17] the rate for *retenciones* was reduced from 6 percent to 3 percent, the number of rates for *detracciones* dropped from five to three, and the number of goods subject to *percepciones* was reduced from 41 to 12.

## Tax Administration

Peru uses a single tax administration to handle the collection of both domestic taxes and custom duties. Created in 1989 after numerous reorganization attempts, SUNAT has become one of the most advanced revenue administrations in the region. Having been granted autonomous agency status in response to the profound deterioration of the tax administration from 1985–90, SUNAT was rebuilt practically from scratch, incorporating a number of professionals from other areas of public service—notably the central bank—who served as the core of a management team committed to excellence in what has become one of Peru's most effective and reputable government agencies.

SUNAT continued its institutional development during the second half of the 1990s when its overall budget stabilized at around 2 percent of total revenue collected. The organizational structure was concentrated around strengthening the Large Taxpayers Unit and developing state-of-the-art IT systems, with support from the Inter-American Development Bank (IDB) and the Inter-American Center for Tax Administration, which succeeded in providing SUNAT with one of the most advanced IT systems in the region.

During the early 2000s, Peru's public administration stagnated. This was in part due to increased restrictions imposed by budgetary regulations regarding salaries and recruitment of new staff, which endured for more than a decade. Restriction also significantly reduced investment funds (thus hindering continuous development and enhancement of IT systems). Nonetheless, one of the most important events in SUNAT's history occurred in 2003, with the merger of the tax and customs administrations into a single agency.

A new round of reforms began in 2010. Key priorities included the development of a new career system for staff; better integration of core revenue administration functions (collections, audit, arrears management, risk management, and taxpayer services) for both domestic taxes and customs, moving away from the organizational model that kept these areas separate; and the implementation of the corporate IT strategy.

All of these objectives were included in the Revenue Administration Modernization Law unanimously passed by Congress in December 2011. Moreover, in line with the government's commitment to increase the tax-to-GDP ratio in the medium term, the Ministry of the Economy and Finance passed a number of administrative measures in mid-2012 designed to give SUNAT

[17]Three special schemes apply to tax revenue in Peru: *retenciones, detracciones,* and *percepciones*. Under the *retenciones* scheme, large taxpayers must deduct 3 percent in withholding in payments to VAT registered traders and pay it to the Treasury; sellers can credit the withholding against their VAT liabilities. Under the *detracciones* scheme, payers also have to make a deduction from payments, but there are several differences from the *retenciones* scheme, including the following: (1) *detracciones* only apply to a certain group of goods and services, (2) the rate of the *detraccion* withholding varies according to the activity, and (3) the withholding of *detracciones* can be used to cancel any kind of tax liabilities. Under the *percepciones* scheme, large taxpayers (and customs) have to apply an additional VAT rate in their sales to VAT registered traders (who can credit it against their VAT liabilities).

increased powers to enforce taxpayer compliance. All these measures were made an integral part of SUNAT's compliance management program for the period 2012–14.

In the wake of these legislative changes, SUNAT has been undergoing a period of profound change. This was signaled by implementation in 2012 of the CIP, a comprehensive redesign of SUNAT's organizational structure to achieve a more balanced integration of the two lines of business, implementation of the new career system for SUNAT staff (developed with IDB technical assistance), identification and design of a comprehensive IDB technical assistance project that will support the development of the new IT strategy starting in mid-2015, and implementation of a new coordinated border management strategy.

Going forward, a key priority is implementation of an integrated control strategy for the VAT. This strategy should be based on strengthening taxpayer registration and tax document authorization through risk analysis, focusing VAT audits on the validity of the input tax, establishing an IT system for checking VAT suppliers, using all the information from withholding mechanisms, and addressing the abuse of fake invoices. This would also support the rationalization measures already initiated, contribute to the maturity of the tax system, and lessen reliance on supplementary schemes such as VAT withholding schemes.

## POTENTIAL TO FURTHER INCREASE REVENUE AND THE QUALITY OF THE TAX SYSTEM

### Main Problems and Challenges

Peru has come a long way in improving the efficiency and fairness of the tax system and its administration. Today the country has a modern tax system based on a GST and income taxes without cascading taxes and with low trade taxes. Several exemptions and inefficient taxes have been eliminated or significantly reduced. Going forward, the challenges that remain to be addressed include the following:

- *Low level of tax effort.* Tax collection (including social contributions) reached a little over 18.7 percent of GDP in 2013. This is relatively low compared to other countries with similar levels of development (Table 8.3). The current Peruvian tax system yields 53 percent of the maximum level of its potential revenue.[18] This somewhat weak tax effort can be explained by inefficiency in collection (noncompliance)[19] and by exemptions (tax expenditure),[20] although a reduction in GST noncompliance and in tax expenditure raised revenue in recent years and partially compensated for the loss of revenue from the opening of the economy and the elimination of about 70 inefficient taxes. As mentioned above, other pillars of the tax system, such as tax rates and the PIT allowance, are near standards of the region. On the other hand, the design of the excise tax must continue to be improved so as to fully internalize the effect of externalities generated by the consumption of certain goods.

[18]Employing a stochastic frontier analysis (Fenochietto and Pessino 2013) allows for estimating a maximum level of revenue that is possible (i.e., the frontier) for a country's given economic and social characteristics. By comparing actual revenue with this tax capacity, what is called the "tax effort" is obtained. Hence, a tax effort of 53 percent means that a country today collects 53 percent of what it could potentially collect.

[19]Using the national account method, SUNAT estimated that the GST gap was reduced from 46.3 percent of potential tax revenue in 2001 to 29 percent in 2012 due to improvements in tax administration.

[20]Tax expenditures represent the revenue forgone from preferential tax treatments, relative to a reference tax system (or benchmark). Due to different benchmarks and different methodologies, a comparison between studies is not always meaningful. Peru has estimated tax expenditures since the beginning of the 2000s. The estimates are included transparently in a chapter of the budget (since 2003) that allows parliamentarians to discuss the fiscal cost of tax incentives and exemptions they have approved. The level of tax expenditures in Peru was estimated by SUNAT at 2.01 percent of GDP for 2014 (SUNAT 2012).

TABLE 8.3

Tax Efforts in Countries of the Region

| | Country | Year | Total Revenue[1] | GDP per Capita[2] | Tax Effort | Tax Capacity |
|---|---|---|---|---|---|---|
| 1 | Guatemala | 2013 | 11.4 | 7,063 | 0.39 | 28.9 |
| 2 | Dominican Republic | 2013 | 14.8 | 11,323 | 0.42 | 35.4 |
| 3 | Panama | 2012 | 16.9 | 17,627 | 0.44 | 38.6 |
| 4 | El Salvador | 2013 | 17.3 | 7,515 | 0.47 | 37.0 |
| **5** | **Peru** | **2013** | **17.2** | **11,400** | **0.53** | **32.4** |
| 6 | Paraguay | 2013 | 16.4 | 7,787 | 0.53 | 30.6 |
| 7 | Chile | 2012 | 21.3 | 21,049 | 0.55 | 38.9 |
| 8 | Costa Rica | 2012 | 21.2 | 13,158 | 0.59 | 35.7 |
| 9 | Nicaragua | 2013 | 20.6 | 4,425 | 0.60 | 34.6 |
| 10 | Colombia | 2013 | 20.2 | 11,977 | 0.61 | 33.4 |
| 11 | Honduras | 2011 | 18.5 | 4,345 | 0.63 | 29.3 |
| 12 | Jamaica | 2011 | 23.3 | 8,485 | 0.63 | 37.0 |
| 13 | Argentina | 2011 | 34.7 | 15,501 | 0.67 | 52.0 |
| 14 | Guyana | 2012 | 22.4 | 6,054 | 0.68 | 32.7 |
| 15 | Uruguay | 2013 | 26.6 | 18,966 | 0.74 | 35.9 |
| 16 | Brazil | 2013 | 29.6 | 14,555 | 0.87 | 34.2 |
| Unweighted Average without Peru | | | 21.0 | 11,322 | 0.59 | 35.6 |

Source: IMF staff estimates based on the methodology of Fenochietto and Pessino (2013).
[1]Include taxes and social contributions.
[2]Purchasing power parity–weighted.

- *A complex tax system.* Further simplification will be important to facilitate better tax administration, reduce evasion and avoidance, enhance revenue mobilization, and increase efficiency. An area where complexity has been reduced, as described earlier, is in the withholding schemes of *retenciones*, *detracciones*, and *percepciones* (which collect some 23 percent of total revenue). But these regimes could still benefit from further improvements. Finally, the tax system needs to be stabilized by reducing the number of changes and limiting them to those that are essential or will simplify the tax system.
- *Keeping pace with international tax developments.* Future reforms need to respect the principles of efficiency, neutrality, fairness, and revenue adequacy, while taking into consideration the importance of macrofiscal sustainability and increased productivity—a great challenge in emerging countries such as Peru. Beyond this, the country needs to continue adapting the tax system to the advances of globalization and a world economy in which international transactions have multiplied exponentially and are being made by companies and linked international conglomerates. The emergence of double-taxation problems, international avoidance via tax havens, fiscal competition to attract capital and investment, and the digital economy are among the new challenges that need to be tackled. Naturally, improvement will be an ongoing process and new challenges will continue to arise as the economy's structure evolves.
- *International taxation and international tax avoidance pose particular challenges for Peru.* The design of Peru's tax system should be reformed to deal with the cross-country spillovers derived from other countries' national tax structures and practices, and tax competition across countries. Domestic and international instruments should be put in place to create a coherent set of effective measures against avoidance.
- *Level of tax exemptions.* Reducing the number of tax exemptions will also improve the quality of the tax system. Tax expenditure review is an important instrument to identify possible options to increase revenue, and to reassess the efficiency and fairness of the tax system. For instance, some exemptions from the GST have a regressive impact (those on food and other goods and services mostly consumed by high-income individuals). There is also scope to eliminate regional GST exemptions and channel the increased revenue toward

poverty relief programs in these same regions. Tax exemptions should be focused more on direct taxes to promote investment in technology and research and development.

- *Further improvement in tax administration.* Although improvements in tax administration have helped reduce GST compliance in recent years, further efforts should be made to strengthen tax administration. Key priorities include better integrating core revenue administration functions for both domestic taxes and customs, implementing a new corporate IT strategy, reinforcing procedures to prevent abuse of SUNAT's broad control powers, implementing an integrated control strategy for the GST, and deepening tax and customs compliance actions based on risk.
- *High levels of tax arrears.* The level of accumulated tax debt is very high, and an excessive level of arrears can affect the credibility of the entire tax administration. The total stock today is higher than one year of revenue. The debt stock should be reduced by writing off very old debt that cannot be recovered (for instance, because the company has gone bankrupt or the taxpayer has died). However, even the best controls will not be effective if taxpayers know that, in the end, they will not have to pay the total amount owed, or that they may have to do so only after many years.

The reforms above should be implemented not only to improve revenue mobilization, but also because they can help enhance growth. Reducing exemptions and loopholes that forgo revenue with little social benefit can simplify taxation and increase its equity and efficiency. Reducing compliance will increase the equity of the tax system by diminishing the gap between those who pay taxes and those who do not. In fact, the challenge of tax policy and administration design is to define a fine line between raising the necessary revenue and accomplishing this in the least distortionary way, while making the system fair and legitimate in the view of taxpayers. With its recent advances in the tax area, Peru is well placed to tackle these challenges in the near future.

## CONCLUSIONS

Peru today has a modern tax system based on the GST and income taxes and a relatively efficient tax and customs administration. Policies have moved in the right direction, and the administration has a clear strategic plan, qualified tax officials, operational plans, and performance indicators. Nonetheless, there is room for improvement without increasing tax rates by reducing noncompliance and tax expenditure still further and, in particular, by aligning policies and administrative procedures with international standards.

Key priorities for tax policy include maintaining international standards and strengthening measures to deal with international taxation, continuing to simplify withholding schemes (or eliminate them if possible), stabilizing the tax system by reducing the number of changes, rationalizing regional exemptions from the GST, and improving the specification of excise tax rates in order to fully cover the cost of externalities.

For tax and customs administration, key priorities include better integrating core revenue administration functions, implementing a new corporate IT strategy and integrated control for the VAT, reinforcing procedures to prevent abuse of SUNAT's broad control powers, reducing tax arrears and tax debt, and deepening tax and customs compliance actions based on risk assessments. Basically, a proper risk analysis management model should be applied to help not only to simplify the tax system but also to reinforce and enhance efficiency in the control and audit of tax programs.

Beyond achieving these priority reforms, it will continue to be important that Peru's tax system—both policies and administration—remain in line with best practices in taxation and consistent with international standards (such as those of the Organisation for Economic Co-operation Development) in order to continue to contribute to the stability, transparency, predictability, and competitiveness of the Peruvian economy.

# ANNEX 8.1

ANNEX TABLE 8.1.1

Central Government Tax Revenue, Social Contributions, and Nontaxes

| | 2003 | 2004 | 2005 | 2006 | 2007 | 2008 | 2009 | 2010 | 2011 | 2012 | 2013 | 2014 |
|---|---|---|---|---|---|---|---|---|---|---|---|---|
| | Millions of Nuevos Soles | | | | | | | | | | | |
| **Total (I + II + III)** | **31,132** | **34,954** | **39,924** | **51,154** | **58,253** | **65,596** | **60,274** | **73,147** | **85,589** | **95,919** | **102,089** | **108,515** |
| **I. Central Government Tax Revenue** | **27,576** | **31,149** | **35,568** | **45,813** | **52,381** | **58,328** | **52,651** | **64,505** | **75,591** | **84,149** | **89,397** | **95,389** |
| Taxes on Income | 7,972 | 9,026 | 11,188 | 18,414 | 22,847 | 24,146 | 20,346 | 25,802 | 33,628 | 37,278 | 36,512 | 40,157 |
| Taxes on Production and Consumption | 18,719 | 20,783 | 22,489 | 25,674 | 29,636 | 35,139 | 33,769 | 40,309 | 45,258 | 49,075 | 53,417 | 55,613 |
| *Of which* | | | | | | | | | | | | |
| General Sales Tax | 14,116 | 16,203 | 18,302 | 21,517 | 25,258 | 31,587 | 29,520 | 35,536 | 40,424 | 44,042 | 47,819 | 50,352 |
| Excises | 4,526 | 4,469 | 4,066 | 4,042 | 4,291 | 3,459 | 4,145 | 4,668 | 4,718 | 4,918 | 5,480 | 5,135 |
| Import Duties | 2,550 | 2,744 | 3,143 | 2,847 | 2,198 | 1,911 | 1,493 | 1,803 | 1,380 | 1,526 | 1,706 | 1,790 |
| Other Taxes | 1,408 | 2,111 | 2,865 | 3,260 | 3,796 | 4,317 | 4,382 | 4,538 | 5,032 | 6,851 | 9,025 | 8,537 |
| *Of which* | | | | | | | | | | | | |
| Banking Transaction Tax | | 650 | 706 | 843 | 1,031 | 1,138 | 968 | 944 | 395 | 106 | 134 | 153 |
| Temporal Tax on Net Assets | | | 1,073 | 1,040 | 1,483 | 1,761 | 1,722 | 1,788 | 2,293 | 2,439 | 2,776 | 3,513 |
| Special Tax on Mining | | | | | | | | | | 442 | 337 | 372 |
| Special Scheme for Small Taxpayers | 75 | 72 | 73 | 80 | 82 | 91 | 98 | 108 | 118 | 133 | 147 | 158 |
| Other Taxes Collected by SUNAT | 302 | 345 | 477 | 524 | 573 | 635 | 690 | 793 | 1,063 | 2,634 | 4,469 | 4,340 |
| Tax Refunds | −3,073 | −3,517 | −4,116 | −4,382 | −6,097 | −7,184 | −7,339 | −7,947 | −9,707 | −10,584 | −11,264 | −10,708 |
| **II. Social Contributions** | **3,502** | **3,741** | **4,023** | **4,879** | **5,245** | **6,768** | **7,244** | **7,957** | **8,979** | **10,185** | **11,303** | 11,893 |
| **III. Nontaxes** | **54** | **64** | **332** | **462** | **627** | **500** | **379** | **685** | **1,019** | **1,590** | **1,389** | **1,234** |

(Continued)

**ANNEX TABLE 8.1.1 *(continued)***

## Central Government Tax Revenue, Social Contributions, and Nontaxes

| | 2003 | 2004 | 2005 | 2006 | 2007 | 2008 | 2009 | 2010 | 2011 | 2012 | 2013 | 2014 |
|---|---|---|---|---|---|---|---|---|---|---|---|---|
| | Percent of Total | | | | | | | | | | | |
| **Total (I + II + III)** | **100.0** | **100.0** | **100.0** | **100.0** | **100.0** | **100.0** | **100.0** | **100.0** | **100.0** | **100.0** | **100.0** | **100.0** |
| **I. Central Government Tax Revenue** | **88.6** | **89.1** | **89.1** | **89.6** | **89.9** | **88.9** | **87.4** | **88.2** | **88.3** | **87.7** | **87.6** | **87.9** |
| Taxes on Income | 25.6 | 25.8 | 28.0 | 36.0 | 39.2 | 36.8 | 33.8 | 35.3 | 39.3 | 38.9 | 35.8 | 37.0 |
| Taxes on Production and Consumption | 60.1 | 59.5 | 56.3 | 50.2 | 50.9 | 53.6 | 56.0 | 55.1 | 52.9 | 51.2 | 52.3 | 51.2 |
| *Of which* | | | | | | | | | | | | |
| General Sales Tax | 45.3 | 46.4 | 45.8 | 42.1 | 43.4 | 48.2 | 49.0 | 48.6 | 47.2 | 45.9 | 46.8 | 46.4 |
| Excises | 14.5 | 12.8 | 10.2 | 7.9 | 7.4 | 5.3 | 6.9 | 6.4 | 5.5 | 5.1 | 5.4 | 4.7 |
| Import Duties | 8.2 | 7.9 | 7.9 | 5.6 | 3.8 | 2.9 | 2.5 | 2.5 | 1.6 | 1.6 | 1.7 | 1.6 |
| Other Taxes | 4.5 | 6.0 | 7.2 | 6.4 | 6.5 | 6.6 | 7.3 | 6.2 | 5.9 | 7.1 | 8.8 | 7.9 |
| *Of which* | | | | | | | | | | | | |
| Banking Transaction Tax | | 1.9 | 1.8 | 1.6 | 1.8 | 1.7 | 1.6 | 1.3 | 0.5 | 0.1 | 0.1 | 0.1 |
| Temporal Tax on Net Assets | | | 2.7 | 2.0 | 2.5 | 2.7 | 2.9 | 2.4 | 2.7 | 2.5 | 2.7 | 3.2 |
| Special Tax on Mining | | | | | | | | | | | | |
| Special Scheme for Small Taxpayers | 0.2 | 0.2 | 0.2 | 0.2 | 0.1 | 0.1 | 0.2 | 0.1 | 0.1 | 0.1 | 0.1 | 0.1 |
| Other Taxes Collected by SUNAT | 1.0 | 1.0 | 1.2 | 1.0 | 1.0 | 1.0 | 1.1 | 1.1 | 1.2 | 2.7 | 4.4 | 4.0 |
| Tax Refunds | −9.9 | −10.1 | −10.3 | −8.6 | −10.5 | −11.0 | −12.2 | −10.9 | −11.3 | −11.0 | −11.0 | −9.9 |
| **II. Social Contributions** | **11.2** | **10.7** | **10.1** | **9.5** | **9.0** | **10.3** | **12.0** | **10.9** | **10.5** | **10.6** | **11.1** | **11.0** |
| **III. Nontaxes** | **0.2** | **0.2** | **0.8** | **0.9** | **1.1** | **0.8** | **0.6** | **0.9** | **1.2** | **1.7** | **1.4** | **1.1** |

| | Percent of GDP | | | | | | | | | | | |
|---|---|---|---|---|---|---|---|---|---|---|---|---|
| **Total (I + II + III)** | **15.2** | **15.4** | **16.2** | **17.8** | **18.2** | **18.4** | **16.5** | **17.4** | **18.2** | **18.9** | **18.7** | **18.8** |
| **I. Central Government Tax Revenue** | **13.4** | **13.7** | **14.4** | **15.9** | **16.4** | **16.4** | **14.4** | **15.4** | **16.1** | **16.6** | **16.3** | **16.6** |
| Taxes on Income | 3.9 | 4.0 | 4.5 | 6.4 | 7.1 | 6.8 | 5.6 | 6.1 | 7.2 | 7.3 | 6.7 | 7.0 |
| Taxes on Production and Consumption | 9.1 | 9.1 | 9.1 | 8.9 | 9.3 | 9.9 | 9.3 | 9.6 | 9.6 | 9.7 | 9.8 | 9.7 |
| *Of which* | | | | | | | | | | | | |
| General Sales Tax | 6.9 | 7.1 | 7.4 | 7.5 | 7.9 | 8.9 | 8.1 | 8.5 | 8.6 | 8.7 | 8.7 | 8.7 |
| Excises | 2.2 | 2.0 | 1.6 | 1.4 | 1.3 | 1.0 | 1.1 | 1.1 | 1.0 | 1.0 | 1.0 | 0.9 |
| Import Duties | 1.2 | 1.2 | 1.3 | 1.0 | 0.7 | 0.5 | 0.4 | 0.4 | 0.3 | 0.3 | 0.3 | 0.3 |
| Other Taxes | 0.7 | 0.9 | 1.2 | 1.1 | 1.2 | 1.2 | 1.2 | 1.1 | 1.1 | 1.3 | 1.7 | 1.5 |
| *Of which* | | | | | | | | | | | | |
| Banking Transaction Tax | 0.0 | 0.3 | 0.3 | 0.3 | 0.3 | 0.3 | 0.3 | 0.2 | 0.1 | 0.0 | 0.0 | 0.0 |
| Temporal Tax on Net Assets | 0.0 | 0.0 | 0.4 | 0.4 | 0.5 | 0.5 | 0.5 | 0.4 | 0.5 | 0.5 | 0.5 | 0.6 |
| Special Tax on Mining | 0.0 | 0.0 | 0.0 | 0.0 | 0.0 | 0.0 | 0.0 | 0.0 | 0.0 | 0.1 | 0.1 | 0.1 |
| Special Scheme for Small Taxpayers | 0.0 | 0.0 | 0.0 | 0.0 | 0.0 | 0.0 | 0.0 | 0.0 | 0.0 | 0.0 | 0.0 | 0.0 |
| Other Taxes Collected by SUNAT | 0.1 | 0.2 | 0.2 | 0.2 | 0.2 | 0.2 | 0.2 | 0.2 | 0.2 | 0.5 | 0.8 | 0.8 |
| Tax Refunds | −1.5 | −1.5 | −1.7 | −1.5 | −1.9 | −2.0 | −2.0 | −1.9 | −2.1 | −2.1 | −2.1 | −1.9 |
| **II. Social Contributions** | **1.7** | **1.6** | **1.6** | **1.7** | **1.6** | **1.9** | **2.0** | **1.9** | **1.9** | **2.0** | **2.1** | **2.1** |
| **III. Nontaxes** | **0.0** | **0.0** | **0.1** | **0.2** | **0.2** | **0.1** | **0.1** | **0.2** | **0.2** | **0.3** | **0.3** | **0.2** |
| GDP in Millions | 205,379 | 227,683 | 247,084 | 287,715 | 319,693 | 355,709 | 365,055 | 419,693 | 469,854 | 508,318 | 546,944 | 576,119 |

Source: IMF staff with data from *Superintendencia Nacional de Aduanas y de Administración Tributaria.*

# ANNEX 8.2. CHANGES IN MINERAL TAXATION

**ANNEX TABLE 8.2.1**

**Summary of Mineral Taxation in Selected Countries**

| Country | Corporate Income Tax | Royalty Rate | Import Duties | Dividend Withholding Tax | Interest Withholding Tax | Other Charged |
|---|---|---|---|---|---|---|
| Peru | 30 percent (32 percent for companies with a stability contract) | 1–12 percent varies with operating margin; tax base is operating profit | Exempt | 4.1 percent | 4.99 percent | 8 percent workers profit share with base of net income before tax. Special Mining Tax of 2–8.4 percent and Special Mining Duty of 4–13.12 percent, with both varying with operating margin and a base of operating profit. |
| Chile | 22.5 percent; incrementally increasing to 27 percent by 2018 | 0–14 percent based on production level and operating margin; tax base is an adjusted corporate income tax base | 6 percent | 35 percent; corporate income tax is creditable; reduced to 10 percent with treaty | 4 percent | Worker profit sharing of 35 percent of pretax income or 25 percent premium on employee base salary up to a maximum of 4.75 percent of minimum salaries. |
| Australia–Western Australia | 30 percent | 2.5 percent (gold and silver)<br>7.5 percent (gems and precious stones)<br>5–7.5 percent (iron ore)<br>AUD1/ton (nonexported coal); 7.5 percent (exported coal)<br>5 percent (copper concentrate); 2.5 percent (copper in metallic form) | Concessions apply if values > $10 million | 0 percent; 30 percent if on previously untaxed profit | 10 percent | – |
| Canada–British Columbia | A combined federal and provincial tax rate of 26 percent | 2 percent on net current proceeds; 13 percent on net revenue | 0–8 percent based on good | 25 percent; reduced to 15 percent by treaty | 25 percent; reduced to 10 percent by treaty | – |

Source: IMF, Fiscal Affair Department's Fiscal Analysis of Resource Industries database.

**ANNEX TABLE 8.2.2**

**Peru: Revenues from Mining** *(Millions of nuevos soles)*

| Mining Revenue | 2007 | 2008 | 2009 | 2010 | 2011 | 2012 | 2013 |
|---|---|---|---|---|---|---|---|
| Corporate Income Tax (advanced payments) | 6,439 | 6,056 | 2,609 | 4,831 | 6,290 | 5,393 | 2,922 |
| Corporate Income Tax (clearing) | 2,264 | 688 | 409 | 787 | 1,474 | 1,064 | 399 |
| Mining Royalties | 519 | 445 | 338 | 646 | 841 | 584 | 517 |
| Special Mining Tax | – | – | – | – | 59 | 442 | 337 |
| Tax Lien | – | – | – | – | 136 | 942 | 809 |
| Value-added Tax | 817 | 797 | 632 | 1,038 | 1,442 | 1,318 | 1,176 |
| Personal Income Tax | 642 | 743 | 968 | 1,153 | 1,607 | 1,595 | 1,411 |
| Temporary Tax on Net Assets | 105 | 110 | 103 | 128 | 162 | 226 | 254 |
| Other Tax Revenues | 494 | 592 | 137 | 196 | 224 | 599 | 682 |
| Tax Refunds | –425 | –352 | –905 | –994 | –1,045 | –1,959 | –2,707 |
| Other Nontax Revenues | 861 | 807 | 122 | 179 | 99 | 216 | 210 |
| **Total** | | **9,885** | **4,828** | **8,124** | **11,612** | **10,667** | **6,114** |
| *Percentage of GDP* | 3.7 | 2.8 | 1.3 | 1.9 | 2.5 | 2.1 | 1.1 |
| *Percentage of General Government Revenues* | 16.7 | 12.5 | 6.7 | 9.3 | 11.4 | 9.4 | 5.1 |

Source: Ministry of the Economy and Finance.

Reforms in mineral taxation have been a priority under the administration of President Ollanta Humala. In 2013, Peru's mining sector (mineral and hydrocarbon) accounted for 12 percent of GDP, about 70 percent of total exports (of which minerals accounted for 61 percent), and 12 percent of total fiscal revenues (3.5 percent of GDP). Fiscal revenue from mining (i.e., copper, gold, lead, zinc, iron, and tin) accounted for about 60 percent of total revenue from mining.[21]

The mining taxation reform approved in September 2011 aimed to increase progressivity and public revenues while preserving the competitiveness of the sector (Annex Table 8.2.1). Up until then, Peru's mineral taxation regime had been comprised mainly of the CIT and royalties based on operating margins (1–3 percent) introduced under the 2004 Mining Royalties Law. The last reforms included the following: (1) new royalties based on operating profits of 1–12 percent to replace the sales-based royalties for companies with no stability contracts with the government, and (2) a new special mining tax—as revenue for the central government—levied on a sliding scale between 2–8.4 percent of operating margins.

Changes have been constrained by stability agreements and the regional distribution of mineral revenue. The new special voluntary levy aims to increase the contribution from companies with stability contract agreements and replaces the voluntary contribution paid in the past. To attract multinational mining companies, tax stability agreements were offered to mining companies in the mid-1990s to ensure a stable legal, tax, and administrative framework. Companies that signed stability agreements pay an additional 2 percent in income tax as an extra charge. Under the voluntary contribution scheme—introduced for regional development in 2006—the amount transferred could be up to 3.75 percent of profits after tax (2.75 percent for the local fund and 1 percent for the regional government fund). During 2007–10, resources transferred from these companies amounted to S/. 2 billion.

The new measures were projected to raise an additional US$1 billion annually (about ½ percent of GDP, at current commodity prices), which will help fund infrastructure and social projects and close gaps in those areas. However, because the prices of metals started to decline in 2012, the actual intake was not as high as expected (Annex Table 8.2.2).

[21] See Chapter 7, "Fiscal Framework Alternatives for a Resource-Rich Country."

# REFERENCES

Acosta-Ormaechea, S., and Y. Yoo. 2012. "Tax Composition and Growth: A Broad Cross-Country Perspective." Working Paper 12/257, International Monetary Fund, Washington, DC.

Arnold, J. 2008. "Do Tax Structures Affect Aggregated Economic Growth? Empirical Evidence from a Panel of OECD Countries." OECD Economics Department Working Paper No. 643, Organisation for Economic Co-operation and Development, Paris.

Fenochietto, R., and C. Pessino. 2013. "Understanding Countries' Tax Effort." Working Paper 13/244, International Monetary Fund, Washington, DC.

## CHAPTER 9

# Modernization of Peru's Public Financial Management Systems

MARIO PESSOA, ISRAEL FAINBOIM, AND ALMUDENA FERNÁNDEZ

*Peru has implemented major public financial management reforms over the past 15 years in order to maintain a sustainable fiscal position, effectively allocate financial resources, and efficiently provide public goods and services. The reforms have aimed at adopting good international practices. One of Peru's objectives is to become a member of the Organisation for Economic Co-operation and Development in the coming years, and the reforms will be important to demonstrate the country's capacity to have in place robust and transparent public financial management systems. The main reforms include:*

- *Adoption of fiscal rules and enhancement of fiscal transparency*
- *Establishment of medium-term fiscal and budget frameworks and gradual implementation of a medium-term expenditure framework and results-based budgeting*
- *Modernization of the treasury and debt directorates and improvements in cash and debt management*
- *Assessment of operational risks and establishment of a business continuity plan*
- *Improvements in public investment management*
- *Modernization of the financial management information system*
- *Reorganization of the Ministry of Economy and Finance*

Many of these reforms were supported by the Fiscal Affairs Department (FAD) of the IMF through technical assistance provided in the last decade. This chapter describes the reforms and assesses their progress, and in an Annex it summarizes the technical assistance provided by the FAD.

## FISCAL RULES AND TRANSPARENCY

Peru has had steadily declining debt and a noteworthy strengthening of its fiscal accounts since the introduction of fiscal rules in 2000. This success can be attributed to a prudent fiscal policy and establishment of a robust fiscal framework. The current fiscal framework is embedded in the 2013 Law to Strengthen Fiscal Responsibility and Transparency (LFRTF), which is supported by four pillars:

- *Numerical fiscal rules* that can be classified into three main categories: budget balance, expenditure rules, and debt rules. Rules vary in terms of scope and coverage and are applied to three different levels of government: the nonfinancial public sector, central (or national) government, and subnational governments (regional and local).
- *A Fiscal Stabilization Fund* (FEF), which is endowed with any fiscal surplus generated by the Treasury (ordinary resources), 10 percent of privatization proceeds, and 10 percent of concessional fees, with a cap of 4 percent of GDP.
- *A Fiscal Council* to work as an independent oversight mechanism for the fiscal rules. The council has not yet been established.

- *The multiannual macroeconomic framework* (MMM),[1] which makes three-year macroeconomic projections of revenue, expenditure, public investment, public debt, and other macroeconomic variables, and presents some assessments of fiscal risks and tax expenditures.

The LFRTF aims to ensure a fiscal balance or surplus over the medium term, allowing for moderate fiscal deficits only in periods of lower growth. Each quarter, the Ministry of the Economy and Finance (MEF) publishes reports detailing the execution of the fiscal rules.

## Fiscal Rules

The LFRTF defines multiple fiscal rules. The primary expenditure of the nonfinancial public sector cannot exceed the limit defined by the MEF according to the guidelines established by the MMM. The limit is defined for three years and is revised annually for the preparation of the budget. In the event that accrued expenditure is smaller than the projection, this difference can be used in the following year if the amount is less than 0.2 percent of GDP. In the event that the GDP gap is larger than 2 percent of potential GDP, the difference can be used transitorily as a countercyclical measure but cannot be larger than 0.5 percent of GDP. In case new tax measures are implemented that affect revenues by more than 0.3 percent of GDP, expenditures can be modified in the same amount. There are also rules to limit increases in expenditures during election years and a ceiling on the increase of expenditure on wages and salaries that cannot be larger than potential GDP growth. For subnational governments, debt cannot be larger than 100 percent of total recurrent revenues of the last four years. Subnational governments can raise external debt only to finance investment projects, and the debt has to be approved by the MEF when the guarantee is provided by the central government. Corrective measures and escape clauses are also contemplated in the event that significant deviations occur caused by national emergencies or international crises, or when negative economic growth is observed.

## Fiscal Stabilization Fund

The FEF has accumulated US$9.1 billion (0.4 percent of GDP at end-2014). Resources of the FEF are deposited at the central bank (*Banco Central de Reserva del Perú* [BRCP]) or abroad under similar rules as those for international reserves. The FEF is subject to a cap of 4 percent of GDP, with any excess allocated to debt reduction. Its resources may only be used when the revenue shortfall (in percent of GDP) is more than 0.3 percent of the average ratio of the last three years or under the escape clauses of the LFRTF. No more than 40 percent of total funds can be used in a given year.

## Fiscal Council

Alongside the fiscal rules, the LFRTF mandates the creation of a Fiscal Council, which has not yet been established. A well-designed and independent Fiscal Council would strengthen the credibility of the fiscal framework. A council's influence comes from its mandate to produce and publish independent and authoritative fiscal analysis, which enhances transparency and increases the accountability of decisions made by policymakers. The LFRTF sets out four broad tasks for the Fiscal Council, requiring it to issue reports and opinions on (1) amendments and enforcement of the fiscal rules, (2) the government's fiscal projections set out in the MMM, (3) the evolution of short- and medium-term public finances, and (4) the methodology for calculating the structural balance, potential GDP, and export prices.

[1]The MMM includes a Medium-Term Fiscal Framework and a Medium-Term Budget Framework.

# MEDIUM-TERM FRAMEWORKS AND RESULTS-BASED BUDGETING

## Medium-Term Fiscal and Budget Framework

The MEF has had a comprehensive medium-term fiscal and budget framework in place since 2000. The MMM is published in May of each year and is an essential part of the budget cycle for determining expenditure and borrowing ceilings. It is revised in August when the budget proposal is submitted to the Congress. Before being approved by the Council of Ministers and published, the MMM is reviewed by the BCRP, which issues an opinion about its consistency.

The MMM presents an array of information, including budget execution data from previous years and estimates of current and projected fiscal information and other macroeconomic aggregates for the next three years. The fiscal policy guidelines are explicitly detailed. In this regard, the 2012 Law No. 29854 improved the MMM framework by incorporating macrofiscal targets based on the definition of structural balance over the cycle.

The MMM is used to determine the fiscal envelope of the annual budget and budget ceilings. The budget, which is regulated by the constitution, must be submitted to the Congress in late August and should be made consistent with the MMM.

## Medium-Term Expenditure Framework

A pilot medium-term expenditure framework (MTEF) was formulated for the first time in September 2012 for a period of four years (2013–16), covering the central and regional governments. The 2014–17 MTEF also includes some aggregate data for local governments.[2] The MTEF establishes the global spending ceiling, as well as of the main policies, consistent with the macrofiscal situation, and is in line with the programs defined under the "budget for results" initiative. It also aims to incorporate the budgetary impact of public investments.

The MTEF takes into consideration parameters defined by the MMM and the projects included in the Public Investment Program. However, full coordination among these frameworks has not been achieved yet.

A guideline for the formulation of the MTEF has been issued. For centrally collected revenues (main taxes and royalties), there is a formula to calculate the projected revenues. The executing units can estimate the revenues directly generated by them using the same macrofiscal parameters as the MMM. For expenditures, parameters are defined for each item of expenditure at the most aggregate level of the budget classifier (salaries, goods and services, interest, etc.). For investment projects, only viable projects included in the national system of public investment (SNIP) can be included in the MTEF.

The budgetary programs allow for costing the budget, taking into consideration the production of goods and services expected to be provided in future years. Therefore, expected production growth influences increases in the budget. In contrast, other activities not associated with the programs are subject to parameters defined by the MEF for each generic category of expenditure.

In 2013, for the first time, the 2013–16 MTEF was prepared using a module of the financial management information system (SIAF). This allowed for capturing information by program for the next three years using the same budget structure and classifier. This approach will facilitate the preparation of the budget for the next cycle because most of the information categories will be prepopulated.

[2]The 2014–17 MTEF is available at https://mef.gob.pe/contenidos/presu_publ/pres_multi/Presupuesto_Multianual_2014_2016.pdf.

## Results-Based Budgeting

Peru has made significant progress in developing results-based budgeting since 2000. Its implementation can be divided into three periods: before 2007, between 2007 and 2011, and after 2011.

Before 2007, several initiatives were developed that focused on the development of strategic planning, prioritization of some programs (whose budgets were protected from cuts), and the definition and review of the quality of information on a few performance indicators.

After 2007, the effort was systematized by the adoption of a legal framework establishing results-based budgeting. Concepts and methods were defined, monitoring and evaluation stages were introduced, and the new system is being gradually adopted throughout the public sector. In 2011, the program concept structure was refined and the logical framework for defining programs was adopted. Progress has been achieved in developing strategic plans, defining and structuring programs, selecting indicators, and monitoring and evaluating programs to improve their design and management.

Advances in the adoption of results-based budgeting can be attributed to the commitment of the budget directors, political support by the authorities (which has ensured the continuity of the reforms), and technical and financial support provided by donors and multilateral agencies (especially the Inter-American Development Bank [IDB] and the German Technical Cooperation).

### *Planning*

Since 2000, the government has adopted Sector Strategic Multi-Year Plans, Institutional Strategic Plans, and annual Institutional Operational Plans. In 2011, the Bicentennial Plan (*Plan Peru 2021*) was designed, becoming the country's first long-term strategic plan.

### *Structuring Programs and Indicators*

Since 2001, some programs have been defined as priorities for the government and protected against discretionary budget reductions, although no performance indicators were defined at that time. In 2004, some social programs were defined as priorities. In 2006, the number of priority programs was increased to 9 and in 2007 to 11.

The results-based budgeting implementation plan was developed in 2007 with the support of the German Technical Cooperation. It proposed a gradual implementation of this tool. It was initially based on a few strategic programs that corresponded mostly to the priority actions linked to the protected programs.

The budget law of 2007 included a chapter on results-based budgeting that laid the foundations for the reform.

Strategic budget programming was formalized in the 2008 budget, and guidelines were published for the design of pilot programs based on the logical framework approach. Methodological guidelines for strategic programming were also developed. Strategic budget programming used a methodology similar to that developed by the health sector, because this sector had management experience considered useful for results-based budgeting. The proposed methodology was developed based on three diagnostic levels or "models" (conceptual, explanatory, descriptive) and then the design of the program was proposed based on an additional "model," the logical framework approach.

The strategic budget programming methodology was used until 2011. At that time, it covered 24 programs representing 14 percent of the budget. Institutional programs were also established as part of results-based budgeting, to identify the programs created by entities through a supreme decree or any other norm ranked as law.

The use of two instruments for budget planning (strategic budget programming and institutional programs) using similar methodologies and approaches created some confusion. This situation led the MEF to review the methods and procedures developed under results-based budgeting. The reorganization occurred as part of the reorganization of the Budget Department (DGPP) in 2010–11. This reform allowed more staff to be dedicated to the development of the new budget framework and tools. The review of the methodology resulted in the following changes:

- The strategic budget programming tool and the institutional programs were discontinued and replaced by budgetary programs.
- Two additional categories of programs were created: (1) administrative actions related to human resource and financial management of the entity, and (2) budgetary allocations that do not result in products (e.g., for debt service and pensions).
- The emphasis on multisectoral programs was reduced.
- A single methodology for program design, the logical framework approach, was adopted.
- All entities were required to create a unit responsible for the design and implementation of the budgetary programs.
- The requirement to present ex ante evidence to justify the causal link between programs and objectives was weakened and the use of ex post evidence was allowed, recognizing that in many cases there is no a priori concluding evidence.

The budget programming guideline defined the participation of regional and local governments in preparation of the 2013 budget. In the budgetary programs that comprised the participation of the three levels of government, it was required that a territorial coordinator for the institution (*pliego* in Peru) responsible for the program, a regional coordinator, and a local coordinator be assigned to work together to define the necessary actions to improve the management of the budgetary program.

Four aspects of the guidelines for the identification and design of the budgetary programs have been developed over the past two years (2014–15): (1) the approach to facilitate territorial coordination, (2) guidelines for selecting public investment projects, (3) improvements in monitoring and evaluating the budgetary programs, and (4) improvement in the budgetary program medium-term planning.

Although the legal mandate defining the rules and procedures to prepare a results-based budget was established in 2007 by the annual budget law, the results-based budgeting guideline is currently included in the General Law of the Public Budget System (Law No. 28411 of 2004, updated). Also, since 2012, the programs and their components (activities, products) have been part of the programmatic and functional structure of the budget.

### *Monitoring and Evaluation of Indicators and Program Evaluations*

In 2004, the DGPP started tracking existing indicators related to budgetary targets and strategic plans. Since 2009, the financial execution and physical targets of products and activities have been monitored, as well as the financial execution of the programs.

The 2007 Budget Law adopted a System for Monitoring and Evaluation of Public Expenditure, and the MEF was assigned to implement it. Two new evaluation tools were introduced in the law: evaluations of the design and execution of the budgetary programs (EDEPs), and impact evaluations. The EDEPs were to be used to adjust the design, processes, and/or management of the programs and to support the budget requests (jointly with the use of performance indicators). The MEF adopted a similar evaluation approach used in Chile and Colombia.

The methodology for evaluating the design and execution of the budget includes preparing an evaluation report and defining a matrix of commitments to improve performance. Commitments

**TABLE 9.1**

**Advances in the Development of Results-Based Budgeting in Peru**

| Item | 2008 | 2009 | 2010 | 2011 | 2012 | 2013 | 2014 | 2015 |
|---|---|---|---|---|---|---|---|---|
| Number of Programs | 5 | 9 | 15 | 24 | 59 | 67 | 73 | 85 |
| Percent of Program Budgets (national government) | 6.8 | 7.4 | 14.4 | 16.9 | 45.9 | 48.4 | 48.6 | na |
| Percent of Program Budgets (regional governments) | 8.6 | 13.6 | 13.1 | 19.4 | 52.5 | 63.6 | 69.7 | na |
| Percent of Program Budgets (local governments) | 0.0 | 0.0 | 0.0 | 8.2 | 33.2 | 33.4 | 37.9 | na |
| Percent of Program Budgets (total)[1] | 5.7 | 7.0 | 11.8 | 15.8 | 44.5 | 48.1 | 50.6 | na |
| Number of Entities with Program Budgeting (national government) | 0 | 1 | 3 | 3 | 17 | 28 | 23 | na |
| Number of Entities with Program Budgeting (regional governments) | 0 | 0 | 0 | 0 | 0 | 2 | 4 | na |
| Number of Programs with Performance Indicators (national government) | 5 | 6 | 13 | 15 | 20 | 20 | | na |
| Number of Programs Linked with National Plans | 0 | 0 | 0 | 0 | 59 | 67 | 73 | na |
| Number of Programs with Territorial Coordination | 4 | 8 | 12 | 19 | 30 | 41 | 49 | na |
| Number of Programs Evaluated for Design and Budget Execution | 4 | 10 | | 10 | | 16 | 11 | |
| Impact Evaluations | | | | | | | 4 | 6 |

Source: Budget Department; and Inder Gley Delgado, 2013, "Avances y Perspectives en la Implementacion del Presupuesto por Resultados eu Perú," Pontipieia Universidad Catálica del Perú.

Note: na = not available.

[1]Excludes debt, pensions, and contingent reserves.

are defined based on the recommendations of the evaluation. There is then a formal negotiation between the entity responsible for the program evaluated and the DGPP.

In 2007, the methodology for the EDEP was designed. It has been applied since 2008 to programs, activities, or projects. Institutional evaluations have been carried out since 2009, and impact evaluations started in 2010. The EDEPs are carried out by three independent evaluators selected through public procurement.

Another noteworthy achievement has been the development of an information technology (IT) application called RESULTA that provides information on progress in the indicators of products and results of the different programs in an interactive way.

## *Reporting and Accountability*

The General Law of the Public Budget System sets out the obligation to prepare a semiannual Financial Execution and Physical Implementation Report to be sent to the Congress and the Comptroller General. The independent evaluations are also sent to Congress together with the commitments made by the evaluated entities to address the shortcomings identified. Since 2012, a report on progress in implementing results-based budgeting has been included in a chapter of the explanatory preamble of the draft budget proposal.

## *Progress in Implementing Reforms*

*Plan Peru 2021* gave the budgetary programs a policy framework that did not exist before and guided the effort to align the programs with the strategic guidelines set forth in the plan. In addition, *Plan Peru 2021* has sought to improve the consistency between the medium-term programs and the Sector Strategic Multi-Year Plans. However, these procedures are not yet fully adopted and standardized.

One significant achievement of the implementation of results-based budgeting is the gradual expansion of budgetary programs as a percentage of the budget. From 5 pilot programs in 2008, the number of programs reached 85 in 2015 with coverage of more than 50 percent of the budget (Table 9.1).

### *Challenges*

Multiyear planning has advanced substantially but has not yet been fully consolidated. *Plan Peru 2021* is an important mechanism to relate national priorities with sectoral plans and foster better coordination between planning (national, sectoral, institutional) and budgetary programs. Newly created instruments (*Plan Peru 2021* and the budgetary programs) still coexist with other methodologies (Sector Strategic Multi-Year Plans and Institutional Operational Plans), generating some duplication and overstretching limited resources.

Sectoral plans are not prepared using the same calendar and methodologies. While some ministries (such as the Ministry of Education) have updated Sector Strategic Multi-Year Plans, others (such as the Ministry of Health) are still in the preparation stage or have not even started. In addition, some ministries (the Ministry of Health and Ministry of Housing, Construction and Sanitation) have long-term plans that have not been updated. In addition, there is limited capacity in the public sector to design and implement programs, as well as a lack of experience in medium-term budgeting and in identifying performance indicators for some programs.

Finally, the use of performance information is limited in most ministries. In principle, performance information is intended to guide policymakers in assessing and reshaping programs and policies. But Peru has a long way to go in this regard, as this has been done only in a few cases. Performance information is still rarely used to support planning, design, and evaluation of budgetary programs.

## TREASURY MANAGEMENT

Peru has improved Treasury management since 2006, implementing key reforms such as the creation of a Treasury Single Account (TSA), better cash forecasting through the adoption of econometric and other forecasting methods, creation of a FEF for saving structural surplus cash, and development of Treasury instruments such as short-term Treasury bills (T-bills) and repos to facilitate active cash management.

### Building a Treasury Single Account: Coverage, Design, and Operation

The Treasury System Law enacted in 2006 gave the Peruvian Treasury the powers needed to centralize all financial resources under a TSA, which was created in 2008 and has been gradually expanded since then. By 2014, approximately 80 percent of cash flows financing the budget were flowing into the TSA main account. Other additions to the TSA in recent years have included resources directly collected by the national and regional governments, the Municipal Compensation Fund (*Foncomun*), earmarked resources for universities, donations from the European Commission, and loans from the World Bank and the IDB.

The model adopted to manage the earmarked resources separates the authorization to spend from the authorization to pay, in line with international practices. Along those same lines, local governments have the ownership of the resources transferred to them, but the actual resources are deposited in the TSA. Those resources are kept as notional subaccounts in the TSA, but within the banking system, as their recording in the financial management system (SIAF) awaits a banking module to be implemented in the future SIAF-II.

The spending units still hold balances in the banking system and there is still work to be done to incorporate those resources into the TSA and close the respective bank accounts. The most substantive resources not yet included in the TSA are those from the Social Security Fund (ESSALUD), the Public Pensions Fund (ONP), resources collected directly by local governments, and domestic and external loans for projects. The resources of public enterprises are not part of the TSA. This is also in line with international practice. The General Directorate of Debt and Treasury (DGETP) will use the same model it uses for earmarked resources for directly collected resources.

The design of the TSA has improved gradually over time, but still needs streamlining. Additional reforms are required in terms of the location of the TSA, the existence of multiple bank accounts, and the absence of a Treasury module in the SIAF to manage the TSA more efficiently. The law refers to the TSA as a collection of Treasury bank accounts. There are also references in the law to the Main Account, and its location is identified as the *Banco de la Nación* (BN), a public bank that lends only to public employees and pensioners. According to the law, the TSA should include all the accounts (including the Main Account) for which the Treasury is the holder and in which the resources are centralized and administered. Most revenues are collected and paid through the BN. The sums held in the bank's head account are mostly swept back into the Treasury's accounts at the central bank (BCRP) at the end of the day. So, the balances in the central bank (BCRP) in effect constitute the TSA.

A large number of accounts are still at the BN for collection purposes, and there are also a large number of bank accounts at the BCRP. For instance, each of the Treasury's resources (ordinary resources, directly collected resources, earmarked resources, etc.) is maintained in different bank accounts at the BCRP. These bank accounts are adopted as a mechanism for recording the transactions and balances in the BN and the BCRP, as the Treasury does not have available a banking module in SIAF that would record transactions and replace all bank accounts by accounting (or virtual) subaccounts.

Revenues are collected through the banking system and transferred to the BN. The tax agency (*Superintendencia Nacional de Administración Tributaria* [SUNAT]) remunerates the collection services via a number of days in which the balances are kept at the commercial banks (days of reciprocity). Currently the number of days is between one and three, depending on the type of payment and location of the commercial bank branch.

Payments are made through a bank account (a subaccount of the TSA) that only records debits for each of the payments registered in SIAF during the day by the spending units. At the end of the day, the BN withdraws from the TSA the amount equivalent to all payments ordered.

Even though electronic payments are growing in importance, checks and similar financial instruments are still used. Electronic payments to government suppliers are mandatory for national and regional governments and are being extended to local governments. In 2013, such payments represented 12 percent of these expenditures. Electronic payments of salaries and pensions currently represent 19 percent of the total.

Almost all cash under the control of the DGETP is held at the BCRP, with only small balances in the BN. These balances were substantial a few years back due to the commodities boom and before the FEF was created to invest the structural cash surplus, but they are rapidly decreasing now. Most of the balances are held in demand deposits at the BCRP, earning interest defined by the central bank usually below market rates. Small sums are in time deposits. These rates paid by the BCRP are established on a discretionary basis by its Committee of Monetary and Currency Exchange Operations, reflecting the BCRP's internal policies. The BN pays an interest rate on the balances maintained as a cash buffer lower than the rate paid by the BCRP.

## Cash Forecasting

A more structured cash forecasting system for the DGETP has been gradually introduced during the last few years. It includes application of econometric models,[3] more frequent updates of forecasting (from quarterly to monthly updates), and an increase in the forecasting horizon (rolling

[3] Even though the usual recommendation to prepare cash forecasts is to use the historical interyear patterns (and econometric models only for forecasting the annual values), complemented with information from the spending units on large expenditures (particularly investments), Peru has been obtaining satisfactory results using time series models and other econometric models.

monthly forecasts are produced for a year) and frequency (daily forecasts are now produced for the next three months, also rolled forward).

The DGETP prepares separate revenue forecasting according to the category of revenues (ordinary, earmarked, own revenues). For ordinary revenues, autoregressive time series models have been developed for the monthly flow of revenues received by SUNAT for the main components (such as tax revenues or custom duties). They are backed up by elasticity-based models of the individual taxes.

Similar work has been done for daily forecasts, but this is more complicated because taxpayers are required to pay each tax according to specific schedules. Currently, daily cash forecasting for three months is prepared using stress scenarios and adopting the most prudent scenarios to avoid overdrafts.

The forecasts of earmarked resources are done also by component: *Foncomun*, *canon*, royalties, *Focam*, several specifically earmarked funds such as the Fund for Performance Incentives, and others. All of these components (with the exception of the earmarked funds) have a trend component and a stationary component, and forecasting aims to capture both components.

The DGETP has been using autoregressive time series models to forecast expenditures. Monthly forecasts of the main expenditures funded by ordinary resources are produced using econometric time series analysis, while the minor components are forecasted using moving averages, rates of growth, and other simple methods. Monthly forecasts of expenditures funded by earmarked resources and directly collected resources are also produced separately and use econometric time series analysis. Daily forecasts are produced in aggregate form using time series analysis in an inter-annual form. Some work has also been done on different economic categories of expenditure.

Finally, there are as yet no IT systems to support cash flow forecasting. New cash flow forecasting infrastructure will be needed to support more active cash management. The DGETP has undertaken some initial analyses regarding the databases to be used to store forecasts (the databases are still maintained in Excel) and ways of transferring and sharing forecast material. This has included drawing on information available within the BN, although this is mostly very short term. However, the IT function within the MEF has now been asked formally to look at options. The DGETP is exploring the use of SharePoint as a way to collect and share forecast material with the spending units and SUNAT (a similar approach has been taken by the Treasuries in Argentina, Chile, and Mexico).

## Active Cash Management

There is currently limited active cash flow management. Most government resources are invested in deposits at the BCRP, with small amounts in the BN. Since 2005, there has been no shortage of liquidity to finance the budget. The government's cash balances at the BCRP were very large as of 2013.

Active cash management is nevertheless still important. It allows for smoothing cash flows at the TSA to get better returns for the investment of excess cash and for identifying that part of surplus cash that could be considered as "structural" and in turn managed for longer-term objectives, therefore earning a higher return.

Peru has advanced in this area since 2012. A number of amendments to facilitate active cash management were made to the Treasury System Law, as enacted through the 2012 Budget Law. Currently, the MEF has the capacity to:

- Carry out a range of financial operations that contribute to the development of the financial market. This includes issuance of Treasury bills (Treasury bills were last issued in 2003–04) and bonds, the use of repo, and other financial instruments, including derivatives.
- Carry out similar operations to maintain and capitalize a Secondary Liquidity Reserve to cope with situations of financial instability affecting the availability of resources for the implementation of the budget or the liquidity of the credit and securities markets that the Treasury ordinarily uses to raise funds.

As a result, Treasury bills have been issued since 2013, when changes in the tax law put them on the same footing as the BCRP's certificates of deposit. They have been used to develop the market, but not for short-term financing needs. The MEF also decided to issue Treasury bonds, intercalating their issuance with that of Treasury bills.[4]

In addition, a Repo Law approved in June 2013 allows for the use of repos by the Treasury for cash smoothing and for investment of cash surpluses. The DGETP has also produced action plans to develop the money market and the secondary bond market, with a number of important initiatives, one of which is to widen the category of primary dealers/market makers. Also, in May 2015 the Treasury conducted the first auction of resources (excess cash) to be placed in the financial system.

Work has been done as well to identify the target minimum daily cash buffer to be maintained at the BN. Referred to as the "security deposit," the buffer is designed to provide coverage against the risks of cash flow deficits resulting from greater payment execution and/or lower revenue collection. The security deposit is maintained in the BN, and its objective is to minimize the expected value of overdraft costs (the BN offers an overdraft line of credit to the DGETP) and the opportunity costs of maintaining funds in an account at the BN that are remunerated at a lower rate than in other options.

The Secondary Liquidity Reserve mentioned above was also established to assist in programming and monthly cash management, and also to serve as a liquidity buffer when there is a substantial decrease in ordinary taxes, the liquidity of securities, or credit. The maintenance of this reserve is an obligation of the DGETP.[5]

Finally, the DGETP has prepared an annual multiyear strategy for financial asset and liability management and created a committee to manage assets and liabilities. The Strategy for Global Asset and Liability Management for 2014–17 established the following financial policy guidelines: (1) deepen the government domestic bond market and increase the share of public debt in nuevos soles and implement a repo market, (2) maintain liquidity reserves to be prepared for situations of economic and financial instability, (3) increase the return on public funds, and (4) improve the infrastructure required for the government domestic bond market. In addition, an MEF Committee for Asset and Liability Management started operating in 2014. Its main task is making decisions on financing and investment of excess cash.

## Coordination between the DGETP and the Central Bank and Agreements with the Banco de la Nación

Active cash management requires strong coordination between the BCRP and the Treasury, as any operation undertaken by the Treasury can affect money supply, the money and capital markets, and the effectiveness of monetary policy. It also requires clear and sound agreements with the BN and the commercial banks, because they provide banking services to the Treasury and the Treasury can invest excess cash in bank deposits.

---

[4]The Treasury is currently issuing Treasury bills at 3, 6, 9, and 12 months. Treasury bills at 3 and 9 months are issued the first Tuesday of each month and those for 6 and 12 months are issued the third Tuesday of each month. The Treasury bills were offered initially at rates higher than those on term deposits and with similar expirations. Stockbrokers agreed to charge very low fees for buying Treasury bills during the initial years. Also, the minimum amount to be purchased is low, favoring the participation of individuals in the market.

[5]Three models were used to calculate the reserve level in order to reduce the risk of under- or overestimations: (1) a Monte Carlo simulation; (2) an econometric model (ordinary least squares [OLS] model) based on estimates of the elasticity of revenues to macroeconomic variables and on exogenous variables that were assumed to follow their behavior during the 2008 crisis; and (3) an error correction model (MCE), where the residuals of the OLS model were used to capture the long-term relationship between the variables that explain the amounts collected. The exogenous variables were simulated using the same criteria as in the OLS model. According to the models, the lowest level of annual revenue that will be reached with a 95 percent confidence is between S/. 78.8 billion and S/. 87.6 billion.

There is already a memorandum of understanding (MoU), formalized by a 2010 ministerial resolution, on the terms and conditions for the DGETP's deposits held at the BCRP. There are a number of other MoUs, or exchanges of letters, on detailed arrangements for the structure of accounts, among other things.

There is a separate MoU between the DGETP and the BN that covers only the rate of interest that the bank pays on balances. It is defined as the rate on overnight deposits, as published by the BCRP, less an allowance for the additional reserve requirement applied to deposits. The BN provides a range of services to the DGETP.

## OPERATIONAL RISK MANAGEMENT AND BUSINESS CONTINUITY PLANNING

Peru has one of the best business continuity plans in Latin America covering operations related to public finances. Following the restructuring of the MEF in 2012, a Risk Management Department was established.

Business continuity means maintaining the uninterrupted availability of all key business resources required to support essential MEF activities. Business continuity planning is therefore that part of operational risk management that establishes cost-effective measures in case a disruptive event occurs. The plans address the subset of operational risks where environmental factors or poor operational controls raise the potential for loss of or damage to essential operations (including people, information, infrastructure, premises).

The operations of a finance ministry are critical to the entire government because this ministry bears responsibility for the management of substantial government assets and liabilities, and is responsible for the bulk of revenue collection and payment of budget expenditures. The large sums involved mean that any risk exposure can have damaging financial consequences and cause severe reputational and political damage. These situations are even more acute in countries with potential risks from natural disasters. The Peruvian government has serious concerns about a possible sizable earthquake affecting the capital of Lima and its surrounding areas, given the location of the fault line and the time period since the last significant earthquake. The main concern centers on the ability of the MEF, the central bank, and the BN to mobilize and operate if such a disaster occurs.

A number of notable achievements have been made in this area since 2011 based partly on what the BN and BCRP have done in this area. Both the BN and the BCRP have fully implemented business continuity plans to cover their operations if a major disruption happens at their respective primary sites. For example, the BCRP has an alternate site for 80 to 100 staff. Also, the BCRP has developed a system for internal control to ensure the security of information and a continuity plan, with three-month reporting on readiness to handle any adverse event. The MEF is confident that both institutions will be able to cope with a major incident to ensure the continuity of their services to the government payment system.

Regarding the MEF, a risk committee was established in May 2013, chaired by the Minister of Economy and Finance, and periodic meetings have already been held. The business continuity plan is documented in the DGETP's Transactions Continuity Plan. The DGETP and the BN have a joint alternate site located about 15 minutes from their primary site, where critical processes/activities can be managed remotely. The site provides for positions for each of the Treasury, Debt, and Risk Management Divisions, plus has space for an IT office and command center with laptops operated when critical staff members are relocated to the site. The Transaction Continuity Plan has been tested many times in the past couple of years and has worked very well.

An initiative to expand the business continuity plan, including extending it to cover the entire MEF, is under way. The Risk Management Department has established a team, assisted by consultants, to prepare an operational risk management matrix for the entire MEF. The MEF has determined that an alternate site providing scope for close to 200 people or around 10 percent of total staff is needed. Such a facility was identified by the MEF not far from the Army Headquarters and the main offices of the BN.

## PUBLIC INVESTMENT MANAGEMENT

Peru's SNIP, created in 2000, is the main instrument to manage the country's investment projects. SNIP is comprehensive and is mandatory for all projects implemented by the central and subnational governments and public enterprises (the nonfinancial public sector). The system allows for all phases of the project (feasibility, implementation, ex post assessment) to be controlled in a centralized way. During the feasibility phase, alternatives are studied, and project selection is based on the highest expected socioeconomic return. During the implementation phase, the project is further detailed through final studies and the preparation of executive projects. Then, as the project enters the operational and maintenance phases, an ex post assessment is performed.

SNIP is supported by an IT system, the Investment Project Bank, which registers each phase of investment projects from the feasibility study to the ex post evaluation. Project Bank is available to the public for consulting on the status of ongoing projects. The MEF's Directorate General of Investment Policy is responsible for SNIP management, and there is a unit in each ministry and subnational government responsible for operating the SNIP. The system controls five stages of each project: (1) feasibility study, (2) feasibility statement, (3) implementation, (4) monitoring, and (5) assessment. The feasibility phase covers preparation of the project profile and the prefeasibility and feasibility studies. The preparation of the project profile is mandatory. The prefeasibility and feasibility studies may not be required, depending on the characteristics of the project. Provided that the project meets technical and legal requirements, a feasibility statement is issued. At this stage the project is included in the Investment Project's Bank if it is declared viable. Prioritization is done only in relation to projects with a positive feasibility statement. During the implementation phase, the final studies and detailed execution plans are prepared and the project is executed.

Several units are involved in the project approval process: (1) the implementation units propose the projects, (2) sectoral programming and investment offices or regional and local governments evaluate and prepare the feasibility statement,[6] (3) authorities at the different levels of government are responsible for project identification, and (4) implementation units at the different levels of government are responsible for implementation, monitoring, and assessment.

The SNIP IT system provides the following information: (1) project identification, and the SNIP code, location, and unit responsible for managing the project; (2) information on the feasibility study, project objective and justification, area of influence, and targeted beneficiaries; (3) project alternatives recommended for implementation, sustainability analysis, and risk and disaster assessment analysis; (4) identification of project components, project cost, financial plan, and identification of operational and maintenance costs; and (5) funding sources and other information. The project code in the SNIP is the same used in the budget to facilitate monitoring during execution.

The Multiannual Public Investment Program details the implementation of investments for the budget year and projected expenditure for the following three years. Information is recorded

[6] In certain cases, the evaluation of projects depends on the MEF, as in the case of projects proposed by subnational governments that need a central government guarantee.

on the total cost of each project and the amount invested to date. Information on projects is partially available to the public on the SNIP website.[7]

## MODERNIZATION OF THE FINANCIAL MANAGEMENT INFORMATION SYSTEM

Public financial management in Peru relies on a robust set of information systems that are moving toward a more integrated approach. The effort to integrate aims to improve the consistency, opportunity, and reliability of financial information.

The Peruvian public sector financial management information system (SIAF-SP or SIAF I) was implemented in 1999. The system was developed in-house, and the main objective was to integrate the budget, Treasury, and accounting operations related to the execution of revenue collection and budget expenditure. However, the accounting procedures are not completely automated.

There are multiple information systems for public expenditure management that are not always fully interconnected but have been instrumental in improving public financial management as a whole. Among the major systems are the SNIP webpage and its multiple applications (such as SNIP-BP, FONIPREL, etc.), Multiannual Public Investment Program, Budget Execution, Electronic System for Procurement and Contracting (Sistema Electrónico de Contrataciones del Estado) and the Administrative Management System (Sistema Integrado di Gestion Administrativa). These systems support budget preparation and execution at the national, regional, and local levels. At present, there is a good degree of integration with the SNIP, Sistema Electrónico de Contrataciones del Estado, and Sistema Integrado di Gestion Administrativa; however, further integration is needed with other systems.

Since 2010, the MEF, with IDB support, has been implementing SIAF II to modernize the technology platform, increase integration, and improve performance of SIAF I. The first stage is to develop the budget preparation module, which has been operational since 2014, and the second stage will cover budget execution and accounting.

The MEF also developed a module in SIAF I to provide program information for the period 2013–16. The Accounting and Treasury Departments worked together on the convergence of the respective chart of accounts and budget classifiers.

## REORGANIZATION OF THE MINISTRY OF THE ECONOMY AND FINANCE

The MEF was restructured in March 2011. The new organizational structure was put in place with three objectives: (1) modernize the ministry in line with international practices; (2) cope with rapid changes in fiscal decentralization and, as a consequence, increase the MEF's capacity to oversee and better control the finances of local governments; and (3) strengthen the MEF's role in the financial markets and in pension systems.

Before 2011, the MEF was organized basically in two vice ministries (Economy and Finance), with four directorates under the authority of each of them. Under the Vice Ministry of Finance were the General Directorates of Budget, Treasury, Debt, and Accounting; and under the Vice Ministry of the Economy were the General Directorates of Economic and Social Affairs, Multiyear Programming, Revenue Policy, and International Economics, Competitiveness, and Private Investment.

---

[7] See http://www.snip.gob.pe/.

The reorganization merged the Treasury and Debt Directorates (creating the DGETP), created a General Directorate of Public Resources (in charge of personnel and pension issues) under the Vice Ministry of Finance, separated the Directorate of International Economics, Competitiveness, and Private Investment into two directorates, and created three General Directorates under the Vice Ministry of the Economy (Macroeconomic Policy and Fiscal Decentralization, Public Investment, and Financial Markets and Private Pensions). In addition, the internal organization of the Budget Directorate was significantly modified. The next sections focus only on describing the reorganization of the Budget, Treasury, and Debt Directorates.

## Reorganization of the Budget Directorate

The reorganization of the General Budget Directorate was largely due to the need to align it with the strategy to implement results-based budgeting and strengthen budget preparation, monitoring, and evaluation. Six directorates were established: Executive, Legal Issues, Budget Programming and Monitoring, Quality of Public Expenditure, Articulation of the Budget of the Territories, and Thematic Budget.

The main function of the Budget Programming and Monitoring Directorate is the preparation of the public budget in coordination with all directorates. It is also in charge of implementation of a multiyear budget and of expenditure control to maintain fiscal discipline. The functions of the Quality of Public Expenditure Directorate are to methodologically guide and support the entities in designing their budget programs; track the performance of the programs; organize, analyze, and use independent evaluations; and determine management incentives.

The Directorates of Thematic Budget and of Articulation of the Budget of the Territories apply the guidelines issued by the above-mentioned directorates and direct the budget process with a national and a regional development perspective. The different entities have to present and justify their budgets and additional demands of resources to these directorates (supported by the Quality of Public Expenditure Directorate), and they are responsible for verifying the proper prioritization of resources using performance information.

## Reorganization of the Treasury and Public Debt Directorates

The DGETP was reorganized into six main directorates: Analysis and Strategy, Treasury Operations, Risk Management, Market Management, Credit and Budgets, and Programming and Accounting. The structure of the debt management side of the new directorate is broadly in line with international practice, with front, middle, and back offices (that is, the Directorates of Market Management, Analysis and Strategy and Budget, and Programming and Accounting, respectively). In many debt (and cash) management units, the responsibilities of the Risk Management Directorate would be integrated with the debt strategy, financing policy, and reporting responsibilities of the middle office. But it is equally important to give adequate status to the risk management function, which was achieved with the decision to establish a separate directorate for that purpose. In practice, the new directorate works closely with the Analysis and Strategy Directorate, particularly on market and credit risks. Both are also involved in the development of a fully integrated asset and liability management approach to the management of the government's balance sheet.

There are still a few organizational changes that could be pursued in the medium term. For example, the investment of cash resources is currently the responsibility of two directorates, Treasury Operations and Market Management. This is not ideal, considering that it may complicate interaction with the markets.

In addition, lead responsibility for developing cash flow forecasts (revenue and expenditure) should continue with the Directorates of Treasury Operations and Market Management. But the forecast prepared should then be passed to the Directorate of Analysis and Strategy.

The merging of the two directorates had to be accompanied by the creation and reform of several coordination committees, a process that is still in progress. The new committees include a Cash Committee and a Risk Committee. The latter should set policies for the full spectrum of risks as well as establish a policy framework within which individual decisions are taken. This would also include identifying the DGETP's "risk appetite." In practice, that will mean setting risk limits where appropriate (e.g., for credit risk and for some exposures to market risk); establishing a framework for managing operational risks; and, more generally, developing techniques to assess risk trade-offs (e.g., against business or cost objectives) and mitigation priorities.

## TECHNICAL ASSISTANCE PROVIDED BY THE IMF

The IMF's FAD has provided extensive technical assistance to Peru since 2010. Technical assistance projects have also been strongly supported by Japanese (Japan International Cooperation Agency) and Swiss (State Secretariat for Economic Affairs) financial cooperation. The main results of these technical assistance projects are outlined below.

- *Restructuring the MEF:* The FAD advised on the restructuring of the MEF that took place in 2011. The MEF merged the Debt and Treasury General Directorates by creating the DGETP, which is organized under a front, middle, and back offices structure, as described above. In addition, the restructuring created a Risk Management Division, reformed the Cash Management Committee, and created an Asset and Liability Management Committee and Risk Management Committee.
- *Cash planning:* Technical assistance has been provided to improve cash forecasting and planning, develop a programming model to ensure implementation of the budget and reduce the costs of financing the Treasury, and provide advice on liquidity management. A new model for cash planning to improve the quality of the cash flow forecasts prepared by line ministries has also been developed.
- *Treasury single account:* The FAD has provided considerable technical assistance in this area. The consolidation of the TSA has progressed significantly. The government reached a consensus regarding the importance of pooling all resources in the TSA. In 2013, the entities' own revenues were included in the TSA, which represented a major achievement in this area. The SIAF system has also been modified to address Treasury needs to improve the TSA.
- *Business continuity plan and risk management:* The FAD has also provided much technical assistance on preparing a business continuity plan. The Risk Management Division, which has been operational since 2011, defined an operational risk management methodology and a risk management policy in 2012. The risk assessment report was completed in 2014. The division has also prepared a risk assessment matrix on contingent liabilities that was integrated into the MEF's 2012 operational plan. The Risk Management Committee was created by law in 2013 and operational procedures were prepared.
- *Active cash management:* Significant improvements have been made in the area of active cash management, an area where the FAD has provided abundant technical support. In 2011, the DGETP's Director General was appointed as a permanent member of the Cash Committee. The government also passed a law authorizing the Treasury to issue short-term bills and have more active cash management. The purpose is to define a cash buffer for cash management purposes and invest the remaining cash surplus. A study to identify and register contingent liabilities was prepared and the government is also working on the measurement of structural balance sheet risk. A comprehensive asset-liability management strategy was approved, an information system to manage the auctions has been developed, and a new regulation was approved to allow the Treasury to issue short-term bills and undertake repo operations.

- *Medium-term budget framework:* An IMF mission in 2012 provided advice on the preparation of a medium-term budget framework (the MMM). It was recommended that the calendar for preparation of this document be changed to better align it with the budget calendar.
- *Government accounting:* Peruvian authorities are involved in a plan to adopt International Public Sector Accounting Standards (IPSAS). Two IMF missions provided advice on accounting in Treasury operations in accordance with the IPSAS. Peru has already included many IPSAS standards in its national accounting standards, but implementation has not been uniform.
- *Study tours:* Treasury officials have visited the Treasury departments of Colombia, Brazil, Mexico, Spain, Chile, New Zealand, and Argentina as part of study tours to exchange information and learn about international experiences on Treasury reforms in more detail. These visits were important to expand the capacity of Treasury staff and to bring successful experiences to the attention of public financial management reformers.
- *Development of the new Public Sector Financial Management Information System (SIAF II):* The system's conceptual model consists of three macro processes: budget preparation, budget execution, and government accounting. The development of the budget preparation module has been concluded. Technical assistance was provided by the FAD through several long visits by an expert on Integrated Financial Management Information Systems development. The IDB is financing the development of SIAF II. Initially planned to be developed by a software firm, the system is currently being developed through a combination of an in-house and externally developed system.

# CHAPTER 10

# Fiscal Decentralization: Progress and Challenges for the Future

ADRIENNE CHEASTY AND JUAN PICHIHUA

*Launched in 2002, Peru's decentralization reform has succeeded in making important changes but is not yet complete. Spending has been significantly decentralized, but with great variation in quantity and quality across the country. This is partly explained by the assignment of unevenly distributed natural resource revenues to fund spending, and partly by the diversity of Peru's subnational governments, many of which are small (Table 10.1) and have limited capacity. The decentralization of nonmineral revenue has been much slower than the decentralization of spending. Subnational borrowing, while not large enough to be a macroeconomic threat, has led to serious debt problems in some governments. The next round of reforms should consider revisiting the assignment of natural resource revenues, strengthening the efficiency of subnational investment, and addressing the fragmentation of jurisdictions.*

## INSTITUTIONAL FRAMEWORK

Peru has traditionally been politically and administratively centralized, with its economic structure and population concentrated in the capital. Decentralization has long been on the political agenda. An initial attempt was made in 1987, when the country was divided into regions and regional governments were created. These were short-lived, however, and were dissolved in 1992. Almost a decade later, in March 2001, the Congress approved a constitutional reform for decentralization, which again established regional governments with political and administrative autonomy.

This reform organized the country into regions, departments, provinces, and districts. The amended constitution defines Peru as a unitary and decentralized state with three levels of government: national, regional, and local. To date, however, no departments have grouped together to form regions.[1] The regional level currently consists of the departments, in addition to the Constitutional Province of Callao, which has the status of a department. The local level has two sublevels: provincial municipalities and district municipalities.

To fund subnational government responsibilities, the reform provides for regional and local governments to share in transfers from the national government, license fees (canons) and compensation funds (the Regional Compensation Fund, Foncor) for regional governments, and the Municipal Compensation Fund (Foncomun) for municipalities.

Fiscal rules were established for regional and local governments to ensure fiscal sustainability. Law No. 27958, which amended the Law on Fiscal Prudence and Transparency enacted in 2003, permitted regional governments to borrow abroad, though only with a national government guarantee, and introduced two quantitative rules on subnational borrowing and a rule on the

[1]The constitution provides that, by passing a referendum, two or more contiguous departments may join to form a region; contiguous provinces and districts may also change the configuration of their regional administrative units.

**TABLE 10.1**

**Size of Local Jurisdiction by Population, 2012**

| | Districts | | Provinces | |
|---|---|---|---|---|
| **Population** | **Number** | **Cumulative (percent)** | **Number** | **Cumulative (percent)** |
| 0–1,000 | 195 | 11.9 | 0 | 0.0 |
| 1,000–5,000 | 739 | 56.8 | 33 | 16.9 |
| 5,000–10,000 | 337 | 77.4 | 23 | 28.7 |
| 10,000–50,000 | 298 | 95.5 | 92 | 75.9 |
| >50,000 | 74 | 100.0 | 47 | 100.0 |
| **Total** | **1,643** | | **195** | |

Source: National Institute of Statistics and Information Technology.

primary balance.[2] The law provided for the temporary suspension of the Regional and Municipal Compensation Funds as corrective measures in the event of noncompliance with these rules. The Law on Fiscal Decentralization added other fiscal rules to limit spending and short-term subnational borrowing. In all, eight rules were put into place. However, many local authorities were not aware of the existence of the rules, and there were no mechanisms for applying sanctions. Hence compliance has been low, particularly with the spending limits.

Against this backdrop, the recent Law on Strengthening Fiscal Responsibility and Transparency (Law No. 30099), which replaced the Law on Fiscal Responsibility and Transparency, reduced the number of subnational fiscal rules to two. The first rule controls regional and local spending, while the other regulates the amount of subnational borrowing. Sanctions are primarily reputational but also include a restriction on transfers from the Fund for the Promotion of Regional and Local Public Investment (Foniprel). In addition, the subnational governments are required to prepare and submit a Multi-Year Report on Fiscal Management.

After more than a decade of decentralization, there is a perception that the outcomes of the process remain unsatisfactory. Ahmad and Garcia-Escribano (2011), for example, characterized the Peruvian decentralization as incomplete.

## Territorial Fragmentation

The fragmentation of Peru's political and administrative units is a major constraint to achieving effective decentralization, both at the intermediate level (departments) and at the local level (municipalities). Based on the country's current organization in terms of territorial divisions, further progress in decentralization is not feasible. Among the main obstacles are that regional governments in departments have not reached a critical size that would enable them to have a tax base sufficient to facilitate tax decentralization, and that fragmented municipalities have weak management capacity to deliver local services.

Departments are small relative to the size of the country itself and are sparsely populated. Hence, tax decentralization will not be possible until regions with greater fiscal capacity have been formed from existing departments. Not counting Loreto, which has its own specific characteristics due to its location, the average size of a department is 39,800 square kilometers. The smallest department is Tumbes, which has a surface area of just 4,600 square kilometers and approximately 200,000 inhabitants. In addition, population density is fairly low. Excluding the Department of Lima, the departments have an average of 24 inhabitants per square kilometer, with no large cities in Peru's interior.

The local level in Peru is one of the most fragmented in Latin America. Most of the 1,842 districts are sparsely populated, with municipalities averaging fewer than 15,000 inhabitants on average,

---

[2]The rules are as follows: (1) the annual ratio of the stock of total debt and current revenue of subnational governments should not exceed 100 percent, (2) the ratio of annual debt service to current revenue should be less than 20 percent, and (3) the average primary balance for the last three years reported by each regional and local government may not be negative.

**TABLE 10.2**

**Changes in the Decentralization of Spending, 2004–13 *(Percent)***

| | Primary Spending | | | Public Investment Spending | | |
|---|---|---|---|---|---|---|
| Year | National | Regional | Local | National | Regional | Local |
| 2004 | 67.9 | 19.8 | 12.3 | 55.4 | 13.7 | 30.9 |
| 2005 | 66.7 | 20.2 | 13.1 | 52.7 | 15.5 | 31.8 |
| 2006 | 63.3 | 20.4 | 16.3 | 38.8 | 17.4 | 43.8 |
| 2007 | 60.8 | 23.2 | 16.1 | 38.2 | 20.7 | 41.1 |
| 2008 | 56.0 | 22.6 | 21.4 | 34.2 | 18.6 | 47.2 |
| 2009 | 58.7 | 20.1 | 21.2 | 33.0 | 20.2 | 46.8 |
| 2010 | 59.6 | 19.5 | 20.9 | 37.7 | 20.6 | 41.7 |
| 2011 | 61.2 | 19.7 | 19.0 | 42.4 | 20.4 | 37.2 |
| 2012 | 56.4 | 21.2 | 22.5 | 30.9 | 24.3 | 44.7 |
| 2013 | 57.8 | 20.4 | 21.8 | 31.2 | 23.1 | 45.7 |
| Percent Change 2004–13 | –15 | 3 | 77 | –44 | 69 | 48 |

Source: Integrated Financial Management System/Ministry of the Economy and Finance.

the smallest average in Latin America. More than half of districts have fewer than 5,000 inhabitants, and there are even some municipalities with fewer than 200 people. Further, nearly 29 percent of provinces have fewer than 10,000 inhabitants.

Given these numbers, further decentralization to municipalities would be incompatible with maintaining any economies of scale in the local delivery of services. In a country with Peru's income level, it is a struggle to provide funding for municipalities with fewer than 1,000 inhabitants. Nonetheless, although it is clear that some of the municipalities are not viable, in the past two years 15 new municipalities were created, and 14 draft laws were presented in 2013 with the aim of establishing new districts, most in Cajamarca. In contrast, municipalities in Colombia and Chile, which are pursuing similar decentralization processes, have an average size of 41,000 and 47,000 inhabitants, respectively.

## DECENTRALIZATION OF SPENDING, SERVICE DELIVERY, AND INVESTMENT

Peru's decentralization of government spending, especially public investment, has been significant over the past decade. Table 10.2 shows how the shares of the three levels of government have changed, both for primary spending and public investment. Local spending has expanded most rapidly, with local governments' share increasing from 12 percent of primary spending in 2004 to around 22 percent in 2013, a 77 percent increase. The national government's share fell by around 15 percent over the period. In 2004, spending was concentrated at the national level (68 percent), although this figure has since dropped to less than 58 percent.

Public investment spending was decentralized even more rapidly. The national government saw the largest decline in investment (–45 percent) between 2004 and 2013, implying an increase in the share of investment undertaken at regional and local levels, which grew by 68 percent and 48 percent, respectively.

The importance that public investment spending by local governments has taken on is a distinguishing feature of Peru's decentralization. It now exceeds investment by regional governments and accounts for more than 45 percent of total public investment. Its growth is largely explained by the rapid expansion of revenues from license fees and royalties during the commodity price boom of the last decade. These revenues are transferred primarily to local governments in extractive areas, with their use restricted to investment spending, as described below.

These changes have turned subnational governments into important players in the delivery of public services and public investment. The transfer of spending authority has meant that regional and local governments have been assigned, and begun to exercise, sector-specific functions that were previously the responsibility of national-level ministries.[3] This process, which was initially regulated by the then National Council on Decentralization and subsequently by the Decentralization Secretariat under the Office of the Chairman of the Council of Ministers, was accelerated by the "decentralization shock" in 2006, which made it possible to compress the previously set timetable and speed up the transfer of spending authority for health and education. As a result, 93 percent of all sector-specific functions have now been transferred to regional governments.

Spending responsibilities generally follow the principle of subsidiarity. Spending that is the exclusive responsibility of the national government includes national defense and security, foreign affairs, judicial services, legislative functions, and management of public debt. The national government accounts for more than 95 percent of total spending in each of these areas.

The regional level is now responsible for the execution of a large share of the budget in education and health. Regional governments account for 54 percent and 47 percent, respectively, of total government spending on these services. Almost all regional governments have seen increases in these shares, to varying degrees. Tacna's regional government, for example, accounts for 84 percent of spending on health in that department, while Cajamarca accounts for only 49 percent. Similarly, progress in the decentralization of education spending has been most pronounced in San Martín, where the regional government accounts for 78 percent of spending, as opposed to Arequipa, where the regional government accounts for only 46 percent of such spending. An exception is Lima,[4] where these functions are still under the responsibility of ministries.

Although spending on education and health appears in the budgets of the regional governments (Figure 10.1), in practice the regional authorities have little discretion in the use of these funds. The use of the education budget is determined at the national level based on budget programs and strictly earmarked expenditures (primarily wages and salaries). The regional governments, which account for 54 percent of education spending, are responsible primarily for salary expenditures (77 percent), while the national government, which accounts for 37 percent of spending in the education budget, is responsible primarily for expenditures on goods and services (31 percent). Low spending by local governments on education mainly refers to infrastructure, particularly in municipalities where the resources in question are substantial.

For sector-specific functions other than education and health, funding has not yet been established, despite the nominal transfer of spending authority from the national level. The functions affected include environmental regulation, land-use planning, and the promotion of industry, tourism, and fisheries. This is due to the absence of a clear delineation of functions between national-level ministries and the regional level (Ahmad and García-Escribano 2006). It is not clear which level of government is responsible for what, since the functions established by the regulatory framework (especially in the Organic Law on Regional Governments and the Law on the Principles of Decentralization) are not clear regarding who delivers which services. This lack of clarity could result in a duplication of effort, with a consequent waste of resources, or in failure to provide certain services altogether.

## Shortcomings in Local Public Investment

At the local level, decentralization of spending is tied to the delivery of general local services such as public sanitation, maintenance of parks and gardens, and local road construction and maintenance. To a large extent, investment spending at the local level is concentrated primarily

[3] Law No. 28237 on the System for the Accreditation of Regional and Local Governments established criteria and procedures for the transfer of these responsibilities.

[4] In the Department of Lima, the regional level is comprised of the Metropolitan Municipality of Lima, which has the status of a region, and the regional government of Lima Province.

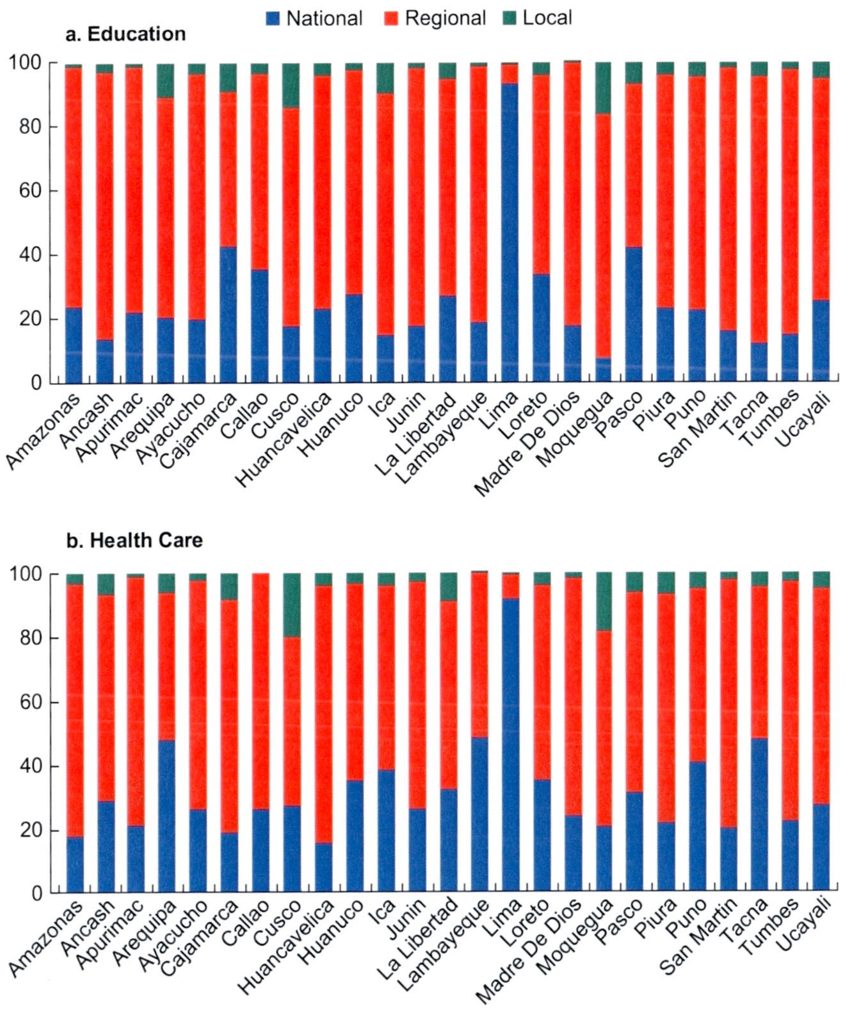


Source: Ministry of the Economy and Finance.

**Figure 10.1** Spending on Education and Health Care in the Departments by Level of Government *(Percent)*

among a small group of local governments that receive enormous resources from license fees and royalties, without consideration of their spending responsibilities or capacity. In other words, the financing has come before the function, contrary to best practices in decentralization. The abundance of resources, sometimes in very small and managerially ill-equipped jurisdictions, has in many cases resulted in suboptimal project choices, waste in outlays, slow execution rates, a buildup of idle balances in the banking system, and temptations for corruption. These problems were noted years back by Prud'homme (1995) and currently pose challenges to the national government's efforts to stimulate the economy and improve infrastructure by boosting investment.

As shown above, the decentralization of public investment has been significant, especially at local levels. Peru's share of subnational investment (64 percent) is now around the average (66 percent) among countries in the Organisation for Economic Co-operation and Development. However, this investment is inefficient and poorly distributed across subnational jurisdictions. The efficiency problems can be traced to local government choices that do not attempt to meet

**TABLE 10.3**

**Distribution of Spending among Departments by Level of Government in 2012 *(Nuevos soles per capita)***

| Department | National | Regional | Local | General |
|---|---|---|---|---|
| Amazonas | 1,153 | 1,252 | 554 | 2,959 |
| Ancash | 699 | 1,360 | 1,119 | 3,177 |
| Apurimac | 1,225 | 1,269 | 728 | 3,221 |
| Arequipa | 1,036 | 868 | 863 | 2,767 |
| Ayacucho | 1,978 | 1,224 | 893 | 4,095 |
| Cajamarca | 953 | 796 | 913 | 2,661 |
| Callao | 2,292 | 1,051 | 489 | 3,831 |
| Cusco | 1,208 | 1,151 | 2,063 | 4,422 |
| Huancavelica | 796 | 1,296 | 1,073 | 3,165 |
| Huanuco | 691 | 899 | 696 | 2,286 |
| Ica | 874 | 809 | 769 | 2,451 |
| Junin | 754 | 736 | 500 | 1,990 |
| La Libertad | 584 | 564 | 683 | 1,832 |
| Lambayeque | 852 | 611 | 468 | 1,931 |
| Lima | 2,842 | 97 | 478 | 3,417 |
| Loreto | 614 | 1,163 | 578 | 2,356 |
| Madre de Dios | 2,787 | 1,925 | 421 | 5,133 |
| Moquegua | 693 | 1,802 | 3,097 | 5,591 |
| Pasco | 788 | 1,277 | 1,215 | 3,280 |
| Piura | 591 | 666 | 683 | 1,939 |
| Puno | 772 | 743 | 719 | 2,234 |
| San Martin | 683 | 1,027 | 618 | 2,327 |
| Tacna | 765 | 1,361 | 1,708 | 3,835 |
| Tumbes | 937 | 1,956 | 967 | 3,860 |
| Ucayali | 615 | 958 | 839 | 2,413 |
| Average | 1,087 | 1,074 | 925 | 3,087 |
| Maximum | 2,842 | 1,956 | 3,097 | 5,591 |
| Minimum | 584 | 97 | 421 | 1,832 |
| Coefficient of Variation | 0.61 | 0.40 | 0.64 | 0.33 |

Source: General Account of the Republic, 2013.
Note: Does not include spending on defense, public debt, and foreign affairs.

needs and fail to align with national priorities. Often, local governments choose to invest in sectors that will generate little welfare gain to the public—even when there is citizen participation in the design. Since the investment is financed mainly by transfers, the public has little incentive to participate or to require accountability for the investment.

## Horizontal Expenditure Imbalance

Peru, like other Latin American countries, has serious horizontal imbalances (Letelier 2012). The uneven distribution of tax bases in Peru—because of the concentration of canon revenues and because economic activity is concentrated in the Department of Lima—implies a high degree of horizontal fiscal imbalance. While the extent of the imbalance cannot be quantified in the absence of information on the fiscal capacity of the subnational jurisdictions, the geographical distribution of spending in departments offers an approximation (Table 10.3). Moquegua, the department with the highest GDP per capita, also has the highest level of government spending per capita (S/. 5,591 per person)—three times higher than the department with the lowest spending level, La Libertad.

The coefficient of variation[5] shows that disparities in departmental spending are most pronounced at the local level (0.64), and somewhat smaller at the regional level (0.40)—with less

[5]The coefficient of variation is a basic measure of dispersion of a probability distribution. It is the standard deviation divided by the mean.

**TABLE 10.4**

**Distribution of Own Revenues by Level of Government in 2004 and 2012** ***(Millions of nuevos soles)***

| Level of Government | 2004 | | 2012 | |
|---|---|---|---|---|
| | Amount | Percent | Amount | Percent |
| Local | 2,079 | 5.0 | 4,816 | 4.2 |
| Regional | 303 | 0.7 | 643 | 0.6 |
| National | 39,110 | 94.3 | 108,333 | 95.2 |
| General | 41,493 | 100.0 | 113,793 | 100.0 |

Sources: Integrated Financial Management System; and Ministry of the Economy and Finance.
Note: Tax revenues, contributions, and other current revenues.

variation if the Department of Lima is excluded. At the national level, spending tends to be more homogeneous (0.33). While the gap between the departments with higher and lower spending levels has narrowed, the position of departments within the distribution has remained the same. Departments with high spending tend to be those with lower poverty rates (Madre de Dios, Moquegua, Tacna, Tumbes, and Lima). Those with lower spending per capita are not necessarily the poorer departments, but those with a high demographic burden.

## ALLOCATION OF SUBNATIONAL REVENUES

Government revenues have remained centralized. The national government continues to generate 95 percent of revenue. The subnational governments that collect their own revenues are mainly local (Table 10.4)—even before the constitutional reform, municipalities had powers allowing them to collect their own revenues. At the regional level, although the regulatory framework provides for revenue-sharing (*coparticipación*) of major national taxes, regional governments' own revenues are currently limited to fees for their services and some other charges. Thus, there has been only a slight decline in the share of revenues collected by local governments since the beginning of decentralization, from 5 to 4.2 percent. Regional governments continue to collect no more than 0.7 percent of total revenues.

### Local Taxes

Local financing is governed by the Law on Municipal Taxation. Local taxes are broken down into tax assessments, charges, and user fees (levies, excise taxes, and contributions for public works).

A particular feature of local finances is that charges and tariffs constitute a significant share of local governments' own revenues, exceeding local taxes in terms of the amount collected. In other words, local governments are more efficient when it comes to the collection of taxes that they impose themselves, such as levies, contributions, charges, and the like. Their collection of own revenues of this kind was double the amount of local taxes collected in 2000 (Alvarado and others 2003). The gap has narrowed since then, but remains significant.

The property tax continues to be the most important local tax, but its share declined considerably from 62 percent in 2004 to 44 percent in 2012. In contrast, there has been a significant increase in the share of the excise tax, which applies to real estate transactions and is easier to collect. The rise in the excise tax is related to growth of the construction industry in major cities, especially in the Lima metropolitan area.

A number of factors contribute to the poor performance of property tax collection. On the one hand, local governments do not have the technical and administrative capacity needed to properly administer and oversee this tax. In light of this, local administrations frequently resort to tax amnesties as a strategy to boost collection rates, although this practice is not sustainable over the long term since it rewards delinquent taxpayers and provides a disincentive for those who pay their taxes on time. On the other hand, local governments lack the basic tools to manage this tax; it is quite rare to find local administrations that have land and property registers, and the few that do exist are out of date and incomplete (Rühling 2008). This is a crucial area for future improvements in the collection of the property tax.

In addition, institutional limitations in the current regulatory framework hinder the improvement of tax collection. The most visible limitation is in determining the tax value of property. This is the responsibility of the Ministry of Housing, which establishes the values for each district depending on the location of the property. This valuation always lags behind values in the real estate market, which results in a substantial reduction in local fiscal capacity. Another limiting factor is the setting of tax rates at the national level without leaving local governments any room to maneuver, even though they have more information about the taxpayers and the ability to use this tax as an instrument for the regulation of urban growth (De Cesare and Smolka 2013). Tax exemptions are another factor limiting collection rates; a number of taxpayers are granted exemptions from payment of all or part of the tax in spite of their ability to pay.

As a result of these various limiting factors, overall tax collection in Peru is fairly low compared to that of other decentralized countries in the region. According to De Cesare (2012), property taxes collected in Peru are around 0.17 percent of GDP, which is quite low when compared to Colombia, for example, even though Colombia's institutional framework for decentralization and intergovernmental organization is fairly similar to Peru's. Colombia's property tax collection is equal to more than 0.7 percent of GDP, or four times that of Peru's. Chile has the best performance in the region, which is related to the central administration of this tax.

## User Charges and Fees

These levies and/or charges are paid for the delivery of an individual public service to a taxpayer. Local governments usually charge levies for services related to public sanitation, such as street cleaning and trash removal, public safety, and the maintenance of public parks and gardens. At the regional level, these revenues are the sole source of the governments' own revenues,[6] and they involve charging levies and tariffs for the delivery of services for which regions are responsible, such as health care, which accounts for 42 percent of the revenue. The income comes primarily from payments by users of regional health care centers and hospitals. Fees for educational services also account for a relatively large share.

To collect these payments at the local level, municipalities have to determine the fee for services, taking into consideration the specific characteristics of each taxpayer. This involves the annual approval of a technical report that explains in detail the cost structure of each service and the methodology to be applied to distribute these costs among taxpayers, thereby establishing the basis for the allocation to each taxpayer. In practice, this exercise is complex and costly.

## Financial Autonomy and Regional Fiscal Space

Given the limited tax decentralization, subnational governments generally have little fiscal autonomy. The greatest autonomy is at the local level: 22 percent of local revenues are these governments' own revenues. The local governments of highly urbanized departments, such as Lima and Callao, have particularly high percentages (65 percent and 39.7 percent, respectively). At the regional level, fiscal autonomy is almost nonexistent, with only 3 percent of revenues coming from regional governments' own sources. The greater local fiscal autonomy can be explained by the fact that local governments have more own sources of financing than at the regional level, and also the power to collect taxes allocated to them.

[6]In the budget terminology, these are referred to as Resources Collected Directly.

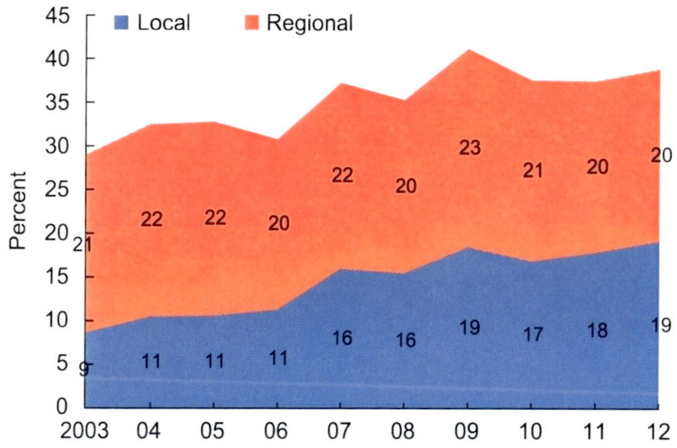


Sources: Ministry of the Economy and Finance; and the National Customs and Tax Administration Supervisory Authority.
Note: Transfers to subnational governments/tax collection by the national government.

**Figure 10.2** Fiscal Transfers as a percentage of Tax Collection from 2003–12

The Law on Fiscal Decentralization envisages a gradual allocation of taxes to regional governments and has identified two stages. During the first stage, resources are to be allocated on the basis of budget transfers through the Regional Compensation Fund, which have been approved under the Law on the Public Budget. The second stage, which awaits the formation of regions, calls for the allocation of 50 percent of the effective collection of the following national taxes in departments: the general sales tax (GST), the selective consumption tax (SCT), and the personal income tax (PIT), which does not include third-category income.

This reallocation would not, in general, improve horizontal tax disparities. The current coefficient of variation across departments, which is equal to 4.2, could decline to just 3.1 (under a hypothetical distribution scenario), but a highly heterogeneous regional distribution of the tax base would remain. Taxpayers continue to be concentrated in Lima Province (with their share falling from 83 to 63 percent). Furthermore, although the department that collects the least (Amazonas) could increase its collection by a factor of more than 10, this figure is fairly low in terms of financing a share of the budget of its regional government. The departments that improve their collection of these taxes are those that account for the largest share of the national GDP: Arequipa, La Libertad, Piura, Lambayeque, and Cusco.

The second stage of decentralization, which provides for revenue-sharing, first requires the formation of regions from the merger of two or more departments. The failure of the referendum in 2005 means that no regions were created, hence the transfer of sources of own revenues remains pending. This is equivalent to keeping the process in its first stage, with regional financing based mainly on fiscal transfers from the national level. The next referendum was initially scheduled for December 2009 but was postponed indefinitely.

## INTERGOVERNMENTAL FISCAL TRANSFERS

Intergovernmental fiscal transfers, which are allocated from the national government to both subnational levels, are the principal source of financing for subnational governments. The proportion of national taxes earmarked for transfer to subnational governments in recent years has been growing. In 2003, intergovernmental fiscal transfers represented 29 percent of total national tax collection, but since 2009 this figure has edged up to around 40 percent (Figure 10.2). This means a growing role of regional and local governments in public spending and consequently in macrofiscal policy.

Since the beginning of the decentralization process, intergovernmental fiscal transfers have taken on unusual importance in subnational public finances. At the regional level, conditional transfers account for around 80 percent of total revenues. Transfers from license fees and royalties (which include various types of canons and canon surcharges, the Camisea Socioeconomic Development Fund, and mining royalties) are the second largest source of financing, accounting for 12.1 percent of total revenues. These transfers are almost three times higher than they were in 2004. Other intergovernmental fiscal transfers, such as customs revenue, which are transferred only to the regional government of Callao, are of marginal importance.

At the local level, intergovernmental fiscal transfers have also become more important, especially as a result of the increase in transfers of canons and royalties. These resources, which are transferred primarily to local governments, accounted for 4.6 percent of total transfers to the local level in 2004. By 2012, their share had risen to more than 42 percent of total transfers. The share of the Municipal Compensation Fund, which represented 86 percent of the transfers to the local level in 2004, has declined, even though its allocation has grown. Other intergovernmental fiscal transfers that have become more important at the local level include transfers of conditional transfers, especially those designated for investment spending, which represent almost 20 percent of the total.

## License Fees (Canons) and Royalties

The canon refers to the transfer of license fees to subnational governments in areas where natural resources are extracted. They start out as a 50 percent share of the income tax paid by extraction companies. There are various types of canons—such as the mining license fee, natural gas license fee, forestry license fee, fishing license fee, and hydroelectric power license fee—and their distribution is regulated by the Law on License Fees. These resources are transferred only to the departments where the production takes place, as provided in Article 77 of the Constitution: "[I]n accordance with the law, the respective districts shall receive an appropriate share of the total revenues and income earned by the state from the extraction of natural resources in each zone in the form of license fees." The distribution within a department is as follows: the regional government receives 25 percent, local governments within the department receive 40 percent, local governments within the province receive 25 percent, and the local government in the area where the extraction takes place receives the remaining 10 percent.[7] The concentration of the distribution means that the license fee is a resource that is very inequitably distributed.

Revenues from extractive industries have mushroomed over the past decade. Between 2004 and 2013, revenues from license fees and royalties more than tripled as a share of GDP (from 0.4 percent of GDP to 1.4 percent). The most significant increase occurred among local governments in producer departments, which receive the largest share of the transfers (they received 1.2 percent of GDP in 2013). The increase means that local governments depend on these resources for more than half of their total revenues (57.9 percent). This dependency makes subnational finances highly vulnerable to developments in commodity markets—a potentially serious problem, given the high volatility and procyclicality in international prices for metals and hydrocarbons.

The increase in these transfers has also created enormous inequalities in terms of access to public resources, especially for public investment. By prioritizing the departments where the

[7]The percentages for the sharing of the petroleum license fees and additional license fees vary by department. In Loreto, 52 percent of these resources are transferred to the regional government, and part of this transfer is determined by the use of credits for regional producers (12 percent). In other departments, the regional governments receive 20 percent, the provincial municipalities receive 20 percent, and the district municipalities 50 percent. Puerto Inca Province in Huánuco is a special case, with the funds being distributed equally among district municipalities in this province, where production takes place.

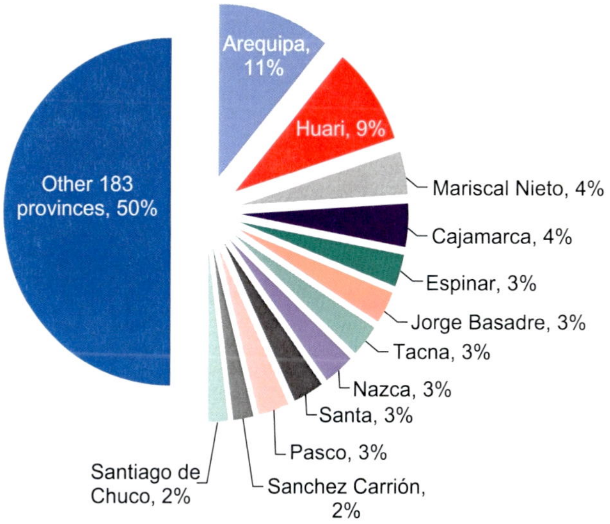


Source: Ministry of the Economy and Finance.

**Figure 10.3** Provincial Allocation of Transfers Based on Mining License Fees, 2012

production takes place, the current distribution rules mean that the resources cannot be shared with other departments. The department receiving the most transfers is Cusco, with a total allocation of S/. 2,658 billion, which is equal to the allocation going to the 18 departments that receive the least. The per capita numbers illustrate the magnitude of these inequalities. Departments where production takes place, such as Moquegua and Cusco, have allocations in excess of S/. 2,432 and S/. 2,044 per person, respectively, compared to departments with extremely small allocations or no allocations at all, such as Lambayeque and Amazonas, which in both cases receive no more than S/. 1 per person.

Inequality in the distribution of the canon and royalties is also pronounced at the local level. Just 12 of the 195 provinces receive 50 percent of mining license fees, with the rest shared among the other 183 provinces (Del Valle 2013; Figure 10.3). Furthermore, among the 12, 3 receive 25 percent of total license fees: Arequipa receives 11 percent, Huari receives 9 percent, and Mariscal Nieto 4 percent. These figures show that even within the departments where production takes place, the mining license fees are concentrated in just a few territories, meaning that the fees are a major cause of inequality.

Besides the inequity of these revenues, their volatility is a problem. The absence of stabilization mechanisms for canons and royalties means that these revenues have been highly procyclical—which represents an argument for not using them to finance subnational governments (Brosio and others 2012). Moreover, the small and unpredictable allocations mean they are ill-suited to financing long-term subnational investments. And the dependence of any local government's canon distribution on the production and profits of enterprises makes revenue projections difficult. Regional and local governments see it as impossible to plan their future resources.

All of this points to problems in the management of local investment due to the atomization of projects, the volatility of income flows, and the lack of capacity needed to bring meaningful projects to completion.

The unexpected jump in mineral resources has meant that regional and local governments in producing areas have not been able to fully spend their revenues. Hence, besides investing in low-quality projects with low social rates of return, subnational governments have been building

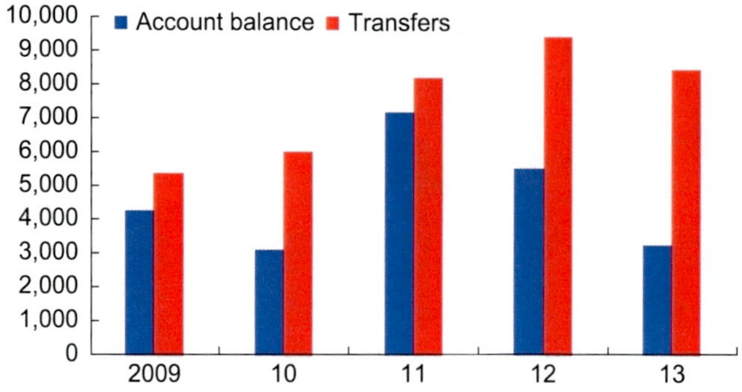


Source: Ministry of the Economy and Finance.

**Figure 10.4** Accumulated Balances of Regional and Local Governments, 2009–13 *(Millions of nuevos soles)*

up large idle balances—income not used during the fiscal year and thus accumulated in their Treasury accounts.[8] These resources could be assigned to other governments with stronger institutional capacity that can deliver higher-return projects.

Figure 10.4 shows the accumulation of balances from 2009 to 2013. In 2011, balances at the end of the year amounted to nearly 90 percent of all of the resources transferred to the jurisdictions that year.

## Compensatory Transfers

The Municipal Compensation Fund is the principal mechanism for equalizing transfers at the local level; allocations are made to all municipalities in Peru as provided by the constitution. The transfers are distributed in accordance with criteria based on equity and compensation, with the aim of ensuring the functioning of all municipalities, and toward this end a minimum allocation amount has been set. It is based primarily on the municipal promotion tax, which is derived from 2 percent of the general sales tax.[9] This is one intergovernmental transfer that does not have conditions for its use, which means that it can pay for either current spending or capital spending depending on the purposes defined by the local governments.

Municipalities' dependence on the Municipal Compensation Fund has declined in recent years. In 2007, 148 municipalities relied on this transfer for more than 75 percent of their total revenues; in 2012, only 12 municipalities were in this position. For most municipalities, the Municipal Compensation Fund represents between 25 percent and 50 percent of their total revenues. The decline in the number of municipalities dependent on this transfer could be linked to improvements in the collection of municipalities' own revenues and an increase in conditional transfers from the central government to small municipalities.

The Municipal Compensation Fund is also to some extent a procyclical transfer, as it is dependent upon the national economic cycle. This has an impact on municipal finances, especially on local governments that rely heavily on the transfer, and on the smallest municipalities in particular.

At the regional level, the Regional Compensation Fund provides for transfers intended to equalize the resource base across regional governments. Its purpose is to distribute resources to regional governments based on criteria of compensation and equity. These transfers have a fixed component and a variable component. The fixed component corresponds to public investment

[8]This accumulation of balances was more common in local than in regional governments.

[9]Other national taxes that contribute to the Municipal Compensation Fund are the vehicle tax and the tax on pleasure boats.

projects of the former Regional Administration Transitional Councils, while the variable component is comprised of 30 percent of resources earned from privatization and concessions, and an additional annual allocation by the national government. The variable component of the Regional Compensation Fund transfer is distributed on the basis of compensatory criteria that take into account poverty indicators and per capita allocation of other noncompensatory transfers (primarily license fees and royalties). The distribution process gives priority to regions in the lower half of the ranking in terms of transfers and in the upper half of the ranking in terms of poverty.

Since 2005, transfers from this fund have been allocated to regional-level public investment spending. For departments, especially those without revenues from license fees and royalties, this transfer finances a considerable share of their public investment. This is the case in Madre de Dios (38.3 percent), Apurímac (30 percent), Amazonas (27 percent), and San Martín (23 percent). The departments receiving smaller allocations from the Regional Compensation Fund are those that bring in more revenue from license fees and royalties (including the customs revenue earned by Callao). In departments such as Cusco, Ancash, Cajamarca, and Tumbes, the share of public investment financed by the Regional Compensation Fund is 2 percent or less. It is clear that this transfer is compensatory, allocating funds to departments that have lower revenue from other types of transfers.

Despite its importance for investment in some regions, the Regional Compensation Fund has become a relatively minor instrument and its distributive capacity is quite limited. This is because the resources assigned to it have dried up. The investment resources that were inherited are almost nonexistent, and the same is true for the revenues from privatization, since this process has come to a halt.

### Other Fiscal Transfers

Other transfers are also allocated to subnational governments, but they are of minor importance, and in some cases temporary. The most significant is the Fund for the Promotion of Regional and Local Public Investment, which was created in 2007 to replace an Intergovernmental Fund for Decentralization that was established under the Law on the Principles of Decentralization but never became operational. The purpose of the Fund for the Promotion of Regional and Local Public Investment is to provide cofinancing for public investment projects of regional and local governments. The funding, which is allocated on a competitive basis, is aimed at narrowing gaps in service delivery and in basic infrastructure. Therefore, poverty levels are an allocation criterion in the project selection process.

Customs revenue is considered a transfer earmarked for the provincial and district municipalities of provinces with customs offices. It is a share of the taxes collected by the customs offices (2 percent of revenues) and is distributed across the municipalities. The Constitutional Province of Callao, which houses the country's main customs office, has a special procedure under which the regional government also shares in these funds. In this case, 45 percent of the transfer is distributed among the districts, 45 percent is allocated to the regional government of Callao, and the remaining 10 percent is transferred to the Education Fund in accordance with Law No. 27613.

## SUBNATIONAL BORROWING

Regional and local governments in Peru may borrow, within the framework of a set of fairly restrictive regulations.[10] The conservative framework was established at a time when public debt

[10] Subnational borrowing is regulated by Law No. 28563, the General Law on the National Borrowing System; the new Law No. 30099, the Law on the Strengthening of Fiscal Responsibility and Transparency; and the organic laws on regional governments and municipalities, among others.

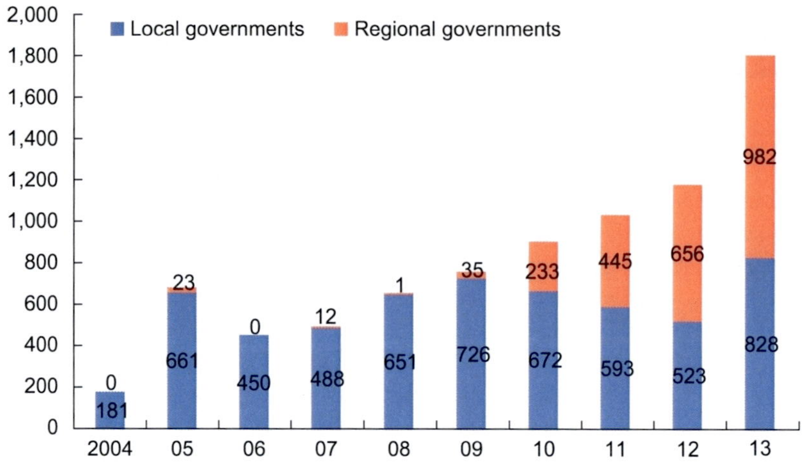


Source: Based on the data from the transparency portal of the Ministry of the Economy and Finance.

**Figure 10.5** Stock of Financial Debt of Subnational Governments from 2004–12 *(Millions of nuevos soles)*

was nearly 50 percent of GDP (Llempén, Morón, and Seminario 2010), so it was of paramount importance to guarantee prudent management of subnational finances without compromising their fiscal equilibrium or functionality.

Three general principles are applied:

- The "golden rule" states that borrowed resources may be used only for investment within the National Public Investment System and under no circumstances may be used for current expenditure.
- Subnational governments may borrow abroad only with a guarantee from the national government.
- The no-bailout clause, which states that the national government will not recognize debts assumed by subnational governments, except those with guarantees.

The stock of subnational debt has grown steadily since 2006. This increase has been driven primarily by regional debt, which has grown as a share of subnational debt since 2009, and by December 2013 exceeded the share of local debt (Figure 10.5). External debt represents 8.7 percent of total subnational debt and 23.6 percent of local debt. The Metropolitan Municipality of Lima is the only local government with external debt.

No domestic private market has yet developed to meet the financing needs of subnational governments (World Bank 2006). As of December 31, 2013, the main lenders were the Ministry of the Economy and Finance and Banco de la Nación, both of which are public entities. Banco de la Nación has become the principal bank lender to subnational governments, providing some 18.6 percent of borrowing. The private national banking sector accounts for 20.2 percent of loans, with just one transaction between the Metropolitan Municipality of Lima and the Continental Bank accounting for more than 50 percent of this lending. International financial institutions such as the World Bank and the Inter-American Development Bank hold nearly 9 percent of the total subnational debt. The only debtor to both of these institutions is the Metropolitan Municipality of Lima, which is the sole entity borrowing abroad.

Borrowing is fairly low compared to current revenues, both at local and regional levels. Taking December 31, 2013, as a reference point, the ratio of financial debt to current revenues at the local level is just 4.5 percent, and at the regional level it is 5.7 percent (Figure 10.6). The geographical distribution of subnational debt shows that local governments have low borrowing

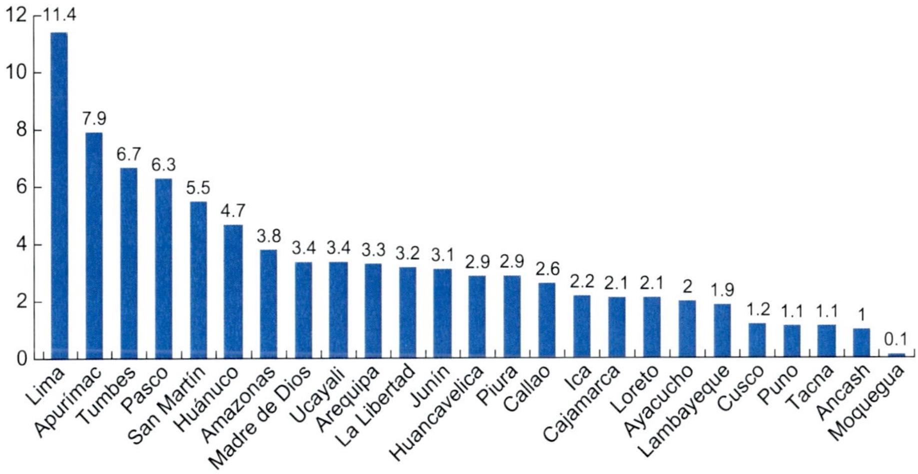


Source: Based on the data from the transparency portal of the Ministry of the Economy and Finance.

**Figure 10.6** Ratio of Debt to Current Revenues of Local Governments, by Department, 2012 *(Percent)*

in terms of this ratio. Excluding the Department of Lima (with a ratio of 11 percent, due primarily to its debt to the Metropolitan Municipality of Lima), which is the principal local government engaged in borrowing, other local governments have an average indicator of no more than 3 percent. Clearly, those that have the lowest levels of debt with respect to current revenues are the departments with transfers of license fees and royalties (canons and royalties), such as Moquegua (0.1 percent), Ancash (1 percent), Tacna (1 percent), and Puno (1.2 percent). At the regional level, debt is higher compared to regional current revenues—with conditional transfers treated as part of their current revenues. Regional governments with debt-to-revenue ratios above 20 percent are Cajamarca, Loreto, and San Martín. By contrast, 14 (more than half) of regional governments report no debt.

Although debt is technically fairly low, there are nevertheless some subnational governments with serious debt problems when other liabilities not included in the debt measure are taken into account, primarily outstanding social security payments, such as health care and pensions, and taxes withheld but not paid.[11] The increase in this other type of debt has come mainly from penalties and interest related to delays in paying the liabilities, a problem that points to shortcomings and precarious financial management in many subnational governments. According to the Report of the Technical Commission for Improvement of the Macrofiscal Framework (Government of Peru 2013), these debts are concentrated among approximately 100 municipalities and two

[11] In accordance with Law No. 30099 (the Law on Strengthening Fiscal Responsibility and Transparency), which replaced the previous Law No. 27245 (the Law on Fiscal Responsibility and Transparency), total debt is the sum of all short-, medium-, and long-term external and domestic liabilities, the disbursements for which have been received and have been documented or, if not, have been recognized and formalized through a corresponding legal standard, excluding deferred income and the provision for social benefits. Total debt also includes liabilities from various operations guaranteed by future revenue streams, whether with or without a guarantee by the national government, such as trust funds, securitization of assets, and the like. The repayable debt applies to balances due both in terms of principal and interest, as well as penalties, that the regional and local governments owe to public entities (SUNAT, the Social Health Insurance, the National Housing Fund, and the Social Security Office). Finally, real debt includes contributions that have not been paid by the subnational governments to pension fund administrators, for which there is a reliable document confirming the existence of both an employment relationship and the withholding of the unpaid social security contribution (e.g., paycheck stubs, payrolls, payments for length of service, unpaid statements, and affidavits acknowledging debt that were required for access to benefits related to installment payments on social security debts in the private pension system).

regional governments. Subnational debt (including other liabilities) is growing as a share of GDP. In 2003, this debt already represented 3 percent of GDP, an amount higher than what was calculated by the World Bank (2006), which placed it at between 1 percent and 1.5 percent.

### The New Fiscal Rule on Subnational Debt

The recent reform of the macrofiscal framework in the Law on Strengthening Fiscal Responsibility and Transparency simplified the fiscal rules governing regional and local public finances. This represented significant progress, since it was a move away from a system with multiple rules and poor compliance to a system focused on greater oversight of subnational borrowing, with two fiscal rules, one of which limits subnational debt.[12]

The new debt rule tackles the problem of other liabilities by including them in its definition of total debt. Starting in 2014, application of the new rules will imply national control of the growth in subnational debt and greater transparency in subnational financial management. The Ministry of the Economy and Finance must report, on a quarterly basis, changes in local debt, including other liabilities and total current revenue of regional and local governments, as well as (aggregate) compliance with the fiscal rule on debt and with convergence targets. Subnational governments are to submit multiyear fiscal management reports to the Ministry of the Economy and Finance; this requirement will be applied gradually to all subnational governments. These reports, with information on the financial situation, will permit better monitoring of subnational governments' fiscal management and the setting of convergence targets for compliance with the fiscal rules.

## MAIN CHALLENGES FOR FISCAL DECENTRALIZATION

While progress with Peru's decentralization agenda has been significant, especially on the spending side, this chapter points to an important agenda of additional reforms needed to complete the process envisaged by the 2002 constitutional reform.

**Address subnational fragmentation.** The most fundamental challenge to further effective decentralization arises from the atomization of subnational governments at both regional and local levels. The small size of jurisdictions makes service delivery difficult and rules out effective collection of own revenues. Moreover, the concentration of canon revenues in a few small low-capacity local governments has impeded the development of infrastructure and in some cases been associated with waste and corruption.

International experience has provided lessons about how to address the fragmentation problem. The common response by countries with atomized municipalities has been to implement forced municipal merger programs. Australia, Sweden, Denmark, and the United Kingdom have implemented this type of reform with positive results. A Law on the Rationalization and Sustainability of Local Administration, which makes provision for the forced merger of municipalities when they are not fiscally viable, is currently under discussion in Spain. Within Peru, consideration might also be given to pursuing the consolidation of departments into regions, in response to the findings of the Technical Commission for the Improvement of the Macrofiscal Framework. Of course, any strategy of this type would need to respect political economy considerations.

Resource-pooling of subnational governments could to some extent mimic the more drastic step of merging jurisdictions. Larger and better-run infrastructure projects could be financed by pooling the canon revenues of the local governments that would benefit from these projects. Consideration should be given to designing a governance structure for such a pooling arrangement that would make it acceptable to local governments (that is, avoid any suggestion that their autonomy would be curtailed).

[12]The new quantitative fiscal rule on subnational borrowing caps total debt and states that the ratio between total debt and average total current revenues over the past four years cannot exceed 100 percent.

**Delineate expenditure responsibilities.** Notwithstanding the successes in devolving education and health functions, further clarifications are needed in the assignment of spending responsibilities. The assignment of other public functions besides education and health needs to be completed, determining which level of government is best positioned to provide each service, while respecting the subsidiarity principle. The right assignment of responsibilities is a prerequisite for the long-term viability of decentralization, because it achieves efficiency by bringing public spending decisions as close as possible to the beneficiary population, while strengthening accountability via a clear definition of the responsibilities of each subnational government. Work will also be needed to make Peru's budgetary and financial management structures consistent with the chosen hierarchy of responsibilities.

**Coordinate shared responsibilities across levels of government.** Subnational governments, and in particular regional governments, have mostly shared responsibilities. This requires close coordination with the national government, which has control over policy-setting, in order to join forces for the efficient delivery of decentralized services. A clear delineation of who is responsible for the regulation, financing, provision, administration, and production of services would make coordination much easier. There have been some early experiences in this area, including work done by the Intergovernmental Commissions on Education and Health Care, which are keeping in close contact with decentralized counterparts. More concrete coordination plans should also be studied—such as the planning contract model used in Colombia, France, and other countries—in order to align efforts at national and regional levels with goals for provision of decentralized public services.

**Align resources with subnational spending needs.** The allocation of resources to subnational governments should reflect (and adequately fund) the spending assignments—that is, finance should follow function (Bahl 2008). Otherwise, resources will be wasted and inequities will build up. Such horizontal imbalances are not only expensive but eventually elicit political backlash. For Peru, this suggests the importance of a reassessment of subnational governments' fiscal needs, in order to avoid an overallocation (in the case of subnational governments that receive canons and royalties) or underallocation.[13] A costing exercise—although unavoidably imperfect—would help to quantify needs, taking into consideration that the cost of providing a public service will differ between, for example, a rural forested area and a coastal city.

**Build subnational administrative capacity.** The recommendations above to merge jurisdictions and reallocate resources away from low-capacity districts originate from fundamental principles of avoiding waste and seeking efficiency from economies of scale. A strengthening of subnational governments' administrative capacity to more effectively manage their finances and deliver services would help achieve these goals, and could to some extent offset problems of small size. Peru's government has been undertaking important efforts in this area and these should be expanded. Stronger capacity would be a prerequisite for further municipal fiscal autonomy.

**Strengthen municipal fiscal autonomy.** Empirical evidence shows that the efficiency and sustainability of decentralization is related to the extent to which subnational governments use own revenues to fund their spending responsibilities. For Peru, this means better exploitation of local tax bases. Local tax collection in Latin America, and especially in Peru, is highly inefficient. Peru is one of the countries with the lowest collection rates in terms of GDP. It would be useful to evaluate the scope for improvements, especially in urban municipalities (major cities), with a view to giving high-capacity jurisdictions greater flexibility to raise tax collection, for instance by modifying levies, tariffs, tax bases, and so on.

**Strengthen the property tax as a major local tax.** The property tax is perhaps the local tax with the most revenue potential, as evidenced by the improvement in these collections since implementation in 2010 of the Municipal Incentives Plan for Property Tax Collection (see Box 10.1). Two

[13]To some extent, a resource-pooling arrangement could substitute for reallocation, since it would reduce the inefficiencies associated with misallocation to too-small jurisdictions.

**BOX 10.1. The Municipal Incentives Plan for Property Tax Collection[1]**

In recent years, and especially since 2010, collection of the property tax in Peru has been improving. This improvement coincides with the implementation in 2010 of the Plan for Incentives to Improve Municipal Management and Modernization.[2] This program, which uses a results-based budgeting approach, aims to improve property tax collection, among other things. Implementation of the incentives to improve collection has produced promising results: the municipalities of Peru's principal as well as smaller cities increased property tax collection by 13 percent in 2012, far above the target (4 percent).

An assessment of the program found all groups of municipalities reporting an increase in tax collection. These results have occurred mainly in the principal cities, where municipalities have seen a reduction in tax evasion and tax arrears following a broader dissemination of tax liabilities, an improvement in notification services, an expansion of the tax base, and an upgrading of the information technology platform. In large population centers, municipalities with more than 500 urban residences have exceeded the targets without having to carry out specific campaigns, suggesting that they are starting from a fairly low collection level. Taxpayers may also have been encouraged to pay the tax by seeing their benefits in some new municipal public works projects.

Despite the program's positive impact, property tax collection in Peru is still quite shaky and at an early stage of development. The municipalities have identified limitations in collection related to weak oversight and control instruments, such as out-of-date data on taxpayer lists (the land and property register), limitations on the use of credit bureaus for small taxpayers, a lack of specialized applications for collection, and the absence of a tax culture.

[1]This box is based on APOYO Consultoría S.A.C. (2013).
[2]It is worth noting that this improvement has also been taking place against the backdrop of the country's sustained economic growth and rising personal income, which in turn is linked with the payment of taxes.

additional sets of reforms could improve property tax collection. The first, which does not depend on local governments, basically entails changing the regulations. It would be important to shift responsibility for the administration of this tax from district governments to the provincial level (Canavire-Bacarreza, Martinez-Vazquez, and Sepúlveda 2011). It would also be essential to impose penalties for harmful practices that undermine collection, such as repeated tax amnesties that reward delinquent taxpayers and deter those who pay their taxes on time. Establishment of a national authority responsible for the development of land and property registers with fiscal data files (as Chile has done) would help expand the tax base. Another option is to develop metropolitan land and property registers, as has been done in Colombia. At the local government level, the oversight of this taxation needs to be strengthened, which will require training personnel in this field. Consolidation of tax administration at the local level would help in that respect, whether these would be semiautonomous (von Haldenwang 2010) or controlled by the local governments.

**Modify the criterion for the distribution of transfers linked to natural resources.** The allocation of canon revenues to subnational governments is a main shortcoming of Peru's decentralization framework. It not only leads to serious horizontal imbalances, it also leaves recipient jurisdictions exceptionally vulnerable to volatility in commodity prices. Any broadening of the distribution beyond the current narrow allocation to producer districts and regions would not only reduce inequality but reduce fiscal risks in producer areas. Moreover, some modification of the distribution criteria *across* departments will be necessary to reduce inequities in access to resources to finance investment. This is the most significant shortcoming of the current system of inter-governmental transfers that needs to be addressed. Other natural resource–producing countries that share this type of income with subnational governments (such as Colombia since 2012 and Brazil since 2013) have successfully undertaken reforms that have improved the equity of distribution.

**Address the volatility and procyclicality of income from canons and royalties.** Much of the financing for subnational investment is hostage to the volatility of income from canons and royalties. Fluctuations in this income create problems for subnational finances such as procyclicality in spending, a buildup of idle balances, and a lack of predictability in the financing of public investment. Dealing with the volatility of these resources calls for recourse to instruments that have been successfully used elsewhere. For example, stabilization funds have been used successfully at the subnational level in the Canadian province of Alberta, and longer-term savings funds, as used in Norway, are options when accumulated funds become large. A pooled savings fund across Peru's subnational governments could provide financing for those jurisdictions with the best investment projects. Those jurisdictions would borrow from the producer-regions accumulating revenues from the canon.

**Reconfigure the Municipal Compensation Fund to better equalize local differences.** The purpose of a compensatory policy at the local level is to guarantee that all inhabitants, regardless of their jurisdiction, have access to public services. The Municipal Compensation Fund (*Foncomun*) would better serve this purpose if two reforms were made, both of which would require changes to the Constitution. First, it should be specified that not all municipalities are entitled to such a resource, especially those able to finance the delivery of services and local investment by strengthening their own revenues. Second, the minimum allocation for low-population municipalities should be removed. It provides an incentive to create new municipalities without the fiscal capacity to provide services. In practice, it acts as a subsidy for jurisdictions that would be better served by a municipality with greater institutional capacity and with economies of scale in service delivery.

**Strengthen the Regional Compensation Fund as a regional-level equalization transfer mechanism.** The Regional Compensation Fund needs to be expanded if it is to fulfill its objectives as a transfer mechanism to equalize access to public investment. There is also a case to extend it to current expenditures in order to close gaps in the delivery of services. This expansion could be linked to budget programs.

## REFERENCES

Ahmad, E., and M. García-Escribano. 2006. "Fiscal Decentralization and Public Subnational Financial Management in Peru." Working Paper 06/120, International Monetary Fund, Washington, DC.

———. 2011. "Constraints to Effective Fiscal Decentralization in Peru." In *Decentralization in Developing Countries: Global Perspectives on the Obstacles to Fiscal Devolution*, edited by J. Martinez-Vazquez and F. Vaillancourt. Cheltenham, UK: Edward Elgar.

Alvarado, B., B. Rivera, J. Porras, and A. Vigil. 2003. "Transferencias intergubernamentales en las finanzas municipales del Perú." El Centro de Investigación de la Universidad del Pacífico, Consorcio de Investigación Económica y Social, U.S. Agency for International Development, Lima.

APOYO Consultoría S.A.C. 2013. "Evaluación final de Resultados del Programa de Modernización Municipal." Unpublished consultancy report, Ministry of the Economy and Finance, Lima.

Bahl, R. 2008. "The Pillars of Fiscal Decentralization." CAF Working Paper 2008/07, Development Bank of Latin America, Caracas.

Brosio, G., A. Cheasty, B. Gruss, and M. Villafuerte. 2012. "The Distribution of Natural Resource Revenues to Subnational Governments." International Monetary Fund, Washington, DC.

Canavire-Bacarreza, G., J. Martinez-Vazquez, and C. Sepúlveda. 2011. "Subnational Revenue Mobilization in Peru." IDB Working Paper 299. Inter-American Development Bank, Washington, DC.

De Cesare, C. 2012. *Improving the Performance of the Property Tax in Latin America. Policy Focus Report.* Cambridge: Lincoln Institute of Land Policy.

———, and M. Smolka. 2013. "Property Tax and Informal Property: The Challenge of Third World Cities." In *A Primer on Property Tax: Administration and Policy*, edited by W. McCluskey, G. Cornia, and L. Walters. Oxford: Blackwell Publishing.

Del Valle, M. 2013. "Ingresos fiscales por explotación de recursos mineros e hidrocarburos en Perú" ("Tax Revenues from the Extraction of Mineral and Hydrocarbon Resources in Peru"). Inter-American Development Bank, Washington, DC.

Government of Peru. 2013. *Report of the Technical Commission for Improvement of the Macrofiscal Framework.* Lima, Peru: Government of Peru.

Letelier, L. 2012. *Teoría y Práctica de la Descentralización Fiscal* (*Theory and Practice of Fiscal Decentralization*). Santiago: Ediciones Universidad Católica de Chile.

Llempén, Z., E. Morón, and C. Seminario. 2010. "Descentralización y desempeño fiscal a nivel subnacional: el caso de Perú." In *Descentralización y sostenibilidad fiscal subnacional: los casos de Colombia y Perú*, edited by M. del Valle and A. Galindo. Washington, DC: Inter-American Development Bank.

Prud'homme, R. 1995. "The Dangers of Decentralization." *World Bank Research Observer* 10 (2): 201–20.

Rühling, M. 2008. "Substitution Effect through Fiscal Transfers: Incidence of the Peruvian Property Tax." PhD Dissertation, University of Potsdam.

Von Haldenwang, C. 2010. "Taxation, Fiscal Decentralization and Legitimacy: The Role of Semi-autonomous Tax Agencies in Peru." *Development Policy Review* 28 (6): 643–67.

World Bank. 2006. "Los retos de la deuda municipal. Causas y propuestas de medidas correctivas" ("The Challenges of Municipal Debt: Causes and Proposed Corrective Measures"). Report No. 35607-PE, World Bank, Washington, DC.

CHAPTER 11

# The Role of Public-Private Partnerships in Closing Infrastructure and Public Services Gaps

GIANCARLO MARCHESI AND ALVARO VALENCIA

*There is a strong relationship between infrastructure and growth as well as a number of social variables. This chapter reviews the different infrastructure gaps in Peru, estimates the extent of those gaps at the sectoral level, and outlines policies and goals to close those gaps. Peru's privatization program in the 1990s constituted an initial effort to strengthen investment in general. More recently, the government has been relatively successful in using two investment approaches to address the country's infrastructure and public services gap: (1) public-private partnerships (PPPs), and (2) the Public Works in Lieu of Taxes (Obras por Impuestos [OxI]) mechanism. Going forward, the government needs to prepare and adopt a national infrastructure plan in line with international best practices.*

## THE IMPORTANCE OF INFRASTRUCTURE

A significant amount of research shows the positive relationship between a country's stock of infrastructure[1] and its economic and social performance (Bonifaz and Urrunaga 2013). Infrastructure has a positive effect not only on economic growth, but also on development in terms of poverty alleviation and income distribution. Chong and Calderón (2001), using cross-country and panel methods, found that both the quantity and quality of physical infrastructure (measured by roads, railways, telecommunications, and energy) are negatively linked with income inequality. The quantitative link tends to be stronger than the qualitative link in developing countries. According to the Asia-Pacific Economic Cooperation (2014), well-designed, sustainable, and resilient infrastructure enhances economic growth, boosts productivity, and promotes job creation. Regional infrastructure also facilitates the smooth flow of goods, services, and people across borders, improves regional connectivity, and promotes sustainable development.

In the case of Peru, Escobal, Saavedra, and Torero (2001) conducted an econometric study to analyze the determinants of poverty and evaluate the effect of the ownership of different assets (including the availability of public services) on the income level of low-income households. The study revealed a significant impact of water and sanitation, electricity, and telecommunications infrastructure on poverty alleviation. In addition, the study found that in urban areas, the availability of telephones had a larger impact on reducing poverty levels than did other types of infrastructure. In rural areas, access to water and sanitation had the largest impact on poverty alleviation, while access to telecommunications was not relevant in explaining poverty levels. Vásquez and Bendezú (2006) found that transportation and telecommunications infrastructure are important in explaining inequality among regions in Peru, while energy infrastructure contributes to reducing

This chapter was prepared with the assistance of Germán Ferreyra.

[1] Infrastructure can be defined as the set of structures and facilities with a long useful life that serve as the basis for the production of goods and services needed for the development of productive, political, social, and personal activities (Inter-American Development Bank 2000).

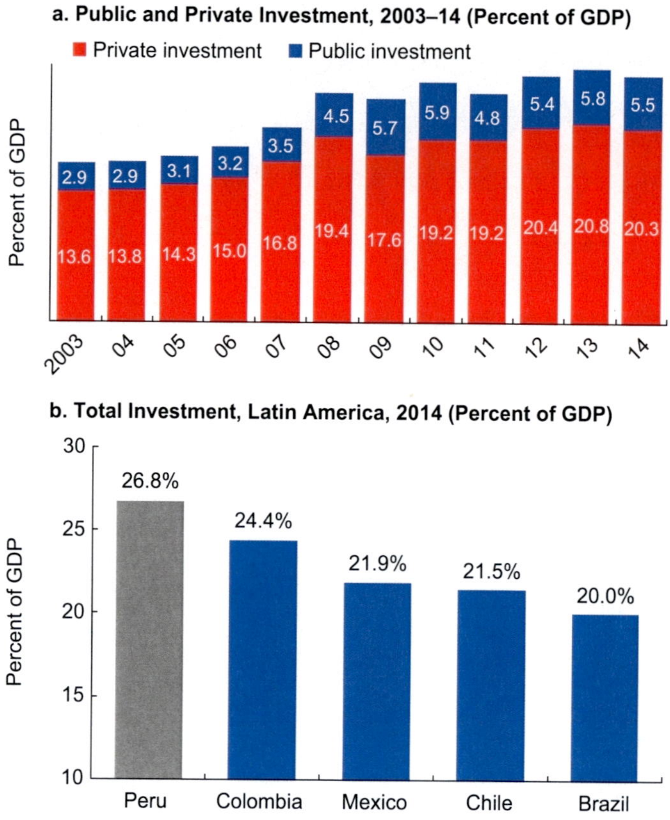


Sources: Central Reserve Bank of Peru (for panel a); and IMF, World Economic Outlook database, April 2015 (for panel b).

Note: Data for Chile and Colombia are IMF staff estimates. Includes change in inventories.

**Figure 11.1** Investment Performance in Peru

regional inequality. Camacho and Sanborn (2008) maintain that because of the strong links between infrastructure, economic growth, development, and even democracy, Peru's government is firmly committed to reducing the existing infrastructure gap in the country as quickly as possible.

## QUANTIFICATION OF THE INFRASTRUCTURE AND PUBLIC SERVICES GAP IN PERU

The Peruvian economy has had solid growth rates since market reforms were implemented in the 1990s, accompanied by strict fiscal and monetary discipline. Strong macroeconomic fundamentals allowed the country to attract significant flows of private investment, especially during the past decade, reaching historic levels (20.8 percent of GDP in 2013) (Figure 11.1a).Total investment (both public and private) also reached historic levels on a national and regional basis (Figure 11.1b).

Moreover, Peru has shown a significant improvement in terms of reducing barriers to business activity, as reflected in its latest position in the World Bank's Doing Business Indicators, which measures the regulations that enhance and constrain business (World Bank 2014a). As Figure 11.2 shows, Peru has gone from ranking 58th (among 178 economies) in 2008 to 35th (among 189 economies) in 2015.

Despite the dynamism shown by private investment in recent years, especially through the PPP approach, along with significant improvements in the business environment, Peru still has an important infrastructure and public services gap that needs to be closed. According to the

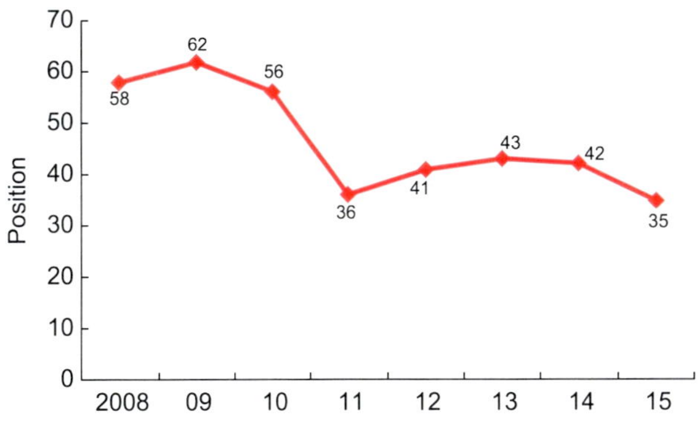


Sources: World Bank, Doing Business Reports (2008–15).

**Figure 11.2** Evolution of Peru in the Doing Business Ranking, 2008–15

**TABLE 11.1**

**Global Competitiveness Index: Infrastructure, Peru**

| Indicator | Ranking Out of 144 Countries |
|---|---|
| **Infrastructure** | 88 |
| **Transport Infrastructure** | 94 |
| Quality of Overall Infrastructure | 105 |
| Quality of Roads | 102 |
| Quality of Railroad Infrastructure | 90 |
| Quality of Port Infrastructure | 87 |
| Quality of Air Transport Infrastructure | 89 |
| Available Airline Seats km/week, millions | 43 |
| **Electricity and Telephony Infrastructure** | 84 |
| Quality of Electricity Supply | 71 |
| Mobile Telephone Subscriptions/100 Population | 97 |
| Fixed Telephone Lines/100 Population | 84 |

Source: World Economic Forum (2014a).

World Economic Forum's *Global Competitiveness Report 2014-2015*, Peru ranks 88th out of 144 countries in terms of infrastructure (World Economic Forum 2014a) (Table 11.1).

On a national level, although there are no official estimates for the infrastructure gap, several studies commissioned or prepared by public entities have estimated the infrastructure gap in different sectors (Figure 11.3). Only some private studies have tried to estimate the national infrastructure gap. For example, using a 10-year horizon, the Association for the Promotion of National Infrastructure (*Asociación para el Fomento de la Infraestructura Nacional)* estimated the national infrastructure gap to be about US$88 billion for 2012–21 (Centro de Investigación de la Universidad del Pacífico and Instituto de Regulación y Finanzas 2012). However, the study seems to underestimate needs in social sectors such as education, health, water and sanitation, and energy. Another study by Bonifaz and Urrunaga (2013) estimates an infrastructure gap of US$200 billion until 2062.[2] However, methodologies are not consistent across studies, so these estimations should not be taken at face value. An official baseline study is needed.

To explain the infrastructure and public services gap in Peru, we use a classification of infrastructure that is based on the main objectives being pursued by the country: economic and social development.[3]

[2] Nonetheless, this estimate considers only four sectors: transportation, water and sanitation, electricity, and telecommunication. It does not include broadband.

[3] A study by the Economic Commission for Latin America and the Caribbean (2004) includes two additional objectives: environmental protection and access to information and knowledge. For the sake of simplicity, the analysis here focuses on economic and social development.

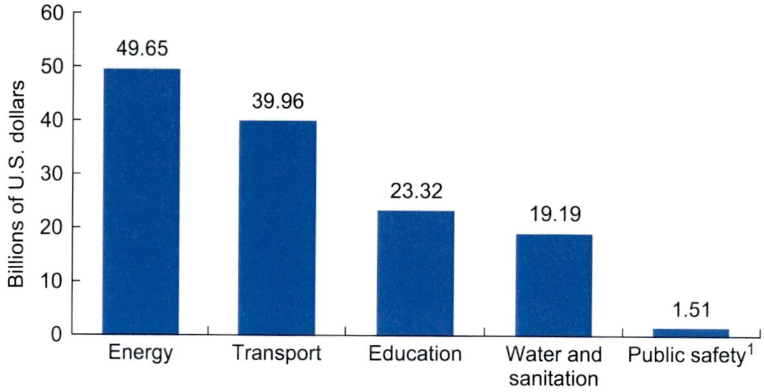


Sources: Energy: Ministry of Energy and Mining (2014); Transport: Ministry of Transport and Communications (2014); Education: Ministry of Education (2013); Water and sanitation: Ministry of Housing, Construction and Sanitation (2014); Justice: Ministry of the Interior and APOYO (2015).

[1]Only considers police stations' infrastructure gap.

**Figure 11.3** Public Entities' Infrastructure Gap Estimates *(Billions of U.S. dollars)*

## Infrastructure for Economic Development

One of the clearest objectives of infrastructure is to boost economic activity by improving the competitiveness of the trade sector. The transmission mechanism between investment in infrastructure, trade, and economic activity is especially true for a country like Peru. According to the Organisation for Economic Co-operation and Development (OECD), the cost and quality of logistics have fundamental implications for sustainable economic growth in Latin America (Organisation for Economic Co-operation and Development, Development Bank of Latin America, and the Economic Commission for Latin America and the Caribbean 2013). If the logistics index (which ranges from 1 to 5) moves up one position, labor productivity gains could amount to 35 percent. In addition, because the share of exports that is logistics-intensive or time-sensitive is three times higher in Latin America than in Organisation for Economic Co-operation and Development economies, the trade and production structure in Latin America is affected considerably by the performance in logistics. Therefore, in order to have a more competitive trade sector, the country needs to invest in trade-related infrastructure such as roads, ports, and airports.

### *Transportation*

According to the Ministry of Transport and Communications (2014), Peru's estimated infrastructure gap in transportation is US$39.9 billion for 2011–31, including US$21.2 billion in investments in roads, US$12.0 billion in railroads, US$3.8 billion in ports, and US$2.9 billion in airports (Figure 11.4).

The current situation of the country's transportation infrastructure is the result of a combination of multiple factors, including:

- *Insufficient maintenance of highways.* For example, Instituto Peruano de Economía (2008) points out that between 1992 and 2005 an estimated US$718.4 million was lost due to the deterioration of 1,357 kilometers of highways because of bad or partial maintenance work.
- *The rapid rise in demand for efficient transportation infrastructure.* During recent years, Peru has experienced strong economic growth that has fostered domestic consumption (the number of vehicles skyrocketed about 350 percent from 1992 to 2012) and foreign trade (from 2003 to 2013 the total value of exports and imports grew 371 percent and

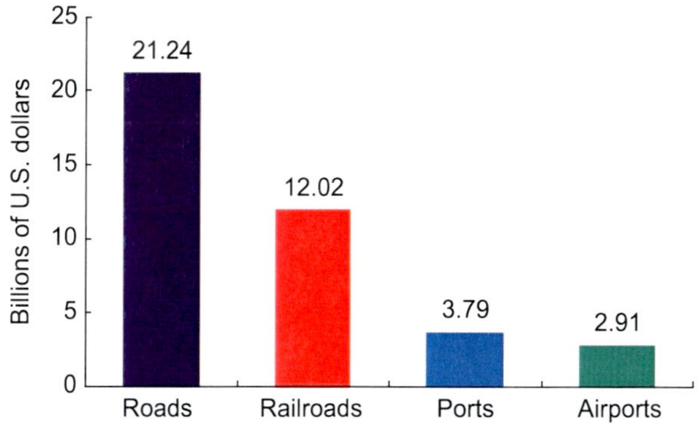


Source: Ministry of Transport and Communications (2014).

**Figure 11.4** Infrastructure Gap in Transportation, 2011–31 *(Billions of U.S. dollars)*

415 percent, respectively). This has exerted tremendous pressure on the existing transportation infrastructure.

Because of the infrastructure deficit, some negative externalities have been generated, representing an obstacle to economic growth. These include:

- *Increased traffic congestion in urban areas.* Exponential growth in the number of automobiles in urban areas, which was not accompanied by a rapid improvement in road infrastructure, has caused congestion and, therefore, losses in productivity. According to Fundación Transitemos (2013), the average traffic speed in Lima is only 14 km/h, which generates economic losses equivalent to US$845 million a year.
- *Loss of competitiveness for the country.* As indicated by the latest Global Enabling Trade Report (World Economic Forum 2014b), Peru ranks 101st among 138 economies in terms of the availability and quality of transportation infrastructure.

To help remedy the above-mentioned problems, the Peruvian government has set the following goals:

- Improve Peru's rankings in the World Economic Forum's Global Competitiveness Report by 2016. By then, Peru should be able to reach the following rankings:
  - 60th in terms of quality of roads
  - 70th in railroad infrastructure
  - 50th in port infrastructure
  - 40th in air transport infrastructure
- Double the length of the national and regional paved-road network from 13,075 kilometers in 2013 to 25,500 kilometers in 2021.
- Have an intelligent transportation system operating in 470 kilometers of highways by 2018.

## *Telecommunications*

According to Centro de Investigación de la Universidad del Pacífico and Instituto de Regulación y Finanzas (2012), the necessary investment to close the telecommunications infrastructure gap is US$19.2 billion for 2012–21, including US$11.9 billion in investments in broadband, US$4.9 billion in mobile telephony, and US$2.4 billion in fixed telephony (Figure 11.5).

As indicated by APOYO (2010), the impact of telecommunication access on the public's welfare has generated growing interest in recent years. Studies have proven the direct relation between the

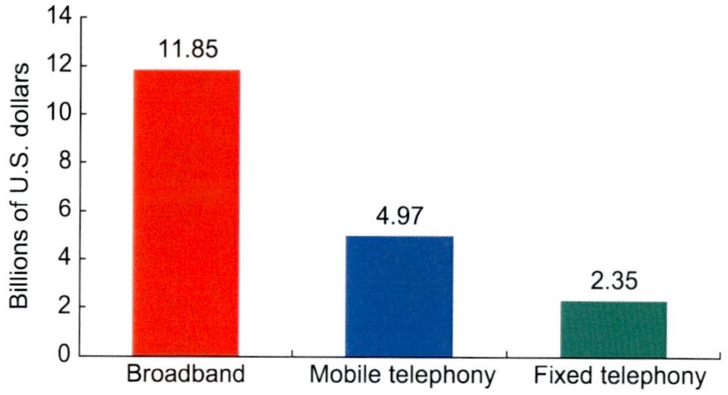


Source: Centro de Investigación de la Universidad del Pacífico and Instituto de Regulación y Finanzas (2012).

**Figure 11.5** Infrastructure Gap in Telecommunications, 2012–21 *(Billions of U.S. dollars)*

availability of telecom services and economic activity. The main consequence of the telecom infrastructure gap is an increased disparity between urban and rural areas. In that regard, in terms of broadband there has been a significant increase in the access of households to the Internet, although it is still quite low (only 33.7 percent of Peruvian households had Internet access in 2013).

The differences between urban and rural areas are of particular note. According to Peru's supervisory authority for private investment in telecommunications, 54.9 percent of households in Metropolitan Lima have Internet access, while in the rural areas the penetration rate is lower than 6 percent (Organismo Supervisor de Inversión Privada en Telecomunicaciones 2014). The situation for fixed lines is not much different. As of September 2014, according to the Instituto Nacional de Estadística e Informática (2014), 26.6 percent of Peruvian households had a fixed-line phone at home. However, while Lima boasts a penetration rate of 52.8 percent, only 2.3 percent of households in rural areas have a fixed-line phone. The picture for mobile telephony is brighter. According to the Instituto Nacional de Estadística e Informática (2014), 85 percent of Peruvian households had mobile phones as of September 2014. Moreover, the difference between metropolitan Lima and the rural areas was not as significant as in broadband and fixed telephony: 91 percent of households in Lima had a mobile phone, compared to 69.8 percent of households in rural areas.

To remedy this situation, the Ministry of Transportation and Communications is implementing a plan to extend the coverage of high-quality, relevant, and efficient telecom services. The target is to fully cover (100 percent) all districts with mobile and/or fixed telephony, as well as Internet service, by 2016.

## *Energy*

The Ministry of Energy and Mining estimates that the necessary investment to close the infrastructure gap in the energy sector will be US$49.6 billion for 2014–25, including US$41.2 billion in investments for hydrocarbons and US$8.4 billion for electricity (Ministry of Energy and Mining 2014) (Figure 11.6).

According to Modi and others (2005), energy has a positive impact not only on productive sectors but also on education, hunger relief, health, gender equality, water and sanitation, and environmental sustainability. Conversely, Saghir (2005) indicates a strong link between lack of access to energy and poverty. One reason is that poor households tend to pay higher prices and use less efficient sources of energy. In Peru, according to data from the Ministry of Development and Social Inclusion, 92.1 percent of households in 2013 had access to electricity from a public network. This is an encouraging statistic, especially when one considers that in 1993 only 54.3 percent of Peruvian households had access to electricity. However, the biggest challenge facing the country is providing access to electricity in rural areas. As highlighted in the National Plan for Rural Electrification for 2013–22, developed by the Ministry of Energy and Mines, factors

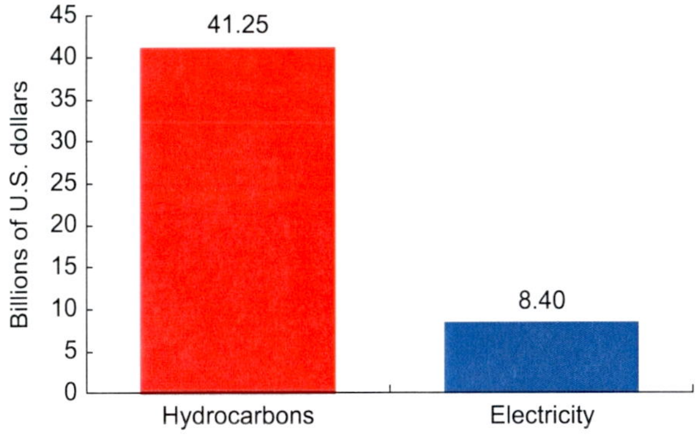


Source: Ministry of Energy and Mining (2014).

**Figure 11.6** Infrastructure Gap in Energy, 2014–25 *(Billions of U.S. dollars)*

like distance, low accessibility, energy consumption per capita, and purchasing power in rural areas make most electrification projects economically and financially unfeasible. Nonetheless, the social return of those projects is actually quite high (Ministry of Energy and Mining 2012).

### *Irrigation*

According to Centro de Investigación de la Universidad del Pacífico and Instituto de Regulación y Finanzas (2012), the necessary investment to close the infrastructure gap in irrigation is US$8.7 billion for 2012–21. This amount includes investments needed to increase agricultural lands. The main obstacle to increase the stock of agricultural land is the lack of water. In order to solve this problem, the Ministry of Agriculture and Irrigation is promoting a US$1.3 billion portfolio of irrigation megaprojects that includes Majes Siguas II, Chavimochic III, and the Olmos Tinajones Project.

## Infrastructure for Social Development

### *Water and Sanitation*

According to the Ministry of Housing, Construction and Sanitation, the necessary investment to attain universal water and sanitation coverage in the country is US$19.2 billion for 2014–21 (Ministry of Housing, Construction and Sanitation 2014). Of that amount, US$13.9 billion is needed to expand coverage and repair sanitation services, while US$4.8 billion is needed to expand coverage and repair potable water services. The remaining US$464 million is for investments to improve the performance of service providers (Figure 11.7).

There is a wealth of literature on the benefits for society derived from the availability of potable water and sanitation. As noted by the Ministry of Housing, Construction and Sanitation (2014), a 2010 declaration by the United Nations stated that access to potable water and sanitation is a human right. This means that governments must guarantee access to those services for every person in their jurisdiction. In the case of Peru, there are still many challenges ahead. As of 2013, 13.9 percent of the population did not have access to potable water, and 32.1 percent did not have access to a sewage system. The problem is particularly serious when the difference between urban and rural areas is considered: 6.7 percent of the population in urban areas does not have access to potable water, while that number goes up to 36.8 percent in rural areas.

The Peruvian government has established the following goals for 2021:

- Expand the coverage and improve the quality and sustainability of potable water services by investing up to US$3.7 billion. The target is to reach a 94 percent coverage rate for access to potable water.

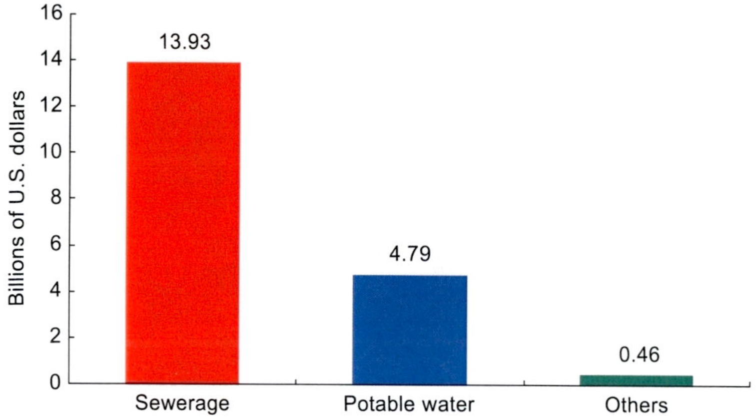


Source: Ministry of Housing, Construction and Sanitation (2014).

**Figure 11.7** Infrastructure Gap in Water and Sanitation, 2014–21 *(Billions of U.S. dollars)*

- Expand coverage and improve the quality and sustainability of sanitation services and residual water treatment by investing up to US$7.7 billion. The target is to provide sanitation services to 82 percent of the population and treat 95 percent of wastewater that ends up in the sewage system.

### *Education, Health, and Public Safety*

According to the Ministry of Education (MINEDU), the necessary investment to close the infrastructure gap in the education sector as of 2013 was US$23.3 billion (MINEDU 2013). In the health sector, Centro de Investigación de la Universidad del Pacífico (2010) estimates the necessary investment to achieve universal health coverage at US$1.1 billion for 2010–15. Finally, in the public safety sector, APOYO (2012) estimates the needed investment to close the deficit in prison infrastructure at US$480 million for 2012–16. In addition, the Ministry of the Interior and APOYO (2015) estimate the needed investment to close the deficit in police stations at US$1.5 billion (Figure 11.8).

The infrastructure gap in education can be traced to the quality of current infrastructure. According to MINEDU (2013), 15 percent of school buildings in the country need to be completely replaced, 75 percent of schools in rural areas do not have basic electricity or water and sanitation services, 56 percent of school buildings are in need of structural rehabilitation to avoid accidents caused by natural disasters, and 92 percent of elementary schools in rural areas do not have Internet access. To help narrow this infrastructure gap, MINEDU is carrying out the National Program for Educational Infrastructure to create incentives for the private sector to get involved in developing educational infrastructure through the PPP modality. MINEDU has a goal for 2021 to build more than 1,130 new schools nationally. Also worthy of mention is the ministry's emphasis on creating what are called "high-performance schools" (*Colegios de Alto Rendimiento*), which provide an integral education to public school's high-performance students from all over the country currently enrolled in the last three years of secondary school. MINEDU expects to invest over US$310 million in the construction of such schools in the Northern, central, and Southern parts of the country.

The health sector faces many challenges as well. According to the Demographic and Family Health Survey (*Encuesta Demográfica y de Salud Familiar*), as of 2013, 17.5 percent of children under 5 years old suffered from chronic malnutrition, and 34 percent of children between the ages of 6 and 59 months suffered from anemia. Only 68.6 percent of children between 18 and

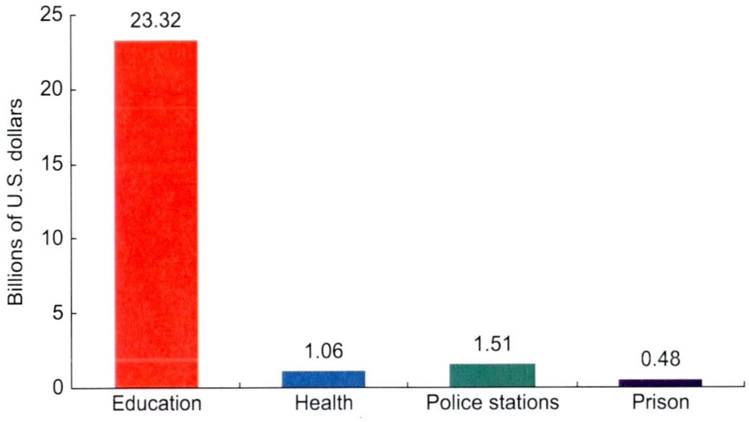


Sources: Ministry of Education (2013); Centro de Investigación de la Universidad del Pacífico (2010); Ministry of the Interior and APOYO (2015); and APOYO (2012).
Note: Estimates for 2012–16 are only for the health sector and prisons.

**Figure 11.8** Infrastructure Gap in Education, Health, and Prisons *(Billions of U.S. dollars)*

29 months old had their complete set of vaccinations, while 65.4 percent of the total population had access to health insurance. To address these daunting challenges, the Peruvian government has set the following ambitious goals for 2021:

- Reduce the child mortality rate from 20 to 15 per 1,000 live births
- Reduce the maternal mortality rate from 103 to 46 per 100,000 live births
- Ensure that 100 percent of the population has access to health insurance

To achieve these goals, the ministry plans to commit investments of US$2.8 billion by 2016, mostly in the construction of national, regional, and provincial hospitals and special projects.

Finally, Peru's prison infrastructure also needs to be upgraded. As of 2013, the total capacity of the country's prisons was 31,452 inmates (Instituto Nacional Penitenciario 2013), but 67,597 people were incarcerated, which amounts to an overpopulation of 115 percent. In addition, according to the 2013 police station census (Ministry of the Interior 2014), more than half of police stations around the country are in poor condition.

To address issues of crime and incarceration, the Ministry of the Interior has set the following goals for 2016:

- Spend 100 percent of budgetary resources allocated to police stations
- Rehabilitate 100 percent of the existing infrastructure
- Interconnect 50 percent of police stations at a national level
- Reduce the incidence of crime from 5.3 per 1,000 inhabitants in 2008 to 3 per 1,000 inhabitants by 2021

## WHAT IS PERU DOING TO ADDRESS ITS INFRASTRUCTURE AND PUBLIC SERVICES GAP?

Since 2008, the Peruvian government has been actively using two investment approaches to address the country's infrastructure and public services gap: PPPs and the Public Works in Lieu of Taxes (OxI) mechanism. These approaches are explained in more detail in the following sections.

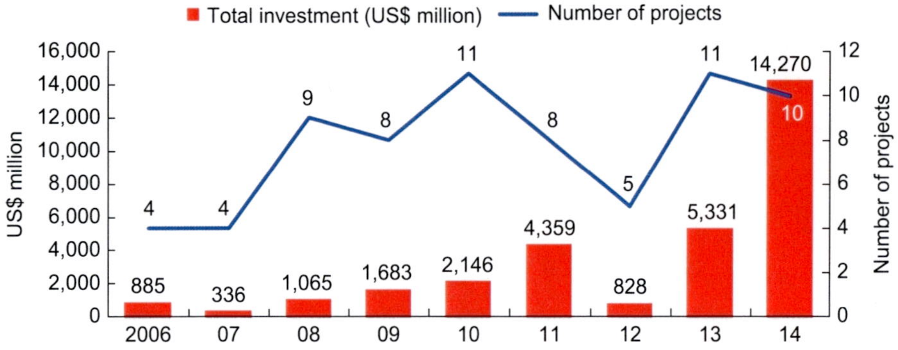


Sources: Ministry of the Economy and Finance; and PROINVERSION.
Note: Amounts in U.S. dollars include the value-added tax.

**Figure 11.9** Projects Awarded through Public-Private Partnerships, 2006–14 *(Millions of U.S. dollars)*

## Public-Private Partnerships

Known in Peru as *Asociaciones Público-Privadas*, PPPs are legally defined as modalities of private investment participation that incorporate experience, knowledge, equipment, and technology. Risks and resources, preferably from the private sector, are distributed. The objective of PPPs is to create, develop, improve, operate, and maintain infrastructure and services that the public sector must provide. Another goal of PPPs is to develop applied research and technological innovation projects.[4]

Peru had its highest level of PPP activity in 2013–14 both in terms of volume and number of projects awarded (Figure 11.9). Also, of the 27 PPP projects awarded during the current administration (August 2011–December 2014) totaling US$20.4 billion (including the value-added tax) in investment commitments, 20 were projects that fell under the self-sustaining category. By sector, transport and energy and hydrocarbons concentrated the largest amounts of investment commitments (over US$6 billion for each sector), due to the 2014 concession of the Metro Line 2 in Lima and Callao and the gas pipeline in southern Peru, respectively (Figure 11.10).

### *Before Public-Private Partnerships: Privatizations and Concessions*

During the first half of the 1990s, the Peruvian government embarked on an ambitious privatization program, recording the second largest volume of transactions in Latin America and profoundly transforming the outlook of the Peruvian economy. Consequently, the weight of the public sector in the economy went from 18.2 percent of GDP in 1980 to 12.2 percent in 2007. The first stage of the program focused purely on privatizations (reaching a peak in the mid-1990s) while the second stage focused on concessions. Privatizations and concessions were both concentrated in telecommunications (telephony), energy, hydrocarbons, finance, transportation (airports, highways, railroads, and ports), tourism, fishing, agribusiness, steel, and, to a lesser extent, water and sanitation (Analistas Financieros Internacionales 2009).

Available statistics show an improvement in the performance of the main privatized sectors. Service coverage improved significantly in the telecommunications, financial, transportation, and energy sectors. Quality indicators also show an improvement in those sectors, as well as mining and hydrocarbons. Both revenues and production increased in practically all privatized sectors, with the profit margins growing especially in energy, mining, and the financial sector. Productivity

[4]As defined by Legislative Decree 1012 and Law 30167. According to the World Bank, PPP is "a long-term contract between a private party and a government entity, for providing a public asset or service, in which the private party bears significant risk and management responsibility, and remuneration is linked to performance" (World Bank 2014b).

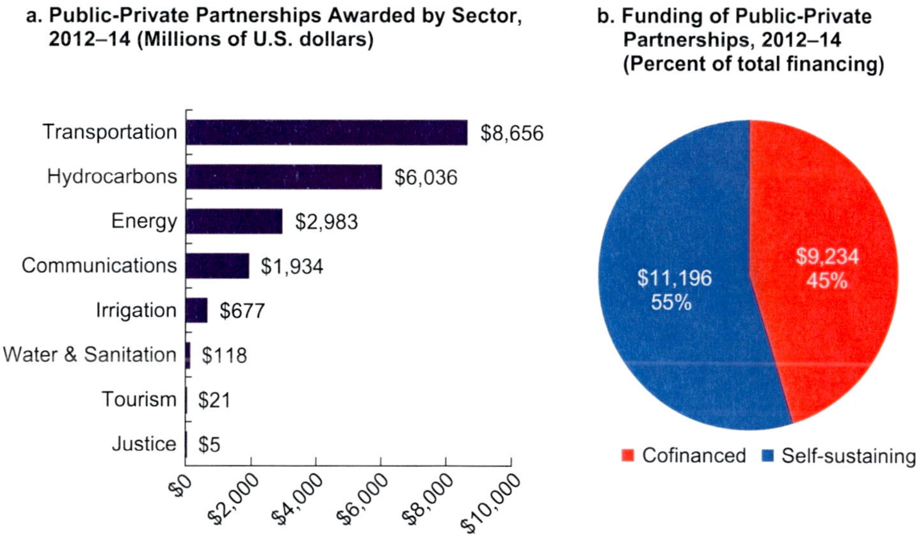


Sources: Ministry of the Economy and Finance; and PROINVERSION.
Note: Amounts in U.S. dollars include the value-added tax.

**Figure 11.10** Breakdown by Sector and Funding of Structure Public-Private Partnerships Awarded, 2011–14 *(Millions of U.S dollars; and percent)*

also increased in telecommunications, roads, and ports. To cite just a few examples of improvements in various sectors:

- The electrification rate increased from 48 percent at the end of the 1980s to 80 percent in 2007.
- The number of fixed telephone lines has increased more than 3.5 times since 1994, and the number of mobile telephones per inhabitant increased from 3 per 100 persons in 1998 to 64 per 100 persons in 2007.
- Total investment commitments in the mining industry represented 4.6 times the transaction amounts.
- Actual investment amounts in the telecommunications and energy sectors surpassed by seven and three times, respectively, the initial investment commitments (Analistas Financieros Internacionales 2009).

When reviewing the evolution of the legal and institutional framework for the promotion of private investment, it is interesting to note that both in the 1970s and 1980s the Peruvian government bet heavily on the nationalization of different multinational enterprises operating in the country. This process reached its peak in 1987, with the failed attempt to nationalize the local banking sector. Consequently, foreign corporations avoided investing in Peru. The new government in 1990 understood it was necessary to foster private investment by creating an adequate legal and institutional framework (Figure 11.11).

In 1991, the Law of Private Investment Promotion in Public Enterprises (Legislative Decree 674) was enacted to promote private investment in enterprises that provided some type of public service. This vital law was the cornerstone for the privatization program, which generated revenues equivalent to US$9.2 billion during the1990s. At the same time, the government created the Commission for the Promotion of Private Investment (*Comisión de Promoción de la Inversión Privada* [COPRI]), as well as Special Committees in charge of conducting the privatization program and assessing which state-owned enterprises needed private sector participation for their modernization. In 1996, the Commission for the Promotion of Private Concessions (PROMCEPRI) was created to promote concessions, which prioritized the development of infrastructure through a bidding process. Taken

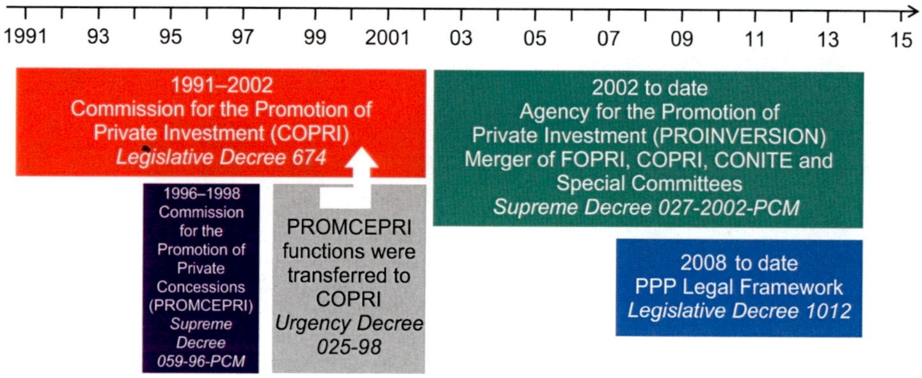


Source: Analistas Financieros Internacionales (2009).

**Figure 11.11** Evolution of the Legal and Institutional Framework: Private Investment Promotion in Peru

together, these measures had a positive impact on infrastructure development, economic growth, local industry, and job creation. In 1998, COFOPRI took over the role of PROMCEPRI.

In 2002, through Supreme Decree 027-2002, COPRI, FOPRI, and other special committees to promote private investment merged to form the Agency for the Promotion of Private Investment (*Agencia de Promoción de la Inversión Privada* [PROINVERSION]). Since then, PROINVERSION has been in charge of promoting the participation of private investment in public services and infrastructure for both public and private initiatives. It also has provided support and specialized technical assistance to public entities that have requested it.

In terms of results, the Peruvian government's decision to promote private investment over the past 25 years paid off handsomely, as it transferred 407 projects that totaled approximately US$59 billion in investment commitments (Table 11.2). The strategy in the 1990s focused on the privatization of inefficient and unprofitable public enterprises. After a wave of privatizations that surpassed US$30 billion in transactions, the Peruvian government—which after a decade of market reforms had by then considerably improved its reputation and risk profile—changed its strategy by switching from privatizations to concessions.

## *Legislative Decree 1012: Streamlining the Process*

In 2008, the government's strategy shifted from traditional concessions to PPPs. With the enactment of Legislative Decree 1012 that year, PPPs took center stage.[5] To date, committed investments under PPPs have totaled over US$28 billion (including the value-added tax). Legislative Decree 1012 defines the criteria for risk allocation among parties, taking into account the public interest and nature of the project.

Legislative Decree 1012 outlines a broad scope both in the level of government involvement and the type of public services and economic sectors involved. Grantors are public entities that belong to the nonfinancial public sector, including the national government (with 18 ministries) and the 25 regional governments, as well as local/municipal governments, decentralized entities, nonfinancial public enterprises, and constitutionally autonomous organizations.

PPPs can be either public or private initiatives, and are classified as either self-sustaining or cofinanced proposals. The former require minimum or no guarantees from the government, or the nonfinancial guarantees have a null or minimal probability (that is, lower than 10 percent) of demanding public resources. Cofinanced proposals are the opposite.

[5] Legislative Decree Number 1012, *Decreto que aprueba la Ley Marco de Asociaciones Público Privadas para la generación de empleo productivo y dicta normas para la agilización de los procesos de promoción de la inversión privada.* Published on May 13, 2008, *Diario Oficial El Peruano.*

**TABLE 11.2**

**Total Investment by Mechanism, 1990–2014**

| Mechanism | Number of Transactions | Total Investment (Millions of U.S. dollars) |
|---|---|---|
| Privatization | 272 | 24,612 |
| Concession | 88 | 32,199 |
| Transfer Options[1] | 23 | 517 |
| Unsolicited Proposals | 7 | 406 |
| FITEL Projects | 11 | 217 |
| Other | 6 | 1,123 |
| **Total** | **407** | **59,075** |

Source: PROINVERSION.
Note: Amounts in U.S. dollars include the value added tax. FITEL = Investment Fund for Telecommunications (*Fondo do Inversion en Telecomunicaciones*).
[1]Exercised and unexercised.

A PPP is considered of national relevance when the total investment commitment is higher than 15,000 taxation units[6] (approximately US$19 million), the project is multisectoral, and the geographical scope involves more than 1 of the 25 regions. The maximum term for a PPP contract according to Article 16 of the PPP law is 60 years. Port concessions have a special legal status that establishes a maximum period of 30 years, extendable to an additional 30 years.[7]

The PPP law defines government guarantees under the financed modality as a way for the private investor to recover the investment in costs or in expenses incurred during the operation and maintenance phase of the project, or as an economic retribution granted by the government for services provided by the concessionaire. Moreover, guarantees can be classified as financial or nonfinancial. The former include total or partial payments that are assumed basically by the grantor. The latter include safeguards stipulated in the contract, derived from risks that are inherent to a PPP project. There is also a limit to guarantees offered by the government. Article 13 of the PPP law stipulates that the present value of the cumulative stock of both the firm commitments and quantifiable contingencies assumed contractually by the Peruvian government, net of revenues, cannot exceed 12 percent of GDP (raised from 7 percent of GDP in December 2014).

### *Cofinanced Private Initiatives*

Legislative Decree 1012 allows for the possibility of receiving unsolicited proposals (or initiatives) from the private sector. These initiatives are also classified as self-sustaining or cofinanced.

Additional Provision 96 of the 2013 National Budget Law created the modality of the cofinanced private initiative (*Iniciativa Privada Cofinanciada* [IPC]). Supreme Decree 005-2013-EF specified its regulation. The main goal of creating IPCs was to foster more direct involvement of the private sector in the development of public infrastructure. The legal framework established in 2013 gave plenty of flexibility to the private sector, but the absence of adequate control mechanisms caused many initiatives to be declared nonviable from a budgetary or technical point of view (Figure 11.12).

### *Recent Modifications to Public-Private Partnerships: Law 30167 and New Regulations*

With the enactment of Law 30167 in March 2014, which modified Legislative Decree 1012 and its new regulation, Supreme Decree 127-2014-EF, a number of adjustments were introduced:

- The definition of PPPs was expanded to other services related to public services and infrastructure, as well as to projects in the field of applied research and technological innovation.

[6]As of 2015, one unit of taxation (*Unidad Impositiva Tributaria*) is equivalent to S/. 3,850 (approximately US$1,240).
[7]According to Article 10, Number 10.3 of the Port Law (*Ley de Puertos*) and Article 50 of its regulation (*Reglamento de Ley de Puertos*).

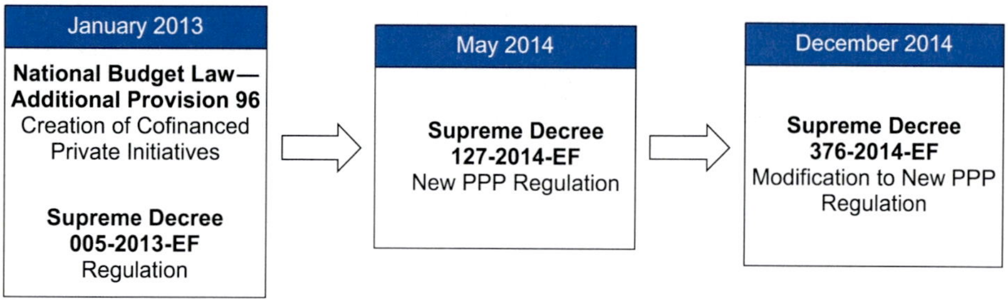


Source: Ministry of the Economy and Finance.
Note: PPP = private-public partnership.

**Figure 11.12** Evolution of Cofinanced Private Initiatives

- One 45-day window at the beginning of the calendar year was established for submitting private cofinanced initiative proposals.
- Sectors are to send their prioritized list of IPCs to PROINVERSION, where a multisectoral list is consolidated and later sent to the Ministry of the Economy and Finance (MEF) for approval of budgetary adequacy.
- The MEF and PROINVERSION established mechanisms for technical assistance to public entities.
- A National Register of PPPs was created to ensure adequate follow-up of the contractual obligations assumed by each government entity.

In December 2014, additional adjustments were introduced as part of the new regulatory framework, Supreme Decree 376-2014-EF. The changes included:

- A better definition of the term "cofinancing," which now refers to any use of public resources and involves the operation phase of the project.
- Optimization of admission, evaluation, and prioritization processes of IPCs with the goal of providing more predictability for the government.

In an effort to promote private investment, the MEF created the Directorate-General of Private Investment Policy and Promotion in May 2014 to design policy and provide technical assistance to public entities regarding the use of the PPP mechanism.

## *Benchmarking and Cross-Country Comparison*

According to the 2014 Latin American and Caribbean Infrascope, Chile, Brazil, Peru, Mexico, and Colombia are the Latin American countries most able to carry out sustainable PPPs to develop infrastructure and increase access to basic services (Economist Intelligence Unit 2015) (Table 11.3). The 2014 Infrascope measures a country's ability to mobilize private investment in infrastructure through PPPs. This report claims that the infrastructure PPP-readiness of Latin America and the Caribbean has improved since the first Infrascope benchmarking study in 2009. In the overall results of the 2014 Infrascope for the region, the country rankings were based on the weighted sum of six category scores: regulatory framework, institutional framework, operational maturity, investment climate, financial facilities, and subnational adjustment. The regulatory and institutional framework categories have had the most significant improvement, as many countries have updated their PPP and concession laws and set up new PPP agencies or specialized units within existing institutions. The regional climate for private infrastructure investment has also strengthened over time.

The results of the assessment suggest that countries can be grouped into four categories: nascent, emerging, developed, and mature (Table 11.4). No country in Latin America and the Caribbean can be strictly classified as "mature" in terms of PPP readiness and capacity (as are, for example, the United Kingdom and Australia). Peru falls under the "developed" category, along with Brazil, Chile, and Mexico, with Chile having the highest score.

**TABLE 11.3**

**Overall Results of the 2014 Latin America and the Caribbean Infrascope**

| Rank | Country | Score[1] |
|---|---|---|
| 1 | Chile | 76.6 |
| 2 | Brazil | 75.4 |
| 3 | Peru | 70.5 |
| 4 | Mexico | 67.8 |
| 5 | Colombia | 61.0 |
| 6 | Uruguay | 52.9 |
| 7 | Guatemala | 46.3 |
| 8 | Jamaica | 44.4 |
| 9 | El Salvador | 41.6 |
| 10 | Costa Rica | 39.0 |
| 11 | Honduras | 37.7 |
| 12 | Paraguay | 37.0 |
| (...) | | |
| 18 | Argentina | 16.0 |
| 19 | Venezuela | 3.2 |

Source: Economist Intelligence Unit (2015).
[1]The index scores countries on a scale of 0 to 100, where 100 represents the ideal environment for public-private partnership projects.

**TABLE 11.4**

**Overview of 2014 Latin America and the Caribbean Infrascope and 2011 Asia Infrascope**

| Stage | Nascent | Emerging | Developed | Mature |
|---|---|---|---|---|
| **Score Range** | **0–29.9** | **30–59.9** | **60–79.9** | **80–100** |
| Latin America and the Caribbean | Argentina<br>Dominican Republic<br>Ecuador<br>Nicaragua<br>Venezuela | Costa Rica<br>El Salvador<br>Guatemala<br>Honduras<br>Jamaica<br>Panama<br>Paraguay<br>Trinidad and Tobago<br>Uruguay | Brazil<br>Chile<br>Colombia<br>Mexico<br>**Peru** | |
| Asia-Pacific (and Benchmark Countries) | Mongolia<br>Papua New Guinea<br>Vietnam | Bangladesh<br>China<br>Indonesia<br>Kazakhstan<br>Pakistan<br>Philippines<br>Thailand | Gujarat state, India<br>Japan<br>Korea | Australia<br>United Kingdom |

Sources: Economist Intelligence Unit (2013, 2015).

## The Role of the Public Works in Lieu of Taxes Mechanism

The OxI mechanism was created by the government in 2008 through Law 29230 to promote the execution of public investment projects (PIPs) at the regional and local levels.[8] It is a form of income tax payment. Rather than being paid in cash to the tax authority, it is paid through the implementation of a PIP. The mechanism is optional and allows regional and local governments and public universities to implement PIPs in their localities without the immediate disbursement of public funds. The private company finances the PIP against the payment of its income tax (up

[8]Law Number 29230. This law promotes public investment at the regional and local levels with the participation of the private sector. Published on May 19, 2008, *Diario Oficial El Peruano.*

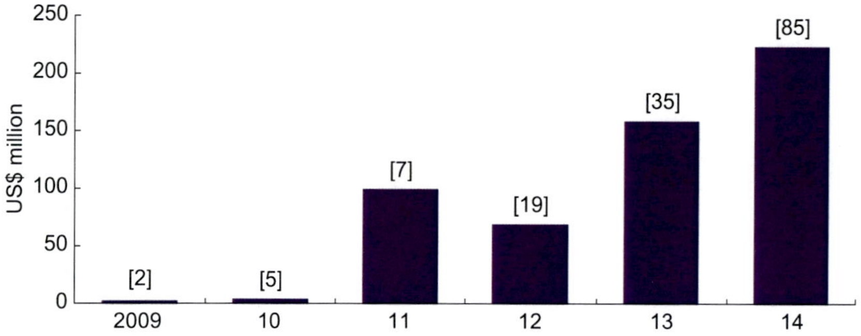


Source: PROINVERSION.
Note: Number of signed agreements in brackets.

**Figure 11.13** Evolution of Public Works in Lieu of Taxes, 2009–14

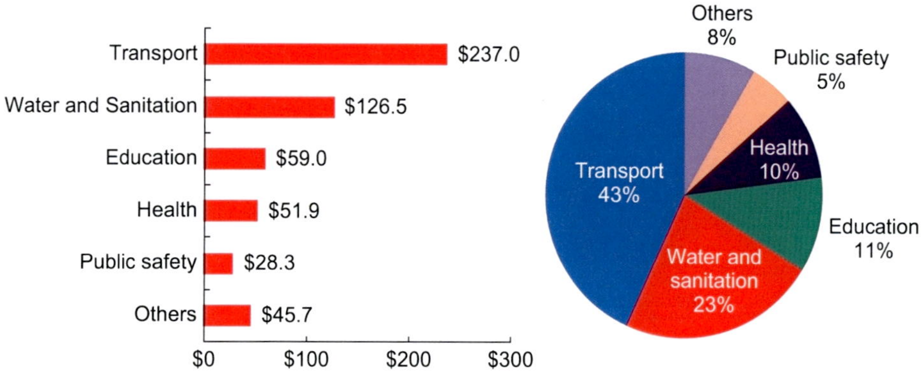


Source: PROINVERSION.

**Figure 11.14** Public Works in Lieu of Taxes: Breakdown by Sector, 2009–14 *(Millions of U.S dollars; and percent of total)*

to 50 percent of last year's income tax) to be paid the next year. Subnational governments and public universities can finance a PIP now and start paying for it 1 year after the PIP is completed, for up to 10 years, with no interest. The financing obtained by subnational entities must be paid back to the national government, with the revenues derived from fees and royalties linked to the exploitation of natural resources such as mining and hydrocarbons.

In a context where revenues from fees and royalties grew at a faster pace than PIP execution, the government welcomed the private sector as a strategic ally to help finance and develop the projects. Viewed as a complement to PPP, the OxI mechanism has been an innovative program, unique in Latin America, due to its simplicity and effectiveness. It has generated a clear and tangible synergy between the subnational governments and private companies, which has ignited public investment, mainly in infrastructure. As a result, the mechanism had committed S/. 1,533 million (US$550 million) in 153 PIPs as of December 2014 (Figures 11.13 and 11.14).

With the goal to further encourage the use of this mechanism, the government made several changes to the legal framework in 2013:

- Public universities were also included in the scope of the mechanism.
- Private companies could finance PIPs not related to infrastructure.
- PIPs could be financed with additional resources coming from social funds such as the Promotion Fund for Public Investment (*Fondo de Promoción de la Inversión Publica Regional y Local*), the Fund for Economic Inclusion in Rural Areas (*Fondo para la Inclusión Económica*

*en Zonas Rurales*), and the Promotion Fund for Irrigation in the Mountains (*Fondo de Promoción del Riego en la Sierra*).

- The Certificate for Regional and Local Public Investment–Treasury (*Certificado Inversión Pública Regional y Local–Tesoro Público*) was made negotiable. Issued by the MEF, this certificate acts as proof of the tax credit to be claimed by the private company in the future.

In addition, the government enacted Law 30264 in November 2014 to allow the use of the OxI mechanism at the national level in sectors such as health, education, tourism, agriculture and irrigation, and public safety, thus broadening the scope of the mechanism.

With regard to the performance of the OxI mechanism, it could be qualified as a success, considering that the goal for 2014 of S/. 500 million (as established in PROINVERSION's Action Plan) was surpassed. In 2014, S/. 634 million (approximately US$220 million) in investments were committed to 85 public projects such as roads and sidewalks, hospitals, schools, water and sanitation, etc. The number of agreements executed in 2014 doubled in comparison to 2013. In addition, 20 private companies, 4 regional governments, and 35 local governments used the OxI mechanism for the first time to develop public projects.

Even given the progress in using this mechanism in recent years, the potential to use it even more in future years is still significant. In 2014, subnational governments and public universities had an overall limit of S/. 26,455 million (approximately US$8.8 billion) to be used under OxI. Thus, only 2 percent of available resources for OxI have been employed so far. Starting in 2015, it is expected that the inclusion of the national government will promote even further use of the OxI mechanism.

## CONCLUSIONS AND LESSONS LEARNED

**How can societal benefits be maximized under the current system?** To maximize the benefits generated by PPPs, Peru needs to continue working on implementing structural reforms in areas such as taxes, labor, and capital markets in order to avoid falling into the middle-income trap.

Among the challenges ahead, the government needs to continue enhancing the legal and institutional framework for compulsory land acquisition, as the acquisition of land and property for the implementation of projects, mostly in transportation, is a recurrent problem. In addition, high-quality valuation practices and standards should be promoted, as they help create an environment of trust for all stakeholders.

**How should the current system be migrated toward consolidated models such as those in the United Kingdom and Canada?** The Peruvian government has acknowledged the need to prepare a national infrastructure plan in line with international best practices. To put things in perspective, estimating the infrastructure gap and subsequently preparing and implementing a national infrastructure plan is a relatively new endeavor even for advanced economies. The UK Treasury, for instance, published its first-ever National Infrastructure Plan in 2010, with updates in the following years. With the National Infrastructure Plan, the government was able to outline its vision for the future of UK infrastructure by taking a holistic view of the challenges ahead and its approach to address them (HM Treasury 2013).

To date, Peru does not have an infrastructure plan per se, only some national plans like the National Development Strategic Plan (Centro Nacional de Planeamiento Estratégico 2015), the Competitiveness Agenda 2014–2018 (Consejo Nacional de la Competitividad 2014) and the Production Diversification National Plan (Ministry of Production 2014). In all these plans, infrastructure is just one component among different priorities. Starting in 2015, Peru will use a prototype of a Multiannual Infrastructure Investment Framework as part of its Report of Fiscal Impact of PPPs (a new report mandated by the modified PPP law in 2014), establishing a baseline for the infrastructure gap and goals for key sectors to be met by the nation's bicentennial (2021). Furthermore, the General Office of the Ministry of Economy and Finance is working on developing a Greenbook and a standardized government guarantee policy, which will be progressively rolled out in 2015 and 2016. Finally, the Peruvian government is working on reducing transaction costs and generating value-for-money by standardizing PPP contracts. By doing this, the government can introduce more accountability and transparency, bring more clarity to the roles and responsibilities of contracting parties, and better assess project risks.

## REFERENCES


Analistas Financieros Internacionales. 2009. "Evaluación del Impacto de las Privatizaciones y Concesiones en el Perú. 1990–2006." PROINVERSIóN, Lima.

APOYO. 2010. "El Impacto de las Telecomunicaciones en el Desarrollo: el Caso de la Telefonía Móvil en el Ámbito Rural." APOYO, Lima.

———. 2012. "Lineamientos para promover la inversión en infraestructura en el Perú: 2012–2016." CAPECO, Lima.

Asia-Pacific Economic Cooperation. 2014. "Infrastructure Public-Private-Partnership, Case Studies of APEC Member Economies. An Outcome of the APEC Finance Ministers' Meeting 2014." APEC Foreign Ministers' Meeting Secretariat.

Bonifaz, José, and Roberto Urrunaga. 2013. "Acortando Brechas en la Infraestructura Pública." In *Cuando Despertemos en el 2062: Visiones del Perú en 50 años,* edited by Bruno Seminario, Cynthia A. Sanborn, and Nikolai Alva. Lima: Universidad del Pacífico.

Camacho, Luis Antonio, and Cynthia A. Sanborn. 2008. "Estado y Democracia: Efectos de la Provisión Pública de Bienestar e Infraestructura sobre la Opinión Pública." *Economía y Sociedad* 69, Lima, Peru.

Centro de Investigación de la Universidad del Pacífico. 2010. *Balance de la Inversión Pública: Avances y Desafíos para Consolidar la Competitividad y el Bienestar de la Población.* Lima: Centro de Investigación de la Universidad del Pacífico.

———, and Instituto de Regulación y Finanzas. 2012. *Por un Perú Integrado: Plan Nacional de Infraestructura 2012–2021.* Lima: Asociación para el Fomento de la Infraestructura Nacional.

Centro Nacional de Planeamiento Estratégico. 2015. "Plan Estratégico de Desarrollo Nacional Actualizado, Perú hacia el 2021. Documento Preliminar." CEPLAN, Lima. http://www.ceplan.gob.pe/documentos/plan-estrategico-desarrollo-nacional-actualizado.

Chong, Alberto, and César Calderón. 2001. "Volume and Quality of Infrastructure and the Distribution of Income: An Empirical Investigation." IDB Research Department, Inter-American Development Bank, Washington, DC.

Consejo Nacional de la Competitividad. 2014. *Agenda de Competitividad 2014-2018. Rumbo al Bicentenario.* Lima: Ministerio de Economía y Finanzas.

Economic Commission for Latin America and the Caribbean. 2004. *Desarrollo de Infraestructura y Crecimiento Económico: Revisión Conceptual.* Santiago: ECLAC.

Economist Intelligence Unit. 2013. *Evaluating the Environment for Public-Private Partnerships in Latin America and the Caribbean. The 2012 Infrascope.* Washington, DC: Multilateral Investment Fund. http://services.iadb.org/mifdoc/website/publications/1869bf57-1d20-46fc-9522-adaffb9e3ff3.pdf.

———. 2015. *Evaluating the Environment for Public-Private Partnerships in Latin America and the Caribbean. The 2014 Infrascope.* New York: Economist Intelligence Unit. http://idbdocs.iadb.org/wsdocs/getDocument.aspx?DOCNUM=39560897.

Escobal, Javier, Jaime Saavedra, and Máximo Torero. 2001. "Distribution, Access and Complementarity: Capital of the Poor in Peru." In *Portrait of the Poor: An Assets-Based Approach,* edited by Orazio P. Attanasio and Miguel Székely. Washington, DC: Inter-American Development Bank.

Fundación Transitemos. 2013. *Hacia una Ciudad para las Personas: Hoja de Ruta para una Movilidad y un Transporte Sostenibles en Lima y Callao al 2025.* Lima: Fundación Transitemos.

HM Treasury. 2013. "National Infrastructure Plan 2013." Government of the United Kingdom.

Instituto Nacional de Estadística e Informática. 2014. "Estadísticas de las Tecnologías de Información y Comunicación en los Hogares." Technical Report No 4, INEI, Lima.

Instituto Nacional Penitenciario. 2013. "Informe Estadístico Penitenciario." Ministry of Justice, Lima.

Instituto Peruano de Economía. 2008. "Lecciones del Mantenimiento de Carreteras en el Perú, 1992–2007." Asociación para el Fomento de la Infraestructura Nacional, Lima.

Inter-American Development Bank. 2000. *Un Nuevo Impulso para la Integración de la Infraestructura Regional en América del Sur.* Washington, DC: Inter-American Development Bank.

Ministry of Education. 2013. "Mecanismos de participación Público-Privadas para la inversión en Educación." http://www.minedu.gob.pe/p/pdf/presentacion_infraestructura.pdf.

Ministry of Energy and Mining. 2012. "Plan Nacional de Electrificación Rural 2013–2022." Ministry of Energy and Mining, Lima.

———. 2014. "Plan Energético Nacional 2014–2025." Ministry of Energy and Mining, Lima.

Ministry of Housing, Construction and Sanitation. 2014. "Plan Nacional de Inversiones del Sector Saneamiento para el Periodo 2014–2021." Ministry of Housing, Construction and Sanitation, Lima.

Ministry of Production. 2014. "Plan Nacional de Diversificación Productiva." Ministry of Production, Lima. http://www.produce.gob.pe/index.php/plan-nacional-de-la-diversificacion-productiva

Ministry of the Interior. 2014. "Elaboración del Plan de Inversiones para el Cierre de Brechas de Infraestructura en Comisarias PNP." Ministry of the Interior and APOYO, Lima.

——— and APOYO. 2015. "Investigación Prospectiva sobre la Criminalidad en el Perú al 2021, y Estimación de la Brecha en Infraestructura de Proyectos Prioritarios y Comisarias en el País." Ministry of the Interior and APOYO, Lima.

Ministry of Transport and Communications. 2014. "Plan de Desarrollo de los Servicios Logísticos de Transporte. Plan de Mediano y Largo Plazo (PMLP)." Ministry of Transport and Communications, Lima.

Modi, Vijay, Susan MacDade, Dominique Lallement, and Jamal Saghir. 2005. "Energy Services for the Millennium Development Goals." World Bank and United Nations Development Programme, Washington, DC, and New York, New York.

Organisation for Economic Co-operation and Development, Development Bank of Latin America, and the Economic Commission for Latin America and the Caribbean. 2013. *Latin American Economic Outlook 2014: Logistics and Competitiveness for Development.* Paris: Organisation for Economic Co-operation and Development Development Centre.

Organismo Supervisor de Inversión Privada en Telecomunicaciones. 2014. "Caracterización de la Demanda de Internet Fijo y Móvil en el Perú: 2012–2013. Un Análisis Descriptivo." Lima, Peru.

Saghir, Jamal. 2005. "Energy and Poverty: Myths, Links, and Policy Issues." *Energy Working Notes* No. 4 (May), World Bank Group. http://siteresources.worldbank.org/INTENERGY/Resources/EnergyWorkingNotes_4.pdf.

Vásquez, Arturo, and Luis Bendezú. 2006. "Inversión en Infraestructura y Desigualdad Regional en el Perú: Nueva Evidencia." In *Inversión en Infraestructura Vial y Crecimiento Económico Regional en el Perú: Un Enfoque Multidimensional.* Lima: Consorcio de Investigación Económica y Social.

World Bank. 2014a. *Doing Business 2015: Going Beyond Efficiency.* Washington, DC: World Bank Group.

———. 2014b. "Public-Private Partnerships: Reference Guide Version 2.0." World Bank Group, Washington, DC. http://documents.worldbank.org/curated/en/2014/01/20182310/public-private-partnerships-referenceguide-version-20.

World Economic Forum. 2014a. *The Global Competitiveness Report 2014–2015.* Geneva: World Economic Forum.

———. 2014b. *The Global Enabling Trade Report 2014.* Edited by Margareta Drzeniek Hanouz, Thierry Geiger, and Sean Doherty. Geneva: World Economic Forum.

CHAPTER 12

# Monetary Policy in a Partially Dollarized Economy: Peru's Experience with Inflation Targeting

ADRIÁN ARMAS, ALEJANDRO SANTOS, AND MELESSE TASHU

*Using empirical analysis, this chapter shows that Peru's inflation-targeting framework has been successful in anchoring inflation expectations, reducing the level and volatility of inflation, reducing the volatility of output growth, and weakening the pass-through of the exchange rate to prices and the pass-through of external interest rates to local interest rates. The design of Peru's inflation-targeting framework, however, differs from conventional inflation-targeting frameworks in that it explicitly takes into account the risks of partial dollarization. The lessons from Peru's experience are that (1) effective monetary policy can be challenging, but is possible in a partially dollarized economy; and (2) foreign exchange intervention can be consistent with and complementary to inflation targeting in a partially dollarized economy.*

Peru has made significant progress in reducing partial dollarization in the 2000s through the use of a voluntary process. The economy became highly dollarized during the 1980s as a consequence of serious macroeconomic mismanagement (Armas and others 2001). By 2000, loans denominated in dollars exceeded 75 percent of total banking loans, but that proportion has declined significantly since then. Despite the progress, financial dollarization remains high, with about 40 percent of credits and deposits at depository institutions denominated in U.S. dollars at end-2013. Estimates also show that transaction dollarization—defined as the use of foreign currency as a means of payments—stands at about 30 percent (Table 12.1).

Partial dollarization—which occurs when some contracts are denominated, prices posted, or payments made in dollars while the local currency remains the exclusive legal tender—poses challenges to the conduct of monetary policy due to its consequences on financial vulnerability. Partial dollarization exposes the balance sheets of firms and households to changes in the exchange rate, is more likely to increase exchange rate pass-through to consumer prices, and exposes the financial system to external shocks. In addition, the effectiveness of monetary policy is generally limited under partial dollarization because the stock of the monetary aggregate under the control of the monetary authority is only a fraction of the relevant monetary stock in the economy.

Notwithstanding these challenges, Peru has been able to stabilize prices through an inflation-targeting regime. It has been more than a decade since Peru introduced an inflation-targeting framework, which has successfully anchored inflation expectations. The design of Peru's inflation-targeting framework, however, differs from that of conventional inflation-targeting frameworks in that it explicitly takes into account, and aims to overcome, the consequences of partial dollarization.

This chapter documents the effectiveness of Peru's inflation-targeting framework in anchoring inflation expectations, reducing the level and volatility of inflation, reducing the volatility of output growth, and weakening the pass-through of the exchange rate to prices and the

**TABLE 12.1**

**Peru: Payment Means in Foreign Currency**
*(Percent of total payments)*

| | 2011 | 2012 | 2013 |
|---|---|---|---|
| Checks | 29.0 | 30.2 | 28.3 |
| Debit Card | 22.7 | 24.1 | 21.6 |
| Credit Card | 12.9 | 16.6 | 18.6 |
| Credit Transfers | 33.0 | 34.6 | 29.7 |
| Direct Debits | 6.7 | 8.0 | 7.6 |
| Automatic Teller Machines | 17.3 | 19.4 | 18.0 |
| Virtual Banking | 34.5 | 38.2 | 35.0 |
| Total | 30.3 | 32.3 | 29.1 |

Sources: Central Reserve Bank of Peru; and authors' calculations.
Note: At the 2012 average exchange rate.

pass-through of external interest rates to local interest rates. Through this analysis, the chapter aims to draw lessons for an optimal monetary policy framework for a partially dollarized economy.

The chapter first discusses conceptual issues regarding the nature and consequences of partial dollarization. It then provides an overview of Peru's experience with partial dollarization and the design of an inflation-targeting framework. The chapter assesses the effectiveness of Peru's inflation-targeting framework and draws lessons for an optimal monetary policy in a partially dollarized economy that may be useful to other partially dollarized emerging market economies.

## PARTIAL DOLLARIZATION AND ITS CONSEQUENCES FOR MONETARY POLICY

In contrast to official dollarization, partial dollarization occurs when some contracts are denominated, prices posted, or payments made in dollars while the local currency remains the exclusive legal tender (Ize 2013). Partial dollarization can be manifested in three forms: financial, transaction, and real dollarization.

- *Financial dollarization*, also known as asset substitution, refers to the use of foreign currency as a store of value or a unit of account for financial contracts. Financial dollarization takes place as a response to high variability in inflation, which affects the differential in variability of returns between domestic currency–denominated assets and foreign currency–denominated assets.
- *Transaction dollarization*, also known as currency substitution, refers to the use of foreign currency as a means of payment. It is common in economies with a high level of inflation, where there is a great opportunity cost of holding domestic currency.
- *Real dollarization* refers to the formal or de facto indexing of local wages or prices to changes in the exchange rate between the domestic currency and the dollar.

The process of dollarization in Peru began in the 1970s due to persistently high inflation and was aggravated during the 1988–90 hyperinflation episode (Quispe 2000). Hyperinflation was brought under control in the early 1990s through broad reform of the financial system and monetary and fiscal policies, but the rate of dollarization remained in the range of 70–80 percent until the early 2000s.

The dedollarization process started in the early 2000s, in particular following implementation of the inflation-targeting framework (Figure 12.1). The process continues today at a steady but slow pace. In particular, financial dollarization, as measured by the ratio of dollar deposits and

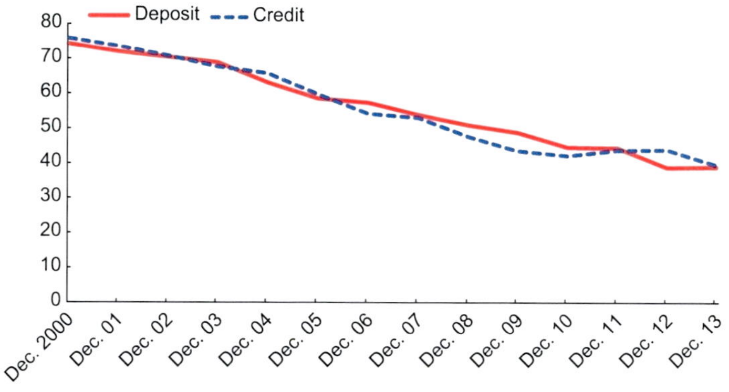


Sources: Central Reserve Bank of Peru; and authors' calculations.
Note: At the December 2011 exchange rate.

**Figure 12.1** Peru: Dollarization at Depository Corporations *(Percent)*

credits at depository institutions, fell from about 75 percent in 2000 to about 40 percent at end-2013. Transactional dollarization, estimated by the ratio of dollar payments and withdrawals from the banking system, was at about 30 percent in recent years, mostly reflecting transactions among firms (historical data are not available).[1] Although there are no direct data, the current rate of real dollarization in Peru is believed to be relatively low based on the estimated small size of the exchange rate pass-through to domestic prices, which is about 0.1 percent (Winkelried 2014).

## Consequences of Partial Dollarization for the Conduct of Monetary Policy

Partial dollarization poses significant challenges to the conduct of independent monetary policy due to its consequences on the exchange rate, interest rate, and prices. The literature identifies at least four consequences of partial dollarization, which in turn pose challenges to the conduct of monetary policy: the balance sheet effect of large changes in the exchange rate, high exchange rate pass-through to domestic prices, high exchange rate volatility, and high pass-through of foreign interest rates to domestic interest rates (Armas, Batini, and Tuesta 2007; Baliño, Bennett, and Borensztein 1999; Leiderman, Maino, and Parrado 2006).

### *Balance Sheet Effect of Large Exchange Rate Depreciations*

In an open nondollarized economy, exchange rate flexibility complements the central bank's effort to stabilize inflation against demand shocks. Consider, for instance, a negative demand shock (leading to a negative output gap) in an inflation-targeting economy. The expected deflationary pressure would prompt the central bank to reduce its policy interest rate in order to boost aggregate demand. The interest reduction would be expected to stimulate aggregate demand both directly and indirectly—that is, directly, through its impact on investment and consumption, and indirectly by encouraging capital outflows and inducing depreciation of the domestic currency, which in turn could complement the direct impact by boosting net exports.

For a financially dollarized economy, however, the indirect impact may not be positive or complementary to the direct impact due to the potential contractionary impact of large exchange rate

[1]A survey by the Central Reserve Bank of Peru (2013) found that about 58 percent of the value of transactions in inputs or supplies among firms as of December 2012 was denominated in foreign currency. The trade and mining sectors had the highest percentages of transactional dollarization, at 80 percent and 75 percent, respectively.

depreciations. Economic agents in a financially dollarized economy may find themselves unable to service their debt during large exchange rate depreciations due to currency mismatches in their balance sheets. As a result, large exchange rate depreciations may lead to credit crunches, which in turn can result in contractionary effects on output, offsetting the initial effects of interest rate cuts (Alvarez-Plata and García-Herrero 2008; Armas, Batini, and Tuesta 2007; Leiderman, Maino, and Parado 2006).

### *High Exchange Rate Pass-Through to Prices*

Empirical evidence shows that exchange rate pass-through to domestic prices is higher for dollarized economies than for nondollarized economies (Alvarez-Plata and García-Herrero 2008; Reinhart, Rogoff, and Savastano 2003). This is particularly true in the case of real dollarization, where changes in the exchange rate are directly reflected in domestic prices and wages, making it harder to anchor inflation expectations. In the case of full real dollarization, monetary policy would be effective only if prices and wages are sticky (Armas, Batini, and Tuesta 2007).

### *High Exchange Rate Volatility*

The exchange rate tends to be highly volatile in partially dollarized economies, in particular if transactional dollarization is high. In that case, demand for foreign/domestic currency may shift easily, often for reasons that are not easily identifiable, due to the high substitutability of the two currencies (Baliño, Bennett, and Borensztein 1999). As a result, the exchange rate tends to be very volatile and inflation expectations are hard to anchor. In the extreme case, where dollars are the only accepted means of payment, monetary policy would be completely ineffective because the relevant interest rate for intertemporal consumption decisions (and thus for aggregate demand) would be interest rates paid on dollar savings (Armas, Batini, and Tuesta 2007; Batini, Levine, and Pearlman 2008). Peru does not have high exchange rate volatility in part because transactional dollarization is relatively low, but also because of frequent foreign exchange interventions by the Central Reserve Bank of Peru (*Banco Central de Reserva del Perú* [BCRP]).

### *High Pass-Through of Foreign Interest Rates to Domestic Interest Rates*

In an open and financially dollarized economy, the close substitution between dollar-denominated and domestic-currency-denominated assets strengthens the links among the international dollar interest rates, the domestic dollar interest rates, and the domestic local currency interest rates (Baliño, Bennett, and Borensztein 1999). The possibility of capital flight following an increase in international dollar interest rates would prompt immediate increases in domestic interest rates. The pass-through depends on the flexibility of the exchange rate; it would be complete in the extreme case where the exchange rate is fixed. In any case, the high pass-through of foreign interest rates to domestic interest rates limits the central bank's ability to influence interest rates on domestic currency, which is key for a successful inflation targeting.

## OPTIMAL MONETARY POLICY UNDER PARTIAL DOLLARIZATION

There is a broad consensus that the previously mentioned consequences of partial dollarization can be overcome and that price stability can be achieved through active monetary policy in partially dollarized economies. The debate, then, is about the design of an optimal monetary policy framework, particularly the degree of exchange rate flexibility.

For highly dollarized economies that are at the initial stage of price stabilization, a fixed exchange rate arrangement is seen as a good choice (Baliño, Bennett, and Borensztein 1999; Batini, Levine, and Pearlman 2008). For partially dollarized economies that have already managed to stabilize inflation, there is a broad consensus that an inflation-targeting framework with a flexible exchange rate arrangement is a better choice (Baliño, Bennett, and Borensztein 1999; De Nicoló, Honohan, and Ize 2003; Ize and Levy-Yeyati 2003). The optimal degree of exchange

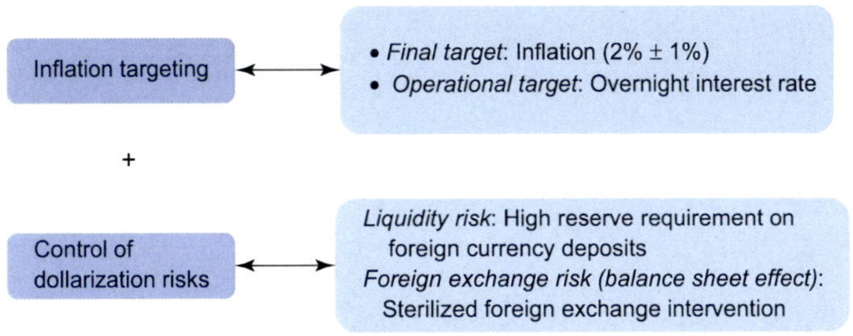


Source: Based on Quispe and Rossini (2010).

**Figure 12.2** Peru: Hybrid Inflation Targeting

rate flexibility is, however, not an easy issue to determine. On the one hand, the balance sheet effect of large changes in the exchange rate calls for the need to smooth exchange rate volatility. On the other hand, it would be difficult to reduce dollarization with a stable exchange rate, as economic agents would not internalize foreign exchange risk and the cost of dollarization.

Authors who emphasize the need to reduce dollarization strongly recommend a freely floating exchange rate. For example, to break the adverse dynamics between rising dollarization and exchange rate rigidities, De Nicoló, Honohan, and Ize (2003) recommend a switch to a freely floating exchange rate arrangement backed by a strong inflation anchor through adoption of full-fledged inflation targeting. Using an analytical model, Ize and Levy-Yeyati (2003) show that for a given variance of inflation, an increase in the variance of the rate of depreciation reduces dollarization by limiting the hedging benefits of dollar assets. The authors conclude that inflation targeting combined with a freely floating exchange rate would reduce financial dollarization by increasing real exchange rate volatility relative to price volatility.[2]

However, other authors argue for exchange rate smoothing due to concerns over the adverse impact (balance sheet impact) of large changes in exchange rate volatility on the effectiveness of inflation targeting. Leiderman, Maino, and Parrado (2006) argue that foreign exchange intervention can be consistent with, and even strengthen, an inflation-targeting framework, as long as the intervention does not target a specific trend for the real exchange rate. Evidence from analytical and empirical models also suggests that exchange rate smoothing is necessary under inflation targeting in partially dollarized or financially vulnerable emerging market economies (Batini, Levine, and Pearlman 2008; García, Restrepo, and Roger 2011).

## Peru's Experience with Inflation Targeting

Peru's inflation-targeting framework, which has been in place since 2002, can best be described as a hybrid regime (Figure 12.2). The implementation of the inflation-targeting framework followed a broad reform of financial, monetary, and fiscal policies in 1991[3] and a decade of a monetary-aggregate-targeting regime[4] that succeeded in reducing and stabilizing inflation resulting from the hyperinflation of the late 1980s (Armas and others 2001). As a result, inflation was already stabilized and low when the inflation-targeting framework was implemented, but dollarization was very high.

The inflation-targeting framework was uniquely designed to take into account the adverse impact of partial dollarization on the effectiveness of monetary policy and promote dedollarization

[2]This conclusion is conditioned on real dollarization being moderate.

[3]The new Central Bank Organic Law, which clearly established maintaining monetary stability as the sole objective of the BCRP, was a key part of these reforms. The law also prohibits the central bank from financing the Treasury or the state development bank.

[4]In particular, the growth of the monetary base was the intermediate target of monetary policy during 1991–2001. The final target of monetary policy evolved from eliminating high inflation during 1991–93 to achieving single-digit inflation during 1994–97, and further to reducing inflation to the international level during 1998–2001.

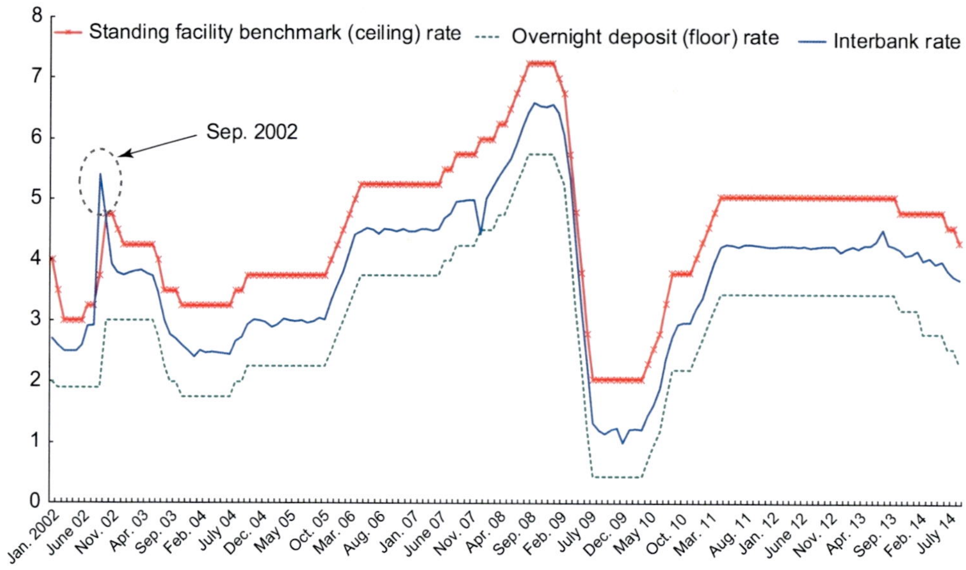


Source: Central Reserve Bank of Peru.

**Figure 12.3** Peru: Interest Rates *(Percent)*

over the long term. More specifically, the inflation-targeting system was implemented in conjunction with relatively active foreign exchange intervention and the use of reserve requirements on foreign currency liabilities. The inflation target was set at a relatively low level (at 2.5 ± 1 percent initially and 2 ± 1 percent since 2007) compared with other emerging market economies in order to anchor Peru's level of medium- to long-term inflation to that of the United States (Armas and Grippa 2006). The purpose was to build public confidence in the local currency against the U.S. dollar and promote dedollarization.

## *Operational Target*

The operational target of the inflation-targeting framework is the overnight interbank rate, as is the case with other inflation targeters. In addition to its obvious advantage of simplicity for communicating the monetary policy stance to the public, targeting the interbank rate has the advantage of promoting dedollarization over the medium to long term by stabilizing and anchoring the short-term interest rate around the policy rate and developing a local currency yield curve. In the absence of a stable and predictable short-term interest rate, there would either be no long-term operation in domestic currency, or its yield would be determined by the foreign interest rate and the expected changes in the exchange rate (Armas and Grippa 2006). The latter in turn implies that inflation expectations would be hard to anchor.

One of the ways in which the design of the inflation-targeting framework in Peru takes into account the risks of financial dollarization is through the escape clause, which allows a temporary closing of the standing facility. This enables the interbank interest rate to overshoot the standing facility benchmark (ceiling) rate in extreme situations when there is a significant exchange rate depreciation pressure that could trigger a balance sheet effect (Armas and Grippa 2006). The objective is to let the interest rate absorb part of the shock and limit the necessary depreciation of the exchange rate, thereby avoiding potential balance sheet effects. In practice, this was implemented only once, in September 2002, following the herd behavior by international investors during the Brazilian presidential election, which led to the first administration of President Luiz Inácio Lula da Silva (Figure 12.3). The accumulation of international reserves since then has allowed BCRP to rely more on sterilized foreign exchange operations during negative shock periods.

## *The Inflation Forecasting System*

The BCRP's inflation forecasting model explicitly takes into account the effects of dollarization on the effectiveness of monetary policy (Armas and Grippa 2006; Quispe and Rossini 2010). This is done by specifying explicit equations for aggregate demand (IS curve) and the exchange rate in addition to the Phillips curve and monetary policy rule equations often used by conventional inflation-targeting central banks. The description of these equations is summarized by Armas and Grippa (2006) as follows:

- The output gap equation, which reflects aggregate demand pressure, has the bilateral real exchange rate and foreign currency interest rate, among others, as explanatory variables. The rationale for including the bilateral real exchange rate is to capture the potential balance sheet effects of large movements in the exchange rate. On the other hand, the foreign currency interest rate is included to capture its impact on consumption and investment decisions in a partially dollarized economy.
- The exchange rate equation relates the spot exchange rate movements to the domestic currency interest rates and foreign currency interest rate, a risk premium, and an inertia term to capture the effects of foreign exchange interventions. Although the exchange rate has a separate equation, it is not directly included in the monetary policy rule equation, implying that monetary policy responds to exchange rate movements only to the extent that it has an impact on inflation (through imported inflation and the effect on the output gap).

## *Controlling the Risks of Financial Dollarization*

The BCRP controls the risks of dollarization—that is, liquidity and foreign exchange risks—through sterilized foreign exchange interventions and active management of reserve requirements on dollar liabilities.

*Foreign exchange intervention.* The BCRP states that the main purpose of its foreign exchange intervention is to contain exchange rate volatility and accumulate international reserves (Rossini, Armas, and Quispe 2014). This implies that the intervention is aimed at avoiding large changes in the exchange rate to prevent balance sheet effects in a partially dollarized economy. Interventions are conducted mostly by buying and selling dollars in the spot market, and in some instances by carrying out swaps and reverse swaps and selling dollar-indexed certificates of deposits. Empirical studies show that the central bank's foreign exchange interventions are effective in containing volatility (Tashu 2014). As a result, Peru's exchange rate has been the most stable among financially open large economies in Latin America (Figure 12.4a).

Foreign exchange intervention has also allowed the BCRP to accumulate the highest level of international reserves (in percent of GDP) in the region. At about 32 percent of GDP, and representing more than five times short-term external debt at end-2013, Peru's level of net international reserves is adequate by any metric (Figure 12.4b). The BCRP considers this as an important self-insurance for the economy against risks associated with partial dollarization.

*Reserve requirement.* Peru has a long history of using reserve requirements. Differential reserve requirements on foreign currency deposits and local currency deposits (higher reserve requirements on foreign currency deposits) have been used since the 1990s to facilitate dedollarization by increasing the cost of financial intermediation in foreign currency. Reserve requirements on foreign currency liabilities are also used as a prudential instrument against foreign currency liquidity and credit risks in the context of partial dollarization. High reserve requirements on foreign currency liabilities have helped to create a liquidity buffer, which is important because the central bank cannot act as a lender of last resort in foreign currency. The buffer is part of the central bank's international foreign currency reserves; it constitutes about 20 percent of total net international reserves (Armas, Castillo, and Vega 2014). The contribution of private banks to the international reserves also helps minimize the moral hazard problem often associated with banks' suboptimal risk assessment in the presence of large international reserves.

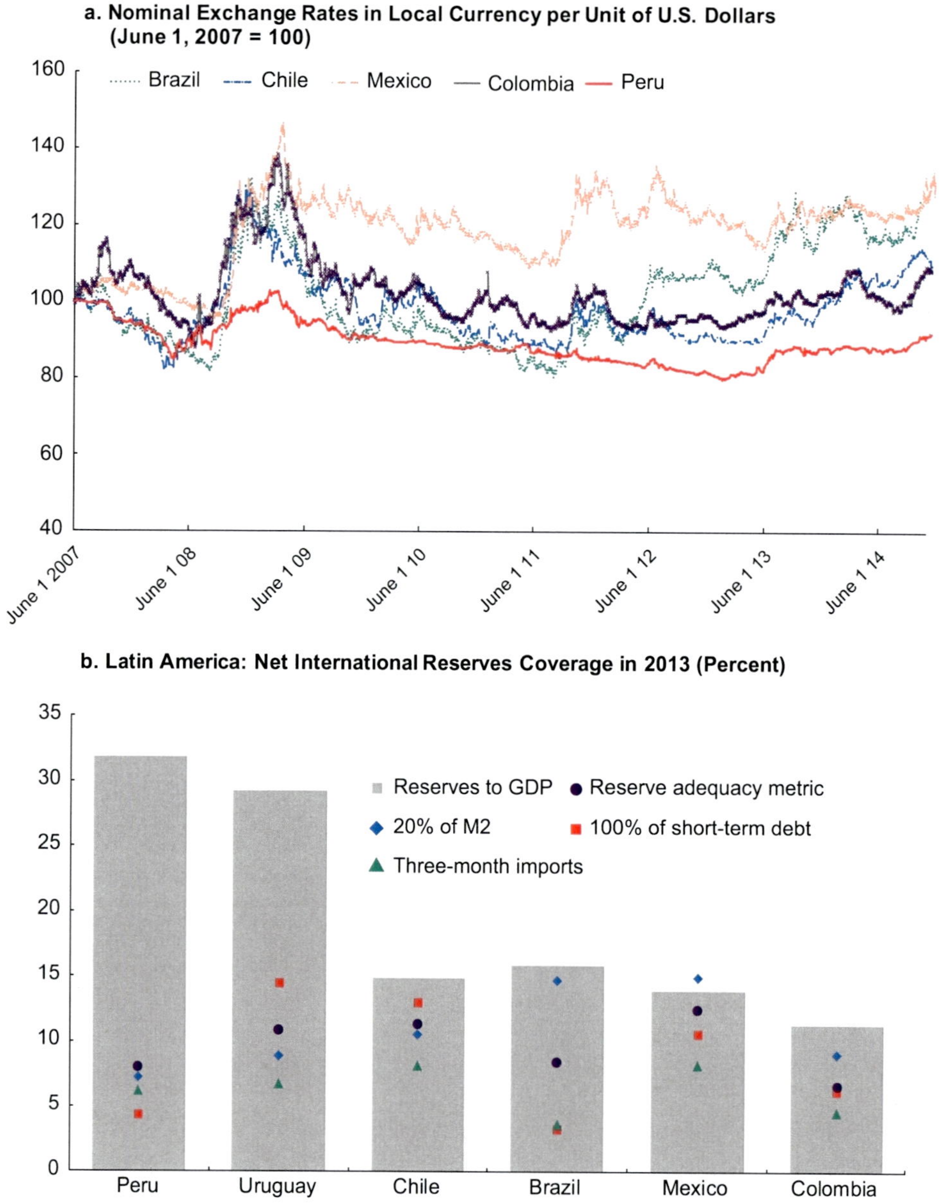


Sources: Haver Analytics; IMF, Reserve Adequency database; and IMF staff calculations.

**Figure 12.4** Exchange Rates and Reserve Adequacy in Selected Latin American Economies

In recent years, reserve requirements have also been used as a countercyclical credit-controlling tool in the face of surges in capital inflows.[5] Faced with the challenges of the global financial cycle (easy money) from 2010 to early 2013, which threatened to compromise the independence and effectiveness of conventional monetary policy in emerging market economies,[6] the BCRP used reserve requirements as the first line of defense. The use of reserve requirements has helped the central bank overcome the trade-off between managing capital flows and controlling inflation or overheating risks. Changes in the reserve requirement are expected to affect credit growth, and hence overheating risks, through at least two channels:

- First, reserve requirements affect supply for credit through their impact on banks' loanable funds and liquidity.
- Second, reserve requirements affect demand for credit by raising lending rates. High reserve requirements reduce banks' financial margin, and banks may in turn raise their lending rate (or reduce deposit rates) to preserve their margins. Empirical analysis by Armas, Castillo, and Vega (2014) provides statistical evidence that reserve requirement changes made in 2010 were successful in increasing lending rates, reducing deposit rates, and reducing credit growth.

### *Lessons from Peru's Experience*

Peru's experience with inflation targeting shows that effective monetary policy is possible under partial dollarization. However, the design of the inflation-targeting framework needs to take into account the risks of dollarization. Armas and Grippa (2006) and Rossini, Armas, and Quispe (2014) argue that the BCRP's success in controlling the foreign exchange and liquidity risks associated with partial dollarization through sterilized foreign exchange intervention and the use of reserve requirements is key to the effectiveness of Peru's inflation-targeting framework.

## ASSESSING THE EFFECTIVENESS OF PERU'S INFLATION-TARGETING POLICY

The success of an inflation-targeting framework can be assessed by its effectiveness in reducing the level of inflation, reducing inflation and output volatility, anchoring inflation expectations, limiting the exchange rate pass-through to consumer prices, and limiting the foreign interest rate pass-through to local interest rates. The empirical difficulty in making such assessments is finding a valid counterfactual. There are two options often used by empirical studies: the country's own history prior to implementation of the policy, and other countries that have not implemented inflation targeting. Both of these comparators are used in this study.

For Peru's preinflation-targeting history, the sample period is limited to 1992–2001, as the period prior to 1992 was characterized by high levels of macroeconomic volatility, including hyperinflation. Since the objective of monetary policy during 1992–2001 was reducing and stabilizing inflation through the control of monetary aggregates, this analysis could be equivalent to comparing the effectiveness of the inflation-targeting regime relative to the monetary-targeting

[5]Surges in capital inflows are often associated with excessive credit growth and overheating risks. A monetary policy response to such overheating risks—by raising the policy rate—may not be effective because high interest rates can attract further capital inflows. Financial dollarization amplifies the ineffectiveness of conventional monetary policy during such episodes, as demand for credit can switch to foreign currency, which does not respond to changes in the monetary policy rate, as the depreciation of the foreign currency and the very low international interest rate make foreign currency credits cheaper.

[6]Rey (2013) argues that exchange rate flexibility cannot insulate economies from the global financial cycle, and that independent monetary policies are possible if and only if the capital account is managed directly or indirectly. The author recommends capital controls, macroprudential policies, and limits on leverage by financial intermediaries as instruments to weaken the potency of the global financial cycle.

**TABLE 12.2**

**Impact of Inflation Targeting**

| | Percent of Deposit Dollarization | | Average Level of Inflation | | Inflation Volatility | | Growth Volatility[1] | |
|---|---|---|---|---|---|---|---|---|
| | 2001–02 | 2012–13 | 1992–2001 | 2002–13 | 1992–2001 | 2002–13 | 1992–2001 | 2002–13 |
| Latin American Inflation Targeters | | | | | | | | |
| *Peru* | *71.3* | *39.0* | *19.9* | *2.9* | *3.1* | *0.7* | *9.7* | *2.8* |
| Brazil[2] | — | — | 268.8 | 6.0 | ... | 2.2 | 5.1 | 3.6 |
| Chile | — | — | 5.2 | 3.2 | 0.6 | 1.1 | 3.4 | 4.0 |
| Colombia | — | — | 10.5 | 4.5 | 2.0 | 0.5 | 1.1 | 1.0 |
| Mexico | — | — | 10.0 | 4.2 | 44.5 | 1.2 | 5.6 | 2.8 |
| Financially Dollarized Economies | | | | | | | | |
| Minimum | 51.2 | 34.5 | 11.9 | 2.4 | 1.2 | 0.7 | — | 2.8 |
| Median | 67.7 | 47.8 | 52.2 | 5.4 | 7.3 | 6.1 | — | 4.6 |
| Maximum | 86.7 | 72.7 | 1,037.5 | 10.3 | 381.8 | 12.2 | — | 18.8 |

Source: Authors' calculations based on data from various sources.
[1] Many of the dollarized economies do not have sufficient data prior to 2001.
[2] Inflation volatility was not computed for 1992–2001 due to the hyperinflation during the first half of the 1990s. Inflation volatility for 2002–13 is computed based a generalized autoregressive conditional heteroskedasticity model on the sample 1996:Q1–2014:Q2.

regime. However, it is important to underline that some of the results could be biased because the starting point for the two regimes was different. While the monetary-targeting regime was introduced at a time of high inflation, the inflation-targeting regime was introduced at a time when inflation was already low and the central bank had an established reputation. In addition, the BCRP made changes in the design of its monetary framework in order to be able to adopt an inflation-targeting regime. For instance, the central bank began to announce an annual inflation target in 1994, and it started making changes in its monetary procedures in 1997 to allow for future stabilization of the interbank rate.

For noninflation-targeting comparator countries, the prevalence of financial dollarization around the time when Peru implemented the inflation-targeting framework is used as a key criterion. The purpose is to assess the effectiveness of Peru's inflation-targeting framework in the context of financial dollarization. In this regard, the selected economies are taken as a proxy for the counterfactual of Peru's inflation-targeting implementation. Consequently, seven emerging market economies (Bulgaria, Croatia, Georgia, Macedonia, Paraguay, Turkey, Uruguay) were selected based on availability of quarterly data on inflation and growth and the closeness of their degree of financial dollarization in 2001–02 to that of Peru. None of these countries are inflation targeters except Turkey, which introduced an inflation-targeting framework in 2006, and Paraguay, which introduced inflation targeting in 2013.

In addition, the performance of Peru's inflation-targeting framework is compared with other frameworks in the region, including those of Brazil, Chile, Colombia, and Mexico, to determine if financial dollarization affected the relative performance of Peru's inflation-targeting framework.

## Reducing the Level and Volatility of Inflation

Peru's level of inflation was already almost at zero when the inflation-targeting framework was implemented. However, this was mainly due to an aggregate demand shock, reflecting the impact of successive external shocks (the Asian crisis in 1997, the Russian/Brazilian crisis in 1998–99, and the Argentine crisis in 2001). However, a comparison of the average level of Peru's inflation in the decades before and after implementation of the inflation-targeting framework shows a clear indication of the effectiveness of the framework. Peru's inflation during 1992–2001 averaged about 20 percent, second highest among regional comparators only to Brazil, which suffered hyperinflation in the first half of the 1990s (Table 12.2).

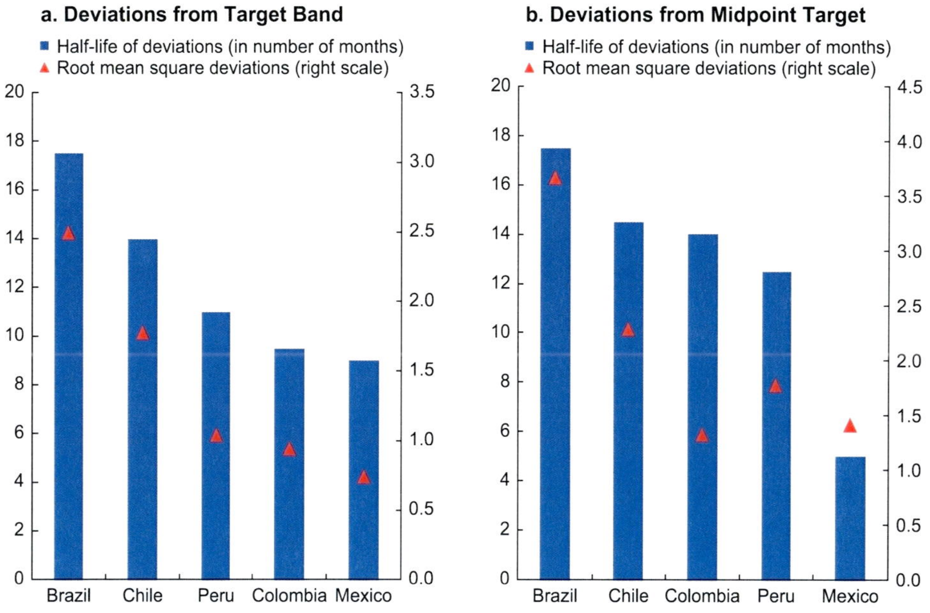


Source: Haver Analytics; IMF desk reports; and authors' estimates.

**Figure 12.5** Inflation Devations from Cantral Bank Targets in Latin America, 2002–13

Following implementation of the inflation-targeting framework, Peru's average yearly inflation fell to 2.9 percent in 2002–13, within the central bank's target range, and has been the lowest in the region and one of the lowest among financially dollarized economies. Deviations of annual inflation from the central bank's target have been limited to the effects of temporary supply-side and exogenous shocks.

Measured by the root mean square deviations of year-over-year monthly inflation from the central bank's target rates during 2002–13, the performance of Peru's inflation-targeting framework is average by regional standards. The root mean square deviations of Peru's inflation, both from the midpoint and band targets of the central bank, are lower than those of Brazil and Chile, but higher than those of Colombia and Mexico. The persistence or the half-life of inflation deviations in Peru is estimated at about 11 months for deviations from the target band and about 12½ months for deviations from the midpoint target, which are shorter than that of Brazil and Chile but longer than that of Mexico (comparison with Colombia is mixed) (Figure 12.5).[7]

Comparing Peru's volatility of inflation and output during the inflation-targeting period with its record during the decade prior to the introduction of the inflation-targeting framework, and with the records of comparator groups, also points to the potential effectiveness of Peru's framework.[8] The volatility of both inflation and growth in Peru declined following the introduction of the inflation-targeting framework and were the lowest among regional inflation targeters and noninflation-targeting, financially dollarized economies after introduction of the framework (Table 12.2).

[7]The half-life of inflation deviations is estimated from a vector autoregression model of each country's inflation deviations, following Murray and Papell (2002), over the sample period 2002–13 (monthly data). A vector autoregression model was used, instead of a simple AR(1) or an augmented Dicky-Fuller specification, due to a higher order of autocorrelation in inflation deviations.

[8]The volatility, of inflation and growth, was computed based on a generalized autoregressive conditional heteroskedasticity (1, 1) model for individual countries.

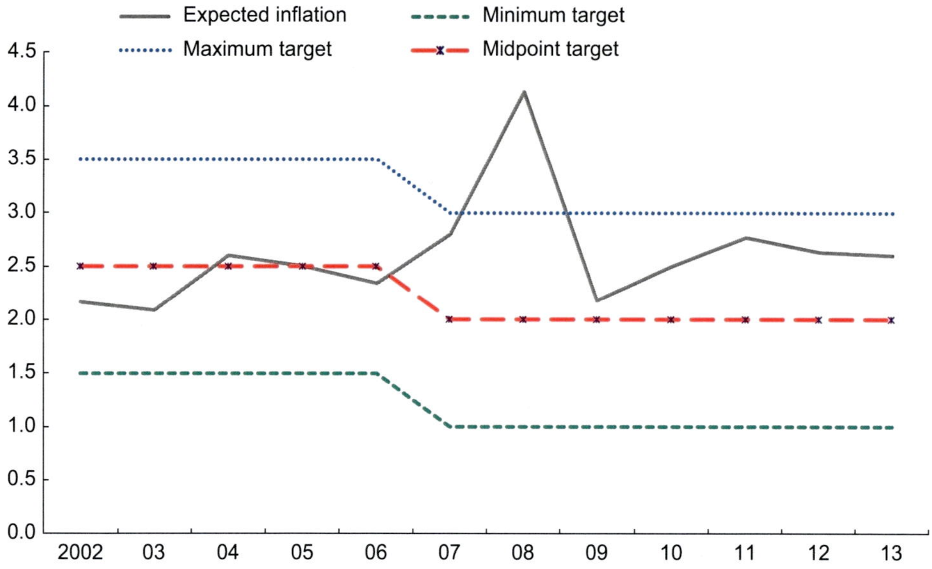


Source: Central Reserve Bank of Peru.

**Figure 12.6** Peru: Inflation Targeting and Expectations *(Percent)*

Following introduction of the inflation-targeting framework, another noticeable development in Peru was the significant reduction in the rate of financial dollarization. At the time when the inflation-targeting framework was introduced, Peru had one of the highest rates of financial dollarization among the group of selected financially dollarized economies. Following the introduction of the framework, however, Peru recorded the sharpest rate of reduction (45 percent decrease) in financial dollarization between 2001–02 and 2012–13. Today, it has among the lowest rates of financial dollarization among the same group of countries. Inflation targeting might have contributed to Peru's relative success in reducing financial dollarization, although it is not possible to attribute the success solely to inflation targeting because other measures, including the development of a local currency securities market and increased exchange rate flexibility, were implemented concurrently.

## Anchoring Inflation Expectations

Peru's inflation-targeting framework has successfully anchored inflation expectations. With the exception of 2008, following the global commodity price shock, inflation expectations have for the most part been well anchored within the central bank's target range (Figure 12.6).

### *Containing Exchange Rate and Interest Rate Pass-Through*

A vector autoregression model estimation of inflation with the exchange rate, the output gap, and international prices[9] shows that the pass-through of the exchange rate to consumer prices abated following the introduction of the inflation-targeting framework. In particular, the exchange rate

[9]The sample period is 1992:Q1–2001:Q4 for the preinflation-targeting period, and 2002:Q1–2014:Q2 for the post-inflation-targeting period. For the impulse response function, the variables were ordered as follows: international prices, exchange rate, output gap, and the domestic consumer price index. To ensure stationarity, all variables except the output gap are expressed as first differences (growth rates over the previous quarter). International prices refer to prices of oil and food. In the first sample (the preinflation-targeting period), the world price of oil was found to be statistically more important (significant), whereas the world price of food became more important in the second sample (the postinflation-targeting period). Statistically insignificant world prices were dropped from the corresponding models to save degrees of freedom, since the sample sizes are already short.

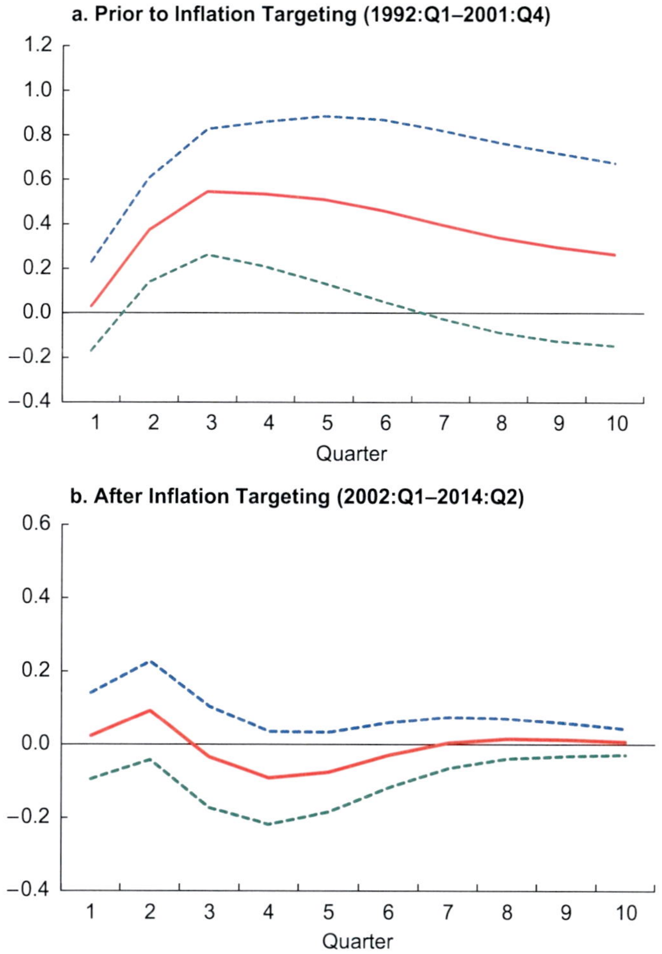


Source: Authors' calculations.

**Figure 12.7** Responses of Inflation to Cholesky One Standard Deviation Innovations of Changes in the Exchange Rate with a 95 Percent Confidence Interval

had a positive and statistically significant impact on inflation in the sample prior to implementation of the inflation-targeting framework, but not in the sample after implementation of the framework (Figure 12.7). Using a rolling vector autoregression model, Winkelried (2014) also shows a significant reduction in the exchange rate pass-through after introduction of inflation targeting in Peru.

Although there is no sufficient interest rate data for a regression analysis prior to the inflation-targeting framework, a graphical presentation shows a clear break in the relationship between the local currency and foreign currency domestic interest rates following implementation of the framework (Figure 12.8). Before implementation of the inflation-targeting framework, the local currency interbank interest rate was very volatile and comoved with the foreign currency interbank interest rate, which in turn is driven by external factors. Following introduction of the inflation-targeting framework, however, the local currency interbank interest rate became very stable, comoving with the central bank's reference rate, while the foreign currency interbank rate continued to be volatile and vulnerable to external shocks. This provides clear evidence of the effectiveness of Peru's inflation-targeting framework in stabilizing local currency interest rates by providing an anchor, that is, the reference rate.

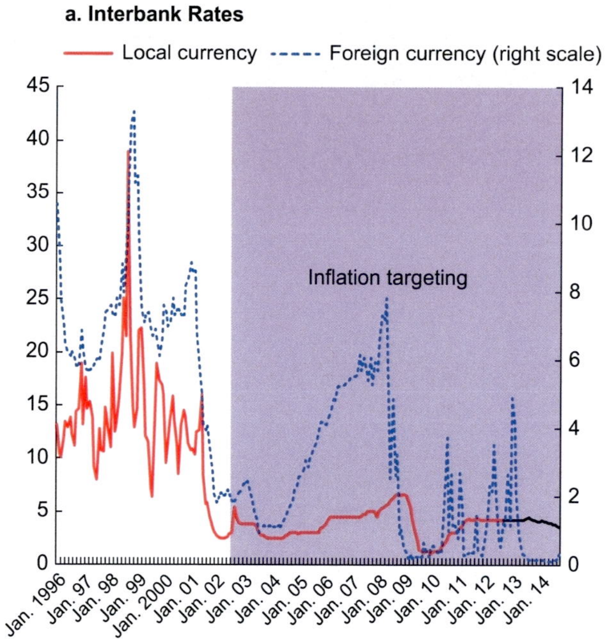


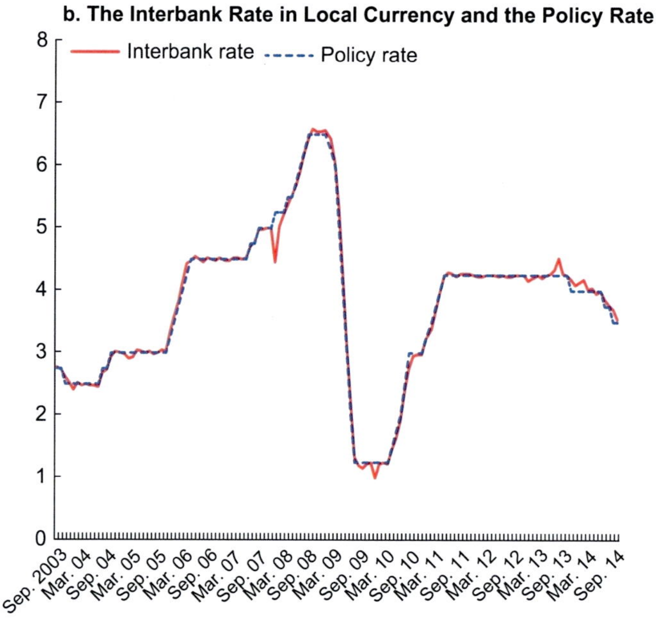


Source: Central Reserve Bank of Peru.

**Figure 12.8** Peru: Interest Rates *(Percent)*

## CONCLUSIONS

This chapter has attempted to draw lessons for an optimal monetary policy design in a partially dollarized economy based on a literature review and the experience of Peru. The chapter also assessed the effectiveness of Peru's inflation-targeting framework.

The empirical assessment shows that Peru's inflation-targeting framework has succeeded in anchoring inflation expectations, reducing inflation and output volatility, and reducing the exchange rate pass-through to domestic prices and the foreign interest rate pass-through to local currency domestic interest rates. The performance of Peru's inflation-targeting framework is comparable to that of nondollarized inflation-targeting frameworks in the region, indicating that the BCRP has successfully overcome the limitations of financial dollarization with regard to conducting independent monetary policy.

The design of Peru's inflation-targeting framework, however, differs from conventional inflation-targeting frameworks in that it explicitly takes into account the risks of partial dollarization. It has been implemented in conjunction with sterilized foreign exchange intervention and reserve requirements on foreign currency liability to contain the foreign exchange and liquidity risks associated with financial dollarization.

The lessons from Peru's experience are that (1) effective monetary policy can be challenging, but is possible in a partially dollarized economy; and (2) foreign exchange intervention can be consistent with and complementary to inflation targeting in a partially dollarized economy.

## REFERENCES

Alvarez-Plata, Patricia, and Alicia García-Herrero. 2008. "To Dollarize or De-dollarize: Consequences for Monetary Policy." DIW Berlin Discussion Paper 842, German Institute for Economic Research, Berlin, Germany.

Armas, Adrián, Nicoletta Batini, and Vicente Tuesta. 2007. "Peru's Experience with Partial Dollarization and Inflation Targeting." Working Paper No. 2014-0003, Central Reserve Bank of Peru, Lima, Peru.

Armas, Adrián, Paul Castillo, and Marco Vega. 2014. "Inflation Targeting and Quantitative Tightening: Effects of Reserve Requirements in Peru." Country Report No. 07/53, International Monetary Fund, Washington, DC.

Armas, Adrián, and Francisco Grippa. 2006. "Inflation Targeting in a Dollarized Economy: The Peruvian Experience." In *Financial Dollarization: The Policy Agenda*, edited by Adrián Armas, Alain Ize, and Eduardo Levy-Yeyati. New York: Palgrave MacMillan.

Armas, Adrián, Francisco Grippa, Zenón Quispe, and Luis Valdivia. 2001. "De metas monetarias a metas de inflación en una economía con dolarización parcial: el caso Peruano." Economic Study No. 7, Central Reserve Bank of Peru, Lima, Peru.

Baliño, Tomás J. T., Adam Bennett, and Eduardo Borensztein. 1999. *Monetary Policy in Dollarized Economies.* Occasional Paper 171. Washington, DC: International Monetary Fund.

Batini, Nicoletta, Paul Levine, and Joseph Pearlman. 2008. "Optimal Exchange Rate Stabilization in a Dollarized Economy with Inflation Targets." Working Paper 2008-004, Central Reserve Bank of Peru, Lima, Peru.

Central Reserve Bank of Peru. 2013. "Inflation Report: Recent Trends and Macroeconomic Forecasts 2013-2015." Lima, September.

De Nicoló, Gianni, Patrick Honohan, and Alain Ize. 2003. "Dollarization of the Banking System: Good or Bad?" Working Paper 03/146, International Monetary Fund, Washington, DC.

García, Carlos J., Jorge E. Restrepo, and Scott Roger. 2011. "How Much Should Inflation Targeters Care about the Exchange Rate?" *Journal of International Money and Finance* 30: 1590–617.

Ize, Alain. 2013. "Financial Dollarization." In *The Evidence and Impact of Financial Globalization*, edited by Gerard Caprio, Jr. Boston: Elsevier.

———, and Eduardo Levy-Yeyati. 2003. "Financial Dollarization." *Journal of International Economics* 59: 323–47.

Leiderman, Leonardo, Rodolfo Maino, and Eric Parrado. 2006. "Inflation Targeting in Dollarized Economies." In *Financial Dollarization: The Policy Agenda*, edited by Adrián Armas, Alain Ize, and Eduardo Levy-Yeyati. New York: International Monetary Fund and Palgrave MacMillan.

Murray, Christian J., and David H. Papell. 2002. "The Purchasing Power Parity Persistence Paradigm." *Journal of International Economics* 56: 1–19.

Quispe, Zenón. 2000. "Monetary Policy in a Dollarized Economy." In *Monetary Policy Frameworks in a Global Context,* edited by Lavan Mahadeva and Gabriel Sterne. London and New York: Bank of England and Routledge.

———, and Renzo Rossini. 2010. "Monetary Policy During the Global Financial Crisis of 2007-09: The Case of Peru." BIS Paper 54, Bank for International Settlements, Basel, Switzerland.

Reinhart, Carmen M., Kenneth Rogoff, and Miguel Savastano. 2003. "Addicted to Dollars." NBER Working Paper 10015, National Bureau of Economic Research, Cambridge, Massachusetts.

Rey, Hélène. 2013. "Dilemma not Trilemma: The Global Financial Cycle and Monetary Policy Independence." Paper presented at the Jackson Hole Economic Symposium. http://www.kansascityfed.org/publicat/sympos/2013/2013Rey.pdf.

Rossini, Renzo, Adrián Armas, and Zenón Quispe. 2014. "Global Policy Spillovers and Peru's Monetary Policy: Inflation Targeting, Foreign Exchange Intervention and Reserve Requirements." BIS Paper No. 78, Bank for International Settlements, Basel, Switzerland.

Tashu, Melesse. 2014. "Motives and Effectiveness of Forex Interventions: Evidence from Peru." Working Paper 14/127, International Monetary Fund, Washington, DC.

Winkelried, Diego. 2014. "Exchange Rate Pass-through and Inflation Targeting in Peru." *Empirical Economics* 46 (4): 1181–196.

CHAPTER 13

# Global Policy Spillovers and Peru's Monetary Policy: Inflation Targeting, Foreign Exchange Intervention, and Reserve Requirements

RENZO ROSSINI, ADRIÁN ARMAS, AND ZENÓN QUISPE

*This chapter provides an overview of the monetary policy actions undertaken by the Central Reserve Bank of Peru (Banco Central de Reserva del Perú [BCRP]) that combined its main inflation-targeting framework with sterilized foreign exchange interventions and reserve requirement measures.[1] The aim was to overcome the spillover effects of global policies in order to counter the recessionary implications of the global financial crisis. The chapter provides a rationale for the use of these instruments, as well as empirical evidence on their effectiveness. In general, the results show that sterilized foreign exchange interventions and reserve requirement changes have had the desired effects in limiting spillover effects and smoothing out the interest rate and credit dynamics in dual monetary economies such as Peru.*

As a policy response to the macroeconomic challenges brought about by financial dollarization and its implications for financial vulnerability, the BCRP adopted an inflation-targeting regime in 2002 and became the first monetary authority to implement this framework under a dual monetary system.

Inflation targeting in Peru has a particular design. The BCRP actively intervenes in the foreign exchange market to smooth out exchange rate fluctuations and build international reserves as a self-insurance mechanism against negative external shocks. Since 2008, reserve requirements have been used as an active monetary control tool to moderate the impact of capital flows on domestic credit conditions in both domestic and foreign currency. The BCRP has also set high reserve requirements on foreign currency liabilities as a prudential tool to address liquidity issues and foreign currency credit risk. These additional policy tools have eased the trade-offs that the BCRP faces when implementing standard monetary measures within an inflation-targeting regime that simultaneously takes into account financial dollarization considerations.

The prompt use of reserve requirements in Peru's monetary policy framework has allowed the BCRP to induce the necessary quantitative tightening required to address the domestic spillover effects of the unprecedented quantitative easing (QE) policies implemented by developed countries.

This chapter describes the relevance of reserve requirements as a complementary instrument for monetary policy based on Peru's experience. The chapter starts by providing an overview of Peru's monetary framework, including standard interest rate setting. Next, it evaluates the general implications of the spillover effects of global quantitative monetary policy and examines sterilized foreign exchange intervention. The discussion then turns to the use of reserve requirements as a monetary policy tool, the transmission mechanism of reserve requirement changes, and the control of financial dollarization risks as well as liquidity risks. Finally, the empirical evaluation of reserve requirements policies is carried out and conclusions are presented.

[1]The reserve requirement overview and evaluation is based on Armas, Castillo, and Vega (2014).

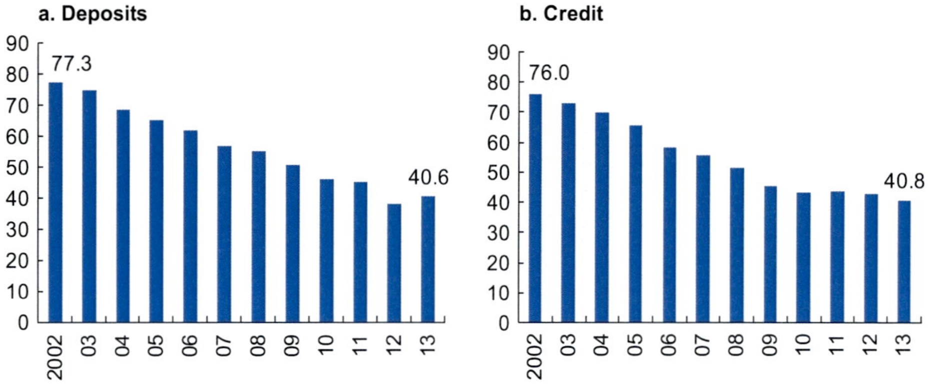


Source: Central Reserve Bank of Peru.

**Figure 13.1** Dollarization Ratios *(Percentage of total)*

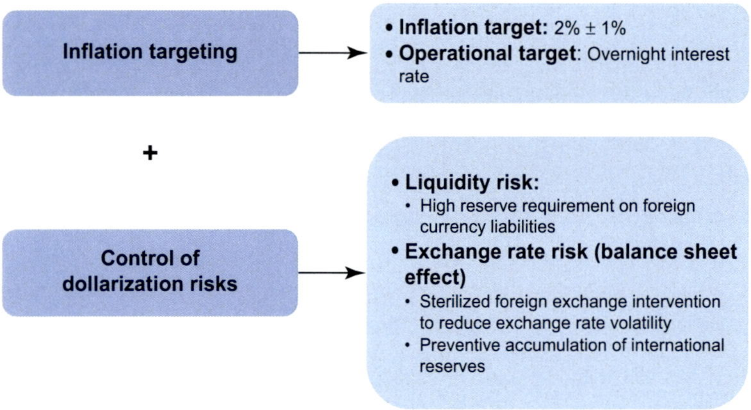


Source: Central Reserve Bank of Peru.

**Figure 13.2** The Inflation-Targeting Plus Dollarization Risk-Control Framework in Peru

## THE MONETARY POLICY FRAMEWORK

In place since 2002, Peru's current monetary policy framework is best characterized as a full-fledged inflation-targeting regime that explicitly takes into account the risks created by financial dollarization. Figure 13.1 shows Peru's high level of financial dollarization. The inflation target is a 2 percent annual increase in the consumer price index, with a tolerance band ranging from 1 percent to 3 percent. Before the adoption of inflation targeting, monetary policy in Peru was implemented through a monetary target framework that used the annual growth rate of the monetary base as an intermediate target and also included instruments such as foreign exchange intervention and high reserve requirements for deposits in foreign currency.

When inflation targeting was adopted, the aforementioned policy tools used to address financial dollarization risks remained in place (Figure 13.2). Webb and Armas (2003) and Armas and Grippa (2005) defined the implementation of the inflation-targeting framework in a financially dollarized economy as a combination of standard interest rate rule setting plus the active use of other instruments to control financial risks.

Since 2008, reserve requirements have been changed frequently to complement changes in the policy interest rate. The main reason for this new role for reserve requirements was the

Source: Armas, Castillo, and Vega (2014).

**Figure 13.3** Quantitative Easing and Quantitative Tightening

unprecedented expansionary monetary policies launched in developed economies, which triggered the zero lower bound for their policy interest rates and the implementation of QE. The central banks of emerging economies had to respond with different actions to deal with the spillover effects of these ultra-easy policies, mainly capital inflows and low international interest rates. Figure 13.3 summarizes the different economic cycles and policy responses of both developed and emerging economies during the QE period.

Since 2008, changes in the marginal and average reserve requirement ratios have been used cyclically in tune with the challenges posed by the new international environment. Reserve requirements have been raised in response to capital inflow episodes, such as in the first quarter of 2008, and then in the second half of 2010, following the announcement of QE:2. Reserve requirements were tightened with the aim of offsetting the impact of capital inflows on credit (particularly in dollars), which also gave the BCRP increased capacity to inject foreign currency liquidity in case of sudden capital flight. Despite Peru's high degree of financial dollarization, this policy framework has proven to be effective in dampening financial risks. In contrast to what happened during the Russian crisis, when a sudden stop in capital flows triggered a credit crunch, Peru's BCRP was better prepared in 2008: high international reserves and higher reserve requirements allowed a massive injection of liquidity into the system and prevented another credit crunch.

Figure 13.4 illustrates how the use of nonconventional monetary policy tools complements the use of the policy rate. Interventions in the foreign exchange market aimed at offsetting excessive exchange rate volatility reduce systemic risks associated with sharp exchange rate depreciations, whereas the use of high and cyclical reserve requirements in foreign currency contributes to curbing systemic liquidity risks associated with financial dollarization.

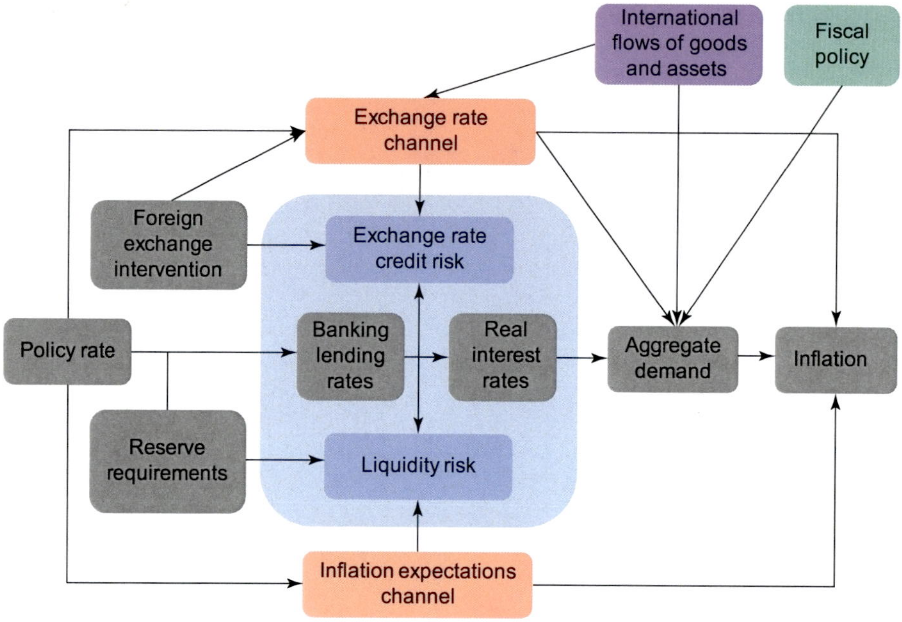


Source: Central Reserve Bank of Peru.

**Figure 13.4** Peru's Monetary Policy Framework

## Standard Interest Rate Setting under Peru's Inflation Targeting, 2002–12

The operational target of monetary policy is the short-term interest rate. Like any other central bank with an inflation-targeting regime, the BCRP uses this operational target to deliver the monetary policy stance to the market. A central bank tends to increase its policy interest rate to fight inflationary pressures during periods of high inflation or output gap levels; conversely, when inflation is below the central bank's target and the output gap is negative, the central bank tends to cut its policy rate. However, in a financially dollarized economy, interest rate setting also has to take into account how financial dollarization affects the transmission mechanism of monetary policy. The BCRP addresses this issue by using an inflation forecasting model (*Modelo de Proyección Trimestral*) that explicitly takes into account the impact of dollarization on credit market conditions and on the dynamics of the exchange rate and inflation (Winkelried 2013). In this model, dollarization reduces the impact of monetary policy on inflation and the output gap, since a large depreciation not only typically generates a positive impact on exports, but also triggers a negative impact on the financial position of firms with currency mismatches. Thus, with financial dollarization, the typical expansionary effect of the exchange rate channel after the implementation of a policy-easing measure is considerably reduced when there is a sharp depreciation. The expansionary net export effect will prevail over the balance sheet effect when depreciation is low. The *Modelo de Proyección Trimestral* takes into account the impact of both reserve requirement changes and interventions in the foreign exchange market on the dynamics of interest rates and the exchange rate.

Figure 13.5 shows the evolution of the policy rate, the output gap, and core inflation since 2004. As can be seen, the policy rate has actively responded to the evolution of both inflation and the output gap. In particular, this has been the case for indicators such as core inflation and inflation expectations during episodes characterized by important changes. Estimations of the policy rule for 2002–09 show that the policy rate not only meets Taylor's principle, but also that the central bank gives more importance to reducing inflation volatility than output gap volatility. The

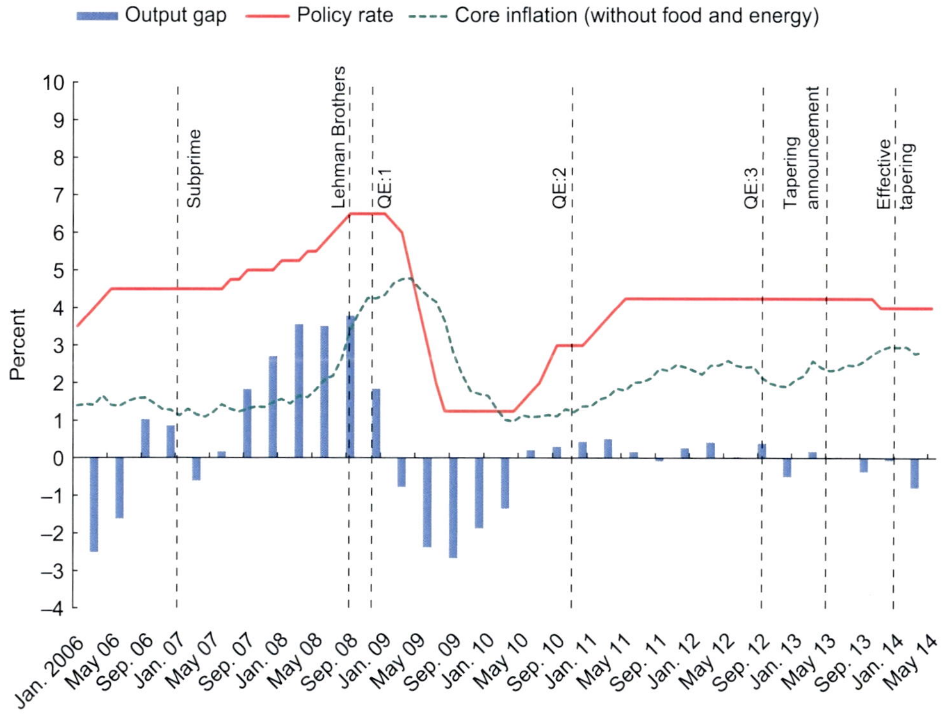


Source: Central Reserve Bank of Peru.
Note: QE = quantitative easing.

**Figure 13.5** Evolution of the Policy Rate, Output Gap, and Core Inflation

estimations reported by Salas (2011) show that the interest rate response to inflation is close to 1.9 and the response to output is close to 0.5.[2]

Two episodes clearly highlight the BCRP's active response to changes in the expected rates of inflation and the output gap. The first started in July 2007, when the central bank began to raise interest rates in response to a persistent rise in inflation. During that period, the BCRP increased its reference interest rate eight times, from 4.5 percent to 6.5 percent (a total of 200 basis points). The second episode followed the collapse of Lehman Brothers in the United States. The BCRP cut the policy interest rate aggressively, from 6.5 percent to 1.25 percent in six months. The policy rates cuts were effective in reducing interest rates not only in the money market, but also in the rest of the financial system. For example, the average interest rate on loans with maturities up to 360 days fell from 15.5 percent to 11.1 percent between January and December 2009.

## GLOBAL POLICY SPILLOVERS AND THE PERUVIAN CAPITAL MARKET

The collapse of Lehman Brothers ushered in the spread of the subprime crisis to emerging economies, first through higher yields on emerging sovereign bonds, which in the case of Peru were around 10 percent for a few weeks (Figure 13.6). That was the first stress test for sovereign bonds, which began to be used in Peru at the same time as the inflation-targeting scheme.

[2]These values correspond to the mode of the posterior distribution of the parameters. The corresponding confidence intervals located these parameters between 1.23 and 2.4 for the case of the interest rate response to core inflation and between 0.3 and 0.6 for the case of the output gap.

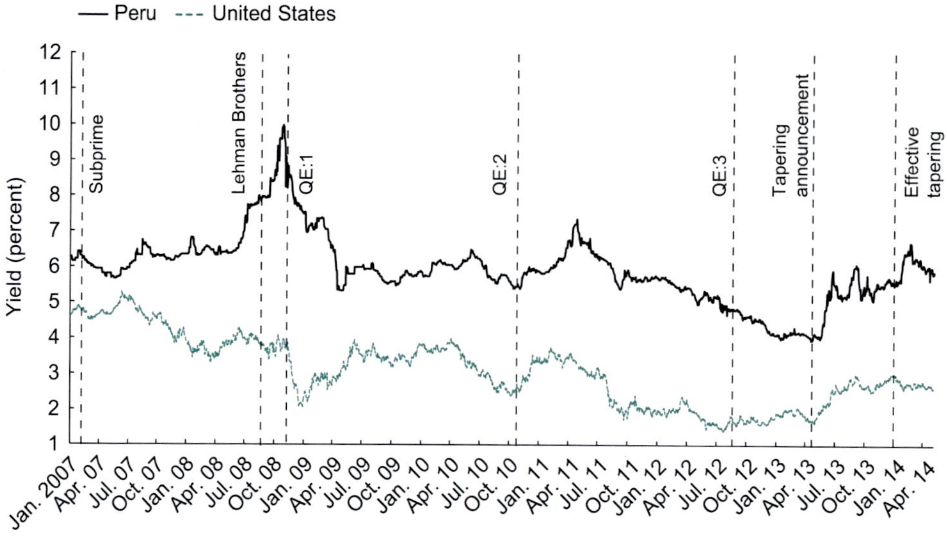


Sources: Central Reserve Bank of Peru; and the Federal Reserve System.
Note: QE = quantitative easing.

**Figure 13.6** Ten-year Sovereign Bond Yield Curves in Peru and the United States *(Percent)*

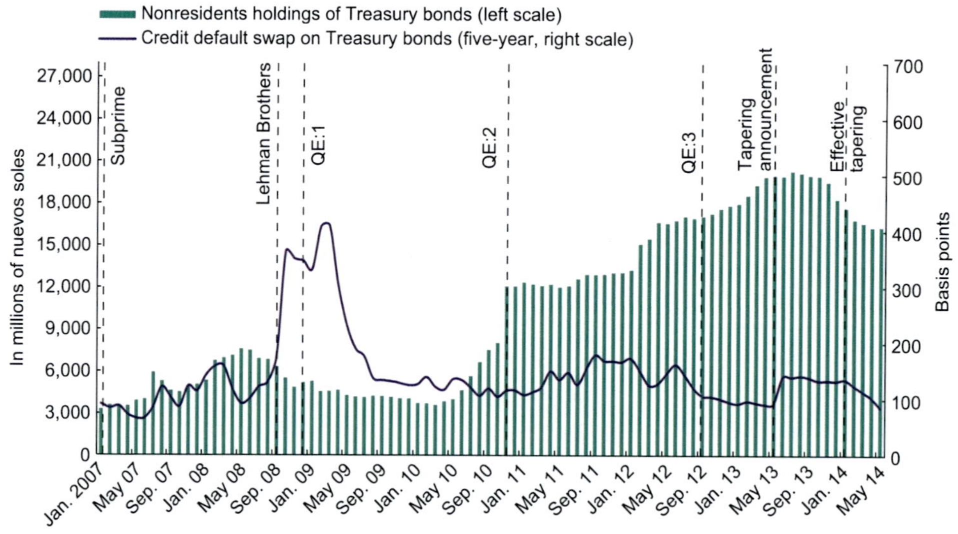


Source: Central Reserve Bank of Peru.
Note: QE = quantitative easing.

**Figure 13.7** Nonresidents' Holdings of Peruvian Treasury Bonds, and Credit Default Swap Spreads

The QE policy led in the developed world by the Federal Reserve generated capital flows toward emerging market economies, attracted by the nominal rates on domestic Treasury bonds. This trend was clear in Peru starting in October 2010, with the Federal Reserve's QE:2, and then even clearer with QE:3 (Figure 13.7). For the first time in Peru's history, most of the holders of Treasury bonds denominated in domestic currency were foreigners.

In May 2013, with Chairman Ben Bernanke's hint that the Federal Reserve would start tapering its asset purchase program, the yield on Peru's 10-year Treasury bonds jumped from around

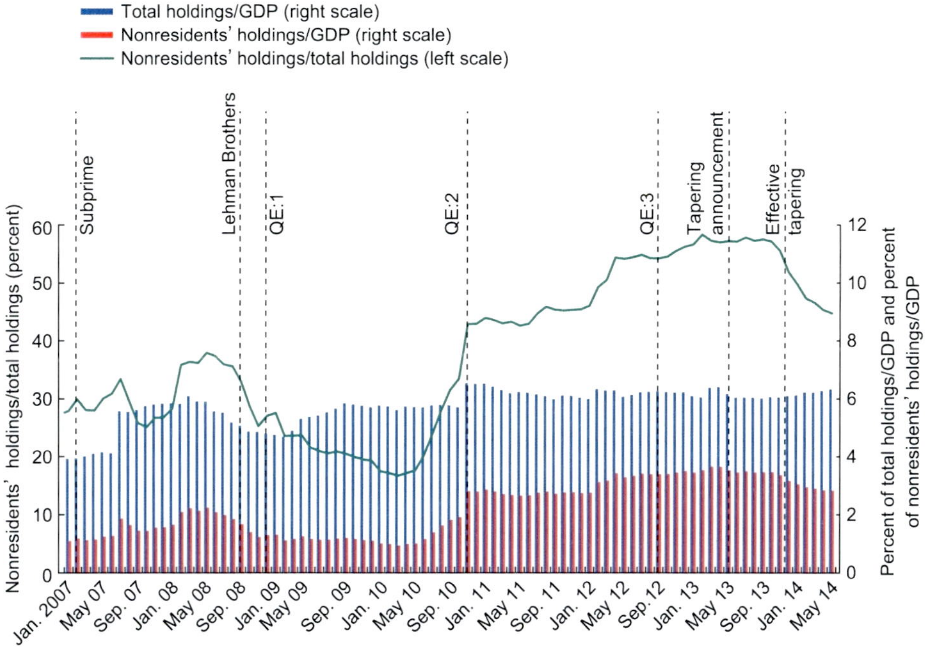


Source: Central Reserve Bank of Peru.

**Figure 13.8** Nonresidents' Holdings of Treasury Bonds in Percentages of Total Holdings and GDP

4 percent to 6 percent (Figure 13.6), with no restrictions in terms of nonresident holdings of Treasury bonds. However, after the tapering process started in January 2014, there was some movement away from sovereign bonds, despite the reduction of the corresponding credit default swap spreads (Figure 13.7).

Nonresidents' shift away from Peruvian Treasury bonds did not imply a higher risk for Peru's economy, as domestic institutional investors absorbed the remaining bonds and the fiscal position was sound (a fiscal surplus of 0.9 percent of GDP in 2013, the highest in Latin America) and very liquid (public sector deposits at the BCRP amounted to 12 percent of GDP). The government continued issuing Treasury bonds that were widely accepted by capital markets. The stock of Treasury bonds increased from 6 percent of GDP in June 2013 to 6.3 percent in May 2014 (Figure 13.8).

## STERILIZED FOREIGN EXCHANGE INTERVENTIONS

In the case of Peru, the main purpose of foreign exchange intervention is to reduce exchange rate volatility and accumulate international reserves in order to prevent balance sheet effects, given the partially dollarized financial position of the domestic private sector. Dollarization magnifies the reaction of financial intermediaries to sharp movements in their funding or high exchange rate volatility. As a result, the economy is prone to credit booms and busts associated with flows of foreign currency deposits, foreign credit lines, or other capital flows. It is also prone to exchange rate movements affecting the quality of the credit portfolio. Thus, dollarization distorts the transmission mechanism of monetary policy and increases liquidity and solvency risks within the financial system.

Foreign exchange interventions are carried out avoiding any signaling regarding the level of, or a possible ceiling or floor for, the exchange rate. They also help to reduce extreme volatilities of the exchange rate preventing balance sheet effects (Figures 13.9 and 13.10). Since the

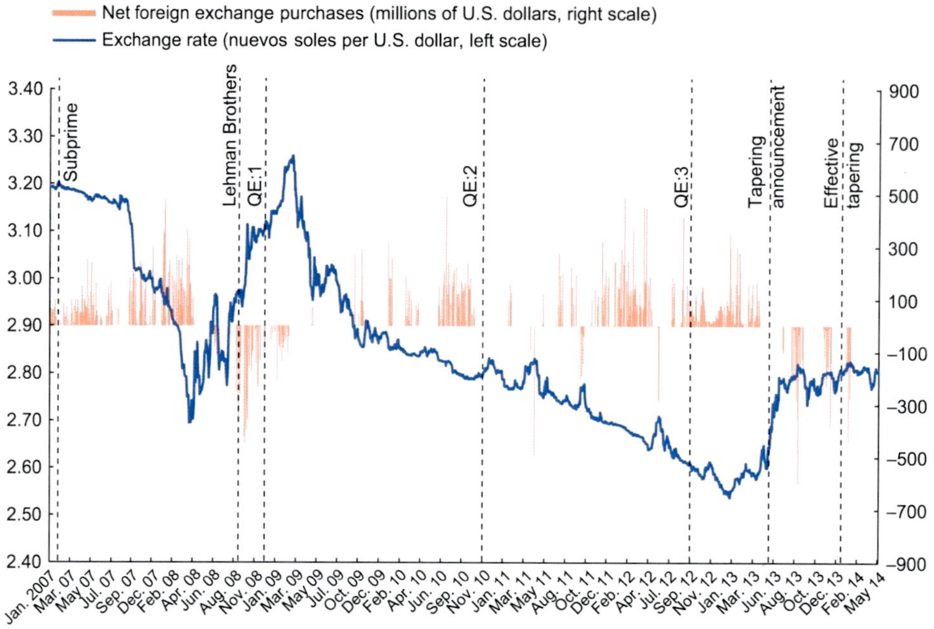


Source: Central Reserve Bank of Peru.
Note: QE = quantitative easing.

**Figure 13.9** Nominal Exchange Rate and Net Foreign Exchange Market Intervention *(U.S. dollars)*

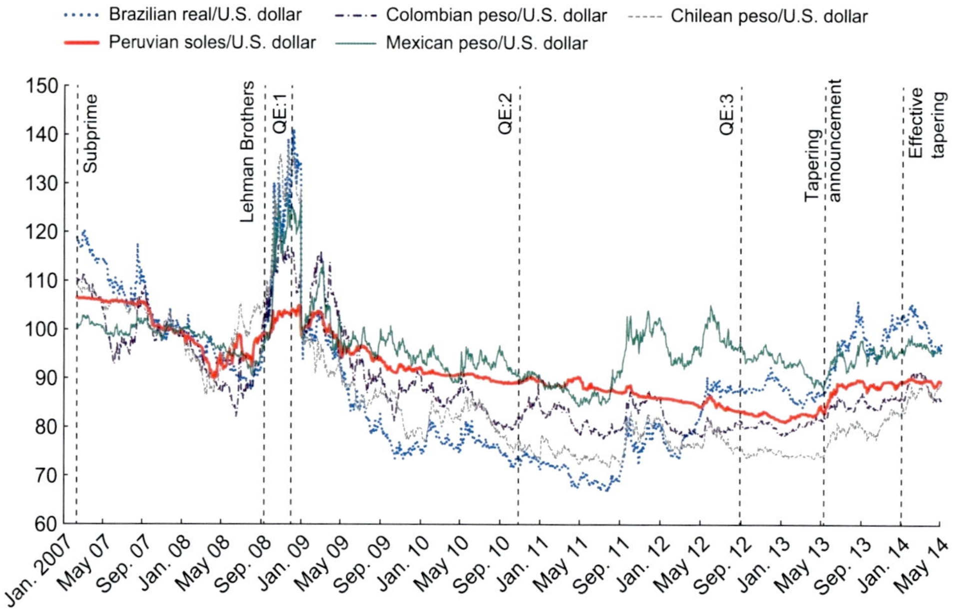


Source: Central Reserve Bank of Peru.
Note: QE = quantitative easing.

**Figure 13.10** Latin American Nominal Exchange Rate Indices *(December 31, 2008 = 100)*

TABLE 13.1

Balance Sheet of Peru's Central Bank as of December 2013 *(Percentage of GDP)*

| Assets | | Liabilities | |
|---|---|---|---|
| **International reserves** | **31.8** | **Treasury deposits** | **11.9** |
| | | In domestic currency | 6.7 |
| | | In foreign currency | 5.3 |
| | | **Reserve requirements** | **11.0** |
| | | In domestic currency | 4.1 |
| | | In foreign currency | 6.9 |
| | | **Central bank instruments** | **3.7** |
| | | **Currency in circulation** | **5.1** |

Source: Central Reserve Bank of Peru.

beginning of the BCRP's interventions under a floating exchange rate system (1990), these operations have been carried out in a discretionary manner. This approach seems to serve Peru's economy well, as opposed to rules-based intervention.

Interventions are made by purchasing or selling dollars in the spot market and carrying out swaps and reverse swaps, which are used mainly when banks may be forced to translate pressures from the nondeliverable forward market into the spot market. In this regard, a swap operation with the BCRP can provide temporary coverage against nondeliverable forward market risks.

In highly dollarized economies, it is convenient to build up international reserves to ring-fence the economy against risks associated with financial dollarization. Every economic crisis in Peru from the Great Depression until 1990 was initiated by balance of payment problems. Given that historical background, international reserves as a self-insurance mechanism against international liquidity shortages are a key element of monetary policy design. These cases fall into the category of structural conditions for reserve accumulation. However, the recent need for reserve accumulation is partially associated with important short-term capital flows due to the very accommodative stance of monetary policy in the developed world, which in fact should be considered cyclical. International reserves help a country preserve economic and financial stability, as they guarantee foreign currency availability in unusual situations, such as possible significant withdrawals from the financial system or temporary external shocks that could generate imbalances in the real sector and feed back into expectations. Additionally, adequate foreign exchange reserves help to reduce the country risk (and improve the associated credit ratings), thereby providing firms with better conditions to access international capital markets (Rossini, Quispe, and Rodríguez 2011).

As shown in the BCRP balance sheet, international reserves are funded mainly by public sector deposits and reserve requirements (Table 13.1). BCRP securities and currency in circulation also funded the international reserve accumulation, but to a lesser degree. To sterilize the liquidity created by foreign exchange interventions, the BCRP issues its own certificates, currently with maturities of up to 18 months and auctioned on a daily basis. These certificates are complemented by banks' reserve requirements and Treasury deposits. Table 13.1 summarizes the 2013 BCRP balance sheet in percentages of GDP. It shows that 11.9 percent of liabilities are represented by sterilization through Treasury deposits (associated with a solid fiscal position), 11 percent by reserve requirements, 3.7 percent by BCRP certificates, and 5.1 percent by currency in circulation accounts (Rossini, Quispe, and Serrano 2013).

## THE CENTRAL BANK'S USE OF RESERVE REQUIREMENTS

The BCRP uses reserve requirements mainly for monetary control, limiting dollarization risks, and increasing the maturity of banks' external leverage.

### Reserve Requirements as an Active Monetary Control Tool

Nonconventional instruments such as reserve requirements have been used in Peru since the 1990s to preserve the transmission channels of monetary policy and prevent systemic risks associated mainly with exchange rate mismatches and liquidity risks created by financial dollarization. The scope and use of reserve requirements have changed in recent years. Before the adoption of inflation targeting, and in response to high financial dollarization, reserve requirements on foreign currency obligations were higher than on domestic currency obligations. Differential rates encourage banks to internalize the risk of granting dollar-denominated loans to economic agents that do not generate dollar incomes, and to create a foreign exchange liquidity buffer to reduce systemic liquidity risks, given that the BCRP cannot act as lender of last resort in foreign currency. During this period, reserve requirements were not used cyclically and only targeted domestic sources of bank funding.

In recent years, reserve requirements have been used by the BCRP to complement its short-term interest rate. As such, they have helped break the trade-off between macro and financial stability. In particular, the reserve requirement–induced quantitative tightening dampened the expansionary effects of capital inflows on domestic credit conditions and, through this channel, also reduced the output gap and inflationary pressures. In the presence of the reserve requirement policy, this quantitative tightening effect on the output gap implies that the policy rate may not need to rise as much. Therefore, the use of quantitative tightening in a situation where there are persistent capital inflows, and in a still underdeveloped local capital market, is analogous to fiscal policy tightening that also allows a lower policy rate and a less appreciated domestic currency. As such, it introduces a new dimension in the policy mix that must also take into account the relationship between reserve requirements and policy rates.

In addition, if there are massive capital inflows or very low international interest rates, financial dollarization strengthens the spillover from expansionary international monetary conditions to the domestic financial system, which weakens domestic monetary policy. This occurs because the demand for credit switches toward foreign currency credit. Under these conditions, higher reserve requirements on dollar liabilities contribute to moderating the spillover effect of international financial conditions on domestic markets, thereby strengthening the transmission of domestic interest rate policy (Figure 13.11). The use of reserve requirements also contributes to monetary policy effectiveness. In credit market segments where the risk premium is high, lending rates are less sensitive to the policy rate, whereas changes in reserve requirements, which operate through changes in financial intermediation margins, have a larger impact on lending rates.

Countercyclical reserve requirements can help offset credit expansions by reducing the amount of banks' loanable funds as a proportion of total bank assets. Massive capital inflows until April 2013 due to hitting the zero lower bound in advanced economies (including QE, Operation Twist, and the massive injection of liquidity by the European Central Bank at a rate of 1 percent) brought about new macroeconomic and financial stability challenges. This time, the preemptive use of nonconventional tools by the BCRP helped create a smoother credit cycle, as compared with the 2007–08 episode (Figures 13.12 and 13.13). The use of nonconventional policy instruments such as reserve requirements and foreign exchange market interventions not only helped mitigate the foreign currency–induced credit and liquidity risks created by financial dollarization, it also contributed to breaking the trade-off between reducing domestic demand pressures and attracting capital flows. The trade-off takes place when the policy rate is increased to face domestic demand pressures amid episodes of strong capital flows.

An increase in the reserve requirement ratio implies that banks must raise liquid assets to meet the new policy requirement. This tends to reduce credit growth, particularly when banks cannot

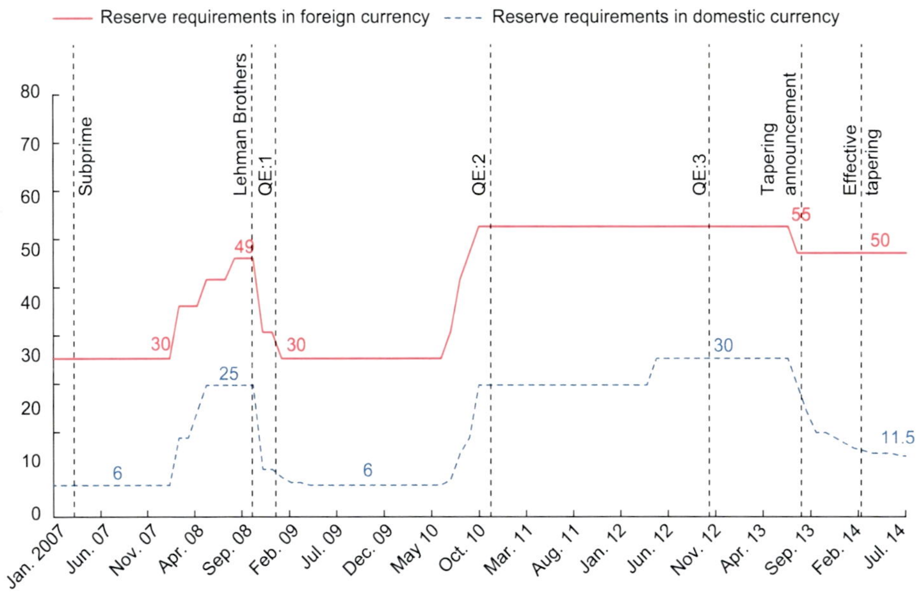


Source: Central Reserve Bank of Peru.
Note: QE = quantitative easing.

**Figure 13.11** Reserve Requirements in Domestic and Foreign Currency *(Percentage of total liabilities subject to reserve requirements)*

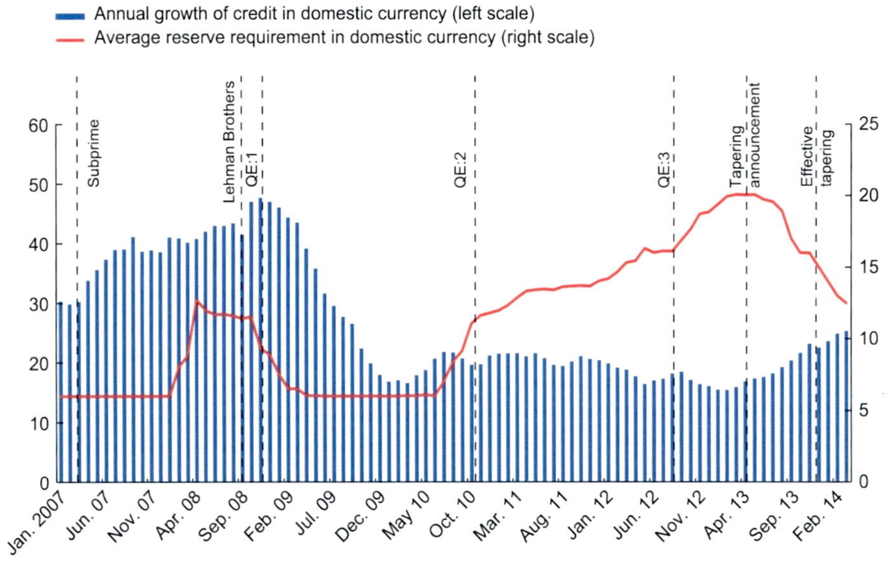


Source: Central Reserve Bank of Peru.
Note: QE = quantitative easing.

**Figure 13.12** Banking System Domestic Currency Credit to the Private Sector and Average Reserve Requirements in Domestic Currency *(Percent)*

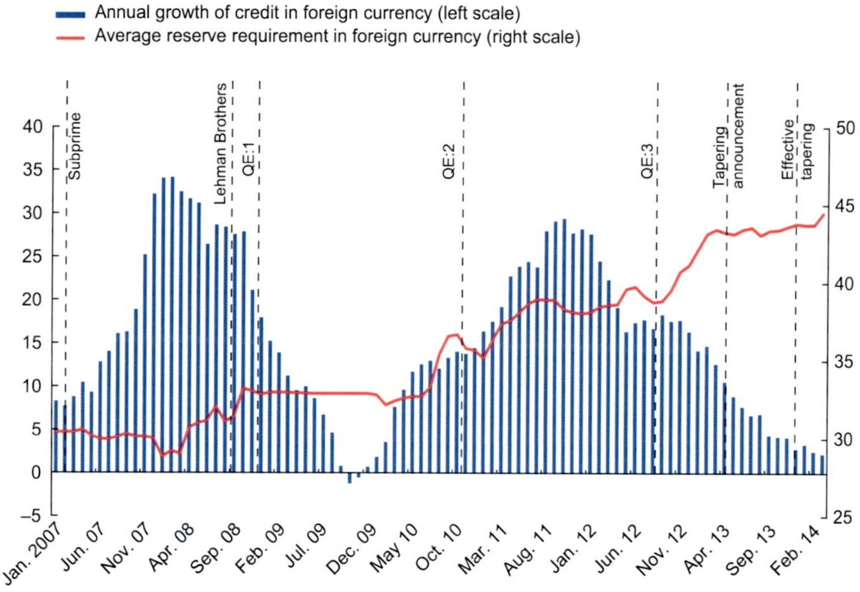


Source: Central Reserve Bank of Peru.
Note: QE = quantitative easing.

**Figure 13.13** Banking System Foreign Currency Credit to the Private Sector and Average Reserve Requirements in Foreign Currency

replace liabilities subject to reserve requirements with other sources of funding, like long-term foreign liabilities (Figure 13.14).[3] This is more likely the case for small financial institutions with limited access to international financial markets. Thus, by increasing reserve requirements during episodes of capital inflows and credit expansions, the BCRP seeks to reduce the probability of liquidity stress scenarios in the financial system. Higher reserve requirements induce private banks to increase their availability of liquid assets, which also reduces their capacity to expand credit, particularly in foreign currency. Hence, reserve requirements generate buffer stocks of liquidity in both domestic and foreign currency.

The quantitative effect of this mechanism depends both on the duration and intensity of reserve requirements increases and on the way this policy is implemented (Céspedes, Chang, and Velasco 2012). Figures 13.12 and 13.13 show a different behavior of credit and liquid assets during 2007 and 2008, when credit growth accelerated and liquid assets decreased despite the increase in reserve requirements in both domestic and foreign currencies. During this period, the increase in reserve requirements was much milder and shorter-lived than the increase since 2010. The effectiveness of reserve requirements was rather limited during this episode. Also during this period, the increase in reserve requirements was implemented only through increases in marginal rates and not through increases in the average reserve requirement rate. This distinction is important because an increase in the average reserve requirement rate has a stronger impact on banks' credit supply than an increase in the marginal rate, because the former is not contingent on the growth of bank deposits, as is the case for marginal reserve requirements. Tovar, García-Escribano, and Vera-Martin (2012) provide empirical evidence on the effectiveness of average over marginal reserve requirements. This implies that when the BCRP increases average reserve requirements, banks must increase their liquid assets even when deposits are not increasing.

[3]In Peru, long-term foreign liabilities are not subject to reserve requirements up to a limit of 2.2 times the bank's net worth.

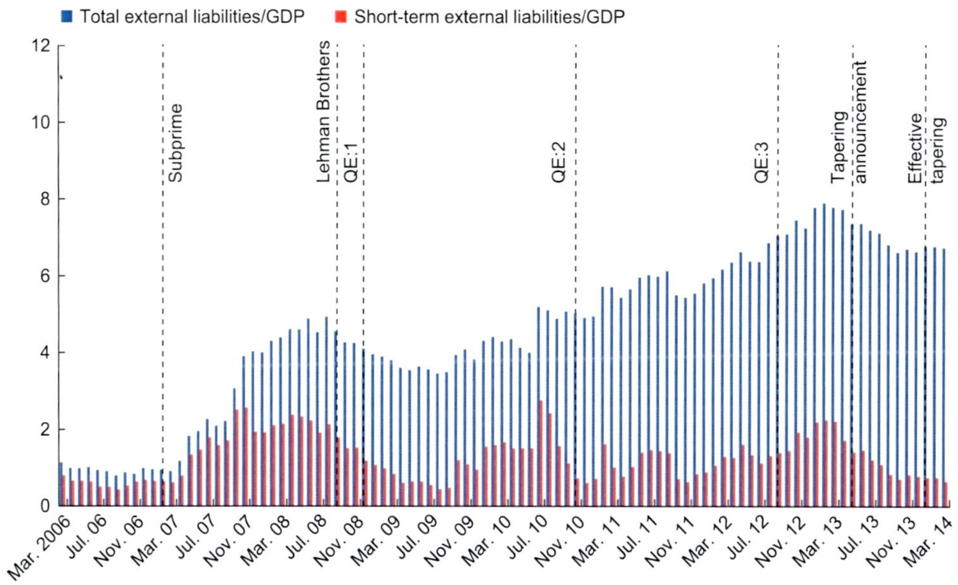


Source: Central Reserve Bank of Peru.
Note: QE = quantitative easing.

**Figure 13.14** Banking System Foreign Liabilities *(Percent of GDP)*

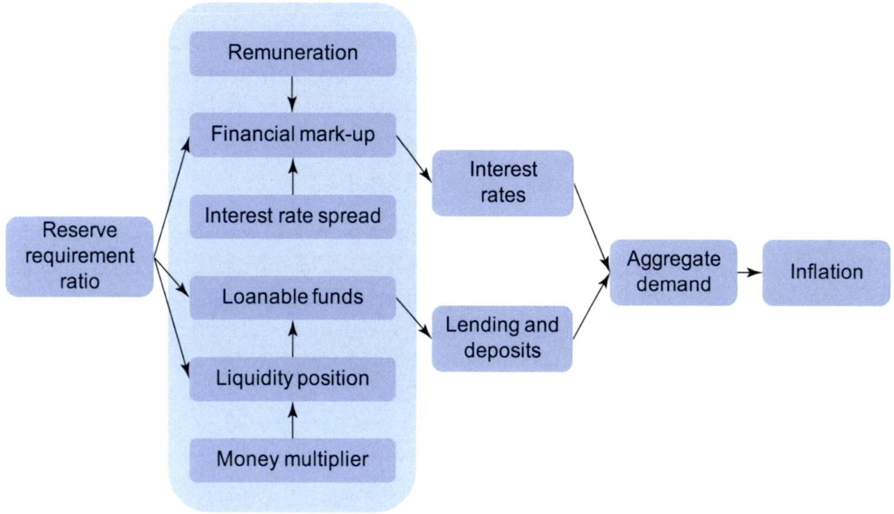


Source: Central Reserve Bank of Peru.

**Figure 13.15** The Transmission Mechanism of Changes in Reserve Requirement Ratios

## *The Transmission Mechanism of Reserve Requirement Changes*

Reserve requirements affect money and credit conditions through a number of channels. A simple mechanism is described here. As Figure 13.15 shows, the first aim of reserve requirements is to reduce financial entities' primary loanable funds. Lower loanable funds imply lower liquidity and credit, which in turn has an impact on aggregate expenditure and inflation. This mechanism is more effective when the balance of liquid assets held by financial entities is low.

Second, higher reserve requirements reduce banks' financial margins. Banks will seek to preserve them by widening the spread between lending and deposit rates (León and Quispe 2010; Montoro and Moreno 2011). They can achieve this by raising lending rates, reducing deposit rates, or both (Terrier and others 2011). Higher market interest rates induce economic agents to reduce their expenditure, thereby attenuating inflationary pressures.

Regarding empirical evidence, there are virtually no references to Peru before 2008, given that reserve requirements were not an active monetary policy tool. The initial approach when the BCRP started to use reserve requirements actively was to calibrate their impact through an accounting procedure that operated through banks' financial margins (León and Quispe 2010). In particular, the prior was that the demand for credit was relatively inelastic to changes in the interest rate, mainly for small and medium firms.

It was also clear that the effectiveness of the reserve requirement tool would depend on the degree of liquid substitute assets or external funding from foreign financial institutions. Data for the 2008–12 events showed that this prior was not far from actual figures. The inflation forecasting model (*Modelo de Proyección Trimestral*) assumes that changes in this instrument increase bank lending rates. The estimated impact of a 1 percent rise in the average reserve requirement ratio is about 0.3 percent on average domestic currency lending rates and 0.1 percent on foreign currency lending rates. The low pass-through from reserve requirements to foreign currency lending rates is explained by the larger set of alternative sources of funding available to corporate firms in foreign currency.

In practice, the implementation of monetary policy within a dual currency economy not only requires forecasting of inflation conditional on the policy rate instrument, it also needs a continuous assessment of risks and vulnerabilities created by financial dollarization under the baseline scenario. Nonconventional policy instruments are then set to curb those risks. For instance, if the baseline scenario assumes a period of capital inflows and persistent low international interest rates, then two risks arise: (1) the risk of a rapid expansion of dollar-denominated loans and (2) a more intense use by local banks of short-term loans from foreign banks. In this case, a rise in reserve requirements on foreign currency liabilities is also considered as a policy option in the baseline scenario.

## Controlling Dollarization Risks with Reserve Requirements

The discussion on the relevance of nonconventional policies as tools to prevent systemic risks and preserve financial stability has become more intense as a result of the global financial crisis. In developed economies, financial asset prices such as stocks and bonds are an element in the policy transmission mechanism. In contrast, emerging economies' shallow capital markets limit the role of financial asset prices in monetary policy transmission. In this group of economies, the most important asset price is the exchange rate. This is the case of financially dollarized economies like Peru.

Financial dollarization generates systemic risks in at least two crucial dimensions. First, by reducing the central bank's ability to act as lender of last resort, financial dollarization increases the likelihood of a liquidity shortage in the financial system. Second, since banks lend in foreign currency to nontradable firms, financial dollarization also creates currency mismatches, which magnify foreign currency–induced credit risks. A common feature of these two additional sources of financial vulnerability implied by financial dollarization is that both generate negative externalities that justify policy intervention. They can also trigger potential nonlinear dynamics with undesirable consequences for financial stability that in turn require the introduction of precautionary policy measures. In this regard, the availability of adequate international reserves is key to providing liquidity to the markets during episodes of financial stress. As shown in the BCRP balance sheet (see Table 13.1), the international reserves are funded by deposits from the public sector, reserve requirements, central bank securities, and currency in circulation.

The key externality at play with financial dollarization is a nonpecuniary one (which was common before the creation of central banks). When banks intermediate in foreign currency, they do not take into account the fact that they are operating under a system without a lender of last resort in that currency. Banks assume that when they need foreign currency, they will be able to obtain it from the interbank market (local or international) at the market interest rate (related of course to the policy rate of the foreign currency issuer). However, this may not be the case, particularly if all banks experience the same type of liquidity shortage.

### Liquidity Risk and the Lender of Last Resort in Foreign Currency

This was the case in Peru during the 1998 Russian crisis, when the shock triggered a sudden stop and quickly damaged banks' foreign currency positions, particularly those banks that took considerable short-term loans from the international financial system. During this episode, banks were not able to obtain foreign currency even at very high short-term interest rates. As a consequence, several banks had to abruptly curtail credit. The average local interbank rate in dollars was 8 percent in July 1998 (240 basis points over one-month Libor) and soared to 12.9 percent by October (760 basis points over one-month Libor).

The rationale for the need for high reserve requirements on foreign currency deposits, which strongly emphasizes the need to provide adequate international liquidity to the financial system during periods of financial distress, was fundamental in diminishing the impact of the sudden stop during the late 1990s financial crisis. Thus, under financial dollarization, preventive policy is required because private banks hold too little foreign currency liquidity. Higher reserve requirements on foreign currency liabilities, along with the accumulation of international foreign reserves, contribute to reducing the adverse impact of this externality. A historical reference of a financial system operating without a lender of last resort (like the financial dollarization case) was in the nineteenth and early twentieth centuries, when bank-run episodes were frequent across the world. In the United States, banks were required to keep a 25 percent reserve against deposits (National Bank Act of 1863). However, the role of reserve requirements decreased over time after the creation of the Federal Reserve in 1913 (Goodfriend and Hargraves 1987).

Reserve requirements on foreign currency liabilities have three desirable effects that help deal with financial distortions. First, reserve requirements send a signal to financial intermediaries that foreign currency liabilities are riskier than their domestic currency counterparts and, thus, reserve requirements help banks internalize dollarization risks. By setting higher reserve requirement ratios on foreign currency liabilities, the BCRP increases the cost of providing foreign currency loans, thereby reducing the incentives for banks to intermediate in foreign currency, particularly in those credit market segments where borrowers have few alternative sources of funding. Second, reserve requirements reduce the likelihood of bank runs because economic agents realize that the banking system has a large pool of foreign currency–denominated liquid assets. Reserve requirements on foreign currency deposits amount to about 20 percent of total international reserves, 50 percent of total foreign currency credit, and 44 percent of overall liabilities subject to reserve requirements. And third, reserve requirement policy contributes to increasing the amount of international liquidity in the financial system when necessary. This level of liquidity allows the central bank to act as lender of last resort in foreign currency by providing foreign currency whenever it is needed. By cutting reserve requirements, the central bank can inject liquidity into the financial system and reduce pressures on the interest rate.

### Credit Risk Induced by Currency Mismatches

The existence of currency mismatches in the balance sheet of domestic agents generates an externality to the financial system, because agents either do not properly internalize the foreign currency–induced risk or engage in moral hazard behavior. Even nontradable firms that set prices in foreign currency do not realize that the nature of the mismatch is a real one. In other words, a negative shock to the economy that results in a depreciation of the real exchange rate increases the real debt of nontradable firms (net present value of cash in dollars will fall). There is also an externality that operates through the payments system: by taking dollar-denominated loans, an individual firm increases its default risk. However, it also increases the default risk of other firms that are linked to the first firm through the payments system. Banks do not properly internalize the complex degree of links between firms, and consequently do not charge the right risk premium when granting dollar-denominated loans to firms in the nontradable sector. In this case, a sharp and unexpected depreciation of the exchange rate can trigger negative balance sheet effects that spill across the payments system to a large set of firms, unduly affecting the credit quality of banks' assets.

It is worth mentioning that it is not only a sharp depreciation of the domestic currency that generates systemic risks in a financially dollarized economy, but also a strong and transitory appreciation. A persistent and sharp appreciation of the domestic currency reduces the real value of firms' debt and may also encourage further appreciation expectations. As a result, firms may perceive that borrowing in foreign currency is cheaper, leading them to increase their currency mismatches and, through this channel, the cost of a sudden exchange rate reversal. Policy measures such as additional provisioning for dollar-denominated loans, higher reserve requirements for foreign currency liabilities, and foreign exchange intervention to smooth out exchange rate fluctuations contribute to dampening this type of credit risk.

### Reserve Requirements as an Instrument to Increase Maturities and Moderate Banks' External Leverage

Higher reserve requirements on both foreign currency short-term external liabilities and deposits not only increase the cost of dollar-denominated loans, but also induce banks to lengthen the maturity of their external liabilities and increase the availability of international liquidity. In 2007, the BCRP extended the use of reserve requirements to banks' short-term foreign liabilities.[4] As a result, banks had the incentive to lengthen the maturities of their foreign currency liabilities, which reduced their vulnerability to sudden capital stops. Currently, a 50 percent special reserve requirement is in place for local banks' obligations to foreign banks with maturities of less than two years. Moreover, banks increased the average maturity of their foreign liabilities from two years in 2007 to four years in 2009. This special reserve requirement has also been used cyclically. The BCRP raises its level in periods of abundant capital inflows and reduces it in response to capital outflows.

Crucially, after the collapse of Lehman Brothers, the limited exposure of local banks to sudden stops of capital flows allowed banks to maintain their supply of credit, which limited the impact of this shock on the local financial system. More recently, as a result of greater international financial integration and historically low world interest rates, short-term capital flows[5] as well as firms' and banks' foreign liabilities (particularly bonds) have increased their share in the capital account. In order to limit overborrowing, the BCRP set an additional reserve requirement (1) when the stock of long-term foreign liabilities and bonds exceeds 2.2 times a bank's net worth, and (2) when credit growth in foreign currency exceeds a given limit established by the BCRP. Furthermore, in 2013, with the aim of reinforcing credit dedollarization, the BCRP introduced additional reserve requirements for financial institutions that grant foreign currency loans above certain prudential limits.

## MEASURING THE EFFECTS OF RESERVE REQUIREMENTS

This section presents the effect of reserve requirement policy applied to both domestic and foreign currency bank liabilities on interest rates and credit. There has been an active stance in policies aimed at reducing currency and term mismatches in the public sector, as well as in the

[4]The BCRP had extended the use of reserve requirements to banks' foreign liabilities in 2004.

[5]Nondeliverable forward operations with nonresident investors and purchases of public debt instruments denominated in domestic currency.

**TABLE 13.2**

**Indicators of Macro Vulnerability**

| | | | Unit | 2003 | 2008 | 2013 |
|---|---|---|---|---|---|---|
| Central Bank | 1 | GDP/international reserves | Number of times | 6.0 | 4.1 | 3.2 |
| | 2 | M2/international reserves | Number of times | 1.0 | 0.9 | 1.2 |
| | 3 | (Short-term foreign liabilities + amortization on external debt)/NIR | Percent | 13.6 | 27.0 | 12.7 |
| Banking System | 4 | Dollarization of banking credit | Percent | 76.0 | 54.8 | 45.3 |
| | 5 | Short-term banks' foreign liabilities/ banking credit | Percent | 4.9 | 5.3 | 2.7 |
| | 6 | Short-term banks' liabilities (deposits + credit lines)/required reserves | Number of times | 3.1 | 2.5 | 1.7 |
| Public Sector | 7 | Dollarization of public debt | Percent | 84.9 | 62.5 | 44.5 |
| | 8 | Nonresidents' holdings of local public debt/public sector deposits in the central bank | Percent | 0.0 | 21.7 | 31.0 |
| | 9 | Average maturity of the public sector debt | Years | 7.6 | 11.2 | 12.5 |

Source: Central Reserve Bank of Peru.

financial and nonfinancial private sector. The different indicators of vulnerability to external capital account events shown in Table 13.2 indicate that active fiscal and central bank policies have aimed at reducing the impact of credit and exchange rate risks.

Econometric evaluation of policy is difficult due to the identification problem. The usual tool in the monetary policy literature is to identify monetary policy through structural vector autoregressions. The vector autoregression procedure is sound in a conventional monetary policy setting where the policy rate dynamically interacts with inflation, economic activity, and the exchange rate. In the analysis of unconventional monetary policy, however, it is important to account for episodes of policy interventions characterized by policy on-off situations. For those cases, Pesaran and Smith (2012) propose a policy evaluation exercise where the effectiveness of policy changes can be directly measured. The idea is to compare observed outcomes after a policy change against a counterfactual generated by an econometric forecast conditional on the policy not being implemented. Pesaran and Smith (2012) show that the conditional forecasts can be generated by a reduced-form equation linking outcomes to both policy and controls invariant to policy.

All that is required to follow the policy assessment exercise by Pesaran and Smith (2012) is to define outcomes and instruments. The choice must have the special feature that the instrument needs to be "off" and then "on" for a reasonable amount of time. Three such episodes are identified by Armas, Castillo, and Vega (2014): (1) the increase in the marginal reserve requirement for domestic currency deposits from 6 percent to 25 percent since July 2010; (2) the increase in the marginal reserve requirement for foreign currency deposits from 30 percent to 55 percent since July 2010;[6] and (3) the increase in reserve requirements on banks' short-term external debt from 30 percent to 60 percent since July 2010. According to Pesaran and Smith (2012), what is needed is a reduced-form equation such as:

$$y_t = \pi_1 x_t + \pi_2' W_t + \upsilon_{yt}, \tag{13.1}$$

where $y_t$ is an outcome variable, $x_t$ is the policy instrument, and $W_t$ is a vector of control variables invariant to ad hoc policy changes. The set of outcome variables is given by the levels of outstanding credit denominated in domestic and foreign currency, lending and deposit interest rates in

[6]An initial tightening episode started in February 2008 and went until May 2008. However, this tightening was quickly reversed after the Lehman Brothers collapse, and thus it cannot be used in this exercise.

**TABLE 13.3**

**Pesaran-Smith (2012) Policy Effectiveness Statistics**

| | Mean Effect ($\hat{d}_H$) | Policy Effectiveness Statistic ($P_H$) | *P*-value | Expected Sign |
|---|---|---|---|---|
| Bank Lending Rates in Nuevos Soles | 0.001 | 6.47 | 0.00 | Yes |
| Bank Lending Rates in U.S. Dollars | 0.006 | 1.57 | 0.06 | Yes |
| Bank Deposit Rates in U.S. Dollars | −0.009 | −3.19 | 0.00 | Yes |
| Bank Lending in Nuevos Soles | −0.019 | −0.57 | 0.28 | Yes |
| Bank Lending in U.S. Dollars | −0.008 | −0.49 | 0.31 | Yes |
| Banks' Short-term External Debt as a Ratio of Total External Debt | −0.300 | 3.20 | 0.00 | Yes |

Source: Armas, Castillo, and Vega (2014).

both currencies, and the ratio of short-term to long-term external debt of banks. Candidates for control variables include, first, a set of external variables including the U.S. federal funds rate, the VIX, the trade-weighted U.S. dollar index, the 10-year U.S. Treasury bond yield, and the slope of the U.S. yield curve. A second set of control variables includes variables affected mostly by external conditions (terms of trade, the Emerging Market Bond Index, domestic primary output) or by the trend financial development (number of employees, number of branches). The key assumption is that these sets of control variables are invariant to policy. To make inferences, a mean effect quantity is constructed through the following equation:

$$\hat{d}_H = \hat{\pi}_1 \left[ \frac{1}{H} \sum_{h=1}^{H} \left( x_{T+h} - x_{T+h}^0 \right) \right], \tag{13.2}$$

where $\hat{\pi}_1$ is the estimated policy coefficient, $H$ is the number of periods over which the specific level of policy tightening has been effective, $x_{T+h}$ represents the observed policy trajectory from period $T$ onward, and $x_{T+h}^0$ is the counterfactual policy trajectory from period $T$ onward. The number of periods the policy stance lasted is $H = 22$ months.

Next, Pesaran and Smith (2012) propose a policy-effectiveness test statistic given by

$$\mathcal{P}_H = \frac{\hat{d}_H}{\hat{\sigma}_{v_y}} \sim^a N(0,1), \tag{13.3}$$

where $\hat{\sigma}_{v_y}$ is the standard error of the policy reduced-form regression. Namely, if the mean effect $\hat{d}_H$ is relatively large compared to the standard error of the forecasting equation, then it is likely that the policy effect is significant.

## Results

The main empirical results of Armas, Castillo, and Vega (2014) are presented in Table 13.3. In general, the effect of reserve requirement changes that took place in 2010 proved to have indeed increased lending interest rates and reduced deposit rates. The effect on bank interest rates implies that an increase in reserve requirements induces bank interest rate spreads to widen, as described earlier in this chapter, and consistent with effects generally expected in the literature (Montoro and Moreno 2011; Terrier and others 2011).

Furthermore, there is evidence that the effect on credit works as expected. This is inconsistent with the results obtained by Pérez and Vega (2014), who show that a 1 percentage increase in the reserve requirement ratio has a 0.4 effect on credit growth within six months. The last empirical result presented here (Table 13.4) relates to the impact of an increase in reserve requirements on banks' short-term external debt. The evidence shows that this policy produced a shift in banks' external debt toward long-term maturities and away from short-term ones.

TABLE 13.4

Dynamic Effects of a 1 Percentage Point Reduction of Reserve Requirements in Domestic Currency

| | 3 Months | 6 Months | 9 Months | 12 Months | 18 Months | 24 Months |
|---|---|---|---|---|---|---|
| Banking Sector Lending in Domestic Currency | 0.26*** | 0.4*** | 0.36 | 0.29 | 0.18 | 0.09 |
| Interest Rate Spread | 0.07*** | −0.14* | −0.14 | −0.14 | −0.11 | −0.08 |

Source: Perez and Vega (2014).
Note: * Denotes significance at the 10 percent level and *** at the 1 percent level.

## CONCLUSIONS

Nonconventional policy tools such as reserve requirements are being used actively by many central banks in emerging market economies. The evidence provided by Peru's experience shows that this is an effective tool to reduce the trade-offs that expansionary monetary policies in developed economies are creating in emerging market financial systems. In particular, reserve requirements can dampen the credit cycles in periods of capital inflows and reduce their expansionary effects on domestic aggregate demand. Also, when reserve requirements are applied to foreign currency bank liabilities, they can contribute to increasing the availability of international liquidity in the financial system, and consequently help to reduce the impact of capital outflows on the domestic financial system.

This chapter has presented counterfactual exercises by Armas, Castillo, and Vega (2014) and following Pesaran and Smith (2012) to quantify the effect of a marginal reserve requirement tightening over the period July 2010 to April 2012. The effects on interest rates and credit levels are measured. As with any other form of tax, reserve requirements generate efficiency costs, which can affect the degree of financial development. However, when financial frictions pervade, these costs are of second-order magnitude compared to the benefits of active use of reserve requirements that reduces the probability of a financial crisis. In this regard, reserve requirement calibration needs to take into account these costs to define both the magnitude and the duration of this type of nonconventional policy instruments. In economies like Peru, where domestic capital markets are not well developed, reserve requirements can also speed up the development of these markets by increasing the cost of financial intermediation through the banking system. However, they can also increase the incentives for firms to use more external funding.

The aforementioned costs can be reduced by spreading out the burden of prudential regulation among a larger set of instruments, such as cyclical capital requirements and dynamic provisioning, and, in the case of financially dollarized economies, additional capital requirements for loans in dollars. The central bank has to continuously assess the efficacy of reserve requirements as prudential instruments and revert them when necessary. For instance, in Peru, reserve requirements on short-term bank liabilities were reduced in 2012 for liabilities related to trade finance so as to avoid a replacement of banking credit with offshore credit lines. Peru's experience also shows that central banks need to closely monitor the impact of this type of instrument in order to minimize its potential costs. Close coordination with the regulatory authority is also necessary so as to complement reserve requirements with the use of other instruments aimed at reducing systemic risks, such as countercyclical provisioning and capital requirements, as well as a higher capital requirement for foreign loans.

## REFERENCES

Armas, A., P. Castillo, and M. Vega. 2014. "Inflation Targeting and Quantitative Tightening: Effects of Reserve Requirements in Peru." Working Paper 003–014, Central Reserve Bank of Peru, Lima.

Armas, A., and F. Grippa. 2005. "Targeting Inflation in a Dollarized Economy: the Peruvian Experience." RES Working Paper 4423, Inter-American Development Bank Research Department, Washington, DC.

Céspedes, L. F., R. Chang, and A. Velasco. 2012. "Is Inflation Targeting Still on Target?" NBER Working Paper No. 18570, National Bureau of Economic Research, Cambridge, Massachusetts.

Goodfriend, M., and M. Hargraves. 1987. "A Historical Assessment of the Rationales and Functions of Reserve Requirements." In *Monetary Policy in Practice,* edited by M. Goodfriend. Richmond, Virginia: Federal Reserve Bank of Richmond.

León, D., and Z. Quispe. 2010. "El encaje como instrumento no convencional de política monetaria." *Revista Moneda* 143, Central Reserve Bank of Peru, Lima.

Montoro, C., and R. Moreno. 2011. "The Use of Reserve Requirements as a Policy Instrument in Latin America." *BIS Quarterly Review* (March), Bank for International Settlements, Basel, Switzerland.

Perez, F., and M. Vega. 2014. "Efectos dinámicos de las tasas de encaje en el Perú." Unpublished, Central Reserve Bank of Peru, Lima.

Pesaran, M., and R. Smith. 2012. "Counterfactual Analysis in Macroeconometrics: An Empirical Investigation into the Effects of Quantitative Easing." Unpublished, Cambridge University, Cambridge, England.

Rossini, R., Z. Quispe, and D. Rodríguez. 2011. "Capital Flows, Monetary Policy and Forex Intervention in Peru." BIS Paper No 57, Bank for International Settlements, Basel, Switzerland.

Rossini, R., Z. Quispe, and E. Serrano. 2013. "Foreign Exchange Intervention in Peru." BIS Paper No. 73, Bank for International Settlements, Basel, Switzerland.

Salas, J. 2011. "Estimación Bayesiana de un modelo macroeconómico simple para una economía pequeña, abierta y parcialmente dolarizada." *Revista de Estudios Económicos* 22: 41–62.

Terrier, G., R. Valdes, C. Tovar, J. Chan-Lau, C. Fernández-Valdovinos, M. García- Escribano, C. Medeiros, M-K. Tang, M. Vera-Martin, and C. Walker. 2011. "Policy Instruments to Lean Against the Wind in Latin America." Working Paper 11/159, International Monetary Fund, Washington, DC.

Tovar, C., M. García-Escribano, and M. Vera-Martin. 2012. "El crecimiento del crédito y la efectividad de los requerimientos de encaje y otros instrumentos macroprudenciales en América Latina." *Revista Estudios Económicos* 24: 45–64.

Webb, R., and A. Armas. 2003. "Monetary Policy in a Highly Dollarized Economy: The Case of Peru." In *Challenges to Central Banking from Globalized Financial Systems,* edited by P. Ugolini, A. Schaechter, and M. Stone. Washington, DC: International Monetary Fund.

Winkelried, Diego. 2013. "Modelo de Proyección Trimestral del BCRP: Actualización y Novedades." *Revista Estudios Económicos* 26: 9–60.

# CHAPTER 14

# Capital Flows, Monetary Policy, and Foreign Exchange Intervention in Peru

RENZO ROSSINI, ZENÓN QUISPE, AND DONITA RODRÍGUEZ

*This chapter explains the main features of sterilized interventions in the foreign exchange market by the Central Reserve Bank of Peru (Banco Central de Reserva del Perú [BCRP]), in a context of an economy with a financial system that operates with two currencies.*[1] *The interventions took place in an environment in which the BCRP developed a policy framework based on a risk management approach that balanced the vulnerabilities associated with partial dollarization of the banking system with the incorporation of nonconventional policy tools such as intervention in the foreign exchange market, accumulation of international reserves, application of different forms of reserve requirements, and different forms of liquidity sterilization. This policy framework controlled the risks of deterioration in the quality of bank assets linked to the balance sheet effects of sharp movements in the exchange rate on the partially dollarized nonfinancial private sector portfolio of assets and liabilities. The policy framework also kept the conventional transmission mechanism with the short-term interest rate as the operational instrument to control inflation, and isolated the Peruvian economy from the effects of the global financial crisis in such a way that Peru was able to recover growth with low inflation and avoid major disruptions from the surge of capital inflows.*

In an environment of partial dollarization, the possibility that local banks can extend credit in foreign currency complicates the normal transmission mechanisms of monetary policy. On the one hand, the policy rate cannot affect these flows and their interest rate. On the other hand, a sharp depreciation can produce a credit contraction resulting from deterioration in the quality of bank assets linked to balance sheet effects on the partially dollarized nonfinancial private sector portfolio of assets and liabilities.

As a result of the risks and vulnerabilities related to partial dollarization, the BCRP has adopted a policy framework that adds several instruments to the conventional policy rate as a tool. These instruments can be grouped as quantitative or nonconventional. For example, higher reserve requirements on short-term foreign exchange liabilities are used to modulate this source of credit, and the BCRP also intervenes in the foreign exchange market, sterilizing excess liquidity with its own instruments that are restricted to local participants. Foreign exchange intervention aims to reduce the volatility of the exchange rate and accumulate international reserves, without any type of signaling or commitment about the level or tendency of the exchange rate.

This policy framework allowed the BCRP to prevent major disruptions and maintain the flow of credit during the global financial crisis. The conventional transmission mechanism is also in place, with the interest rate as the instrument to control inflation.

This chapter discusses four issues related to this policy framework, with the first issue being the selection of a discretionary type of foreign exchange intervention vis-à-vis a rule-based one.

[1]This chapter was first presented at the Bank for International Settlements Meeting of Deputy Governors, Basel, February 17–18, 2011.

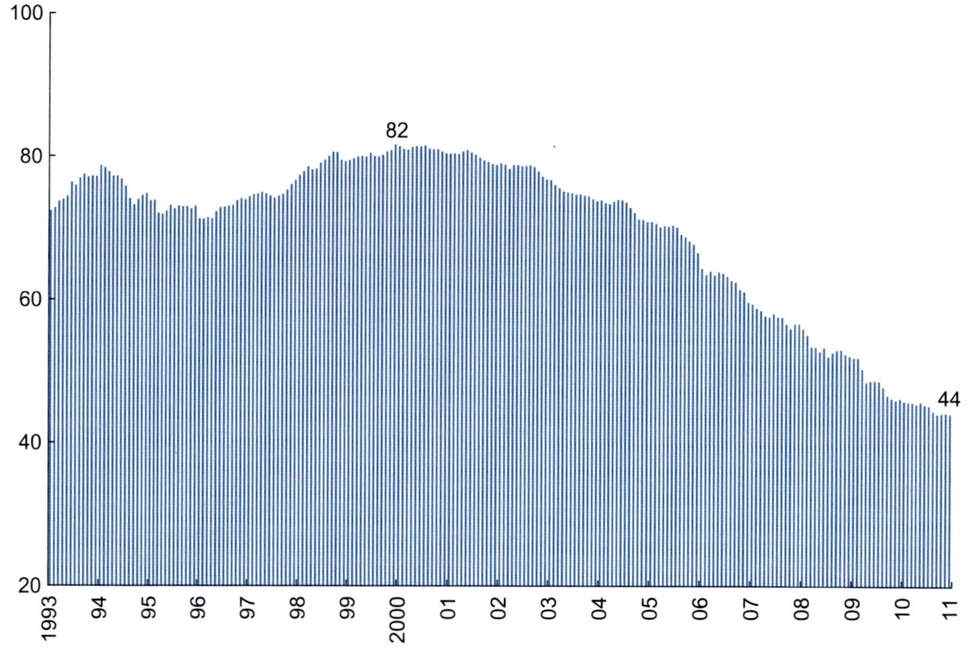


Source: Authors' calculations.

**Figure 14.1** Peru: Credit Dollarization, 1993–2010 *(Percent of total credit)*

Second, the chapter examines sterilization with respect to its cost, the instruments used, and the degree of access to nonresidents. The chapter then looks at the use of reserve requirements as a complement to the conventional policy rate tool, before turning to the issue of competitiveness in an environment marked by strong capital flows.

## MONETARY POLICY UNDER PARTIAL DOLLARIZATION

Persistently high inflation and severe macroeconomic imbalances in Peru during the 1970s and 1980s, along with the lack of inflation-adjusted instruments, led households to hold foreign currency as a store of value. This process of financial dollarization increased significantly during the hyperinflation of 1988–90. In the years that followed, a wide-ranging package of financial system and monetary and fiscal policy reforms were introduced to stabilize the economy. After achieving macroeconomic stabilization during the 1990s, the BCRP implemented a fully fledged inflation-targeting regime in 2002 with an initial point target of 2.5 percent, and since 2007 a continuous point target of 2 percent, both with a tolerance range of ±1 percent. As a result, during the past decade the average annual inflation rate has been 2.3 percent. However, despite improved economic conditions and stable macroeconomic fundamentals during the past 20 years, inertia, transaction costs, and still-underdeveloped capital markets explain the slow but continuous decline of the share of deposits and credits in dollars, from a peak of 82 percent in 1999 to 44 percent in 2010 (Figure 14.1).

Dollarization magnifies the reaction of financial intermediaries to sharp movements in their funding or to high exchange rate volatility. As a result, the economy is prone to credit booms and busts associated with flows of foreign currency deposits, foreign credit lines, or other capital flows. It is also prone to exchange rate movements that affect the quality of the credit portfolio.

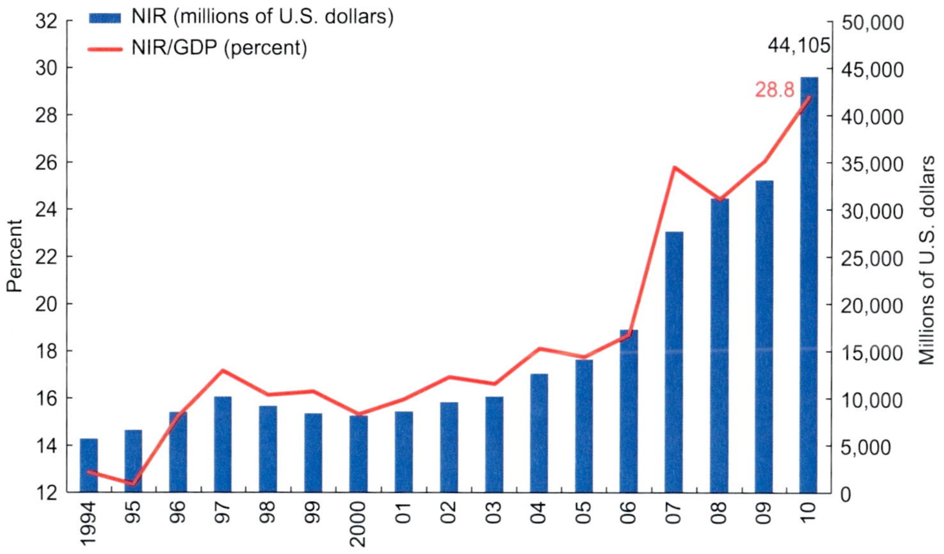


Source: Central Reserve Bank of Peru.
Note: NIR = net international reserves.

**Figure 14.2** Peru: Net International Reserves *(Millions of U.S. dollars and as a percent of GDP)*

Dollarization therefore alters the transmission mechanism of monetary policy and increases the liquidity and solvency risks of the financial system because:

- The maturity mismatch generated in foreign currency introduces higher liquidity risks.
- Solvency risk increases when the assets of nonfinancial economic agents are mainly denominated in domestic currency, while their liabilities are denominated in dollars.

After various external shocks, especially the Russian crisis of 1998, the BCRP designed an action plan to prevent a credit contraction during events of financial stress. Thereafter, the monetary policy framework in Peru, in addition to the common features of an inflation-targeting regime, began to include a set of measures to deal with the risks of financial dollarization. The strategy included three levels of liquidity: accumulation of international reserves by the BCRP, high liquidity requirements of financial intermediaries, and a solid public sector financial position resulting from disciplined and coordinated fiscal policy. In line with this strategy, international reserves increased from 12.9 percent of GDP in December 1994 to 28.8 percent in December 2010 (Figure 14.2).

The set of monetary policy instruments can be separated into the normal price instrument of the interest rate and nonconventional quantitative instruments such as the reserve requirement or the structure of the central bank balance sheet. The importance of the latter group of policies has gained attention with the innovative actions performed by central banks during the subprime financial crisis aimed at avoiding or limiting a collapse of credit. The motivation to consider measures that act more directly on credit flows—rather than waiting for the more indirect impact through changes in interest rates—is that during credit booms or crunches, short-term interest rates became less effective in signaling the stance of the monetary policy to financial intermediaries. These intermediaries become insensitive to policy actions based on movements in the interest rate, but more inclined to react to changes in expectations and risk appetite.

The quantitative instruments are part of a more ample risk management approach of monetary policy that includes preventive and corrective measures oriented toward avoiding a credit

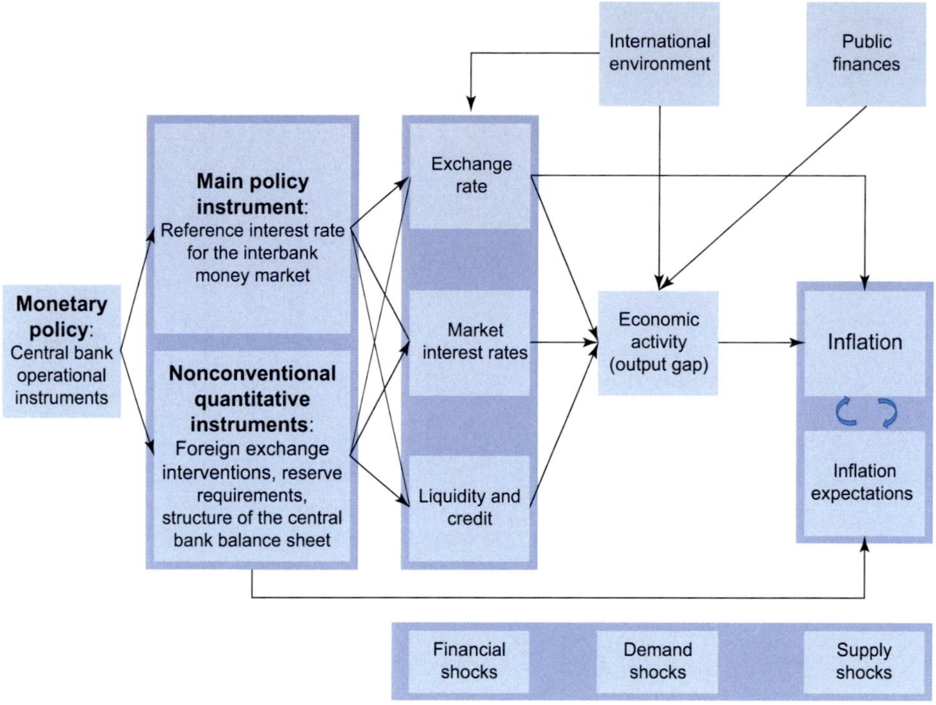


Source: Central Reserve Bank of Peru.

**Figure 14.3** Monetary Policy Transmission Mechanisms

boom or crunch and preserving the transmission mechanisms of monetary policy and financial stability. Figure 14.3 illustrates the common transmission mechanism of monetary policy that uses changes in the short-term interest rate to control inflation by influencing the output gap, but adding the effect of nonconventional quantitative policies affecting banking credit, and in this way also affecting the output gap and the inflation rate.

## FOREIGN EXCHANGE INTERVENTION

Interventions in the foreign exchange market by the BCRP aim to reduce the volatility of the exchange rate without signaling or committing to a certain exchange rate level. A predictable exchange rate would in practice transform the exchange rate system into a type of pegged system, thus ensuring success of one-sided bets by speculators and negating the value of the intervention. One way to avoid predictability and to reinforce the central bank's commitment only to price stability is to use a rule-based type of intervention based, for example, on preannounced amounts of foreign exchange purchases in the market. However, it is possible that different events can make intervention either unnecessary or insufficient, forcing the bank to abandon or change the rule. An alternative type of intervention is one that is more discretionary. Under this approach, having a clear idea that it is important to avoid signaling an exchange rate, the central bank is able and willing to engage in foreign exchange operations without a preannounced amount of operations.

The main type of foreign exchange intervention is through direct operations with commercial banks in the spot market and at the prevailing exchange rate (Armas 2004). The BCRP can also make swaps through temporary purchases or sales of foreign currency, using an auction procedure.

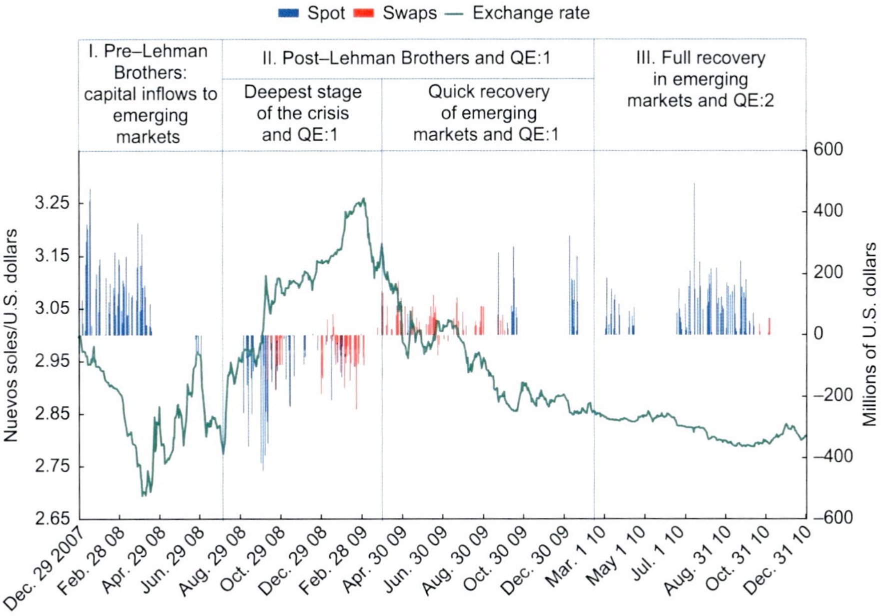


Source: Authors' calculations.
Note: QE = quantitative easing.

**Figure 14.4** Peru: Exchange Rate and Central Bank Net Foreign Exchange Intervention *(Exchange rate in nuevos soles per U.S. dollar; foreign exchange interventions in millions of U.S. dollars)*

The latter instrument is used when the forward market in foreign currency is putting pressure on the exchange positions of local banks. It is also important to consider that at maturity the swaps can either be renewed or exercised, with both possibilities having the same characteristics as an intervention in the market.

Figure 14.4 illustrates the momentum and types of foreign exchange intervention of the BCRP together with the evolution of the exchange rate since 2007. Three clear episodes can be identified: before the collapse of Lehman Brothers, after the collapse, and after the announcement of the second round of quantitative easing by the Federal Reserve. The figure also identifies direct intervention in the foreign exchange spot market and placements or maturing swap operations. During these three stages, the BCRP did not attempt to reverse the tendencies, but rather to reduce the degree of volatility. It can also be seen that the daily amount of interventions does not follow any particular type of rule.

Table 14.1 shows the three recent stages of surges and contractions of capital flows, how they materialized in the exchange markets, and the amount of foreign exchange intervention by the BCRP. The amount of purchases was US$8.7 billion before the Lehman Brothers collapse. During the period of acute crisis in the last quarter of 2009, following the collapse of Lehman Brothers, the BCRP sold US$4.8 billion (or US$8 billion if we include the US$3.2 billion in balances at maturity of swaps). The amount of purchases then rose to US$6.5 billion (including US$200 million in swaps) with the arrival of signals of normalization and the announcement and implementation of the second round of quantitative easing.

The BCRP's foreign exchange intervention has been effective in reducing the volatility of the nuevo sol. As Figure 14.5 shows, the Peruvian currency has been very stable in comparison with those of other countries in the region. The coefficient of variability has been close to 5 percent, whereas for other economies it has reached values between 8 percent and 13 percent.

**TABLE 14.1**

**Peru: Spot and Forward Exchange Markets** *(Millions of U.S. dollars)*

| | Pre–Lehman Brothers | Post–Lehman Brothers | |
|---|---|---|---|
| | Capital Inflows to Emerging Markets (Jan 2008–Apr 2008) | Deepest Stage of the Crisis and QE:1 (Oct 2008–Mar 2009) | Full Recovery in Emerging Markets and QE:2 (Jun 2010–Dec 2010) |
| **Pension Funds** | **−1,596** | **2,541** | **−768** |
| Spot | −171 | 968 | 332 |
| Forward | −1,425 | 1,573 | −1,100 |
| **Nonresident Investors** | **−1,013** | **1,944** | **−1,871** |
| Spot | −2,388 | 1,604 | −1,932 |
| Forward | 1,376 | 339 | 61 |
| **Other Residents** | **−6,119** | **3,499** | **−3,830** |
| Private, Nonfinancial | −6,119 | 2,489 | −4,450 |
| Financial Institutions | −1 | 1,010 | 619 |
| **Central Bank Interventions** | **8,728** | **−7,984** | **6,469** |

Source: Authors' calculations.
Note: Positive figures imply net demand; negative figures imply net supply positions. QE = quantitative easing.

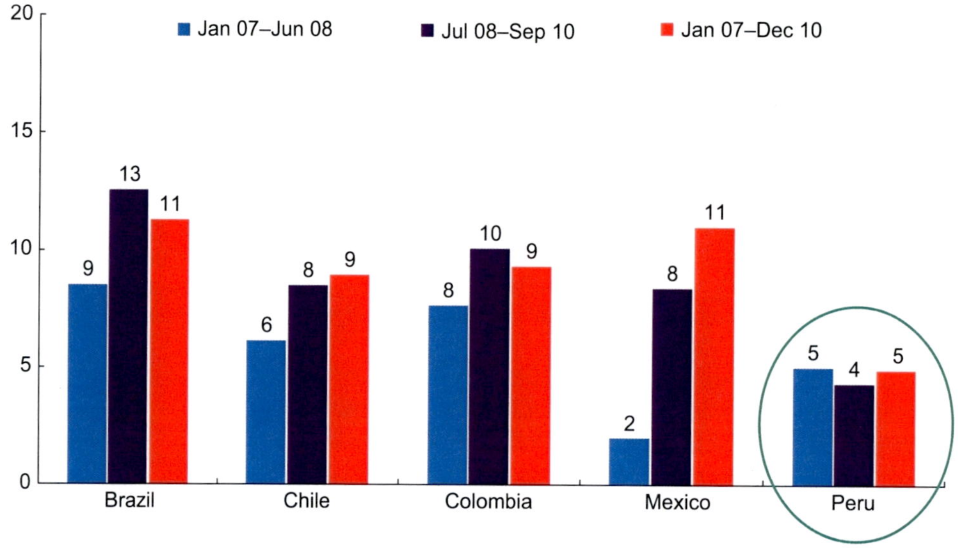


Source: Authors' calculations.

**Figure 14.5** Nominal Exchange Rate *(Variability coefficient, standard deviation/average)*

## STERILIZATION

To avoid side effects of foreign exchange intervention on the ability to control inflation, the central bank needs a sufficient capacity for sterilization. There are two crucial factors that helped to accomplish this goal in the case of Peru: a solid fiscal position and the increasing demand for a monetary base. Table 14.2 presents a simplified balance sheet of the BCRP that shows that fiscal deposits in the central bank represent 10 percent of GDP, which is close to 35 percent of international reserves. The fiscal contribution to sterilize the liquidity created by intervention in the exchange rate market also helps reduce pressure on the real exchange rate.

Sterilized interventions should not affect the ability to use the short-term interest rate as a policy tool. To assess the impact of foreign exchange intervention on the variability of the interest rate, we computed a ratio indicating the volatility of the interbank interest rate relative to the

**TABLE 14.2**

**Balance Sheet of the Central Reserve Bank of Peru as of January 2011**
*(Percent of GDP)*

| Assets | | Liabilities | |
|---|---|---|---|
| Net international reserves | 28.8% | Treasury deposits | 10.3% |
| | | Central bank securities | 1.8% |
| | | Term deposits of banks | 4.2% |
| | | Reserve requirements | 6.1% |
| | | Other liabilities | 1.0% |
| | | Currency (notes and coins) | 5.4% |

Source: Central Reserve Bank of Peru.

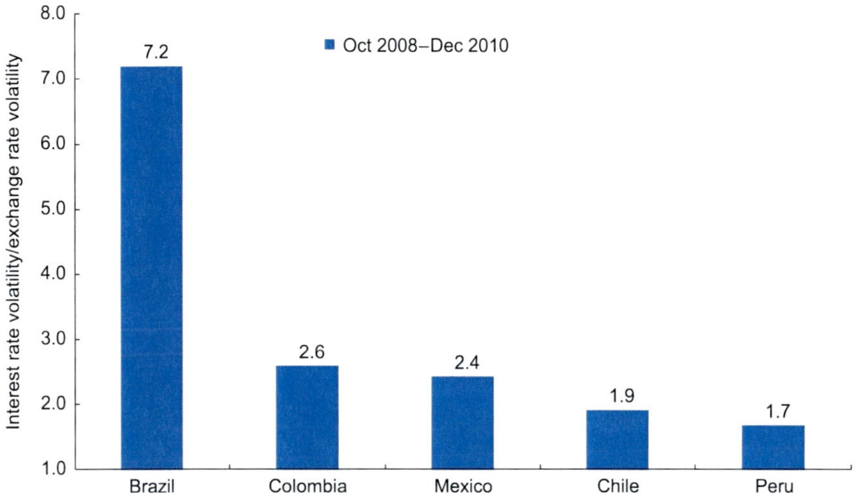


Source: Authors' calculations.

**Figure 14.6** Volatility of Interest Rates Relative to Volatility of Exchange Rates

variability of the exchange rate in different economies with floating exchange rates. Figure 14.6 indicates that Peru has the lowest ratio.

Another concern about sterilization is the financial cost from the carry cost or interest rate differential from returns of international reserves with the interest rate paid to the different liabilities of the central bank (Rossini, Quispe, and Gondo 2008). In a situation with higher local interest rates, the central bank could face financial losses. One component that eases this burden is the currency, which is a liability free of interest rate. As shown in Figure 14.7, the return on foreign assets held by the BCRP exceeds the average cost of its liabilities.[2]

Finally, an important issue with sterilized interventions is that they can create an incentive to attract further capital inflows due to the interest rate differential between the local and international interest rates. This possibility could neutralize monetary policy either by paralyzing the use of the policy rate or by attracting further foreign financing. These capital flows have an additional incentive, which is the expectation of appreciation of the local currency.

[2] With respect to exchange rate losses that can be generated by a currency appreciation on international reserves valued in local currency, there is not a consensus about the accounting treatment of this valuation effect. Some central banks record it in their profit and losses report, while others record it in a separate item in the capital account. From an economic point of view, the change of valuation in local currency of international reserves is not relevant. For example, it would be meaningless to record and distribute dividends originated in a depreciation of the currency that increased the nominal amount of international reserves.

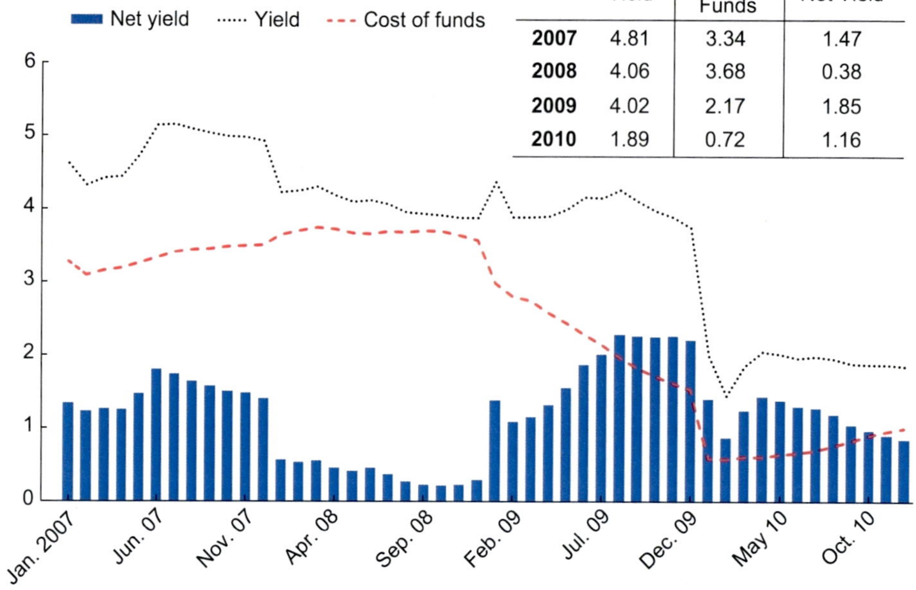


| | Yield | Cost of Funds | Net Yield |
|---|---|---|---|
| **2007** | 4.81 | 3.34 | 1.47 |
| **2008** | 4.06 | 3.68 | 0.38 |
| **2009** | 4.02 | 2.17 | 1.85 |
| **2010** | 1.89 | 0.72 | 1.16 |

Source: Authors' calculations.

**Figure 14.7** Central Bank Net International Reserve Yields and Cost of Funds *(Percent)*

The surges of capital inflows before the collapse of Lehman Brothers and the effects of the second round of qualitative easing in Peru resulted in the growth of demand for different financial instruments in local currency by nonresident participants, including the sterilization papers of the central bank. To avoid the circularity of sterilized intervention attracting more capital inflows, the central bank implemented three measures: (1) imposition of a 4 percent fee for the purchase or sale of BCRP paper to participants different than local financial institutions in order to reduce resale to nonresident players, (2) an increase to 120 percent of the reserve requirement on deposits in local currency to nonresident agents, and (3) substitution of certificates for term deposits as an instrument of sterilization to avoid the resale of other instruments in local currency to nonresident agents, and their subsequent replacement by BCRP paper.

Other macroprudential measures were put in place by Peru's Superintendency of Banking, Insurance, and Private Pension Funds and by the Treasury. The former cut the limit for the long position in net foreign position for banks from 75 percent to 60 percent, limited the amount of daily and weekly foreign exchange operations by pension funds, and recently prepublished a norm that limits the long position in derivatives for banks to 40 percent of their net worth.

For its part, the Treasury has taxed the capital gains generated by forward contracts with a rate of 30 percent, and recently issued bonds in the international markets denominated in domestic currency but paid in foreign currency. This operation increased the demand for foreign currency by domestic agents that purchased those bonds. The BCRP increased the limit on foreign investment of pension funds from 17 percent to 30 percent in 2010.

## RESERVE REQUIREMENTS

The accumulation of liquid foreign currency by financial intermediaries has been determined mainly by macroprudential policies. In particular, the BCRP uses reserve requirements to manage capital flows and at the same time accumulate a buffer stock of international reserves. For instance, during the capital-inflow episode of the first quarter of 2008, the central bank raised

**TABLE 14.3**

## Peru: Monetary Policy Interest Rate and Reserve Requirement Ratios, 2002–11 *(Percent)*

| | | Reserve Requirements Ratios | | | | | | | |
|---|---|---|---|---|---|---|---|---|---|
| | | | | | | Foreign Currency | | | |
| | | | Domestic Currency | | | General Regime | | External Liabilities | |
| | Monetary Policy Interest Rate: Reference Rate for the Interbank Money Market | Legal Minimum Required Ratio | Marginal Requirement for Deposits | Policy Increases in the Average Ratio | Required Ratio for Nonresidents | Marginal Requirement for Deposits | Policy Increases in the Average Ratio | Short Term | Long Term |
| **I. Pre-Lehman Brothers: Capital Inflows and Inflationary Pressures in Emerging Markets** | | | | | | | | | |
| May 2006 | 4.50 | 6.00 | | | | 30.00 | | 30.00 | 30.00 |
| Jul. 2007 | 4.75 | 6.00 | | | | 30.00 | | 30.00 | 30.00 |
| Sep. 2007 | 5.00 | 6.00 | | | | 30.00 | | 30.00 | — |
| Jan. 2008 | 5.25 | 6.00 | | | | 30.00 | | 30.00 | — |
| Mar. 2008 | 5.25 | 8.00 | 15.00 | | 15.00 | 40.00 | | 40.00 | — |
| Apr. 2008 | 5.50 | 9.00 | 20.00 | | 40.00 | 45.00 | | 45.00 | — |
| Jun. 2008 | 5.75 | 9.00 | 20.00 | | 40.00 | 45.00 | | 45.00 | — |
| Jul. 2008 | 6.00 | 9.00 | 25.00 | | 120.00 | 49.00 | | 49.00 | 9.00 |
| Aug. 2008 | 6.25 | 9.00 | 25.00 | | 120.00 | 49.00 | | 49.00 | 9.00 |
| Sep. 2008 | 6.50 | 9.00 | 25.00 | | 120.00 | 49.00 | | 49.00 | 9.00 |
| **II. Post-Lehman Brothers and QE:1** | | | | | | | | | |
| Post-Lehman Brothers: Deepest Stage of the Crisis and QE:1 | | | | | | | | | |
| Oct. 2008 | 6.50 | 9.00 | | | 120.00 | 35.00 | | — | — |
| Dec. 2008 | 6.50 | 7.50 | | | 35.00 | 30.00 | | — | — |
| Feb. 2009 | 6.25 | 7.50 | | | 35.00 | 30.00 | | — | — |
| Mar. 2009 | 6.00 | 6.00 | | | 35.00 | 30.00 | | — | — |
| Post-Lehman Brothers: Quick Recovery of Emerging Markets and QE:1 | | | | | | | | | |
| Apr. 2009 | 5.00 | 6.00 | | | 35.00 | 30.00 | | — | — |
| May 2009 | 4.00 | 6.00 | | | 35.00 | 30.00 | | — | — |
| Jun. 2009 | 3.00 | 6.00 | | | 35.00 | 30.00 | | — | — |
| Jul. 2009 | 2.00 | 6.00 | | | 35.00 | 30.00 | | — | — |
| Aug. 2009 | 1.25 | 6.00 | | | 35.00 | 30.00 | | — | — |
| Dec. 2009 | 1.25 | 6.00 | | | 35.00 | 30.00 | | — | — |
| Feb. 2010 | 1.25 | 6.00 | | | 35.00 | 30.00 | | 35.00 | — |
| **III. Post-Lehman Brothers: Full Recovery in Emerging Markets and QE:2** | | | | | | | | | |
| May 2010 | 1.50 | 6.00 | | | 35.00 | 30.00 | | 35.00 | — |
| Jun. 2010 | 1.75 | 6.00 | | | 35.00 | 30.00 | | 35.00 | — |
| Jul. 2010 | 2.00 | 7.00 | | | 40.00 | 35.00 | | 40.00 | — |
| Aug. 2010 | 2.50 | 8.00 | 12.00 | | 50.00 | 45.00 | 0.10 | 50.00 | — |
| Sep. 2010 | 3.00 | 8.50 | 15.00 | | 120.00 | 50.00 | 0.20 | 65.00 | — |
| Oct. 2010 | 3.00 | 9.00 | 25.00 | | 120.00 | 55.00 | 0.20 | 75.00 | — |
| Nov. 2010 | 3.00 | 9.00 | 25.00 | | 120.00 | 55.00 | | 75.00 | — |
| Dec. 2010 | 3.00 | 9.00 | 25.00 | | 120.00 | 55.00 | | 75.00 | — |

Sources: Authors' calculations.

the reserve requirements in domestic and foreign currency, combining this policy with a series of other measures aimed at discouraging holdings of central bank instruments by nonresident investors. The rate of marginal reserve requirements in domestic currency was raised from 6 percent to 25 percent (Table 14.3), the rate of reserve requirements for deposits of nonresidents was raised to 120 percent, and the rate of marginal reserve requirements in foreign currency was raised from 30 percent to 49 percent.[3]

[3] During the intensification of the global financial crisis in the last quarter of 2008, the reserve requirements were reduced in order to avoid a credit contraction.

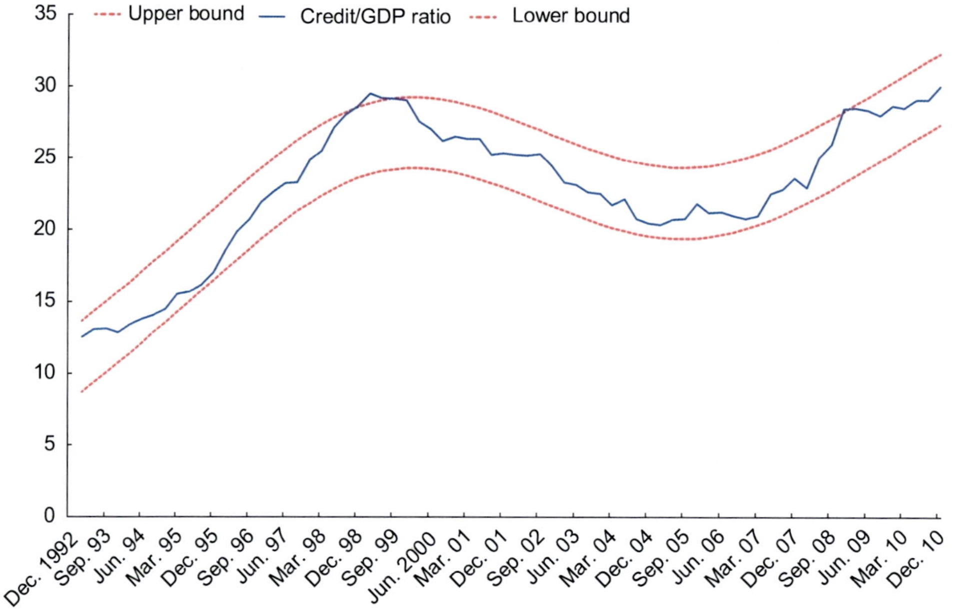


Source: Authors' calculations.

**Figure 14.8** Peru: Credit/GDP Ratio, 1993–2010 *(Annual ratios from quarterly data, in percent)*

In addition, due to the quantitative easing measures in the developed world, there was a resurgence of capital inflows during the second half of 2010. In this case, the BCRP reinstated its reserve requirement policies, raising the requirement to 25 percent in domestic currency, 55 percent in foreign currency, and 75 percent for external short-term liabilities of the financial system. It also reinstated the reserve requirement ratio for domestic currency deposits of non-resident investors to 120 percent. Noting greater dynamism of lending to the domestic market from domestic bank subsidiaries abroad, the BCRP also included their liabilities within the total liabilities subject to reserve requirements.[4]

Rossini and Quispe (2010) describe the credit crunch in Peru in 1999–2001 as being caused by the combination of an initial surge of capital inflows and a subsequent expansion of banking credit, followed by a sharp contraction of credit produced by a sudden stop of capital flows and a sharp currency depreciation caused by the 1998 Russian crisis. Figure 14.8 shows the evolution of banking credit as a proportion of GDP, including a band of ±2 standard deviations of the credit-to-GDP ratio over the sample constructed around a series smoothed by a Hodrick-Prescott filter, which can be used to identify periods of excessive credit expansion or contraction. Following the recovery from the financial crisis, credit has been evolving within this band.

## REAL EXCHANGE RATES

The nominal appreciation of the exchange rate caused by capital inflows raised concerns about the negative effect of this situation on the tradable sectors. To assess this impact, we studied data of the real exchange rate and evaluated the deviations from the equilibrium real exchange rate. In both cases, the surge of capital inflows has not involved a major negative effect on competitiveness for Peru.

[4]In September 2007, the central bank eliminated the reserve requirements for external loans with two-year or longer maturities of commercial banks in order to extend their maturities. The longer-term external funding of banks increased from 17 percent of total external funding in October 2007 to 50 percent in December 2007.

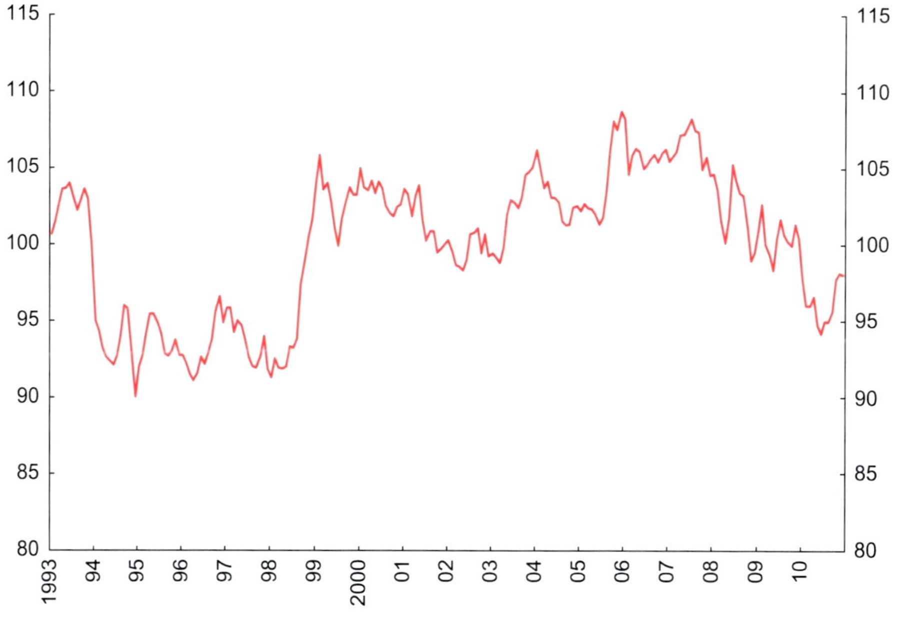


Source: Authors' calculations.

**Figure 14.9** Effective Real Exchange Rate *(Index based on 1993–2010 average = 100)*

**TABLE 14.4**

**Coefficient of Variability of the Real Effective Exchange Rate** *(Percent)*

| Country | Dec 1994–Dec 2010 | Jan 2001–Dec 2010 | Country | Dec 1994–Dec 2010 | Jan 2001–Dec 2010 |
|---|---|---|---|---|---|
| Brazil | 21.3 | 22.7 | United States | 8.0 | 7.8 |
| Czech Republic | 20.9 | 11.5 | Israel | 9.2 | 6.3 |
| South Africa | 14.1 | 12.2 | Thailand | 10.2 | 7.0 |
| Korea | 11.9 | 11.9 | Euro area | 7.3 | 5.3 |
| Indonesia | 19.1 | 7.8 | Chile | 7.7 | 6.9 |
| Philippines | 11.6 | 11.3 | Sweden | 7.7 | 5.4 |
| Australia | 12.3 | 10.5 | India | 4.6 | 4.5 |
| Canada | 10.8 | 9.9 | Malaysia | 9.5 | 3.7 |
| Japan | 13.9 | 9.0 | Switzerland | 4.9 | 4.0 |
| United Kingdom | 9.3 | 9.7 | Singapore | 5.4 | 3.7 |
| Mexico | 12.7 | 8.4 | Peru | **5.1** | **3.6** |

Source: Bank for International Settlements.
Note: Calculations based on the Bank for International Settlements' exchange rate indices.

Figure 14.9 presents the evolution of the index of the effective real exchange rate. The rate was around ±5 percent of the average level over 1993–2010. This relatively stable real exchange rate holds up in international comparisons. In Table 14.4, the comparative coefficient of variability among 22 countries shows that the real effective exchange rate (REER) of the Peruvian currency was the third least volatile from December 1994 to December 2010. Moreover, for a shorter period, from January 2001 to December 2010, Peru had the least volatile REER.

We use the behavioral equilibrium exchange rate method to estimate the equilibrium real exchange rate. Table 14.5 shows the estimated elasticities of the REER from its fundamental determinants.[5] According to the estimations, this approach shows no major misalignments of the REER with respect to its equilibrium path (Figure 14.10).

[5]The calculations are based on Rodriguez (2011).

**TABLE 14.5**

**Empirical Results**

| Fundamental Variable | Elasticity |
|---|---|
| Net Foreign Liabilities/GDP | 0.20 |
| Terms of Trade | −0.24 |
| Trade Liberalization (exports and imports)/GDP | 0.14 |
| Peruvian GDP/GDP of Peru's Trade Partners | −0.30 |
| Public Expenditure/GDP | −0.01 |
| Credit Dollarization Ratio | 0.08 |

Source: Authors' calculations.

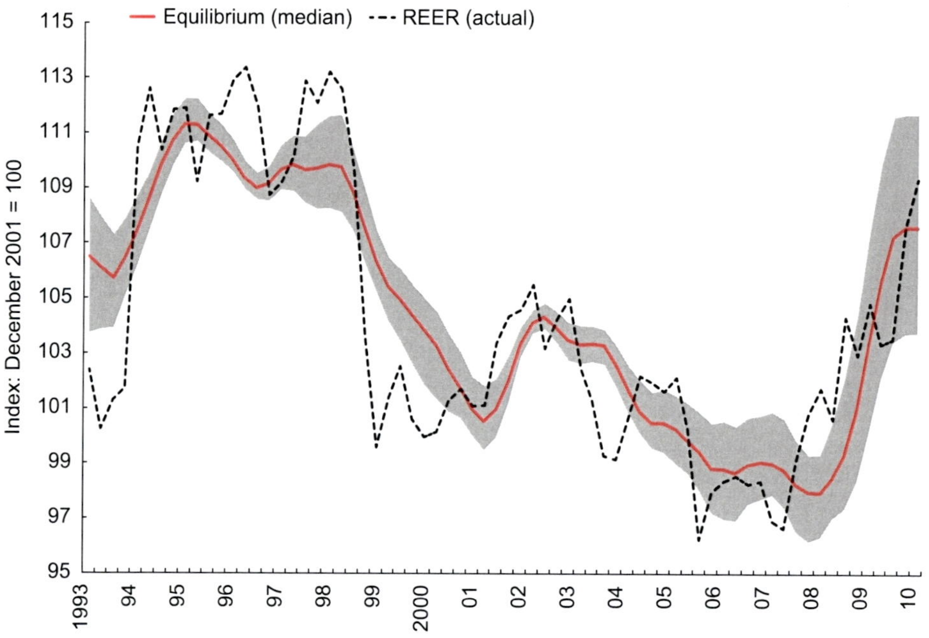


Source: Authors' calculations.
Note: REER = real effective exchange rate.

**Figure 14.10** Peru: Behavioral Equilibrium Exchange Rate

# CONCLUSIONS

Peru's central bank has developed a policy framework based on a risk management approach. In this sense, the vulnerabilities associated with partial dollarization of the banking system have been taken into account in adding nonconventional policy tools such as intervention in the foreign exchange market, accumulation of international reserves, and application of different forms of reserve requirements and liquidity sterilization. With this policy framework, the Peruvian economy was relatively isolated from the effects of the global financial crisis and able to recover growth with low inflation and avoid major disruptions from the surge of capital inflows.

## REFERENCES

Armas, A. 2004. "Forex Interventions in Peru: 2002-2004." BIS Paper 24, Bank for International Settlements, Basel, Switzerland.

Rodriguez, Donita. 2011. "The Determinants of the Equilibrium Real Exchange Rate in Peru." Working Paper, Central Reserve Bank of Peru, Lima.

Rossini, R., and Z. Quispe. 2010. "Monetary Policy during the Global Financial Crisis of 2007-2009: The Case of Peru." BIS Paper 54, Bank for International Settlements, Basel, Switzerland.

Rossini, R., Z. Quispe, and R. Gondo. 2008. "Macroeconomic Implications of Capital Inflows in Peru: 1991–2007." BIS Paper 44, Bank for International Settlements, Basel, Switzerland.

CHAPTER 15

# The Peruvian Financial System from 1990–2014: Balancing Development and Financial Stability

Javier Poggi, Lucia Romero, Manuel Luy, and Narda Sotomayor

*After a period of severe financial turmoil in the late 1980s, the Peruvian economy stabilized in the early 1990s, which has allowed for healthy growth of the financial system over the past 25 years. This chapter analyzes the developments of the financial system over that period and explains the advances from the regulatory perspective. Enormous progress has been made in the areas of growth, diversification, expansion of new markets, and financial inclusion, with some international best practices adapted to the Peruvian context. Progress was achieved in a stable environment of prudential regulation, ensuring the sustainability of the gains and forming the basis for solid economic development. However, there remains considerable room for innovation, further development of new markets, efficiency gains, and higher levels of financial inclusion.*

The aim of the chapter is to review developments in Peru's financial system over the past 25 years from two perspectives. First, a historical perspective describes the significant changes that have occurred in the scope and functioning of the financial system as well as its risk profile. This reflects a great capacity to deal with adverse scenarios, giving Peru an exceptional level of financial stability, which is an essential ingredient for sound and sustainable economic growth. Second, a regulatory perspective shows how a strong regulatory framework adapted to Peru's circumstances has been built. The regulatory framework developed by the Superintendency of Banking, Insurance, and Private Pension Funds (*Superintendencia de Banca, Seguros y AFP* [SBS]) has adapted international standards to the local risk environment and supplemented them with innovative regulatory proposals to manage risks relevant to Peru's markets, even though these risks have not been sufficiently addressed at the international level. The comprehensiveness of Peru's regulations makes them a standard for prudential regulation in Latin America.

This chapter starts by describing the development of Peru's financial system over the past 25 years, highlighting the major changes that have occurred in recent years in terms of diversified growth, development of new markets (particularly the dynamism of the microfinance sector), extension of investment portfolio maturities, and dedollarization of the economy. The chapter then covers regulatory issues, highlighting the adoption of international best standards reinforced with ad hoc prudential regulations tailored to the specific characteristics of the national financial system. The chapter describes the strengths of Peru's current financial system and then provides some final comments.

## DEVELOPMENT OF THE FINANCIAL SYSTEM

The Peruvian financial system was in a state of collapse in 1990. The system consisted mainly of the subsidized development bank and a mutual housing program, both of which were practically bankrupt as a result of hyperinflation and interest rate controls. Hyperinflation, together with the freezing of foreign currency certificates of deposit and the attempt to nationalize the commercial banking system in the second half of the 1980s, led to massive capital outflows and a significant increase in financial informality. The financial system was reduced to a minimum, access to credit was almost nonexistent for most of the population, and there was a major credit crunch that prevented the financing of even the most important economic activities.

In 1991, the government launched a major process of economic reform, including reform of the financial system. The country's new constitution and the revamped General Law on the Financial System and Insurance System sought to promote free competition, with the state playing a secondary role, and establish a level playing field for domestic and foreign investment to encourage the entry of intermediaries with more advanced technologies. In addition, the public's right to freely hold foreign currency was guaranteed and banks were given the freedom to set interest rates, commissions, and fees. This led to the development of efficient financial intermediation in line with the characteristics and needs of the Peruvian economy, and laid the foundation for sound business growth.

Moreover, passage of a series of laws regarding the Central Reserve Bank of Peru (*Banco Central de Reserva del Perú* [BCRP]), the National Enterprises and Securities Supervisory Commission (now the Superintendency of the Securities Market), and the SBS allowed for the reorganization of these institutions and the creation of conditions to enable regulation and supervision to keep pace with new developments in the market.

In the past 25 years, Peru's financial system has undergone a remarkable transformation. As a result of the new environment that began to take shape in the 1990s and has been continually improved since, the role of the financial system in the economy and the country's development has changed dramatically. Examining what was accomplished will help us understand the evolution of the financial system both in terms of the country's extraordinary growth and the multifaceted transformation that took place.

## Exceptional Financial System Growth

Peru's financial system has grown more than 10 times in the past 20 years. In 1994, the financial system had assets of S/. 21.6 billion (about US$9.8 billion), and by June 2014 those assets exceeded S/. 300 billion (about US$105.7 billion). This growth is equivalent to an average annual rate of 14.2 percent in nominal terms (when inflation was running at about 4 percent on average). Loans and deposits grew at a similar pace, with an average annual growth rate over the past 20 years of 14.9 percent and 13.3 percent, respectively. This growth occurred in a favorable economic environment in which the Peruvian economy grew at average annual rate of 4.7 percent and in which GDP per capita quadrupled.

## Significant Growth in the Household Lending Market

In the first few years after the financial system reform, the loan portfolio was focused on providing short-term financing for business activities. However, conditions were coming together for the expansion of financing to other segments of the market that had previously not been served. Thus, while in 1995, 92 percent of the loan portfolio was devoted to financing business activities and only 8 percent financed individuals and households (6 percent consumer and 2 percent mortgages), by 2005 household financing accounted for 30 percent of loans, chiefly as a result of the growth of mortgage lending. At present, the share of loans to individuals accounts for 34 percent of all financial system loans (18 percent consumer and 15 percent mortgages). Consumer retail lending (by installments) accounts for 60 percent of consumer credit, the credit card market for 34 percent, and the vehicle lending market 6 percent. Two major factors are responsible for this change in the market niches served by the financial system. First, the corporate and large enterprise segments are now able to obtain financing on the international market, both by issuing paper and by borrowing directly from foreign banks. Second, a significant increase in income per capita and employment levels has made it possible to finance households that were previously unable to obtain credit.

## Becoming the World Leader in the Development of Microfinancing

The poor results in the past from direct government intervention in the financial system involved efforts to serve segments of the population not served by traditional banking (either because of geographic location or sector, or because of the size of the productive unit). This led to a different approach to promoting access to financing for low-income segments of the population, especially microenterprises. It was understood that the government should not participate directly in financial intermediation, but that it had a responsibility to provide a legal and regulatory environment that would enable both public and private providers of financial services to develop relevant products and appropriate technologies to serve microenterprises in a profitable and sustainable manner. To that end, the political vision included two key elements: (1) promotion of the involvement of multiple actors and (2) emphasis on the regulation of microcredit activities.

The first element consisted of attracting to the regulated system interested financial service providers—especially those providers with the required know-how—willing to serve the least favored segments of society. Thus, a microfinance sector began to take shape. Its origins date back more than 30 years to the creation of municipal savings and loan banks (the first in 1983) to promote equitable, decentralized growth in Peru. As those banks were not sufficient to serve rural and urban microenterprises throughout the country, specialized private entities started to be created in the mid-1990s. This led to the appearance of rural savings and loan banks owned by local and regional investors, which were called upon to fill the vacuum created by the liquidation of the agricultural bank (*Banco Agrario*). The authorities later promoted the conversion of nongovernmental organizations into regulated entities, the largest nongovernmental organization into a specialized bank, and others under the license of Micro- and Small Enterprise Development Entities. Initially, all these various types of entities were governed by special laws, but pursuant to the General Law on the Financial System and the Insurance System of 1996, microfinance institutions were incorporated into the financial system on the same terms as banking institutions. Since then, they have been governed by the General Law, supplemented by specific laws. The microfinance system is now mature, with a market share slightly above 11 percent in terms of the size of its assets, although it finances 44 percent of financial system borrowers.

The microfinance institutions' main activity has always been to grant loans to microenterprises. As a result of the microfinance institutions' interaction with these enterprises, it was understood that this was a different activity than commercial lending, which should be recognized in the regulations. Thus, for the first time, in August 1997 microcredit was defined in the regulations as a new credit category, covered by the Regulation on Debtor Assessment and Classification and the Provisioning Requirement.[1] It was also specified that the regulation be generally applicable to all financial system enterprises engaged in that activity. The definition of microcredit was modified over time to better reflect market realities and characterize the risks involved, but the criterion of limiting risk was kept unchanged by establishing a debt ceiling for financial system borrowers. At present, microcredit and lending to small enterprises are distinguished from other types of business lending and both benefit from rules that allow for the use of appropriate technologies to serve the recipients of microcredit, who are typically informal borrowers with scant documentation and little or no credit history. The requirements governing the documentation that the customer must submit are minimal, and the criterion for classifying debtor risk is very simple, based solely on the number of days a payment is late. These standards go hand in hand with the

[1] SBS Resolution No. 572-97, amended by SBS Resolution No. 808-2003 and, subsequently, by SBS Resolution No. 11356-2008.

provisioning requirements and with the strict monitoring of portfolio quality, according to which a delay in a microloan installment payment renders the entire microloan delinquent. This way, it is possible to define an adequate regulation for microcredit without sacrificing prudence, as the focus is on limiting risk and, consequently, defining rules consistent with the principle of proportionality. These rules have not only simplified the process of evaluating and classifying loans to microenterprises, they have also expedited approval and reduced the costs of granting and monitoring loans, opening the door to a major expansion of the portfolio. From the regulatory amendment of 1997 to date, the number of micro and small enterprises (MSEs) that have obtained credit from the financial system has grown considerably. Between mid-2002 and mid-2014, the number of MSE borrowers rose from 361,000 to more than 2 million.

In mid-2014, the MSE credit market was served primarily by 39 microfinance entities, as well as by commercial banks, and MSE loans totaled S/. 31,418.8 million. In general, the regulations and standards adopted by the SBS over the past two decades have promoted the democratization of credit, greater competition in the MSE credit market, improved risk management by enterprises, and greater market transparency, which has contributed to the growth of microfinance. This positive environment has been recognized internationally, and Peru has been selected six times in a row as the best environment for the development of microfinance, according to the Economist Intelligence Unit. Moreover, when the Economist Intelligence Unit study[2] was expanded in 2014 to analyze the environment for financial inclusion, Peru once again came out on top.

## Notable Progress on Financial Inclusion

The SBS's interest in microcredit is only the beginning of a more comprehensive vision of financial system development that has been taking shape over time, inspired by international experiences and especially by interactions with the industry. It was understood that although the stability of the financial system is essential, it is also necessary to seek the participation of all segments of the population in the financial system. The benefits of financial inclusion—including the accumulation and profitability of savings, investment financing, coverage, and diversification and reduction of risks—make this a key instrument for achieving greater social inclusion and economic development. Consequently, in the process of seeking a balance between the objectives of stability, integrity, and inclusion, an overall strategy was fine-tuned to promote financial inclusion. This included changes and refinements in the regulatory and supervisory environment as well as specific actions to improve the financial culture of the population.

The objective was to make improvements in the regulatory framework that would encourage the development of products and services (microloans, microinsurance, basic accounts, and e-money) within the means and reach of all, as well as the opening of channels closer to the population that were also inexpensive for service providers.

Toward the mid-2000s, major advances were made in microcredit development and transparency regarding the cost of financial services. However, access to financial services was still limited. At end-2000, there were 1,987 financial system offices and automatic teller machines located in only 8 percent of all districts at the national level, which meant that there were 13 service points for every 100,000 inhabitants. Toward the end of 2005, the number of service points had grown to 3,701, or 22 service points for every 100,000 inhabitants, but they were still concentrated in the largest cities.

The high costs of traditional channels hampered financial system growth, especially in the more remote and less densely populated areas. In response to this problem, the SBS issued a regulation in 2005 authorizing financial institutions to provide services through "correspondent tellers,"[3] which are service points operating in establishments owned by individuals or legal

[2]Economist Intelligence Unit. 2014. *Global Microscope on the Microfinance Business Environment* (2007–14). London, UK: Economist Intelligence Unit.

[3]SBS Circular No. B2147-2005, replaced by SBS Resolution SBS No. 775-2008.

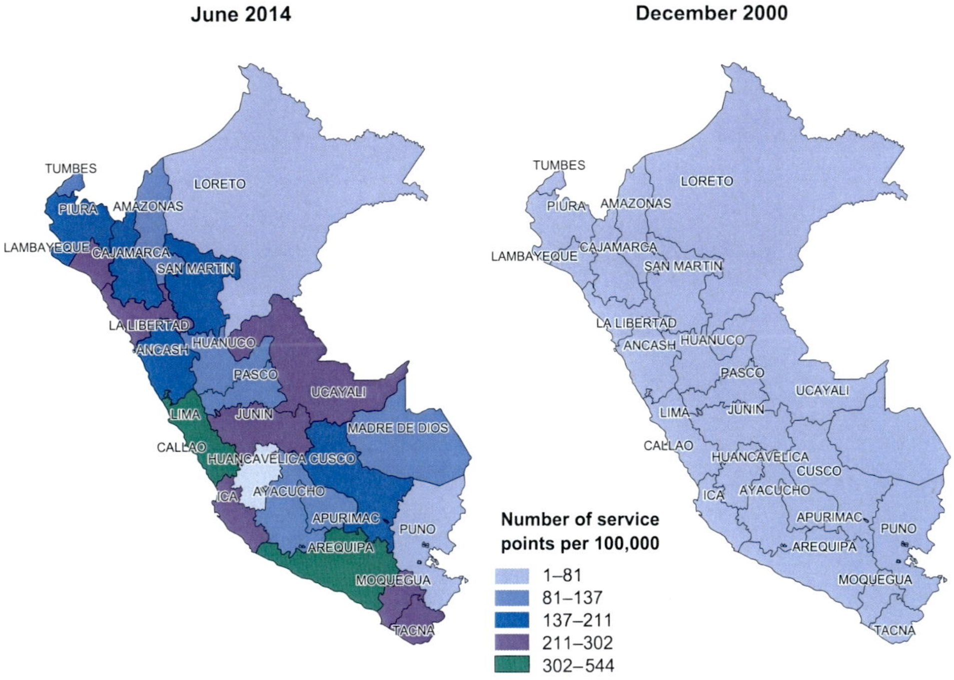


Source: Superintendency of Banking, Insurance and Pension Funds.

**Figure 15.1** Access to Financial Services

entities other than financial entities. These service points are an effective, low-cost instrument for reaching the public. The years following the introduction of correspondent tellers saw remarkable growth of the financial system service network at the national level. By end-2010, access to financial services had improved significantly. The number of financial system service points (offices, automatic teller machines, and correspondent tellers) climbed to 23,748 points (that is, 130 points for every 100,000 inhabitants) and the number of districts in which the financial system had a presence grew to 33 percent of the total. The dynamism created by the increase in correspondent tellers continued between 2010 and 2014, with the number of service points rising to 30,315, representing an increase from 13 to 280 service points for every 100,000 inhabitants over the period, and a financial system presence in a little more than 50 percent of all districts at the national level (Figure 15.1). However, those districts are home to 91 percent of the population.

Although the operations made available through correspondent tellers were initially limited to payments, withdrawals, cash deposits, and transfers, they were gradually expanded. In recent years, the opening of basic savings accounts (in small amounts and with few transactions), handling of e-money transactions, and the distribution of microinsurance have been permitted. The industry has yet to take advantage of this expansion of operations through correspondent tellers.

The improvement in access to financial services was also accompanied by major advances in the use of such services, although that progress is more pronounced for loans. For example, the total number of financial system debtors went from a little more than 1 million in 2000 to more than 6 million in 2014. The percentage of individual debtors relative to the adult population went from 8 percent in 2000 to 17 percent in 2005, 25 percent in 2010, and 30.7 percent in June 2014.

Despite the progress, the gap in financial inclusion is still wide because the factors that affect it are beyond the financial regulator's scope of action. In general, the most difficult remaining

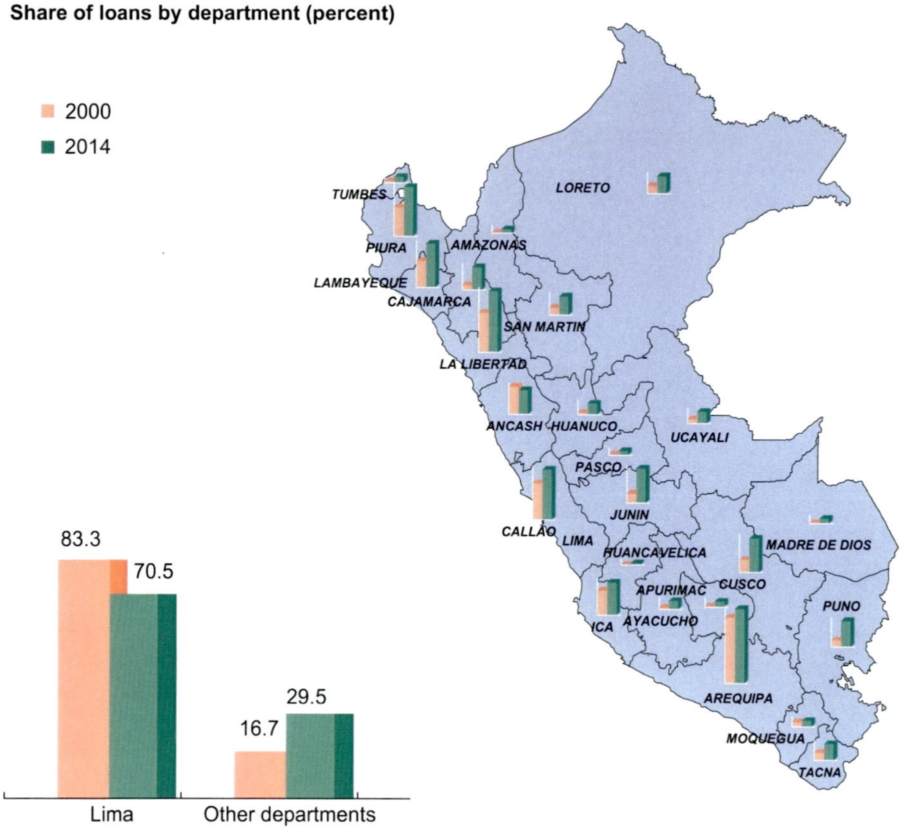


Source: Superintendency of Banking, Insurance and Pension Funds.

**Figure 15.2** Regional Diversification of Loans

challenges—especially that of reaching the poorest and most remote populations—will require a joint effort by the public institutions that represent the various sectors. Consequently, the National Financial Inclusion Strategy that is being developed brings together the Ministry of the Economy and Finance, the Ministry of Development and Social Inclusion, the BCRP, Banco de la Nación, and the SBS.

## Promoting Diversified Growth: Financial Services in the Regions and Sectoral Diversification of Loans

Another important change in expanding the financial system was the transition from growth concentrated in the capital to a higher regional presence of financial institutions. The use of correspondent tellers as a means of providing services, as well as the SBS's authorization for municipal savings and loan banks to operate in areas outside the jurisdiction of their municipality, had a positive impact on the growth dynamic of financial system loans and deposits by geographic area. This trend toward decentralization, seen especially on the credit side, has meant that over the past 15 years, while loans in the Lima Department grew at an annual average rate of 10.4 percent, loans in the rest of the country grew at an annual average rate of 16.5 percent.

Thus, the share of loans in Lima went from 83.3 percent of all loans at the national level at end-2000 to 70.5 percent in June 2014. The average annual growth of deposits in the provinces over the past 15 years was also slightly higher than in Lima (12.8 percent versus 11 percent), so Lima's share of total deposits decreased from 82.3 percent to 81 percent during the period (Figure 15.2).

Lending has also contributed to the productive diversification of the economy. In this regard, it is important to note the decrease over the past 15 years in the share of loans to the primary export sectors, such as fisheries and mining, and the significant increase in the financing of trade and services. There was also a change in the structure of financing in the manufacturing sector, with the textiles and food and beverages subsectors posting the least growth (annual averages of 6 percent and 8 percent, respectively), while the financing of nonmetallic ore production and the manufacture of chemical substances and products posted the most growth.

## Greater Economic Stability Enabled the Financial System to Extend Loan Maturities

The possibility for the financial system to switch to longer maturities led to development of the mortgage loan market, the granting of financial leases, and the expansion of financing for infrastructure investment projects. Thus, while in the 1990s barely 20 percent of all loans had maturities of more than one year, such loans now account for more than 60 percent of the loan portfolio. This development reflects the increased stability of the Peruvian economy and is highly significant because expanding the financing horizon has made many more projects feasible, with obvious benefits for private investment.

## Significant Dedollarization of the Financial System

Another major change in Peru's financial system has been the significant reduction in the dollarization of loans and deposits since 2002. Because of the hyperinflation in the 1980s and early 1990s, hysteresis continued to affect the behavior of economic agents, which kept financial dollarization at high levels for another decade. A combination of various factors explains the dedollarization process observed since then. One contributing factor was the package of macroeconomic stabilization policies that yielded favorable results. In 2002, the BCRP switched its monetary policy to an inflation-targeting framework—initially, the BCRP targeted inflation at 2.5 percent and then in 2007 an inflation target of 2 percent was set, with a range of tolerance of ±1. This made it possible to anchor inflation expectations, keep the floating exchange rate with low volatility, and accumulate a significant quantity of international reserves, which enabled the country to deal with stress situations. Also contributing to these positive developments were the BCRP's required reserve policy and the country's dynamic economic activity during most of the period.

Another contributing factor was the SBS's prudential regulation measures, which addressed the latent risk of high dollarization from two angles. The first aimed to limit the foreign currency exposures of financial system enterprises. A limit was therefore placed on the net derivatives position, which was adjusted gradually with a view to discouraging speculation by institutional agents. The second sought to reduce foreign exchange credit risk, to which end a strategy was developed to create appropriate incentives for enterprises to lend to their customers in the same currency as that in which they generate income, an issue that will be discussed later in this chapter.

Thus, dollarization, which in the early 2000s was close to 80 percent and 73 percent for loans and deposits, respectively, began to descend gradually. It reached its lowest levels in the first half of 2013 for deposits (35 percent) and in mid-2014 for loans (39 percent). For mortgage loans, in particular, the decline in dollarization was much more pronounced, going from a mortgage portfolio almost entirely in dollars (approximately 95 percent of the mortgage portfolio between January 2001 and mid-2006) to 35 percent in 2014. This was attributable both to the impetus given the *MiVivienda* financing program in domestic currency and to the steps taken by the SBS to monitor foreign exchange credit risk, particularly at end-2012. These measures require financial enterprises to make larger capital provisions for mortgage loans issued in foreign currency.

# DEVELOPMENT OF THE FINANCIAL SYSTEM REGULATORY FRAMEWORK

In the early 1990s, the basis for a new legal framework for the Peruvian financial system was set. Based on this new environment, the SBS developed a comprehensive prudential regulatory framework, recently supplemented with an innovative macroprudential regulatory system. Thus, in the 1990s, certain basic elements of prudential regulation were modernized, including essentially a new standard for market and liquidity risk provisions and regulations.

The efforts to strengthen prudential regulation were only a first step and proved insufficient to enable the financial system to avoid—without further complications—the domestic and external economic shocks that significantly affected the Peruvian economy in the late 1990s.

The lessons learned from that experience led to a process of strengthening prudential regulation and resulted in the current regulatory framework of the Peruvian financial system, which today is aligned with international best standards without losing sight of the specific characteristics of the local financial system.

The development of this regulatory framework was based on certain basic principles and thus designed to be:

- Comprehensive, covering all risks related to the functioning of the Peruvian financial system.
- Focused on risk management best practices, that is, requiring financial system enterprises to develop effective risk identification, measurement, management, and monitoring.
- Balanced, in that it seeks to ensure that regulatory requirements are proportional to the scale and complexity of the various institutions that make up the financial system.
- Dynamic, in that it is adaptable to changes occurring in the economic and financial environment that could result in the potential accumulation of financial system risks.
- Forward-looking, in that it promotes the use of tools that enable financial system enterprises to achieve long-term sustainability. In this regard, the latest macroprudential developments have proven to be essential.

As mentioned above, the regulatory framework of the Peruvian financial system was also designed to be sufficiently flexible to ensure that risk management and alignment requirements are properly balanced with opportunities for financial innovation and development.

Below is a summary covering the past 25 years of changes in the legal framework, major normative developments in the regulatory framework currently governing the Peruvian financial system, and independent assessments carried out by international organizations concerning the quality of regulation and supervision in the Peruvian financial system.

## Legal Changes

### *Structural and Financial Liberalization Reforms*

In the early 1990s, a significant change in the legal framework of the financial system paved the way for a process of sustained development. Although this process was not free of problems, it led to the current system, which is both sound and regulated in accordance with international best standards.

The reform consisted of promoting free competition in the financial system, reducing the government's presence, removing interest rate ceilings and direct credit controls, and eliminating subsidized loans for public sector financing. In 1991, a new General Law on the Financial and Insurance System (Decree Law 637) was approved. An important aspect of this law is that the overall operational limit for the Peruvian financial system began to converge with the capital requirement standards of the Basel Committee. The law also created the Deposit Insurance Fund.

The Organic Law of the Superintendency of Banking and Insurance (Decree Law 25987), approved in 1992, preserved the operational, economic, and administrative autonomy of the SBS.

Finally, in 1996, Law 26702, the General Law on the Financial and Insurance System and Organic Law of the Superintendency of Banking and Insurance, was approved. This law amended the legislation governing the financial system, which in recent times had changed rapidly. The law fully incorporated the regulations on credit risks contained in the 1988 Basel Accord and its 1996 amendment concerning market risks. The law helped modernize the system and further strengthened the SBS, making contributions in three areas: consolidated supervision, antimoney laundering rules, and prevention of credit concentration.

Law 26702 stated that the capital-to-risk-weighted assets ratio could not be less than 9.1 percent, slightly more demanding than the ratio of 8 percent specified in the international standards. This minimum requirement constituted recognition that the Peruvian financial system faced greater risks than its developed-country peers. In general, the law adapted the national legislation to the Basel Accord and promoted competition in the financial system.

In general terms, the aim of the financial system reform was to provide a more solid and reliable framework for the development of entities in the system and for the public in general, as well as to promote the emergence of new institutions and instruments for the development of the financial and capital markets.

### *Convergence toward New International Standards*

The General Law on the Financial System and the Insurance System and Organic Law of the Superintendency was amended in 2008 with a view to strengthening the financial system and making it more competitive, implementing Basel II, and enabling the adaptation of the existing regulatory framework for financial services to commitments undertaken in the United States–Peru Trade Promotion Agreement.

Among the main modifications was the change in the prudential legal framework to enable Peru to begin the process of adjustment to the new international standards and embark on a process of harmonization with the frameworks established (or to be established) in other countries. This would minimize regulatory arbitration problems, among other benefits.

These legal modifications enabled the SBS to implement regulatory changes in line with international best standards such as Basel II. These included the incorporation of capital requirements for operational risk and the possibility of using methods based on internal models (for example, the internal ratings–based approach for the capital requirement) and Basel III (for example, the introduction of capital buffers over and above the minimum requirement). In addition, making use of the national discretionary authority provided for in the NCA, the capital requirement under this law was prudentially raised to 10 percent of risk-weighted assets.

## Major Regulatory Developments

### *Provisions*

The rules on provisioning in the Peruvian financial system have evolved over time, from the incorporation of generic provisions in 1997 to the adoption of a dynamic provisioning component in 2008. They are in line with international best standards and include guidelines for the inclusion of local market characteristics.

Various elements of Peru's provisioning rules have made them a key component of the country's prudential framework. Elements that distinguish Peru's rules and reflect its local risk environment include the treatment of collateral and guarantees, risk alignment criteria, and the segmentation of the credit portfolio according to the different types of credit, based on the risk determinants specific to each. This makes it possible to properly segment portfolios with a view to identifying the sensitivity of each to various kinds of shocks and obtain a better approximation of the vulnerabilities of each financial institution.

Since the 1990s, the SBS has been aware that a potential source of risk in the financial system could be associated with a certain level of underprovisioning due to (1) problems in the Peruvian market with proper valuation of various types of collateral that mitigate credit risk and (2) a sudden loss of asset value during periods of economic recession while at the same time liquidation times usually increase. Thus, as a preventive measure to mitigate such risk, Peru's regulations establish provisioning of all loans, even those that are overcollateralized. Typically, the value of collateral or guarantees is deducted from the amount of the debt and the corresponding provisioning rates are applied to the net balance. In such cases, a loan might not be provisioned if it was fully collateralized. In Peru, a provisioning rate is applied to the collateralized portion and a higher rate to the portion of a loan not covered, thus ensuring that all loans have some degree of provisioning to mitigate the effects of insufficient or optimistic valuations of collateral or guarantees.

Another distinctive feature of Peru's regulations comes from the concept of alignment. The payment culture in Peru was weak initially and still needs to be taken into account in the regulatory design. Consequently, regulations require that if a debtor has credit exposures to a number of different institutions, its credit risk rating reflecting payment behavior in a particular financial institution must be informed and considered the same in all the other financial institutions where the debtor also has debts. In other words, the regulations impose a common risk concept for a given debtor, even when the debtor's payment behavior may differ from one institution to another. This encourages a similar payment behavior throughout the financial system and promotes better control of overall credit risk. The inclusion of this element in regulatory design has proven to be sufficiently consistent with actual practices. Various exercises carried out by the SBS show that when a debtor falls behind in a financial institution, it is a very good indicator of the debtor's credit position in the next six months at other institutions.

Regarding the generic provision requirement, until 2008 this provision was the same for different types of debtors (corporate, small and medium enterprises, microenterprise, revolving consumers, etc.), even though it was acknowledged that the implicit risk in these various types of credit was different and that it changed differently over the course of the business cycle. Thus, as a result of the establishment of homogeneous provisioning charges for portfolios with heterogeneous risks, financial institutions specializing in riskier lines of business could have insufficient provisions to cover expected losses in their portfolio, while other institutions with more diversified portfolios could hold provisions larger than their anticipated losses. In other words, risk alignment in the level of required provisions was poor.

In this context, the SBS worked to identify various risk factors in order to be able to differentiate the provisioning requirements and make them more sensitive to risk. As a result of this work, the SBS recognized the heterogeneity of the various types of credit. Credit was therefore divided into eight types, each treated differently. In the business activities segment, there are corporate loans and loans to large, medium, and small enterprises, as well as to microenterprises. In the household segment, there are mortgage loans, revolving consumer loans, and nonrevolving consumer loans. This differentiation is important because it has been proven statistically that the expected losses of those portfolios may differ in both positive and negative stages of the business cycle, so respective provisioning charges therefore should be different. This segmentation also makes it possible to recognize the nature of loans to small and medium enterprises, which, because of their informal nature, cannot be subjected to reporting requirements similar to those applied to a commercial loan. For this reason, a simplified regime was established that facilitates the granting of loans and the monitoring of debtors, without making risk assessment any less strict.

Moreover, the provisioning framework in Peru includes a basic component and a cyclical component that take into account the positive relationship between the business cycle and the credit cycle. In times of economic expansion, buffers are accumulated that can only be used as provisions for portfolio deterioration in negative stages of the business cycle. (The dynamic component of the provisions will be explained in greater detail later in this chapter.)

### *Implementation of Basel II*

In 2003, the SBS created a Special Committee to design a long-term plan for strengthening the financial system with regulatory and supervisory mechanisms to enable implementation of international best standards while at the same time recognize the differences between the global and domestic financial systems. The first task of this committee was to assess the applicability of the New Capital Accord–Basel II (NCA) to the Peruvian financial system.

The committee identified Peru as one of the most advanced countries in the region in terms of implementing and adapting such international regulatory standards. The SBS finished implementing Pillar 1 in 2009, having issued regulations concerning the capital requirement for credit, market, and operational risks that establish different methodologies, including the approaches used in internal models (the internal ratings–based approach and the advanced measurement approach) that financial system enterprises could use to calculate regulatory capital, as well as the conditions governing their use.

The SBS thus aligned itself with the international standards set out in the NCA, but also made certain adjustments in view of the specific risks and circumstances of the Peruvian economy, based on various studies carried out that measured local risks using domestic microdata on the last financial crisis experienced in Peru in the late 1990s.

Although the standardized credit risk approach was implemented in accordance with Basel II guidelines for the calculation of capital requirements using the comprehensive approach, a number of modifications were made in the overall minimum capital requirement and in the weights used for retail banking, based on the loss distribution computed for Peru's business cycle. It was thus determined that the appropriate capital requirement was 10 percent instead of the 8 percent stipulated in the NCA. There were two main reasons for this change: (1) the greater volatility in the loss distribution in an emerging economy such as Peru's, which generates wider tails and, therefore, larger unexpected losses; and (2) a higher risk environment (greater probabilities of default and more severe losses), which requires a higher capital requirement in the standardized approach in order to preserve incentives to migrate toward the internal models on which the NCA is based. Regarding the weights of retail exposures, values of 50 percent for mortgage loans and 100 percent for consumer loans were assigned instead of the 35 percent and 75 percent, respectively, specified in the NCA. In the case of mortgage loans, the approach takes into account the small size and shallowness of the Peruvian real estate market, which could generate more severe losses in the recessionary phase of the business cycle, leading to the adoption of a more conservative value. Unexpected losses were estimated for consumer loans, with the result that the gains generated by the diversification of this type of portfolio, which in Europe justify a smaller risk weighting than for commercial portfolios, were not statistically supported in Peru.

Another relevant difference in the standardized credit risk approach was the establishment of a single weight of 100 percent for commercial loans instead of allowing external risk ratings. This weight was adopted because the local risk rating agencies lacked experience in assessing the solvency of real sector enterprises.

Regarding the internal models approach, a number of changes were also made to adapt the processes of parameter calculation to the Peruvian business cycle. Thus, enterprises wishing to migrate to the basic internal ratings–based approach were required to estimate the probability of default by considering as a minimum an entire business cycle instead of the five years required by the NCA. Those entities wishing to migrate to the advanced internal ratings–based approach are required to have time series for a complete business cycle in order to estimate loss parameters and credit conversion factors. This is based on evidence of greater volatility in the business cycles of emerging economies (such as Peru) than in developed economies. Consequently, given the greater fluctuations, it is essential that more data be included in the estimation in order to obtain consistent and efficient estimates.

As for Pillar 2, financial system enterprises have been required for several years to carry out an Internal Capital Adequacy Assessment Process, incorporating risks in addition to those targeted in Pillar 1 such as individual, geographic, and sectoral concentration risk; interest-rate risk in the banking book; and market concentration risk. In this process, given the heterogeneity of the entities in the Peruvian financial system, the authorities put in place a standardized methodology for assessing these additional risks that could be used by enterprises lacking the necessary infrastructure to make their own economic capital calculations. In addition, since 2014, financial institutions have been required to conduct stress tests using three scenarios provided by the SBS: baseline scenario, stress scenario, and severe stress scenario. The results of these tests will be compared with those obtained from the supervisory top-down model that the SBS has been using since 2008 to determine whether there are significant differences and to provide feedback to the institutions.

### *Basel III and Macroprudential Regulation*

To increase the stability of the financial system, the SBS has been implementing the Basel Committee reforms known as Basel III, adapted to local circumstances. The Basel III implementation program in Peru is comprised of three stages: (1) setting buffers that increase the level of capital, (2) monitoring new prudential liquidity standards, and (3) improving capital quality. The first two stages have already been implemented and the third is in the final phase of development.

Regarding the accumulation of buffers that increase the level of capital, the Regulation on the Additional Capital Requirement issued in 2011 establishes capital charges over and above the regulatory minimum. The purpose of this regulation is to establish capital buffers for business cycles and systemic risk (in a manner consistent with Basel III), as well as buffers for other risks such as individual, regional, and sectoral concentration risk, interest rate risk in the banking book, and a buffer for the bank's risk profile. These features are similar to the "conservation buffer" established in Basel III, but make it more risk-sensitive inasmuch as the calculation is different for each entity, based on the above-mentioned risks. These buffers will be fully implemented in 2016 (the timetable began in 2012) and will constitute, for the financial system as a whole, an additional capital requirement of 3.1 percentage points above the regulatory minimum of 10 percent for entities with greater cumulative risk. This will add as many as 6.6 points to the minimum (16.6 percent capital ratio).

The cyclical buffer established by the Peruvian regulation differs in various ways from the standard proposed by Basel in that it is adapted to local risk features and is more risk-sensitive. The first difference is that in Peru, given that all financial institutions are sensitive to the business cycle, the buffer needed to be required of all institutions without exception and not just to internationally active entities as suggested by the scope of application specified in Basel.

The second major difference is that unlike Basel, Peru's required buffer is established by type of exposure. This is because, according to SBS calculations, the sensitivity of the different types of credit is heterogeneous. In other words, an entity that only has revolving consumer loans—which have proven to be those most sensitive to the business cycle—needs to maintain considerably larger buffers than an entity engaged solely in corporate lending. This means that the size of the buffer required of each entity is sensitive to the business cycle and will be substantially larger, for example, in entities specializing in credit cards than in entities with more diversified portfolios or that specialize in corporate lending, although the buffer requirement is the same for each type of loan, regardless of the entity that grants it. Thus, while Basel III proposes a capital increase of 0 percentage points to 2.5 percentage points, based on the situation of the countries in which each entity operates, in Peru, where banking is less international, this buffer is based on the types of credit granted by each entity and requires additional capital charges ranging from 1 to 5 percentage points (Table 15.1).

TABLE 15.1

Additional Business Cycle Capital Requirements in Peru

| | Base | | Cycle | | Total | |
|---|---|---|---|---|---|---|
| **Types of Credit** | **Risk Weight** | **Capital Required** | **Risk Weight** | **Capital Required** | **Risk Weight** | **Capital Required** |
| Corporations | 100 | 10% | 12 | 1.20% | 112 | 11.20% |
| Large Companies | 100 | 10% | 25 | 2.50% | 125 | 12.50% |
| Medium Companies | 100 | 10% | 30 | 3.00% | 130 | 13.00% |
| Small Companies | 100 | 10% | 35 | 3.50% | 135 | 13.50% |
| Micro Companies | 100 | 10% | 40 | 4.00% | 140 | 14.00% |
| Revolving Consumer | 100 | 10% | 55 | 5.50% | 155 | 15.50% |
| Nonrevolving Consumer | 100 | 10% | 35 | 3.50% | 135 | 13.50% |
| Housing Mortgages | 50 | 5% | 15 | 1.50% | 65 | 6.50% |

Source: Superintendency of Banking, Insurance and Pension Funds.

The third difference is the rule of activation and deactivation of the cyclical component. While developed economies use a rule based on the loans-to-GDP ratio gap, Peru's calculations showed that a rule based solely on GDP growth was a better predictor of the business cycle and its impact on the loan portfolio. This way, a GDP growth threshold was calculated, above this threshold a change in the regime occurred in the relationship between output growth and credit growth (5 percent), which could be due to optimism both on the demand and supply sides, which tend to relax the credit origination criteria. The rule, based solely on GDP, works better in an economy such as Peru's, which is in the process of increasing participation in the banking system (the credit-to-GDP ratio is close to 30 percent), so it is only natural that credit would grow faster than GDP. Consequently, the rule on accumulating buffers within the business cycle will be triggered if the moving average of output growth exceeds 5 percent (long-term rule) or if the latest year-on-year growth is not less than 4 percentage points of the preceding year's growth (in order to be able to respond to sudden slowdowns, as in 2009). As Figure 15.3 shows, the cyclical rule worked quite well in addressing the impact of the global financial crisis, and more recently in responding to the slowdown in the Peruvian economy.

The final difference between Peru's regulations and the Basel standard is related to the proportion of the required buffer that must be accumulated when the cyclical rule is activated. Although under Basel, buffers are accumulated gradually, based on the deviation of the gap between the credit-to-GDP ratio and its long-term trend, in Peru the activation rule works as a signal that triggers accumulation of the entire buffer within a maximum period of one year. When an entity needs more time, it must have a compliance plan approved by the SBS. This requirement is based on the recognition that access to deep and developed capital markets is not simple in Peru, and that achieving certain capital goals requires orderly and sustained planning.

The design of the systemic risk buffer is also different from that of Basel. At the international level, this risk requires that globally systemic entities maintain capital buffers, while in Peru the relevant requirement incorporates capital buffers for entities considered systemic from a domestic standpoint. Thus, different capital charges were established for all entities whose assets exceed 3 percent of GDP, based on their external risk rating, market share, and the assets-to-GDP ratio.

As for the other risks covered in the regulation (individual, regional, and sectoral concentration; interest rate risk in the banking book; and the entity's risk propensity), the aim was to introduce into a financial system in which all entities are subject to the Basel II standardized approach the possibility of requiring capital buffers for risks not covered in Pillar 1 of Basel II. In other words, the objective was an approximation in a standardized way of the self-assessment of capital that nevertheless preserves the incentives for developing individual economic capital models, as this allows entities migrating toward the internal ratings–based approach to make their own calculations.

On the subject of monitoring new prudential liquidity standards, the regulation on liquidity risk management augmented the (more structural) liquidity ratios required since the late 1990s with the liquidity coverage ratio, which is a requirement for very short-term liquidity. Although

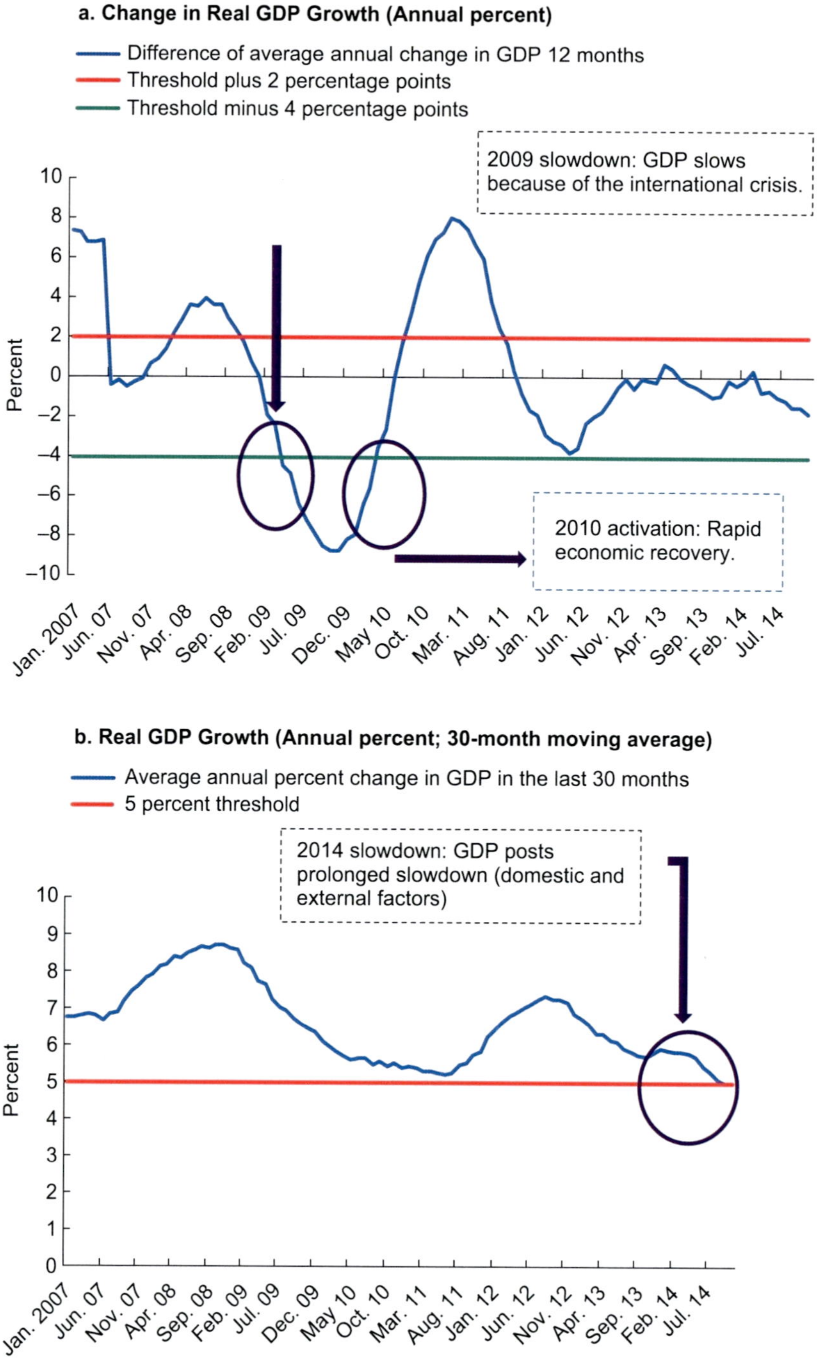


Source: Superintendency of Banking, Insurance and Pension Funds.

**Figure 15.3** Trend of the Cyclical Rule

the liquidity coverage ratio was based on the Basel III proposal, it recognizes that there is greater sensitivity to deposit outflows both in more stable and less stable banks than assumed by Basel, and consequently they are assigned larger weights. Similarly, owing to the shallowness of the Peruvian capital market, certain instruments mentioned in Basel are not recognized as liquid assets and special treatment is given to reserve requirements established by the BCRP. The period granted for adapting to this requirement will end in January 2017.

Regarding capital quality improvement, the SBS has been working on a project to revise its regulatory framework to incorporate the principles established in Basel III. A quantitative impact study is currently being conducted, after which a timetable will be defined that will require the Peruvian financial system to comply as fully as possible with the principles embodied in the international best standards.

In addition to implementing the recommendations proposed in Basel III, the SBS considered it important to augment its system of provisions with a cyclical buffer. Studies of the Peruvian business cycle showed that in the contractionary phase of the cycle, the loss distribution shifted entirely, which caused both the mean and the tail of the distribution to move, increasing both expected and unexpected losses. Therefore, buffers would be required both for provisions and for capital.

As a result, the SBS added a dynamic element to its system of provisions in 2008. The aim of this measure was to accumulate additional provisions during the expansionary phase of the business cycle so that when the cycle reversed, financial institutions would be prepared for a possible reduction in the incomes of economic agents. This cyclical component is added to the provisioning rate applied to loans granted to debtors with normal credit ratings. As in the case of additional business cycle capital requirements, the provisioning buffer is differentiated by type of exposure, requiring larger buffers for segments more sensitive to the business cycle, such as consumer portfolios and the financing of MSEs. The activation and deactivation rule is the same as the rule used for cyclical capital, as explained above.

An important characteristic of this system of cyclical buffers implemented by the SBS is the existence of an established sequence and use for the buffers once the rule is deactivated and the buffers can be used. The provisioning buffer can only be used to cover new provisions due to portfolio deterioration, and only when the provisioning buffer is depleted can 60 percent of the cyclical capital buffer be used. Use of the remaining 40 percent requires SBS authorization.

### *Local Components of Prudential Regulation*

In addition to implementing (with certain adaptations) the standards proposed by Basel III and other internationally agreed-upon macroprudential measures, the SBS has been steadily incorporating regulatory measures concerning local risks to mitigate the potential impact on financial stability.

The main risks identified and currently subject to regulation are the high degree of portfolio dollarization and the limited amount of reliable information on the incomes of a large informal segment of the population. Regarding the former, concern is focused on the financing granted in dollars to borrowers who generate income in nuevos soles; this currency mismatch is known as foreign exchange credit risk. The concern regarding the latter is how to properly manage and mitigate the possibility of excessive retail indebtedness.

**Foreign exchange credit risk.** Although in recent years the trend has been toward constant appreciation of the nuevo sol, there have been episodes of significant depreciations that, if they were to continue, could limit the payment capacity of debtors who generate income in local currency. This, as a result, could lead to losses in the portfolios of financial entities.

For this reason, the SBS developed a regulatory system based on three elements: (1) requirement of a minimum package of management measures to identify, assess, and mitigate foreign exchange credit risk; (2) additional provisions if in the opinion of the supervisor the management measures adopted prove insufficient; and (3) an additional capital requirement for operations subject to foreign exchange credit risk.

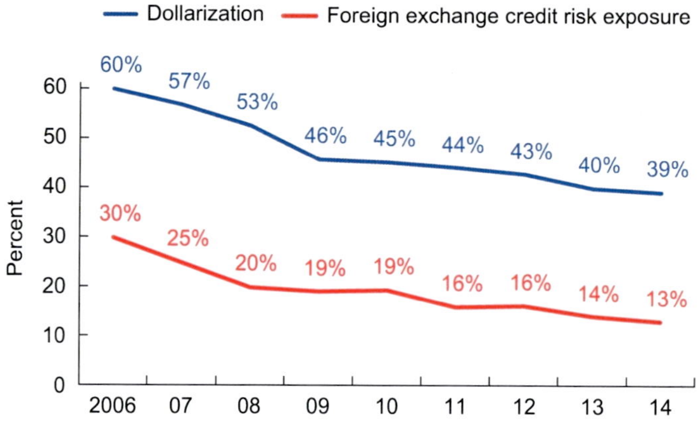


Source: Superintendency of Banking, Insurance and Pension Funds.

**Figure 15.4** Dollarization and Foreign Exchange Credit Risk Exposure

Pursuant to the regulation on the management of foreign exchange credit risk issued in 2005, financial entities are required to identify exposures subject to this type of risk by developing models to assess their debtors' payment capacity following a real depreciation of 10 percent and 20 percent. Thus, if a debtor does not pass the entity's eligibility criteria following such a shock, it is considered vulnerable to foreign exchange credit risk. This exercise is important to make a proper distinction between a dollarized portfolio and a portfolio exposed to foreign exchange credit risk. The debtor could have debt in dollars but not pose a risk of loss to the financial institution, either because it generates income in dollars, is properly hedged against risk, or has a debt-to-income ratio such that it has the capacity to absorb a permanent and significant real devaluation. The procedures for identifying foreign exchange credit risk, carried out by entities and supervised by the SBS, must differentiate the treatment given each of the various types of credit in foreign currency, as each segment requires a different analysis. They must also clearly identify risk-mitigating factors, which can have a positive impact on the probability of debtor default. Financial entities are required to report whether each debtor is exposed to foreign exchange credit risk. As Figure 15.4 shows, the level of exposure to foreign exchange credit risk is significantly lower than the level of loan portfolio dollarization, so that this risk, while still present in the Peruvian financial system, is limited.

After reviewing and monitoring the methodologies used by enterprises to identify foreign exchange credit risk, the SBS requires entities it considers as having insufficient risk management measures to significantly increase their provisions for all regular loans granted in foreign currency.

The SBS also adapted the adjusted exposure formula established in Basel II for the standardized approach to credit risk capital requirements, which includes an increase of 8 percent for exposures subject to foreign exchange credit risk. The minimum capital requirement will thus be 8 percent higher if the debtor is exposed to this type of risk. This value was calculated by determining the marginal losses between debtors exposed to foreign exchange credit risk and those not exposed in a period of high and constant depreciation of the local currency.

**Overindebtedness.** In the context of rapid growth of the Peruvian economy at the start of the 2000s, credit to households grew at rates close to 25 percent between 2003 and 2006. Although this rapid growth was partly attributable to improvements in real income and employment as well as to the robust efforts by the authorities to make the banking system more inclusive, it can also be explained by excessive optimism, as it is particularly difficult to distinguish one factor from another in an economy such as Peru's where informality levels are high. In 2006, the SBS issued a regulation on the potential overindebtedness of retail debtors in order to address the problem. This regulation emphasizes the management of overindebtedness risks. In particular, it makes explicit a set of good management practices from the origination of loans to the process of collecting them. For example, the regulation assesses penalties on entities that do not observe prudential practices such as considering the overall indebtedness of the debtor (and not just the debt associated with the lending institution); performing a complete risk assessment for all types of credit, including increases in lines of credit; maintaining conservative policies regarding the loan-to-value (LTV) ratio for mortgage loans and the loan-installment-to-payment ratio for consumer loans; analyzing harvests; and having in place efficient income forecasting models when required. If a financial entity does not observe all the good practices defined in the regulation, its entire portfolio will be subject to a predetermined increase in provisioning (double the generic provision). For credit cards, a credit conversion factor of 20 percent will also be applied to the unused portion of lines of credit. As a result of that regulation and in a context of international economic deceleration, the growth of credit to households fell to rates in the 15 percent range, and in the case of consumer loans, revolving (credit card) loans were reconfigured as installment loans with the consequent decrease in risk. This is because statistical analyses of Peruvian microdata showed that the probability of default on revolving loans is 75 percent higher than for consumer installment loans.

In view of the economic recovery of Peru in 2010 that saw the economy grow by 8.5 percent and post high growth rates in succeeding years, the SBS decided in 2012 to supplement the above-mentioned measures for mitigating potential overindebtedness with a series of prudential measures that would ensure that new consumer and mortgage loan disbursements be made subject to prudent loan origination criteria in an environment of sustained economic growth and a highly competitive retail credit market.

Differentiated capital requirements were established for mortgage loans based on such factors as the LTV ratio, the recording of properties in public registers (to distinguish finished from future housing), the type of interest rate, the purpose of the mortgage loan (primary residence or other use), and the currency in which the loan was granted. For example, a mortgage loan for a primary residence recorded in public registers in domestic currency, at a fixed interest rate, and with a maximum term of 20 years and an LTV ratio below 90 percent will have a 50 percent risk weight, resulting in a capital charge equal to 5 percent of the loan amount. To retain this same capital requirement, a loan having the same characteristics but in foreign currency will require maintaining an LTV ratio of less than 80 percent. Moreover, if the mortgage loan is granted in foreign currency but is not for a primary residence, the LTV ratio must be less than 65 percent in order to maintain the 5 percent capital requirement. Any deviation from the established prudential standards increases the weight up to 250 percent (25 percent capital charge)—that is, five times more capital than if the prudential criteria were observed.

Capital charges were also established for consumer loans, differentiated on the basis of the residual maturity of the obligations in the case of (nonrevolving) vehicle loans and on the amortization period for revolving loans. A prudential standard established that the term of vehicle loans and other nonrevolving loans would be five and four years, respectively, while the amortization period of revolving loans would be three years. Loans conforming to these prudential standards will have a 100 percent weight and the capital charges will therefore increase to 10 percent of the loan. However, if the standards are not complied with, the risk weight could increase to 250 percent, which would mean a capital charge of 25 percent of the loan (Table 15.2).

The above shows that the aim of local prudential measures is to mitigate risks specific to the Peruvian market by generating sufficient incentives for enterprises to incorporate the cost of risks associated with their decisions and to carefully manage those risks. Since 2013, the growth rates of loans to households have been below 15 percent, so the potential problem of overindebtedness continues to require follow-up and monitoring, but within a more limited framework

**TABLE 15.2**

**New Prudential Capital Requirement**

**Mortgage Loans**

<table>
<tr><th></th><th colspan="2">LTV Ratio</th></tr>
<tr><th>Loan for:</th><th>Nuevos Soles</th><th>U.S. Dollars</th></tr>
<tr><td>Primary Residence</td><td>90%</td><td>80%</td></tr>
<tr><td>Others</td><td>70%</td><td>65%</td></tr>
</table>

<table>
<tr><th rowspan="3">LTV</th><th rowspan="3">Collateral Recorded</th><th colspan="3">Risk Weight</th></tr>
<tr><th colspan="3">Residual Maturity (years)</th></tr>
<tr><th>Up to 20</th><th>20–30</th><th>+30</th></tr>
<tr><td rowspan="2">≤ LTV</td><td>Yes</td><td>50%</td><td>75%</td><td>100%</td></tr>
<tr><td>No</td><td rowspan="2">100%</td><td rowspan="2">150%</td><td rowspan="2">200%</td></tr>
<tr><td rowspan="2">> LTV</td><td>Yes</td></tr>
<tr><td>No</td><td>150%</td><td>200%</td><td>250%</td></tr>
</table>

**Consumer Loans**

<table>
<tr><th rowspan="3">Consumer credit</th><th colspan="4">Risk Weight</th></tr>
<tr><th colspan="4">Residual Maturity/Amortization (years)</th></tr>
<tr><th>Up to 3</th><th>3–4</th><th>4–5</th><th>+5</th></tr>
<tr><td>Vehicle</td><td colspan="3">100%</td><td>250%</td></tr>
<tr><td>Nonrevolving</td><td colspan="2">100%</td><td>150%</td><td>250%</td></tr>
<tr><td>Revolving</td><td>100%</td><td colspan="3">250%</td></tr>
</table>

Source: Superintendency of Banking, Insurance and Pension Funds.
Note: LTV = loan-to-value ratio.

commensurate with the risks it represents. This analysis of overindebtedness is also focused on the MSE segments, which in prior years grew significantly.

## *Brief Summary of the Results of Independent Assessments*

The necessary complement to the degree of progress of the regulatory framework is the effectiveness of supervision aimed at ensuring that the framework is complied with in practice and that prudent risk management is successful. The IMF, together with the World Bank, periodically assesses the quality of regulation and supervision in most countries of the world under the Financial Sector Assessment Program. Peru submitted to such independent assessments in 2000, 2005, and 2010.

The Financial Sector Assessment Programs conclude with a detailed analysis of the degree of compliance with the Bank for International Settlements' Core Principles for Effective Banking Supervision,[4] which constitute the international standard of regulation and supervision requirements for preserving the stability of the financial system. There are 25 principles, but with the first subdivided into six subprinciples, the assessment actually has 30 principles and subprinciples. In 2001, Peru fully or largely complied with two-thirds of these principles and subprinciples. In other words, either Peru was materially noncompliant with 10 principles, or those principles did not represent a material risk at the time. In 2010, in line with the regulatory developments described in this section, as well as developments in the SBS supervisory framework, Peru

[4]In 1999, the Basel Committee established a methodology based on a series of specific criteria for assessing the degree of conformity of each country's banking regulation and supervision with these principles.

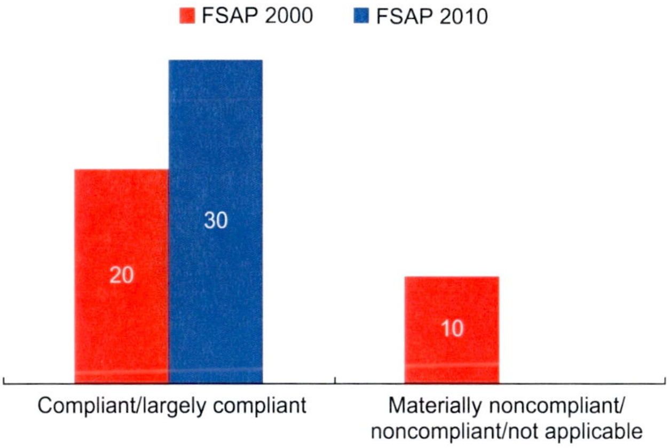


Source: Superintendency of Banking, Insurance and Pension Funds.
Note: FSAP = Financial Sector Assessment Program.

**Figure 15.5** Peru's Compliance with the Basel Committee's Core Principles

received a grade of 100 percent compliant—that is, all the principles were assessed as fully or largely complied with. This demonstrates the remarkable progress Peru has made in the area of banking regulation and supervision, as acknowledged in an independent assessment based on the applicable international best practices.

In 2012, the Basel Committee revised these principles based on the experience of the international financial crisis in 2008–09 and incorporated new and more stringent assessment principles and criteria. Greater emphasis was placed on the topics of corporate governance and macroprudential risk assessment. To date, however, Peru has not been assessed in accordance with these new standards. Nevertheless, in preparation for such an assessment the SBS performed a self-assessment applying the new standards and, on that basis, it is expected that Peru will continue receiving very high marks for compliance with the new principles, as it did in the 2010 assessment (Figure 15.5).

## FINANCIAL SYSTEM STRENGTHS

Thanks to regulations that require enterprises to adopt minimum risk management standards and accumulate buffers to mitigate the negative effects of the economy's ups and downs, the Peruvian financial system is strong and stable. The situation in the wake of the 2008–09 international financial crisis demonstrated that the prudential measures adopted by the Peruvian financial system enabled it to deal satisfactorily with the crisis, as shown by the financial indicators. At present, Peru has a financial system with appropriate liquidity and asset quality levels and a buffer of provisions and capital to meet future contingencies.

The Peruvian financial system is abundantly liquid. Both full-service banks and nonbank enterprises have liquidity ratios (liquid assets as a percentage of liabilities maturing in less than a year) in both currencies that greatly exceed the regulatory minimums. At the end of the first half of 2014, the liquidity ratio in domestic currency for the system as a whole was 30.5 percent (the required minimum is 8 percent) and in foreign currency 53.7 percent (the required minimum is 30 percent), putting the overall liquidity ratio at 41.3 percent. Moreover, the liquidity coverage ratios, which represent the very-short-term liquidity needed to deal with cash outflows in the next 30 days under a stress scenario such as the one proposed in Basel III, are greater than 100 percent for both currencies (the regulatory minimum is 80 percent, and the 100 percent requirement will go into effect in 2017).

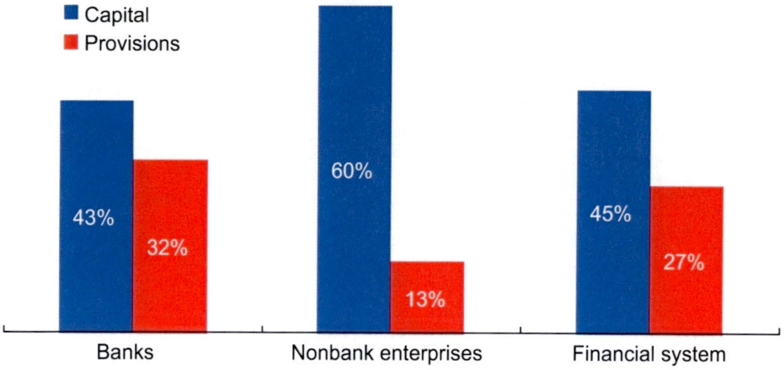


Source: Superintendency of Banking, Insurance and Pension Funds.

**Figure 15.6** Capital and Provisions: Buffers as a Percentage of Regulatory Minimums

The indicators of the quality of financial system assets are highly satisfactory. First, 93.2 percent of all direct and indirect financial system loans were granted to debtors in the normal category and only 2.5 percent to customers classified as having potential problems. In other words, more than 95 percent of borrowers are customers who pay on time or, in the event of a slight delay, have sufficient cash flow to honor their obligations. Second, the delinquency ratio, measured as the portfolio balance in arrears (overdue plus judicial collection) as a percentage of all direct loans, is 2.9 percent, an appropriate level considering that the criterion for classifying a loan as overdue is more conservative than the international standard. For example, the commercial portfolio, which accounts for more than 50 percent of the financial system portfolio, is considered overdue when payment is 15 or more days in arrears. Third, although 39 percent of the loan portfolio is denominated in dollars, only 13 percent of the total portfolio is exposed to foreign exchange credit risk. Moreover, total provisions significantly exceed the balance of the impaired portfolio, so that for each nuevo sol in the overdue portfolio, the system has 1.63 nuevos soles in provisions. This is due essentially to the dynamic component of the provisions, which provides for their accumulation in periods of economic growth to cover portfolio deterioration in negative stages of the business cycle. At end-June 2014, the financial system as a whole had a provisioning buffer in excess of S/. 2 billion, which is 27 percent above the regulatory minimum for banks, while the provisioning buffers are around 32 percent over the minimum required.

Regarding solvency, in June 2014 the financial system had a capital ratio of 14.5 percent (14.3 percent for full-service banks and 16 percent for nonbank enterprises), higher than Basel's regulatory minimums of 10 percent and 8 percent, respectively. This means that the financial system as a whole has a capital buffer of S/. 11.7 billion, which represents about 45 percent of additional capital to deal with possible contingencies, primarily as a result of the capitalization of a significant percentage of the profits earned by enterprises in recent years (between 50 percent and 70 percent) and the issuance of subordinate instruments with very long maturities in order for them to be counted as capital (Figure 15.6).

Finally, it is important to note that most financial system enterprises in Peru are profitable and have been capitalizing a sizable portion of their profits. In June 2014, the annualized profitability of assets in the system as a whole stood at 1.9 percent, while the annualized profitability of capital amounted to 18.4 percent.

## CONCLUSIONS

Although there is considerable room in the Peruvian financial system for innovation, the development of new markets, efficiency gains, and higher levels of financial inclusion, there has been significant progress over the past 25 years in the areas of growth, diversification, development of new markets, and financial inclusion. It is also important to point out that this progress was achieved in a stable environment of prudential regulation, helping to ensure that the gains achieved will be sustainable in the long term and serve as a sound platform for future development. This is evidenced by the financial stability currently enjoyed by the Peruvian financial system, which gives reason to believe that the financial system will continue to evolve in a sound and sustainable manner and contribute to the ongoing development of the Peruvian economy.

## FURTHER READING

Basel Committee on Banking Supervision. 2005. "Basel II: International Convergence of Capital Measurement and Capital Standards: A Revised Framework." Basel, November.

———. 2010. "Guidance for National Authorities Operating the Countercyclical Capital Buffer." Basel, December.

———. 2011. "Basel III: A Global Regulatory Framework for More Resilient Banks and Banking Systems—Revised Version." Basel, June.

Gordy, Michael, and Bradley Howells. 2004. "Procyclicality in Basel II: Can We Treat the Disease Without Killing the Patient?" *Journal of Financial Intermediation* 15(3): 395–417.

Gordy, Michael, and Eva Lutkebohmert. 2003. "A Risk-Factor Model Foundation for Ratings-Based Bank Capital Rules." *Journal of Financial Intermediation* 12: 199–232.

———. 2013. "Granularity Adjustment for Regulatory Capital Assessment," *International Journal of Central Banking* 9(3): 33–71.

Poggi, Javier, Manuel Luy, Sandra Vásquez, and Eduardo Bastante. 2007. "El Nuevo Acuerdo de Capital en Economías Emergentes: El Caso Peruano." *Banco Interamericano de Desarrollo* 85–116.

Repullo, Rafael, and Jesús Saurina. 2012. "The Countercyclical Capital Buffer of Basel III. A Critical Assessment." *The Crisis Aftermath: New Regulatory Paradigms* 45–67.

———, and C. Trucharte. 2010. "Mitigating the Procyclicality of Basel II." *Economic Policy* 659–702.

Saurina, Jesús. 2009. "Dynamic Provisioning. The Experience of Spain." *Crisis Response, Public Policy for the Private Sector, The World Bank,* Note N°7. Washington, DC.

Superintendencia de Banca and Seguros y Administradoras Privadas de Fondos de Pensiones. 1996. "Ley General del Sistema Financiero y del Sistema de Seguros y Orgánica de la Superintendencia de Banca y Seguros." Ley N° 26702.

———. 2006. "Historia de la Supervisión y Regulación Financiera en el Perú."

———. 2008. "Reglamento Para la Evaluación y Clasificación del Deudor y la Exigencia de Provisiones." Resolución SBS N° 11356-2008.

———. 2009. "Reglamento Para el Requerimiento de Patrimonio Efectivo por Riesgo de Crédito." Resolución SBS N° 14354-2009.

———. 2009. "Reglamento Para el Requerimiento de Patrimonio Efectivo por Riesgo Operacional." Resolución SBS N° 2115-2009.

———. 2009. "Reglamento Para el Requerimiento de Patrimonio Efectivo por Riesgo de Mercado." Resolución SBS N° 6328-2009.

———. 2011. "Reglamento Para el Requerimiento de Patrimonio Efectivo Adicional." Resolución SBS N° 8425-2011.

———. 2013. "Reglamento de Apertura, Traslado o Cierre de Oficinas, Uso de Locales Compartidos, Cajeros Automáticos y Cajeros Corresponsales." Resolución SBS N° 6285-2013.

———. 2014. "Perú: Indicadores de Inclusión Financiera de los Sistemas Financiero, de Seguros y de Pensiones." Superintendencia de Banca, Seguros y AFP, June.

Wezel, Torsten, Michel Canta, and Manuel Luy. 2014. "A Practical Example of the Nonperforming Loans Proyejction Approach to Stress Testing." In L. L. Ong, editor. *A Guide to IMF Stress Testing: Methods and Models.* Washington, DC: International Monetary Fund, 473–84.

Wezel, Torsten, Jorge A. Chan-Lau, and Francesco Columba. 2012. "Dynamic Loan Loss Provisioning: Simulations on Effectiveness and Guide to Implementation." Working Paper WP/12/110, International Monetary Fund, Washington, DC.

CHAPTER 16

# Drivers of Dedollarization in Peru

Mercedes García-Escribano

*Peru has successfully pursued market-driven financial dedollarization during the past 15 years. Dollarization of credit and deposits of commercial banks—across all sectors and maturities—has declined, with larger declines for commercial credit and time and saving deposits.*[1] *The analysis presented in this chapter confirms that dedollarization has been driven by macroeconomic stability, introduction of prudential policies to better reflect currency risk (such as the management of reserve requirements), and the development of the domestic capital market in nuevos soles. Further dedollarization efforts could focus on three fronts: preserving consolidated macroeconomic stability, including exchange rate flexibility; managing additional prudential measures to further discourage banks from lending and funding in foreign currency; and deepening capital market development in domestic currency.*

Dollarization in Peru has continued to decline gradually since 2010, though it still remains elevated. It constituted 38 percent of credits and 43 percent of deposits as of end-2014. In recent years, the Central Reserve Bank of Peru (*Banco Central de Reserva del Perú*) has adopted a number of measures to encourage greater local currency lending and discourage foreign currency lending and deposit taking. New repo instruments were introduced by the Central Reserve Bank of Peru in 2014 aimed at increasing local currency credits and replacing existing foreign currency loans. Reserve requirements on foreign currency deposits have been gradually increased and augmented by additional requirements on institutions that miss certain dedollarization targets.

Dollarization in Peru started with the inflationary process of the mid-1970s and peaked during the hyperinflation of 1988–90, despite efforts to dedollarize in 1985. With high inflation, the U.S. dollar started to be the preferred means of payments and store of value. Lending institutions also saw that dollars minimized the risk of capital losses. Consequently, financial dollarization rose significantly (Figure 16.1). In 1985, while inflation was high, the government forced the conversion of foreign currency deposits to local currency, resulting in capital flight and financial disintermediation. When the restriction on foreign currency deposits was lifted, redollarization was quick, and by the end of the 1990s about 80 percent of deposits (and credit) were denominated in foreign currency.

Since the introduction of the inflation-targeting regime in early 2000s, Peru has experienced a gradual and sustained market-driven financial dedollarization.[2] Starting in 2001, dollarization of credit declined by nearly 25 percentage points to below 55 percent by end-2009 (Figure 16.1). Dollarization of deposits also declined by a similar amount to about 52 percent, and transaction dollarization also declined and is now minimal (Table 16.1).

Although a great deal of work exists on the financial consequences of dollarization, the empirical literature on the process of dedollarization is scant. Although it is widely accepted that hyperinflation is one of the driving factors in financial dollarization when indexed instruments are not readily available, it is still a puzzle why high ratios of dollarized deposits and loans persist after

[1] Financial dollarization occurs when a large share of residents' assets and liabilities are denominated in foreign currency. Dollarization ratios in this chapter refer to commercial banks, unless noted otherwise.

[2] Other countries in Latin America with widespread dollarization have also experienced a process of market-driven dedollarization during the past 15 years, including Bolivia, Uruguay, and Paraguay.

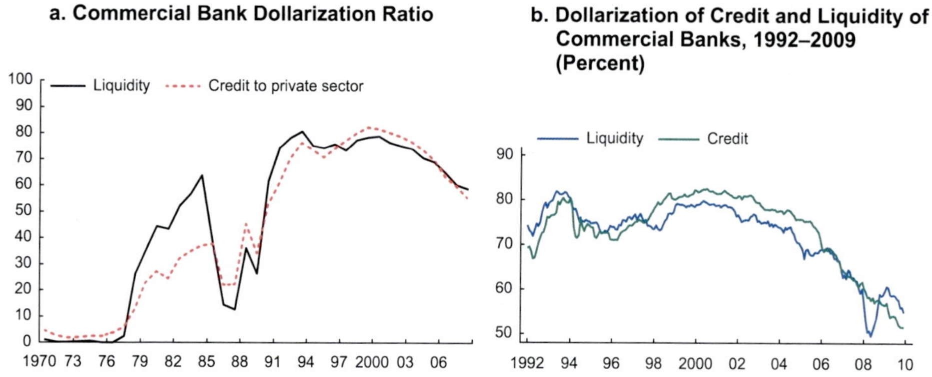


Sources: Central Reserve Bank of Peru; and IMF staff calculations.

**Figure 16.1** Peru: Evolution of Dollarization for Commercial Banks *(Percent)*

**TABLE 16.1**

Dollarized Transactions *(Percentage in value terms of check and cash payment operations made in dollars)*

| | 2003 | 2004 | 2005 | 2006 | 2007 | 2008 | 2009 |
|---|---|---|---|---|---|---|---|
| **Checks**[1] | 26.2 | 26.3 | 25.1 | 24.8 | 24.4 | 19.4 | 18.1 |
| **Cash Withdrawal** | | | | | | | |
| Debit Cards | 21.6 | 17.6 | 13.6 | 12.4 | 8.7 | 4.6 | 5.4 |
| Credit Cards | 11.1 | 9.3 | 6.3 | 5.5 | 4.7 | 3.6 | 3.4 |
| Automatic Teller Machines | 13.4 | 10.7 | 7.8 | 7.9 | 7.0 | 5.3 | 5.3 |

Source: Central Reserve Bank of Peru.

[1] Includes checks cashed at the bank, deposited at the bank, and processed at the electronic clearing house.

periods when inflation has substantially declined. Ize and Levy-Yeyati (2003) developed a model of optimal portfolio choice of risk-averse borrowers and lenders where the equilibrium level of deposit dollarization depends on the relative price and real exchange rate volatility. Specifically, their minimum variance portfolio model implies that if real exchange depreciation is less volatile than inflation, then consumers would prefer the dollar deposit, as it is less risky. The authors tested the model using cross-section data on deposit dollarization for 23 countries. De Nicolo, Honakan, and Ize (2005) and Rennhack and Nozaki (2006) confirm the minimum variance portfolio hypothesis. Another strand of literature highlights the role of currency-blind regulatory frameworks. For example, Broda and Levy-Yeyati (2003) argue that an explicit deposit insurance that applies uniformly across all deposits exacerbates deposit dollarization. Kokenyne and Veyrune (2008) and Erasmus, Leichter, and Menkulasi (2009) review international experience with dedollarization and conclude that dollarization is not easily reversed, even after the underlying causes have been removed. The authors highlight that successful attempts to dedollarize have been market-based and have combined a track record of macroeconomic stability with other policies to enhance the attractiveness of the local currency.

This chapter explores the factors that explain bank dedollarization in Peru during the decade of the 2000s. The chapter examines the contributing role of three groups of factors to the process of banks' dedollarization: macroeconomic stability, prudential regulations, and the development of the domestic capital market in nuevos soles. In contrast with the literature that focuses exclusively on dollarization of overall deposits, this chapter simultaneously examines the dollarization of deposits and credits. By estimating deposits and credits simultaneously, the response of banks to the different factors that may affect dollarization is taken into consideration. The chapter also examines the drivers of dedollarization across categories of deposits and credits.

The findings confirm that bank dedollarization in Peru has been the result of a three-pronged approach. First, macroeconomic stability, proxied by (1) inflation, (2) different measures of exchange rate changes, and (3) sovereign credit risk (Emerging Market Bond Index for Peru) had a significant impact on dedollarization. Second, prudential measures such as the introduction of asymmetric reserve requirements and provisions for currency-induced credit risk had an impact on banks' incentives to borrow and lend in nuevos soles. Finally, the development of the local capital market in nuevos soles had a mixed impact on bank dedollarization. The issuance of long-term treasuries in nuevos soles lowered dollarization of credit, probably by facilitating bank funding and pricing of long-term loans in the Peruvian currency. However, other nuevo sol market instruments led to higher bank dollarization. These may have competed with bank loans in nuevos soles, having an impact on the pool of bank borrowers.

This chapter first describes the dedollarization trend of credit and deposits, and explores in detail the dedollarization of credit by sectors and of deposits by maturity structure. This section decomposes the changes in credit (deposit) dollarization into a within and between component. The chapter then describes the three groups of factors—macroeconomic conditions, regulatory and prudential policy measures, and the development of a capital market in nuevos soles—that could have affected banks' and agents' preferences for borrowing and lending in domestic currency. The chapter models the dedollarization dynamics using a vector autoregression approach and identifies the factors that have boosted dedollarization in recent years. Based on the empirical findings, the chapter then outlines measures that could help further deepen and consolidate dedollarization.

## DEDOLLARIZATION—STYLIZED FACTS

### Dedollarization by Type of Credit and Deposits

Financial dedollarization in Peru has been a gradual process since the early 2000s.[3] A sharp deposit dedollarization took place in late 2007, and that was quickly reversed following the collapse of Lehman Brothers (Figure 16.2a). The return to trend dedollarization during 2008 resulted from an increase in foreign currency deposits, while domestic currency deposits remained stable.

Dollarization varies across types of loans and deposits. Dollarization of loans with longer maturities (mortgage and commercial) is higher than loans with shorter maturities (consumer and small business) (Figure 16.2b). Dollarization of demand and savings deposits, which are more liquid, is lower than that of time deposits (Figure 16.2c).

### Dedollarization between and within Sectors

This section decomposes dedollarization of credit and deposits into a within-and-between component. Time-series data on aggregate credit dollarization captures not only dedollarization within sectors, but also compositional changes of credit among sectors. Similarly, data on aggregated deposit dollarization is influenced by compositional changes among deposits of difference maturity structure. Changes in credit dollarization over time can be decomposed as follows:

$$d_t - d_\tau = \sum_{i=1}^{I} d_{it}\frac{c_{it}}{c_t} - \sum_{i=1}^{I} d_{i\tau}\frac{c_{i\tau}}{c_\tau} = \sum_{i=1}^{I}\left(d_{it} - d_{i\tau}\right)\frac{c_{it}}{c_t} + \sum_{i=1}^{I} d_{i\tau}\left(\frac{c_{it}}{c_t} - \frac{c_{i\tau}}{c_\tau}\right),$$

where $d_{it}$ is dollarization of credit in sector $i$ in year $t$, and $c_{it}$ is the total credit extended to sector $i$ in year $t$. The first term captures the time-series changes in dollarization within sectors. The

[3] To avoid the impact of valuation changes, deposits and credits in foreign currency are evaluated at a constant exchange rate.

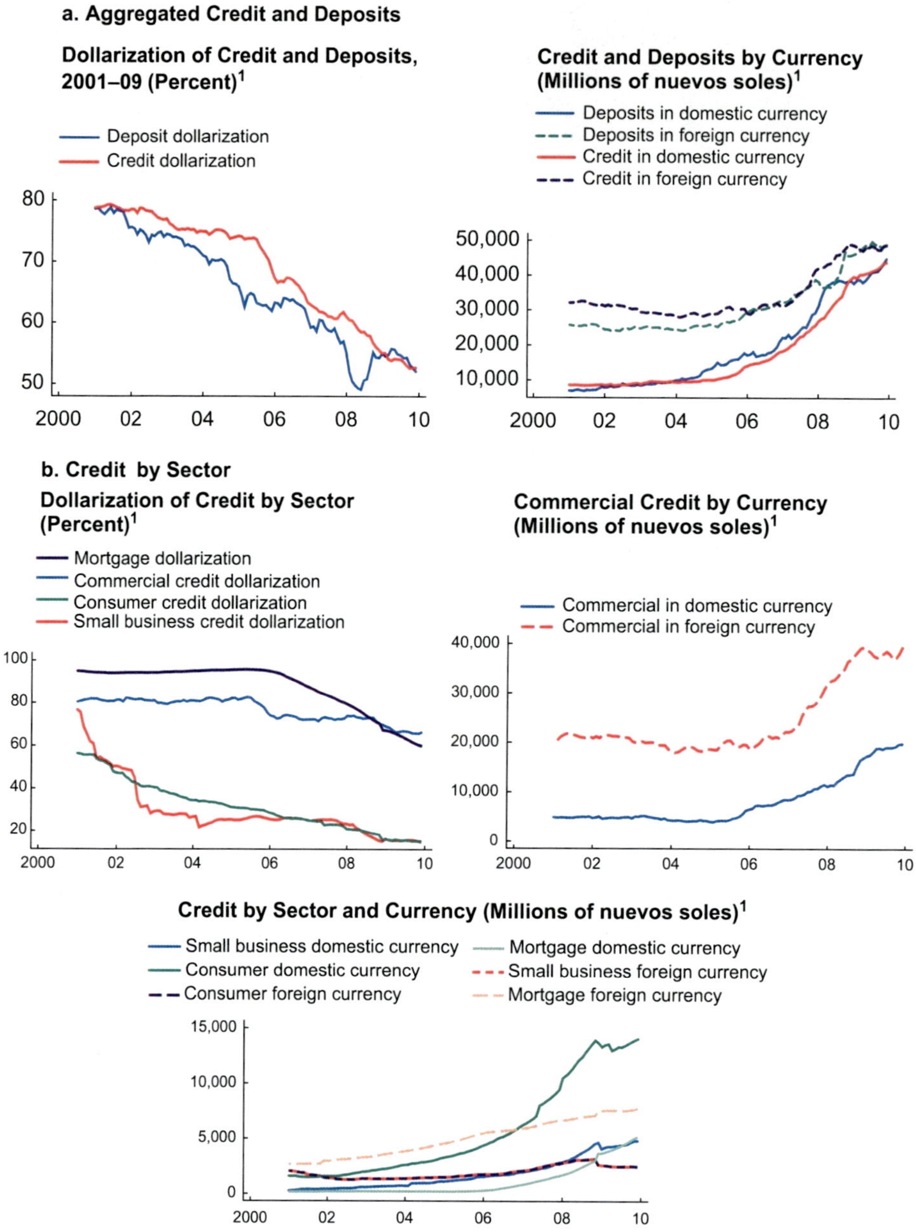


**Figure 16.2** Peru: Dedollarization of Credit by Sectors and of Deposits by Maturity *(continued)*

second term captures the effect of changes in credit composition. A similar decomposition can be done for deposits.

Dedollarization has been driven mainly by changes within each type of credit and deposits. The decomposition of credit dedollarization through time into within-and-between components shows that credit dedollarization has mostly been driven by within-sector dedollarization (Table 16.2a). The analysis also indicates that commercial sector dedollarization explains the bulk of total dedollarization. All commercial sectors—with the exception of fishing, mining, and electricity/water/gas—contributed to the commercial credit dedollarization process (Annex 16.1). The within-and-between decomposition for deposit dedollarization reveals that dedollarization within maturity explains almost all the decline in deposit dollarization (Table 16.2b).

c. Deposits Across Maturity Loans

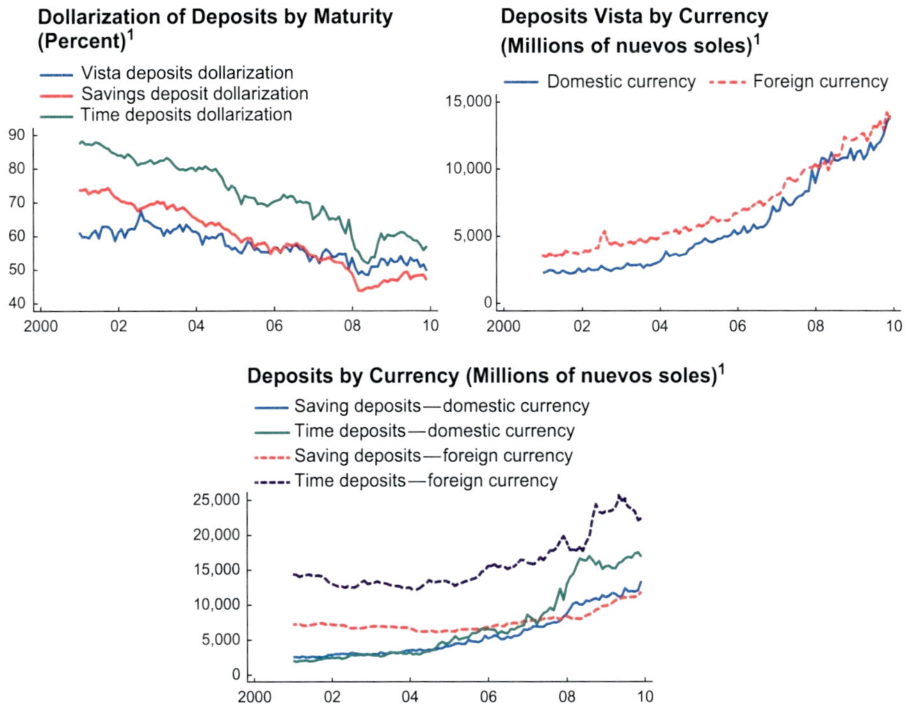


Sources: Central Reserve Bank of Peru; Superintendency of Banking, Insurance and Private Pension Funds; and IMF staff calculations.
[1] Foreign-currency credit and deposits evaluated at constant exchange rate.

**Figure 16.2** *(continued)*

**TABLE 16.2**

## Peru: Decomposition of Dedollarization into within and between Components *(Percent)*

**a. Credit**[1]

| | Dollarization | | Share in Total Credit | | 2001–09 | | |
|---|---|---|---|---|---|---|---|
| Sectors | 2001 | 2009 | 2001 | 2009 | Between Effect | Within Effect | Total Effect |
| Commercial | 80.8 | 66.5 | 79.0 | 62.8 | −10.7 | −11.3 | −22.0 |
| Small Business | 50.3 | 15.3 | 2.6 | 6.0 | 0.5 | −0.9 | −0.4 |
| Consumer | 47.8 | 14.9 | 9.0 | 17.5 | 1.3 | −3.0 | −1.7 |
| Mortgage | 94.1 | 59.9 | 9.4 | 13.7 | 2.5 | −3.2 | −0.7 |
| Total | 78.3 | 53.5 | 100 | 100 | −6.4 | −18.4 | −24.8 |

**b. Deposits**[1]

| | Dollarization | | Share in Total Deposits | | 2001–09 | | |
|---|---|---|---|---|---|---|---|
| Maturities | 2001 | 2009 | 2001 | 2009 | Between Effect | Within Effect | Total Effect |
| Saving | 71.7 | 46.9 | 32.1 | 27.6 | −2.1 | −8.0 | −10.1 |
| Time | 84.6 | 57.1 | 48.9 | 42.9 | −3.4 | −13.4 | −16.8 |
| Total | 75.5 | 52.1 | 100 | 100 | −0.3 | −23.1 | −23.5 |

Sources: Central Reserve Bank of Peru; Superintendency of Banking, Insurance and Private Pension Funds; and IMF staff calculations.
[1] Credit and deposits in foreign currency are evaluated at a constant nominal exchange rate.

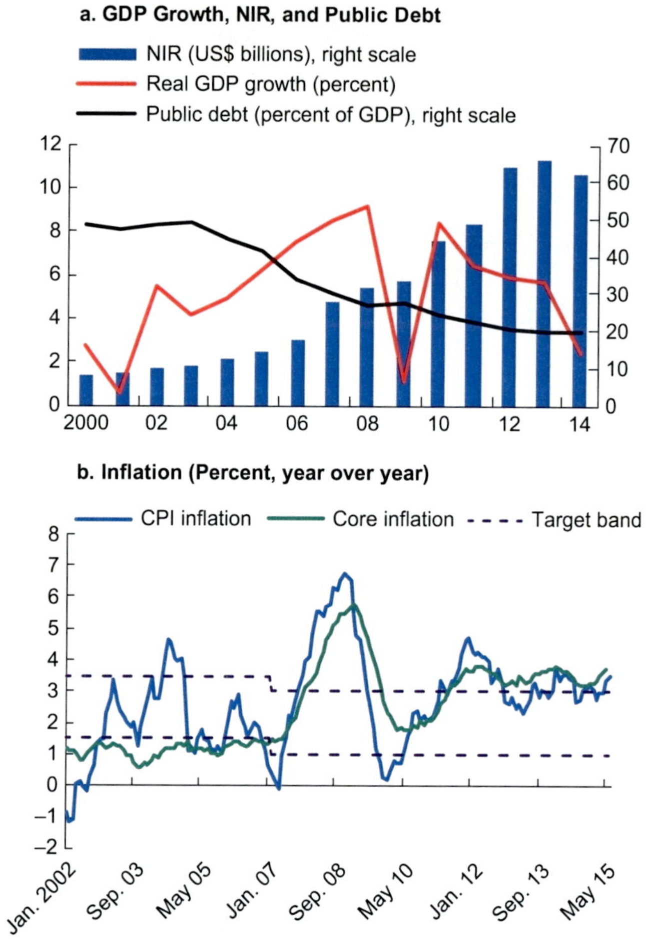


Sources: Central Reserve Bank of Peru; Haver Analytics; and IMF staff calculations.
Note: CPI = consumer price index; NIR = net international reserves.

**Figure 16.3** Peru: Macroeconomic Performance, 2000–15

# CONTRIBUTING FACTORS AND MEASURES

## Macro Preconditions—Successful Implementation of Stabilization Policies

Dedollarization in Peru has followed the successful implementation of macroeconomic stabilization policies. Taking advantage of buoyant economic conditions in recent years, the Peruvian government pursued large fiscal surpluses (of 2 percent to 3.3 percent of GDP per year) from 2006–08. As a result, public debt has been reduced below 30 percent of GDP, one of the lowest levels in the region (Figure 16.3a). Under the inflation-targeting framework introduced in 2002—initially with a target of 2.5 percent with a band of ±1 percent and since 2007 lowered to 2 percent with a band of ±1 percent—the Central Reserve Bank of Peru has successfully contained inflation within the inflation target band and anchored expectations (Figure 16.3b). Moreover, the central bank has built a significant buffer of international reserves, providing credible assurance of its ability to provide support in case of stress.[4] Finally, as a result of stringent prudential regulations, Peru's financial sector is sound, as shown by its resilience during the global financial crisis.

[4] Net international reserves increased from US$9.6 billion in 2002 to US$33.1 billion in 2009.

Markets have acknowledged Peru's outstanding performance. Peru was granted investment grade by Fitch and Standard & Poor's in April and July 2008, respectively, and by Moody's in December 2009, consolidating its standing among major emerging market economies. In May 2010, Peru's Emerging Market Bond Index stood at about 210 basis points compared to 410 basis points for Latin America as a whole.

## Prudential Measures

Several prudential measures introduced during the period of analysis helped the dedollarization process by lowering banks' incentives to borrow and lend in foreign currency. These measures include:[5]

- *Reserve requirements.* The difference between the reserve requirements on foreign currency deposits and domestic currency deposits changed during the period of analysis (Figure 16.4a). The remuneration that the central bank pays on reserves changed as well. Figure 16.4b illustrates the evolution of the remuneration rate for deposits in both currencies above the 6 percent level (which is the current level of nonremunerated reserve requirement applied to all deposits).
- *Provisioning requirements.* Since mid-2006, banks have had to carry out a routine evaluation of currency risks, or alternatively, set up a reserve ranging from 0.25 percent to 1 percent of the credit in foreign currency that has not been evaluated.[6] Since 2009, additional provisions for foreign currency risk as a percent of total provisions have been marginal.

Additional prudential measures linked to currency exposures that are in place but were not modified during the period of analysis include:

- *Liquidity requirements.* Banks are required to hold liquid assets equivalent to at least 8 percent in domestic currency and 20 percent in foreign currency of all their liabilities maturing during the next 12 months.
- *Banks' net open position.* In addition to limiting banks' foreign currency exposure, Peru has capital requirements on open foreign exchange positions. The limit on banks' long (short) open position was changed to 75 (15) percent of capital in February 2010 from a previous limit of 100 (10) percent of capital.[7]

## Development of a Capital Financial Market in Nuevos Soles

Peru has been actively developing its public and private debt market in domestic currency in recent years.

- *Domestic public debt market.* In 2003, Peru launched a market-making program with the objective of developing a market for domestic public debt, consisting mainly of fixed-rate instruments in domestic currency.[8,9] In line with this objective, Peru's public debt

[5] In addition to the financial prudential measures listed below, other regulatory measures may have had an impact on the demand for local currency. In particular, the Consumer Protection Law was amended in 2004 to force retailers and wholesalers to list prices in domestic currency. However, the law leaves agents free to list prices also in dollars.

[6] Cayazzo and others (2006) indicate that among 17 surveyed countries that are partially dollarized, only Peru reports requiring higher provisions for foreign currency loans relative to domestic currency ones.

[7] Cayazzo and others (2006) indicate that Poland, Singapore, and Sweden have capital charges on foreign exchange exposures. Argentina, Bolivia, Chile, Costa Rica, Honduras, and Uruguay only have limits on these exposures. The other countries among the 17 surveyed, including Peru, have both capital charges and limits on foreign currency exposures.

[8] Ministerial Resolution 106-2003, Supreme Decree 189-2004, and Supreme Decree 137-2005.

[9] The two types of domestic public bonds (known as *soberanos*) are the fixed-coupon *tasa fija* (fixed-rate) bonds and the inflation-adjusted valor adquisitivo constante bonds. *Tasa fija* bonds are the most liquid instruments and represent nearly 90 percent of *soberanos*.

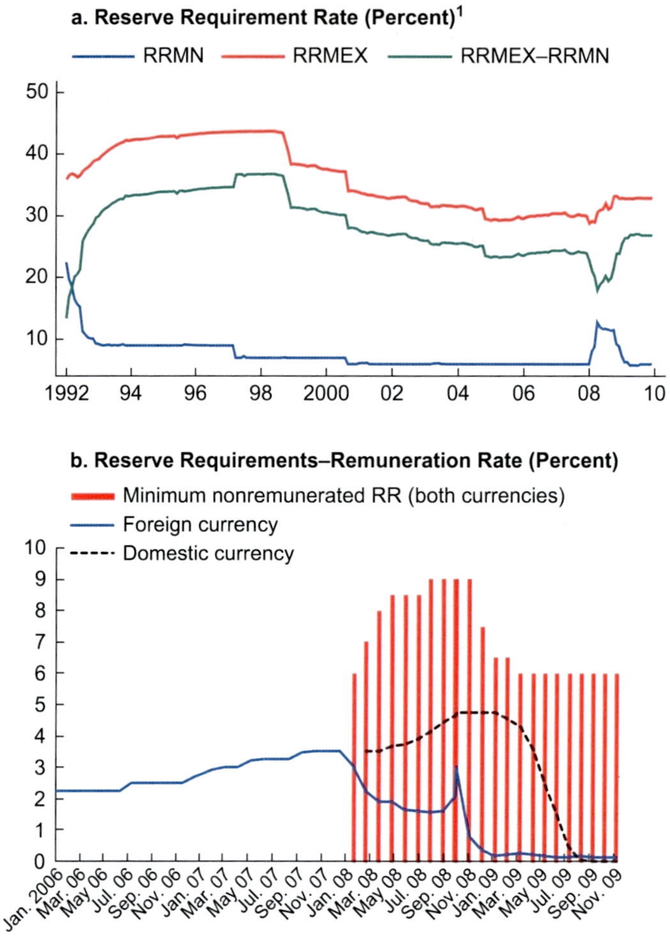


Sources: Central Reserve Bank of Peru; and IMF staff calculations.

Note: In percent of liabilities subject to reserve requirements. MEX = foreign currency; MN = domestic currency; RR = reserve requirements.

**Figure 16.4** Peru: Reserve Requirements

management strategy has been focused on developing a yield curve of government bonds in nuevos soles and reducing the share of public debt denominated in foreign currency (Figure 16.5a). As a result, government bonds in nuevos soles have gained liquidity and the yield curve has been extended considerably.[10,11]

- *Private debt market.* Private bond issuances in local currency have also increased substantially in recent years (Figure 16.5b).

[10] As of February 2010, the longest maturity of fixed-rate government paper in domestic currency was 32 years, as opposed to 5 years in 2003. The valor adquisitivo constante curve extends up to 39-year tenors, but has limited liquidity, as the total outstanding amount is US$700 million.

[11] Reflecting the availability of domestic debt instruments in nuevos soles, the portfolio of local pension funds (AFPs) denominated in dollars declined to 32 percent in November 2008 from 50 percent in 2000, then increased to 41 percent in December 2009 as the limits on AFP foreign investments were raised. AFPs hold more than 50 percent of the stock of *soberanos*, followed by foreign investors (21 percent), local banks (15 percent), and insurance companies (4 percent).

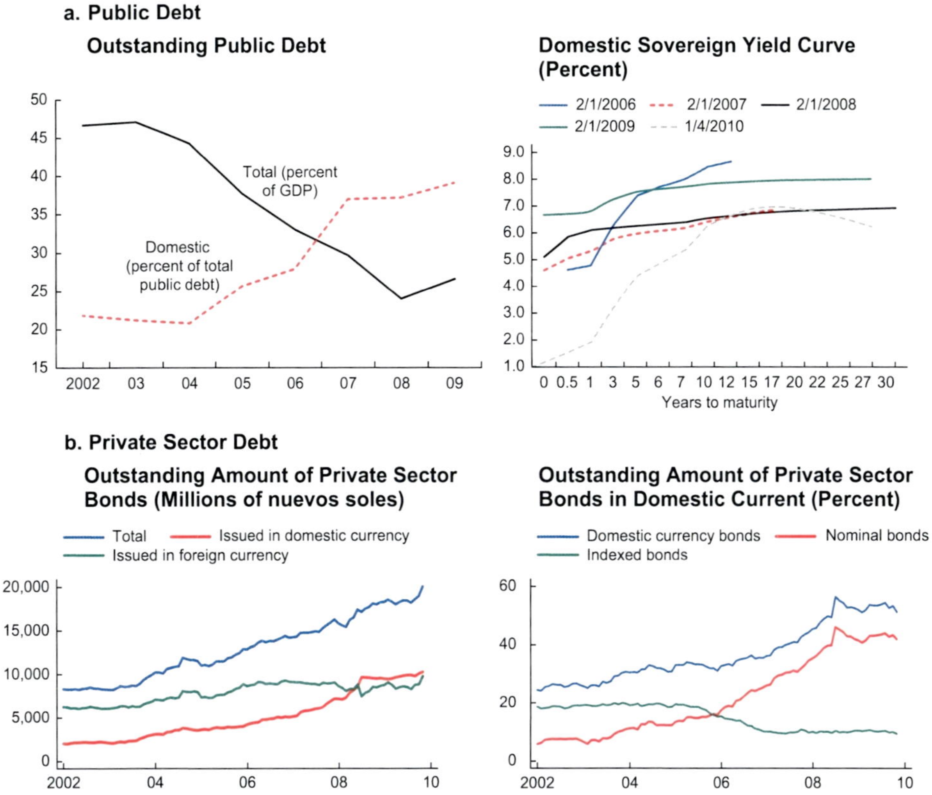


Sources: Central Reserve Bank of Peru; Superintendency of Banking, Insurance and Private Pension Funds; and IMF staff calculations.

**Figure 16.5** Peru: Development of Debt Market in Domestic Currency

## UNDERSTANDING DEDOLLARIZATION

Dollarization reflects the choice of currency by depositors, borrowers, and banks. Dollarization of credits and deposits reflects the equilibrium in the credit and deposit markets: banks supply loanable funds and demand deposits, and the private sector demands credit and provides funding. Banks, in turn, are active intermediaries between creditors and depositors. Data on quantities of credit and deposits and on lending and deposit rates correspond to the equilibrium in these markets (Figure 16.6). The vertical axis of Figures 16.6c and 16.6d depict the ratio of lending (deposit) rates in foreign to domestic currency.

Peru's dedollarization process is consistent with a shift of both demand of credit and supply of deposits toward nuevos soles. The null hypothesis of stable demand would imply that dollarization of credit (deposits) and the ratio of lending (active) rates in foreign to domestic currency negatively covary.[12] Shaded areas in Figure 16.6c appear to be consistent with rejecting the null, thereby with a shift in the demand of credit toward nuevos soles particularly for commercial loans

---

[12] The hypothesis of stable demand for credit in dollars implies that

$$(d_{it} - d_{i\tau})(r_{it} - r_{i\tau}) < 0, \text{ where } d_{it} = \frac{c_{it}^{foreign}}{c_{it}}, r_{it} = \frac{i_{it}^{foreign}}{i_{it}^{domestic}},$$

where $i_{it}$ is the lending rate to sector $i$ in year $t$.

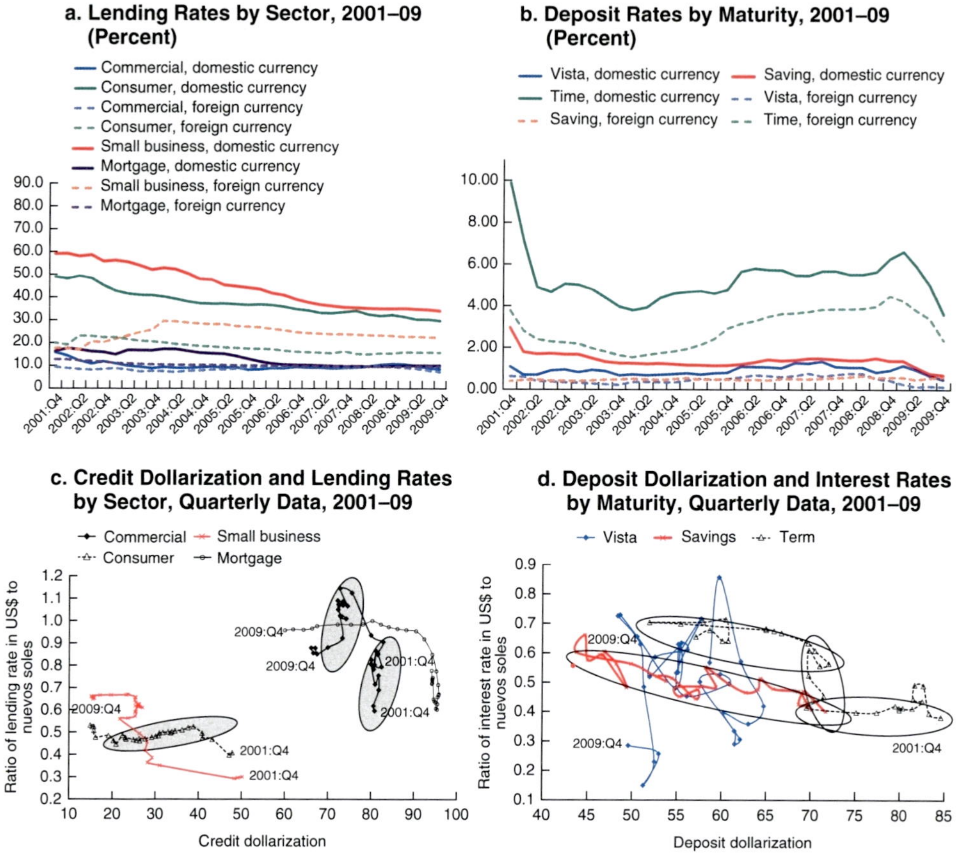


Sources: Central Reserve Bank of Peru; and IMF staff calculations.

**Figure 16.6** Peru: Credit and Deposit Markets—Quantities and Prices

since 2006. Other patterns, such as those highlighted in the deposits market, would be consistent with supply shifts.

A vector autoregression (VAR) approach allows for modeling the dynamics between dollarization of credits and deposits. Such an approach avoids imposing a particular structure on credit and deposit dollarization. It permits capturing (1) the simultaneous determination of credit and deposit dollarization, (2) the response to exogenous factors that are demand or supply shifters, and (3) the dynamics of credit and deposit dollarization.[13]

Two VAR specifications are estimated using monthly data for the period 2001–09. The first specification includes dollarization of total credit and total deposits, both in first differences, as endogenous variables. The second includes six endogenous variables, in first differences: dollarization of commercial credit, consumer credit, mortgages, demand deposits, savings deposit, and time deposits.[14] Both specifications include a set of exogenous variables to proxy macrostability, changes to prudential measures, and development of the capital market in nuevos soles. Annex 16.2 presents the definition of the exogenous variables (Annex Table 16.2.1), and the endogenous

[13] Granger causality was verified from deposit to credit dollarization.

[14] All series are valued at the constant nominal exchange rate. The series of total credit and deposit dollarization used for the analysis in this section are constructed using December 2008 weights to avoid composition changes among types of credit and types of deposits. Cointegration tests were performed in both specifications but rejected. Cointegration tests allowing for structural breaks were not performed, as the period under analysis is characterized by macroeconomic stability and coincides with the introduction of the inflation-targeting framework. Dollarization series in first differences are I(0) processes.

and exogenous data series (Annex Figure 16.2.1).[15] Further work could model some of the exogenous variables as endogenous.

The VAR estimation results of the aggregate model are presented in Annex Table 16.2.2. Annex Figure 16.2.2 depicts, for several of the exogenous variables, the impact of a unit increase to the exogenous variables on credit and deposit dollarization over time. The findings are:

- *Macroeconomic variables.* Inflation is not significant, suggesting that it is not an important driver of dollarization once inflation and expectations are well contained—as was the case in Peru during the estimation period. Appreciation spikes are important for explaining dedollarization of credits and deposits. An appreciation spike equivalent to appreciations greater than 1 percent for two consecutive months results in a decline of the dollarization rate of 0.5 percentage points over time (Annex Figure 16.2.2). After controlling for sharp exchange rate movements, the remaining exchange rate variability further helps to lower dollarization of credit. Under historical variability of the exchange rate over the last two years, the decline in credit dollarization will be 2.5 percentage points per year. The inclusion of Emerging Market Bond Index changes in the regression measures the impact of macroeconomic stability not reflected in exchange rate movements.
- *Market development.* The issuance of long-term Treasury bonds in nuevos soles fosters dedollarization, as the development of a nuevo sol yield curve helps bank funding and pricing of long-term credit in this currency. Results indicate that as the share of private sector bonds issued in domestic currency increases, dollarization of credit increases as well. This could be due to the fact that this variable is capturing instruments competing with bank lending in nuevos soles, and as a consequence dollarization of banking credit rises. However, overall credit in nuevos soles in the economy increases.

The VAR specification with disaggregated credit and deposits confirms the findings of the aggregate model and provides further insights on the drivers of dedollarization. Results are presented in Annex Table 16.2.3, and a selection of dynamic multipliers is included in Annex Figure 16.2.3. The results can be summarized as follows:

- *Macroeconomic variables.* Consistent with the aggregate model, exchange rate spikes matter for dedollarization. Appreciation spikes foster dedollarization of commercial credit, while depreciation spikes are associated with higher dollarization of mortgages. Once we control for sharp exchange rate movements, volatility of the exchange rate lowers dollarization of commercial credit. Inflation seems to promote dollarization of time deposits.
- *Prudential variables.* Higher reserve requirement spreads lower dollarization, specifically for commercial credit. The introduction of higher provisions for foreign currency loans helped lower dollarization of mortgages, but this result merits further analysis as the dummy variable could be capturing other events that took place around the time this measure was introduced, such as the reduction in the inflation-targeting band in 2007.[16]
- *Market development.* The issuance of long-term Treasury bonds in nuevos soles promotes dedollarization of credit. The coefficients on Treasury bonds with terms of 10–15 years and 15–20 years are significant for commercial credit. As found in the aggregate model, the increase in the share of bonds issued in nuevos soles raises dollarization of credit, particularly credit extended to the commercial sector, which supports the explanation that some of the private debt instruments issued in nuevos soles compete with bank loans in nuevos soles.

[15] A dummy variable for the 2004 legal change forcing retailers to list prices in domestic currency was tested as an explanatory variable but it was not significant; thus, this variable was not included in the set of exogenous variables used in this chapter.

[16] The provision of credit risk guarantees by the government-sponsored housing program (*MiVivienda*) for new mortgages denominated in foreign currency extended by financial institutions was discontinued in January 2008. Therefore, this change in *MiVivienda* is not driving the results.

## NEXT STEPS

A range of measures could play a role in consolidating and deepening the dedollarization process in Peru.

- *Macroeconomic-related measures.* Reflecting strengthened institutions and a track record of prudent policies, the inflation-targeting framework and consolidated policy credibility have been key to keeping inflation expectations well anchored, which is essential to the dedollarization process. Moreover, the successful policy response during the global financial crisis further increased currency credibility. In this context, some further exchange rate flexibility, while avoiding extreme depreciations, could foster the dedollarization process.
- *Prudential measures.* Regulatory measures can also promote funding and lending in domestic currency. Provisions and capital requirements for foreign currency lending to unhedged domestic borrowers could be periodically reassessed to ensure that the foreign exchange credit risk remains well internalized. The development of mortgage-covered bonds in nuevos soles, which is being promoted by the Peruvian authorities, will help banks finance mortgages in nuevos soles.[17]
- *Development of a capital market in nuevos soles.* Deepening long-term funding and pricing in nuevos soles will enhance dedollarization, which would be supported by further improving the yield curve of *soberanos* and developing the repo market and the fixed-floating swap curve. The development of long-term nuevo sol instruments indexed to the consumer price index could promote dedollarization through the "solarization" of pensions.[18]

## CONCLUSIONS

Peru has successfully pursued market-driven financial dedollarization during the past 15 years that has been based on a three-pronged approach: ensuring macroeconomic stability, effectively managing reserve requirements and introducing other prudential policies to better reflect currency risk, and developing a capital market in nuevos soles. As a result, dollarization ratios of credit and deposits have declined across all sectors and maturities, with larger declines for commercial credit and time and saving deposits.

Based on the results, the road ahead to further deepen dedollarization could focus on three fronts. Maintaining macroeconomic stability, including exchange rate flexibility, and strengthening institutional credibility could induce further credit dedollarization. Additional prudential measures could further discourage lending and funding in foreign currency. Finally, the capital market in domestic currency is still narrow, and although its development could compete with bank loans, overall it will help financial dedollarization.

## ANNEX 16.1. DECOMPOSITION OF COMMERCIAL AND SMALL BUSINESS SECTOR DEDOLLARIZATION

During the period 2001–09, all commercial and small business sectors in Peru, with the exception of fishing, mining, and electricity/water/gas, were dedollarized (Annex Figure 16.1.1).

[17] Currently, the interest rate on mortgages in nuevos soles is fixed for the first five years and then converts to a variable rate that changes with the Limabor.

[18] Currently, regulation allows insurance companies to offer pensions in either dollar or nuevo sol valor adquisitivo constante, but in practice, most pensions (about 95 percent) are denominated in dollars because there is very limited availability of nuevo sol valor adquisitivo constante instruments in the market. An alternative approach to promote dedollarization of pensions would entail changing the legislation to permit the "solarization" of pensions, in other words, the denomination of pensions in nominal nuevos soles. Insurance companies would then be able to offer pensions in nuevos soles adjusted with a fixed-actor, while hedging themselves with bonds in nominal nuevos soles.

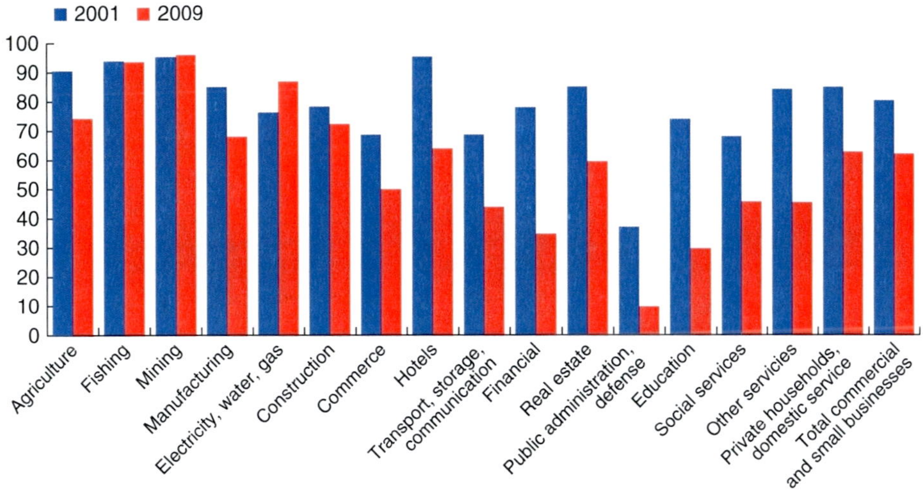


Sources: Superintendency of Banking, Insurance and Private Pension Funds; and IMF staff calculations.

**Annex Figure 16.1.1** Peru: Dollarization by Commercial Sector, 2001 and 2009

**ANNEX TABLE 16.1.1**

**Peru: Decomposition of Dedollarization across Commercial Sectors** *(Percent)*

| | Dollarization | | Share in Total Credit | | 2001–09 | | |
|---|---|---|---|---|---|---|---|
| **Sector** | **2001** | **2009** | **2001** | **2009** | **Between Effect** | **Within Effect** | **Total Effect** |
| Agriculture | 90.1 | 73.8 | 3.2 | 2.7 | –0.4 | –0.4 | –0.9 |
| Fishing | 93.4 | 93.1 | 2.7 | 1.3 | –1.4 | 0.0 | –1.4 |
| Mining | 94.9 | 95.5 | 6.3 | 3.9 | –2.3 | 0.0 | –2.3 |
| Manufacturing | 84.6 | 67.5 | 22.7 | 18.3 | –3.7 | –3.1 | –6.8 |
| Electricity, Water, Gas | 75.8 | 86.4 | 3.4 | 4.4 | 0.8 | 0.5 | 1.3 |
| Construction | 77.7 | 71.8 | 2.9 | 1.9 | –0.8 | –0.1 | –0.9 |
| Commerce | 68.1 | 49.3 | 18.4 | 14.0 | –3.0 | –2.6 | –5.6 |
| Hotels | 95.0 | 63.3 | 1.5 | 1.5 | 0.0 | –0.5 | –0.5 |
| Transport, Storage, Communication | 68.1 | 43.1 | 4.4 | 6.1 | 1.2 | –1.5 | –0.4 |
| Financial | 77.6 | 33.9 | 3.2 | 2.7 | –0.4 | –1.2 | –1.6 |
| Real Estate | 84.5 | 58.7 | 6.1 | 5.4 | –0.6 | –1.4 | –2.0 |
| Public Administration, Defense | 36.3 | 8.8 | 0.9 | 0.3 | –0.2 | –0.1 | –0.3 |
| Education | 73.4 | 28.9 | 0.5 | 0.9 | 0.3 | –0.4 | –0.1 |
| Social Services | 67.5 | 44.9 | 0.4 | 0.3 | –0.1 | –0.1 | –0.2 |
| Other Servicies | 83.7 | 44.7 | 2.1 | 1.9 | –0.1 | –0.7 | –0.9 |
| Private Households, Domestic Service | 84.4 | 62.0 | 2.8 | 2.9 | 0.1 | –0.7 | –0.6 |
| **Total Commercial and Small Businesses** | **79.8** | **61.4** | **81.6** | **68.6** | **–10.4** | **–12.7** | **–23.0** |

Sources: Superintendency of Banking, Insurance and Private Pension Funds; and IMF staff calculations.
Note: Credits in foreign currency are evaluated at a constant nomimal exchange rate.

The decomposition of dedollarization between and within components shows that half of the dedollarization in the commercial and business sectors is explained by the decline in dollarization within sectors, with manufacturing, commerce, and real estate contributing the most (Annex Table 16.1.1).

# ANNEX 16.2. EXOGENOUS VARIABLES AND DATA SERIES

**ANNEX TABLE 16.2.1**

## Definition of Exogenous Variables

| | |
|---|---|
| **Macrostability Variables** | |
| $inflation_t$ | Sum over *t* and *t* – 1 of the monthly percentage change of the consumer price index |
| $d_t^{appreciation}$ | Dummy equal to 1 if depreciation in *t* and *t* – 1 exceeds 1 percent; zero, otherwise[1] |
| $d_t^{depreciation}$ | Dummy equal to 1 if appreciation in *t*, and *t* – 1 exceeds 1 percent; zero, otherwise[1] |
| $e_t$ | Sum over *t* and *t* – 1 of the monthly percentage change of the nominal exchange rate |
| $s_t$ | Standard deviation of daily percentage change of the nominal exchange rate over 90 days |
| $\Delta embi_t$ | First-difference of the Emerging Market Bond Index Peru, divided by 100 |
| **Prudential Variables** | |
| $\Delta\ RR_t$ | Difference over *t* and *t* – 2 of the spread between the reserve requirement rate in foreign currency to the rate in domestic currency (in percent) |
| $d_t^{2006}$ | Dummy equal to 1 starting in mid-2006 until mid-2007 to reflect the introduction of higher provisions for foreign currency loans; zero, otherwise |
| **Nuevos Soles Capital Market Variables** | |
| $\Delta$ *share bonds in soles* | First difference of the percentage of the stock of private sector bonds denominated in local currency |
| $d_t^{10-15}$ | Dummy equal to 1 if during that month a Treasury bond maturing in 10 up to 15 years was issued; zero, otherwise |
| $d_t^{15-20}$ | Dummy equal to 1 if during that month a Treasury bond maturing in 15 up to 20 years was issued; zero, otherwise |
| $d_t^{20}$ | Dummy equal to 1 if during that month a Treasury bond maturing in 20 or more years; zero, otherwise |

Source: Authors.

Note: The exogenous variables are I(0) processes.

[1] According to the definition for the depreciation and appreciation dummies, there are 7 episodes of depreciation and 10 episodes of appreciation in the estimation sample consisting of 94 observations.

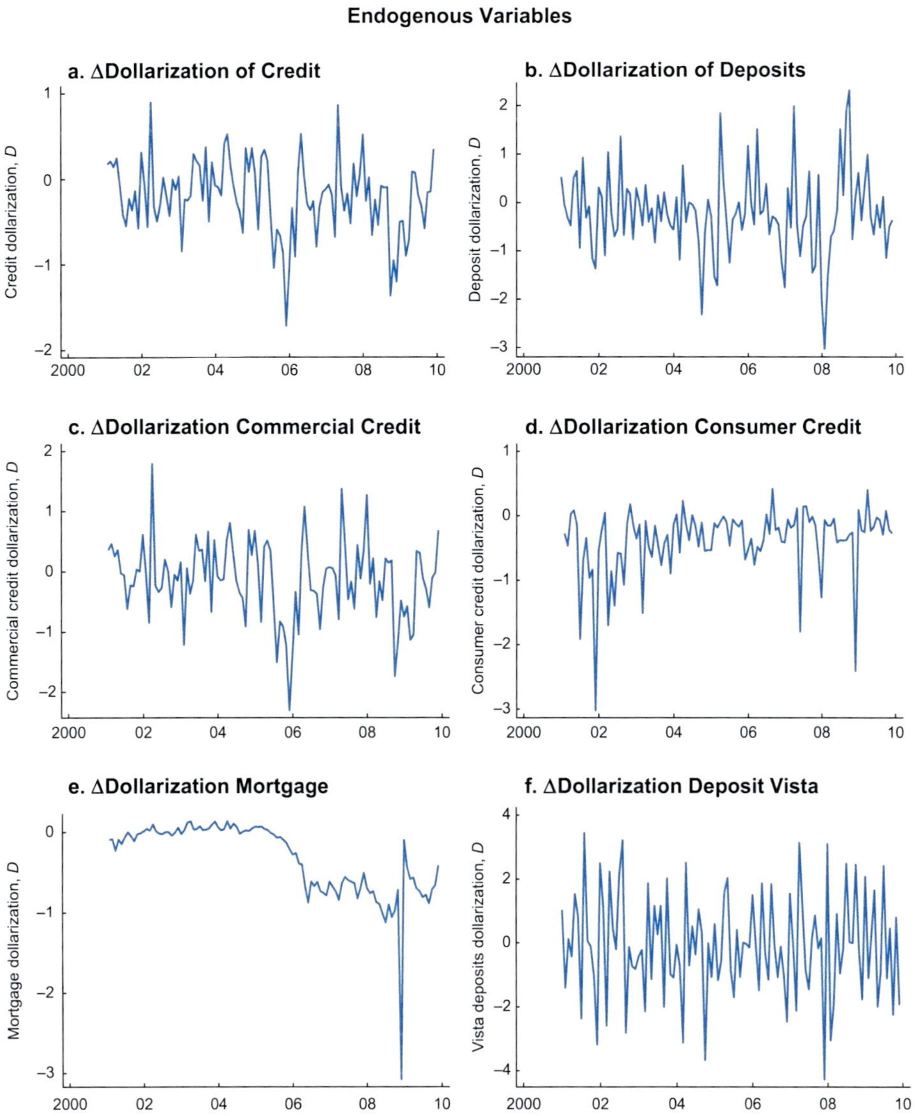


Source: IMF staff calculations.

**Annex Figure 16.2.1** Data for the Empirical Analysis *(continued)*

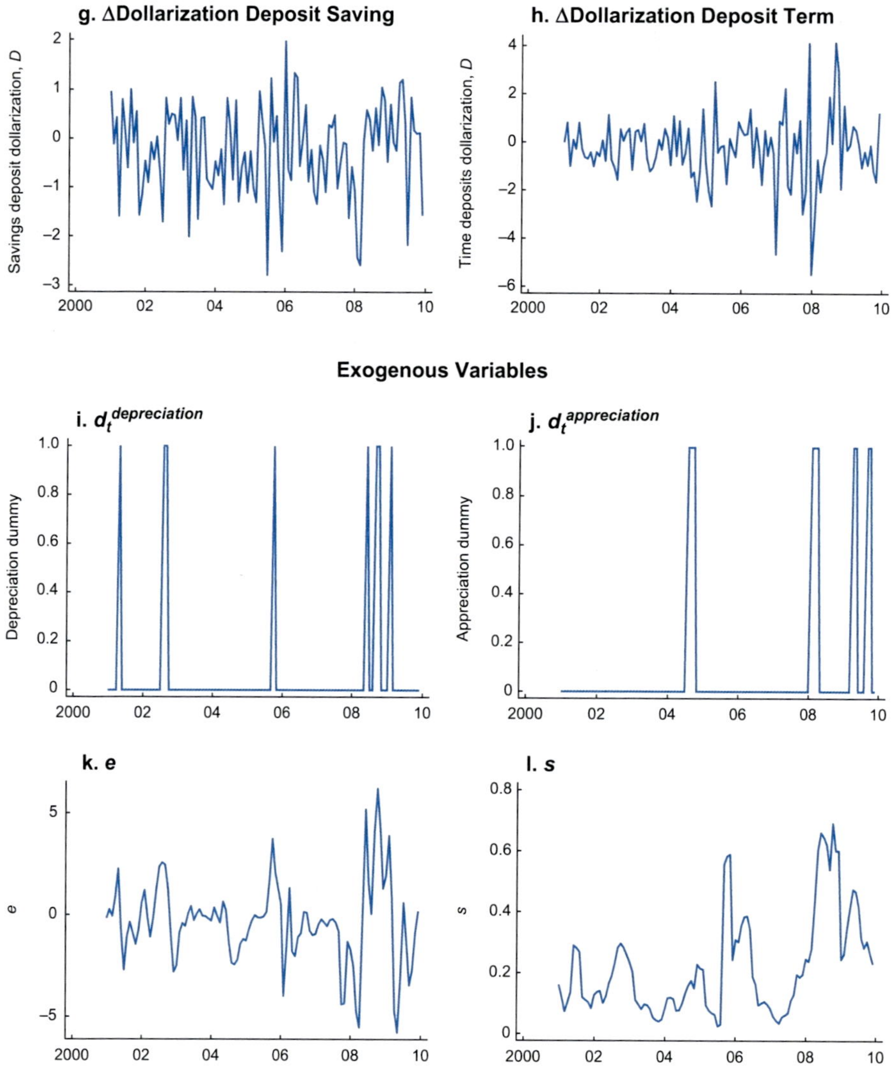


**Annex Figure 16.2.1** *(continued)*

**Exogenous Variables**

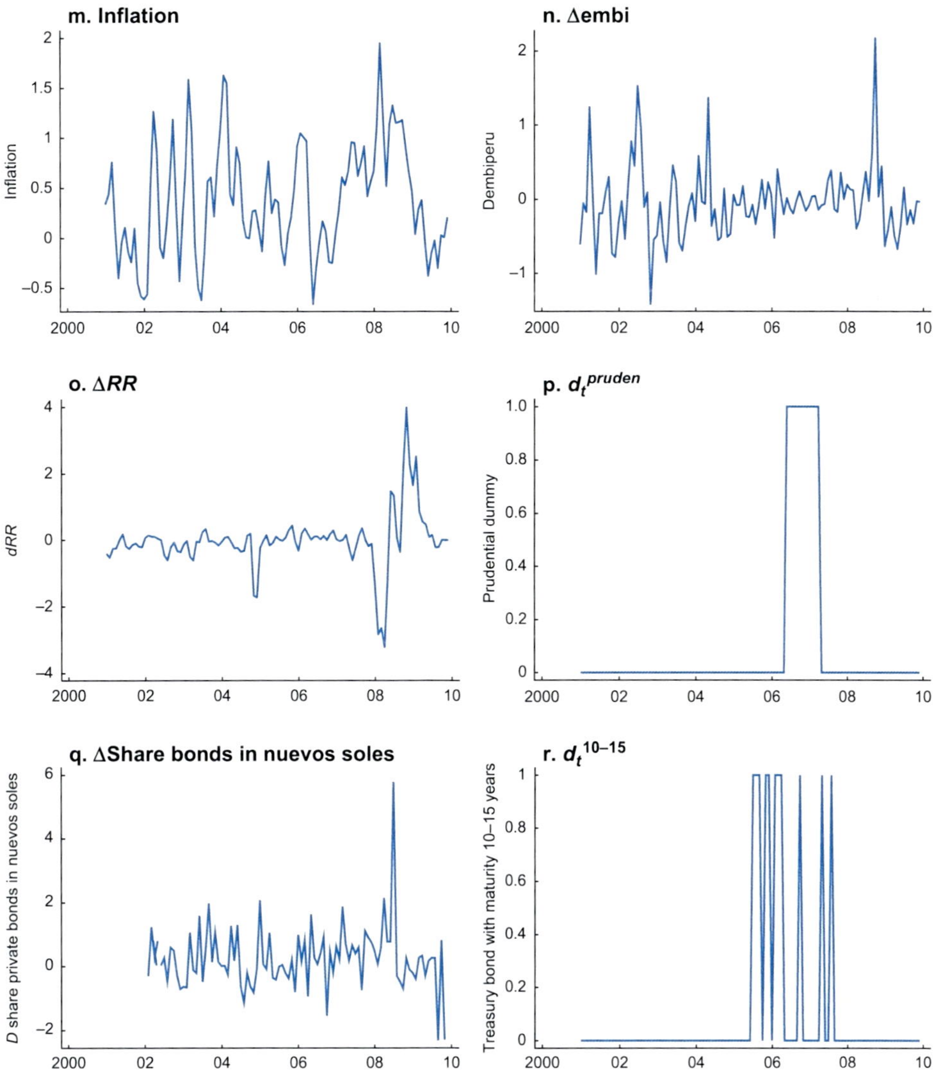


**Exogenous Variables**

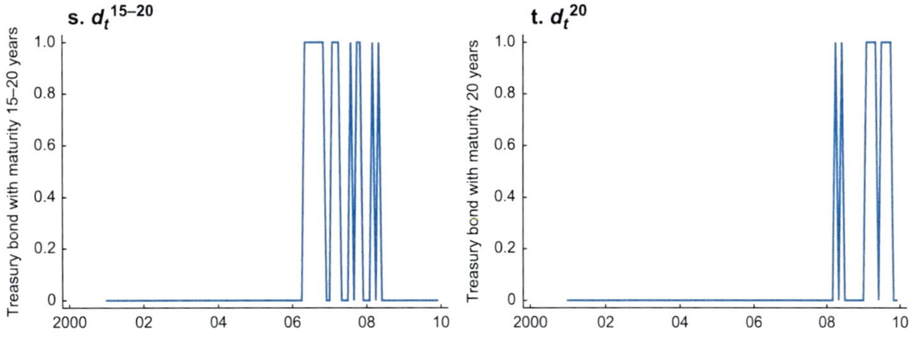


**Annex Figure 16.2.1** *(continued)*

**ANNEX TABLE 16.2.2**

## Results of Aggregate Vector Autoregression Model

| | (1) | (2) | (3) | (4) | (5) | (6) | (7) | (8) |
|---|---|---|---|---|---|---|---|---|
| | $\Delta dol^{credit}_t$ | $\Delta dol^{deposit}_t$ | $\Delta dol^{credit}_t$ | $\Delta^{deposit}_t$ | $\Delta dol^{credit}_t$ | $\Delta dol^{deposit}_t$ | $\Delta dol^{credit}_t$ | $\Delta dol^{deposit}_t$ |
| $\Delta dol^{credit}_{t-1}$ | 0.16* | −0.42** | 0.12 | −0.34 | 0.08 | −0.34 | 0.02 | −0.42* |
| | (0.10) | (0.20) | (0.10) | (0.21) | (0.10) | (0.22) | (0.10) | (0.23) |
| $\Delta dol^{credit}_{t-2}$ | 0.14 | 0.10 | 0.13 | 0.12 | 0.12 | 0.09 | 0.09 | 0.08 |
| | (0.10) | (0.20) | (0.10) | (0.20) | (0.10) | (0.21) | (0.10) | (0.22) |
| $\Delta dol^{deposit}_{t-1}$ | 0.05 | 0.03 | 0.06 | −0.02 | 0.08 | −0.01 | 0.09* | 0.01 |
| | (0.05) | (0.09) | (0.05) | (0.10) | (0.05) | (0.11) | (0.05) | (0.11) |
| $\Delta dol^{deposit}_{t-2}$ | −0.08** | −0.07 | −0.07 | −0.12 | −0.02 | −0.13 | −0.03 | −0.13 |
| | (0.04) | (0.09) | (0.05) | (0.10) | (0.05) | (0.10) | (0.05) | (0.11) |
| **Macrostability** | | | | | | | | |
| $inflation_t$ | −0.01 | 0.13 | −0.04 | 0.17 | −0.09 | 0.20 | −0.09 | 0.22 |
| | (0.07) | (0.14) | (0.07) | (0.14) | (0.08) | (0.17) | (0.08) | (0.17) |
| $d_t^{appreciation}$ | −0.41** | −0.59* | −0.43*** | −0.59* | −0.45*** | −0.57 | −0.45*** | −0.72* |
| | (0.16) | (0.34) | (0.16) | (0.34) | (0.17) | (0.36) | (0.17) | (0.38) |
| $d_t^{depreciation}$ | 0.27 | 0.49 | 0.25 | 0.56 | 0.32 | 0.51 | 0.27 | 0.41 |
| | (0.19) | (0.40) | (0.19) | (0.40) | (0.21) | (0.44) | (0.21) | (0.46) |
| $e_t$ | −0.09*** | 0.05 | −0.08** | 0.02 | −0.09** | 0.01 | −0.08** | 0.01 |
| | (0.03) | (0.06) | (0.03) | (0.07) | (0.03) | (0.07) | (0.04) | (0.08) |
| $s_t$ | −0.43 | 0.47 | −0.47* | 0.45 | −0.54* | 0.36 | −0.49* | 0.34 |
| | (0.27) | (0.56) | (0.27) | (0.56) | (0.28) | (0.60) | (0.28) | (0.62) |
| $\Delta embi$ | 0.00 | 0.07 | 0.01 | 0.07 | −0.01 | 0.10 | 0.00 | 0.15 |
| | (0.09) | (0.18) | (0.09) | (0.18) | (0.09) | (0.20) | (0.09) | (0.20) |
| **Prudential** | | | | | | | | |
| $\Delta RR_t$ | | | −0.06 | 0.17 | −0.10 | 0.17 | −0.10 | 0.14 |
| | | | (0.07) | (0.14) | (0.07) | (0.14) | (0.07) | (0.15) |
| $d^{2006}$ | | | −0.20 | 0.05 | −0.23* | 0.07 | −0.24 | 0.21 |
| | | | (0.13) | (0.26) | (0.13) | (0.28) | (0.17) | (0.37) |
| **Capital Market Development** | | | | | | | | |
| *Δ share bonds in nuevos soles* | | | | | 0.07* | −0.01 | 0.06 | −0.03 |
| | | | | | (0.04) | (0.09) | (0.04) | (0.09) |
| $d^{10-15}$ | | | | | | | −0.31** | −0.25 |
| | | | | | | | (0.13) | (0.28) |
| $d^{15-20}$ | | | | | | | −0.01 | −0.17 |
| | | | | | | | (0.15) | (0.33) |
| $d^{20}$ | | | | | | | −0.13 | 0.18 |
| | | | | | | | (0.15) | (0.34) |
| *Constant* | −0.07 | −0.42*** | −0.02 | −0.45*** | 0.00 | −0.46*** | 0.03 | −0.43** |
| | (0.07) | (0.15) | (0.07) | (0.15) | (0.08) | (0.17) | (0.08) | (0.18) |
| Observations | 105 | 105 | 105 | 105 | 94 | 94 | 94 | 94 |
| *R*-squared | 0.27 | 0.21 | 0.39 | 0.83 | 0.40 | 0.85 | 0.39 | 0.86 |

Source: IMF staff calculations

Note: Standard errors in parentheses. *** $p<0.01$, ** $p<0.05$, * $p<0.1$.

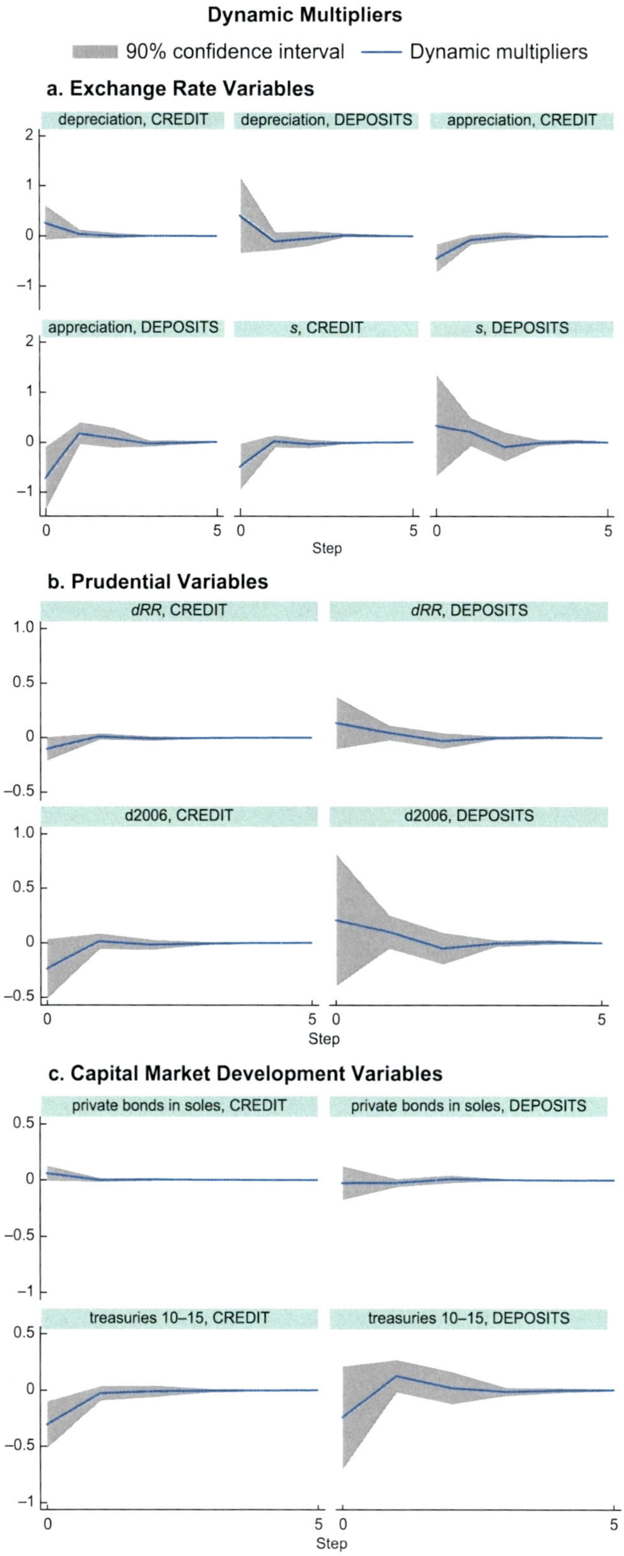


Source: IMF staff calculations.

Note: Panels by impulse variable and response variable.

**Annex Figure 16.2.2** Aggregate Model: Dynamic Impact of Selective Exogenous Variables

**ANNEX TABLE 16.2.3**

## Results of Six Variable Vector Autoregression Specifications

| | (1) $\Delta dol^{commercial}_t$ | (2) $\Delta dol^{consumption}_t$ | (3) $\Delta dol^{mortgage}_t$ | (4) $\Delta dol^{vista}_t$ | (5) $\Delta dol^{saving}_t$ | (6) $\Delta dol^{time}_t$ |
|---|---|---|---|---|---|---|
| $\Delta dol^{commercial}_{t-1}$ | −0.03 | 0.02 | −0.04 | −0.07 | −0.2 | −0.43 |
| | (0.10) | (0.08) | (0.05) | (0.26) | (0.16) | (0.27) |
| $\Delta dol^{commercial}_{t-2}$ | 0.07 | 0.19*** | 0.07 | −0.09 | −0.01 | 0.12 |
| | (0.09) | (0.07) | (0.05) | (0.23) | (0.14) | (0.24) |
| $\Delta dol^{consumption}_{t-1}$ | 0.35** | −0.1 | −0.1 | −0.2 | 0.19 | 0.03 |
| | (0.14) | (0.11) | (0.07) | (0.35) | (0.22) | (0.37) |
| $\Delta dol^{consumption}_{t-2}$ | −0.19 | 0.14 | −0.04 | −0.19 | 0.21 | −0.02 |
| | (0.12) | (0.09) | (0.06) | (0.29) | (0.18) | (0.30) |
| $\Delta dol^{mortgage}_{t-1}$ | −0.34* | −0.12 | 0.16* | −0.84* | −0.28 | 0.01 |
| | (0.18) | (0.13) | (0.09) | (0.45) | (0.28) | (0.47) |
| $\Delta dol^{mortgage}_{t-2}$ | −0.12 | 0.17 | 0.41*** | 0.76* | 0.34 | 0.67 |
| | (0.18) | (0.14) | (0.09) | (0.46) | (0.28) | (0.48) |
| $\Delta dol^{vista}_{t-1}$ | −0.03 | −0.02 | −0.01 | −0.53*** | 0.13** | 0.07 |
| | (0.04) | (0.03) | (0.02) | (0.10) | (0.06) | (0.10) |
| $\Delta dol^{vista}_{t-2}$ | −0.02 | −0.13*** | −0.04** | −0.28*** | 0.03 | −0.05 |
| | (0.04) | (0.03) | (0.02) | (0.10) | (0.06) | (0.10) |
| $\Delta dol^{saving}_{t-1}$ | 0.28*** | 0.04 | 0.03 | 0.09 | −0.32*** | 0.31 |
| | (0.07) | (0.06) | (0.04) | (0.18) | (0.11) | (0.19) |
| $\Delta dol^{saving}_{t-2}$ | −0.04 | 0.02 | 0 | −0.27* | −0.17* | 0.26 |
| | (0.06) | (0.05) | (0.03) | (0.16) | (0.10) | (0.16) |
| $\Delta dol^{time}_{t-1}$ | 0.05 | 0 | 0.03 | 0.30*** | 0.21*** | −0.25** |
| | (0.04) | (0.03) | (0.02) | (0.10) | (0.06) | (0.10) |
| $\Delta dol^{time}_{t-2}$ | 0.01 | −0.04 | −0.03 | 0.23** | 0.08 | −0.23** |
| | (0.04) | (0.03) | (0.02) | (0.11) | (0.06) | (0.11) |
| **Macrostability** | | | | | | |
| $inflation_t$ | −0.10 | −0.07 | −0.07 | −0.40 | −0.17 | 0.93*** |
| | (0.11) | (0.08) | (0.06) | (0.28) | (0.17) | (0.29) |
| $d^{appreciation}_t$ | −0.62** | 0.20 | 0.02 | −0.22 | −0.31 | −1.04 |
| | (0.25) | (0.18) | (0.12) | (0.62) | (0.38) | (0.64) |
| $d^{depreciation}_t$ | 0.23 | 0.31 | 0.37** | 0.65 | 0.64 | 0.95 |
| | (0.31) | (0.23) | (016) | (0.78) | (0.47) | (0.80) |
| $e_t$ | −0.11** | −0.01 | 0.02 | 0.08 | −0.01 | −0.01 |
| | (0.05) | (0.04) | (0.03) | (0.13) | (0.08) | (0.13) |
| $s_t$ | −1.24*** | −0.12 | −1.03*** | −1.66 | 0.92 | 0.64 |
| | (0.45) | (0.33) | (0.23) | (1.13) | (0.69) | (1.17) |
| $\Delta embi$ | 0.23* | −0.16* | −0.18*** | 0.79** | −0.39** | 0.16 |
| | (0.13) | (0.10) | (0.06) | (0.32) | (0.20) | (0.33) |
| **Prudential** | | | | | | |
| $\Delta RR_t$ | −0.28*** | 0.1 | 0 | −0.01 | 0.14 | 0.28 |
| | (0.10) | (0.07) | (0.05) | (0.25) | (0.15) | (0.26) |
| $d^{2006}_t$ | −0.31 | −0.1 | −0.23* | −0.71 | −0.27 | 1.10* |
| | (0.25) | (0.18) | (0.13) | (0.62) | (0.38) | (0.65) |
| **Capital Market Development** | | | | | | |
| *Δ share bonds in nuevos soles* | 0.15*** | −0.05 | 0 | 0.13 | −0.02 | −0.08 |
| | (0.06) | (0.04) | (0.03) | (0.15) | (0.09) | (0.15) |
| $d^{10-15}$ | −0.53*** | 0.2 | 0.04 | −0.21 | −0.61** | −0.1 |
| | (0.18) | (0.13) | (0.09) | (0.44) | (0.27) | (0.46) |
| $d^{15-20}$ | −0.38* | 0.37** | −0.11 | 0.53 | 0.22 | −0.42 |
| | (0.23) | (0.17) | (0.11) | (0.57) | (0.35) | (0.59) |
| $d^{20}$ | −0.36 | 0.19 | −0.08 | 0.79 | 0.11 | 0.4 |
| | (0.23) | (0.17) | (0.11) | (0.56) | (0.34) | (0.59) |
| *Constant* | 0.31** | −0.36*** | 0.08 | 0.22 | −0.25 | −0.69* |
| | (0.15) | (0.11) | (0.07) | (0.37) | (0.23) | (0.39) |
| Observations | 94 | 94 | 94 | 94 | 94 | 94 |
| $R$-squared | 0.48 | 0.37 | 0.75 | 0.42 | 0.41 | 0.31 |

Source: IMF staff calculations.

Note: Standard errors in parentheses. *** $p < 0.01$, ** $p < 0.05$, * $p < 0.1$.

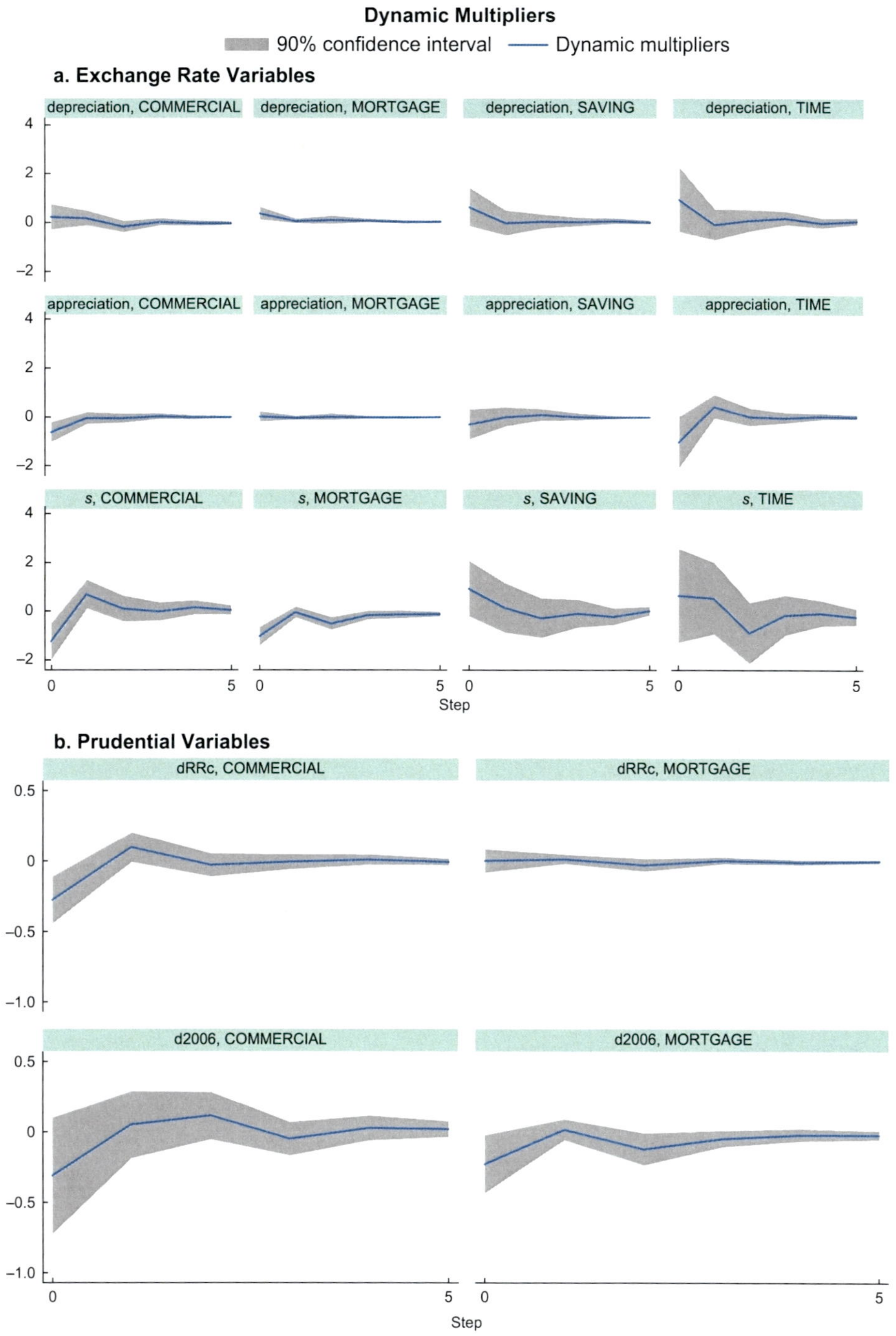


Source: IMF staff calculations.

Note: Panels by impulse variable and response variable.

**Annex Figure 16.2.3** Six-Variable Model: Dynamic Impact of Selective Exogenous Variables *(continued)*

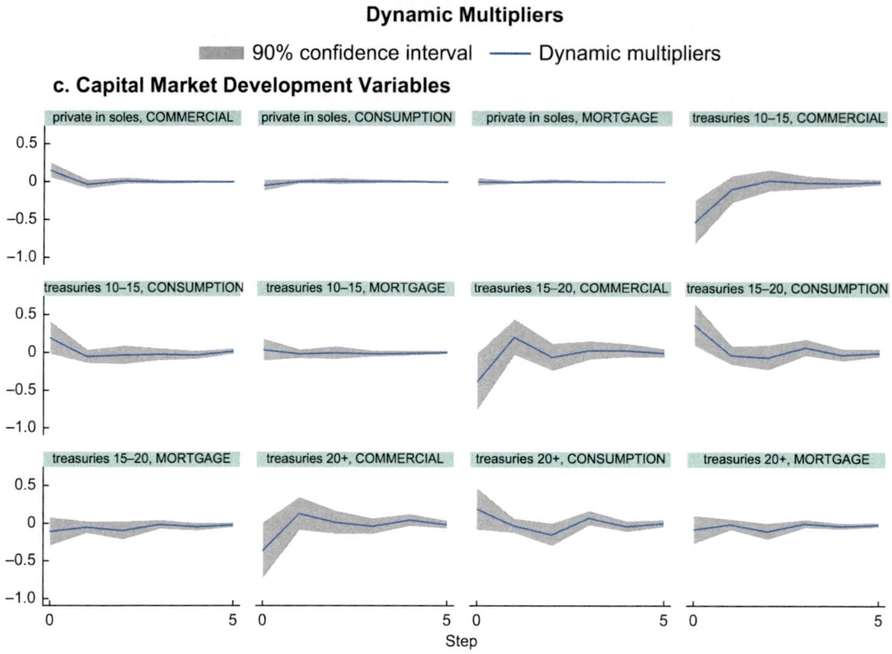


**Annex Figure 16.2.3** *(continued)*

# REFERENCES

Broda, C., and E. Levy-Yeyati. 2003. "Endogeneous Deposit Dollarization." Staff Report 160, Federal Reserve Bank of New York.

Cayazzo, J., A. G. Pascual, E. Gutierrez, and S. Heysen, "Toward an Effective Supervision of Partially Dollarized Banking Systems." Working Paper WP/06/32, International Monetary Fund, Washington, DC.

De Nicolo, P. Honokan, and A. Ize. 2005. "Dollarization of Bank Deposits: Causes and Consequences." *Journal of Banking and Finance* 29: 1697–727.

Erasmus, L., J. Leichter, and J. Menkulasi. 2009. "Dedollarization in Liberia—Lessons from Cross-country Experience." Working Paper 09/37, International Monetary Fund, Washington, DC.

Ize, A., and E. Levy-Yeyati. 2003. "Financial Dollarization" *Journal of International Economics* 59: 323–47.

Kokenyne, A., and R. Veyrune. 2008. "Dedollarization." Unpublished.

Rennhack, R., and M. Nozaki. 2006. "Financial Dollarization in Latin America." In *Financial Dollarization—The Policy Agenda,* edited by A. Armas, A. Ize, and E. Levy. New York: Palgrave Macmillan for the International Monetary Fund.

## CHAPTER 17

# Banking Sector Spreads and Bank Competition in Peru

KEVIN ROSS AND JUAN ALONSO PESCHIERA

*The profitability of Peru's banking system improved markedly over the past decade—in line with the country's strong economic performance—as banks (both foreign and domestic) entered and exited the industry. Throughout this consolidation, effective interest rate spreads for the banking system remained relatively stable and elevated.*[1] *To many observers, this signaled a lack of competition or the existence of other impediments that reduced the efficiency of financial intermediation. However, the analysis in this chapter of banks' financial statements indicates that effective spreads actually varied substantially among banks depending upon their asset size and ownership status. Interest rate regressions suggested that increases in system-wide concentration levels did indeed raise spreads. However, banks that gained market share ended up lowering effective spreads, implying competitive behavior.*

High interest rates spreads in the banking system adversely affect domestic savings and investment, and can be interpreted as an indicator of a lack of competition and efficiency. In Peru and the rest of Latin America, it was generally believed that financial liberalization, macroeconomic stability, strengthened market-based supervision, and new banking entrants would increase competition and reduce bank spreads toward industrial-country levels. But although bank spreads in Peru have indeed moderated relative to the 1990s, they still remain relatively high and have not declined as much as expected given the country's solid economic growth performance, implementation of structural reforms, and major advances in banking supervision.

In this context, this chapter examines the source of Peru's effective interest spreads through accounting decompositions, financial ratio analysis, and spread regressions.[2] Banks play an important intermediation role by transforming customer deposits into loans. While interest rate spreads reflect this risk-taking role, their level and evolution also contains information regarding regulation and operating costs as well as management decisions—all of which can be evaluated by accounting decompositions. Viewed from a slightly different angle, banks make profits through the use of leverage and an efficient deployment of their assets and operations. In this context, an examination of financial ratios focused on profit creation provides a complementary view to interest rate decompositions, and allows for a deeper understanding of spreads. Finally, interest rate regressions offer a direct way to estimate the influence of risk, costs, bank concentration, and market power factors on spreads.

This chapter starts by providing background information and stylized facts before reporting the results of the interest rate decompositions. The chapter describes the outcome of financial statement analysis on key profitability ratios and then presents the results from basic interest rate regressions formulated to test hypotheses regarding spreads and bank concentration. Conclusions from the study are then presented.

[1]The terms "interest rate spreads" and "interest rate margins" are used interchangeably in this chapter.

[2]See Afanasieff and others (2002), Brock and Franken (2003), Estrada, Gomez, and Orozco (2006), and Gelos (2006) for an analysis of banking spreads in other Latin American countries.

## BACKGROUND AND STYLIZED FACTS

In the late 1990s, Peru's economy and banking system were affected by several large shocks. Crises in Asia in 1997 and Russia in 1998 caused a sudden stop and a reversal of capital flows, which weakened the currency and private sector balance sheets and in turn caused credit portfolios to deteriorate. Lower export prices and El Niño effects also affected production and reduced incomes, weakening domestic demand and further worsening the quality of credit portfolios.

These factors, coupled with some political instability, resulted in a banking crisis. With balance sheets severely destabilized, 6 of Peru's 26 banks left the system in 1999. In 2000, two banks failed, and two more were taken over by the country's banking supervision authority (*Superintendencia de Bancas, Seguro, y AFP* [SBS]). In November 2000, the Peruvian government launched a financial system restructuring program (*Programa de Consolidación del Sistema Financiero*). The program extended a $200 million credit line to the deposit insurance system (*Fondo de Seguro de Depósitos*), financed by issuing Treasury bonds, to be used in the restructuring of financial institutions. The program centered on subsidizing the purchase by stronger institutions of institutions estimated to have negative value. In addition, the government launched two more programs at a cost of $500 million to refinance agricultural and commercial loans.

The government's financial sector restructuring program successfully accelerated the banking sector consolidation process. Further exits and mergers occurred during 2001–06 such that there were only 11 banks in operation by end-2006. During 2007–08, foreign banks such as Santander, Deutsche Bank, and Mexico's Azteca bank entered the Peruvian market. Moreover, two smaller financial cooperatives were transformed into retail banks specializing in consumer credit linked to retail department stores (i.e., Banco Falabella and Banco Ripley). In 2009, Scotia acquired Banco del Trabajo (a microfinance specialist) and in 2013 Banco GNB from Colombia acquired HSBC banking assets in Peru, while Banco Cenosud from Chile entered the market. These operations left the banking system with 16 institutions, a configuration that remained in place as of end-2014.

The restructuring process has resulted in a more concentrated system, which has eased somewhat in recent years (Figure 17.1). Concentration ratios based on the top three (four) banks in terms of asset size increased from 66 (74) percent in 2000 to 78 (87) percent in 2007, before falling back down to 72 (84) percent in 2014. Herfindahl indices were between 0.16 and 0.18 (moderate concentration) from 2000–03, and remained above 0.20 (signaling high concentration) thereafter. Foreign ownership or control of total banking system assets has remained relatively stable at around 50 percent since 2002.

To date, the empirical evidence on the relationship between banking system concentration and competition in Peru is inconclusive. Rojas (2000) found that banking concentration, credit risk, and country risk were the main factors behind Peru's high banking spreads in the 1990s. Using data from 1995–2004, Espino and Carrera (2005) also indicated that banking interest rate spreads in Peru were positively affected by a lack of bank competition. However, Morón, Tejada, and Villacorta (2010) found evidence of intense banking competition by product line (e.g., mortgages, leasing) in Peruvian banks, suggesting that while overall system concentration may be high, it has not resulted in collusive anticompetitive practices.

Peru's banking system today stacks up very favorably in international comparisons. Figure 17.2 presents a number of financial soundness indicators using 2014 data for a variety of South American countries. Profitability ratios—return on assets (RoA) and return on equity (RoE)—are solid. Like many of its peers, the Peruvian banking system is well funded through internal sources, with deposit-to-loan ratios near 100 percent. Thus, although some Peruvian banks do tap foreign financing sources, there is no overreliance on external financing of basic loan operations. Raw capital ratios in Peru are 10 percent, resulting in a leverage ratio similar to regional

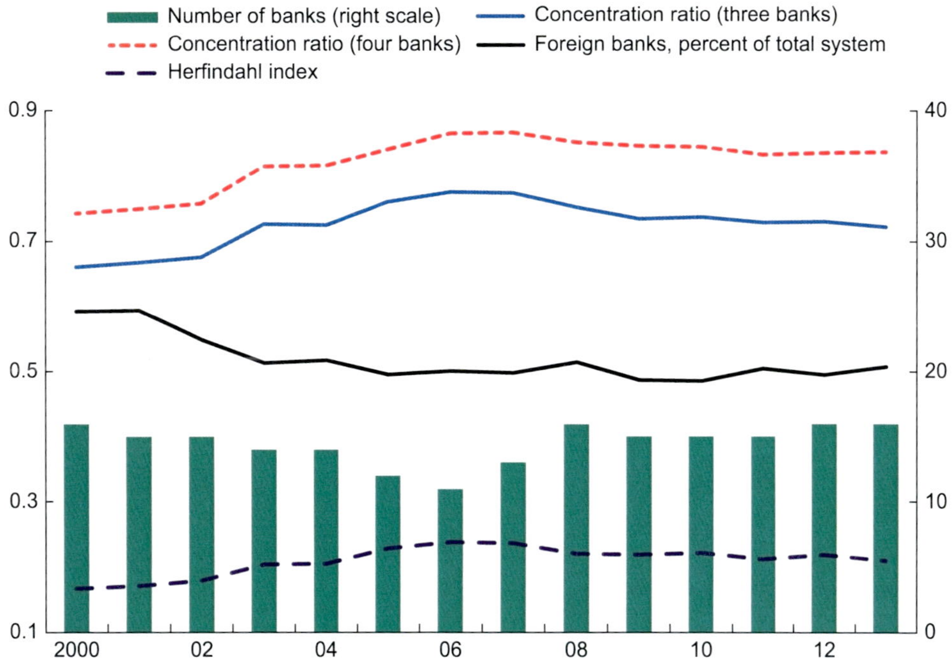


Sources: Peru's banking supervision authority (*Superintendencia de Bancas, Seguro, y AFP*); and IMF staff estimates.

**Figure 17.1** Peru: Banking Sector Concentration and Ownership

averages. At the same time, regulatory tier 1 risk-weighted capital ratios in Peru (not shown here) are near 14 percent—which is at the regional average.

While the level of nonperforming loans has increased recently, it still remains relatively low and is amply provisioned for. Financial sector deepening indicators such as private banking credit to GDP and broad money stock to GDP are well below middle-income averages. However, this also implies that the banking system has sufficient room to expand.[3] At first blush, efficiency indicators across countries suggest personal expenses in Peruvian banks may take up an inordinately large portion of noninterest costs. However, these expenses are still rather small in comparison to banks' gross income levels—suggesting that labor costs are broadly in line with peer groups. Finally, dollarization levels of both assets and liabilities within the Peruvian system remain elevated (see Chapters 15 and 16).[4]

Efforts to improve transparency and limit excessive commission and fee charges are ongoing. In 2012, the SBS banking regulator undertook a comprehensive review of existing regulations focused on information transparency for users of financial products. As a result of that review, a number of reforms were implemented to improve access to information on interest rates, fees and commissions, and other expenses, and to prohibit certain excessive charges. These efforts led to cancelling 938 commissions lines usually charged for various financial products. The SBS has noted that the process is ongoing and that it expects to further streamline the commissions charged to users of financial products. This may reduce the noninterest income of banks going forward.

[3]Fitch Ratings (2012) has noted that *demographic* penetration (number of branches per 100,000 inhabitants) and *geographic* penetration (number of branches per square kilometer) are comparatively low in Peru compared with other countries in the region. Considering Peru's relatively large rural population, an efficient expansion of banking services into these regions will require selecting the right distribution mechanisms.

[4]The Central Reserve Bank of Peru announced in late 2014 that it will evaluate various measures to reduce dollarization in 2015.

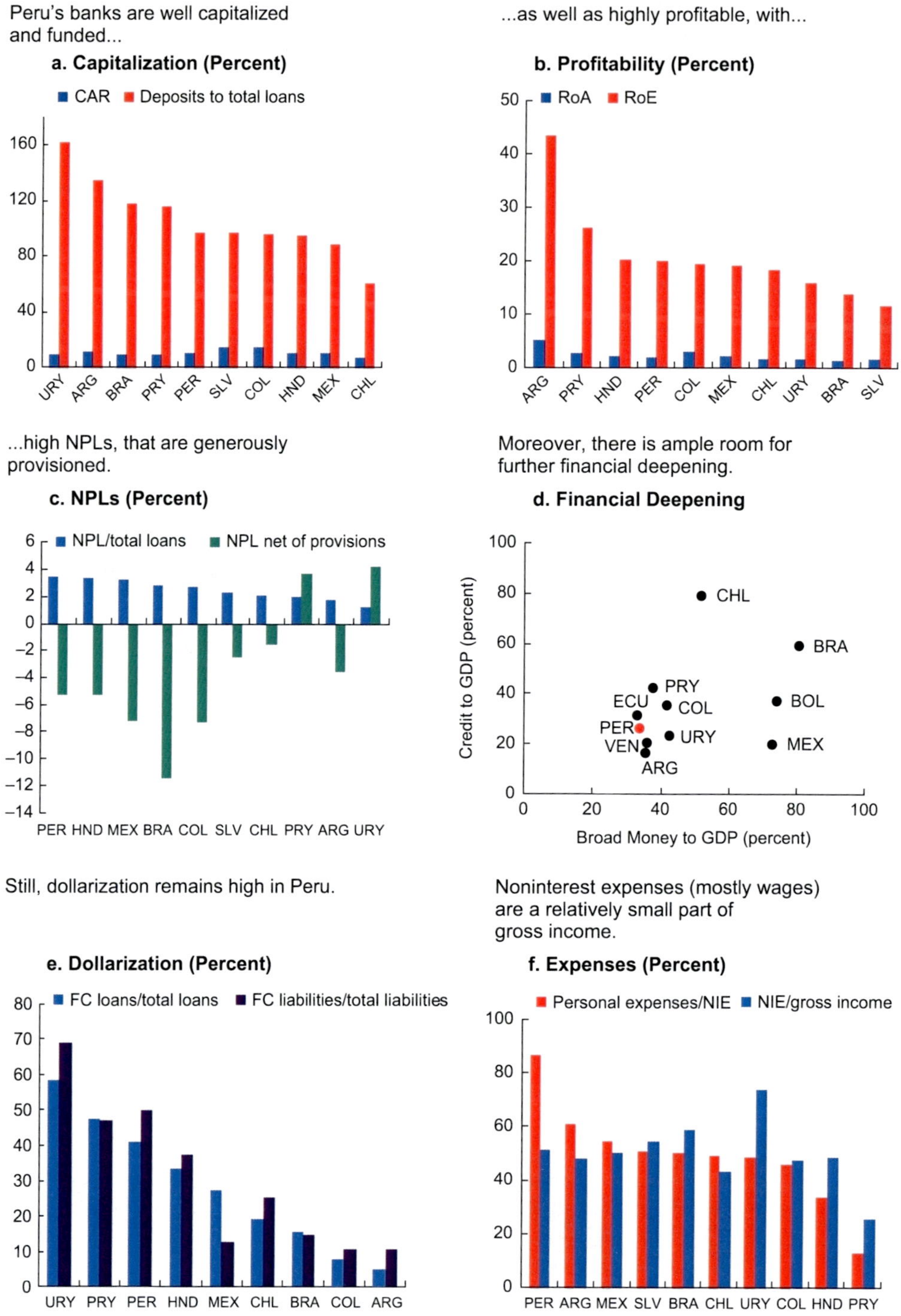


Sources: IMF, Financial Soundness Indicators, International Financial Statistics, and World Economic Outlook databases.

Note: See page vii for a list of three-letter country codes used in this volume. CAR = capital asset ratio; FC = foreign currency; NIE = noninterest expenses; NPL = nonperforming loan; RoA = return on assets; RoE = return on equity.

**Figure 17.2** Banking Sector Indicators, 2013

**TABLE 17.1**

**Quality of Legal Framework and Credit Information, 2014**

| | Ranking on Credit[1] | Strength of Legal Rights Index (0–10)[2] | Depth of Credit Information Index (0–8)[3] | Public Registry Coverage (% of Adults) | Private Bureau Coverage (% of Adults) |
|---|---|---|---|---|---|
| Argentina | 71 | 2 | 8 | 41.2 | 100.0 |
| Bolivia | 116 | 0 | 7 | 15.1 | 39.0 |
| Brazil | 89 | 2 | 7 | 52.5 | 63.6 |
| Chile | 71 | 4 | 6 | 44.7 | 8.8 |
| Colombia | 2 | 12 | 7 | 0.0 | 87.0 |
| Ecuador | 89 | 1 | 8 | 0.0 | 73.0 |
| El Salvador | 71 | 3 | 7 | 28.2 | 32.0 |
| Honduras | 7 | 9 | 8 | 21.8 | 36.1 |
| Mexico | 12 | 8 | 8 | 0.0 | 100.0 |
| Paraguay | 71 | 2 | 8 | 22.8 | 45.5 |
| Peru | 12 | 8 | 8 | 33.5 | 100.0 |
| Uruguay | 52 | 4 | 8 | 84.6 | 100.0 |
| Venezuela | 104 | 1 | 7 | 0.0 | 28.7 |
| **Average** | **...** | **4.3** | **7.5** | **26.5** | **62.6** |

Source: World Bank (2015).
[1] Getting credit, overall ranking. Higher value reflects lower rank.
[2] Higher scores measure degree to which collateral and bankruptcy laws protect rights of borrowers and lenders, and thus facilitate lending.
[3] Higher scores indicate greater accessibility of credit information.

The overall quality of the credit framework in Peru is robust. Table 17.1 presents data from the World Bank's 2014 Doing Business Indicators on the ease of getting credit in a number of South American countries. Peru's credit system was ranked 12th out of 185 countries, above most of its regional comparators. This index is based on two subcomponent indicators related to the protection of legal rights and depth of available credit information. The legal framework, whereby the rights of borrowers and lenders with respect to secured transactions are protected, was rated an 8 on a scale of 10 (with 10 being the highest)—again above average. The overall depth of available information (coverage, scope, and accessibility) is viewed very favorably as well. The private bureau and public registry credit coverage in Peru is also above norms.

## INTEREST RATE DECOMPOSITIONS

In general, banks require a combination of effective interest and noninterest rate margins to cover costs and earn a profit. With noninterest rate margins determined by price-setting behavior on bank services (fees and commissions), the various factors that determine effective interest rate spreads can be assessed through simple accounting decompositions.[5] Using balance sheet and income statement data, the effective interest rate spread can be decomposed into the following components:[6]

$$(i_l - i_d) = [rr + p + oc + prov + tax + d] - nnii + e \qquad (17.1)$$

where $i_l$ is the average effective interest rate charged on loans, $i_d$ is the average effective interest rate provided on deposits, $rr$ is the required reserves/deposits, $p$ is the profit margin/deposits, $oc$ is the overhead costs/deposits, $prov$ is the provisions/deposits, $tax$ is the tax payments/deposits, $d$ is the deposit insurance costs/deposits, $nnii$ is the net noninterest income/deposits, and $e$ is the residual errors that arise from combining flow and stock data.

[5] See IMF (2004) for a full derivation. In the analysis, we use annual income and balance sheet data from the SBS.

[6] It can be difficult to discern the true level of interest-bearing assets and liabilities to use in the calculation of the effective lending and deposit interest rates. Thus the error term can be large.

**TABLE 17.2**

**Interest Rate Spread Decompositions: Total Banking System**

| | 2000 | 2001 | 2002 | 2003 | 2004 | 2005 | 2006 | 2007 | 2008 | 2009 | 2010 | 2011 | 2012 | 2013 |
|---|---|---|---|---|---|---|---|---|---|---|---|---|---|---|
| Effective Interest Margin | 6.9 | 6.8 | 7.6 | 7.5 | 7.7 | 6.9 | 7.1 | 6.3 | 6.1 | 7.5 | 7.8 | 7.3 | 7.6 | 7.6 |
| Reserve Requirements | 2.4 | 2.6 | 2.1 | 1.9 | 1.9 | 1.6 | 1.8 | 1.6 | 1.8 | 1.8 | 1.6 | 2.1 | 2.3 | 2.6 |
| Deposit Insurance | 0.2 | 0.2 | 0.2 | 0.2 | 0.1 | 0.1 | 0.1 | 0.1 | 0.1 | 0.1 | 0.1 | 0.1 | 0.1 | 0.1 |
| Operational Costs | 7.2 | 5.9 | 6.0 | 6.0 | 5.8 | 4.8 | 5.1 | 4.4 | 4.1 | 4.7 | 4.1 | 4.6 | 4.6 | 4.4 |
| Provisions | 5.1 | 1.4 | 1.5 | 1.1 | 1.0 | 0.7 | 0.9 | 1.1 | 1.2 | 1.9 | 1.5 | 1.5 | 1.8 | 1.7 |
| Profit | 0.6 | 0.7 | 1.3 | 2.2 | 2.6 | 3.4 | 3.7 | 3.8 | 3.9 | 4.1 | 3.8 | 3.8 | 3.5 | 3.3 |
| Taxes | 0.2 | 0.2 | 0.3 | 0.8 | 1.2 | 1.1 | 1.3 | 1.2 | 1.2 | 1.3 | 1.2 | 1.0 | 0.9 | 0.9 |
| **Total Cost Factors** | **15.8** | **11.0** | **11.5** | **12.1** | **12.5** | **11.7** | **12.9** | **12.2** | **12.2** | **13.9** | **12.2** | **13.1** | **13.2** | **12.9** |
| Noninterest Income | 7.6 | 4.3 | 4.7 | 4.5 | 4.6 | 4.6 | 4.7 | 4.7 | 4.9 | 4.6 | 3.9 | 4.2 | 4.1 | 3.7 |
| Residual | (1.3) | 0.1 | 0.8 | (0.1) | (0.3) | (0.2) | (1.2) | (1.2) | (1.3) | (1.7) | (0.5) | (1.5) | (1.5) | (1.7) |

Source: IMF staff estimates.

The decomposition indicates that effective interest rate spreads ($i_l - i_d$) will increase as bank costs (from reserve requirements, operations, provisions, taxes, and deposit insurance) and profits increase, and fall with higher amounts of noninterest income.

System-wide accounting interest rate spread decompositions from 2000–13 are provided in Table 17.2, and lead to the following conclusions:

- Operational costs and profits are the two main factors behind effective interest rate margins.
- Effective interest margins increased as the system consolidated and the economy expanded. After declining during the financial crisis, margins have returned to about 7½ percent.
- Since 2000, noninterest income has remained around 4½ percent, with a marked decline within the last year. This may reflect regulatory pressure to reduce the charges on nonlending banking services.
- The relative stability of total cost factors—at around 10–13 percent—hides the fact that operational costs have gradually declined from above 7 percent in 2000 to around 4½ percent in 2013.
- Profits and associated tax costs increased until the start of the global financial crisis in 2009, partially offsetting operational cost improvements.
- Since 2009, provisions and reserve requirement costs—reflecting monetary policy decisions—have also increased as tax and operational costs moderated.

Interest rate decompositions across various bank subgroupings reveal substantial differences. Figures 17.3 and 17.4 graphically present the interest rate decompositions for the total banking system, as well as for two separate comparative groupings: (1) the largest three banks (by asset size) versus the other banks in the system[7] and (2) foreign versus domestic banks. The main outcome is that margins and costs of the smaller bank grouping (other) are markedly different from the three largest banks:

- *Regarding effective interest spreads,* smaller banks generally tended to increase their margins, reaching a spread of about 12–13 percent. In contrast, the spreads of the largest three banks

[7]The results using a four largest versus smaller bank decomposition are very similar.

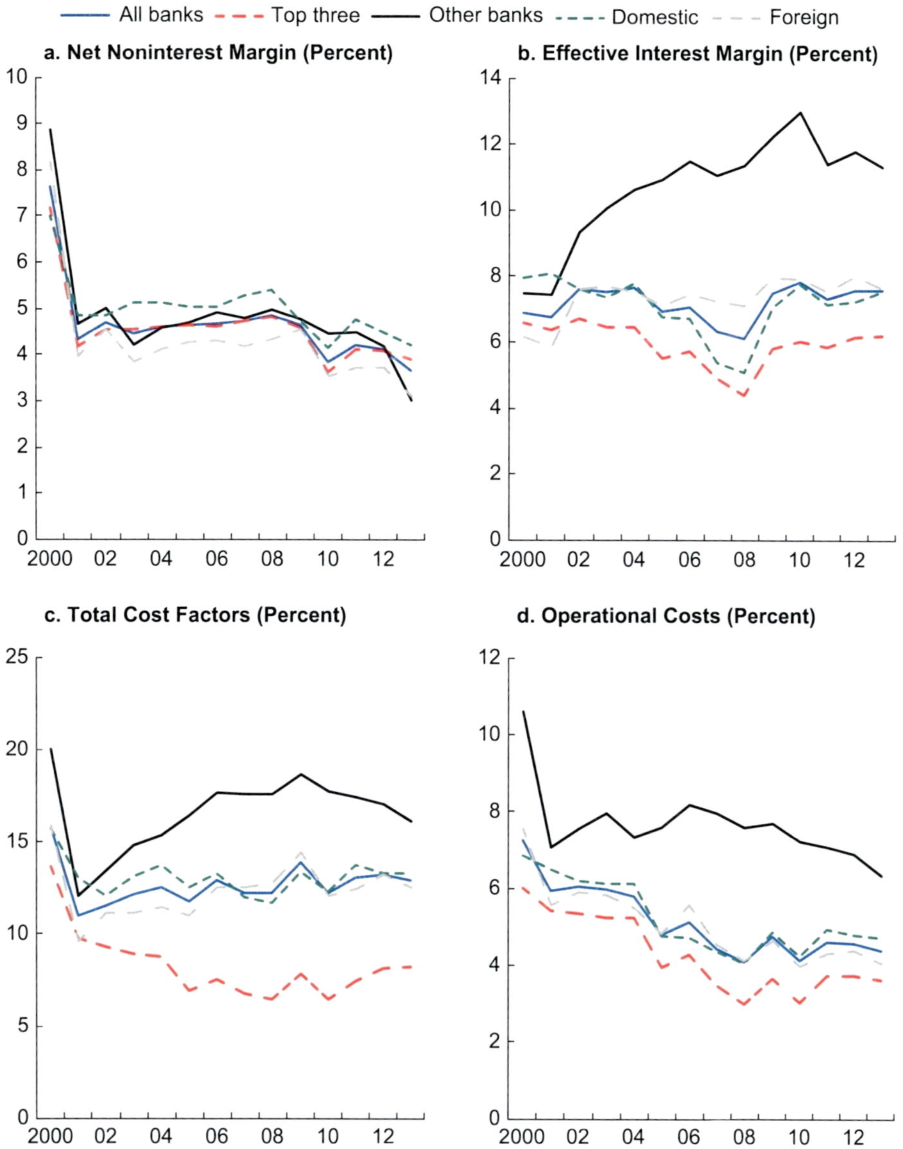


Sources: Data from Peru's banking supervisory authority (*Superintendencia de Bancas, Seguro, y AFP*); and IMF staff estimates.

**Figure 17.3** Peru: Interest Rate Spread Decompositions, 2000–13

fell to 4.5 percent in 2008–09 before returning to 6 percent by end-2013. Outside of the 2008–09 period, both foreign and domestic banks achieved margins of about 7.5 percent.

- *Noninterest margins* for domestic banks tended to be 1 percentage point higher than for foreign banks. By size, the margins of smaller banks were about ½ percentage point higher than those of the three largest banks.
- Smaller banks' markedly higher *expenses* (of 15–20 percent) were driven by higher operational costs (7–8 percent), reserve requirements (2.5–3.5 percent), and provisions

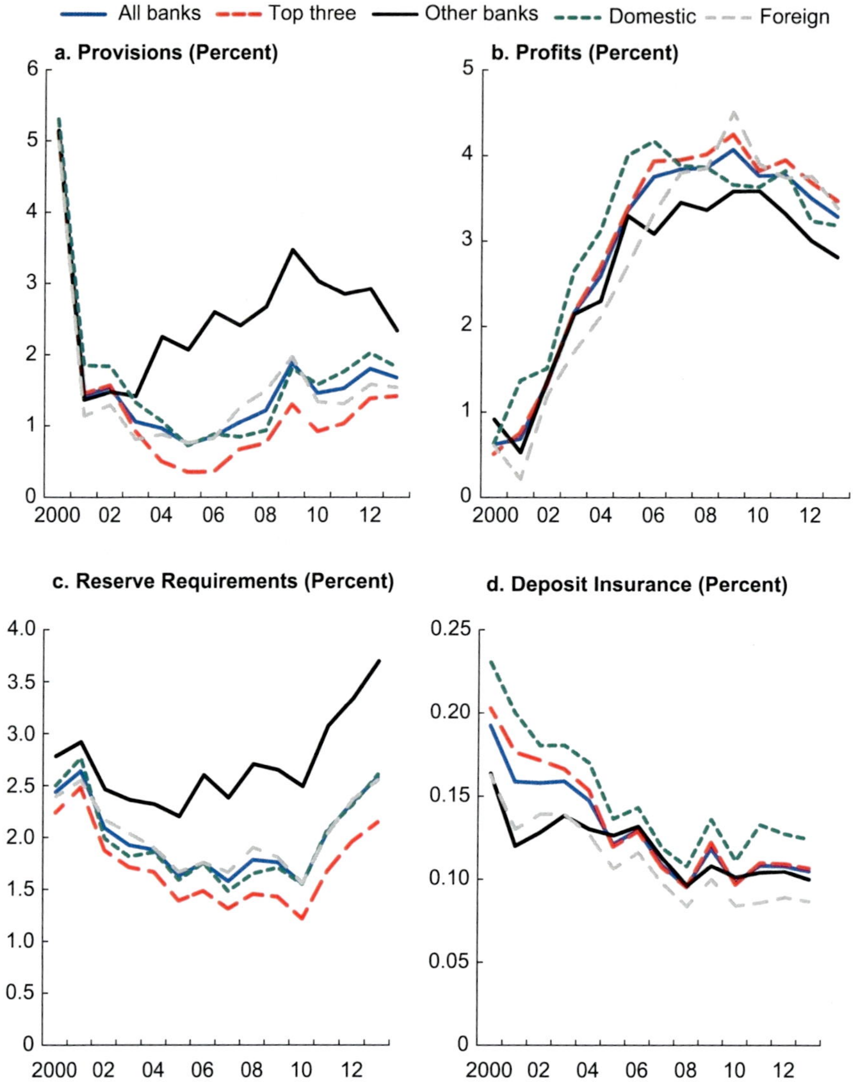


Sources: Data from Peru's banking supervisory authority (*Superintendencia de Bancas, Seguro, y AFP*); and IMF staff estimates.

**Figure 17.4** Peru: Interest Spread Decompositions, 2000–13

(2–3 percent), with the remainder taken up by profits (2–3 percent). It would appear that any operational cost savings these smaller banks achieved since 2007 have been taken up by higher provisions and reserve requirements, and offset by lower noninterest margins. The largest three banks reported much lower operational costs and provisions than smaller banks, while the breakdown and evolution between foreign and domestic banks was very similar. Profits for large and foreign banks tend to exceed the profitability of small and domestic banks.

## FINANCIAL STATEMENT ANALYSIS

Financial statement analysis focuses on three key financial ratios.[8] These ratios are the RoE, RoA, and net interest margin (NIM), each of which can be further decomposed into two separate ratios. To assess profitability of the system, it is important to analyze these ratios and their subcomponents to provide insights into banking sector performance and management over time.

- *RoE is the ratio between after tax earnings (EAT) and book value of equity (BE).* It presents the earnings per unit of invested capital, making it a universally comparable indicator for measuring the profitability of investment. RoE consists of three components: (1) tax policy ($TP = EAT/EBT$), (2) financial leverage ($LEV = T/BE$), and (3) RoA ($RoA = EBT/TA$). RoA changes are often the main cause of changes in a bank's performance, whereas tax policy and leverage effects should be relatively stable.

$$RoE = TP \times LEV \times RoA \tag{17.2}$$

- *A bank's RoA can be further disaggregated into three components:* (1) burden ($B = NNIR/TA$), (2) earning assets ratio ($EAR = EA/TA$), and (3) NIM ($NIM = (IR - IE)/EA$). Burden measures the success in maintaining control over operating costs. It is normal for the bank's burden to have a negative value, since noninterest revenues (*NNIR*, revenues from fees and commissions) are not able to cover all nonincome-related costs. Earning asset ratios usually have a minor role in determining changes in *RoA,* but are a good indicator for analyzing the strategic focus of individual banks. The *NIM* reveals the net income from investing through borrowed funds.

$$RoA = B + EAR \times NIM \tag{17.3}$$

- *Finally, the NIM can also be decomposed into three variables:* (1) return on earning assets ($REA = IR/EA$), (2) cost of liabilities ($COL = IE/L$), and (3) liabilities to earning assets ($LEA = L/EA$). The return on earning assets directly connects earning assets and interest revenue, and is a measure of the average rate of lent funds. *COL* is an indicator of the average price of borrowed capital, while *LEA* measures the intensity of the bank's investment activities.

$$NIM = REA - COL \times LEA \tag{17.4}$$

Table 17.3 presents the financial statement analysis for the whole banking system. RoE has steadily increased, peaking at 27 percent in 2008 before falling back to 20 percent in 2013. The main driver of banking sector profitability has been a greater generation of RoA, which have gone from about ½ percent to above 3 percent as the burden of administrative expenses has fallen dramatically and as the percentage of assets deployed has increased. However, the peak in RoE was strongly influenced by a spike in leverage at the peak of the economic expansion in 2007–08. Tax policy effects were actually a drag on profits until 2005, with a notable increase in after-tax earnings in 2011–13. Finally, it appears that NIMs have been relatively stable—with offsetting

---

[8] Variables not defined in the text are EBT, earnings before tax; TA, total assets; IR, interest revenue; IE, interest expense; and EA, earning assets.

**TABLE 17.3**

**Peru: Financial Statement Analysis of Banking System**

| | 2000 | 2001 | 2002 | 2003 | 2004 | 2005 | 2006 | 2007 | 2008 | 2009 | 2010 | 2011 | 2012 | 2013 |
|---|---|---|---|---|---|---|---|---|---|---|---|---|---|---|
| **Return on Equity** (TP x LEV x RoA) | **0.03** | **0.04** | **0.08** | **0.11** | **0.11** | **0.21** | **0.22** | **0.25** | **0.27** | **0.22** | **0.22** | **0.22** | **0.21** | **0.20** |
| Tax Policy (EAT/EBT) | 0.73 | 0.76 | 0.74 | 0.61 | 0.54 | 0.67 | 0.66 | 0.68 | 0.70 | 0.68 | 0.68 | 0.75 | 0.75 | 0.73 |
| Financial Leverage (TA/E) | 10.5 | 10.3 | 10.1 | 9.8 | 9.6 | 10.8 | 10.5 | 11.4 | 12.1 | 9.8 | 10.5 | 9.9 | 10.0 | 10.3 |
| Return on Assets (EBT/TA) | 0.00 | 0.01 | 0.01 | 0.02 | 0.02 | 0.03 | 0.03 | 0.03 | 0.03 | 0.03 | 0.03 | 0.03 | 0.03 | 0.03 |
| **RoA** (NNIR/TA + EA/TA × NIR/EA) | **0.00** | **0.01** | **0.01** | **0.02** | **0.02** | **0.03** | **0.03** | **0.03** | **0.03** | **0.03** | **0.03** | **0.03** | **0.03** | **0.03** |
| Burden (NIR – NIE/TA) | −0.03 | −0.03 | −0.03 | −0.03 | −0.03 | −0.02 | −0.02 | −0.02 | −0.01 | −0.02 | −0.02 | −0.03 | −0.03 | −0.03 |
| Earnings-to-Assets Ratio (EA/TA) | 0.54 | 0.59 | 0.60 | 0.64 | 0.65 | 0.65 | 0.72 | 0.76 | 0.73 | 0.76 | 0.67 | 0.75 | 0.72 | 0.72 |
| NIM (IR – IE/EA) | 0.07 | 0.07 | 0.08 | 0.08 | 0.08 | 0.07 | 0.07 | 0.06 | 0.06 | 0.07 | 0.08 | 0.07 | 0.08 | 0.08 |
| **NIM** (REA – (COL x LEA) | **0.07** | **0.07** | **0.08** | **0.08** | **0.08** | **0.07** | **0.07** | **0.06** | **0.06** | **0.07** | **0.08** | **0.07** | **0.08** | **0.08** |
| REA (IR/EA) | 0.16 | 0.14 | 0.11 | 0.10 | 0.10 | 0.09 | 0.10 | 0.09 | 0.10 | 0.10 | 0.09 | 0.09 | 0.10 | 0.10 |
| Cost of Liabilities (IE/L) | 0.06 | 0.04 | 0.02 | 0.02 | 0.02 | 0.02 | 0.03 | 0.03 | 0.03 | 0.02 | 0.01 | 0.02 | 0.02 | 0.02 |
| Liabilities to Earning Assets (L/EA) | 1.7 | 1.5 | 1.5 | 1.4 | 1.4 | 1.4 | 1.3 | 1.2 | 1.3 | 1.2 | 1.4 | 1.2 | 1.3 | 1.3 |

Source: IMF staff estimates.
Note: COL = cost of liabilities; E = earnings; EA = earning assets; EAT = earnings after tax; EBT= earnings before tax; IE = interest expense; IR = interest revenue; L = liabilities; LEA = liabilities to earning assets; LEV = financial leverage: NIE = noninterest expenses; NIM = net interest margin; NIR = noninterest revenues; NNIR = net noninterest revenues; REA = return on earning assets; RoA = return on assets; TA = total assets; TP = tax policy.

movements in the cost of funds and return on earning assets—with a minor improvement in investment intensity.

The evolution of financial ratios is markedly different between smaller and larger banks (Figures 17.5 and 17.6). The smaller bank grouping generated much larger NIMs, but due to a worsening of their administrative burden, they experienced a smaller improvement in their RoA.[9] Moreover, due to lower use of leverage and an average tax policy effect, the smaller banks reported a smaller increase in bank profitability or RoE. Foreign banks also tended to do a better job than domestic banks in generating RoA, but have not reduced their administrative burden until recently. Thus, until 2008 the RoA for foreign banks was better than domestic banks. Since 2008, domestic banks' RoA have worsened in line with a worsening of their administrative burdens. Still, overall profitability or RoE are better for domestic banks due to their greater use of leverage.

[9]The profit margins from the interest rate decompositions reflect earnings before taxes, and have been scaled by deposits. As noted above, financial ratio analysis allows a more precise view on the generation of earnings and profits.

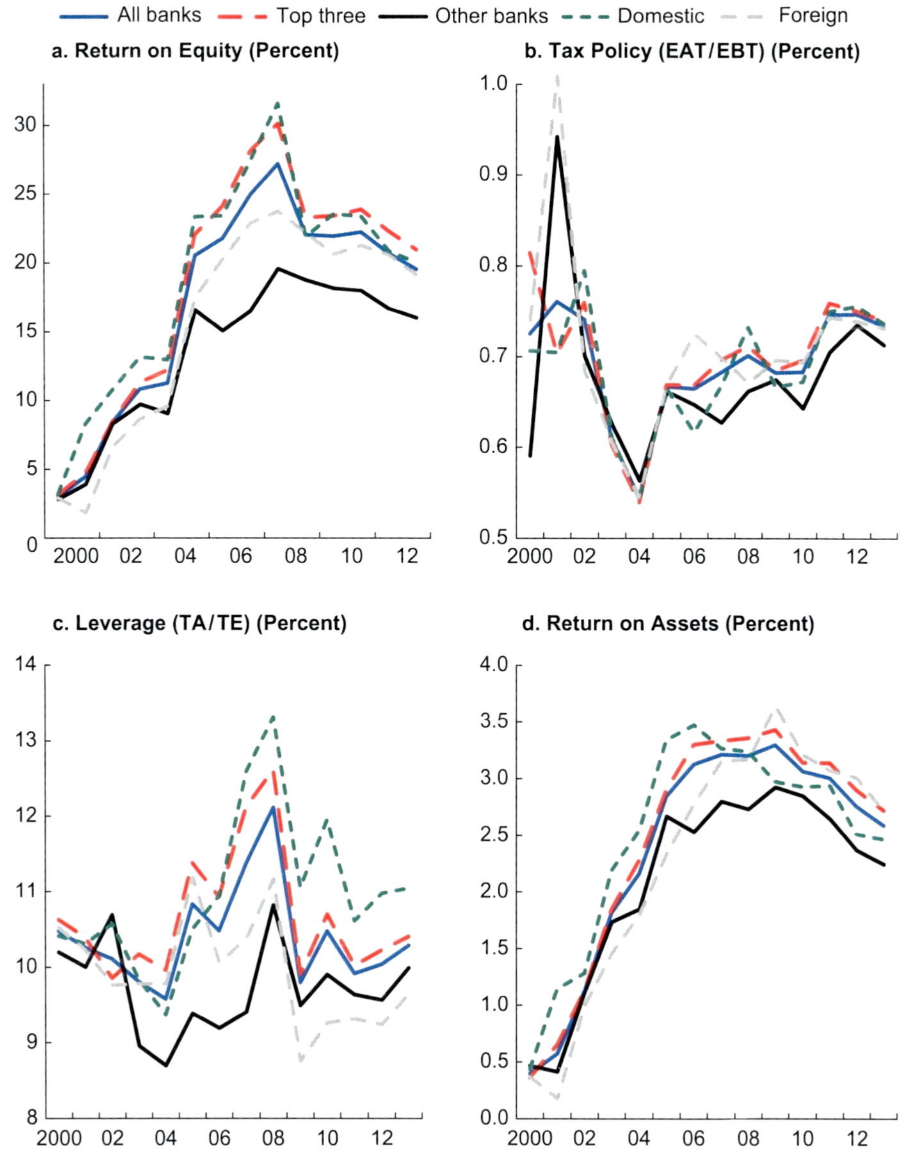


Sources: Data from Peru's banking supervisory authority (*Superintendencia de Bancas, Seguro, y AFP*); and IMF staff estimates.
Note: EAT = earnings after tax; EBT= earnings before tax; TA = total assets; TE = total equity.

**Figure 17.5** Peru: Financial Statement Analysis, 2000–13

## INTEREST RATE REGRESSIONS

Estimation of the interest rate spread panel regressions broadly follows the framework of Espino and Carrera (2005). Using monthly data (December 2001 to December 2013) provided by the SBS, we estimated the following equation:[10]

$$\begin{aligned} Spread_{it} = {} & \alpha + \beta_1 NPL_{it} + \beta_2 Liq_{it} + \beta_3 MR_{it} + \beta_4 Cost_{it} + \beta_5 Share_{it} + \beta_6 IC3_t \\ & + \beta_7 Libor_t + \beta_8 ER_t + \beta_9\, Inf_t + \varepsilon_t. \end{aligned} \tag{17.5}$$

[10] All estimations are done using the EVIEWS econometric statistical package, using unbalanced panel data regression techniques assuming fixed effects. Robust estimators were calculated using White cross-sectional seemingly unrelated regression model corrections to ensure robust standard errors.

The dependent variable is the effective interest rate spread (*Spread*), as defined previously. The main explanatory variables reflect credit and market risks, as well as operating and liquidity costs, and all should positively affect interest margins. For example, as nonperforming loans (*NPL*) increase, banks would have an incentive to increase margins in order to better reflect actual credit risks. Similarly, an increase in the liquidity asset ratio (*Liq*), calculated as liquidity over total assets, represents a lost opportunity cost of undertaking financial intermediation and would increase margins. Market risk (*MR*) is defined as each bank's disposable investment over its total assets, while (*Cost*) is administrative costs over total assets. Two other variables, market share (*Share*) and the bank concentration ratio (*IC3*), are also employed in separate regressions to test if banks' market power or concentration in the system have an impact on margins. The general assumption is that both variables should increase margins. Additional macroeconomic conditioning variables—the three-month London interbank offered rate (LIBOR), domestic inflation (*Inf*), and the nuevo sol–U.S. dollar exchange rate—are also included.

Table 17.4 presents the two panel regression estimates and results in the following findings:

- The main result is that the key explanatory variables—credit and market risks, and liquidity and operational costs—are all positive (in line with theory) and highly significant. These are the foremost factors behind effective interest rate spreads.
- The coefficient estimate for the bank concentration variable (*IC3*) is also positive, and indicates that for every 1 percentage point increase in system-wide bank concentration, the effective interest rate margin rises by 0.074 percentage points. This estimate is more than double the 0.033 estimated coefficient reported by Espino and Carrera (2005) using quarterly data from 1995 to 2004.

**TABLE 17.4**

## Interest Spread Regressions

| | Regression 1 (Market Share) | Regression 2 (Bank Concentration) |
|---|---|---|
| $NPL_t$ | 0.0955 | 0.1059 |
| (*t*) | (9.3) | (9.6) |
| $LIQ_t$ | 0.0914 | 0.1001 |
| (*t*) | (6.8) | (7.8) |
| $MR_t$ | 0.2012 | 0.1954 |
| (*t*) | (8.5) | (8.4) |
| $COST_t$ | 0.9850 | 1.0373 |
| (*t*) | (8.4) | (9.4) |
| $LIBOR_t$ | −0.0018 | −0.0025 |
| (*t*) | (−6.2) | (−6.3) |
| $ER_t$ | −0.0001 | −0.0001 |
| (*t*) | (−0.8) | (−0.5) |
| $INF_t$ | −0.0023 | −0.0027 |
| (*t*) | (−7.3) | (−8.0) |
| C | 0.0625 | −0.0073 |
| (*t*) | (5.7) | (−0.3) |
| $SHARE_t$ | −0.1623 | … |
| (*t*) | (−2.9) | … |
| $IC3_t$ | … | 0.0725 |
| (*t*) | … | (2.6) |
| $R^2$ | 0.9527 | 0.9526 |
| *Prob* (*F*) | 0 | 0 |
| Number of Banks | 15 | 15 |
| Observations | 1,291 | 1,291 |

Sources: Peru's banking supervisory authority (*Superintendencia de Bancas, Seguro, y AFP*); and IMF staff estimates.

Note: *t*-statistics are below the estimated coefficients. Robust unrelated regression panel-corrrected standard errors methods.

- The coefficient for an individual bank's market share, however, is negative and implies that for every 1 percentage point increase in a bank's market share, the effective interest rate margin falls by 0.16 percentage points. This result may seem counterintuitive, but stems from the fact that the larger banks that have gained market share have been the institutions that have experienced lower effective interest rate margins, while the smaller banks that have lost market share have increased margins.
- Finally, the results of the macro conditioning variables are somewhat surprising. The exchange rate has no impact on margins—which is unexpected if uncovered interest rate parity holds. Also, the LIBOR coefficient, a proxy for the cost of external funding, is negative (although significant).

## CONCLUSIONS

The Peruvian banking system compares very well with other Latin American systems. Banks are well capitalized, have ample access to deposit funding sources, and follow prudent provisioning policies. Most importantly, the credit delivery system is very healthy. Nevertheless, Peru's consolidation process has resulted in a more concentrated banking system with slightly lower levels of foreign participation. An open question is whether an absence of spread reduction for the system as a whole reflects a lack of competition in the sector. The panel regressions indicated that increases in system-wide concentration levels did raise spreads, but also implied that banks that gained market share ended up lowering effective spreads.

While effective interest rate spreads for the system as a whole have been stable, they have varied widely among certain bank groupings. Surprisingly, both interest and noninterest spreads as well as the return on interest-earning assets on a system-wide basis have remained relatively constant throughout Peru's banking consolidation process and as the economy has rapidly expanded. For the most part, banks' profits rapidly increased due to reductions in personnel and administrative expenses. Moreover, a greater deployment of interest-earning assets and an environment in which the cost of funds is lower also helped to bolster profits. Most striking, the experience and behavior of smaller banks has been significantly different from that of the three largest banks. The smaller banks achieved much higher spreads, and while they also raised profits substantially, they have not been able to control costs to the same degree as larger banks. Finally, when split between domestic and foreign banks, the differences in outcomes appears much smaller.

## REFERENCES

Afanasieff, Tarsila S., Priscilla M. Villa Lhacer, and Marcio I. Nakane. 2002. "The Determinants of Bank Interest Spreads in Brazil." Central Bank of Brazil Working Paper No. 46, Banco Central do Brasil, Brasília, Brazil (August).

Brock, Philip, and Helmut Franken. 2003. "Measuring the Determinants of Average and Marginal Bank Interest Rate Spreads in Chile, 1994–2001." *Economia Chilena* 6 (3): 45–65.

Espino, Freddy, and Cesar Carrera. 2005. "Concentración bancaria y margen de las tasas de interés en Perú." Economic Studies of the Central Reserve Bank of Peru, Lima.

Estrada, Dario, Esteban Gomez, and Ines Orozco. 2006. "Determinants of Interest Rate Margins in Colombia." Economic Study No. 393, Banco de la Republica de Colombia, Bogotá, Colombia.

Fitch Ratings. 2012. "Efficiency in Andean Banks." September 13. www.fitchratings.com.

Gelos, Gaston R. 2006. "Banking Spreads in Latin America." Working Paper, 06/44, International Monetary Fund, Washington, DC.

International Monetary Fund. 2004. "Bank Profitability and Competition." Technical Note, Financial Sector Assessment Program Update, Republic of Kazakhstan, Country Report No. 04/336, International Monetary Fund, Washington, DC.

Morón, Eduardo, Johanna Tejada, and Alonso Villacorta. 2010. "Competencia y Concentración en el Sistema Financiero en el Perú." Universidad del Pacifico Discussion Document DD/10/03, Lima.

Rojas, Jorge. 2000. "Trends in Peruvian Bank Spreads," In *Why So High? Understanding Interest Rate Spreads in Latin America*, edited by Philip Brock and Liliana Rojas-Suarez. Washington, DC: Inter-American Development Bank.

Superintendencia de Bancas, Seguro, y AFP. 2000–2013. Annual Reports. Lima, Peru.

World Bank. 2015. 2014 Doing Business Indicators. World Bank, Washington, DC. http://www.doingbusiness.org/data.

## CHAPTER 18

# Institutional Frameworks for Macroprudential Policy: Considerations for Peru

MERCEDES VERA MARTIN

*Peru has been a leader in adopting and shaping macroprudential policy in the region. However, the underlying institutional framework is relatively informal and involves independent institutions, with the objective of achieving financial stability. There is no institution with a clear mandate to conduct macroprudential policy, despite its relevance since the 2008–09 global financial crisis. International experience with the institutional framework has varied since the crisis, but has included setting up committees dedicated to eliminating the institutional boundaries between the central bank and the financial regulatory agencies. This chapter tries to apply international experience to the case of Peru and sketches out the possible creation of a financial stability council to enhance the effectiveness of macroprudential policy and its coordination with other macro policies. Such a council could facilitate the integration of macroprudential policies in the policy toolkit, and enhance their complementary role with macroeconomic and microprudential policies.*

Embedding a macroprudential perspective into the policy framework is one of the lessons of the 2008–09 global financial crisis. The crisis highlighted the potential force of financial and real sector interactions. Macroeconomic policies and microprudential frameworks have limitations in identifying and managing systemic risk, as they may fail to identify or appropriately handle financial excesses or adverse shocks that pose a risk to the financial system and the economy as a whole. Consequently, a number of countries have been reviewing their institutional frameworks for financial stability to support developing a macroprudential policy function. The challenge is how to put in place a broader framework of macroprudential policy to preserve financial stability by assessing and managing systemic risk and its potential amplifying effects in the financial sector early on. In some cases, this involves rethinking the appropriate institutional boundaries between the central bank and financial regulatory agencies. Macroprudential policy can be a useful element of the policy toolkit and complement other macroeconomic policies, mainly to support leaning against the wind and dealing with volatile capital inflows in the context of open capital accounts (Terrier and others 2011).

A strong institutional framework will facilitate the effective conduct of macroprudential policy. In principle, effective arrangements that promote preventive actions by the authorities are desirable for all countries, although it is important that such arrangements take into account country-specific circumstances. Country experiences seem to suggest that complex and fragmented institutional structures can create frictions in risk identification and mitigation that can reduce the effectiveness of macroprudential policy. Also, to support accountability, it may be desirable to identify lead authorities or a policymaking committee to which a mandate and powers are allocated to conduct macroprudential policy. In general, central banks are well positioned to take a leading role given their experience and capacity in risk assessment and the need for coordination with monetary policy.

This chapter suggests ways to enhance coordination for the conduct of macroprudential policy in Peru, taking into account recent cross-country experiences. In order to improve systemic risk oversight and monitoring, advanced and emerging market countries have been adopting financial stability responsibilities, usually through more structured frameworks that outline mandates and roles. A formalized institutional framework would facilitate the conduct of macroprudential policy to more effectively manage systemic risks and enhance the role of macroprudential policy in the policy toolkit. Such structures will need to support effective identification of risks through access to information, provide incentives for the timely and effective use of policy tools, and support coordination across policy while preserving the autonomy of established policy functions.

## CONDUCT OF MACROPRUDENTIAL POLICY: CURRENT INSTITUTIONAL FRAMEWORK

The Peruvian authorities have been very proactive in implementing macroprudential instruments to support financial and macroeconomic stability. The Central Reserve Bank of Peru (*Banco Central de Reserva del Perú* [BCRP]) has used reserve requirements to manage liquidity in the financial system, both during the upturn and downturn, and as a complement to the conduct of monetary policy. The Superintendency of Banking, Insurance and Private Pension Funds (*Superintendencia de Bancas, Seguro, y AFP* [SBS]) has implemented measures to smooth the procyclicality of financial services (through dynamic provisioning since end-2008) and internalize foreign exchange credit risks (additional provisions and capital, and limits to the foreign exchange derivative position). The SBS has also analyzed interconnectedness of financial institutions. In July 2010, the SBS issued regulations to impose additional capital requirements taking into account the economic cycle and concentration risks.

In Peru's current legal framework, financial stability objectives are not explicitly allocated, but rather implicitly established in the objectives of the different economic authorities. Responsibility for financial stability is not explicitly assigned to any particular institution in the legal or regulatory frameworks, but it is clearly a collective goal for the financial authorities, including the BCRP, SBS, and the Ministry of the Economy and Finance (MEF). The BCRP has clear involvement in financial stability issues through its mandate to ensure monetary stability (see below), and more specifically to ensure the stability of the payment systems, and ultimately through its role as a lender of last resort. The SBS, which is the microprudential regulator, is responsible for the health of financial institutions and the stability of the financial sector as a whole. The role of the MEF in the conduct of macroprudential policy could be seen as more passive during normal times and more active during crisis times, as decisions potentially have a fiscal cost.

The BCRP and SBS have clear roles in preserving financial stability—Peru is clearly a case of "twin-peaks" in financial stability policy design. Both are constitutionally independent institutions with explicit mandates: the BCRP for preserving monetary stability and the SBS for monitoring and supervising financial institutions.

- ***BCRP.*** With its objective to preserve monetary stability (Constitution, Article 84), the BCRP has as its functions to regulate currency and credit in the financial system, manage international reserves, issue currency and coins, and inform the country about financial conditions. In addition, the Central Bank Board is in charge of establishing, regulating, and modifying reserve requirements of financial institutions and the payment system (Organic Law, Article 24.c and d, respectively).
- ***SBS.*** The SBS is in charge of monitoring and supervising banking enterprises, insurance companies, private pension funds, other deposit-taking institutions, and companies that are determined by law (for example, because of relevant linkages to the financial sector) (Article 87 of the Constitution). In its supervisory responsibilities, the SBS has the objective of

protecting the interests of the public in the sphere of the financial and insurance systems (Article 345 of the General Law of the Financial System and Private Pension Funds, and Organic Law for the Supervision of the Banking Sector and Insurance). Article 347 of the same law notes that the SBS is responsible for defending the interests of the public and for safeguarding the economic and financial strength of the entities under its control.

On prudential grounds, both institutions oversee the financial sector, providing relevant information to the public. The BCRP prepares a financial stability report on a biannual basis that discusses recent economic and financial developments, including the challenges and risks ahead. The information is processed by the central bank's financial sector unit, with limited participation of SBS staff. The SBS publishes monthly bulletins on balance sheets, income statements, and risk assessments (credit, liquidity, operational) of banking institutions, pension funds, microfinance institutions, and insurance companies. Recent efforts by the stock market regulator (*Superintendencia de Mercado de Valores*) to gather corporate sector financial information are also valuable.

As a result of the 2008–09 global financial crisis, Peru's policy coordination has been enhanced, but remains voluntary. At the technical level, coordination is currently done through a voluntary consultative committee established in 2008 in light of the crisis, with the participation of the MEF, SBS, and BCRP. Created to manage the effects of the crisis, the committee has evolved to discuss other issues that require interinstitutional coordination and is not necessarily circumscribed to financial stability. Its biweekly meetings are followed up by a meeting at the highest level to discuss policy coordination. This voluntary arrangement hinders establishing an overall macroprudential perspective on the policy framework. Decisions seem to be made piecemeal, which could lead to delays in policy action. The committee has no mandate for financial stability and therefore lacks accountability.

The institutional setup could be enhanced to facilitate information sharing, analysis of systemic risks in the economy, and actions and accountability. No specific institution has a clear mandate to analyze systemic risk in the economy or the conduct of macroprudential policy. Challenges remain in designing macroprudential policy with a broad and systematic perspective to ensure an integrated evaluation of financial and economic vulnerabilities and sufficient oversight of systemic risks, and to prevent delays in implementing new measures. Greater cooperation would facilitate the integration of macroprudential policies in the policy toolkit and enhance the complementary role of those policies with macroeconomic and microprudential policies. At a more operational level, information sharing could be enhanced to facilitate a better understanding of risks and to establish feedback loops between the financial and real sectors of the economy with the aim of better managing plausible sources of systemic risk (that could rise outside the regulated financial system). In this context, efforts to enhance understanding of a detailed balance sheet of the economy with expanded sectoral analysis would help in assessing interconnectedness, maturity mismatches, and foreign exchange risks in the context of an economy that is still dollarized.[1]

## INTERNATIONAL EXPERIENCE IN ENHANCING INSTITUTIONAL FRAMEWORKS

Since the 2008–09 global financial crisis, a number of countries have reviewed their institutional frameworks for financial stability to develop the macroprudential policy function. Keeping in mind that no universal recipe for the institutional setup exists, and that country-specific features need to be accounted for, it is strongly recommended that countries undertake such efforts to

[1] For example, see Lima and others (2005) for a detailed balance sheet analysis for Colombia.

enhance preventive action. Given the incipient experience, however, the discussion about the institutional framework for macroprudential policy is still mostly at the conceptual level, which hinders any empirical assessment of the effectiveness of different arrangements.

Efforts have been diverse in scope, from setting up dedicated committees to eliminating institutional boundaries between the central bank and the financial regulatory agencies. Nier and others (2011) summarize recent trends, noting that institutional arrangements are shaped by country-specific circumstances, including the initial legal framework, the culture of coordination, and the need for accountability. The authors identify seven models according to the degree of institutional integration of the central bank and supervisory agencies, the ownership of the macroprudential mandate, the role of the Treasury, the separation of policy decisions and control over instruments, and the existence of a separate body coordinating across policies (Table 18.1). Together with Iceland and Switzerland, Peru has the least institutional integration between the central bank and the financial regulatory functions, with multiple agencies sharing the macroprudential mandate and no formal role for the Treasury in macroprudential policy.

Central banks are always represented and often play a leading role. It is desirable for the central bank to play an important role in macroprudential policy because of its experience and expertise in the assessment of macroeconomic and financial developments, its available resources, and its role in ensuring the stability of payment systems and being the lender of last resort (IMF 2011, 2013, 2014). The spectrum of responsibilities varies depending on the institutional arrangements, ranging from the central bank being responsible for the macroprudential mandate to sharing responsibilities with other supervisory institutions.

In practice, there are different institutional arrangements with differing types of involvement by the central bank. Some countries where the central bank has regulatory and supervisory powers have assigned the macroprudential mandate to the central bank (Czech Republic, Ireland, New Zealand, Singapore). In other countries (Malaysia, the United Kingdom), macroprudential policy is assigned to a committee within the central bank to facilitate coordination with the monetary policy mandate, foster an open discussion about different trade-offs, and create dedicated decision-making structures. In still other countries, macroprudential policy is assigned to a committee outside the central bank, with the central bank participating in the committee (Australia, France, Mexico, the United States).[2]

Existing and emerging frameworks usually include powers to communicate risk warnings and to recommend the adjustment of regulatory instruments. Examples include the ability to issue nonbinding recommendations to other authorities—powers extended, for example, to the European Systemic Risk Board, the Financial Policy Committee (FPC) in the United Kingdom, and the Financial Stability Oversight Council in the United States. Recommendations are often subject to a "comply or explain" mechanism, and sometimes strengthened with the ability to publish recommendations.

Predictably, powers to set and adjust instruments directly are most common where the macroprudential mandate and control over the instruments fall under the same authority. This is also the case when a central bank also serves as financial supervisor. Mechanisms to assign specific instruments to a new macroprudential body are also being developed in some cases but remain less common. For example, the new UK arrangement envisages the FPC being able to issue binding directions on specific macroprudential instruments.[3] Where responsibility for the operation

---

[2]In the United States, the Federal Reserve is 1 of the 10 voting members of the Financial Stability Oversight Council but is in charge of regulation of the systemically important banks and nonbanks, as designated by the council.

[3]Legislation in the United Kingdom called for the Financial Services Authority to be dismantled and a new subsidiary of the central bank, called the Prudential Regulatory Authority, to be created to supervise banks and insurers. The central bank established the FPC to identify and reduce looming threats to financial stability. The governor chairs the FPC and the board of the Prudential Regulatory Authority in addition to his or her traditional duties as head of the central bank and the Monetary Policy Committee.

**TABLE 18.1**

## Stylized Institutional Models for Macroprudential Policy

| Features of the Model | Model 1 | Model 2 | Model 3 | Model 4 | Model 5 | Model 6 | Model 7 | Model R 1 |
|---|---|---|---|---|---|---|---|---|
| 1. Institutional integration of central bank and supervisory agencies | Full (at a central bank) | Partial | Partial | Partial | No | No (Partial*) | No | No |
| 2. Ownership of macroprudential policy mandate | Central bank | Committee "related" to central bank | Independent committee | Central bank | Multiple agencies | Multiple agencies | Multiple agencies | Committee (multinational; regional) |
| 3. Role of Ministry of Finance/Treasury/ government | No (Active*) | Passive | Active | No | Passive | Active | No | Passive (European Commission; Economic and Financial Committee) |
| 4. Separation of policy decisions and control over instruments | No | In some areas | Yes | In some areas | No | No | No | Yes |
| 5. Existence of separate body coordinating across policies | No | No | No (Yes*) | No | Yes | Yes (de facto**) | No | No |
| Examples of specific model countries/regions | Czech Republic, Ireland (new), Singapore* | Malaysia, Romania, Thailand, United Kingdom (new) | Brazil,* France, United States | Belgium (new), The Netherlands, Serbia | Australia | Canada, Chile, Hong Kong SAR,* Korea,** Lebanon Mexico | Iceland, Peru Switzerland | European Union (European Systemic Risk Board) |

Source: Nier and others (2011).
Note: For each model (column), asterisks are used, when necessary, to identify alternative specifications of individual model features. Countries that apply these alternative specifications are identified with the same asterisks in the last row of the column.

of the new macroprudential tools remains ill-defined, clear assignments are needed to facilitate the willingness to act.

Well-defined objectives within the chosen institutional framework can help prevent inaction. Under the general principle that macroprudential policy should not substitute for policy action in other areas, clear objectives enhance the governance structure for the conduct of macroprudential policy and are considered the starting point for a framework that facilitates decision making. Clear objectives can also facilitate the allocation of responsibilities and identify the trade-offs in the pursuit of financial stability vis-à-vis other policy objectives.

A main challenge is to establish accountability in the absence of an easily measurable metric of success. The challenge is often compounded by the presence of multiple agencies in macroprudential policymaking that may differ in their primary objective and/or other views. Transparency and clear communication of policy decisions to the public are central elements of accountability. This is a strategy that could be expanded by including ex ante statements of strategy, publication of records of meetings, and annual performance statements with an ex post assessment of policy effectiveness. In some cases, there is also accountability to Parliament. The European Union establishes accountability for the European Systemic Risk Board to the European Parliament. In the United Kingdom, the FPC's Financial Stability Report is presented to Parliament. The U.S. structure combines both strong reporting requirements to Congress and Financial Stability Oversight Council members' obligation to individually attest that they believe that the proper actions are being taken to support financial stability.

## MOVING FORWARD: ADAPTING THE INSTITUTIONAL FRAMEWORK IN PERU

Governance structures for macroprudential policy need to support an alignment of goals, instruments, and know-how as well as operational autonomy from the government. Mandates should be realistic and avoid a false sense of precision, given the difficulties in addressing systemic risk. Control over instruments should be commensurate with the control of mandates in order to enhance accountability. And given the especially long lag between the build-up of systemic risk and its materialization, and the political economy of economic booms, operational autonomy from the government is important. In this regard, clearly distinguishing between the setups for macroprudential policy and for crisis management can reduce the need for strong Treasury involvement.

A formalized institutional setup would facilitate monitoring systemic risks more effectively, bring about better design of macroprudential policies in response to evolving financial vulnerabilities, and enhance analysis and coordination across institutions. As a starting point, enhancing information sharing would facilitate a better and shared understanding of systemic macrofinancial linkages. But it will also be important to adopt a more robust institutional mechanism (see below) to ensure a methodical approach to the analysis of systemic risks in the Peruvian economy. That analysis should go beyond financial sector surveillance and include potential financial activities out of the purview of regulations and other plausible sources of systemic risks.

Different configurations for the assignment of the macroprudential policy function among agencies will call for different governance arrangements. These will differ in terms of decision making, autonomy, and accountability arrangements. The range of the institutional framework for macroprudential policy could then be seen as a shared responsibility across agencies, reside in a separate macroprudential agency with decentralized implementation, or be the sole responsibility of the central bank (which may or may not have a separate microprudential regulator).

An institutional arrangement for macroprudential policymaking should strive to be conducive to effective mitigation of systemic risk. This involves having a clear objective, providing incentives and tools for authorities to take timely action with that objective, supporting accountability and transparency of decisions, and ensuring effective coordination across policy areas that have a bearing on financial stability. The authorities will need to take into consideration that the analysis underlying macroprudential policy shares characteristics with analysis used for microprudential policy (to understand the risks of systemically important institutions), and for monetary and fiscal policy (to understand the implications of different financial structures). Some aspects of the analytical underpinning macroprudential policy, however, are also specific to the task, such as issues of financial interconnectedness.

## Enhancing Coordination

Given the current legal framework, a possible step would be to form a macroprudential or financial stability council. The council could institutionalize the current informal setting, go beyond individuals' willingness to coordinate, and fit with the structure of having multiple bodies with a financial stability mandate.[4] A financial stability council should go beyond its "key person" and voluntary nature, as well as extend its mandate across the political cycle, without jeopardizing the operational autonomy and independence of each agency. A key step is to recognize financial stability coordination as its sole mandate. Given that decision-making powers would be distributed among several agencies and have no control over instruments, the council could help coordinate several agencies—such as the central bank, the microprudential regulator, the securities market regulator, and the ministry of finance—in the design of macroprudential policy. Instruments, however, would remain under the control of individual institutions.

The council could help the authorities raise awareness about potential risks, facilitate consensus-building on the appropriate policy mix, and identify overlaps and gaps in monitoring vulnerabilities. It could be the venue for joint analysis and peer pressure. In addition, the council would have the advantage of overseeing the potential for regulatory arbitrage, helping to identify the most appropriate tools. Europe and the United States have adopted a peer review and recommendation approach that enables members of their councils to retain autonomy over their sphere of responsibility. In those instances, in order to make the council operational and form the basis for effective coordination while respecting the agencies' autonomy, recommendations are hardened through a "comply-or-explain" obligation upon recipient of a recommendation, which could ultimately be made public.

While helpful at enhancing coordination, the proposed financial stability council also has some shortcomings. The council will not have an explicit mandate on financial stability issues nor control over instruments, which could result in a lack of accountability and delays in action because the council would not have powers to direct members' actions. However, despite difficulties defining specific objectives for financial stability, the council's role in clarifying mandates and articulating financial stability policy could help enhance financial surveillance. In the search for an operational definition of financial stability, countries have considered defining it in terms of preconditions (New Zealand), outcomes such as either the absence of problems or smooth functioning (India), robustness to shocks (Norway), or a multidimensional objective (Deutsche Bundesbank, United Kingdom).[5]

Information and analytical expertise relevant to macroprudential policy should be readily available to the macroprudential structure. When information is already collected through reporting channels (regulatory returns, onsite examinations, or information from payment systems), the framework could govern the access rights for the macroprudential authority. The arrangements for sharing information are often complex, since they involve confidential and market-sensitive information, but clear memoranda of understandings should facilitate cooperation among the

[4] Box 18.1 outlines the terms of reference for a proposed financial stability council in Peru.

[5] For details, see Ingves (2011, Box 1).

**BOX 18.1. Proposed Terms of Reference for a Financial Stability Council in Peru**

**Mandate**

The mandate of the Financial Stability Council would be surveillance of systemic risk and oversight for the stability of the financial system as a whole. The council could clarify the responsibility of financial stability in the current regulatory framework and be in charge of coordinating the design of macroprudential policies over the medium term. Earlier crises have shown that there is a need not only to "do more of the same," but also to address new questions and challenges that are constantly emerging.

**Responsibilities**

The council's responsibilities would include (1) monitoring systemic risk in the economy by analyzing the procyclicality of financial services and interconnectedness of the economy as a whole; (2) identifying vulnerabilities that could pose systemic risks; (3) monitoring changes in the condition of sectoral balance sheets (including corporates and households) and developments in credit and asset markets, all of which have the potential to affect the level and distribution of systemic risk within the economy; (4) designing early warning systems for systemic risk and incorporating economy-wide stress-testing analysis; (5) coordinating macroprudential policy with macroeconomic and microprudential policies; and (6) determining new data requirements for the analysis of systemic risks, while serving as a forum for information and data sharing among institutions.

**Structure**

The council would be a consultative (nonexecutive) committee with representatives at the highest level—including the finance minister, the president of the Central Reserve Bank of Peru, the director of the Superintendency of Banking, Insurance and Private Pension Funds, and the president of the Stock Market Superintendency. The council would be supported by a technical committee with meetings held on a biweekly basis. Recommendations would be considered and eventually implemented by the competent institutions.

Source: IMF (2011).

different agencies. The council should also have the power to request information directly from private firms when relevant information is not readily available to the macroprudential authority through other means (for example, foreign exchange exposures of corporates).

The stronger the legal framework that establishes the coordinating committee, the stronger its institutional setup. In the case of Mexico, an executive order established the Financial Stability Committee (Box 18.2). The Financial Stability Oversight Council in the United States—established by Title I of the Dodd-Frank Wall Street Reform and Consumer Protection Act—was signed into law by President Barack Obama on July 21, 2010. In Australia, the Council of Financial Regulators is the coordinating body for the main financial regulatory agencies. Its setup is as an informal body and provides a flexible, low-cost approach to coordination among the main financial regulatory agencies. The council is nonstatutory and has no regulatory functions separate from those of its members.[6]

The central bank should play a prominent role in the financial stability council because of its role in price stability and as a lender of last resort. Financial stability can affect the macroeconomic environment, with consequences for economic activity, price stability, and the monetary policy transmission mechanism. Central banks are the ultimate source of liquidity for the economy, and an appropriate liquidity provision is also crucial for financial stability. The performance

[6]In September 2008, Australia's council members released a joint memorandum of understanding (MOU) dealing specifically with financial crisis management arrangements. The MOU builds on the cooperative arrangements that have been in place for a number of years and which have been set out in bilateral MOUs signed between various members of the council. The MOUs also establish regular bilateral coordination arrangements that aim, among other things, to ensure close consultation and to avoid overlaps and gaps in regulatory coverage. See http://www.rba.gov.au/fin-stability/reg-framework/cfr.html.

## BOX 18.2. From Coordination to a Fully Integrated Macroprudential Framework

### Mexico: Enhancing Coordination

*Origin:* Mexico's financial stability council is a consultative committee responsible for the assessment, analysis, and institutional coordination of financial stability issues.

*Objective:* Promote financial stability, prevent disruptions in the functioning of the financial system, and, when such disruptions occur, minimize their impact. The council is in charge of identifying conditions that could jeopardize the adequate functioning of the financial system and the country's economic development, as well as proposing policies and solutions to address such situations. The council is required to respect the independence of each of its institutional members.

*Functions:* (1) Identify potential risks to financial stability and recommend and coordinate policies, measures, or actions that need to be undertaken by the institutions that are represented on the council; (2) act as a consultative organ for the executive on topics related to financial stability; (3) prepare an annual report on financial stability that includes a diagnosis by the council and presents the activities it has undertaken; and (4) conduct any necessary actions to reach its main objectives.

*Structure:* The council is led by the finance minister, and its other members are the deputy finance minister, Bank of Mexico governor, three central bank deputy governors, and the heads of the securities and banking regulator (*Comisión Nacional Bancaria y de Valores*), insurance regulator (*Comision Nacional de Seguros y Fianzas*), pension regulator (*Comisión Nacional del Sistema de Ahorro para el Retiro*), and deposit insurance agency (*Instituto para la Protección al Ahorro Bancario*). With regular quarterly meetings, the council can also invite individuals from public and private institutions (under confidentiality agreements).

*Technical committee:* The council is supported by a technical committee responsible for proposals and recommendations on issues of financial stability or crisis resolution. For that purpose, the technical committee gathers all economic and financial information required for the analysis and assessment of financial stability.

*Working groups:* The council has created four working groups to (1) standardize and gather information on relevant issues related to monitoring financial stability, (2) establish a framework to identify financial vulnerability, (3) design the metrics and methodologies for systemic risk measurement, and (4) ensure that financial market participants access sufficient and relevant information for decision making and present an annual report on financial sector stability.

### United Kingdom: Toward an Integrated System

*Origin:* The 2009 Banking Act gave the Bank of England (BoE) a statutory financial stability objective and created a new Financial Stability Committee (FSC) to advise on and monitor the nature and implementation of the BoE's financial stability strategy. The BoE then became responsible for microprudential and macroprudential regulation to avoid gaps in responsibilities and regulatory powers. This architecture ensures that macroprudential regulation is coordinated effectively with the prudential regulation of individual firms.

*Functions:* The FSC controls macroprudential tools to ensure that systemic risks to financial stability are dealt with.

*Structure:* The majority of the FSC's members are BoE executives who bring the expertise and understanding of the financial system that only a central bank can provide. The current governor and deputy governors for financial stability and monetary policy are joined by a new deputy governor for prudential regulation, as well as two other BoE executives. The FSC also includes external members to ensure a wider perspective, including representatives from other regulatory bodies and from the markets themselves.

*Accountability:* The FSC is designed as a transparent and accountable institution with appropriate lines of accountability into the Court of Directors of the BoE and the Treasury, as well as broader accountability to Parliament.

*Prudential regulation:* A subsidiary of the BoE—the Prudential Regulation Authority—is responsible for prudential regulation of all deposit-taking institutions, insurers, and investment banks. The Prudential Regulation Authority has a board chaired by the governor of the BoE and a chief executive who is also the deputy governor for prudential regulation.

*Coordination:* The FSC is able, within the remit of macroprudential policy, to require the Prudential Regulation Authority to take regulatory action with respect to all firms. It may also suggest amendments to rules to make the system more resilient. The FSC can also exercise similar macroprudential controls over the new consumer protection and markets authority in the context of macroprudential tools.

Source: IMF (2011).

of the monetary policy functions provides the central bank with a macroeconomic focus and an understanding of financial market functioning and infrastructure that are needed for macroprudential policy. Placing the monitoring and management of systemic risks at the central bank would benefit the analysis through important synergies, given the central banks' comparative advantage in understanding feedback loops between the financial sector and the real economy. However, safeguards need to be in place to ensure the autonomy of the central bank in the conduct of monetary policy.

The participation of the MEF in the financial stability council needs to be safeguarded to avoid pressures from the political cycle. The MEF's involvement in the council would reflect the role of the ministry in crisis resolution, given its responsibility for the use of public funds. It thus needs to have a role in the preamble of designing prudential policy. Finance ministries are often involved in setting objectives and priorities for macroprudential policy, and have an important role if changes in legislation are expected to be needed to mitigate systemic risk (for example, with respect to expanding the perimeter of regulation). However, mechanisms to isolate the macroprudential policy framework from pressures linked to the political cycle are important, especially because of the asymmetry between the visibility and time profile of costs and benefits of macroprudential policy. The costs of macroprudential measures (restrictions on certain activities) are felt immediately, whereas benefits (lower incidence of financial stress) accrue over the longer term and are hard to measure.

The SBS brings the expertise of the microprudential regulator, with a clear advantage in terms of instrument design and interconnectedness—the cross-sectional dimension of systemic risks. While analysis and decision making can be centralized in a council, implementation cannot. Separate macroprudential policy instruments do not exist in significant scale or reach, and implementation must use instruments primarily assigned to other policy objectives. In this regard, the settings for the relevant microprudential instruments can be supplemented by an additional macroprudential overlay, and the SBS has control over numerous instruments. For example, the SBS has worked on interconnectedness, and the measures requesting additional capital requirements take into account this element (via concentration risks and size).

The involvement of Peru's stock market regulator (the *Superintendencia de Mercado de Valores*) is more related to structural aspects of macroprudential policy. Many of the tools deployed by securities market regulators (such as product disclosure, settlement arrangements, and market access rights) are likely to be relevant to macrofinancial stability policy objectives. Further, securities markets often span the regulatory perimeter, while the corporate sector can also become a source of systemic risk, as seen in Brazil and Mexico in the wake of the 2008–09 financial crisis.

## CONCLUSIONS

Formalizing an institutional setup for macroprudential policy in Peru could enhance the regular analysis of systemic risks in the economy and facilitate information sharing, actions, and accountability. Although Peru has been at the forefront of implementation of macroprudential instruments, the institutional framework is relatively informal and involves independent institutions with a general mandate for financial stability. The setup lacks clear mandates on macroprudential policy, and could be prone to inaction. A financial stability council could facilitate the integration of macroprudential policies in the policy toolkit and enhance their complementary role with macroeconomic and microprudential policies.

A council could help the authorities form a consolidated appreciation of systemic risks, foster consensus on the appropriate policy mix, and identify and monitor vulnerabilities. It could also help the authorities identify overlaps and gaps in monitoring vulnerabilities. Information and analytical expertise relevant to macroprudential policy should be readily available to the macroprudential structure. The central bank needs to play a prominent role in the financial stability council because of its central role in price stability and as a lender of last resort. The participation of the MEF in the council would need to be protected to avoid pressures from the political cycle.

## REFERENCES

Ingves, S. 2011. "Central Bank Governance and Financial Stability: A Report by a Study Group." Bank of International Settlements, Basel (May). http://www.imf.org/external/pubs/ft/wp/2006/wp0605.pdf.

International Monetary Fund. 2011. "Macroprudential Policy: An Organizing Framework." Policy Paper, International Monetary Fund, Washington, DC (March). http://www.imf.org/external/np/pp/eng/2011/031411.pdf.

———. 2013. "Key Aspects of Macroprudential Policy." Policy Paper, International Monetary Fund, Washington, DC (June). http://www.imf.org/external/np/pp/eng/2013/061013b.pdf.

———. 2014. "Staff Guidance Note on Macroprudential Policy." International Monetary Fund, Washington, DC (June). http://www.imf.org/external/np/pp/eng/2014/110614.pdf.

Lima, Juan Manuel, Enrique Montes, Carlos Varela, and Johannes Wiegand. 2005. "Sectoral Balance Sheet Mismatches and Macroeconomic Vulnerabilities in Colombia, 1996–2003." Working Paper 06/05, International Monetary Fund, Washington, DC.

Nier, E., J. Osinski, L. I. Jacome, and P. Madrid. 2011. "Towards Effective Macroprudential Policy Frameworks: An Assessment of Stylized Institutional Models." Working Paper 11/250, International Monetary Fund, Washington, DC.

Terrier, G., R. Valdes, C. Tovar, J. Chan-Lau, C. Fernandez-Valdovinos, M. Garcia-Escribano, C. Medeiros, M. Tang, M. Vera Martin, and C. Walker. 2011. "Policy Instruments to Lean against the Wind in Latin America." Working Paper 11/159, International Monetary Fund, Washington, DC.

# CHAPTER 19

# Trade Evolution and Policy Challenges

Yu Ching Wong

*Peru has been experiencing high and stable economic growth since the mid-2000s, largely underpinned by prudent macroeconomic management and favorable terms of trade. Buoyant commodity prices, especially for copper and gold, have benefited Peru both in terms of expanding exports and attracting mineral-related foreign direct investment (FDI). Greater diversification of products and trading partner concentration could go a long way toward reducing Peru's exposure to commodity boom-and-bust cycles and help put economic growth firmly on a sustainable path.*

Peru's trade openness has risen significantly over the past decade. Trade openness—measured as the ratio of the sum of exports and imports to GDP—increased to 47 percent of GDP in 2011, a significant increase from the 27 percent level in 2002. This upward trend in trade openness was underpinned by an expansion of exports, which increased seven times in nominal terms during 2000–11, on the back of the global commodity price boom. The international price of copper—one of the country's key exports—rose by nearly 400 percent from 2000–11. Imports as a share of GDP also surged rapidly during 2007–08, fueled by buoyant domestic demand and FDI inflows. Peru's exports and imports contracted sharply during the global financial crisis in 2008–09, with a negative terms-of-trade shock of about 17 percent. However, by 2011, Peru's trade-to-GDP ratio had largely recovered to the precrisis peak. Trade liberalization and the establishment of free trade agreements with its key trading partners have also helped increase Peru's trade openness.[1] Among the LA6 economies,[2] Peru achieved the largest gain in trade openness during the 2000–11 period, emerging as the third most open economy to trade in 2011 (Figure 19.1).[3]

Higher openness was accompanied by a rising share in world trade. The share of Peru's exports in world exports increased from 0.11 percent in 2000 to 0.28 percent in 2011. This represented an expansion of about 2½ times, and was larger than any other LA6 economy (as a group, the LA6 increased on average by 1½ times during the same period). At the same time, the share of

This chapter was originally included as part of the Selected Issues paper of the IMF's 2013 Article IV Consultation in Peru and is based on data up to 2011. Although the chapter remains valid as an analysis of the behavior of Peruvian exports during the commodity price boom, the commodity cycle has come to an end and export prices, compared to 2011 averages, have fallen by approximately 23 percent, led by declines in key export prices such as copper (–40 percent) and gold (–20 percent). In addition, several trading partners (particularly other emerging markets) have weakened, affecting nontraditional exports. These developments have led to a deterioration of Peru's trade accounts since 2011.

[1] At present, Peru has 10 bilateral free trade agreements with Canada, Chile, China, Cuba, Mexico, Panama, Singapore, Korea, Thailand, and the United States, and regional agreements with the European Free Trade Association, Andean Community, European Union, and Southern Cone Common Market. Several other free trade agreements (including with the Trans-Pacific Partnership) are in the pipeline, about to enter into force, or being negotiated.

[2] The LA6 are Brazil, Chile, Colombia, Mexico, Peru, and Uruguay.

[3] Some of the recent gain in trade openness could be viewed as reversing a previous decline. Peru's trade represented 34 percent of GDP in the early 1980s but declined thereafter to around 14 percent of GDP in 1987–89, a level below comparator countries. Structural impediments appear to be the major constraints to increasing trade, including limited investment outside of the mining and gas sectors, high logistics costs, and transportation-related problems (IMF 2004).

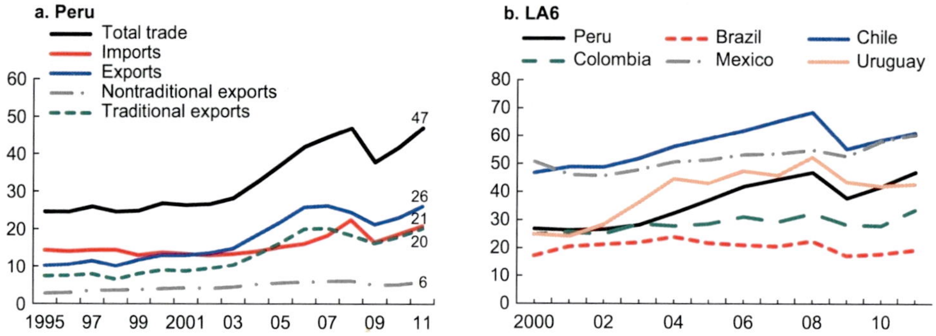


Sources: Central Reserve Bank of Peru; IMF, World Economic Outlook database; and IMF staff calculations.
Note: LA6 = Brazil, Chile, Colombia, Mexico, Peru, and Uruguay.

**Figure 19.1** Peru and the LA6: Trade Openness

Peru's imports almost doubled from 0.12 percent of world imports in 2000 to 0.22 percent in 2011, a pace of expansion that topped LA6 economies during the period (Figure 19.2).

Peru has gained world market share in mineral products since the mid-2000s. Its exports of nonferrous metals and ores expanded rapidly, reaching an export market share of 2 percent of world exports in 2011 (from 1.2 percent in 2000). That figure is still low, however, compared to other countries in the region: the shares of Brazil and Chile in world exports of nonferrous metals and ores were 5¾ percent and 5½ percent, respectively, in 2011. Peru's exports of primary commodities, while smaller than other large Latin American primary commodity exporters such as Brazil (which holds 5 percent of world exports), have also gained world market share, rising steadily to about 0.5 percent of world exports in 2011 from about 0.3 percent in the early 2000s. However, the rise in Peru's share of world imports was largely a reflection of the rising demand for primary commodities and manufactures (see Figure 19.2).

This chapter provides an overview of the main characteristics of Peru's trade boom during 2000–11, with the objective of analyzing some of its principal trends and structural changes. The chapter first examines the evolution of Peru's mining exports during the past decade, which has been supported more by the rise in international metal prices than by volume growth, and trends toward higher product concentration in mining. The chapter then focuses on Peru's increasing exposure to China through trade linkages and their implications, before turning to some considerations on the merits of greater diversification in trade and economic structure that could help reduce vulnerabilities to adverse external shocks to commodity exports.

## RIDING THE COMMODITY PRICE BOOM

The mining sector is shaping the pattern of economic development in Peru. The sector's share of GDP has more than doubled from about 5½ percent in 2000 to 12 percent since 2006 at current prices. However, while the mining sector has become a larger part of the economy, real growth in the sector slowed to an annual average of 2.2 percent from 2006–11 (from 7.2 percent in 2000–05) (Table 19.1). The GDP share of the agriculture and fishing sector (8.5 percent in 2000 to 6.9 percent in 2011) and the tertiary sector (62 percent in 2000 to 57 percent in 2011) both declined at current prices, while the secondary sector remained at around 24 percent.[4] In part due to Peru's rich resource endowment and the positive terms-of-trade shock, this pattern of economic development comes in contrast to many emerging and developing economies, which experienced a decline in the share of primary sectors in the process of industrialization as

[4]The secondary sector is comprised of manufacturing, utilities, and construction.

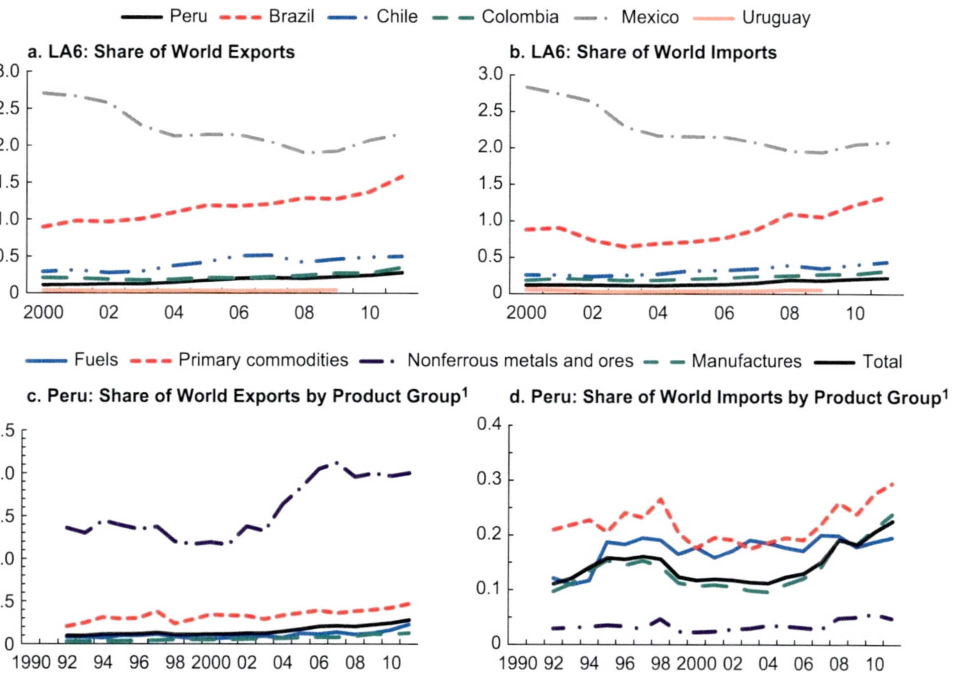


Sources: UN, Commodity Trade Statistics database; World Bank, World Integrated Trade Solution database; and IMF staff calculations.
Note: LA6 = Brazil, Chile, Colombia, Mexico, Peru, and Uruguay.
[1] The product groups are the sum of one-digit Standard International Trade Classification (STIC) (Revision 3) export data as follows: fuels (SITC 3), primary commodities (SITC 0, 1, 2, –27, –28), nonferrous metals and ores (SITC 68, 27, 28), and manufactures (SITC 5, 6, 7, 8, 9, –68).

**Figure 19.2** Peru and the LA6: World Trade Integration

**TABLE 19.1**

Peru: Real GDP and Mining Sector GDP Growth *(Percent change; in constant 1994 prices)*

| | 1992–99 | 2000–05 | 2006–11 |
|---|---|---|---|
| Total GDP | 4.4 | 4.0 | 72 |
| *Of which:* Contribution by Mining | 0.3 | 0.4 | 0.1 |
| Mining GDP | 7.3 | 7.2 | 2.2 |
| Share of Mining GDP (percent) | 4.8 | 6.2 | 5.6 |

Sources: National Statistics Institute; and IMF staff calculations.

production and employment expanded first to the secondary sector and then to the services sector as the economy moved up the value-added chain.

The share of traditional exports increased steadily over 2000–11, reflecting expansion of mining exports. Traditional exports increased by 7½ times in dollar terms during 2000–11 to US$36 billion in 2011, representing 77 percent of total exports (20 percent of GDP), up from about 70 percent to total exports in 2000. About three-quarters of the expansion came from the growth in mining exports. Nontraditional exports accounted for the remaining 23 percent of exports (6 percent of GDP) in 2011 (Figure 19.3).[5]

[5] In Peru's trade statistics, traditional exports refer to the aggregate category of fishing products (fish oil and fishmeal), agricultural products (mainly coffee), mineral products, and petroleum and natural gas. Nontraditional exports are a range of newer products that are also mostly resource-intensive, but with higher value added, including other agriculture, textiles, chemicals, and fabricated metal products and machinery.

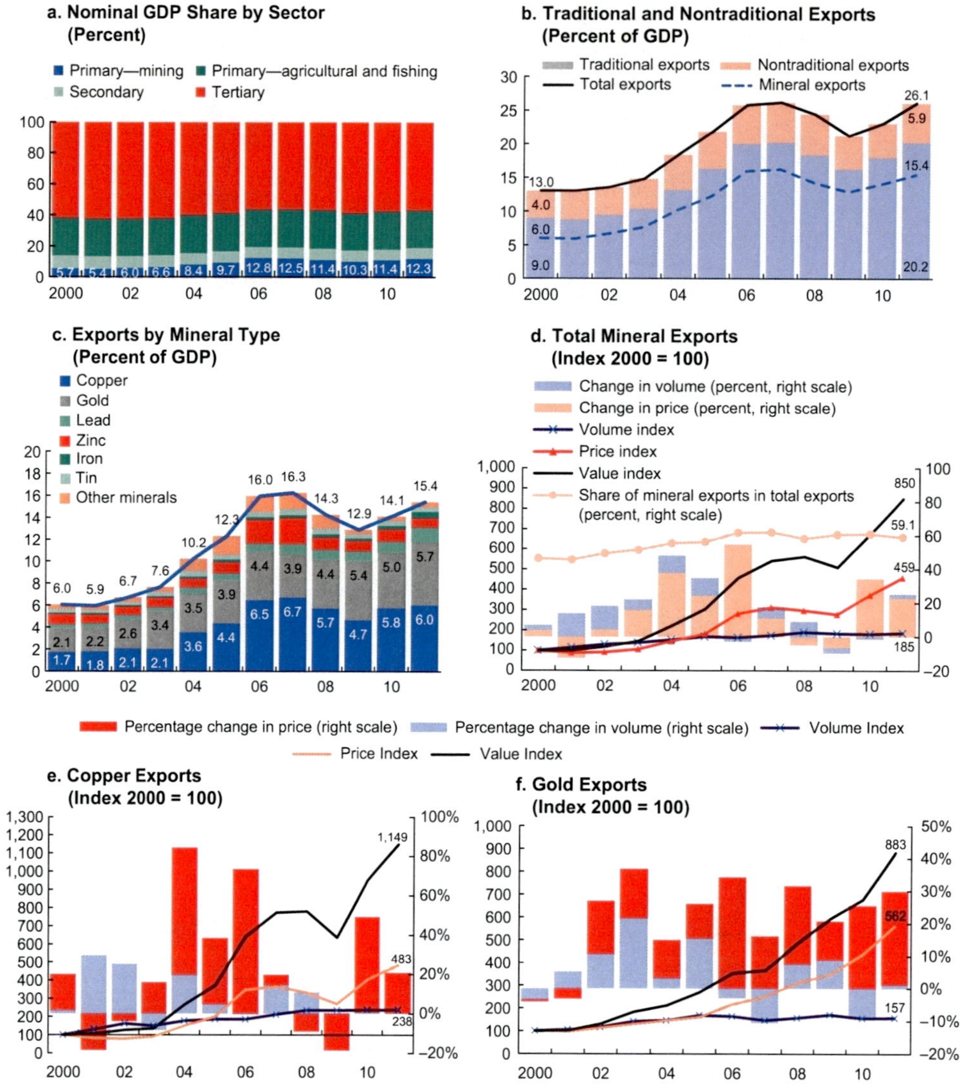


Sources: Central Reserve Bank of Peru; and IMF staff calculations.

**Figure 19.3** Peru: Mining Production, Mineral Exports, and Traditional and Nontraditional Exports, 2000–11

Multiple metal exports have helped reduce vulnerabilities. Mining exports increased 8½ times over from 2000 to 2011 and reached US$27 billion in 2011, accounting for 60 percent of total exports and 15½ percent of GDP in 2011. Although Peru exports six key metals, the export structure has become more concentrated in copper and gold, which account for 23 percent and 22 percent of total exports, respectively. Gold and copper account for close to 80 percent of mineral exports and 12 percent of GDP. The low correlation of gold prices with other metal prices has helped reduce somewhat the impact of the negative terms-of-trade shock.[6] During the global financial crisis, the decline in the value of copper exports of close to 20 percent in 2009—copper prices plummeted by about 20 percent with nearly unchanged export volume—was

[6]Gold prices continued to rise, despite a decline in other metals prices, during the 2008–09 crisis. This is partly attributed to the status of gold as a safe-haven asset—gold prices tend to increase in uncertain times or adverse economic conditions.

partially offset by an increase in the value of gold exports of 22 percent in 2009 driven by both higher prices and volumes (see Figure 19.3).

Export price growth has dwarfed export volume growth in the mining sector. A key feature of the rapid expansion in Peru's mining exports during the past decade was that it was mostly due to higher prices and less from higher volume. Metal exports increased by 8½ times in dollar terms during 2000–11, with prices contributing 2½ times more than volumes to the growth of export values. More specifically, the volume of copper exports increased by less than 2½ times (to 1.3 million metric tons) against a surge in copper prices of close to 5 times during the period. For gold, the volume change was smaller, with an expansion of 57 percent (to 6.4 million troy ounces) against the effect of a 5½ times increase in gold prices (see Figure 19.3). Given that global metal prices are projected to remain largely flat in the medium term, further growth in the value of mining exports would hinge on volume gain through construction of new mines or expansion of existing ones.

Although nontraditional exports grew at healthy rates as a result of rising volume, their share is still limited due to the booming prices in traditional exports. Nontraditional exports increased by five times during 2000–11 to US$10 billion in 2011 (30 percent of total exports or 6 percent of GDP). Even though they grew at an average 24 percent per year starting in 2003 (excluding the temporary decline in 2009 associated with the global crisis), nontraditional exports remained at 5–6 percent of GDP due to the rapid pick-up in traditional exports with surging mineral prices. Two major product categories—textiles, and agriculture and livestock—continued to account for half of total nontraditional exports.

Agricultural exports emerged as the key nontraditional export, surpassing textiles and apparel. Exports of agricultural and livestock expanded by an annual average of about 20 percent from 2000–11, reaching close to 30 percent of total nontraditional exports in 2011 (from less than 20 percent in 2000). In contrast, textiles and apparel exports increased by an annual average of about 10 percent from 2000–11, and their share declined to below 20 percent of total nontraditional exports in 2011 (Figure 19.4). Textile exports accounted for only about US$2 billion or 4 percent of total exports (1 percent of GDP). These recent trends largely reflect the gain in export competitiveness in Peruvian vegetables and fruits, with the notable example of asparagus, which has emerged as one of the country's main nontraditional exports.[7] While unfavorable exchange rate movements are often cited as one of the factors impeding the growth of the textiles and apparel sector, market analysts also highlighted factors such as a shortage of skilled labor, high logistics costs, and a lack of brand names as impediments faced by textile and apparel firms in further expanding exports.

Export concentration has risen as a result of the commodity price boom. In Peru, the top 15 export product categories at the three-digit Standard International Trade Classification (SITC) level accounted for more than 80 percent of total exports (Table 19.2). The products are concentrated in agriculture, mining, and fuels, in part reflecting commodity price increases, with only 1 of the top 15 export categories being a manufactured product. This is also consistent with the comparative analysis indicating that Peru has a comparative advantage in 15 categories, mostly in agricultural and mining products, measured at the SITC two-digit level (Annex Table 19.1.1). Similarly, export concentration increased, indicating declining diversification during the past decade, similar to the trend observed in other primary-commodity exporters among the LA6 economies (Figure 19.5).[8]

---

[7]Asparagus exports from Peru totaled US$480 million (0.3 percent of GDP) in 2011. Almost half was exported to the United States, with the rest exported mostly to European markets.

[8]As measured by the Hirschman Herfindahl index, which is the sum squared of each product in total exports. A country with a perfectly diversified export portfolio will have an index close to zero, whereas a country that exports only one product will have a value of one.

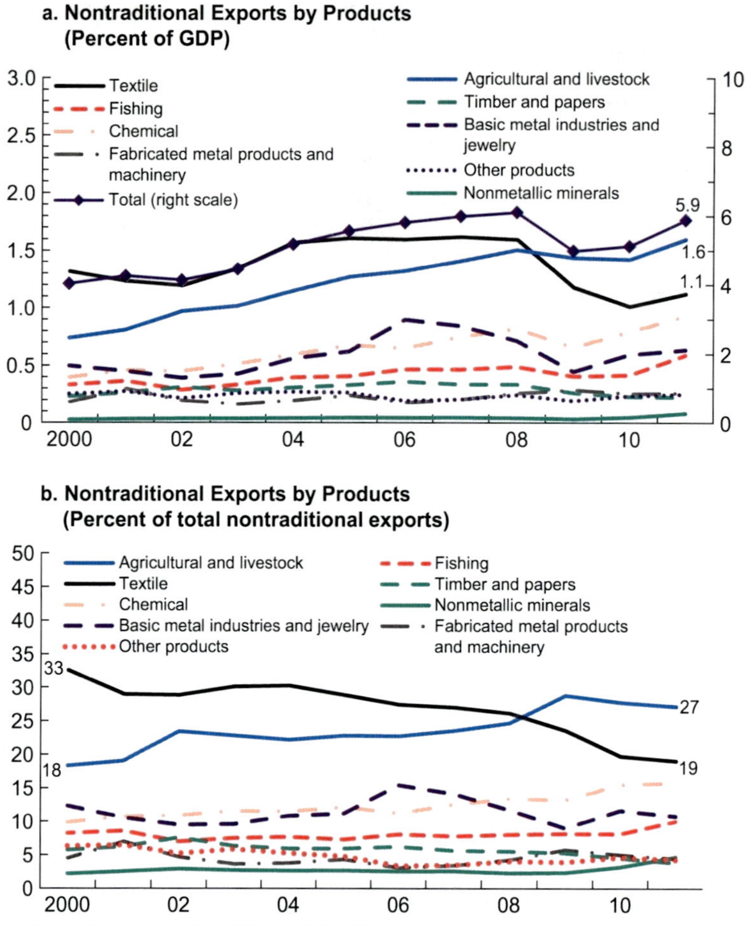


Sources: Central Reserve Bank of Peru; and IMF staff calculations.

**Figure 19.4** Peru: Nontraditional Exports

**TABLE 19.2**

## Peru: Top Exports by Product, 2005–11

| Rank as of 2011 | Category | SITC | Product | Share of Total Exports 2005 | Share of Total Exports 2011 | Millions of U.S. Dollars 2011 |
|---|---|---|---|---|---|---|
| 1 | Others | 971 | Gold nonmonetary excluding ore | 17.9 | 21.8 | 9,931 |
| 2 | Crude materials | 283 | Copper ores/concentrates | 8.2 | 17.1 | 7,800 |
| 3 | Crude materials | 287 | Base metal ore/conc nes | 12.5 | 7.9 | 3,606 |
| 4 | Nonferrous metals | 682 | Copper | 12.4 | 7.3 | 3,326 |
| 5 | Fuels | 334 | Heavy petrol/bitum oils | 7.7 | 6.4 | 2,934 |
| 6 | Agriculture | 081 | Animal feed excluding unmilled cereals | 7.0 | 4.2 | 1,902 |
| 7 | Agriculture | 071 | Coffee/coffee substitute | 1.8 | 3.5 | 1,586 |
| 8 | Fuels | 343 | Natural gas | 0.0 | 2.8 | 1,284 |
| 9 | Crude materials | 281 | Iron ore/concentrates | 1.3 | 2.2 | 1,023 |
| 10 | Agriculture | 057 | Fruit/nuts, fresh/dried | 0.9 | 1.7 | 778 |
| 11 | Miscellaneous manufactures | 845 | Articles of apparel nes | 3.3 | 1.7 | 763 |
| 12 | Crude materials | 289 | Precious metal ore/conc | 0.4 | 1.6 | 738 |
| 13 | Nonferrous metals | 686 | Zinc | 1.2 | 1.4 | 623 |
| 14 | Fuels | 333 | Petrol/bitum oil, crude | 1.1 | 1.3 | 574 |
| 15 | Agriculture | 056 | Vegetable, roots, and tubers, prepared or preserved, nes | 1.2 | 1.1 | 495 |
| | | | Total | 77.0 | 81.9 | 37,364 |

Sources: UN Comtrade; and IMF staff calculations.
Note: nes = not elsewhere specified; SITC = Standard International Trade Classification.

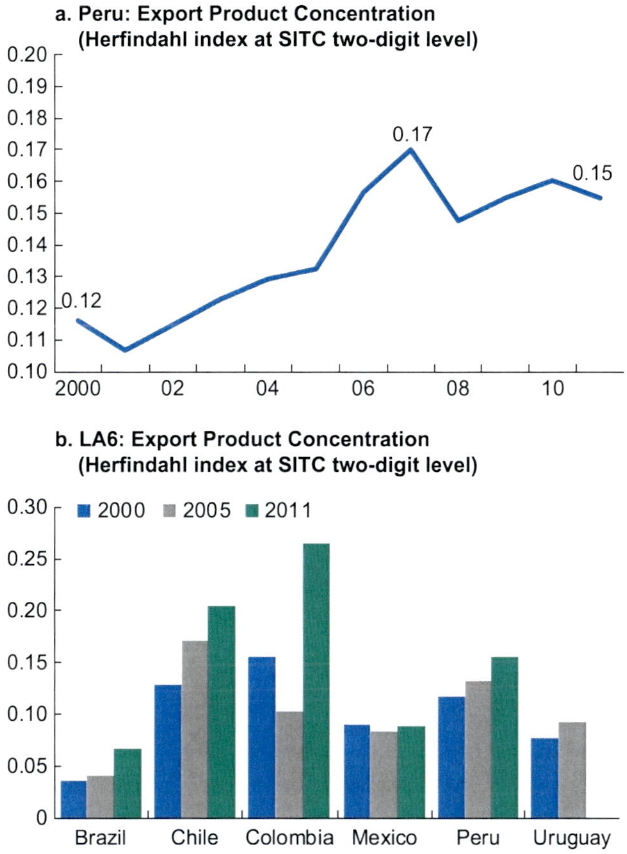


Sources: UN Comtrade; and World Bank, World Integrated Trade Solution database.
Note: Data for 2011 are not available for Uruguay. SITC = Standard International Trade Classification.

**Figure 19.5** Peru and the LA6: Export Product Concentration

## INCREASING TRADE EXPOSURE TO CHINA

Export concentration by destination has declined slightly since the mid-2000s. The top three export destinations accounted for 38 percent of the total in 2011, compared to 48 percent of the total in 2005. However, Peru, like many other emerging economies, relies more than it did a decade ago on China rather than on the United States as both an export market and an import-supplying country. The share of exports to China rose steadily over the past decade to 15 percent of total exports (3.9 percent of GDP), replacing the United States as the largest single export-country destination for Peru in 2011. Interestingly, the declining share of the United States as an export destination (it accounted for close to one-third of total exports as recently as the mid-2000s) has contributed to a marginal decline in export concentration by destination (Figure 19.6).

Exports to China are also concentrated in a relatively narrow range of products, mainly mining exports. The breakdown in Table 19.3 shows that China is among the top three export destinations in 7 of Peru's top 15 export categories, covering about 80 percent of Peru's total exports. All export items are mining products. China alone absorbs about 30 percent of Peru's total copper exports (SITC 283 and 682).

However, import concentration by origin increased from 2005 to 2011 due to the rapid growth of imports from China. Imports from China grew at an average rate of 30 percent from

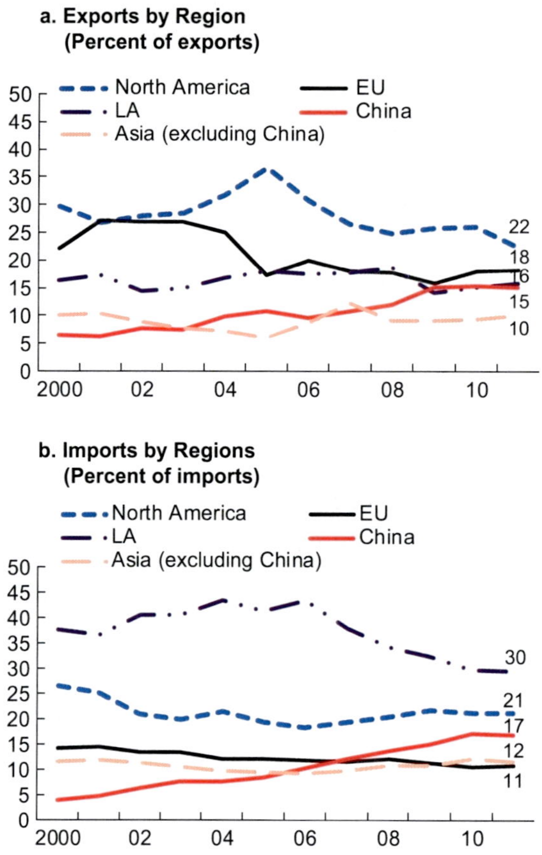


Sources: UN Comtrade; World Bank, World Integrated Trade Solution database; and IMF staff calculations.

Note: EU includes all 27 European Union members; LA consists of the LA6 economies (Brazil, Colombia, Chile, Mexico, Peru, and Uruguay) plus Argentina, Bolivia, Ecuador, Paraguay, and Venezuela; and Asia consists of India, Indonesia, Japan, Hong Kong SAR, Korea, Malaysia, the Philippines, Singapore, and Thailand.

**Figure 19.6** Peru: Major Trading Partners

2001–05 before accelerating to an average of 57 percent during 2006–08 and 2010. By 2011, Peru imported a larger share from China and declining shares from neighboring Latin American countries (Figure 19.6). For instance, in 2011, imports from China accounted for three-quarters of Peru's imports of clothing and accessories (SITC 84), 40 percent of imports of textile yarn and fabric (SITC 65), and half of imports of telecommunication and sound equipment (SITC 76). The rapid gain in import share by China in the apparel sector suggests the intense competition faced by Peruvian suppliers, which has implications on production and in turn export competitiveness.

Like other Latin America primary exporters, Peru has recovered much faster from the global crisis than initially anticipated. The recovery owes much to the stabilizing effects from China as an important source of world growth.[9] However, while China may remain an important driver

[9]Based on a global vector autoregression model for five large Latin American economies (including Peru), Cesa-Bianchi and others (2011) concluded that the long-term impact of a Chinese GDP shock on Latin American economies has increased by three times since the mid-1990s. Winkelried and Saldarriaga (2012) found that about half of the growth reported in Latin American countries over 2000–10 can be attributed to direct and indirect multiplier effects induced by the growth of China.

**TABLE 19.3**

## Peru: Top Exports by Product and by Major Export Destinations, 2011 *(Percent)*

| Rank | SITC | Category | Share of Top Three Export Destinations | | | | | | Herfindahl Index |
|---|---|---|---|---|---|---|---|---|---|
| | | | First | | Second | | Third | | |
| 1 | 971 | Gold nonmonetary excluding ore | Canada | 30.9 | United States | 8.5 | European Union | 2.9 | 0.10 |
| 2 | 283 | Copper ores/concentrates | China | 31.0 | European Union | 28.7 | Japan | 16.8 | 0.22 |
| 3 | 287 | Base metal ore/conc nes | China | 28.5 | Korea | 16.9 | European Union | 13.9 | 0.15 |
| 4 | 682 | Copper | European Union | 28.4 | China | 21.5 | Brazil | 14.4 | 0.17 |
| 5 | 334 | Heavy petrol/bitum oils | United States | 42.6 | Canada | 12.3 | Brazil | 6.1 | 0.21 |
| 6 | 081 | Animal feed excluding unmilled cereals | China | 54.8 | European Union | 14.7 | Japan | 7.1 | 0.33 |
| 7 | 071 | Coffee/coffee substitute | European Union | 59.2 | United States | 23.3 | Colombia | 4.9 | 0.41 |
| 8 | 343 | Natural gas | European Union | 37.8 | Korea | 17.4 | Japan | 17.3 | 0.23 |
| 9 | 281 | Iron ore/concentrates | China | 97.8 | Japan | 2.2 | ... | ... | 0.96 |
| 10 | 057 | Fruit/nuts, fresh/dried | European Union | 48.8 | United States | 25.9 | Hong Kong SAR | 5.2 | 0.31 |
| 11 | 845 | Articles of apparel nes | United States | 51.7 | Venezuela | 20.7 | European Union | 8.2 | 0.32 |
| 12 | 289 | Precious metal ore/conc | European Union | 36.3 | Canada | 21.1 | China | 19.6 | 0.25 |
| 13 | 686 | Zinc | European Union | 22.2 | United States | 21.9 | China | 20.2 | 0.16 |
| 14 | 333 | Petrol/bitum oil, crude | United States | 56.8 | Chile | 36.6 | ... | ... | 0.46 |
| 15 | 056 | Vegetables, roots, and tubers, prepared or preserved, nes | European Union | 47.9 | United States | 39.5 | Brazil | 3.9 | 0.39 |

Sources: UN Comtrade; and IMF staff calculations.

Note: nes = not elsewhere specified; SITC = Standard International Trade Classification.

for global growth, the Chinese economy is expected to shift toward slower but more balanced growth, relying less on investment. This implies that China's commodity demand would change in terms of quantity and composition. In this context, Peru's vulnerability to China is not only related to a possible slowdown but also to the impact of Chinese demand on global commodity prices as development patterns change.

## TOWARD GREATER TRADE DIVERSIFICATION: TURNING COMMODITY DEPENDENCY INTO A BLESSING

Some regard natural resource endowment as a curse—what is known as "Dutch disease"—as commodity price booms tend to lead to a currency appreciation of the primary commodity exporter, which in turn results in crowding out the manufacturing sector.[10] The approach taken by other primary commodity exporters such as Canada highlights that policy can help reduce the adjustment costs and maximize the benefits arising from commodity booms. More specifically, leaning against commodity-driven movements in the nominal exchange rate to support noncommodity exports and domestic producers who face competition from imports would over time result in higher wages and inflation, causing the real exchange rate to appreciate and resulting in the same competitiveness challenge. On the other hand, measures, such as those that aim to capture more value added domestically, increase skills to compete and sustain business investment. Such policies can strengthen the benefits of a resource-rich economy (Bank of Canada 2012).

Greater diversification in products and trading partners could go a long way toward reducing risks to commodity boom-and-bust cycles. Studies have shown that countries with more diversified production structures tend to have lower volatility of output, consumption, and investment and higher resilience to external shocks (Papageorgiou and Spatafora 2012). Trade diversification can be achieved across trading partners and products, the latter through the introduction of new export products, a more balanced mix of existing exports, or fetching higher prices for existing products by upgrading product quality. Bringing about these changes requires upgrading production and trade structure to generate more intersector linkages, and increasing value added by moving up the value chain, which needs to be supported by infrastructure investments and human capacity development.

Higher intraregional and intraindustry trade in Latin America could help to reduce overdependence on China and commodity trade. As a result of historical, institutional, and relative endowments and other factors, intraregional trade accounted for less than 15 percent of Latin America trade in 2011, compared to 44 percent in Asia and 63 percent in the European Union. Preliminary estimates suggest that the share of intraindustry trade in LA6 economies averaged 0.40 in 2011, with Peru (0.30) at the low end and Mexico (0.53) at the high end (Annex Table 19.1.2).[11] In this context, trade diversification could be brought forward through greater division of labor in the production of manufactured goods within the region to meet rising aggregate demand from higher regional economic growth, and by increasing exports to the rest of the world. The gain in export competitiveness in Peruvian fruits and vegetables is an example of the success of diversification by finding niche markets. Efforts to foster FDI inflows in the manufacturing sectors over the medium term and to further enhance market access through free trade agreements are steps in the right direction.

[10] Magud and Sosa (2010) documented that while shocks that trigger foreign exchange inflows appreciate the real exchange rate, generate factor reallocation, and reduce manufacturing output and net exports, there is no evidence in the literature that Dutch disease reduces overall economic growth.

[11] Excluding Uruguay, for which trade data are not available from the UN Commodity Trade database for 2010–11.

In this regard, the expansion of intraregional and intraindustry trade in Asia through "open regionalism" since the mid-1980s also provides some examples of how resource-rich exporting countries such as Peru could diversify their production and trade structure. In response to the rapid appreciation of the Japanese yen since 1985, the shift of labor-intensive manufacturing operations in Asia via Japanese FDI outflows—first to the newly industrialized economies, then to resource-rich countries in the Association of Southeast Asian Nations along with China—resulted in accelerated growth of capital goods exports to these host countries, accompanied by the imports of consumer and intermediate goods to Japan and other advanced economies. The rise of China as "factory Asia" and as the hub of the global product-sharing network further increased intraregional trade flows. Those flows are also enhanced by intraindustry exchange and vertical specialization trade as countries move up the global value chain.[12]

Diversification and structural transformation often have to be underpinned by reforms and policy measures. Other than maintaining prudent macroeconomic policies—including a strong fiscal position and saving some of the mining windfalls—keys to increasing Peru's export competitiveness include implementing broad-based microeconomic measures that focus on eliminating infrastructure bottlenecks, improving the quality of infrastructure, raising educational and skill levels, and fostering an efficient business climate for domestic and foreign investors. In this context, the compilation of competitiveness indicators such as unit labor cost, labor productivity, and wage by sector would facilitate better monitoring of changes in competitiveness. However, Papageorgiou and Spatafora (2012) noted that, based on country experiences, it remains an open issue to what extent industry-focused and narrowly targeted measures have historically helped to underpin diversification efforts.

## CONCLUSIONS

Buoyant commodity prices have benefited Peru both in terms of expanding exports and attracting mineral-related FDI inflows. Nevertheless, trade concentration by product, and to a lesser extent by trading partner, has clearly increased with the commodity price boom. While nontraditional exports grew at healthy rates, they were outpaced by booming traditional exports. Like other Latin American primary commodity exporters, Peru has recovered much faster from the global crisis than initially anticipated despite the lackluster growth recovery in advanced economies. The recovery has been due largely to the stabilizing effects of the emergence of China as the main driver of commodity demand and world growth. Nevertheless, there is a growing consensus that excessive concentration of exports, particularly the concentration in commodities, increases vulnerabilities and could be detrimental to long-term economic development.

Going forward, greater diversification in products and trading partners could go a long way toward reducing Peru's exposure to commodity boom-and-bust cycles and help put economic growth firmly on a sustainable path. In addition to maintaining prudent macroeconomic policies, Peru's efforts to further trade liberalization and enhance market access through free trade agreements are steps in the right direction. The key to consolidating growth over the medium term will include further enhancing structural reforms focused on improving the quantity and quality of infrastructure, raising educational and skill levels, and fostering an efficient business climate for domestic and foreign investors.

[12] Intraindustry trade in Asia increased from about 0.35 in 1992 to about 0.46 in 2005 (IMF 2011).

# ANNEX 19.1

**ANNEX TABLE 19.1.1**

**Peru: Revealed Comparative Advantage, 1995, 2000, 2005, and 2011**

| SITC | Category | 1995 | 2000 | 2005 | 2011 |
|---|---|---|---|---|---|
| 00 | Live animals except fish | 0.2 | 0.2 | 0.2 | 0.1 |
| 01 | Meat and preparations | 0.0 | 0.0 | 0.0 | 0.0 |
| 02 | Dairy products and eggs | 0.1 | 0.1 | 0.6 | 0.5 |
| 03 | Fish/shellfish/etc. | 4.2 | 3.4 | 2.7 | 3.4 |
| 04 | Cereals/cereal preparation | 0.1 | 0.3 | 0.4 | 0.4 |
| 05 | Vegetables and fruit | 2.2 | 3.4 | 3.3 | 3.5 |
| 06 | Sugar/sugar prep/honey | 1.5 | 1.3 | 0.5 | 0.4 |
| 07 | Coffee/tea/cocoa/spices | 9.1 | 8.2 | 6.0 | 7.2 |
| 08 | Animal feed ex unml cer | 32.5 | 40.9 | 23.6 | 10.2 |
| 09 | Miscellaneous food products | 0.4 | 0.4 | 0.3 | 0.3 |
| 11 | Beverages | 0.0 | 0.1 | 0.1 | 0.1 |
| 12 | Tobacco/manufactures | 0.0 | 0.5 | 0.2 | 0.1 |
| 21 | Hide/skin/fur, raw | 0.1 | 0.3 | 0.3 | 0.2 |
| 22 | Oil seeds/oil fruits | 0.0 | 0.1 | 0.0 | 0.0 |
| 23 | Crude/synthetic/reclaimed rubber | 0.0 | 0.0 | 0.0 | 0.0 |
| 24 | Cork and wood | 0.2 | 1.4 | 1.5 | 0.8 |
| 25 | Pulp and waste paper | 0.0 | 0.0 | 0.0 | 0.0 |
| 26 | Textile fibers | 3.1 | 3.5 | 1.7 | 1.1 |
| 27 | Crude fertilizer/mineral | 0.5 | 0.9 | 0.5 | 3.2 |
| 28 | Metal ores/metal scrap | 18.0 | 14.5 | 18.4 | 13.2 |
| 29 | Crude anim/vegetable mater nes | 1.5 | 1.9 | 1.1 | 1.1 |
| 32 | Coal/coke/briquettes | 0.0 | 0.0 | 0.0 | 0.0 |
| 33 | Petroleum and products | 1.1 | 0.7 | 0.9 | 0.7 |
| 34 | Gas natural/manufactured | 0.0 | 0.0 | 0.3 | 2.5 |
| 41 | Animal oil/fat | 30.8 | 51.3 | 37.4 | 19.7 |
| 42 | Fixed vegetable oils/fats | 0.2 | 0.2 | 0.1 | 0.0 |
| 43 | Animal/vegetable oils processed | 0.2 | 0.3 | 0.3 | 0.1 |
| 51 | Organic chemicals | 0.1 | 0.1 | 0.0 | 0.1 |
| 52 | Inorganic chemicals | 0.9 | 1.1 | 1.2 | 1.3 |
| 53 | Dyeing/tanning/color mat | 0.8 | 0.8 | 0.7 | 1.3 |
| 54 | Pharmaceutical products | 0.2 | 0.1 | 0.0 | 0.0 |
| 55 | Perfume/cosmetic/cleanser | 0.5 | 0.8 | 0.7 | 0.4 |
| 56 | Manufactured fertilizers | 0.0 | 0.0 | 0.1 | 0.1 |
| 57 | Plastics in nonprimary form | 0.0 | 0.0 | 0.1 | 0.1 |
| 58 | Plastics in nonprimary form | 0.0 | 0.2 | 0.5 | 0.7 |
| 59 | Chem material/prods nes | 0.1 | 0.2 | 0.2 | 0.1 |
| 61 | Leather manufactures | 0.1 | 0.2 | 0.4 | 0.3 |
| 62 | Rubber manufactures nes | 0.1 | 0.4 | 0.3 | 0.2 |
| 63 | Cork/wood manufactures | 0.2 | 0.4 | 0.3 | 0.2 |
| 64 | Paper/paperboard/article | 0.1 | 0.2 | 0.2 | 0.3 |
| 65 | Textile yarn/fabric/art | 1.0 | 0.7 | 0.4 | 0.5 |
| 66 | Nonmetal mineral manufactures | 0.2 | 0.3 | 0.3 | 0.2 |
| 67 | Iron and steel | 0.0 | 0.3 | 0.1 | 0.1 |
| 68 | Nonferrous metals | 13.1 | 11.8 | 9.1 | 4.1 |
| 69 | Metal manufactures nes | 0.2 | 0.2 | 0.2 | 0.2 |
| 71 | Power generating equipment | 0.0 | 0.0 | 0.0 | 0.0 |
| 72 | Industry special machine | 0.0 | 0.1 | 0.1 | 0.1 |
| 73 | Metalworking machinery | 0.0 | 0.0 | 0.0 | 0.0 |
| 74 | Industrial equipment nes | 0.0 | 0.0 | 0.0 | 0.0 |
| 75 | Office/data-processing machines | 0.0 | 0.0 | 0.0 | 0.0 |
| 76 | Telecommunications equipment | 0.0 | 0.1 | 0.0 | 0.0 |
| 77 | Electrical equipment | 0.0 | 0.0 | 0.0 | 0.0 |
| 78 | Road vehicles | 0.0 | 0.0 | 0.0 | 0.0 |
| 79 | Railway/tramway equipment | 0.0 | 0.0 | 0.0 | 0.0 |
| 81 | Building fixtures, etc. | 0.0 | 0.1 | 0.1 | 0.1 |
| 82 | Furniture/furnishings | 0.0 | 0.1 | 0.1 | 0.1 |
| 83 | Travel goods/handbags/etc. | 0.0 | 0.1 | 0.1 | 0.1 |
| 84 | Apparel/clothing/access | 1.1 | 2.3 | 2.2 | 1.4 |
| 85 | Footwear | 0.0 | 0.1 | 0.1 | 0.1 |
| 87 | Scientific instruments | 0.0 | 0.0 | 0.0 | 0.0 |
| 89 | Misc manufactures nes | 0.6 | 0.4 | 0.5 | 0.2 |
| 97 | Gold nonmonetary excluding ore | 20.6 | 49.2 | 50.7 | 17.3 |

Sources: UN Comtrade; and World Bank, World Integrated Trade Solution database.

Note: Revealed Comparative Advantage $RCA = (Xij / Xit) / (Xnj / Xnt)$ where $X$ represents exports, $i$ is a country, $j$ is a commodity (or industry), $t$ is a set of commodities (or industries), and $n$ is a set of countries. If $RCA > 1$ ($RCA < 1$), the country is said to have a comparative advantage (disadvantage) in the commodity/industry. nes = not elsewhere specified; SITC = Standard International Trade Classification.

**ANNEX TABLE 19.1.2**

## Intraindustry Trade Index for Peru, Brazil, Chile, Colombia, and Mexico, 2011

| SITC | Category | Peru | Brazil | Chile | Colombia | Mexico |
|---|---|---|---|---|---|---|
| 00 | Live animals except fish | 0.7 | 0.1 | 0.9 | 0.4 | 0.3 |
| 01 | Meat and preparations | 0.2 | 0.0 | 1.0 | 0.4 | 0.4 |
| 02 | Dairy products and eggs | 0.9 | 0.5 | 0.7 | 0.2 | 0.2 |
| 03 | Fish/shellfish/etc. | 0.2 | 0.3 | 0.1 | 0.8 | 0.7 |
| 04 | Cereals/cereal preparation | 0.2 | 0.9 | 0.6 | 0.1 | 0.4 |
| 05 | Vegetables and fruit | 0.2 | 0.7 | 0.1 | 0.7 | 0.3 |
| 06 | Sugar/sugar prep/honey | 0.4 | 0.0 | 0.2 | 0.3 | 0.7 |
| 07 | Coffee/tea/cocoa/spices | 0.1 | 0.1 | 0.6 | 0.2 | 0.7 |
| 08 | Animal feed ex unml cer | 0.4 | 0.1 | 0.8 | 0.1 | 0.2 |
| 09 | Miscellaneous food products | 0.3 | 0.9 | 0.8 | 0.6 | 0.9 |
| 11 | Beverages | 0.5 | 0.3 | 0.2 | 0.4 | 0.4 |
| 12 | Tobacco/manufactures | 0.5 | 0.0 | 0.5 | 0.9 | 0.7 |
| 21 | Hide/skin/fur, raw | 0.0 | 0.5 | 0.0 | 0.1 | 0.3 |
| 22 | Oil seeds/oil fruits | 0.0 | 0.0 | 0.7 | 0.1 | 0.0 |
| 23 | Crude/synthetic/reclaimed rubber | 0.0 | 0.4 | 0.0 | 0.0 | 0.8 |
| 24 | Cork and wood | 0.5 | 0.1 | 0.0 | 1.0 | 0.3 |
| 25 | Pulp and waste paper | 0.1 | 0.1 | 0.0 | 0.0 | 0.1 |
| 26 | Textile fibers | 0.6 | 0.5 | 0.4 | 0.1 | 0.4 |
| 27 | Crude fertilizer/mineral | 0.4 | 0.9 | 0.6 | 0.4 | 0.9 |
| 28 | Metal ores/metal scrap | 0.0 | 0.1 | 0.1 | 0.1 | 0.5 |
| 29 | Crude animal/vegetable matter nes | 0.6 | 0.7 | 0.4 | 0.1 | 0.5 |
| 32 | Coal/coke/briquettes | 0.3 | 0.0 | 0.0 | 0.0 | 0.1 |
| 33 | Petroleum and products | 0.8 | 0.9 | 0.1 | 0.2 | 0.7 |
| 34 | Gas natural/manufactured | 0.0 | 0.0 | 0.0 | 0.1 | 0.0 |
| 35 | Electric current | 0.2 | 0.1 | 0.0 | 0.0 | 0.3 |
| 41 | Animal oil/fat | 0.2 | 0.5 | 1.0 | 0.0 | 0.1 |
| 42 | Fixed vegetable oils/fats | 0.0 | 0.6 | 0.6 | 0.7 | 0.2 |
| 43 | Animal/vegetable oils processed | 0.5 | 0.7 | 0.1 | 0.8 | 0.3 |
| 51 | Organic chemicals | 0.3 | 0.7 | 0.5 | 0.2 | 0.4 |
| 52 | Inorganic chemicals | 0.9 | 0.7 | 0.8 | 0.5 | 0.7 |
| 53 | Dyeing/tanning/color materials | 0.9 | 0.5 | 0.2 | 0.7 | 0.5 |
| 54 | Pharmaceutical products | 0.1 | 0.4 | 0.3 | 0.4 | 0.6 |
| 55 | Perfume/cosmetic/cleanser | 0.5 | 1.0 | 0.2 | 1.0 | 0.9 |
| 56 | Manufactured fertilizers | 0.1 | 0.1 | 0.9 | 0.2 | 0.2 |
| 57 | Plastics in primary form | 0.1 | 0.7 | 0.3 | 0.8 | 0.5 |
| 58 | Plastics in nonprimary form | 0.8 | 0.7 | 0.7 | 0.8 | 0.4 |
| 59 | Chemical material/products nes | 0.2 | 0.5 | 0.4 | 0.5 | 0.4 |
| 61 | Leather manufactures | 0.7 | 0.0 | 1.0 | 0.2 | 0.8 |
| 62 | Rubber manufactures nes | 0.3 | 0.8 | 0.4 | 0.3 | 0.5 |
| 63 | Cork/wood manufactures | 0.4 | 0.3 | 0.4 | 0.2 | 0.4 |
| 64 | Paper/paperboard/article | 0.4 | 0.9 | 0.9 | 0.9 | 0.5 |
| 65 | Textile yarn/fabric/art | 0.6 | 0.4 | 0.3 | 0.5 | 0.5 |
| 66 | Nonmetal mineral manufactures | 0.6 | 1.0 | 0.2 | 1.0 | 1.0 |
| 67 | Iron and steel | 0.1 | 0.6 | 0.5 | 0.6 | 0.7 |
| 68 | Nonferrous metals | 0.1 | 0.8 | 0.0 | 0.3 | 1.0 |
| 69 | Metal manufactures nes | 0.3 | 0.8 | 0.5 | 0.4 | 0.7 |
| 71 | Power-generating equipment | 0.1 | 0.8 | 0.1 | 0.1 | 1.0 |
| 72 | Industry special machine | 0.1 | 0.8 | 0.2 | 0.1 | 0.7 |
| 73 | Metalworking machinery | 0.0 | 0.2 | 0.1 | 0.0 | 0.2 |
| 74 | Industrial equipment nes | 0.1 | 0.5 | 0.2 | 0.1 | 0.8 |
| 75 | Office/data-processing machines | 0.0 | 0.1 | 0.1 | 0.0 | 0.9 |
| 76 | Telecommunications equipment | 0.0 | 0.2 | 0.1 | 0.0 | 0.9 |
| 77 | Electrical equipment | 0.1 | 0.3 | 0.2 | 0.4 | 0.9 |
| 78 | Road vehicles | 0.0 | 0.7 | 0.2 | 0.1 | 0.6 |
| 79 | Railway/tramway equipment | 0.6 | 0.7 | 0.2 | 0.0 | 0.8 |
| 81 | Building fixtures, etc. | 0.3 | 0.7 | 0.2 | 0.8 | 0.6 |
| 82 | Furniture/furnishings | 0.3 | 0.9 | 0.2 | 0.8 | 0.6 |
| 83 | Travel goods/handbags/etc. | 0.2 | 0.1 | 0.3 | 0.5 | 0.3 |
| 84 | Apparel/clothing/accessories | 0.5 | 0.2 | 0.3 | 1.0 | 0.7 |
| 85 | Footwear | 0.2 | 0.5 | 0.3 | 0.2 | 0.8 |
| 87 | Scientific instruments | 0.1 | 0.3 | 0.1 | 0.1 | 1.0 |
| 88 | Photographic equipment/clocks | 0.0 | 0.2 | 0.2 | 0.0 | 0.6 |
| 89 | Miscellaneous manufactures nes | 0.6 | 0.5 | 0.4 | 0.5 | 0.7 |
| 96 | Coin nongold noncurrent | 0.0 | 0.0 | 0.0 | 1.0 | 0.1 |
| 97 | Gold nonmonetary excluding ore | 0.0 | 0.0 | 0.0 | 0.0 | 0.1 |

Sources: UN Comtrade; and IMF staff calculations.

Note: Measured by Grubel-Lloyd Index: $IIT_i = ((Export_i + Import_i) - |Export_i - Import_i|)/(Export_i + Import_i)$, where $0 \leq IIT_i \leq 1$. If $IIT_i = 1$ there is only intraindustry trade; conversely, if $IIT_i = 0$, there is only interindustry trade.

$0 \leq IIT_i < 0.5$

$0.5 \leq IIT_i < 1.0$

$IIT_i = 1$

nes = not elsewhere specified; SITC = Standard International Trade Classification.

## REFERENCES

Bank of Canada. 2012. "Dutch Disease." Remarks by Mark Carney, Governor of the Bank of Canada (September 7).

Cesa-Bianchi, Ambrogio, M. Hashem Pesaran, Alessandro Rebucci, and Teng Teng Xu. 2011. "China's Emergence in the World Economy and Business Cycles in Latin America." IDB Working Paper No. 266, Inter-American Development Bank, Washington, DC.

International Monetary Fund. 2004. "Why Are Trade Levels Low in Peru?" in *Peru—Selected Issues.* IMF Country Report No. 04/156, International Monetary Fund, Washington, DC.

———. 2011. "Regional Economic Outlook: Asia and the Pacific." Washington, DC (April).

Magud, N., and S. Sosa. 2010. "When and Why Worry About Real Exchange Rate Appreciation? The Missing Link between Dutch Disease and Growth." Working Paper 10/271, International Monetary Fund, Washington, DC.

Papageorgiou, Chris, and Nicola Spatafora. 2012. "Economic Diversification in LICs: Stylized Facts and Macroeconomic Implications." Staff Discussion Notes No. 12/13, International Monetary Fund, Washington, DC.

Winkelried, Diego, and Miguel Saldarriaga. 2012. "Trade Linkages and Growth in Latin America: A Time-varying SVAR Approach." Working Paper No. 2012–011, Central Reserve Bank of Peru, Lima.

# CHAPTER 20

# Drivers of Peru's Equilibrium Real Exchange Rate: Is the Nuevo Sol a Commodity Currency?

MELESSE TASHU

*This chapter tests the hypothesis of "commodity currency" on the nuevo sol and identifies the drivers of Peru's equilibrium real exchange rate using cointegration analysis. The results show that export commodity prices do not have a statistically significant impact on Peru's real effective exchange rate (REER), suggesting that the nuevo sol is not a commodity currency. Large profit repatriation and foreign exchange intervention have effectively insulated Peru's real exchange rate from the impact of commodity price shocks. The results suggest that Peru's equilibrium real exchange rate is driven by relative productivity and government consumption and that the real exchange rate is broadly in line with fundamentals.*

Because the real exchange rate is the relative price of tradable and nontradable goods in an economy, determining whether that rate is in line with the equilibrium level is important to efficiently allocate resources between the tradable and nontradable sectors.[1] A misaligned real exchange rate—that is, a real exchange rate that deviates substantially from the equilibrium level—could create large macroeconomic imbalances and distort incentives and allocation of resources by sending wrong signals to economic agents.

Although the equilibrium real exchange rate is an unobservable variable, economic theory suggests that it is driven by such observable economic fundamentals as the terms of trade (or the real prices of key export commodities for commodity-dependent economies), productivity of tradables relative to nontradables, government consumption, and the net foreign asset position. For commodity-dependent economies like Peru, in particular, the equilibrium real exchange rate is conjectured to be primarily determined by the real prices of export commodities such that the currencies of these countries are commonly referred to as "commodity currencies" (Bodart, Cabdelon, and Carpantier 2012; Cashin, Cespedes, and Sahay 2004; Chen and Rogoff 2003).

The essential step in estimating the equilibrium real exchange rate is establishing an econometric relationship between the real exchange rate and the fundamentals, which is the main objective of this chapter. In particular, the chapter aims to test whether Peru's real exchange rate is primarily determined by the real prices of key export commodities, as the "commodity currency" hypothesis would suggest. To achieve this objective, the chapter employs the Johansen cointegration method. Robustness of the results is tested with various specifications, including alternative definitions of the real exchange rate and real commodity prices, varying sample sizes, and alternative methodologies.

The chapter also attempts to estimate the path of the notional equilibrium real exchange rate using the estimated long-term cointegration relationship between the real exchange rate and the fundamentals. The equilibrium real exchange rate estimated here, however, does not have a

[1]The terms "real exchange rate" and "real effective exchange rate" are used interchangeably in this chapter. Both terms refer to the exchange rate of the nuevo sol against a basket of currencies of major trading partner countries adjusted for price differentials between Peru and trading partner countries.

normative implication, as it does not necessarily imply optimality from a welfare perspective. A normative assessment of the equilibrium real exchange rate requires making judgments on the optimality of the values of the fundamentals, which is beyond the scope of this chapter.

## THEORETICAL FRAMEWORK

Attempts to model the equilibrium real exchange rate go back to purchasing power parity theory, which states in its absolute form that the exchange rate between currencies of two countries is simply given by the relative price levels expressed in the same currency (that is, generalization of the law of one price). In its relative form, purchasing power parity theory asserts that the percentage change in the exchange rate between two currencies is determined by the inflation differential between the corresponding countries. In its weakest form, the purchasing power parity hypothesis requires deviations from the purchasing power parity real exchange rate to eventually die out and the real exchange rate to be stable, exhibiting a stationary or mean reverting property in the long term (Astorga 2012; Rogoff 1996). If this were true, the equilibrium real exchange rate would be constant and could be represented by the long-term or purchasing power parity real exchange rate. However, the purchasing power parity hypothesis received very little empirical support, especially in the short term, as most studies show that real exchange rate deviations are persistent and the real exchange rate exhibits a unit root process (Astorga 2012; Engel 2000; Meese and Rogoff 1983; Rogoff 1996).

The empirical failure of the theory of purchasing power parity, referred to in the literature as the purchasing power parity puzzle, has led to the hypothesis that the equilibrium real exchange rate could be time-varying, driven by real factors or fundamentals. In a seminal paper on the purchasing power parity puzzle, Rogoff (1996) argued that the high short-term volatility of the real exchange rate and the very slow adjustment of shocks to purchasing power parity are so irreconcilable that the deviations from purchasing power parity must be accounted for by real factors. Such real factors that are hypothesized to drive the equilibrium real exchange rate include the terms of trade (or real prices of commodities for commodity-dependent economies), the relative productivity of tradables to nontradables, government consumption, and the net foreign asset position (Froot and Rogoff, 1995; Montiel, 2007; Ricci, Milesi-Ferretti, and Lee 2013; Rogoff, 1996).

- *Real price of commodities:* While the terms of trade are generally used in real exchange rate models, the real price index of key export commodities is a more relevant variable for commodity-dependent, small, and open economies. As Chen and Rogoff (2003) indicate, aggregate export and import price indices used to construct the terms of trade include goods with sluggish nominal price adjustments and incomplete pass-through, leading to identification problems in econometric estimations. On the contrary, world commodity prices are purely exogenous for small exporting economies, as they are determined on world markets. An increase in commodity prices can lead to wage increases in the commodity sector and across the economy, because labor is assumed to be mobile, leading to an increase in the relative price of nontradables as the price of tradables is determined in the world market and, therefore, to a real exchange rate appreciation (Cashin, Cespedes, and Sahay 2004; Chen and Rogoff 2003).
- *Relative productivity of tradables to nontradables:* According to the Balassa–Samuelson hypothesis (Balassa 1964; Samuelson 1964), an increase in the relative productivity of tradables to nontradables will drive up economy-wide wages, assuming labor is mobile between the two sectors, resulting in a higher relative price of nontradables (that is, a real appreciation).
- *Government consumption:* Higher government consumption is likely to lead to an appreciation of the equilibrium real exchange rate, since government consumption tends to fall

more on nontradables than tradables (Froot and Rogoff 1995; Ricci, Milesi-Ferretti, and Lee 2013; Rogoff 1996).

- *Net foreign asset liability position:* An increase in net foreign liabilities will require a more depreciated real exchange rate to generate the trade surplus necessary to service the external debt (Ricci, Milesi-Ferretti, and Lee 2013; Rogoff 1996).

## EMPIRICAL MODEL AND DATA DESCRIPTION

To test if the nuevo sol is a commodity currency, this chapter follows Chen and Rogoff (2003) and Cashin, Cespedes, and Sahay (2004), who specify the REER as a function only of the real price of commodities. Given Peru's reliance on commodity exports, particular metals such as copper and gold,[2] the hypothesis of commodity currency expects Peru's real effective exchange to be driven primarily by the real price of export commodities. Hence, the regression model takes the following log-linear form:

$$LREER_t = \alpha_0 + \alpha_1 LRP\_COM_t + \mu_t, \tag{20.1}$$

where *REER* is the REER index, which is a trade-weighted and exchange-rate–adjusted ratio of domestic to foreign prices; an increase in the REER is an appreciation. For the robustness exercise, the bilateral real exchange rate index vis-à-vis the U.S. dollar is also used. The source of REER data is the IMF's Information Notice System database, and the real exchange rate is constructed using data on the bilateral exchange rate and prices from the IMF's International Financial Statistics database.

*RP_COM* is the real price of export commodities, constructed as the weighted average world price indices of copper, gold, lead, and zinc (Peru's major export metals) deflated by the manufacturing export unit value index of advanced economies. Metal price indices are obtained from the International Financial Statistics database, and the manufacturing export unit value index is from the IMF's World Economic Outlook database. Other variables include the following: $\mu$ is the stochastic error term, $L$ is the natural logarithm transformation operator, and $t$ is the time index. The nuevo sol would be regarded as a commodity currency if $\alpha_1$ were positive and statistically significant.

To identify the drivers of the equilibrium REER more generally, equation (20.1) is modified by including the remaining fundamentals and is respecified as:

$$LREER_t = \beta_0 + \beta_1 * LRP_{COM\,t} + \beta_2 * LPROD_t + \beta_3 * LGCN_t + \beta_4 * LNFL_t + \varepsilon_t, \tag{20.2}$$

where

- *PROD* is relative productivity. The economy-wide labor productivity of Peru relative to trade-weighted average labor productivity of trading partner countries is used, since data on sectoral productivity are not available. The implicit assumption is that productivity growth is likely to be biased in favor of the tradable sector, meaning that a country with high growth of overall productivity will also exhibit higher productivity growth in the tradable sector relative to the nontradable sector. The source of data is Haver Analytics.
- *GCN* is primary current public sector consumption (spending on wages and salaries and goods and services) as a ratio of Peru's GDP relative to that of trading partner countries.

[2]Metal exports represent about 55 percent of Peru's total export receipts.

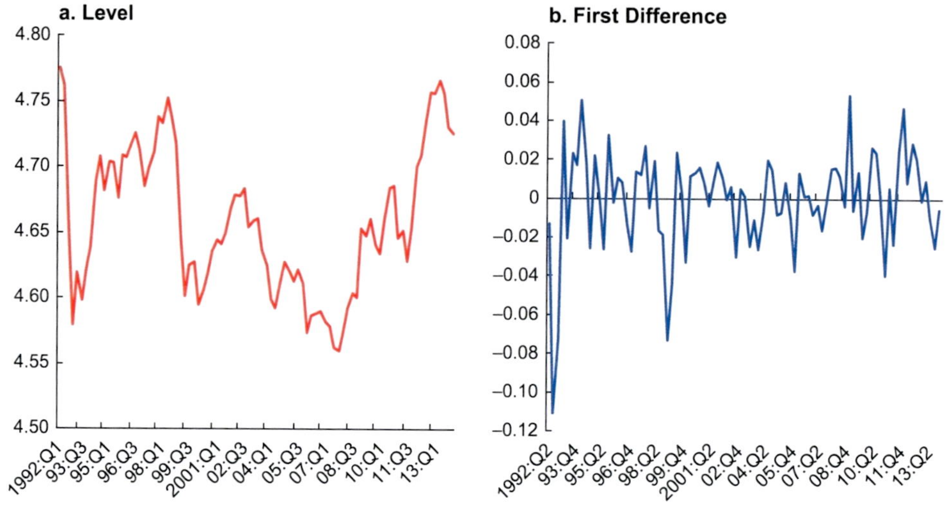


Sources: IMF, Information Notice System database; and author's calculations.

**Figure 20.1** Peru: Real Effective Exchange Rate

Only U.S. data are used in the denominator, as consistent time series data are not available for most other trading partner countries such as China, Brazil, and Chile. Sources of data are the Central Reserve Bank of Peru (*Banco Central de Reserva del Perú* [BCRP]) and the U.S. Bureau of Economic Analysis.

- *NFL* is the stock of net foreign liability at the end of the previous period as a ratio of the previous period's total external trade in goods and services. As alternatives, *NFL* as a ratio of GDP and the cumulative current account balance (as a ratio of trade and GDP) are explored. The source of data is the BCRP.
- $\varepsilon$ is the stochastic error term.
- All other terms are as defined above.

The sample covers quarterly data for the period 1992–2013. The year 1992 was chosen as the beginning of the sample period to avoid potential structural shifts in the real exchange rate data due to changes in the currency prior to 1992 and major stabilization efforts realized since then. Peru's current currency, the nuevo sol, was introduced in July 1991 and has been in use since then. For the robustness exercise, however, annual data for the sample period 1970–2013 and monthly data for the sample period 1992-2013 were also used.

Descriptive analysis of the data shows that Peru's REER is strongly correlated with relative productivity and relative government consumption. On the other hand, the REER does not seem to have a discernible correlation with the real commodity price index, and its correlation with net foreign liability appears to shift from positive prior to 2007 to negative since 2007 (Annex Figure 20.1.1c).

## ESTIMATION METHOD AND RESULTS

### Estimation Method

Examining the data shows that the REER does not seem to exhibit a stationary process, as there is visual evidence of drift in the data (Figure 20.1a). The first difference of the REER, however, clearly portrays a stationary process (Figure 20.1b). This observation is supported by the results of

**TABLE 20.1**

**Real Exchange Rate and Commodity Prices: Alternative Specifications**

| Alternative Specification | Coefficient | *T*-value |
|---|---|---|
| Dynamic Ordinary Least Squares | 0.03 | 1.21 |
| Fully Modified Ordinary Least Squares | 0.02 | 0.43 |
| Bilateral Real Exchange Rate as Dependent Variable | 0.05 | 0.87 |
| Real Price of Copper | 0.02 | 0.73 |
| Terms of Trade | 0.04 | 0.41 |
| Monthly Data: 1992–2013 | 0.03 | 1.17 |
| Annual Data: 1970–2013 | 0.01 | 0.11 |

Source: Author's calculations.

formal unit root tests, which show that Peru's REER follows an I(1) process, and unit root tests for the fundamentals also show that they are all integrated of order one (Annex Table 20.1.1), implying that the proper approach for estimating the REER equation is a cointegration analysis. Hence, the Johansen cointegration method is used to test and estimate cointegration relationships between the REER and the fundamentals. Alternative estimation methods, including the dynamic ordinary least squares, the fully modified ordinary least squares, and the two-stage least squares methods, are also explored to test the robustness of the results to changes in estimation methodology.

## Is the Nuevo Sol a Commodity Currency?

### *Results*

The estimates below suggest that the real price index of commodities does not explain the behavior of the REER (the number in parenthesis is the *t*-value).

$$LREER_t = 4.55 + 0.02{*}LRP\_COM_t. \qquad (20.3)$$
$$(0.793)$$

Although Johansen's trace and maximum eigenvalue tests indicate the presence of cointegration at the 10 percent level (Annex Table 20.1.2a), the estimated coefficient on *LRP_COM* is very small and not statistically significant, ruling out the null hypothesis of a commodity currency. The result is robust to changes in the definition of the real exchange rate (using the bilateral real exchange rate against the U.S. dollar real exchange rate instead of the REER) and the *RP_COM* (using the real price of copper and the terms of trade in place of *RP_COM*), data frequency (using monthly and annual data), estimation method, and sample coverage (Table 20.1). In all cases, the coefficients are positive as expected, but not statistically significant.

The test for linear cointegration in the annual sample yielded no cointegration with coefficients sensitive to changes in specification. Because this might be due to potential structural breaks (regime shifts) due to significant turbulence in the Peruvian economy in the 1980s (including hyperinflation and changes in currency), a Gregory-Hansen (1996) cointegration test with a regime shift was used to test for evidence of a nonlinear cointegration between the REER and *RP_COM*. The result shows evidence of nonlinear cointegration with a regime shift in 1987 at the 10 percent level (Annex Table 20.1.3a). Following this result, a dummy was created for this structural shift and the nonlinear cointegration relationship was estimated using fully modified ordinary least squares with *LRP_COM* and *LRP_COM* interacted with a dummy for a structural shift on the right-hand side. The estimated coefficients were –0.26 for *LRP_COM* and 0.27 for *LRP_COM* interacted with a dummy with a net elasticity of 0.01 after the structural shift, that is, for the period 1987–2013. This is comparable to the sample period of the monthly and quarterly frequency data. Both coefficients were statistically significant, but a Wald restriction test for the sum of the coefficients equals zero could not be rejected at any level of significance (Annex Table 20.1.4c).

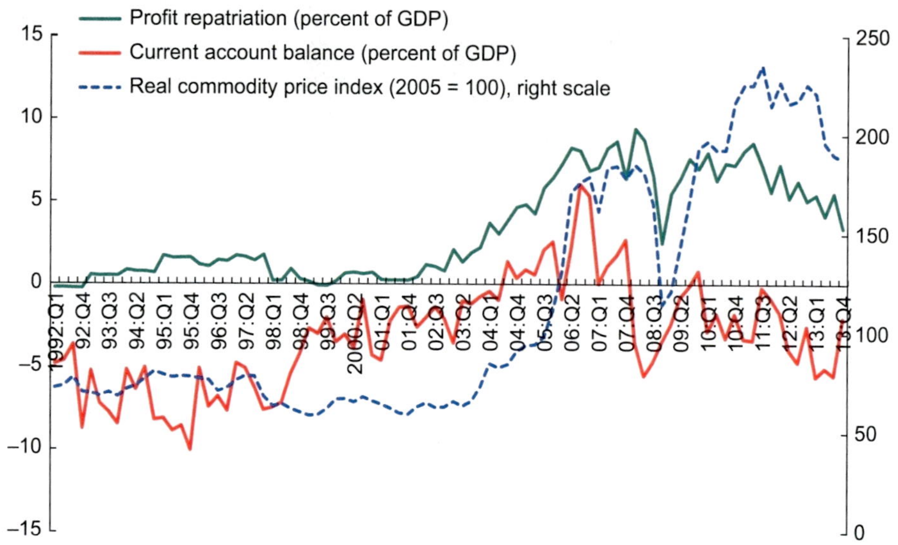


Sources: Central Reserve Bank of Peru; and author's estimations.

**Figure 20.2** Real Price of Commodities, Profit Repatriation, and Current Account Balance

## *Possible Explanations for Why the Nuevo Sol May Not Be a Commodity Currency*

Although most similar studies on other commodity-dependent economies find evidence of commodity currency, Peru was one of the few countries with no such evidence in Cashin, Cespedes, and Sahay (2004) (Annex Table 20.1.5). The absence of a statistically significant long-term relationship between export commodity prices and the REER in an economy that relies heavily on commodities for export, and that faced significant positive commodity price shocks in the study period, is somewhat puzzling. Potential factors that could have weakened the statistical relationship between commodity prices and REER may include large profit repatriation and active foreign exchange intervention.

- *Profit repatriation:* Despite significant price increases for its exports, Peru has run current account deficits during most of the past decade, as large profit repatriations more than offset trade surpluses (Figure 20.2). The mining sector in Peru is operated by the private sector, mostly owned by nonresidents. As a result, most of the profit from the sector is repatriated. During 2003–13, the years identified by Adler and Magud (2013) as the commodity income windfall period, profit repatriation from Peru amounted to about 6 percent of GDP a year on average. This might have weakened the statistical relationship between the commodity prices and the REER, since a large part of the commodity price shock might have been leaked as profit repatriation without having a significant impact on domestic demand. It is true that a large part of the repatriated profit has been reinvested in Peru in the mining sector, but the investments mostly involve imported machinery with limited impact on domestic demand.
- *Active foreign exchange intervention:* Peru's central bank intervenes actively in the foreign exchange market with a stated objective of limiting exchange rate volatility to contain the risks of financial dollarization. Empirical evidence shows that the BCRP's foreign exchange interventions are successful in containing exchange rate volatility (Tashu 2014). On the other hand, Peru has one of the lowest and most stable rates of inflation in the region, thanks to an inflation-targeting framework that has successfully anchored inflation expectations (Armas, Castillo, and Vega 2014; Armas and Grippa 2005).[3] As a result, Peru's real

[3] Although the inflation-targeting framework was introduced in 2002, the monetary-targeting framework, which was in place prior to 2002, is also credited with having reduced and stabilized inflation from the hyperinflation of the 1980s.

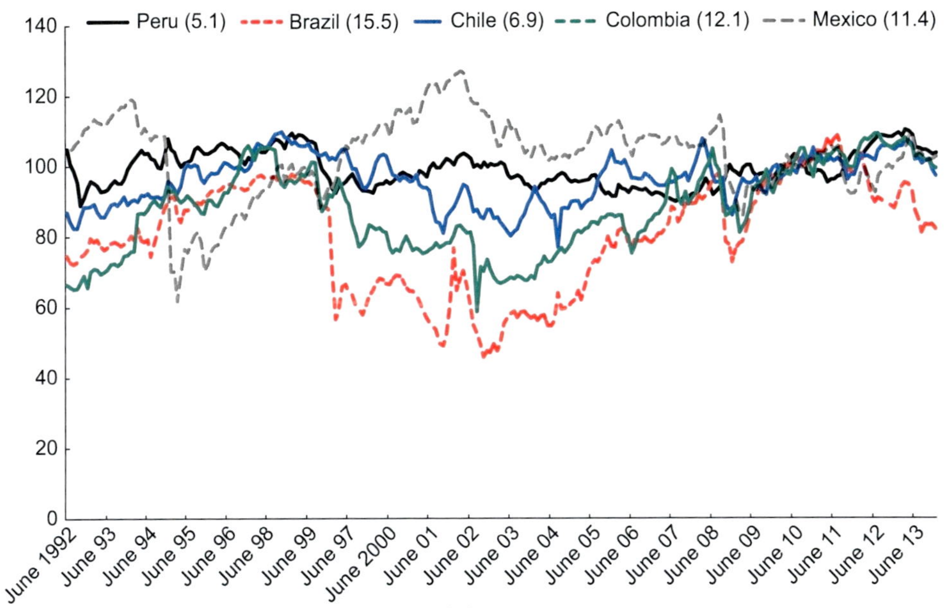


Sources: IMF, Information Notice System database; and author's calculations.
Note: Numbers in parenthesis in front of country names refer to standard deviations of the real effective exchange rate.

**Figure 20.3** Real Effective Exchange Rate Indices in Selected Latin American Economies

exchange rate is the most stable among financially open large Latin American economies (Figure 20.3).

A sustained and sterilized foreign exchange intervention in an inflation-targeting regime appears to have weakened the impact of commodity prices on the real exchange rate.[4] To illustrate this, consider a positive commodity price shock. In an inflation-targeting regime, the central bank could prevent the inflationary pressure from the commodity windfall income by increasing its policy rate, which in turn can lead to an increase in capital inflows. In a freely floating exchange rate regime, the capital inflows would have appreciated the nominal, and hence the real, exchange rate. The BCRP's sterilized foreign exchange intervention has, however, limited the impact of capital inflows on the exchange rate, effectively insulating the real exchange rate from the impact of commodity price shocks.

To test the hypothesis that large profit repatriations and the central bank's foreign exchange interventions could have insulated the REER from the impact of commodity prices, consider a specification where the REER depends on commodity prices, profit repatriation in percent of GDP (*PREP*), and net international reserves (NIR) in percent of GDP (*NIR_GDP*) as a proxy for foreign exchange intervention:[5]

$$LREER_t = \theta_0 + \theta_1 * LRP_{COM\,t} + \theta_2 * LPREP_t + \theta_3 * LNIR\_GDP_t + \varepsilon_t. \quad (20.4)$$

[4]Complementary fiscal policy and the use of reserve requirements have helped the BCRP sustain its sterilized foreign exchange interventions without compromising the health of its balance sheet. For instance, about 37½ percent and 34½ percent of the foreign exchange intervention in 2013 was sterilized by public sector deposits and reserve requirements, respectively, and only about 11½ percent of the intervention was sterilized through central bank instruments (Rossini, Armas, and Quispe 2014). In this regard, the positive commodity price shock, which increased tax revenues from the mineral sector, has helped the Treasury support the central bank's sterilization effort.

[5]The NIR used here excludes valuation effects, so changes in the NIR mostly reflect foreign exchange interventions and other measures aimed at containing exchange rate volatility, such as changes in reserve requirements on foreign currency liabilities.

Profit repatriation (*PREP*) should lead to a depreciation of the nominal and hence the real exchange rate because it increases demand for foreign exchange. As a result, $\theta_2 < 0$. The *NIR_GDP* is also expected to have a negative relationship with the real exchange rate, as an increase in the NIR (foreign exchange purchases by the central bank) and a decrease in the NIR (foreign exchange sales by the central bank) should lead to a depreciation and appreciation of the national currency, respectively, if successful. Hence, $\theta_3 < 0$.

Since changes in commodity prices can also affect the *PREP* and *NIR_GDP*, we can specify the following equations:

$$LPREP_t = \gamma_0 + \gamma_1 * LRP\_COM_t + \varphi_t \tag{20.5}$$

$$LNIR_t = \delta_0 + \delta_1 * LRP\_COM_t + \tau_t \tag{20.6}$$

In equation (20.4), the impact of commodity prices on the REER if we were to hold the *PREP* and *NIR_GDP* constant is $\theta_1$. In reality, however, both the *PREP* and *NIR_GDP* change when commodity prices change. Firms' profits increase as commodity prices increase, implying $\gamma_1 > 0$, and a positive commodity price shock prompts central bank intervention in the foreign exchange market and hence an increase in the NIR, implying $\delta_1 > 0$. As a result, the net impact of commodity prices on the REER is given by $\theta_1 + \theta_2 * \gamma_1 + \theta_3 * \delta_1$), and could be zero, negative, or positive depending on the relative size of the individual coefficients.

Estimation of equations (20.4) to (20.6) using the Johansen cointegration method yields the following results:[6]

$$\underset{}{LREER_t} = 4.22 + \underset{(3.63)}{0.49 * LRP\_COM_t} - \underset{(-1.79)}{0.16 * LPREP_t} - \underset{(-4.89)}{0.56 * LNIR\_GDP_t} \tag{20.7}$$

$$PREP_t = -3.87 + \underset{(5.53)}{1.01 * LRP\_COM_t} \tag{20.8}$$

$$LNIR\_GDP_t = 0.38 + \underset{(5.52)}{0.55 * LRP\_COM_t}. \tag{20.9}$$

The results show that all of the coefficients have the expected sign and are statistically significant at standard levels of significance. Furthermore, the estimate for the net impact of the commodity prices $\theta_1 + \theta_2 * \gamma_1 + \theta_3 * \delta_1$ equals 0.01, which is very low and virtually the same as the estimated coefficient obtained when the REER is regressed only on the commodity prices [equation (20.3)].

Thus, the empirical evidence supports the hypothesis that the commodity price shock has been absorbed mostly by large profit repatriations and sustained foreign exchange intervention, weakening the net impact on the REER. The impact of commodity prices on the REER, if we were to hold profit repatriation constant and assume no foreign exchange intervention, would have been statistically significant with an estimated elasticity of about 0.5. In reality, however, changes in commodity prices have a statistically significant positive impact on profit repatriation and central bank intervention, which in turn negatively affects the REER, neutralizing the initial impact of commodity prices on it.

[6] All of the variables have unit root (Annex Table 20.1.1). The Augmented-Dickey-Fuller test seems to suggest that the log of *NIR_GDP* is I(0) when constant or constant and trend are added. But the Augmented-Dickey-Fuller test is known to have low power; that is, it has a tendency to reject the null hypothesis of I(1) too often when it is true. The more efficient unit root test, the Dickey-Fuller GLS test accepts the null hypothesis at all levels of significance, suggesting that the NIR is I(1). Johansen's Trace and Maximum Eigenvalue cointegration tests show the presence of a statistically significant cointegration vector among the variables in each of the three equations.

## Identifying the Drivers of the Equilibrium Real Exchange Rate

The search for a cointegrating vector between the REER and fundamentals involved an algorithm that (1) discards models that do not have a statistically significant vector, (2) eliminates variables that do not have coefficients with theoretically expected signs or whose inclusion changes the signs of other variables, (3) discards models that do not have a statistically significant error correction term with a negative sign, and (4) maximizes the *R*-square of the error correction model. The net foreign liability was dropped from the chosen model following this algorithm, similar to the results of other studies, including Montiel (2007) and Coudert, Couharde, and Mignon (2011). The test for cointegration among the remaining variables shows a single cointegrating vector at the 10 percent significance level (Annex Table 20.1.2b), which, after normalizing for the coefficient of *LREER*, takes the following form:

$$\underset{}{LREER_t} = 4.74 + \underset{(1.48)}{0.03 * LRP\_COM_t} + \underset{(2.97)}{0.36 * LPROD_t} + \underset{(4.35)}{0.37 * LGCN_t}, \tag{20.10}$$

where the numbers in parentheses refer to *t*-values.

While all of the fundamentals in equation (20.10) have the expected signs on their coefficients, the real price of commodities is not statistically significant, as is the case in equation (20.3). Tests for cointegration restrictions show that *LRP_COM* is not important for the cointegrating vector (Annex Table 20.1.2c). As a result, equation (20.10) is reestimated without *LRP_COM* and the resulting cointegration vector, which becomes statistically significant at the 1 percent level (Table 20.1.2d), and the short-term dynamic equations are shown in equations (20.11) and (20.12), respectively:

$$LREER_t = 4.90 + \underset{(3.57)}{0.48 * LPROD_t} + \underset{(4.32)}{0.39 * LGCN_t} \tag{20.11}$$

$$\begin{aligned} DLREER_t &= \underset{(0.05)}{0.0001} - \underset{(-3.02)}{0.13 * ECM_{t-1}} + \underset{(2.33)}{0.22 * DLREER_{t-1}} \\ &\quad + \underset{(3.60)}{0.45 * DLPROD_{t-1}} - \underset{(-2.92)}{0.09 * DLGCN_{t-1}}, \end{aligned} \tag{20.12}$$

where *D* stands for the first difference, the subscript (–1) refers to the first lag, and *ECM* stands for the error correction term, which is the error term of equation (20.11). Numbers in parenthesis are *t*-values.

Accordingly, relative productivity and government consumption are the main drivers of the equilibrium REER in Peru. The coefficient on the error correction term in the dynamic equation is –0.13 and is statistically significant at 1 percent, implying that about 13 percent of deviations of the REER from the long-term equilibrium would be corrected after one quarter. The half-life of a shock to the REER, calculated as log(0.5)/log(1 – 0.13), is estimated at about five quarters, which is consistent with the results of other empirical studies. Both productivity and government consumption are also significant in the short-run dynamic model [equation (20.12)], the latter with an unexpected negative sign.

The above result is robust to changes in specifications (Table 20.2). The exception is when annual data for 1970–2013 are used, which show a statistically significant *RP_COM,* but the elasticity remains very small (0.03).[7]

[7]The results for the annual data are obtained following the procedure described above, that is, testing for cointegration with regime shift using the Gregory-Hansen (1996) test and estimating the long-term relationship using nonlinear fully modified ordinary least squares (Annex Tables 20.1.3b and 20.1.4b, c). In this case, the break was identified as 1988/89.

TABLE 20.2

The Real Exchange Rate and Fundamentals: Alternative Specifications

| Alternative Specification | *LRP_COM* | *LPROD* | *LGCN* |
|---|---|---|---|
| Two-stage Least Squares | 0.01 | 0.43 | 0.14 |
| (Using First Lags as Instruments) | (0.52) | (8.59) | (2.09) |
| Dynamic Ordinary Least Squares | 0.02 | 0.36 | 0.15 |
| | (0.95) | (3.63) | (1.95) |
| Fully Modified Ordinary Least Squares | 0.01 | 0.36 | 0.11 |
| | (0.83) | (4.20) | (1.71) |
| Bilateral Real Exchange Rate as Dependent Variable[1] | ... | 0.92 | 0.41 |
| | | (3.32) | (2.87) |
| Real Price of Copper | 0.02 | 0.40 | 0.41 |
| | (1.05) | (3.08) | (4.38) |
| Terms of Trade | 0.05 | 0.43 | 0.41 |
| | (0.65) | (3.12) | (4.22) |
| Annual Data: 1970–2013[2] | 0.03 | 0.19 | 0.19 |
| | (2.95) | (9.26) | (8.62) |

Source: Author's calculations.
Note: Numbers in parenthesis are *t*-values.
[1] *RP_COM* is dropped from the bilateral real exchange rate model as it carries a theoretically wrong sign.
[2] Net foreign liability also becomes significant with a theoretically expected negative sign and elasticity of 0.06. The trade openness index, which has not been included in the quarterly data since Peru liberalized its external trade in 1991, is also included in the annual sample (Annex Table 20.1.4b, c).

## Is the Real Effective Exchange Rate Misaligned?

While a proper estimation of the equilibrium real exchange rate requires a multicountry panel regression analysis similar to the IMF's external balance assessment (Phillips and others 2013), the estimated long-term relationship between the REER and statistically significant fundamentals is used to estimate the notional path of the equilibrium REER. The idea is to evaluate how much the actual REER is aligned with the path of the REER predicted by the estimated long-term cointegration relationship [equation (20.11)] and the values of statistically significant fundamentals. In theory, the equilibrium REER is the value of the REER predicted by the "sustainable" or "steady-state" values of the fundamentals (Montiel 2007). Hence, the fundamentals are filtered by the Hodrick-Prescott filter to remove cyclical components and estimate their sustainable components.

The actual, fitted, and equilibrium REER are presented in Figure 20.4a along with the estimated misalignment in Figure 20.4b. The fitted value tracks the actual REER very well, indicating a very good fit to data. As a result, the statistical error of the estimated equilibrium REER is likely to be negligible.

The estimated results show that, over the past decade, Peru's REER appears to have been broadly in line with the fundamentals, with the exception of mild misalignments in some years. In particular, the REER was:

- Mildly undervalued during 2004–07 by 2¼ percent on average. The REER depreciated about 4 percent during this period, while the equilibrium REER depreciated about 2 percent as the impact of large retrenchments in government consumption (relative to the United States) more than offset the impact of improvements in relative productivity (Table 20.3 and Figure 20.5).
- Consistent with the equilibrium REER in 2008.
- Mildly overvalued during 2009–13 by about 4¾ percent on average. This possibly occurred because the massive capital inflow, which caused a significant REER appreciation (14 percent), was driven not only by Peru's fundamentals, which justified only 9 percent equilibrium REER appreciation, but also by global push factors. However, a large part of the misalignment, which peaked in the first quarter of 2013 at 8¾ percent, was corrected in the

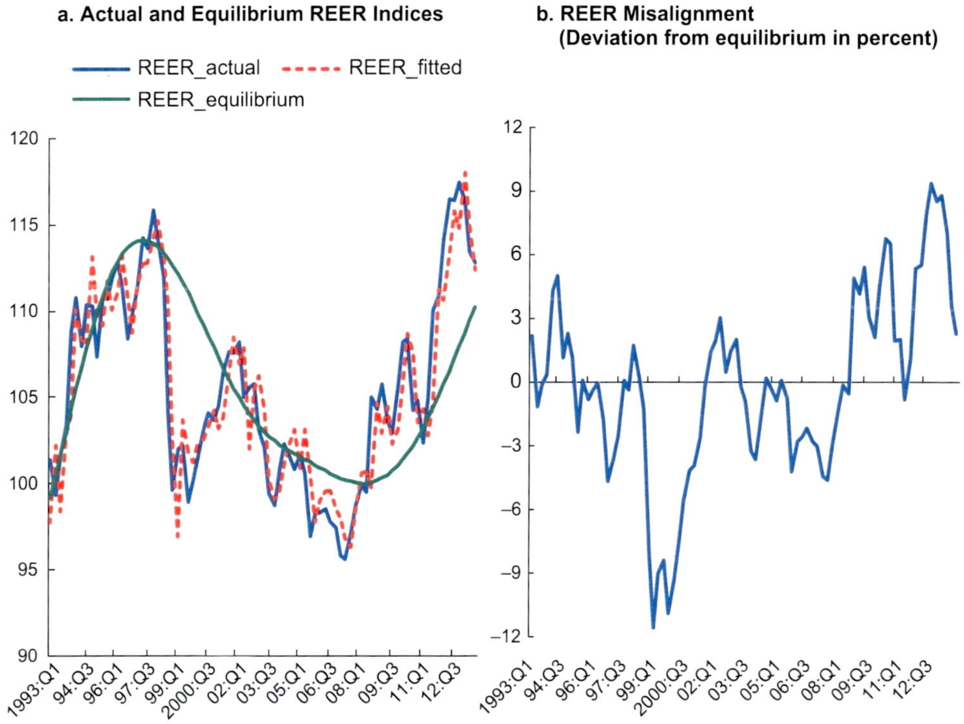


Sources: IMF, Information Notice System database; and author's calculations.
Note: REER = real effective exchange rate.

**Figure 20.4** Peru: Equilibrium Real Effective Exchange Rate

second half of 2013 as the nuevo sol depreciated following the Federal Reserve's announcement of monetary policy tapering (Table 20.3 and Figure 20.5).

It is important to note that this assessment does not necessarily have a normative value, as a REER close to its equilibrium level may still reflect distortions in the fundamentals (Phillips and others 2013). A normative assessment of the equilibrium REER requires making judgments on the appropriateness of the fundamentals from a welfare perspective, which is beyond the scope of this chapter.

## CONCLUSIONS

This chapter has conducted a cointegration analysis to test the hypothesis of the commodity currency and identify the drivers of Peru's equilibrium real exchange rate. The first part of the empirical analysis involved testing the "commodity currency" hypothesis on the nuevo sol. The results show that the real price index of Peru's export commodities does not have a statistically significant impact on the REER, suggesting that the nuevo sol is not a commodity currency. This appears puzzling for a country that relies heavily on metal commodities for its exports. The analysis showed empirically that large profit repatriation and the BCRP's active foreign exchange intervention could have mitigated the impact of commodity prices on the REER.

The second part of the empirical analysis identified the main drivers of the equilibrium REER from a pool of economic fundamentals that include the real price of commodities, Peru's productivity relative to that of trading partners, the Peruvian government's consumption relative to that of its trading partners, and the net foreign liability. The results show that only productivity and government consumption, both relative to that of trading partners, have statistically

**TABLE 20.3**

**Actual and Estimated Equilibrium Real Effective Exchange Rate**

| Year | Actual | Equilibrium | Misalignment |
|---|---|---|---|
| 2004 | 100.8 | 102.1 | −1.3 |
| 2005 | 100.0 | 101.4 | −1.4 |
| 2006 | 98.2 | 100.8 | −2.6 |
| 2007 | 96.5 | 100.2 | −3.7 |
| 2008 | 100.8 | 100.0 | 0.7 |
| 2009 | 104.1 | 100.4 | 3.7 |
| 2010 | 106.6 | 101.6 | 5.0 |
| 2011 | 105.5 | 103.5 | 1.9 |
| 2012 | 114.5 | 106.1 | 7.9 |
| 2013 | 115.0 | 109.1 | 5.4 |

Source: Author's calculations.

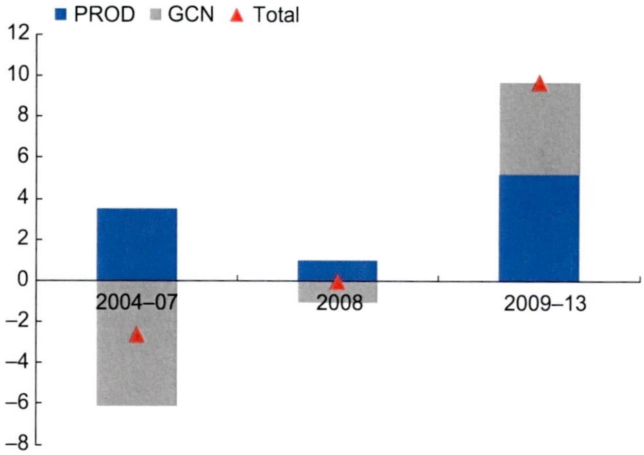


Source: Author's calculations.
Note: GCN = primary current public sector consumption; PROD = relative productivity.

**Figure 20.5** Contributions of Fundamentals to Changes in the Equilibrium Real Effective Exchange Rate

significant relationships with the REER, suggesting that the equilibrium REER is driven only by these two fundamentals.

The equilibrium REER was estimated based on the cointegrating relationship between the REER and the statistically significant fundamentals. The results show that Peru's REER is broadly in line with the notional equilibrium level predicted by the "sustainable" values of the fundamentals. The REER was mildly overvalued in the years following the 2008–09 global financial crisis, which is not surprising given the surge in capital inflows triggered mostly by easy monetary policy in advanced economies. But the recent depreciation of the REER following the Federal Reserve's announcement of unconventional monetary policy tapering in May 2013 appears to have mostly corrected the overvaluation. This does not necessarily imply that all is well with the level of the real exchange rate from a welfare perspective, as the equilibrium REER itself could be the result of distortions in the fundamentals (suboptimal levels of government consumption, for instance). Making such a normative assessment requires determining the optimal or "welfare maximizing" levels of the fundamentals, which is beyond the scope of this chapter.

The results of the analysis of the equilibrium REER need to be interpreted only as indicative, since a proper exchange rate assessment requires a panel data–based analysis, in line with the IMF's External Balance Assessment, to deal with technical problems associated with small sample size and potential structural breaks.

# ANNEX 20.1

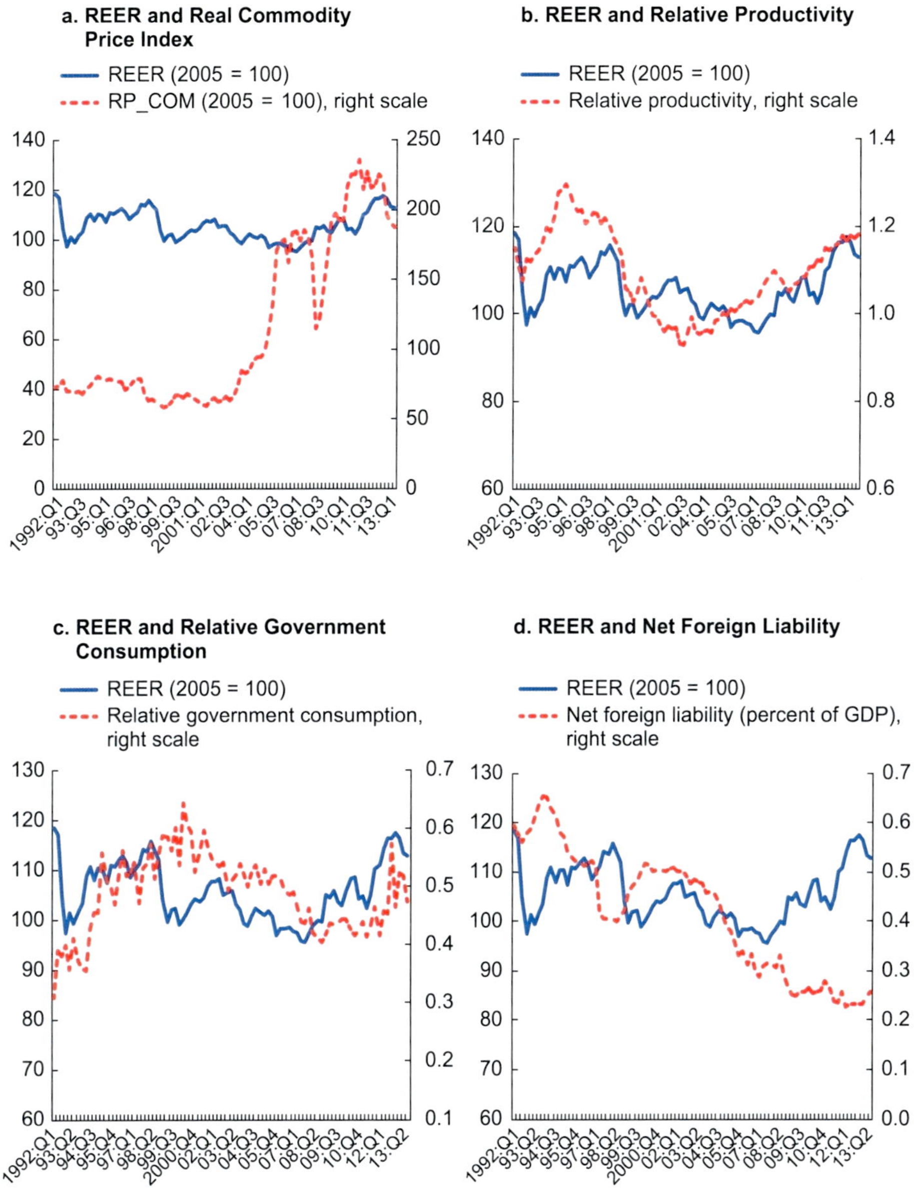


Sources: Central Reserve Bank of Peru; IMF, Information Notice System and World Economic Outlook databases; U.S. Bureau of Economic Analysis; and author's calculations.

Note: REER = real effective exchange rate.

**Annex Figure 20.1.1** Peru: The Real Effective Exchange Rate and the Fundamentals

**ANNEX TABLE 20.1.1**

## Unit Root Test Results

| Variable | | ADF *t*-Statistic | | | DF-GLS *t*-Statistic | | |
|---|---|---|---|---|---|---|---|
| | | None | Constant | Constant and Trend | Constant | Constant and Trend | Remarks |
| Real Effective Exchange Rate | Level | −0.24 | −2.59 | −2.44 | −1.36 | −1.71 | *I(1)* |
| | Difference (1st) | −7.51 | −7.46 | −7.53 | −7.01 | −7.58 | |
| Real Bilateral Exchange Rate | Level | −0.20 | −2.37 | −1.70 | −1.24 | −1.37 | *I(1)* |
| | Difference (1st) | −6.93 | −6.89 | −6.96 | −6.73 | −7.01 | |
| Real Price Index of Export Commodities | Level | 0.84 | −0.73 | −2.13 | −0.41 | −1.76 | *I(1)* |
| | Difference (1st) | −6.75 | −6.80 | −6.79 | −6.84 | −6.84 | |
| Real Price of Copper | Level | 0.57 | −0.89 | −2.54 | −0.65 | −1.87 | *I(1)* |
| | Difference (1st) | −7.01 | −7.02 | −7.01 | −7.06 | −7.07 | |
| Terms of Trade | Level | 0.06 | −1.78 | −2.41 | −1.78 | −2.19 | *I(1)* |
| | Difference (1st) | −6.38 | −6.34 | −6.29 | −6.21 | −6.24 | |
| Relative Productivity | Level | −0.57 | −0.93 | −0.54 | −0.91 | −0.73 | *I(1)* |
| | Difference (1st) | −8.01 | −7.98 | −7.99 | −2.50 | −6.19 | |
| Relative Government Consumption | Level | −1.05 | −2.44 | −2.51 | −0.48 | −1.11 | *I(1)* |
| | Difference (1st) | −15.08 | −15.03 | −17.08 | −1.67 | −3.46 | |
| Net Foreign Liability[1] | Level | −0.95 | −0.65 | −1.44 | 0.53 | −1.43 | *I(1)* |
| | Difference (1st) | −6.97 | −7.36 | −7.32 | −7.38 | −7.33 | |
| Net International Reserves[2] | Level | 2.50 | −4.46 | −4.35 | 0.94 | −1.03 | *I(1)* |
| | Difference (1st) | −6.34 | −6.81 | −7.14 | −4.53 | −5.60 | |
| Profit Repatriation[2] | Level | −0.58 | −1.50 | −2.38 | −0.90 | −2.51 | *I(1)* |
| | Difference (1st) | −12.16 | −12.12 | −12.10 | −11.93 | −11.63 | |
| *Critical Values* | | | | | | | |
| | *1%* | *−2.59* | *−3.51* | *−4.07* | *−2.59* | *−3.63* | |
| | *5%* | *−1.95* | *−2.90* | *−3.46* | *−1.95* | *−3.07* | |
| | *10%* | *−1.61* | *−2.59* | *−3.16* | *−1.61* | *−2.78* | |

Source: Author's calculations.
Note: The null hypothesis is unit root in all cases and is accepted for *t*-statistics greater than corresponding critical values. All variables are expressed in natural logarithmic form. ADF = augmented-Dickey-Fuller test; DF-GLS = Dickey-Fuller GLS test.
[1]As a ratio of previous period's total external trade in goods and services.
[2]In percent of GDP.

**ANNEX TABLE 20.1.2**

## Johansen Cointegration Tests between the Real Effective Exchange Rate and the Fundamentals

**(a) Cointegration between *LREER* and *LRP_COM***

*Unrestricted Cointegration Rank Test (Trace)*

| Hypothesized Number of CE(s) | Eigenvalue | Trace Statistic | Critical Value | Probability[1] |
|---|---|---|---|---|
| None* | 0.147 | 14.960 | 15.495 | 0.060 |
| At Most 1 | 0.015 | 1.304 | 3.841 | 0.254 |

*Unrestricted Cointegration Rank Test (Maximum Eigenvalue)*

| Hypothesized Number of CE(s) | Eigenvalue | Maximum-Eigen Statistic | Critical Value | Probability[1] |
|---|---|---|---|---|
| None* | 0.146826 | 13.6561 | 14.2646 | 0.0622 |
| At Most 1 | 0.015048 | 1.30398 | 3.841466 | 0.2535 |

**(b) Cointegration among *LREER, LRP_COM, LGCN,* and *LPROD_M***

*Unrestricted Cointegration Rank Test (Trace)*

| Hypothesized Number of CE(s) | Eigenvalue | Trace Statistic | Critical Value | Probability[1] |
|---|---|---|---|---|
| None* | 0.266075 | 46.37389 | 47.85613 | 0.0684 |
| At Most 1 | 0.120272 | 19.76994 | 29.79707 | 0.4385 |
| At Most 2 | 0.071095 | 8.749647 | 15.49471 | 0.3891 |
| At Most 3 | 0.027603 | 2.407229 | 3.841466 | 0.1208 |

**ANNEX TABLE 20.1.2** ***(Continued)***

## Johansen Cointegration Tests between the Real Effective Exchange Rate and the Fundamentals

*Unrestricted Cointegration Rank Test (Maximum Eigenvalue)*

| Hypothesized Number of CE(s) | Eigenvalue | Maximum-Eigen Statistic | Critical Value | Probability[1] |
|---|---|---|---|---|
| None* | 0.266075 | 26.60395 | 27.58434 | 0.0663 |
| At Most 1 | 0.120272 | 11.02029 | 21.13162 | 0.6453 |
| At Most 2 | 0.071095 | 6.342418 | 14.2646 | 0.5697 |
| At Most 3 | 0.027603 | 2.407229 | 3.841466 | 0.1208 |

**(c) Cointegration Restriction Tests**

| Null Hypothesis | Restricted Log-Likelihood | LR Statistic | Degrees of Freedom | Probability |
|---|---|---|---|---|
| Coefficient on *LRP_COM* is Zero | 650.3344 | 1.920112 | 1 | 0.1658 |
| Coefficient on *LPROD* is Zero ** | 649.2462 | 4.096616 | 1 | 0.0430 |
| Coefficient on *LGCN* is Zero*** | 645.7832 | 11.02264 | 1 | 0.0009 |

**(d) Cointegration among *LREER, LGCN,* and *LPROD_M***

| Hypothesized Number of CE(s) | Eigenvalue | Trace Statistic | Critical Value | Probability[1] |
|---|---|---|---|---|
| None *** | 0.236197 | 37.57606 | 29.79707 | 0.0052 |
| At Most 1 | 0.103207 | 14.40381 | 15.49471 | 0.0725 |
| At Most 2 ** | 0.056874 | 5.035806 | 3.841466 | 0.0248 |

*Unrestricted Cointegration Rank Test (Maximum Eigenvalue)*

| Hypothesized Number of CE(s) | Eigenvalue | Maximum-Eigen Statistic | Critical Value | Probability[1] |
|---|---|---|---|---|
| None ** | 0.236197 | 23.17225 | 21.13162 | 0.0255 |
| At Most 1 | 0.103207 | 9.368004 | 14.2646 | 0.2568 |
| At Most 2 ** | 0.056874 | 5.035806 | 3.841466 | 0.0248 |

**(e) *LREER, LRP_COM, LPROFIT,* and *LNIR_GDP***

*Unrestricted Cointegration Rank Test (Trace)*

| Hypothesized Number of CE(s) | Eigenvalue | Trace Statistic | Critical Value | Probability[1] |
|---|---|---|---|---|
| None ** | 0.3317 | 54.1336 | 47.8561 | 0.0115 |
| At Most 1 | 0.1118 | 20.2804 | 29.7971 | 0.4040 |
| At Most 2 | 0.0752 | 10.3257 | 15.4947 | 0.2565 |
| At Most 3* | 0.0438 | 3.7582 | 3.8415 | 0.0525 |

*Unrestricted Cointegration Rank Test (Maximum Eigenvalue)*

| Hypothesized Number of CE(s) | Eigenvalue | Maximum-Eigen Statistic | Critical Value | Probability[1] |
|---|---|---|---|---|
| None *** | 0.331698 | 33.85326 | 27.58434 | 0.0069 |
| At Most 1 | 0.111755 | 9.954619 | 21.13162 | 0.7489 |
| At Most 2 | 0.075207 | 6.567558 | 14.2646 | 0.5415 |
| At Most 3* | 0.043754 | 3.758178 | 3.841466 | 0.0525 |

**(f) *LNIR_GDP* and *LRP_COM***

*Unrestricted Cointegration Rank Test (Trace)*

| Hypothesized Number of CE(s) | Eigenvalue | Trace Statistic | Critical Value | Probability[1] |
|---|---|---|---|---|
| None *** | 0.247573 | 24.18814 | 15.49471 | 0.0019 |
| At Most 1 | 0.003496 | 0.294206 | 3.841466 | 0.5875 |

*Unrestricted Cointegration Rank Test (Maximum Eigenvalue)*

| Hypothesized Number of CE(s) | Eigenvalue | Maximum-Eigen Statistic | Critical Value | Probability[1] |
|---|---|---|---|---|
| None *** | 0.247573 | 23.89393 | 14.2646 | 0.0011 |
| At Most 1 | 0.003496 | 0.294206 | 3.841466 | 0.5875 |

**(g) *LPROFIT* and *LRP_COM***

*Unrestricted Cointegration Rank Test (Trace)*

| Hypothesized Number of CE(s) | Eigenvalue | Trace Statistic | Critical Value | Probability[1] |
|---|---|---|---|---|
| None ** | 0.155422 | 16.85422 | 15.49471 | 0.031 |
| At Most 1 | 0.031229 | 2.665094 | 3.841466 | 0.1026 |

*Unrestricted Cointegration Rank Test (Maximum Eigenvalue)*

| Hypothesized Number of CE(s) | Eigenvalue | Maximum-Eigen Statistic | Critical Value | Probability[1] |
|---|---|---|---|---|
| None* | 0.155422 | 14.18913 | 14.2646 | 0.0514 |
| At Most 1 | 0.031229 | 2.665094 | 3.841466 | 0.1026 |

Source: Author's calculations.

Note: * denotes rejection of the hypothesis at 10 percent level, ** denotes rejection of the hypothesis at 5 percent level, and *** denotes rejection of the hypothesis at 1 percent level. CE = cointegration equation.

[1]MacKinnon-Haug-Michelis (1999) *p*-values.

**ANNEX TABLE 20.1.3**

## Gregory-Hansen Test for Cointegration with Regime Shift: Annual Sample, 1970–2013

**(a) *LREER* and *LRP_COM***

| | Test Statistic | Shift Year | Asymptotic Critical Values 1% | 5% | 10% |
|---|---|---|---|---|---|
| ADF | −4.70* | 1987 | −5.47 | −4.95 | −4.68 |
| $Z_t$ | −4.75* | 1987 | −5.47 | −4.95 | −4.68 |
| $Z_a$ | −30.34 | 1987 | −57.17 | −47.04 | −41.85 |

**(b) *LREER* and All Fundamentals[1]**

| | Test Statistic | Shift Year | Asymptotic Critical Values 1% | 5% | 10% |
|---|---|---|---|---|---|
| ADF | −7.08*** | 1988 | −6.92 | −6.41 | −6.17 |
| $Z_t$ | −6.24* | 1989 | −6.92 | −6.41 | −6.17 |
| $Z_a$ | −30.34 | 1989 | −90.35 | −78.52 | −75.56 |

Source: Author's calculations.
Note: The null hypothesis is "no cointegration." * denotes null hypothesis rejected at 10 percent significance level, and *** denotes null hypothesis rejected at 1 percent significance level. ADF = augmented-Dickey-Fuller test.
[1]Includes *LRP_COM, LPROD, LGCN,* and *LNFL.*

**ANNEX TABLE 20.1.4**

## Estimating Nonlinear Cointegration Using the Fully Modified Ordinary Least Squares Method: Annual Sample, 1970–2013

**(a) *LREER* and *LRP_COM***

$LREER = a(1) * LRP\_COM + a(2) * LRP\_COM \times RS1987 + a(3)$

| Coefficient[1] | Coefficient | Standard Error | Probability |
|---|---|---|---|
| *a(1)* | −0.26 | 0.12 | 0.0349 |
| *a(2)* | 0.27 | 0.02 | 0.0000 |
| *a(3)* | 4.59 | 0.54 | 0.0000 |

**(b) *LREER* and All Fundamentals**

$$LREER = b(1)*LRP\_COM + b(2) * LRP\_COM \times RS1988 + b(3) * LGCN + b(4) * LGCN \times RS1988 + b(5) * LPROD$$
$$+ b(6) * LPROD \times RS1988 + b(7) * LNFL + b(8) * TRADE\_OPEN + b(9)$$

| Variable[2] | Coefficient | Standard Error | Probability |
|---|---|---|---|
| *b(1)* | −0.16 | 0.01 | 0.0000 |
| *b(2)* | 0.19 | 0.00 | 0.0000 |
| *b(3)* | −0.44 | 0.03 | 0.0000 |
| *b(4)* | 0.63 | 0.04 | 0.0000 |
| *b(5)* | −0.76 | 0.04 | 0.0000 |
| *b(6)* | 0.95 | 0.04 | 0.0000 |
| *b(7)*[3] | −0.06 | 0.01 | 0.0000 |
| *b(8)*[3,4] | 0.52 | 0.01 | 0.0000 |
| *b(9)* | 4.01 | 0.04 | 0.0000 |

**(c) Wald Coefficient Restriction Tests**

| Null Hypothesis | Value | *t*-Statistic | Probability |
|---|---|---|---|
| $a(1) + a(2) = 0$ | 0.01 | 0.11 | 0.9100 |
| $b(1) + b(2) = 0$ | 0.03 | 2.95 | 0.0057 |
| $b(3) + b(4) = 0$ | 0.19 | 9.26 | 0.0000 |
| $b(5) + b(6) = 0$ | 0.19 | 8.62 | 0.0000 |

Source: Author's calculations.
[1]*RS1987* refers to a dummy for regime shift in 1987, identified by the Gregory-Hansen test (Annex Table 20.1.3a).
[2]*RS1988* refers to a dummy for regime shift in 1988, identified by the Gregory-Hansen test (Annex Table 20.1.3b).
[3]LNFL and *TRADE_OPEN* (dummy for trade openness) show no change in the sign of their coefficients when interacted with *RS1988*. As a result, they are included without interactions.
[4]*TRADE_OPEN* was not included in the cointegration test in Annex Table 20.1.3b, because the Gregory-Hansen test does not allow for more than four right-side variables and dummy variables.

**ANNEX TABLE 20.1.5**

## Empirical Evidence on Commodity Currency

| Authors (year) | Countries | Sample | Method | Elasticity on Commodity Prices | Definition of Commodity Prices |
|---|---|---|---|---|---|
| Chen and Rogoff (2003) | Australia, Canada, New Zealand | Quarterly: year varies | Time series cointegration | Australia (0.4), Canada (0.4), and New Zealand (0.6) | Real commodity prices |
| Cashin, Cespedes, and Sahay (2004) | 58 commodity-exporting countries, including Peru | Monthly: 1980–2002 | Time series cointegration | Median = 0.4; terms of trade not important for Peru | Real commodity prices |
| Ferreyra and Salas (2006) | Peru | Quarterly: 1980–2005 | Time series cointegration | 0.3 | Terms of trade |
| Montiel (2007) | Argentina, Bolivia, Brazil, Chile, Paraguay, Uruguay | Annual: 1969–2005 | Time series cointegration | Terms of trade important only for Argentina (1.7), Bolivia (0.6), and Uruguay(0.6) | Terms of trade |
| Iossifov and Loukoianova (2007) | Ghana | Quarterly: 1984–2006 | Time series cointegration | 0.4 | Real commodity prices |
| Astorga (2012) | Argentina, Brazil, Chile, Colombia, Mexico, Venezuela | Annual: 1900–2000 | Time series cointegration | Argentina (0.4), Brazil (0.2), Chile (0.1), Colombia (0.4), Mexico (not significant), Venezuela (0.1) | Terms of trade |
| Coudert, Couharde, and Mignon (2011) | 52 commodity exporters | Annual: 1980–2007 | Panel cointegration | 0.4 | Real commodity prices |
| Bodart, Cabdelon, and Carpantier (2012) | 42 commodity-dependent countries | Monthly: 1980–2009 | Panel cointegration | 0.2 | Real commodity prices |
| Ricci, Milesi-Ferretti, and Lee (2013) | 48 industrial and emerging countries | Annual: 1980–2004 | Panel cointegration | Advanced countries (0.8) | |
| Emerging market countries (0.5) | Real commodity prices | | | | |
| Phillips and others (2013) | 40 advanced and emerging market countries | Annual: 1990–2010 | Panel ordinary least squares (fixed effect) | 0.1 | Real commodity prices |

## REFERENCES


Adler, Gustavo, and Nicolas E. Magud. 2013. "Four Decades of Terms-of-Trade Booms: Saving-Investment Patterns and a New Metric of Income Windfall." Working Paper 13/103, International Monetary Fund, Washington, DC.

Armas, Adrian, Paul Castillo, and Marco Vega. 2014. "Inflation Targeting and Quantitative Tightening: Effects of Reserve Requirements in Peru." Working Paper 2014-003, Central Reserve Bank of Peru, Lima.

Armas, Adrian, and Francisco Grippa. 2005. "Targeting Inflation in a Dollarized Economy: The Peruvian Experience." IDB Working Paper 538, Inter-American Development Bank, Washington, DC.

Astorga, Pablo. 2012. "Mean Reversion in Long-Horizon Real Exchange Rates: Evidence from Latin America." *Journal of International Money and Finance* 31: 1529–550.

Balassa, Bela. 1964. "The Purchasing Parity Doctrine: A Reappraisal." *Journal of Political Economics* 72 (6): 584–96.

Bodart, V., B. Cabdelon, and J. F. Carpantier. 2012. "Real Exchange Rates in Commodity Producing Countries: A Reappraisal." *Journal of International Money and Finance* 31: 1485–502.

Cashin, Paul, Luis Felipe Cespedes, and Ratna Sahay. 2004. "Commodity Currencies and the Real Exchange Rate." *Journal of Development Economics* 75 (1): 239–68.

Chen, Yu-chin, and Kenneth S. Rogoff. 2003. "Commodity Currencies." *Journal of International Economics* 60 (1) Special Issue: 133–60.

Coudert, Virginie, Cecile Couharde, and Valerie Mignon. 2011. "Does Euro or Dollar Pegging Impact the Real Exchange Rate? The Case of Oil and Commodity Currencies." *World Economy* 34 (9): 1557–592.

Engel, Charles. 2000. "Long-run PPP May Not Hold After All." *Journal of International Economics* 57: 243–73.

Ferreyra, Jesus, and Jorge Salas. 2006. "Tipo de cambio real de equilibrio en el Peru: modelos BEER y construccion de bandas de confianza." BCRP Working Paper Series 2006-006, Central Reserve Bank of Peru, Lima.

Froot, Kenneth, and Kenneth Rogoff. 1995. "Perspectives on PPP and Long-run Real Exchange Rates." In *The Handbook of International Economics*, edited by Gene Grossman and Kenneth Rogoff. Amsterdam: North-Holland.

Gregory, Allan W., and Bruce E. Hansen. 1996. "Residual-Based Tests for Cointegration in Models with Regime Shifts." *Journal of Econometrics* 70: 99–126.

Iossifov, Plamen, and Elena Loukoianova. 2007. "Estimation of a Behavioral Equilibrium Exchange Rate Model for Ghana." Working Paper 07/155, International Monetary Fund, Washington, DC.

MacKinnon, James G., Alfred A. Haug, and Leo Michelis. 1999. "Numerical Distribution Functions of Likelihood Ratio Tests for Cointegration." *Journal of Applied Econometrics* 14: 563–77.

Meese, Richard A., and Kenneth Rogoff. 1983. "Empirical Exchange Rate Models of the Seventies: Do They Fit Out of Sample." *Journal of International Economics* 14: 3–24.

Montiel, Peter J. 2007. "Equilibrium Real Exchange Rates, Misalignment and Competitiveness in the Southern Cone." ECLAC Macroeconomic Development Series 62, Economic Commission on Latin America and the Caribbean, Santiago.

Phillips, Steven, Luis Catão, Luca Ricci, Rudolfs Bems, Mitali Das, Julian Di Giovanni, D. Filiz Unsal, Marola Castillo, Jungjin Lee, Jair Rodriguez, and Mauricio Vargas Ricci. 2013. "The External Balance Assessment (EBA) Methodology." Working Paper 13/272, International Monetary Fund, Washington, DC.

Ricci, Luca Antonio, Gian Maria Milesi-Ferretti, and Jaewoo Lee. 2013. "Real Exchange Rates and Fundamentals: a Cross-Country Perspective." *Journal of Money, Credit and Banking* 45 (5): 845–65.

Rogoff, Kenneth. 1996. "The Purchasing Power Parity Puzzle." *Journal of Economic Literature* 34: 647–68.

Rossini, Renzo, Adrian Armas, and Zenon Quispe. 2014. "Global Policy Spillovers and Peru's Monetary Policy: Inflation Targeting, Foreign Exchange Intervention and Reserve Requirements." BIS Paper No. 78, Bank for International Settlements, Basel.

Samuelson, Paul. 1964. "A Theoretical Note on Trade Problems." *Review of Economics and Statistics* 46 (12): 145–54.

Tashu, Melesse. 2014. "Motives and Effectiveness of Forex Interventions: Evidence from Peru." Working Paper 14/7, International Monetary Fund, Washington, DC.

CHAPTER 21

# Motives and Effectiveness of Foreign Exchange Interventions: Evidence from Peru

MELESSE TASHU

*This chapter empirically assesses the motives and effectiveness of foreign exchange intervention in Peru. While the Central Reserve Bank of Peru states that its foreign exchange interventions are directed only toward containing excessive volatility, the results of this chapter show that, in practice, the interventions seem to have been aimed at "leaning against the wind" as well. The results also show that foreign exchange sales, but not purchases, react to volatility, indicating asymmetry in the central bank's reactions to episodes of appreciation and depreciation pressures. Similarly, the chapter documents evidence of assymetry in the effectiveness of the foreign exchange interventions.*

Capital flows to Peru have increased significantly in recent years, reflecting both push factors (easy money in advanced economies) and pull factors (strong fundamentals of the Peruvian economy). While a large share of these flows is foreign direct investment, the growing size and volatility of portfolio and short-term flows is a source of concern, as these often lead to the buildup of risks and vulnerabilities in the financial system.

While using prudential measures to contain the buildup of financial and macroeconomic risks, the Central Reserve Bank of Peru (*Banco Central de Reserva del Perú* [BCRP]) relies on a daily basis on foreign exchange intervention to safeguard the foreign exchange market against the pressures from large and volatile capital flows. In 2013 alone, the BCRP intervened with foreign exchange purchases of US$5.2 billion through April and with foreign exchange sales of a similar amount between July and December in the spot market, reflecting the volatility of capital flows. The BCRP intervened with a stated objective of containing volatility in the foreign exchange market. The pattern of its intervention, however, suggests that "leaning against the wind"—that is, limiting the pace of appreciations and depreciations—could also be another objective of the intervention.

This chapter aims to assess empirically the motives and effectiveness of foreign exchange interventions in Peru. Effectiveness is assessed not only against officially stated objectives but also against other motives empirically revealed by the data. In this regard, the chapter estimates a reaction function of the BCRP in order to identify the revealed motives of its interventions and to address the simultaneity problem between foreign exchange interventions and exchange rates. In doing so, the chapter also tests if there is asymmetry in the BCRP's responses to appreciation and depreciation pressures and if there is asymmetry in the effectiveness of interventions between foreign exchange purchases and sales.

The chapter employs an innovative empirical approach to address the potential simultaneity problem between foreign exchange intervention and exchange rate movements. In particular, the chapter devises instrumental variables based on information on the specific timing of foreign exchange interventions by the BCRP and the intradaily exchange rate data. Although the BCRP's foreign exchange intervention is not preannounced, intervention decisions are made every day by a committee that meets between 11:30 a.m. and 1:00 p.m. Hence, the chapter uses exchange rate movements before 11:30 a.m. to estimate the BCRP's reaction function and uses the predicted values of the likelihood of foreign exchange interventions from the estimated reaction function as instruments for foreign exchange intervention in the exchange rate equations. The dependent variables of the exchange rate equations in the second-stage regression are changes in the level and volatility of the exchange rate between the afternoon and morning trading sessions.

The chapter first examines capital flows and foreign exchange interventions in Peru, followed by a discussion of methodological issues. The data and estimation results are then presented along with the conclusions drawn from them.

## CAPITAL FLOWS AND FOREIGN EXCHANGE INTERVENTIONS

Peru's significant amount of net capital flows averaged about 8 percent of GDP a year from 2010–13, well above the regional average (about 5 percent of GDP),[1] and above Peru's own average of about 6 percent over the past decade. Gross inflows amounted to about 9½ percent of GDP a year during 2010–13 (Figure 21.1). This surge in capital flows reflects both push and pull factors. In advanced economies, interest rates hit bottom and monetary aggregates jumped significantly following the global financial crisis, pushing a glut of financial flows to emerging market economies.[2] Meanwhile, Peru has become an increasingly attractive destination for capital flows, with its record of high economic growth (about 6½ percent a year during the past decade), strong terms of trade, and sound monetary and fiscal policies.

The increase and volatility of portfolio and short-term capital flows to Peru have raised concerns even though a large share of the flows is foreign direct investment. Despite the authorities' efforts to encourage capital outflows to ease appreciation pressures (including by increasing the limits on external investment by pension fund managers), net portfolio inflows have continued to rise as Peruvian firms' demand for external financing has increased to take advantage of low global interest rates. External bond issuance by Peruvian firms doubled to US$6.5 billion in 2013 (3.2 percent of GDP) from US$3 billion in 2012 (1.5 percent of GDP).

Empirical evidence shows that surges in capital inflows are associated with excessive expansion of credit, asset price bubbles, real exchange rate appreciation, and current account deteriorations, which are likely to lead ultimately to financial and economic crisis (Cardarelli, Elekdag, and Kose 2010; Furceri, Guichard, and Rusticelli 2012; Reinhart and Reinhart 2008). While avoiding capital control measures, the Peruvian authorities implemented preventive measures, including accumulating international reserves, strengthening macroprudential policies, and encouraging capital outflows to avoid the buildup of vulnerabilities associated with capital flows. Consequently, early signs of overheating—including credit growth of over 20 percent and significant appreciation of stock and housing prices in 2011—moderated toward the end of 2012 despite the continuation of capital inflows.

On a daily basis, however, the authorities use foreign exchange intervention to safeguard the foreign exchange market and the financial system from the impact of high and volatile capital flows. Peru's foreign exchange market is an interbank market based primarily on spot transactions. The derivatives market is not well developed and is limited to very small forwards and options transactions. Trading in the spot market is also thin. Consequently, modest changes in capital flows can generate volatilities in the foreign exchange market (Figure 21.2), with potential effects on balance sheets and the buildup of vulnerabilities in the financial system due to relatively

[1]The average net capital flows to Brazil, Chile, Colombia, Mexico, and Uruguay.

[2]The Federal Reserve's tapering of purchase of securities starting in the second half of 2013 has already slowed the pace of capital flows to emerging market economies, including Peru.

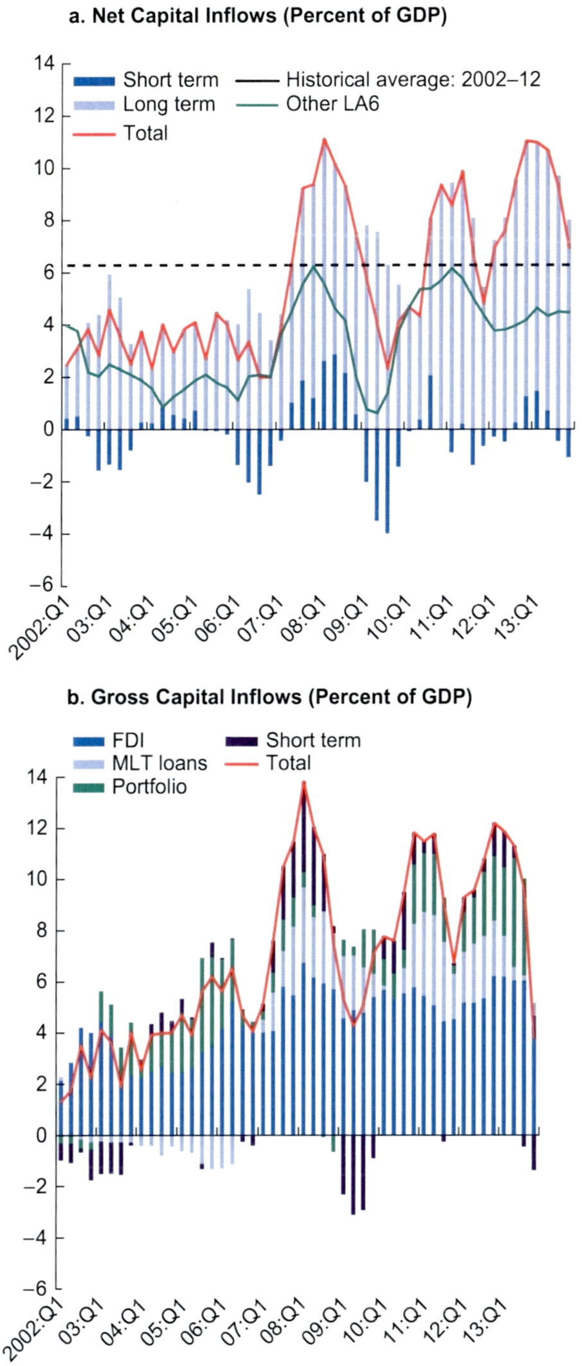


Sources: Central Reserve Bank of Peru; Haver Analytics; and author's estimates.
Note: FDI = foreign direct investment; LA6 = Brazil, Chile, Colombia, Mexico, Peru, and Uruguay; MLT = medium and long term.

**Figure 21.1** Capital Flows, Four-Quarter Moving Sum

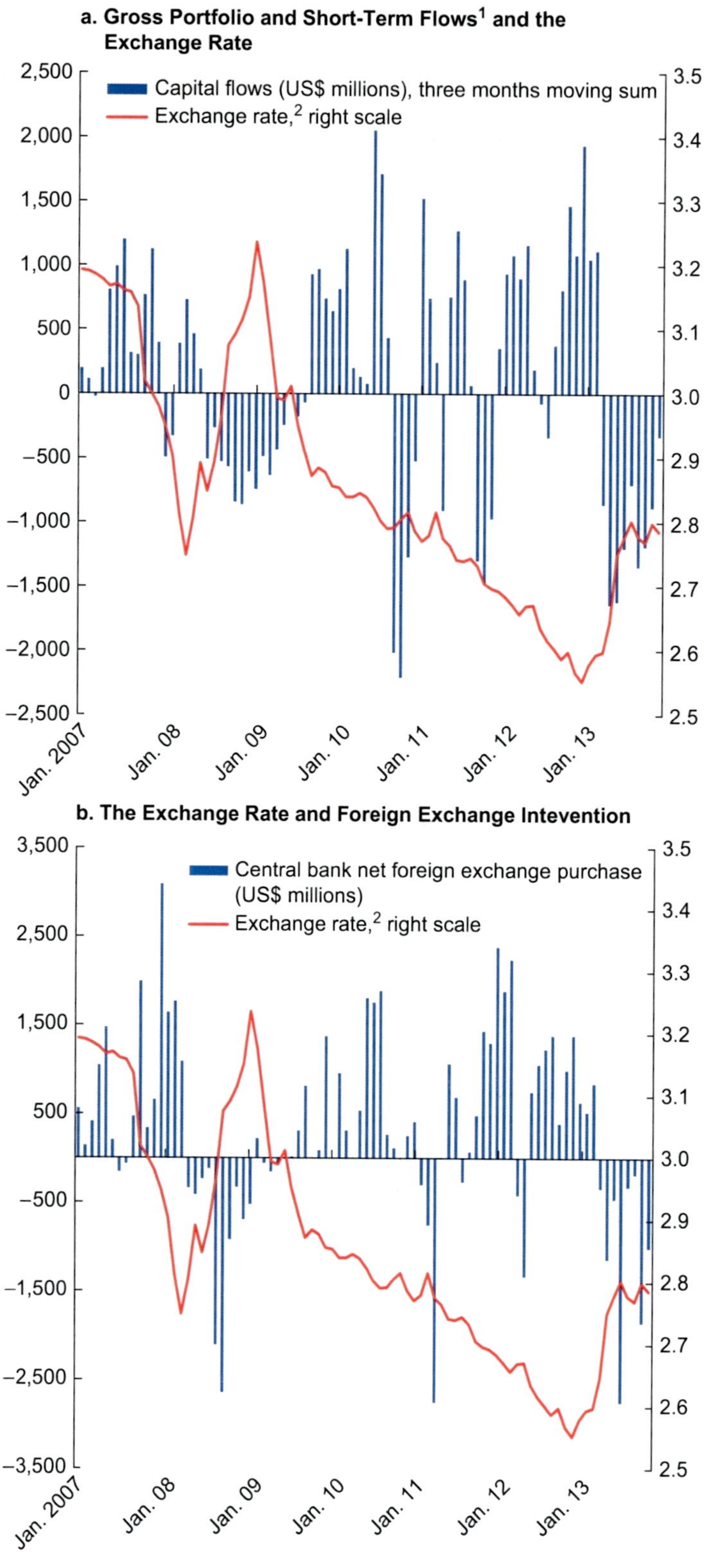


Sources: Central Reserve Bank of Peru; Haver Analytics; and IMF staff estimates.

[1] Because monthly balance of payments data are not available, monthly portfolio flows are proxied by EFBR bond and equity flows, and short-term flows are constructed as the change in the short-term external liability position of commercial banks.

[2] Exchange rate is nuevos soles/U.S. dollars.

**Figure 21.2** Capital Flows, Exchange Rate, and Foreign Exchange Intervention high financial dollarization.[3] As a result, the BCRP tries to reduce exchange rate volatility by intervening in the foreign exchange market.

Interventions are conducted mainly in the spot market and occasionally by making swaps and sales of dollar-indexed securities (equivalent to selling foreign exchange forward) (Rossini, Quispe, and Rodriguez 2013; Rossini, Quispe, and Serrano 2013). By and large, foreign exchange interventions by the BCRP are not preannounced.[4] Foreign exchange interventions during recent episodes of capital inflows have led to reserve accumulation. Net international reserves stood at about US$65.7 billion (about 32½ percent of GDP) as of end-2013. These interventions were mostly sterilized through issuance of BCRP securities, Treasury deposits, and reserve requirements. BCRP securities denominated in local currency are sold to financial institutions and have a return of about 4 percent. (In addition, a 4 percent fee is charged on transfers of the securities to nonfinancial entities to ensure that they do not attract further capital inflows from nonresidents.) The BCRP has also sold foreign exchange during times of depreciation pressures such as following the Lehman Brothers crisis, the euro zone crisis, and more recently following the Federal Reserve's announcement of unconventional monetary policy tapering. Foreign exchange sales are also sterilized (local currency liquidity injected) mainly through swaps and repos.

Foreign exchange interventions absorb a significant amount of foreign exchange pressures. A Foreign Exchange Market Pressure Index[5] is used to break down by the pressures on the exchange rate and the net international reservess (Figure 21.3). The Foreign Exchange Market Pressure Index shows that foreign exchange interventions absorb a significant share of the pressure from capital flows, although the authorities continue to allow for increasing exchange rate flexibility. While the increases in foreign exchange reserves during periods of high capital inflows can in principle be the result of a reserve buildup, recent foreign exchange interventions in Peru seem to have been motivated mainly toward easing the pressure on the exchange rate. For instance, the net international reserves was already high at end-2011, and foreign exchange interventions since then could have most likely been conducted to ease foreign exchange pressures.

Statistical evidence suggests that containing volatility may not be the only objective of foreign exchange intervention in Peru. The BCRP's foreign exchange intervention prior to May 2013 was concentrated on foreign exchange purchases, and after May 2013 on foreign exchange sales, indicating that foreign exchange interventions might be aimed at more than just containing volatility. In other words, the pattern of the BCRP's intervention may indicate attempts to lean against the wind or limit the rate of appreciations or depreciations. Empirical studies have also found evidence that the deviation of the exchange rate from its trend induces foreign exchange intervention in Peru (Gonzalez 2009; Humala and Rodriguez 2009). Furthermore, contrary to the stated objective, the BCRP's intervention during September 2012–April 2013 appears to have increased volatility.

---

[3]Despite significant progress in reducing financial dollarization over the past decade, credit and deposit dollarization remain high at around 40 percent.

[4]The exception is between September 2012 and April 2013, when the BCRP purchased foreign exchange almost on a daily basis after announcing in August 2012 that it would purchase more stable amounts of foreign exchange even during days of depreciating pressures, while keeping the amounts of intervention unannounced. The decision was taken due to concerns of predictable appreciating pressure on the nuevo sol and the strategy sought to generate higher exchange rate volatility (BCRP 2012; Rossini, Quispe, and Serrano 2013).

[5]The index tries to measure exchange rate and reserve accumulation pressures. It is calculated as the sum of the percentage change in the exchange rate and the percentage change in reserves, following the empirical literature (Aizenman and Hutchison 2012; Cardarelli, Elekdag, and Kose 2010). The exchange rate is defined, for this purpose, in terms of U.S. dollars per nuevos soles so that the pressure on the exchange rate has the same sign as the pressure on foreign exchange reserves.

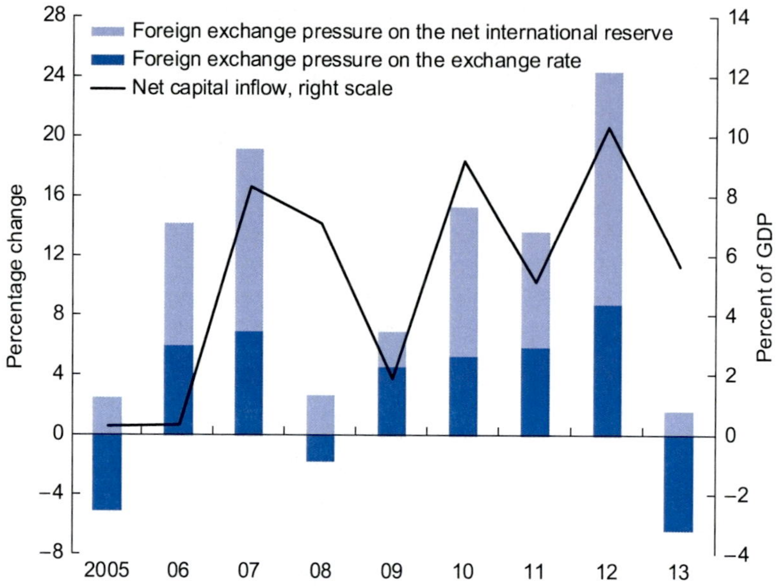


Sources: Central Reserve Bank of Peru; and IMF staff estimates.

**Figure 21.3** Capital Flows, Exchange Rate, and Foreign Exchange Intervention

This chapter investigates the motives and effectiveness of foreign exchange interventions in Peru. To achieve these goals, the chapter proceeds in two steps. First, the BCRP's reaction functions are estimated separately for foreign exchange purchases and sales to shed light on the motives of interventions, which may vary between episodes of appreciations and depreciations. Second, the likelihoods of interventions, predicted from the first-stage regressions, are used as instrumental variables for foreign exchange interventions (to overcome potential simultaneity biases) in the exchange rate equations.

## METHODOLOGY

The literature identifies two channels through which a sterilized intervention can affect the level of the exchange rate: the portfolio balance and signaling effects.[6] According to the portfolio balance approach, sterilized intervention alters the composition of agents' portfolios as central banks buy/sell domestic assets in their sterilization effort, and thereby the relative prices of domestic- and foreign currency–denominated assets, assuming that these assets are imperfect substitutes in investors' portfolios (Dominguez and Frankel 1993; Sarno and Taylor 2001). Alternatively, foreign exchange intervention could work through the signaling channel if central bank interventions are perceived by private agents as a signal for a future policy stance or as a means of disseminating information about exchange rate fundamentals, assuming the central bank has superior information (Dominguez and Frankel 1993; Kearns and Rigobon 2005; Sarno and Taylor 2001).

Efforts to empirically test the impact of foreign exchange interventions on the exchange rate are often hampered by potential simultaneity biases. While intervention could affect the exchange

[6] Dominguez (2003, 2006) also shows how intervention can affect the intradaily exchange rate returns through a third channel, the microstructure channel. This approach shows how heterogeneity among traders, based on their differences in understanding and interpreting information revealed through central bank information, can affect the short-term value and volatility of the exchange rate.

rate, the decision to intervene is not independent of movements in the exchange rate (Disyatat and Galati 2007; Dominguez and Frankel 1993; Galati, Melick, and Micu 2005; Kearns and Rigobon 2005). Even after the central bank has decided to intervene, the timing and amount of the intervention depends on the reaction of the exchange rate to the initial intervention (Disyatat and Galati 2007; Kearns and Rigobon 2005).

A common solution to the simultaneity problem is the use of lagged intervention variables (Baillie and Osterberg 1997; Broto 2012; Dominguez and Frankel 1993; Guimaraes and Karacadag 2004). But this method may underestimate the true impact of interventions, as part of the impact may be reflected through lagged values of the dependent variables, which are often included among the explanatory variables (Galati, Melick, and Micu 2005). Furthermore, central banks often intervene with the aim of influencing not only future movements but also contemporaneous movements of the exchange rate.

Another approach employed in recent empirical studies is event study–style regressions. This method attempts to address the simultaneity problem by precisely identifying the time of intervention and relating it to the exchange rate returns using very high-frequency intradaily data (Dominguez 2003, 2006).[7] However, this method may not resolve the simultaneity problem if central banks base their intervention decisions on intradaily exchange rate movements or volatility (Dominguez 2003). That said, there is evidence that central banks are more likely to base their intervention decisions on longer-term objectives, although the size of the interventions may be determined by market reactions to the initial interventions (Neely 2001).[8] Unfortunately, this method demands very high-frequency (minute-by-minute) data on exchange rates and interventions, which are not publicly available for Peru.

A third approach to addressing the simultaneity bias is by using an instrumental variable method, which involves estimating a central bank's reaction function and using predicted values of intervention from the estimated reaction function as an instrument for intervention in the exchange rate equation (Adler and Tovar 2011; Disyatat and Galati 2007; Galati, Melick, and Micu 2005; Kearns and Rigobon 2005). The common practice is to use lagged values of the exchange rate in an ordinary least squares estimation of the central bank's reaction function. The exclusion of the contemporaneous values of the exchange rate could, however, create an omitted variable bias, although the bias could be trivial because there is no empirical evidence of persistence in exchange rate moments (Galati, Melick, and Micu 2005).[9]

This chapter employs an instrumental variable estimation method to assess the effectiveness of foreign exchange intervention in Peru. However, unlike the common practice of using lagged exchange rates in the reaction functions, the chapter uses same-day exchange rates, taking advantage of intradaily exchange rate data availability and the approximate timing of foreign exchange interventions. The foreign exchange market in Peru operates between 9:00 a.m. and 1:30 p.m. local time, and decisions on foreign exchange interventions are made every day by a committee that meets between 11:30 a.m. and 1:00 p.m. (Lahura and Vega 2013), indicating that interventions are conducted after 11:30 a.m.[10] On the other hand, intradaily exchange rate data are

[7] Dominguez (2003, 2006) runs regressions of five-minute exchange rate returns (mean and volatility) on (time-stamped to the nearest five-minute) signed intervention and other announcement dummy variables.

[8] Two-thirds of 22 central banks surveyed by Neely (2001) indicated that they intervened in the foreign exchange market to align the exchange rate to "fundamental values," and about 90 percent of them indicated that the purpose of their intervention was to resist short-term trends. But 95 percent of the respondents reported that market reactions to their initial intervention sometimes or always affected the size of the intervention.

[9] Consequently, the correlation between the included lagged moments and the omitted contemporaneous moments is likely to be negligible.

[10] The decision to intervene in the afternoon may also be motivated by the fact that most foreign exchange dealers aim to close their positions by the end of the trading day, leading to an increased flow of transactions during the closing hours. The author thanks Marco Ortiz and Fernando Perez Forero of the BCRP for pointing this out.

publicly available for three specific points in time: market opening (around 9:00 a.m.), 11:00 a.m., and market closing (1:30 p.m.). The chapter uses exchange rate movements during the morning session to estimate the BCRP's reaction function. Predicted values of the likelihoods of foreign exchange interventions from the BCRP's reaction function are then used as instruments for foreign exchange interventions in the regressions for changes in the exchange rate (both the level and volatility) between the afternoon and morning sessions.

The assumption is that the BCRP makes intervention decisions after observing the behavior of the exchange rate during the morning trading session. This method minimizes the possibility of omitted variable bias in the second stage of the regressions. Furthermore, interventions are used in the form of dummy variables, since the daily dollar amounts of interventions may depend on market reactions to the initial interventions and hence may create a simultaneity bias. The model also assumes that intervention decisions by the central bank are completely unanticipated by the market; otherwise, expectations for intervention could affect the behavior of the exchange rate in the morning trading session and create simultaneity bias. This assumption is consistent with the BCRP's discretionary intervention strategy, except during September 2012–April 2013.

In particular, the BCRP is assumed to intervene in the foreign exchange market when the level and volatility of the exchange rate deviate from implicit target ranges following the standard literature (Disyatat and Galati 2007; Galati, Melick, and Micu 2005; Sarno and Taylor 2001).[11] The likelihood of the central bank's intervention depends on the extent of the deviations. This can be represented by the following equation:

$$INT_t = \alpha_0 + \alpha_1\left(s_t - s_t^*\right) + \alpha_2\left(\sigma_{S_t} - \sigma_{S_t}^*\right) + \varepsilon_t, \quad (21.1)$$

where *INT* is the dummy for intervention (1 when the BCRP intervenes, 0 otherwise), $st$ and $s_t^*$ are logs of the actual and target levels of the nuevo sol/U.S. dollar exchange rate, $\sigma s$ and $\sigma_S^*$ are the actual and target volatility of the exchange rate, $\varepsilon$ is the random error term, and $t$ is the time index.

For each period, the BCRP is assumed to set its target ranges for the level and volatility of the exchange rate based on historical averages. The main results of this chapter are obtained based on exchange rate level and volatility targets estimated by a one-year simple moving average, but the exercise is replicated with a six-month simple moving average and one-year rolling Hodrick-Prescott filtered average targets (for the level of exchange rate only) to test if the results are robust to changes in the time length and method of averaging.

Equation (21.1) is estimated using a probit model for foreign exchange purchases and sales separately to capture the potential asymmetry in the BCRP's reactions to episodes of appreciations and depreciations.[12] For foreign exchange sales, *INT* is a dummy variable with 1 on days of foreign exchange sales and 0 otherwise. Similarly, for the equation for foreign exchange purchases, *INT* equals 1 on days of foreign exchange purchases and 0 otherwise. There is empirical evidence on asymmetry of central bank intervention in the foreign exchange market (Lahura and Vega 2013; Pontines and Rajan 2011; Ramachandran and Srinivasan 2007). For instance, volatility is likely to be more of a concern and a reason for intervention during episodes of depreciations than

[11] International reserve accumulation could be another potential motive for foreign exchange purchases, but this is not included in our model because the central bank is less likely to have a daily target for international reserves. Furthermore, since international reserves were already high in Peru, it is less likely to be a principal motive for foreign exchange intervention during the sample period of this study, in particular in 2012 and 2013.

[12] A single equation for intervention, defined as a multinomial dummy of 1 for foreign exchange purchases, 0 for no intervention, and −1 for foreign exchange sales, is also estimated using a multinomial logistic regression as a robustness exercise for the test of asymmetry in the central bank's reaction to episodes of appreciation and depreciation (results are discussed later in the chapter).

during episodes of appreciations, as the former are often associated with anxiety in the financial market. On the other hand, motives for intervention during episodes of appreciation are likely to be reserve accumulation and leaning against the wind to prevent real exchange rate appreciations and current account deficit deterioration. The fact that central banks of developing countries have a limit on foreign exchange sales (due to the zero lower bound on foreign exchange reserves), but can purchase foreign exchange without limit (at least in principle), can be another source of asymmetric central bank intervention.[13]

The intervention rules are defined as follows:

- *The BCRP intervenes to prevent excessive appreciations and depreciations.* The BCRP's tolerable range is assumed to be the target exchange rate, estimated by historical average, plus or minus one standard deviation. The BCRP intervenes to prevent excessive appreciations if the exchange rate during the morning trading session[14] falls below the lower bound of its tolerable range (defined here as the historical average minus one standard deviation). It also intervenes to avoid excessive depreciations if the exchange rate during the morning trading session exceeds the upper bound of its tolerable range (defined here as the historical average plus one standard deviation).[15]

  Consequently, the exchange rate gap (deviation) is derived as follows:

$$(s_t - s_t^*) = \begin{cases} (s_t - s_t^{*u})\, \textit{if the exchange rate rises above the upper bound} \\ (s_t^{*l} - s_t)\, \textit{if the exchange rate falls below the lower bound} \end{cases}$$

  where $\alpha_1$ is expected to be positive in both cases, since the likelihood of intervention increases with the increasing exchange rate gap.

- *The BCRP intervenes to contain excessive volatility.* Intervention takes place if the volatility of the morning trading session (as measured by the square root of the squared deviation of the morning session exchange rate from the weekly average exchange rate) exceeds the historical average weekly standard deviation. A higher volatility gap is expected to increase the likelihood of intervention.

Predicted values of interventions (estimated likelihoods of intervention) from the above regressions are used as instrumental variables for foreign exchange intervention in the exchange rate equations below [equations (21.2) and (21.3)]. Both estimated likelihoods of foreign exchange purchases and sales enter the equations for the level and volatility of the exchange rate in addition to control variables (other potential factors that could affect the daily variability of the exchange rate). The dependent variables are defined as the differences between the afternoon session levels and the corresponding morning session levels.[16]

$$\Delta er\_pm_t = \beta_0 + \beta_1 INT\_pur_t + \beta_2 INT\_\mathrm{sale}_t + \beta_3 Control_t + \varepsilon_t \tag{21.2}$$

$$\Delta vol\_pm_t = \gamma_0 + \gamma_1 INT\_pur_t + \gamma_2 INT\_\mathrm{sale}_t + \gamma_3 Control_t + \mu_t, \tag{21.3}$$

[13] The author thanks Marco Ortiz and Fernando Perez Forero of the BCRP for pointing this out.

[14] Due to lack of higher frequency data, the morning session exchange rate is calculated as the average of the opening (9:00 a.m.) and the 11:00 a.m. exchange rates.

[15] In a similar setup, Galati, Melick, and Micu (2005) uses the historical average ±1.5 standard deviation as target bounds for the yen/U.S. dollar exchange rate. Given the low variability of the nuevo sol/U.S. dollar rate, this chapter tightens the target bound to ±1 standard deviation, although the model is reestimated using a ±1.5* standard deviation target bound to see if the results are sensitive to the width of the target bound.

[16] Due to data limitations, the 1:30 p.m. (closing) exchange rate is used as the afternoon session exchange rate.

where $\Delta er\_pmt$ is the difference between the closing exchange rate and the exchange rate at 11:00 a.m., and $\Delta vol\_pm_t$ is the difference between the afternoon session volatility and the morning session volatility.[17] $INT\_purt$ is the dummy for a foreign exchange purchase, $INT\_sale_t$ is the dummy for a foreign exchange sale, and *Control* is the other control variables as defined below.

$INT\_pur_t$ and $INT\_sale_t$ enter the regression equations separately to test for potential asymmetric responses to foreign exchange purchases and sales. Asymmetric responses may result if foreign exchange purchases and foreign exchange sales signal different information to the market (Lahura and Vega 2013). For instance, foreign exchange purchases during episodes of appreciation may be perceived as an effort by the central bank to build international reserves. Such accumulation of international reserves may in turn attract more capital inflows, due to improved self-insurance against external shocks, and weaken the effectiveness of the foreign exchange intervention. On the other hand, foreign exchange sales by the central bank during episodes of depreciation can be effective because the intervention may be perceived by the market as a signal that the central bank is attempting to correct misalignments in the exchange rate. Empirical evidence for asymmetric effects of foreign exchange interventions has been found by Lahura and Vega (2013) for Peru and Broto (2012) for Brazil, Chile, Colombia, and Peru.

In theory, control variables include the unexpected components of major economic data announcements (surprises), measured by the differences between the officially announced data and the corresponding average analyst estimates just before the announcement (Disyatat and Galati 2007; Dominguez 2003, 2006; Galati, Melick, and Micu 2005). However, the announcements of major economic news in Peru and the United States (economic growth, consumer price index, unemployment, and the policy rate), with the exception of GDP growth in Peru, are made either early in the morning or after the foreign exchange market closes, and are not expected to have differential impacts on morning and afternoon exchange rate variability. The Peruvian authorities announce monthly economic growth data sometime around noon and, as a result, the difference between the announced GDP growth rate and the average estimates before the announcement (in absolute value terms for the volatility equation) are included in equations (21.2) and (21.3). In addition, indicators for regional and global factors are included. The change in the Chicago Board of Exchange Market Volatility Index (VIX) between the opening and closing quotes is included in the volatility regression to capture the impact of global market volatility, which is expected to be positive.[18] On the other hand, the daily change (between market opening and closing) in the common factor (principal component) of LA6 exchange rates is included in the exchange rate equation to capture the impact of regional factors, such as the impact of commodity prices, which is also expected to be positive.[19]

## DATA AND ESTIMATION RESULTS

Data on daily (11:00 a.m. and 1:30 p.m.) exchange rates and daily foreign exchange interventions are from the online statistical database of the BCRP. Data for the opening session exchange rate for Peru, exchange rates for other LA6 economies, and analysts' consensus estimates of GDP are from Bloomberg. Finally, VIX are from the Chicago of Board Options Exchange online

[17]The afternoon session volatility is measured by the square root of the squared deviation of the afternoon session exchange rate from the weekly average exchange rate.

[18]Ideally, the changes in the VIX should have been between the 11:00 a.m. and 1:30 p.m. quotes to match the changes in the dependent variables. But minute-by-minute historical quotes are not available for the period covered in this chapter.

[19]The LA6 are Brazil, Chile, Colombia, Mexico, Peru, and Uruguay.

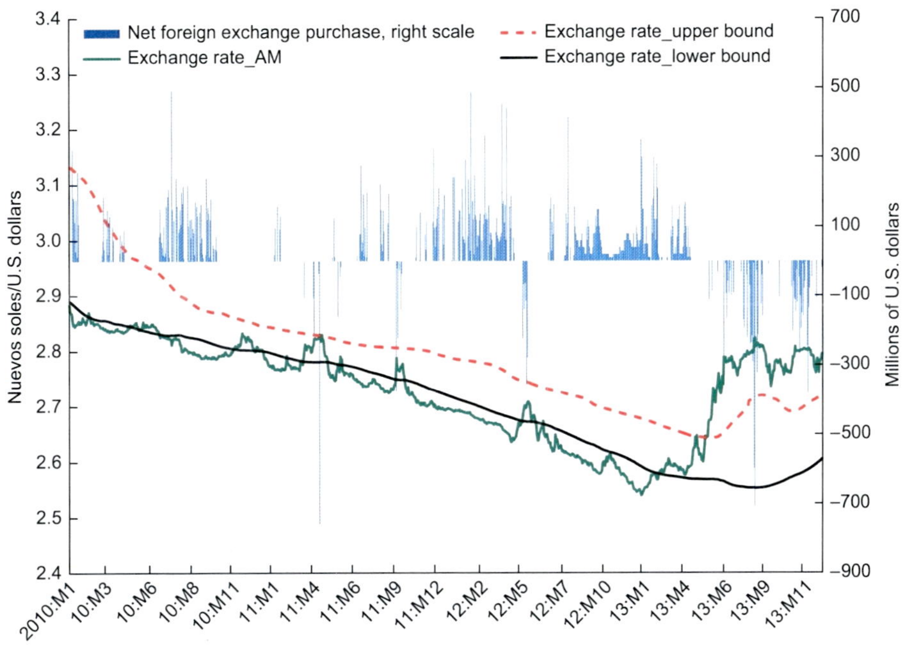


Sources: Central Reserve Bank of Peru; and IMF staff estimates.

**Figure 21.4** Exchange Rates and Foreign Exchange Intervention

database. The sample covers daily data for four years (January 2010–December 2013) and includes a total sample of 982 observations.[20]

Statistical analysis of the exchange rate and intervention data suggests that intervention decisions are prompted mainly by the deviations of the level of the exchange rate from a notional target range. In particular, foreign exchange purchases are strongly associated with the deviation of the level of the exchange rate from the lower bound of the BCRP's tolerable range (Figure 21.4). However, foreign exchange sales are conducted during episodes of exchange rate depreciations even when the level of the exchange rate falls within the target range, possibly due to volatility concerns. In general, volatility is high during periods of depreciations as shown by the widening of the target range in the second half of 2013.

Foreign exchange purchases seem to be driven primarily by the deviation of the exchange rate from the BCRP's notional tolerable range (leaning against the wind). About 91 percent of the foreign exchange purchases were conducted during days when the level of the morning session exchange rate fell below the lower bound of the notional tolerable range. Less than 5 percent of the foreign exchange purchases were conducted on days when only exchange rate volatility deviated from the target, whereas the level of the exchange rate remained within target (Figure 21.5).

However, leaning against the wind does not seem to be the only target of foreign exchange sales. Compared to foreign exchange purchase days, a lower proportion (75 percent) of the foreign exchange sales was conducted on days when the morning session exchange rate deviated from the upper bound of the BCRP's notional tolerable range. On the other hand, a relatively large share of the foreign exchange sales (about 20 percent) were conducted on days when the exchange rate volatility deviated from the target while the level remained within the BCRP's tolerable range (Figure 21.6).

[20] Of the 982 observations, the BCRP purchased foreign exchange on 354 days (36 percent of total observations), sold foreign exchange on 81 days (8¼ percent of total observations), and did not intervene on 534 days (55½ percent of total observations).

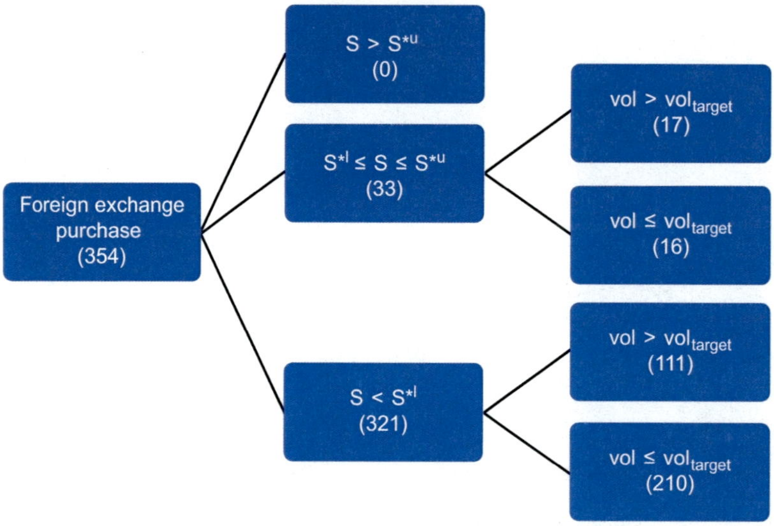


Sources: Central Reserve Bank of Peru; and author's calculations.
Note: Numbers in parentheses indicate the number of intervention days during the sample. $S^{*l}$ and $S^{*u}$ represent the lower and upper bounds, respectively, of the Central Reserve Bank of Peru's tolerable range for the level of the exchange rate.

**Figure 21.5** Characterization of Foreign Exchange Purchases by the Central Reserve Bank of Peru, January 2010–December 2013

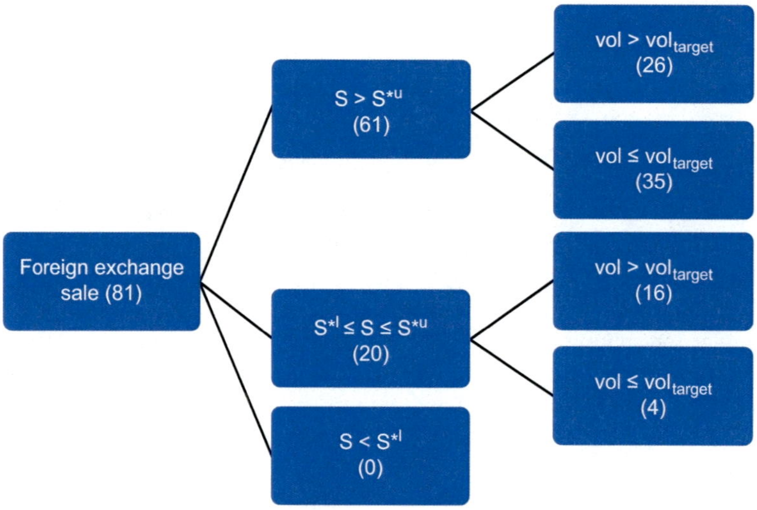


Sources: Central Reserve Bank of Peru; and author's calculations.
Note: Numbers in parentheses indicate the number of intervention days during the sample. $S^{*l}$ and $S^{*u}$ represent the lower and upper bounds, respectively, of the Central Reserve Bank of Peru's tolerable range for the level of the exchange rate.

**Figure 21.6** Characterization of Foreign Exchange Sales by the Central Reserve Bank of Peru, January 2010–December 2013

TABLE 21.1

Probit Regression Results for the Probability of Foreign Exchange Intervention

| (a) Foreign Exchange Purchases | | | (b) Foreign Exchange Sales | |
|---|---|---|---|---|
| **Independent Variable** | **(1)** | **(2)** | **Independent Variable** | **Coefficient** |
| Foreign exchange purchase_first lag | 1.613<br>(11.60)*** | 1.511<br>(10.73)*** | Foreign exchange sale_first lag | 1.143<br>(5.42)*** |
| Foreign exchange purchase_second lag | 0.525<br>(3.76)*** | 0.398<br>(2.79)*** | Foreign exchange sale_second lag | 0.711<br>(3.24)** |
| Excessive appreciation | 31.437<br>(6.64)*** | 29.139<br>(5.79)*** | Excessive depreciation | 12.823<br>(6.36)*** |
| Excessive volatility | −0.110<br>(−1.11) | −0.215<br>(−1.90)* | Excessive volatility | 0.304<br>(3.72)*** |
| Excessive appreciation* dummy for intervention policy change | —<br>— | 306.325<br>(2.44)** | Constant | −2.280<br>(−18.81)*** |
| Excessive volatility* dummy for intervention policy change | —<br>— | −0.695<br>(−1.17) | | |
| Constant | −1.766<br>(−16.93)*** | −1.710<br>(−16.10)*** | | |
| *Model statistics* | | | *Model statistics* | |
| Number of observations | 960 | 960 | Number of observations | 960 |
| LR-$\chi^2$ (4) | 632.4*** | 663.0*** | LR-$\chi^2$ (4) | 249.5*** |
| Pseudo-$R^2$ | 0.50 | 0.52 | Pseudo $R^2$ | 0.49 |

Source: Author's estimations.

Note: Purchase and sale of foreign exchange are represented by dummy variables with values of 1 when there was purchase (sale) and 0 otherwise. Equations (21.1) and (21.2) are without and with intervention policy change dummy interaction, respectively. Numbers in parentheses are *z*-values. * Significant at the 10 percent level, ** significant at the 5 percent level, and *** significant at the 1 percent level.

## The BCRP's Reaction Functions

The BCRP's reaction functions are estimated by probit regressions. The estimated regressions seem to explain intervention decisions very well. The likelihood ratio statistics and the Pseudo $R^2$ values are large, indicating strong goodness of fit. Two-day lags of the dependent variables are found to be statistically significant, indicating the tendency for intervention clustering (Table 21.1).

The results provide strong evidence that the BCRP intervenes to prevent excessive appreciations and depreciations (deviations from the notional tolerable range). Deviations of the level of the exchange rate from the lower and upper bounds of the BCRP's notional tolerable range are positively and significantly associated with foreign exchange purchases and sales, respectively indicating that such deviations prompt foreign exchange interventions (Table 21.1). But the BCRP's reaction to volatility appears to be asymmetric. While the deviation of the exchange rate volatility from the BCRP's target is positively and significantly associated with foreign exchange sales, its correlation with foreign exchange purchases is negative but not statistically significant. This suggests that excessive exchange rate volatility seems to be more of a concern for the BCRP during episodes of depreciations.

Regression (2) in Table 21.1 was estimated with the addition of a dummy for intervention policy change, interacted with excessive exchange rate appreciation and exchange rate volatility, to test if the BCRP's preannouncement of interventions in August 2012 was associated with a change of its reactions to exchange rate movements.[21] The results do not change in a significant way. The BCRP's reaction to excessive appreciation remains statistically significant. Its reaction to excessive volatility remains negative, but becomes weakly significant, suggesting that the BCRP

[21]The dummy takes 1 during September 2012–April 2013, the appreciation episode when the central bank's new intervention strategy was applied, and 0 otherwise.

**TABLE 21.2**

**Estimated Effects of Foreign Exchange Intervention on the Level and Volatility of the Exchange Rate**

| | Change in the Level of the Exchange Rate | | | Change in Volatility of the Exchange Rate | | |
|---|---|---|---|---|---|---|
| **Explanatory Variables** | **(1)** | **(2)** | **(3)** | **(1)** | **(2)** | **(3)** |
| Foreign exchange purchase | 0.018 | 0.018 | 0.027 | −0.073 | −0.077 | −0.128 |
| | (1.41) | (1.49) | (1.73)* | (−2.21)** | (−2.33)** | (−3.08)*** |
| Foreign exchange sale | −0.138 | −0.138 | −0.137 | −0.124 | −0.135 | −0.143 |
| | (−2.68)*** | (−2.70)*** | (−2.68)*** | (−1.86)** | (−2.00)** | (−2.12)** |
| Foreign exchange | 0.113 | 0.115 | 0.115 | — | — | — |
| sale_first lag | (2.20)** | (2.25)** | (2.27)** | — | — | — |
| Change in ER_LA[1] | — | 0.013 | 0.013 | — | — | — |
| | — | (4.48)*** | (4.47)*** | — | — | — |
| GDP surprise[2] | — | −0.006 | −0.007 | — | −0.006 | −0.005 |
| | | (−0.28) | (−0.30) | | (−0.1) | (−0.08) |
| Absolute value of change in | — | — | — | — | −0.011 | −0.011 |
| the VIX | — | — | — | — | (−1.01) | (−0.97) |
| Likelihood of foreign | — | — | −0.015 | — | — | 0.093 |
| exchange purchase interacted with dummy for intervention policy change | — | — | (−0.89) | — | — | (2.02)** |
| Constant | −0.002 | −0.003 | −0.004 | 0.113 | 0.126 | 0.132 |
| | (−0.32) | (−0.38) | (−0.53) | (6.16)*** | (5.68)*** | (5.90)*** |
| *Model statistics* | | | | | | |
| Number of observations | 979 | 979 | 979 | 980 | 980 | 980 |
| F-statistic | 3.59*** | 6.25*** | 5.34*** | 3.16** | 1.84* | 2.29** |
| Adjusted $R^2$ | 0.008 | 0.026 | 0.026 | 0.004 | 0.003 | 0.007 |

Source: Author's estimations.

Note: The table estimates use the instrumental variable (two-stage least-squares) method. Predicted values of foreign exchange purchase and sale from regressions (a) and (b) of Table 21.1 are used as instruments for foreign exchange purchase and sale, respectively. Equation (21.1) is the baseline regression, equation (21.2) includes control variables, and equation (21.3) includes interaction of foreign exchange purchases with a dummy for intervention policy change on top of control variables. Numbers in parentheses are *t*-values. * significant at the 10 percent level, ** significant at the 5 percent level, and *** significant at the 1 percent level. VIX = Chicago Board Options Exchange Volatility Index.

[1]Change in the principal component of exchange rates in the LA6 (Brazil, Chile, Colombia, Mexico, Peru, Uruguay).

[2]The difference between actual real GDP growth and consensus estimates prior to data release. Entered in absolute value in the volatility equations.

might have intervened out of a concern for too low volatility, which is not in line with its general stated objective.

The results of the BCRP's estimated reaction function are robust to changes in estimation methodology. For instance, the main results remain unchanged when a single equation reaction function, instead of separate reaction functions for foreign exchange purchases and sales, is estimated using a multinomial logistic regression (Annex 21.1).[22] In particular, the odds of foreign exchange purchases are affected only by excessive appreciations, but the odds of foreign exchange sales are affected both by excessive depreciations and volatility.

## Effects of Foreign Exchange Interventions

Instrumental variable estimates for the level and volatility of the exchange rate provide evidence of asymmetric effects of foreign exchange interventions on exchange rate variability (Table 21.2). Three regressions are estimated for each change in the level and volatility of the exchange rate. Regression (1) includes only foreign exchange intervention variables (foreign exchange purchases

[22]The dependent variable is a dummy that takes 1 for foreign exchange purchases, –1 for foreign exchange sales, and 0 for no intervention. Multinomial logistic regression, instead of multinomial probit, was used because no convergence was achieved using multinomial probit regression.

and sales),[23] whereas regression (2) includes other control variables. Regression (3) includes interaction of a dummy variable for intervention policy change with a foreign exchange purchase.

According to the results, there is no strong statistical evidence to suggest that foreign exchange purchases by the BCRP are successful in preventing an appreciation of the exchange rate, as the likelihood of foreign exchange purchases is either statistically insignificant [regressions (1) and (2)] or only weakly significant [regression (3)]. But the likelihood of foreign exchange purchases has a statistically significant and negative impact on volatility, indicating the foreign exchange purchase by the BCRP reduces volatility. In other words, although the BCRP's objective for intervention during episodes of appreciation is to lean against the wind, it ends up reducing volatility without having a significant impact on the level of the exchange rate.

On the other hand, foreign exchange sales appear to be successful not only in reducing volatility, but also in preventing the depreciation of the exchange rate, although some of the effects appear to reverse the following day. These results are consistent with findings of Lahura and Vega (2013)[24] that foreign exchange sales are more successful in preventing depreciation than foreign exchange purchases in preventing appreciation. With the exception of the first lag of foreign exchange sales, lags of foreign exchange intervention are not found to be statistically significant, indicating that the effects of interventions are short lived.

Unfortunately, the overall fits of the estimated models are not good, as is the case with similar empirical studies on exchange rates. The variables included in this chapter explain very little about exchange rate variability. This is partly because not all potential determinants are included due to limitations on daily data, but it also reflects the difficulty of explaining exchange rate variability. Among the control variables, only the common factor (principal component) of the exchange rates of LA6 economies became statistically significant, reflecting the importance of regional common factors such as the impact of commodity prices.

The results are robust to changes in the definition of the target and tolerable range of the exchange rate. The above regressions were reestimated for the target exchange rate defined as a six-month moving average and a one-year Hodrick-Prescott rolling filtered average, and for the tolerable range defined as a one-year historical average ±1.5 times the standard deviation. The results both for the BCRP's reaction function and the exchange rate regressions, presented in Annexes 21.2 to 21.4, show that the conclusions drawn above are robust to changes in the definition of the target and tolerable range of the exchange rate. The only exception is that volatility became statistically significant in the foreign exchange purchase equation when the BCRP's tolerable range is broadened to a one-year historical average e±1.5* standard deviation, in particular in the second regression. But the coefficient remains negative, still supporting the hypothesis of asymmetric BCRP reaction.

## CONCLUSIONS

This chapter has presented empirical evidence of the asymmetry in the BCRP's reactions to appreciation and depreciation pressures. While foreign exchange purchases are driven mainly by excessive appreciation of the exchange rate, foreign exchange sales respond to both excessive exchange rate volatility and excessive depreciation of the exchange rate. This implies that exchange rate volatility may be more of a concern for the BCRP during depreciation pressures than during appreciation pressures. In all regressions, excessive volatility is negatively associated with the likelihood of foreign exchange purchases by the BCRP, and in some of the regressions it becomes

[23] Statistically significant variables in regressions (1) and (2) of Table 21.1 are used as instruments for the likelihood of foreign exchange sales and purchases, respectively.

[24] The authors employ event study regressions and structural vector autoregressions.

statistically significant, albeit weakly. This indicates that the BCRP might have intervened against very low volatility during appreciation episodes. This latter result is consistent with the BCRP's public statements in August 2012 that it was concerned by the low volatility and persistent appreciation of the nuevo sol, and with its decision to preannounce foreign exchange purchases of stable amounts even during days of depreciations.

Although foreign exchange sales seem to be effective in preventing depreciation, there is not sufficient statistical evidence to support the success of foreign exchange purchases. The results show that foreign exchange sales by the BCRP are effective in reducing the level and volatility of the exchange rate. Foreign exchange purchases do not have statistically significant effects on the level of the exchange rate, but they do have an unintended statistically significant negative impact on exchange rate volatility. The results also show that the BCRP's preannouncement of its interventions in August 2012 did not change the effectiveness of the intervention.

Since interventions can be costly, the BCRP needs to target its interventions where they are most effective.[25] In this regard, the results of this chapter imply that:

- Foreign exchange sales by the central bank can be warranted during periods of depreciation pressures if there are concerns over excessive volatility and depreciation. The statistical evidence in this chapter shows that foreign exchange sales are effective in reducing the excessive volatility and depreciation of the nuevo sol. But since these effects are found to be short lived, interventions should not aim at preventing the depreciating trend of the exchange rate, which ought to be driven by fundamentals.
- Foreign exchange purchases by the central bank during periods of appreciation pressures are warranted mostly if volatility is a concern.[26] If reducing volatility is not the objective, as the results of this study indicate, foreign exchange purchases could perpetuate the appreciation by reducing volatility and encouraging a one-sided bet on the domestic currency.

[25]The cost of sterilization in 2012 was estimated at about ½ percent of GDP.

[26]Building international reserves can also be a reason for intervention during episodes of appreciations, although this is less likely to be the case in Peru recently.

# ANNEX 21.1. SINGLE EQUATION REGRESSION OF THE REACTION FUNCTION OF THE CENTRAL RESERVE BANK OF PERU

**ANNEX TABLE 21.1.1**

Multinomial Logistic Regression of Foreign Exchange Intervention

| | (1) | | (2) | |
|---|---|---|---|---|
| **Independent Variable** | **Foreign Exchange Sale** | **Foreign Exchange Purchase** | **Foreign Exchange Sale** | **Foreign Exchange Purchase** |
| Intervention_first lag | −1.531 | 2.636 | −1.529 | 2.439 |
| | (−4.49)*** | (11.04)*** | (−4.49)*** | (10.15)*** |
| Intervention_second lag | −0.798 | 0.853 | −0.797 | 0.634 |
| | (−2.30)** | (3.57)*** | (−2.30)** | (2.63)*** |
| Deviation from target (appreciation) | −71511 | 45.131 | −73835 | 38.394 |
| | (−0.02) | (5.12)*** | (−0.01) | (4.09)*** |
| Deviation from target (depreciation) | 14.940 | −9406 | 14.850 | −9170 |
| | (4.08)*** | (−0.00) | (4.06)*** | (−0.00) |
| Volatility | 0.285 | −0.130 | 0.284 | −0.300 |
| | (1.82)** | (−0.68) | (1.81)** | (−1.39) |
| Deviation from target (appreciation)* | — | — | 56546 | 519.424 |
| dummy for intervention policy change | — | — | (0.01) | (2.39)** |
| Volatility* dummy for intervention | — | — | −1.783 | −1.453 |
| policy change | — | — | (−0.42) | (−1.39) |
| Constant | −2.703 | −2.668 | −2.693 | −2.516 |
| | (−9.22)*** | (−12.63)*** | (−9.19)*** | (−11.78)*** |
| *Model statistics* | | | | |
| Number of observations | 980 | | 980 | |
| LR-$\chi^2$ (10) | 877.12*** | | 909.20*** | |
| Pseudo-$R^2$ | 0.50 | | 0.52 | |

Source: Author's estimations.

Note: The dependent variable is a dummy taking values of 1 for foreign exchange purchase, −1 for foreign exchange purchase sale, and 0 otherwise. The base outcome is no intervention. Equations (21.2) and (21.2) are without and with, respectively, intervention policy change dummy interaction. Numbers in parentheses are *z*-values. * Significant at the 10 percent level, ** significant at the 5 percent level, and *** significant at the 1 percent level.

# ANNEX 21.2. THE EXCHANGE RATE TARGET ESTIMATED BY SIX-MONTH MOVING AVERAGE EXCHANGE RATE

### ANNEX TABLE 21.2.1

**Probit Regression Results for the Probability of Foreign Exchange Intervention**

**(a) Foreign Exchange Purchases**

| Independent Variable | (1) | (2) |
|---|---|---|
| Foreign exchange purchase_first lag | 1.635 | 1.548 |
| | (11.75)*** | (11.05)*** |
| Foreign exchange purchase_second lag | 0.569 | 0.464 |
| | (4.07)*** | (3.28)*** |
| Excessive appreciation | 47.200 | 45.548 |
| | (6.31)*** | (5.81)*** |
| Excessive volatility | −0.110 | −0.217 |
| | (−1.13) | (−1.94)* |
| Excessive appreciation* dummy for intervention policy change[1] | — | — |
| | — | — |
| Excessive volatility* dummy for intervention policy change | — | 0.630 |
| | — | (1.59) |
| Constant | −1.669 | −1.639 |
| | (−17.76)*** | (−17.29)*** |
| *Model statistics* | | |
| Number of observations | 980 | 898 |
| LR-$\chi^2$ | 642.5*** | 484.87*** |
| Pseudo-$R^2$ | 0.50 | 0.44 |

**(b) Foreign Exchange Sales**

| Independent Variable | Coefficient |
|---|---|
| Foreign exchange sale_first lag | 1.430 |
| | (7.48)*** |
| Foreign exchange sale_second lag | 1.010 |
| | (5.11)** |
| Excessive depreciation | 7.461 |
| | (2.73)*** |
| Volatility | 0.220 |
| | (2.71)*** |
| Constant | −2.022 |
| | (−21.12)*** |
| *Model statistics* | |
| Number of observations | 980 |
| F-statistic | 217.62*** |
| Adjusted $R^2$ | 0.39 |

Source: Author's estimations.

Note: Purchase and sale of foreign exchange are represented by dummy variables with values of 1 when there was purchase (sale) and 0 otherwise. Equations (21.1) and (21.2) are without and with intervention policy change dummy interaction, respectively. Numbers in parentheses are *z*-values.

* Significant at the 10 percent level, ** significant at the 5 percent level, and *** significant at the 1 percent level.

[1]Dropped from equation (21.2) as it predicts success perfectly.

**ANNEX TABLE 21.2.2**

## Estimated Effects of Foreign Exchange Intervention on the Level and Volatility of the Exchange Rate

| | Change in the Level of the Exchange Rate | | | Change in Volatility of the Exchange Rate | | |
|---|---|---|---|---|---|---|
| **Explanatory Variables** | **(1)** | **(2)** | **(3)** | **(1)** | **(2)** | **(3)** |
| Foreign exchange purchase | 0.017 | 0.017 | 0.025 | −0.090 | −0.094 | −0.127 |
| | (1.32) | (1.39) | (1.70) | (−2.73)*** | (−2.84)*** | (−3.28)*** |
| Foreign exchange purchase | −0.133 | −0.126 | −0.126 | −0.170 | −0.179 | −0.181 |
| sale | (−3.07)*** | (−2.94)*** | (−2.94)*** | (−2.40)** | (−2.51)** | (−2.53)** |
| Foreign exchange purchase | 0.110 | 0.105 | 0.105 | — | — | — |
| sale_first lag | (2.55)*** | (2.44)** | (2.45)** | — | — | — |
| Change in ER_LA[1] | — | 0.013 | 0.013 | — | — | — |
| | — | (4.36)*** | (4.36)*** | — | — | — |
| GDP surprise[2] | — | −0.007 | −0.008 | — | −0.006 | −0.005 |
| | | (−0.33) | (−0.35) | | (−0.09) | (−0.08) |
| Absolute value of change in | — | — | — | — | −0.012 | −0.011 |
| the VIX | — | — | — | — | (−1.05) | (−0.98) |
| Likelihood of foreign | — | — | −0.017 | — | ... | 0.079 |
| exchange purchase | — | — | (−0.98) | — | ... | (1.67)* |
| interacted with dummy for | | | | | | |
| intervention policy change | | | | | | |
| Constant | −0.002 | −0.002 | −0.003 | 0.123 | 0.136 | 0.138 |
| | (−0.29) | (−0.33) | (−0.41) | (6.64)*** | (6.18)*** | (6.23)*** |
| *Model statistics* | | | | | | |
| Number of observations | 979 | 979 | 979 | 980 | 980 | 980 |
| F-statistic | 4.10*** | 6.36*** | 5.46*** | 5.08*** | 2.82** | 2.81** |
| Adjusted $R^2$ | 0.010 | 0.027 | 0.027 | 0.008 | 0.007 | 0.009 |

Source: Author's estimations.

Note: Estimated using the instrumental variable (two-stage least-squares) method. Statistically significant variables in regressions (1) and (2) of Table 21.2.1 are used as instruments for likelihood of foreign exchange sales and purchases, respectively. Equation (21.1) is the baseline regression, equation (21.2) includes control variables, and equation (21.3) includes interaction of foreign exchange purchases with dummy for intervention policy change on top of control variables. Numbers in parentheses are *t*-values. * Significant at the 10 percent level, ** significant at the 5 percent level, and *** significant at the 1 percent level. VIX = Chicago Board Options Exchange Volatility Index.

[1]Change in the principal component of exchange rates in the LA6 (Brazil, Chile, Colombia, Mexico, Peru, Uruguay).

[2]The difference between actual real GDP growth and consensus estimates prior to data release. Entered in absolute value in the volatility equations.

# ANNEX 21.3. THE EXCHANGE RATE TARGET ESTIMATED BY ONE-YEAR AVERAGE ROLLING HODRICK-PRESCOTT FILTERED EXCHANGE RATE

### ANNEX TABLE 21.3.1

**Probit Regression Results for the Probability of Foreign Exchange Intervention**

| (a) Foreign Exchange Purchases | | | (b) Foreign Exchange Sales | |
|---|---|---|---|---|
| **Independent Variable** | **(1)** | **(2)** | **Independent Variable** | **Coefficient** |
| Foreign exchange purchase_first lag | 1.620 | 1.519 | Foreign exchange sale_1st lag | 1.072 |
| | (11.65)*** | (10.80)*** | | (5.34)*** |
| Foreign exchange purchase_second lag | 0.531 | 0.405 | Foreign exchange sale_2nd lag | 0.660 |
| | (3.80)*** | (2.85)*** | | (3.16)** |
| Excessive appreciation | 31.935 | 29.668 | Excessive depreciation | 13.784 |
| | (6.73)*** | (5.88)*** | | (7.01)*** |
| Excessive volatility | −0.115 | −0.220 | Volatility | 0.283 |
| | (−1.16) | (−1.94)* | | (3.52)*** |
| Excessive appreciation* dummy for intervention policy change | — | 323.227 | Constant | −2.254 |
| | — | (2.39)** | | (−19.14)*** |
| Excessive volatility* dummy for intervention policy change | — | −0.675 | | |
| | — | (−1.14) | | |
| Constant | −1.773 | −1.720 | | |
| | (−17.31)*** | (−16.52)*** | | |
| *Model statistics* | | | *Model statistics* | |
| Number of observations | 980 | 980 | Number of observations | 980 |
| LR-$\chi^2$ (4) | 648.38*** | 6678.62*** | F-statistic | 260.23*** |
| Pseudo-$R^2$ | 0.51 | 0.53 | Adjusted $R^2$ | 0.47 |

Source: Author's estimations.

Note: Purchase and sale of foreign exchange are represented by dummy variables with values of 1 when there was purchase (sale) and 0 otherwise. Equations (21.1) and (21.2) are without and with intervention policy change dummy interaction, respectively. Numbers in parentheses are *z*-values.

* Significant at the 10 percent level, ** significant at the 5 percent level, and *** significant at the 1 percent level.

**ANNEX TABLE 21.3.2**

## Estimated Effects of Foreign Exchange Intervention on the Level and Volatility of the Exchange Rate

| | Change in the Level of the Exchange Rate | | | Change in Volatility of the Exchange Rate | | |
|---|---|---|---|---|---|---|
| **Explanatory Variables** | **(1)** | **(2)** | **(3)** | **(1)** | **(2)** | **(3)** |
| Foreign exchange purchase | 0.018 | 0.019 | 0.027 | –0.072 | –0.077 | –0.128 |
| | (1.42) | (1.49) | (1.72)* | (–2.20)** | (–2.32)** | (–3.07)*** |
| Foreign exchange sale | –0.138 | –0.137 | –0.136 | –0.124 | –0.135 | –0.143 |
| | (–2.68)*** | (–2.69)*** | (–2.67)*** | (–1.86)** | (–2.00)** | (–2.12)** |
| Foreign exchange sale_first lag | 0.113 | 0.114 | 0.115 | — | — | — |
| | (2.20)** | (2.25)** | (2.26)** | — | — | — |
| Change in ER_LA[1] | — | 0.013 | 0.013 | — | — | — |
| | — | (4.45)*** | (4.44)*** | — | — | — |
| GDP surprise[2] | — | –0.007 | –0.007 | — | –0.006 | –0.005 |
| | | (–0.30) | (–0.32) | | (–0.10) | (–0.08) |
| Absolute value of change in the VIX | — | — | — | — | –0.011 | –0.016 |
| | — | — | — | — | (–1.03) | (–1.49) |
| Likelihood of foreign exchange purchase interacted with dummy for intervention policy change | — | — | –0.015 | — | — | 0.093 |
| | — | — | (–0.88) | — | — | (2.02)** |
| Constant | –0.002 | –0.003 | –0.004 | 0.113 | 0.126 | 0.132 |
| | (–0.33) | (–0.38) | (–0.53) | (6.15)*** | (5.68)*** | (5.90)*** |
| *Model statistics* | | | | | | |
| Number of observations | 979 | 979 | 979 | 980 | 980 | 980 |
| F-statistic | 3.59*** | 6.20*** | 5.30*** | 3.14** | 1.83* | 2.28** |
| Adjusted $R^2$ | 0.008 | 0.026 | 0.026 | 0.004 | 0.003 | 0.007 |

Source: Author's estimations.

Note: Estimated using the instrumental variable (two-stage least-squares) method. Statistically significant variables in regressions (1) and (2) of Table 21.3.1 are used as instruments for likelihood of foreign exchange sales and purchases, respectively. Equation (21.1) is the baseline regression, equation (21.2) includes control variables, and equation (21.3) includes interaction of foreign exchange purchases with a dummy for intervention policy change on top of control variables. Numbers in parentheses are *t*-values. * Significant at the 10 percent level, ** significant at the 5 percent level, and *** significant at the 1 percent level. VIX = Chicago Board Options Exchange Volatility Index.

[1]Change in the principal component of exchange rates in the LA6 (Brazil, Chile, Colombia, Mexico, Peru, Uruguay).

[2]The difference between actual real GDP growth and consensus estimates prior to data release. Entered in absolute value in the volatility equations.

# ANNEX 21.4. TOLERABLE RANGE DEFINED AS ONE-YEAR HISTORICAL AVERAGE EXCHANGE RATE ±1.5 TIMES STANDARD DEVIATION

### ANNEX TABLE 21.4.1

**Probit Regression Results for the Probability of Foreign Exchange Intervention**

**(a) Foreign Exchange Purchases**

| Independent Variable | (1) | (2) |
|---|---|---|
| Foreign exchange purchase_first lag | 1.691 (12.27)*** | 1.625 (11.75)*** |
| Foreign exchange purchase_second lag | 0.606 (4.39)*** | 0.524 (3.75)*** |
| Excessive appreciation | 41.367 (5.01)*** | 34.138 (3.81)*** |
| Excessive volatility | −0.170 (−1.75)* | −0.246 (−2.26)** |
| Excessive appreciation* dummy for intervention policy change[1] | — — | — — |
| Excessive volatility* dummy for intervention policy change | — — | 0.375 (0.87) |
| Constant | −1.544 (−18.25)*** | −1.500 (−17.61)*** |
| *Model statistics* | | |
| Number of observations | 980 | 896 |
| LR-$\chi^2$ (4) | 627.7*** | 461.24*** |
| Pseudo-$R^2$ | 0.49 | 0.42 |

**(b) Foreign Exchange Sales**

| Independent Variable | Coefficient |
|---|---|
| Foreign exchange sale_first lag | 1.391 (7.21)*** |
| Foreign exchange sale_second lag | 0.972 (4.91)** |
| Excessive depreciation | 9.592 (3.44)*** |
| Volatility | 0.244 (3.12)*** |
| Constant | −2.034 (−21.04)*** |
| *Model statistics* | |
| Number of observations | 980 |
| F-statistic | 222.06*** |
| Adjusted $R^2$ | 0.40 |

Source: Author's estimations.

Note: Purchase and sale of foreign exchange are represented by dummy variables with values of 1 when there was purchase (sale) and 0 otherwise. Equations (21.1) and (21.2) are without and with intervention policy change dummy interaction, respectively. Numbers in parentheses are *z*-values.

* Significant at the 10 percent level, ** significant at the 5 percent level, and *** significant at the 1 percent level.

[1] Dropped from equation (21.2) because it predicts success perfectly.

**ANNEX TABLE 21.4.2**

## Estimated Effects of Foreign Exchange Intervention on the Level and Volatility of the Exchange Rate

| | Change in the Level of the Exchange Rate | | | Change in Volatility of the Exchange Rate | | |
|---|---|---|---|---|---|---|
| **Explanatory Variables** | **(1)** | **(2)** | **(3)** | **(1)** | **(2)** | **(3)** |
| Foreign exchange purchase | 0.015 | 0.016 | 0.024 | −0.082 | −0.086 | −0.123 |
| | (1.20) | (1.25) | (1.57) | (−2.48)** | (−2.58)** | (−3.08)*** |
| Foreign exchange sale | −0.136 | −0.130 | −0.130 | −0.180 | −0.189 | −0.192 |
| | (−3.08)*** | (−2.98)*** | (−2.98)*** | (−2.58)*** | (−2.68)*** | (−2.72)*** |
| Foreign exchange | 0.107 | 0.103 | 0.103 | — | — | — |
| sale_first lag | (2.42)** | (2.35)** | (2.36)** | — | — | — |
| Change in ER_LA[1] | — | 0.013 | 0.013 | — | — | — |
| | — | (4.37)*** | (4.36)*** | — | — | — |
| GDP surprise[2] | — | −0.007 | −0.008 | — | −0.007 | −0.006 |
| | | (−0.33) | (−0.34) | | (−0.12) | (−0.10) |
| Absolute value of change in | — | — | — | — | −0.011 | −0.011 |
| the VIX | — | — | — | — | (−1.03) | (−0.96) |
| Likelihood of foreign | — | — | −0.017 | — | — | 0.078 |
| exchange purchase | — | — | (−0.96) | — | — | (1.68)* |
| interacted with dummy for | | | | | | |
| intervention policy change | | | | | | |
| Constant | −0.001 | −0.001 | −0.002 | 0.121 | 0.134 | 0.137 |
| | (−0.16) | (−0.18) | (−0.29) | (6.53)*** | (6.09)*** | (6.17)*** |
| *Model statistics* | | | | | | |
| Number of observations | 979 | 979 | 979 | 980 | 980 | 960 |
| F-statistic | 4.05*** | 6.35*** | 5.45*** | 4.92*** | 2.72** | 2.72** |
| Adjusted $R^2$ | 0.010 | 0.027 | 0.027 | 0.008 | 0.007 | 0.009 |

Source: Author's estimations.

Note: Estimated using the instrumental variable (two-stage least-squares) method. Statistically significant variables in regressions (1) and (2) of Table 21.4.1 are used as instruments for likelihood of foreign exchange sales and purchases, respectively. Equation (21.1) is the baseline regression, equation (21.2) includes control variables, and equation (21.3) includes interaction of foreign exchange purchases with a dummy for intervention policy change on top of control variables. Numbers in parentheses are *t*-values. * Significant at the 10 percent level, ** significant at the 5 percent level, and *** significant at the 1 percent level. VIX = Chicago Board Options Exchange Volatility Index.

[1]Change in the principal component of exchange rates in the LA6 (Brazil, Chile, Colombia, Mexico, Peru, Uruguay).

[2]The difference between actual real GDP growth and consensus estimates prior to data release. Entered in absolute value in the volatility equations.

## REFERENCES

Adler, Gustavo, and Camilo E. Tovar. 2011. "Foreign Exchange Intervention: A Shield Against Appreciation Winds?" Working Paper No. 11/165, International Monetary Fund, Washington, DC.

Aizenman, Joshua, and Michael M. Hutchison. 2012. "Exchange Market Pressure and Absorption by International Reserves: Emerging Markets and Fear of Reserve Loss during the 2008–2009 Crisis" *Journal of International Money and Finance* 31: 1076–91.

Baillie, Richard T., and William P. Osterberg. 1997. "Why Do Central Banks Intervene?" *Journal of International Money and Finance* 16: 909–19.

Banco Central de Reserva del Peru. 2012. "Inflation Report: Recent Trends and Macroeconomic Forecasts 2012–2014." December, Lima.

Broto, Carmen. 2012. "The Effectiveness of Forex Interventions in Four Latin American Countries." *Emerging Markets Review* 17: 224–40.

Cardarelli, R., Selim Elekdag, and M. Ayhan Kose. 2010. "Capital Inflows: Macroeconomic Implications and Policy Responses." *Economic Systems* 34 (4): 333–56.

Disyatat, Piti, and Gabriele Galati. 2007. "The Effectiveness of Foreign Exchange Intervention in Emerging Market Countries: Evidence from the Czech Koruna." *Journal of International Money and Finance* 26 (3): 383–402.

Dominguez, Kathryn M.E., 2003. "The Market Microstructure of Central Bank Intervention." *Journal of International Economics* 59 (1): 25–45.

———. 2006. "When Do Central Bank Interventions Influence Intra-Daily and Longer-Term Exchange Rate Movements?" *Journal of International Money and Finance* 25 (7): 1051–071.

———, and Jeffrey A. Frankel. 1993. "Does Foreign-Exchange Intervention Matter? The Portfolio Effect." *American Economic Review* 83: 1356–369.

Furceri, Davide, Stephanie Guichard, and Elena Rusticelli. 2012. "The Effect of Episodes of Large Capital Inflows on Domestic Credit." *North American Journal of Economics and Finance* 23 (3): 325–44.

Galati, Gabriele, William Melick, and Marian Micu. 2005. "Foreign Exchange Market Intervention and Expectations: the Yen/Dollar Exchange Rate." *Journal of International Money and Finance* 24 (6): 982–1011.

Gonzalez, Maria. 2009. "Disentangling the Motives for Foreign Exchange Intervention in Peru." Country Report No. 09/41, International Monetary Fund, Washington, DC.

Guimaraes, Roberto F., and Cem Karacadag. 2004. "The Empirics of Foreign Exchange Intervention in Emerging Market Countries: The Cases of Mexico and Turkey." Working Paper 04/123, International Monetary Fund, Washington, DC.

Humala, Alberto and Gabriel, Rodriguez. 2009. "Foreign Exchange Intervention and Exchange Rate Volatility in Peru." BCRP Working Paper No. 2009–008, Central Reserve Bank of Peru, Lima.

Kearns, Jonathan, and Roberto Rigobon. 2005. "Identifying the Efficacy of Central Bank Interventions: Evidence from Australia and Japan." *Journal of International Economics* 66 (1): 31–48.

Lahura, Erick, and Marco Vega. 2013. "Asymmetric Effects of FOREX Intervention Using Intraday Data: Evidence from Peru." BIS Working Paper No. 430, Bank for International Settlements, Basel.

Neely, Christopher J. 2001. "The Practice of Central Bank Intervention: Looking Under the Hood." *Review/ Federal Reserve Bank of St. Louis* 83 (3): 1–10.

Pontines, Victor, and Ramkishen S. Rajan. 2011. "Foreign Exchange Market Intervention and Reserve Accumulation in Emerging Asia: Is There Evidence of Fear of Appreciation?" *Economics Letters* 111 (3): 252–55.

Ramachandran, M., and Naveen Srinivasan. 2007. "Asymmetric Exchange Rate Intervention and International Reserve Accumulation in India." *Economics Letters* 94 (2): 259–65.

Reinhart, Carmen M., and Vincent R. Reinhart. 2008. "Capital Flow Bonanzas: An Encompassing View of the Past and Present." NBER Working Paper No. 14321, National Bureau of Economic Research, Cambridge, Massachusetts.

Rossini, Renzo, Zenón Quispe, and Donita Rodríguez. 2011. "Capital Flows, Monetary Policy and Forex Intervention in Peru." In "The Influence of External Factors on Monetary Policy Frameworks and Operations," p. 261. BIS Papers No. 57, Bank for International Settlements, Basel, Switzerland.

Rossini, Renzo, Zenon Quispe, and Enrique Serrano. 2013. "Foreign Exchange Intervention in Peru." In "Market Volatility and Foreign Exchange Intervention in EMEs: What Has Changed?" BIS Papers No. 73, p. 243, Bank for International Settlements, Basel, Switzerland.

Sarno, Lucio, and Mark P. Taylor. 2001. "Official Intervention in the Foreign Exchange Market: Is It Effective and, If So, How Does It Work?" *Journal of Economic Literature* 39 (3): 839–68.

CHAPTER 22

# Measuring External Risks for Peru: Insights from a Macroeconomic Model for a Small, Open, and Partially Dollarized Economy

FEI HAN

*This chapter quantifies the effects of external risks for Peru, giving particular attention to two major external risks: the investment slowdown in China and monetary policy tightening in the United States. In particular, a macroeconomic model for a small, open, and partially dollarized economy is developed and estimated for Peru to measure risk spillovers and simulate domestic macroeconomic responses in different scenarios with these two external risks. The simulation results suggest that Peru's output is vulnerable to both risks, particularly U.S. monetary policy tightening. Simulations also highlight the importance of higher exchange rate flexibility and a lower degree of dollarization, which could help mitigate the negative spillover effects of these external risks.*

As a small and open economy, Peru is exposed to external shocks from its major trading partners, particularly China. China is one of Peru's main trading partners and was its largest export destination during 2011–12 (Figure 22.1a). In particular, 17 percent of Peru's total exports went to China in 2012 (about 4 percent of GDP), of which 81 percent were metals (Figure 22.1b). According to data from the UN Commodity Trade Statistics, over a third of Peru's copper exports, 64 percent of gold exports, and 22 percent of other mineral commodities went to China during 2008–12 (Figure 22.1c). However, China's mineral imports from Peru, including copper and gold, still represent a relatively small share of China's total mineral imports (Figure 22.1d).

As a partially dollarized economy, Peru is exposed to monetary policy shocks in the United States. By end-2013, about 38 percent of banking system liquidity and 42 percent of bank credit to the private sector in Peru were denominated in foreign currency, reflecting high financial dollarization (Figure 22.2a). Not surprisingly, Peru's short-term interest rate denominated in U.S. dollars is highly correlated with the U.S. federal funds rate (Figure 22.2b).[1] Thus, U.S. monetary policy shocks that affect the federal funds rate might lead to a significant impact on the dollar-denominated domestic interbank interest rate and, hence, economic activity.

The IMF's 2012 and 2013 Spillover Reports identified China's investment slowdown and U.S. monetary policy normalization as two of the major global risks going forward (IMF 2012, 2013). The 2012 Spillover Report found that China has significant spillover effects on its main trading partners and on world prices, mainly through investment, which has been a key driver of China's economic growth and lower external surpluses. In particular, as mentioned in the 2012 Spillover Report, "a slowdown in China's investment growth, while desirable to rebalance demand towards consumption in the medium term, could in the interim hit partners and world prices, especially if the adjustment were to be sharp and disorderly." Furthermore, prompt normalization of U.S.

[1]The correlation between the U.S. dollar–denominated interest rate in Peru and the U.S. federal funds target rate was 0.9 during 2000–13.

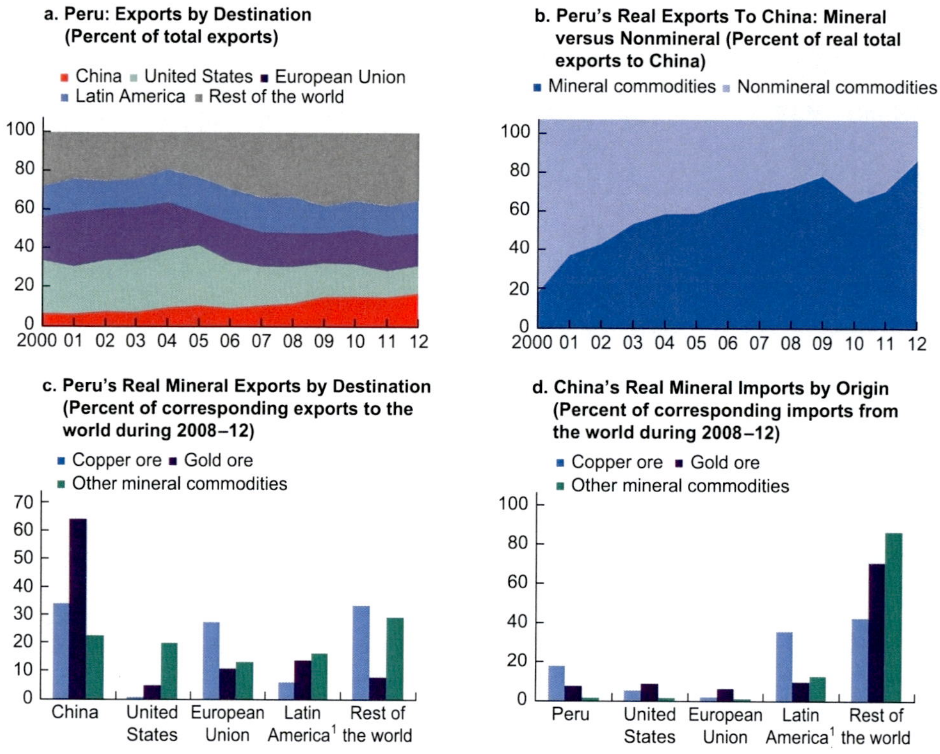


Sources: IMF, International Financial Statistics database; UN Comtrade; and IMF staff calculations.
Note: Latin America comprises LA6 (Brazil, Chile, Colombia, Mexico, Peru, Uruguay) plus Argentina, Bolivia, Ecuador, Paraguay, and Venezuela.
[1]Excluding Peru.

**Figure 22.1** Peru's Trading Partners

monetary policy was also identified as one of the other main global spillover risks in the 2013 Spillover Report. As the U.S. economy recovers, monetary policy should be tightened, and this will likely lead to capital flows into the United States and higher interest rates across the world, slowing economic growth. As a partially dollarized, small, and open economy, Peru's exposure to the U.S. monetary policy shock might be larger than that of a typical nondollarized, small, and open country.

There is limited literature quantifying the exposure of Peru to China's investment slowdown or U.S. monetary policy tightening. Salas (2010) proposed a simple macroeconomic model resembling the Quarterly Projection Model developed by the Central Reserve Bank of Peru (*Banco Central de Reserva del Perú* [BCRP]), but no external shocks were considered. Ahuja and Nabar (2012) measured the spillover effects of China's investment slowdown on main commodity exporters by estimating the direct trade exposures of each commodity exporter to China. However, as found in Annex IV of the IMF Staff Report for the 2013 Article IV Consultation with Peru (IMF 2014), the main transmission channel of China's spillovers to Peru is through China's impact on world metal prices, and hence Peru's terms of trade and economic activity (income effect), instead of the direct trade channel.

This chapter uses a new Keynesian macroeconomic model for a small, open, and partially dollarized economy to estimate and simulate Peru's macroeconomic and policy responses to a temporary slowdown in China's investment growth and a continued tightening of U.S. monetary policy. In particular, the chapter develops a simple new Keynesian type macroeconomic model consisting of an aggregate demand equation (or IS curve), an expectations-augmented Phillips curve, a Taylor-type monetary policy rule, and an uncovered interest parity (UIP) condition

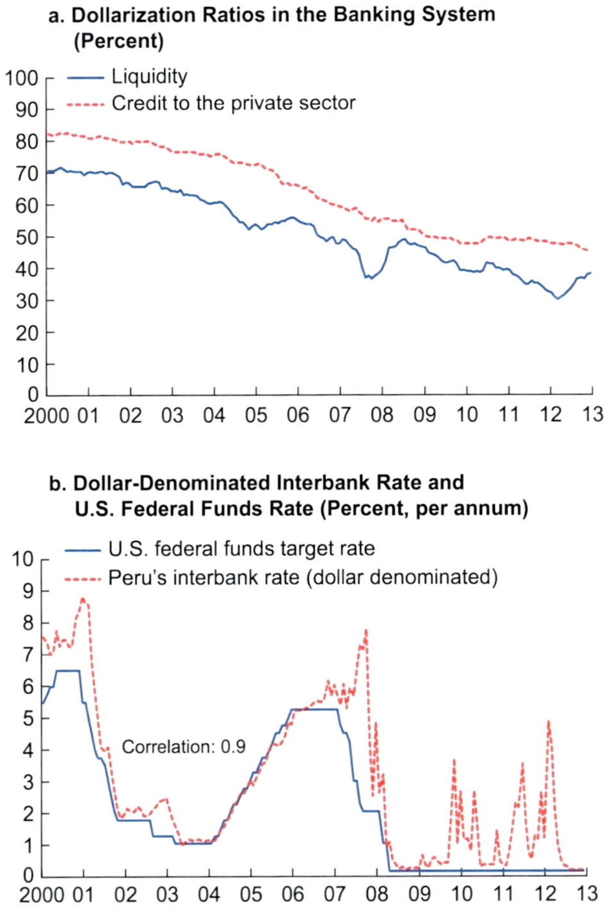


Sources: Central Reserve Bank of Peru; and Haver Analytics.

**Figure 22.2** Peru: Exposure to Shocks from U.S. Monetary Policy

based on a similar model proposed by Salas (2010). To be consistent with the 2012 and 2013 IMF Spillover Reports, the chapter considers a temporary slowdown in China's investment growth and continued tightening of U.S. monetary policy as the external shocks. In the model, Chinese and U.S. variables are treated exogenously.[2] In addition, the model assumes that the spillovers from China's investment slowdown are mainly transmitted through global metal prices and trade linkages, and the spillovers from U.S. monetary policy tightening are mainly transmitted through Peru's short-term interest rate denominated in U.S. dollars and trade linkages. The model is then estimated to quantitatively measure these spillover channels, simulated under different scenarios to generate the macroeconomic and policy responses.

An investment slowdown in China would have a significantly negative impact on world metal prices, and hence Peru's terms of trade, economic growth, and other core macroeconomic variables. More specifically, the model estimates suggest that a decrease in China's investment growth by one standard deviation is likely to cumulatively reduce Peru's terms of trade (in gap terms) and output gap by about 2 percentage points and 0.2 percentage points, respectively, over the year after the shock. The effect dies out in about three years.

[2]This chapter does not use a two-region framework such as the one developed by Berg, Karam, and Laxton (2006b), because the outward spillovers from Peru to China and the United States seem to be quite limited.

Continued tightening of U.S. monetary policy would have significantly negative and long-lasting spillover effects on Peru's U.S. dollar–denominated short-term interest rate, and hence economic growth and other core macroeconomic variables. In particular, simulations using the estimated model suggest that, depending on the magnitude and persistence of the U.S. monetary policy shock, the costs to Peru's economic activity might be larger and more persistent than those from China's investment slowdown, partly due to the nontemporary feature of the shock.

Greater exchange rate flexibility is likely to mitigate the impact of both external shocks. By allowing more room for the exchange rate to fluctuate, Peru can better use it as the first line of defense against external shocks, and significantly reduce their adverse impact. Simulations with the macroeconomic model suggest that a more flexible nominal exchange rate (as a result, for instance, of less foreign exchange intervention) is likely to reduce the spillover effects of the two external shocks on Peru's output gap, particularly over the first year after the shock.[3]

Less dollarization can also reduce the exposure of Peru to U.S. monetary policy tightening, and might be even more effective than a more flexible exchange rate. Considering the potential balance sheet effects of a more flexible exchange rate,[4] macroprudential policies directed toward reducing credit dollarization, such as reserve requirements on foreign currency–denominated deposits and short-term external liabilities,[5] might be more desirable for policymakers. This chapter's model simulations with less dollarization suggest that these macroprudential measures could be even more effective than allowing the nominal exchange rate to fluctuate more widely.

The next section of this chapter presents the macroeconomic model, followed by a description of the data and estimation strategy of the model and the estimation results. The chapter then discusses the simulation exercises conducted in three scenarios: a baseline scenario, a China scenario (where China's investment growth slows down temporarily), and a China and U.S. scenario (where, on top of the China scenario, the U.S. short-term interest rate rises permanently). More simulation exercises are then conducted to examine the roles that exchange rate flexibility and dollarization can play. The final section of the chapter presents conclusions.

## A MACROECONOMIC MODEL FOR A SMALL, OPEN, AND PARTIALLY DOLLARIZED ECONOMY

A new Keynesian macroeconomic model for Peru is developed to analyze the macroeconomic responses in the context of a small, open, and partially dollarized economy. The model is based on a general equilibrium and rational expectations model developed by Salas (2010) and Berg, Karam, and Laxton (2006a, 2006b), which can be characterized by a core set of behavioral equations. Since the model is relatively small compared to the traditional dynamic stochastic general equilibrium models, and yet has a well-grounded economic interpretation (Berg, Karam, and Laxton 2006a, 2006b), it has been used by the BCRP for policymaking. The model has four building blocks: (1) an IS curve or aggregate demand equation, (2) an expectations-augmented Phillips curve or aggregate supply equation, (3) a Taylor-type monetary policy rule for the short-term interest rate, and (4) a UIP condition. Three features of the model are worth noting. First, in the context of a small and open economy, terms-of-trade and foreign output are included as exogenous variables in the aggregate demand equation. Second, in a partially dollarized economy, agents can take loans in U.S. dollars. Thus the U.S. dollar–denominated short-term interest

[3]The effectiveness of a more flexible exchange rate depends on the assumption of the degree of flexibility, as will be discussed later in this chapter.

[4]The balance sheet effects associated with large exchange rate fluctuations have been analyzed in many studies. As shown by Calvo and Reinhart (2002) and Reinhart and Reinhart (2008), exchange rate depreciation can reduce the ability to repay foreign currency–denominated debt.

[5]See García-Escribano (2010) for a detailed discussion on Peru's prudential measures for dedollarization.

rate also enters the aggregate demand equation as an exogenous variable. Third, to capture the foreign exchange interventions conducted by the central bank, a backward-looking behavior in the determination of the exchange rate expectations is considered in the model.[6]

## Aggregate Demand

The aggregate demand or IS curve describing the dynamics of the output gap ($y_t$) is characterized in equation (22.1).

$$y_t = a_y y_{t-1} + a_r \left(\beta_r r_t + \beta_{r\$} r_t^{\$}\right) + a_{tot} \left[\beta_{tot} ToT_t + \left(1 - \beta_{tot}\right) ToT_{t-1}\right] + a_q q_t + a_{y^*} y_t^* + \varepsilon_t^y. \quad (22.1)$$

In this equation, $r_t$ is the real interest rate in local currency and $r_t^{\$}$ is the real interest rate in U.S. dollars. Their effects on the output gap are affected by a common coefficient $a_r$ and idiosyncratic coefficients, or weighting parameters, $\beta_r$ and $\beta_r\$$. $ToT_t$ is the terms-of-trade gap, that is, the gap for international relative prices,[7] and this captures the indirect spillover channel from China to Peru. It is assumed that both contemporaneous and lagged terms of trade could directly affect the current output gap, and $\beta_{tot}$ is the weighting parameter for the current terms-of-trade gap. $q_t$ is the gap for the real effective exchange rate (REER).[8] The external demand measured by the foreign output gap, $y_t^*$, is also considered. It is assumed that Peru, as a small and open economy, does not affect its terms or trade or external demand. In other words, the terms of trade and external demand in equation (22.1) are exogenous variables. Finally, the disturbance term $\varepsilon_t^y$ denotes a demand shock. Annex 22.1 provides a detailed description of the data.

## Expectations-Augmented Phillips Curve

A standard new Keynesian aggregate supply equation or expectations-augmented Phillips curve characterizing inflation ($\pi_t$) is specified in equation (22.2).

$$\pi_t = b_\pi \pi_{t-1} + b_{\pi^e} E_t\left(\pi_{t+1}\right) + b_y y_t + b_m \left(\pi_t^m + s_t - s_{t-1}\right) + \varepsilon_t^\pi. \quad (22.2)$$

In this equation, inflation has both backward- and forward-looking behaviors, indicated by the two components, $\pi_{t-1}$ and $E_t(\pi_{t+1})$, respectively, where $E_t(\pi_{t+1})$ is the inflation expectation. $\left(\pi_t^m + s_t - s_{t-1}\right)$ is imported inflation measured in local currency, computed as the sum of imported inflation $\pi_t^m$ (measured in U.S. dollars), and the nominal exchange rate variation, $(S_t - S_{t-1})$. The disturbance term $\varepsilon_t^\pi$ represents a supply shock.

## Monetary (Interest Rate) Policy Rule

A Taylor-type monetary policy rule characterizing the determination of the short-term nominal interest rate ($i_t$) is specified in equation (22.3).

$$i_t = c_i i_{t-1} + \left(1 - c_i\right)\left\{\bar{i} + c_y y_t + c_\pi \left(\pi_t - \bar{\pi}\right) + c_{\pi^e}\left[E_t\left(\pi_{t+1}\right) - \bar{\pi}\right]\right\} + \varepsilon_t^i. \quad (22.3)$$

[6]Central banks in several partially dollarized economies actively intervene in the foreign exchange market in order to prevent the balance sheet effects stemming from large exchange rate fluctuations; see Calvo and Reinhart (2002) and Reinhart and Reinhart (2008).

[7]All the gap variables in this chapter are computed with the Hodrick-Prescott (HP) filter.

[8]The REER is also included here because Peru's terms of trade and REER are not highly correlated, and thus seem to contain differentiated information. An increase in the REER indicates a real appreciation vis-à-vis its trading partners.

In this equation, $\bar{i}$ is the steady-state nominal interest rate or the neutral rate, and $\bar{\pi}$ is the inflation target. Following Barro (1989), interest rate smoothing is considered when the central bank determines the interest rate, as indicated by its first lag, $i_{t-1}$. In addition, the interest rate also responds to output gap $y_t$ and the deviations of inflation $\pi_t$ and expected inflation $E_t(\pi_{t+1})$ from the inflation target $\bar{\pi}$. Thus, the interest rate has a forward-looking behavior, as both inflation and inflation expectations are anchored by this policy rule. The disturbance term $\varepsilon_t^i$ denotes a monetary policy shock.

## Uncovered Interest Rate Parity Condition

The nominal exchange rate $S_t$ is determined by the uncovered UIP, as expressed in equation (22.4).

$$4\left[E_t\left(s_{t+1}\right)-s_t\right]=i_t-i_t^*+\varepsilon_t^s. \tag{22.4}$$

In equation (22.4), the expected quarterly exchange rate variation $[E_t(S_{t+1}) - S_t]$ is multiplied by four to be transformed into an annual term, which is equal to the differential between the interest rate in local currency and the interest rate in foreign currency (or U.S. dollars, in this chapter) plus an error term $\varepsilon_t^s$. Following Salas (2010), we assume that the exchange rate expectation $E_t(S_{t+1})$ is determined by a weighted average of a backward-looking component ($S_{t-1}$) and a forward-looking component ($S_{t+1}$), as specified in equation (22.5), which is in line with the authorities' objective of interventions to reduce the excess volatility of the exchange rate.

$$E_t\left(s_{t+1}\right)=\gamma s_{t-1}+(1-\gamma)s_{t+1}+\varepsilon_t^e. \tag{22.5}$$

The parameter $\gamma$ (between 0 and 1) implicitly measures the extent to which the exchange rate is smoothed by the central bank's foreign exchange interventions. More specifically, the higher the value of $\gamma$, the higher the degree of exchange rate smoothing.

In addition, following Salas (2010), the REER (in gap terms) in equation (22.1) is determined by its first lag, nominal exchange rate variation, and the differential between domestic and foreign inflation, as specified in equation (22.6).

$$q_t=d_q q_{t-1}+d_s\left(s_t-s_{t-1}\right)+d_\pi\left(\pi_t^*-\pi_t\right)+\varepsilon_t^q, \tag{22.6}$$

where $\pi_t^*$ is foreign inflation and the disturbance term $\varepsilon_t^q$ denotes a shock to the REER.

Finally, the real interest rates $r_t$ and $r_t^{\$}$ in the aggregate-demand equation [equation (22.1)] are linked to the domestic nominal interest rates $i_t$ and $i_t^*$ in local currency and U.S. dollars, respectively, by the Fisher equation.

$$r_t = i_t - E_t(\pi_{t+1})$$

$$r_t^* = i_t^* + E_t\left(s_{t+1}\right)-E_t\left(\pi_{t+1}\right).$$

## External Shocks

The terms of trade, external demand, and interest rate in U.S. dollars are the main exogenous variables in this model and the main channels through which external shocks spill over to Peru.

We assume that the terms-of-trade gap follows an AR(1) process with world metal prices as an exogenous variable.

$$ToT_t=\rho_{tot}ToT_{t-1}+\rho_m M_t+\varepsilon_t^{tot}. \tag{22.7}$$

In equation (22.7), $M_t$ is the world metal price (in gap terms), and $\varepsilon_t^{tot}$ is the disturbance term or the terms-of-trade shock stripping out the shocks to world metal prices.

We also assume that the domestic nominal interest rate in U.S. dollars, $i_t^*$, follows an AR(1) process with the U.S. federal funds rate $FFR_t$ as an exogenous variable, as presented in equation (22.8).[9]

$$i_t^* = \rho_i i_{t-1}^* + \rho_f FFR_t + \varepsilon_t^{i^*}. \quad (22.8)$$

External demand $y_t^*$ is approximated by a trade-weighted average of Peru's top three trading partners' output gaps, including the United States, China, and the euro area, as specified in equation (22.9).

$$y_t^* = w_t^{US} y_t^{US} + w_t^{EA} y_t^{EA} + w_t^{CHN} y_t^{CHN}. \quad (22.9)$$

In equation (22.9), $y_t$ is the output gap of each of these three economies and $w_t$ is the trade weight between each of the three economies and Peru (summing up to 1).

China's investment slowdown is transmitted through its impact on China's output and world metal prices. There are mainly two channels for the transmission of this shock in the model. First, as discussed above, China's investment slowdown directly affects China's growth and output gap $y_t^{CHN}$, and thus external demand $y_t^*$ according to equation (22.9) (the direct channel). Second, China's investment slowdown puts downward pressures on world metal prices ($M_t$) and Peru's terms of trade according to equation (22.7) (the indirect channel).

U.S. monetary policy tightening is transmitted through its impact on Peru's dollar-denominated nominal interest rate. This is mainly characterized by equation (22.8). It should be noted that, for simplicity, the second-round impact of U.S. monetary tightening on Peru through its impact on its own output is not considered in this chapter. While this is a shortcoming of the model, this assumption is motivated by the fact that the United States accounted for less than 20 percent of Peru's total trade during 2011–12. If this second-round adverse impact were to be taken into account, the actual spillovers might be even larger than our model estimates.[10]

## DATA AND ESTIMATION

The model is estimated with quarterly data over the sample period 2000:Q1–2013:Q3.[11] It has six endogenous variables: output gap, inflation, interbank interest rate in local currency, nominal exchange rate (quarterly rate of change), REER gap, and terms-of-trade gap. All the gap variables are computed with the HP filter. Expected inflation $E_t(\pi_{t+1})$ is proxied by the one-year-ahead inflation expectation, obtained from the BCRP's macroeconomic expectation survey.[12] Inflation is computed as the seasonally adjusted annualized rate, and the inflation target $\bar{\pi} = 2$ according

---

[9]The coefficient estimates would still be consistent even if the interest rates were integrated of order 1.

[10]Since this chapter is mainly interested in the impact of the rise in the U.S. (short-term) interest rate, we define the U.S. scenario as one without higher demand for Peru's exports. However, if we were to define the U.S. scenario as higher interest rates and higher demand for Peru's exports (due to the Federal Reserve's announcement that the monetary policy tightening will be conditional on improved economic indicators), then the actual impact might be smaller than the projections in this chapter.

[11]Except equation (22.8), which is estimated with data over 2000:Q1–2009:Q1, before the federal funds target rate hit the zero lower bound.

[12]The inflation expectations in the survey are end-of-year expectations. We adopt the BCRP's weighting scheme to compute the one-year-ahead expected inflation.

to the BCRP.[13] Annex 22.1 provides a detailed description of the data and their sources. Finally, the model is estimated as a system using the generalized method of moments, and the endogenous variables are instrumented by their first lags in the estimation to avoid the endogeneity problem. The weighting parameters $\beta_r$, $\beta_{r\$}$, and $\beta_{ToT}$ are not estimated but calibrated following Salas (2010): $\beta_r = 0.3$, $\beta_{r\$} = 0.15$, and $\beta_{tot} = 0.48$.[14]

Estimation results are presented in Annex Tables 22.1.1 to 22.1.4. Since the level of dollarization has been trending down and the share of Peru's exports to China has increased more notably since the mid-2000s (see Figure 22.1a), we also use a subsample 2005:Q1–2013:Q3 in the estimation as a robustness check to the full-sample estimates, whereas the results are qualitatively similar. Several points are worth mentioning. First, the coefficient estimates all have the expected signs and are in line with Salas (2010). Second, world metal prices are statistically significant in terms of driving Peru's terms-of-trade dynamics, which confirms other empirical findings.[15] Third, the U.S. federal funds rate has a significant impact on Peru's dollar-denominated nominal interest rate, which is consistent with the high correlation between these two series, as shown in Figure 22.2. Fourth, although local currency–denominated and dollar-denominated interest rates seem to have an insignificant impact on Peru's output gap, the impact becomes significant if more observations are included.[16] This suggests a downward sloping IS curve for Peru, and thus implies that the U.S. monetary policy tightening is likely to have a significant impact on Peru's real economy. Last but not least, similar to Salas (2010), we also find a significantly high degree of exchange rate smoothing, which might be partly due to the BCRP's foreign exchange interventions.

## SCENARIOS AND SIMULATIONS

This section conducts simulations using the estimated model to examine the macroeconomic responses in three different scenarios over 2013:Q4–2018:Q4. The first is a baseline scenario with the IMF's baseline projections.[17] The second is the China scenario where the investment growth rate of China declines temporarily by one standard deviation from the baseline in 2015:Q1.[18] The third is the China and U.S. scenario where, on top of the China scenario, the U.S. federal funds target rate starts to rise in 2015:Q2 following the projections made by Carpenter and others (2013). The simulation horizon is 2013:Q4–2018:Q4.

Assumptions of the external variables in the baseline scenario mainly come from IMF projections, except China's real GDP growth and the U.S. federal funds rate. We assume that the annual growth rate of Chinese real GDP stays at 7½ percent and the federal funds target rate remains unchanged at 0.15 percent per annum throughout the simulation horizon. The other external variables, including world metal prices, foreign inflation (proxied by world inflation), and the

[13]The annual inflation target has been 2 percent (with a tolerance band of ±1 percentage point) since 2007. However, the target was 2½ percent (with a tolerance band of ±1 percentage point) during 2002–06, and the target range was 3½–4 percent and 2½–3½ percent in 2000 and 2001, respectively. For simplicity, we follow Salas (2010) and assume that the annual inflation target is 2 percent over our entire sample period from 2000–13.

[14]These values of the calibrated parameters are also in line with the ones in the Quarterly Projection Model developed by the BCRP (Macroeconomic Models Department 2009).

[15]These values of the calibrated parameters are also in line with the ones in the Quarterly Projection Model developed by the BCRP (Macroeconomic Models Department 2009).

[16]However, due to data availability of the other variables, we cannot estimate the entire model with the extended sample period.

[17]Except the assumptions of China's real GDP growth and the U.S. federal funds rate; see the detailed assumptions in the following paragraph.

[18]This is a one standard deviation negative temporary shock to China's investment growth in one quarter, equivalent to a 2.5 percent decline in China's investment levels from the baseline. This shock is the same as the shock to China's investment growth considered in the IMF's 2012 Spillover Report for a better comparison (IMF 2012).

output gaps of the United States and euro area, are obtained from the IMF's World Economic Outlook database projections. Imported inflation (measured in U.S. dollars) and expected inflation are obtained from the projections included in IMF (2014).

The China scenario assumes a one standard deviation (temporary) decline in China's investment growth compared to the baseline scenario in 2015:Q1.[19] This shock has a negative impact on world metal prices and China's output gap, as expected (Annex Figure 22.1.1). First, we estimate the impact on world metal prices using a simple vector autoregression with exogenous variables, which includes the growth of China's real investment in fixed assets (FAI) and world metal price inflation as endogenous variables, and U.S. and euro area real GDP growth as exogenous variables. The estimates suggest that a one standard deviation decline in China's real FAI growth is likely to reduce world metal prices by 3¼ percent over a year, similar to the finding in IMF (2013) and Ahuja and Nabar (2012).[20] World metal price inflation returns to its baseline level after about two years. Second, to estimate the impact of this shock on China's output gap, we estimate another simple vector autoregression with exogenous variables model with China's real FAI and GDP growth as endogenous variables, and U.S. and euro area real GDP growth as exogenous variables. The estimates suggest that the shock reduces China's real GDP growth by 0.3 percentage points cumulatively after one year.[21] Finally, the assumptions for the other external variables remain the same as those in the baseline scenario.

The China and U.S. scenario assumes that, besides the assumptions in the China scenario, the federal funds target rate starts to rise gradually in 2015:Q2, following the projections made by Carpenter and others (2013). In this scenario, the federal funds target rate is assumed to increase linearly by 107 basis points over the first year (2015:Q2–2016:Q2) and another 107 basis points over the second year (2016:Q2–2017:Q2), then plateau when it reaches 4 percent per annum in 2018:Q4 (Annex Figure 22.1.1). With these dynamics, the impact on Peru's dollar-denominated interest rate is significant (almost one to one) and long lasting.

## China Scenario

Simulation results suggest that a one standard deviation negative shock to China's investment growth is likely to reduce Peru's output gap by about 0.6 percentage points cumulatively over the simulation horizon. The simulated dynamics for the main endogenous variables (in deviations from the baseline scenario) are shown in Annex Figure 22.1.2. The shock is estimated to reduce Peru's terms-of-trade gap by about 4 percentage points over the simulation horizon, and thus widen Peru's negative output gap, mainly through the income effect.[22] The output gap returns to its baseline level about three years after the shock.

The shock has a negligible impact on inflation, the nominal interest rate, and the exchange rate. Year-on-year inflation declines by only 0.03 percentage points at the peak over the simulation horizon, reflecting the well-anchored inflation expectation. The nominal interest rate in local currency is lowered by six basis points at the peak as a response to the widened negative output gap. In particular, exchange rates (both nominal and real) only depreciate slightly, reflecting a high degree of exchange rate smoothing, which is similar to the finding of Salas (2010). This might be partly due to the foreign exchange interventions conducted by the BCRP.

[19] Following Ahuja and Nabar (2012), we use real investment in fixed assets as a proxy for real investment due to the availability of quarterly data for investment.

[20] See Table 24A.2 in Ahuja and Nabar (2012). The estimated impact on world metal prices is then transformed into the impact on the gap of world metal prices by computing the new trend of metal prices with the HP filter.

[21] The estimated impact is then transformed into the impact on China's output gap by computing the new potential output with the HP filter.

[22] The shock also reduces China's output gap and affects Peru's output gap through the direct trade channel captured by $y^*$. However, this channel is not the main spillover channel, as found in IMF (2014).

## China and U.S. Scenario

In this scenario, Peru's output gap is reduced by about 2½ percentage points cumulatively over the simulation horizon and continues to widen. The shock is estimated to raise Peru's dollar-denominated interest rate by about 100 basis points one year after the shock, and thus reduce Peru's output gap significantly in terms of both magnitude and persistence. The output gap does not return to its baseline level within the simulation horizon, partly due to the long-lasting feature of this federal funds rate shock (see Annex Figure 22.1.1).

The shock has a much larger impact on inflation, the nominal interest rate, and the exchange rate than the shock to China's investment slowdown. In particular, exchange rates (both nominal and real) depreciate substantially according to the UIP and much more than in the China scenario.[23] As a result of the shock and these relatively large depreciations, inflation first declines and then starts to rise two years after the shock. However, the impact on year-on-year inflation is still limited (the peak impact is less than 0.2 percentage points), partly due to the well-anchored expected inflation. The nominal interest rate in local currency is lowered further by 3 basis points at the peak compared to the China scenario due to a larger (negative) output gap.

## The Role of Exchange Rate Flexibility

Greater exchange rate flexibility is likely to mitigate the impact of external shocks on output, but a large depreciation might put upward pressure on inflation. In order to better examine the role of exchange rate flexibility in the model, we make the nominal exchange rate (EXR) in the model exogenous by replacing the UIP condition (4) and the formation of exchange rate expectation (5) with exogenously specified dynamics of the EXR. Purchasing power parity is assumed to hold over the simulation horizon; the projected EXR is taken as our baseline. We then contrast this baseline EXR with a more-depreciated EXR path where the EXR converges exponentially toward its historical average during 2002–13.[24] Compared to the endogenous EXR in the China and U.S. scenario (Annex Figure 22.1.2), this "depreciated EXR" path assumes more rapid depreciations at the beginning but slower depreciations later on (Annex Figure 22.1.3), which shows simulation results based on these two exogenous EXR paths. Three observations are worth mentioning. First, due to a relatively large depreciation in 2015:Q1, the output gap starts to rise at the beginning but turns negative as the shocks unwind. Second, a more depreciated EXR path can reduce the decline in the output gap by about 0.4 percentage points cumulatively over the simulation horizon in both scenarios. Third, inflation is under pressure in the first year after the shocks due to the "front-loaded" depreciation,[25] and as a response, the interest rate in local currency shoots up by about 25 basis points at the same time.

## The Role of Dollarization

A lower degree of dollarization significantly reduces the adverse impact of the shock to the U.S. federal funds rate, without inducing substantial inflationary pressures. The parameter $\beta_{r\$}$ can be interpreted as a rough measure of the degree of dollarization. In an extreme case where $\beta_{r\$} = 0$, the model becomes a standard macroeconomic model for a small and open economy without dollarization, and there is no direct impact of the federal funds rate on domestic economic activity. Based on this observation, we can lower the degree of dollarization by assigning a smaller

[23]The nominal exchange rate depreciates by about 9 percent by end-2018 in the China and U.S. scenario, compared to a depreciation of only 0.2 percent in the China scenario.

[24]This is merely an illustrative assumption of a more flexible EXR, since the EXR does not generally have the mean-reverting property. This more-depreciated assumption translates to about an 11 percent depreciation compared to the baseline EXR over the simulation horizon.

[25]The peak impact on year-on-year inflation is about ½ percentage points in both scenarios.

value to $\beta_{r\$}$. A simulation exercise is done with $\beta_{r\$} = 0.075$, half of the calibrated value (Annex Figure 22.1.4). Four points are worth noticing. First, the lower degree of dollarization does not affect the China scenario. Second, the decline in the output gap in the China and U.S. scenario is significantly reduced by about 1 percentage point cumulatively over the simulation horizon, and the output gap starts to converge toward its baseline level. Third, depreciations of both nominal and real EXRs are similar to those in Annex Figure 22.1.2. Fourth, year-over-year inflation is slightly higher than in the high dollarization case, but is only 0.2 percentage points above the baseline scenario at the peak. As a result, the interest rate in local currency does not decrease as much as in the high dollarization case.

## CONCLUSIONS

This chapter finds that Peru's economic activity is vulnerable to both China's investment slowdown and continued tightening of U.S. monetary policy, a larger and long-lasting impact from the latter. A macroeconomic model for a small, open, and partially dollarized economy was developed and estimated to simulate the impact of these two external risks. The simulation results suggest that (1) a one standard deviation temporary decline in China's investment growth is likely to reduce Peru's output gap by about 0.2 percentage points cumulatively one year after the shock, and (2) a rising U.S. federal funds rate as of 2015:Q2 (increasing by some 100 basis points per year) might have substantial and persistent effects on Peru's output.

Greater exchange rate flexibility or less dollarization could enhance Peru's resilience against external risks. Simulations with a more flexible exchange rate produce smaller negative spillovers to Peru for both external risks. One of the findings of this chapter, as well as certain other studies such as Salas (2010), is the significant exchange rate smoothing achieved by the BCRP's frequent interventions in the foreign exchange market. Thus, less foreign exchange intervention might lower the degree of exchange rate smoothing and increase the flexibility of the exchange rate. Furthermore, this chapter finds that less dollarization can reduce the negative spillovers of U.S. monetary policy tightening more effectively than greater exchange rate flexibility. Macroprudential policy directed toward reducing credit dollarization, such as reserve requirements on foreign currency–denominated deposits and short-term external liabilities, might be more desirable for policymakers in terms of reinforcing Peru's resilience to external interest rate shocks.

# ANNEX 22.1

## Data

| Variable | Data and Source |
|---|---|
| Output gap | GDP (millions of 1994 nuevos soles), seasonally adjusted by Haver Analytics. Gap computed with the Hodrick-Prescott filter. Source: Haver Analytics. |
| Terms-of-trade gap | Export price index relative to import price index (1994 = 100, quarterly average, seasonally adjusted). Gap computed with the Hodrick-Prescott filter. Source: Central Reserve Bank of Peru. |
| Real effective exchange rate gap | Gap computed with the Hodrick-Prescott filter. Source: IMF, Information Notice System database. |
| Foreign output gap | A weighted average of the output gaps of the United States, euro area, and China using trade shares between each of the three economies with Peru as the weights. Sources: IMF, World Economic Outlook and International Financial Statistics databases. |
| Inflation | Consumer price index inflation (December 2001 = 100, quarterly average, seasonally adjusted). Source: Central Reserve Bank of Peru. |
| Imported inflation | Computed with the import price index (1994 = 100, quarterly average, seasonally adjusted). Source: Central Reserve Bank of Peru. |
| Foreign inflation | World inflation (quarterly average, seasonally adjusted). Source: IMF, International Financial Statistics database. |
| World metal price gap | World metal price index (2005 = 100, quarterly average, seasonally adjusted). Source: IMF, International Financial Statistics database. |
| Nominal interest rate in local currency | Interbank interest rate (quarterly average). Source: Central Reserve Bank of Peru. |
| Nominal interest rate denominated in U.S. dollars | U.S. dollar–denominated interbank interest rate (quarterly average). Source: Central Reserve Bank of Peru. |
| Nominal exchange rate | Quarterly average. Increase denotes depreciation. Source: Central Reserve Bank of Peru. |
| U.S. federal funds rate | Quarterly average. Source: Haver Analytics. |
| Expected inflation | One-year-ahead inflation expectations (quarterly average). Source: Macroeconomic Survey of the Central Reserve Bank of Peru. |
| Expected nominal exchange rate | One-year-ahead expectations of nominal exchange rate (quarterly average). Source: Macroeconomic Survey of the Central Reserve Bank of Peru. |
| China's investment in fixed assets | Source: National Bureau of Statistics of China. |

**ANNEX TABLE 22.1.1**

### Estimation Results: Aggregate Demand Equation

$$y_t = a_y y_{t-1} + a_r\left(\beta_r r_t + \beta_{r^\$} r_t^\$\right) + a_{tot}\left[\beta_{tot} ToT_t + (1-\beta_{tot}) ToT_{t-1}\right] + a_q q_t + a_{y^*} y_t^* + \varepsilon_t^y$$

| Parameter | GMM Estimates | Standard Error | GMM Estimates (2005:Q1–2013:Q3) | Posterior Mode in Salas (2010) |
|---|---|---|---|---|
| **Estimated Parameters** | | | | |
| $a_y$ | 0.71*** | 0.08 | 0.65*** | 0.49 |
| $a_r$ | −0.26 | 0.36 | −0.97*** | −0.28 |
| $a_{tot}$ | 0.03*** | 0.01 | 0.02** | 0.04 |
| $a_q$ | −0.04 | 0.14 | 0.08 | −0.06 |
| $a_{y^*}$ | 0.31* | 0.17 | 0.86*** | 0.08 |
| **Calibrated Parameters** | | | | |
| $\beta_r$ | 0.3 | — | 0.3 | 0.3 |
| $\beta_{r\$}$ | 0.15 | — | 0.15 | 0.15 |
| $\beta_{tot}$ | 0.48 | — | 0.48 | 0.48 |

Source: IMF staff estimates.
Note: *, **, and *** indicate statistical significance at the 10 percent, 5 percent, and 1 percent levels, respectively. GMM = generalized method of moments.

**ANNEX TABLE 22.1.2**

## Estimation Results: Expectations-Augmented Phillips Curve

$$\pi_t = b_\pi \pi_{t-1} + b_{\pi^e} E_t\left(\pi_{t+1}\right) + b_y y_t + b_m \pi_t^m + \varepsilon_t^\pi$$

**Estimated Parameters**

| Parameter | GMM Estimates | Standard Error | GMM Estimates (2005:Q1–2013:Q3) | Posterior Mode in Salas (2010) |
|---|---|---|---|---|
| $b_\pi$ | 0.12** | 0.05 | 0.15 | 0.65 |
| $b_{\pi^e}$ | 0.21*** | 0.02 | 0.19*** | 0.30 |
| $b_y$ | 0.10*** | 0.03 | 0.14*** | 0.10 |
| $b_m$ | 0.06*** | 0.01 | 0.06*** | 0.05 |

Source: IMF staff estimates.
Note: *, **, and *** indicate statistical significance at the 10 percent, 5 percent, and 1 percent levels, respectively.
GMM = generalized method of moments.

**ANNEX TABLE 22.1.3**

## Estimation Results: Monetary Policy Rule

$$i_t = c_i i_{t-1} + \left(1 - c_i\right)\left\{\bar{i} + c_y y_t + c_\pi\left(\pi_t - \bar{\pi}\right) + c_{\pi^e}\left[E_t\left(\pi_{t+1}\right) - \bar{\pi}\right]\right\} + \varepsilon_t^i$$

**Estimated Parameters**

| Parameter | GMM Estimate | Standard Error | GMM Estimates (2005:Q1–2013:Q3) | Posterior Mode in Salas (2010) |
|---|---|---|---|---|
| $c_i$ | 0.73*** | 0.04 | 0.73*** | 0.66 |
| $c_y$ | 0.70*** | 0.26 | -0.09 | 0.51 |
| $c_\pi$ | 0.71* | 0.41 | 5.54 | — |
| $c_\pi^e$ | 0.15 | 0.28 | -0.20 | 1.93 |
| $\bar{i}$ | 3.30*** | 0.38 | 3.07*** | — |

Source: IMF staff estimates.
Note: *, **, and *** indicate statistical significance at the 10 percent, 5 percent, and 1 percent levels, respectively.
GMM = generalized method of moments.

**ANNEX TABLE 22.1.4**

## Estimation Results: Exchange Rate Expectation Equation

$$E_t\left(s_{t+1}\right) = \gamma s_{t-1} + \left(1 - \gamma\right) s_{t+1} + \varepsilon_t^e$$

**Estimated Parameters**

| Parameter | GMM Estimate | Standard Error | GMM Estimates (2005:Q1–2013:Q3) | Posterior Mode in Salas (2010) |
|---|---|---|---|---|
| $\gamma$ | 0.61** | 0.26 | 0.73*** | 0.66 |

Source: IMF staff estimates.
Note: *, **, and *** indicate statistical significance at the 10 percent, 5 percent, and 1 percent levels, respectively.
GMM = generalized method of moments.

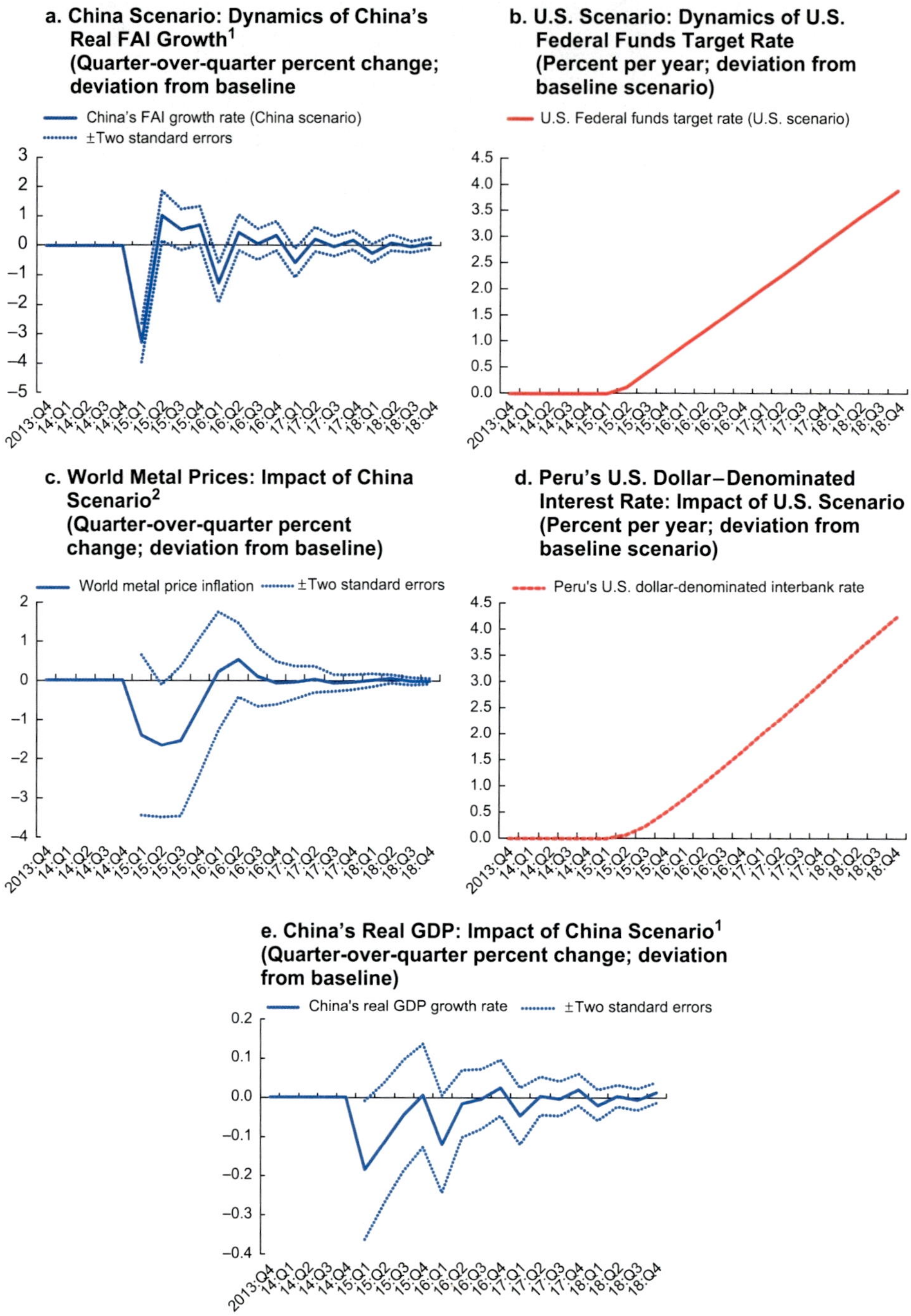


Sources: Central Reserve Bank of Peru; Haver Analytics; IMF, Global Assumptions, International Financial Statistics, Information Notice System, and World Economic Outlook databases; National Institute of Statistics; and IMF staff estimates.

Note: Panels b and d based on vector autoregressions with exogenous variables. Three different scenarios of external shocks are considered in this simulation exercise over the simulation horizon of 2013:Q4–2018:Q4: (1) Baseline scenario: mainly assumptions from the IMF's World Economic Outlook database and IMF (2014). (2) China scenario: A one standarddeviation temporary decline in China's investment growth in 2015:Q1 compared to the baseline scenario. (A one standard deviation decline in growth is equivalent to a 2.5 percent decline in China's investment levels from the baseline scenario.) (3) U.S. scenario: The federal funds target rate starts to rise in 2015:Q2 and follows the projections made by Carpenter and others (2013). FAI = real investment in fixed assets; VARX = vector autoregressive model with exogenous variables.

[1]Impulse responses of China's real GDP growth to a one standard deviation shock to the FAI growth in 2015:Q1 estimated with a VARX model including China's real FAI and GDP growth as endogenous variables and U.S. and euro area real GDP growth as exogenous variables. Lag length is chosen according to the AIC. Shocks are identified in the VARX by the Cholesky decomposition and the impulse responses are not affected by the Cholesky ordering.

[2]Impulse responses of China's FAI growth to its own one standard deviation shock in 2015:Q1 estimated with a VARX model including China's FAI growth rate and world metal price inflation as endogenous variables and U.S. and euro area real GDP growth as exogenous variables. Lag length is chosen according to the Akaike's information criterion. Shocks are identified in the VARX by the Cholesky decomposition and the impulse responses are not affected by the Cholesky ordering.

**Annex Figure 22.1.1** External Shocks and Simulation Scenarios

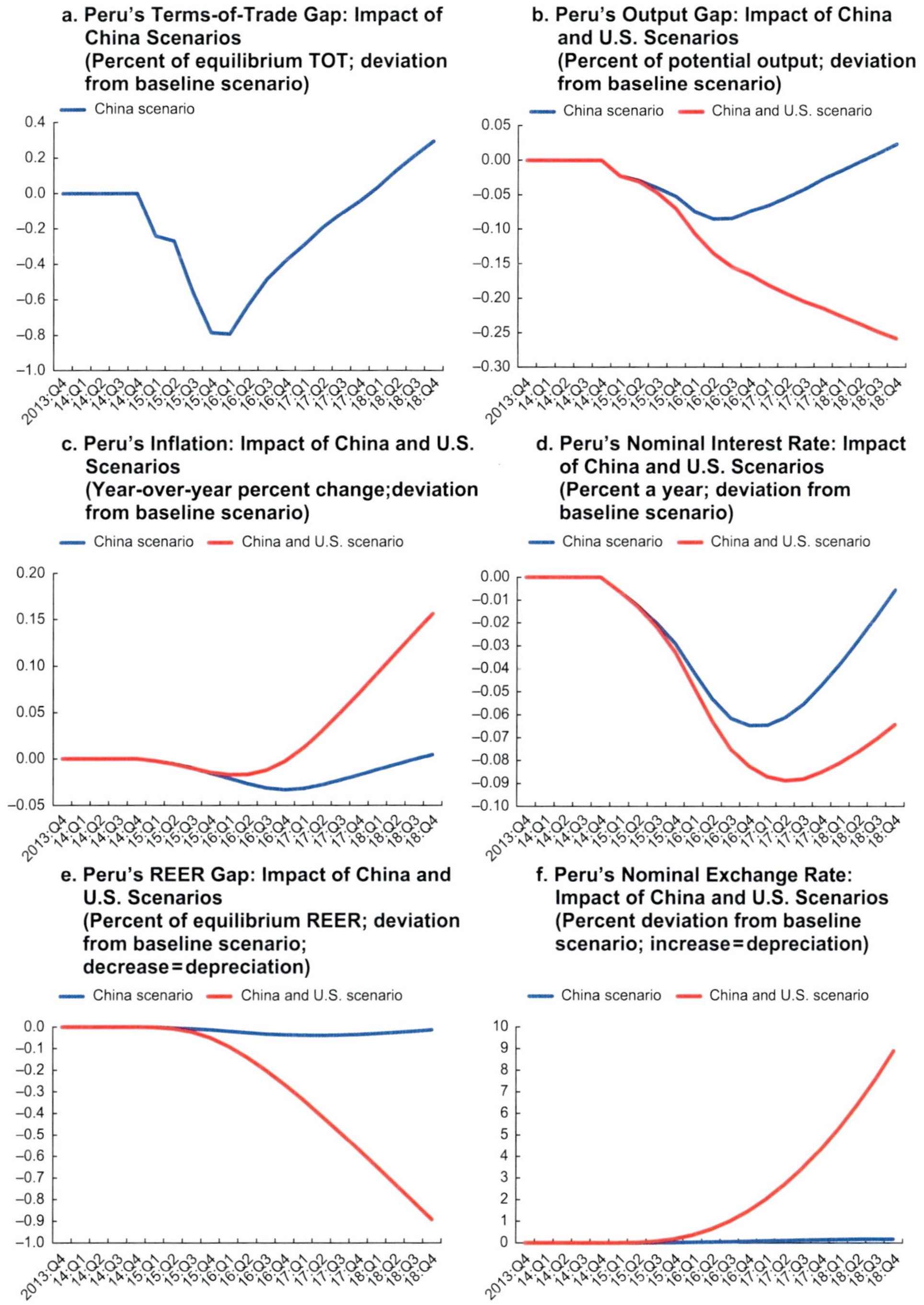


Sources: Central Reserve Bank of Peru; Haver Analytics; IMF, International Financial Statistics, Information Notice System, and World Economic Outlook databases; National Institute of Statistics; and IMF staff estimates.

Note: Three different scenarios of external shocks are considered in this simulation exercise over the simulation horizon of 2013:Q4–2018:Q4: (1) Baseline scenario: mainly assumptions from the IMF's World Economic Outlook database and IMF (2014). (2) China scenario: A one standard deviation temporary decline in China's investment growth in 2015:Q1 compared to the baseline scenario. (A one standard deviation decline in growth is equivalent to a 2.5 percent decline in China's investment levels from the baseline scenario.) (3) China and U.S. scenario: On top of the assumptions in the China scenario, the U.S. federal funds target rate starts to rise in 2015:Q2 and follows the projections made by Carpenter and others (2013). REER = real effective exchange rate; TOT = terms of trade.

**Annex Figure 22.1.2** Peru's Macroeconomic Responses: Impact of External Shocks

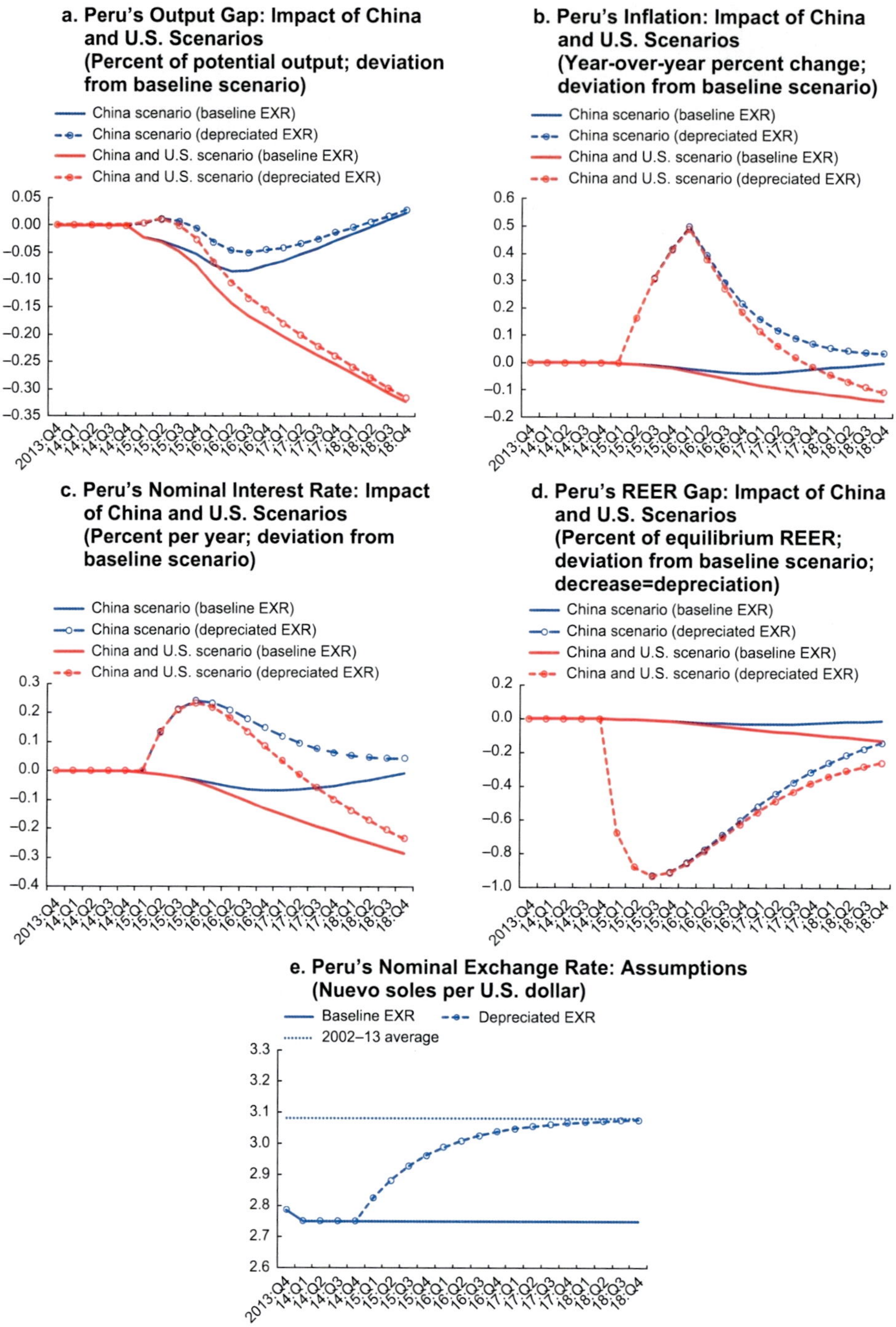


Sources: Central Reserve Bank of Peru; Haver Analytics; IMF, International Financial Statistics, Information Notice System, and World Economic Outlook databases; National Institute of Statistics; and IMF staff estimates.

Note: Nominal EXR is assumed to be exogenous in this simulation exercise over the simulation horizon of 2013:Q4–2018:Q4. Three different scenarios of external shocks and two different EXR dynamics are considered and specified as follows: (1) Baseline scenario: mainly assumptions from the IMF's World Economic Outlook database and IMF (2014). (2) China scenario: A one standard deviation temporary decline in China's investment growth in 2015:Q1 compared to the baseline scenario. (A one standard deviation decline in growth is equivalent to a 2.5 percent decline in China's investment levels from the baseline scenario.) (3) China and U.S. scenario: On top of the assumptions in the China scenario, the U.S. federal funds target rate starts to rise in 2015:Q2 and follows the projections made by Carpenter and others (2013). (4) Baseline EXR is calculated assuming that the purchasing power parity holds during 2014:Q1–2018:Q4. (5) EXR starts to depreciate gradually toward its 2002–13 average when China's investment growth declines in 2015:Q1. EXR = exchange rate; REER = real effective exchange rate.

**Annex Figure 22.1.3** Peru's Macroeconomic Responses with Exogenous Exchange Rate: Impact of External Shocks

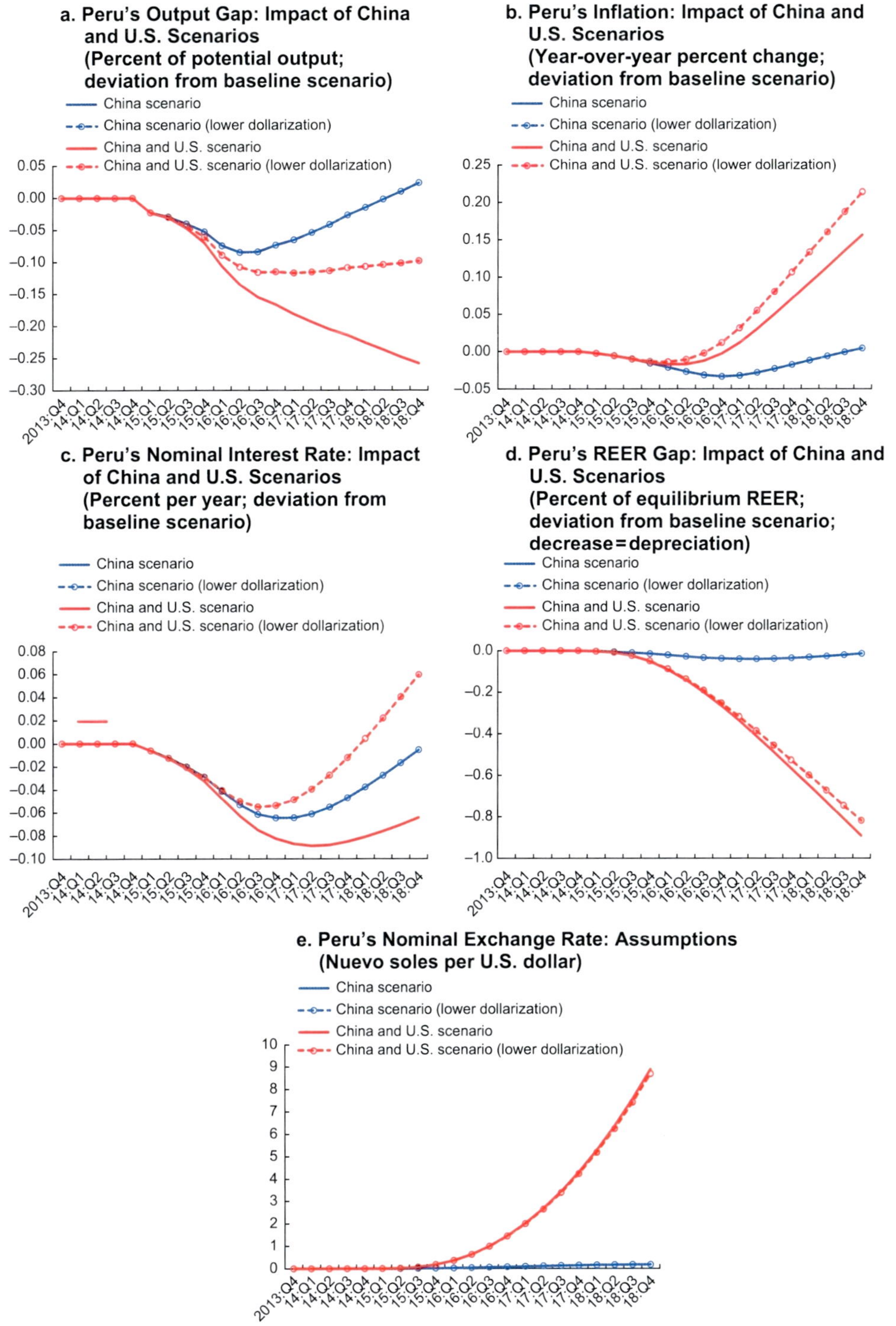


Sources: Central Reserve Bank of Peru; Haver Analytics; IMF, International Financial Statistics, Information Notice System, and World Economic Outlook databases; National Institute of Statistics; and IMF staff estimates.

Note: A lower degree of dollarization in this simulation exercise is characterized by a smaller value of the calibrated parameter $\beta_{r\$}$ in the model. More specifically, $\beta_{r\$}$ is set to be a half of the calibrated value, that is, 0.075. In addition, three different scenarios of external shocks are considered in this simulation exercise over the simulation horizon of 2013:Q4–2018:Q4. (1) Baseline scenario: mainly assumptions from the IMF's World Economic Outlook database and IMF (2014). (2) China scenario: A one standard deviation temporary decline in China's investment growth in 2015:Q1 compared to the baseline scenario. (A one standard deviation decline in growth is equivalent to a 2.5 percent decline in China's investment levels from the baseline scenario.) (3) China and U.S. scenario: On top of the assumptions in the China scenario, the U.S. federal funds target rate starts to rise in 2015:Q2 and follows the projections made by Carpenter and others (2013). REER = real effective exchange rate.

**Annex Figure 22.1.4** Peru's Macroeconomic Responses with a Lower Degree of Dollarization: Impact of External Shocks

## REFERENCES

Ahuja, A. and M. Nabar. 2012. "Investment-Led Growth in China: Global Spillovers." Working Paper 12/267, International Monetary Fund, Washington DC.

Barro, R. J. 1989. "Interest-Rate Smoothing." NBER Working Paper No. 2581, National Bureau of Economic Research, Cambridge, Massachusetts.

Berg, A., P. Karam, and D. Laxton. 2006a. "A Practical Model-Based Approach to Monetary Policy Analysis—Overview." Working Paper 06/80, International Monetary Fund, Washington, DC.

———. 2006b. "Practical Model-Based Monetary Policy Analysis—A How-To Guide." Working Paper 06/81, International Monetary Fund, Washington, DC.

Calvo, G. A., and C. M. Reinhart. 2002. "The Fear of Floating." *The Quarterly Journal of Economics* 117 (2): 379–408.

Carpenter, S. B., J. E. Ihrig, E. C. Klee, D. W. Quinn, and A. H. Boote. 2013. "The Federal Reserve's Balance Sheet and Earnings: A Primer and Projections." Finance and Economics Discussion Series Working Paper No. 2013–1, U.S. Federal Reserve, Washington, DC.

García-Escribano, M. 2010. "Peru: Drivers of De-dollarization." Working Paper 10/169, International Monetary Fund, Washington, DC.

International Monetary Fund. 2012. "Spillover Report" (July 9). http://www.imf.org/external/np/pp/eng/2012/070912.pdf.

———. 2013. "IMF Multilateral Policy Issues Report: 2013 Spillover Report" (August 1). http://www.imf.org/external/np/pp/eng/2013/070213.pdf.

———. 2014. "Peru: Staff Report for the 2013 Article IV Consultation." Country Report 14/21 (January 24). http://www.imf.org/external/pubs/ft/scr/2014/cr1421.pdf.

Macroeconomic Models Department. 2009. "Modelo de Proyección Trimestral del BCRP." BCRP Working Paper No. 2009–006, Central Reserve Bank of Peru, Lima.

Reinhart, C., and V. Reinhart. 2008. "Capital Inflows and Reserve Accumulation: The Recent Evidence." NBER Working Paper No. 2581, National Bureau of Economic Research, Cambridge, Massachusetts.

Salas, J. 2010. "Bayesian Estimation of a Simple Macroeconomic Model for a Small Open and Partially Dollarized Economy." BCRP Working Paper No. 2010-007, Central Reserve Bank of Peru, Lima.

CHAPTER 23

# Advances and Challenges in Social Policies

YU CHING WONG

*Significant progress has been made in reducing poverty and income inequality in Peru over the past decade. Poverty and inequality indicators improved thanks to a combination of high growth, macroeconomic stability, job creation, increased incomes, and strengthened social policies. The authorities have expressed their commitment to more socially inclusive growth. A new Ministry of Social Inclusion was created in 2011 for that purpose, and the budget has devoted an increasing amount of resources for socially inclusive initiatives. However, much remains to be done in specific areas such as gender inequality and social disparities between rural and urban populations. Further enhancing the efficiency of social spending through better targeted social programs and continuing to raise more resources to increase social expenditure will be key for Peru to achieve socially inclusive growth.*

This chapter reviews progress as measured by different social indicators in Peru, compares those indicators with regional and nonregional peers, and examines the policy challenges to achieve more socially inclusive growth. The next section reviews the performance of Peru's key social indicators in comparison with other emerging market economies in Latin America and other peer countries. The chapter then reviews Peru's key challenges to further reduce intracountry or regional disparities in poverty levels and in meeting basic needs. The chapter presents a snapshot of public social expenditure in Peru and summarizes the authorities' priorities and action plans—as announced at the start of President Ollanta Humala's administration in 2011—to achieve key social targets by 2016. The chapter also highlights the efforts needed to increase the size and efficiency of social expenditure inputs, before presenting some conclusions.

## COMPARISONS OF PERU'S SOCIAL INDICATORS WITH SELECTED LATIN AMERICAN COUNTRIES

Growth and macroeconomic stability in Peru over the past 10 years have contributed to a significant reduction in poverty.[1] Peru's economic growth has been one of the strongest among the LA6 countries in the region,[2] with purchasing power parity GDP per capita expanding on average by 6 percent during 2000–14 (Figure 23.1). Against this backdrop, poverty in Peru, as measured by the international benchmark of the share of the population living on less than $2 (purchasing power parity) a day, was reduced by two-thirds during 2000–12 (Figure 23.2). This largely reversed an increase in poverty during 1990–2000, as poverty reduction was slow in response to economic expansion in the 1990s and poverty increased in the wake of the Asian crisis that

The author would like to thank Madelyn Estrada and Zulima Leal for outstanding research assistance.

[1] Social indicator data from the World Bank and the United Nations Development Programme are used for cross-country comparisons with Peru.

[2] The LA6—Brazil, Chile, Colombia, Mexico, Peru, and Uruguay—are the Latin American economies with more integrated and developed financial markets that follow inflation targeting as the monetary framework.

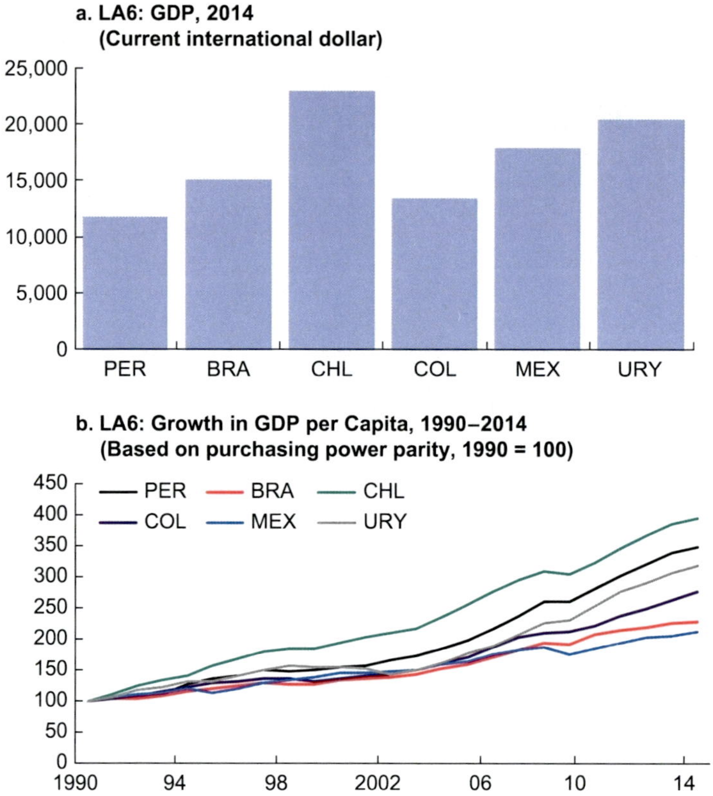


Source: IMF, World Economic Outlook database.
Note: LA6 = Brazil (BRA), Chile (CHL), Colombia (COL), Mexico (MEX), Peru (PER), and Uruguay (URG).

**Figure 23.1** Peru and Selected Latin American Countries: GDP per Capita (2014) and GDP per Capita Growth

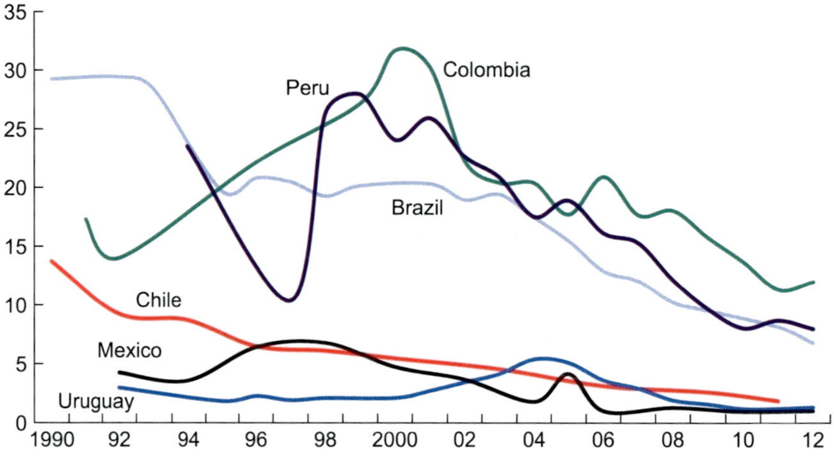


Source: World Bank, World Development Indicators database (World Data Bank; January 30, 2015).
Note: Poverty headcount ratio at $2 a day (purchasing power parity).

**Figure 23.2** Peru and Selected Latin American Countries: Poverty Rate

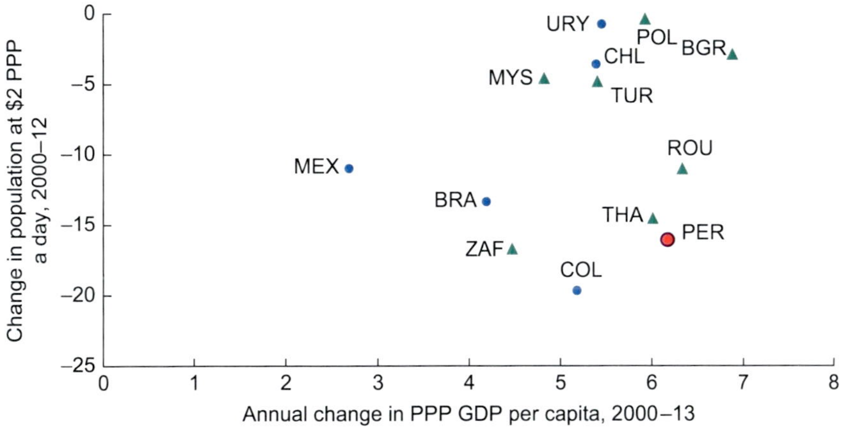


Sources: IMF, World Economic Outlook database; and World Bank, World Development Indicators.
Note: LA6 (Brazil, Chile, Colombia, Mexico, Peru, Uruguay) and peer comparators Bulgaria, Malaysia, Romania, South Africa, Thailand, and Turkey. See page vii for country abbreviations used in this figure. PPP = purchasing power parity.

**Figure 23.3** Poverty Reduction and Change in GDP Per Capita, 2000–13

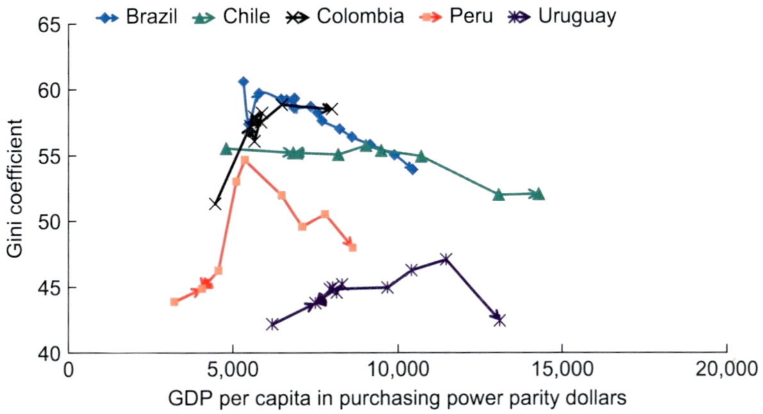


Sources: IMF, World Economic Outlook database; and World Bank, World Development Indicators database.

**Figure 23.4** Increase in GDP per Capita Has Helped to Reduce Income Inequality (1990–2009)

affected Peru. Among the LA6 economies, Peru's poverty level is below that of Colombia, but above the levels of the other four countries (on a purchasing power parity $2 per day poverty line basis; see Figure 23.3).

Peru has also achieved important progress in reducing income inequalities (Figure 23.4). Income inequality declined steadily as income per capita rose, with the Gini coefficient declining to 45 percent in 2012, representing an improvement of about 11 percentage points since the late 1990s. Peru ranks second among the LA6 in the measure of income inequality by the Gini coefficient, although Latin American countries are among the most unequal in the world.[3,4]

Peru has also seen strong improvements in a large number of key social indicators, with steady progress in human development. Peru ranked 82nd out of 187 countries (44th percentile) on the

[3]Peru ranks 27th in income inequality out of 129 countries with data on the Gini coefficient. For the top 55 countries with the highest income inequality, 22 are countries from Latin America and Caribbean (United Nations Development Programme 2013).

[4]Peru ranked the sixth lowest (Haiti, 26 percent; Honduras, 67 percent; Bolivia, 71 percent; Nicaragua, 74 percent; and Paraguay, 82 percent) among countries in Latin America and the Caribbean.

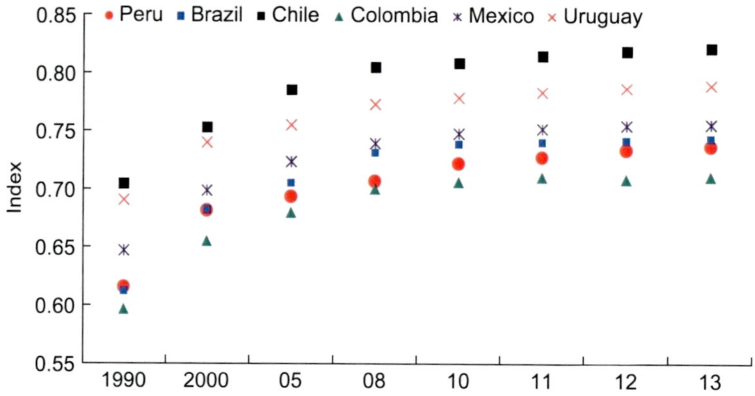


Source: United Nations Development Programme, Human Development Index.
Note: Chile (41st) is in the category of "Very High Human Development"; Uruguay (50th), Mexico (71st), Brazil (79th), Peru (82nd), and Colombia (98th) are in the category of "High Human Development" in 2013.

**Figure 23.5** LA6: Human Development Index Rankings

United Nations Development Programme's Human Development Index in 2013 (Figure 23.5). In terms of relative ranking, the score represents a slight improvement compared to Peru's performance since 2005 (46th percentile) but largely on par with that in 2000 (43th percentile).

Peru's performance on other social indicators, especially health and education, are also comparable to LA6 countries (Figure 23.6). For instance, Peru achieved impressive progress in reducing infant mortality by more than half from 2003–13, to 13 per 1,000 live births. However, Peru still has room for improvement compared to other LA6 countries in terms of access to improved rural water sources (only available to 72 percent of the rural population), and adult literacy rates (Figure 23.6). Secondary and tertiary education enrollments are not particularly low when compared with other countries, but progress in the past decade has been slow.

## INTRACOUNTRY DISPARITIES

Peru has a ways to go in improving gender inequalities (Figure 23.7). The country ranked 77th out of 152 countries (51st percentile) in 2013 on the Human Development Gender Inequality Index, a composite measure that shows inequality in achievements between women and men in reproductive health, empowerment, and the labor market. In particular, Peru's maternal mortality rate of 67 per 100,000 live births (albeit a declining trend since the late 2000s) is still high among the LA6. Also, only 83 percent of childbirths are attended by skilled health personnel in Peru, the lowest among the LA6.[5]

Reducing widespread rural poverty remains a major policy challenge in Peru. The rural population accounts for a quarter of the country's total population, but 49 percent of the poor were concentrated in rural areas in 2013 (Table 23.1).[6] While 5 percent of the national population fell below the extreme poverty line in 2013, 16 percent of Peruvians in rural areas were living in

[5]In fact, Peru ranked the sixth lowest among countries in Latin America and the Caribbean. The lowest were Haiti, 26 percent; Honduras, 67 percent; Bolivia, 71 percent; Nicaragua, 74 percent; and Paraguay, 82 percent.

[6]With increasing urbanization, 75 percent of Peru's population resided in urban areas and only 25 percent in rural areas in 2013 (Instituto Nacional de Estadística e Informática 2014). By national definition in Peru, households are classified as "poor" if their total expenditures are lower than the cost of a basic food basket plus an estimate of nonfood expenditures, and as "extremely poor" if their total expenditures are lower than the cost of a basic food basket. In 2013, the threshold was defined at 292 nuevos soles per capita per month for poverty and 155 nuevos soles per capita per month for extreme poverty (Instituto Nacional de Estadística e Informática 2010).

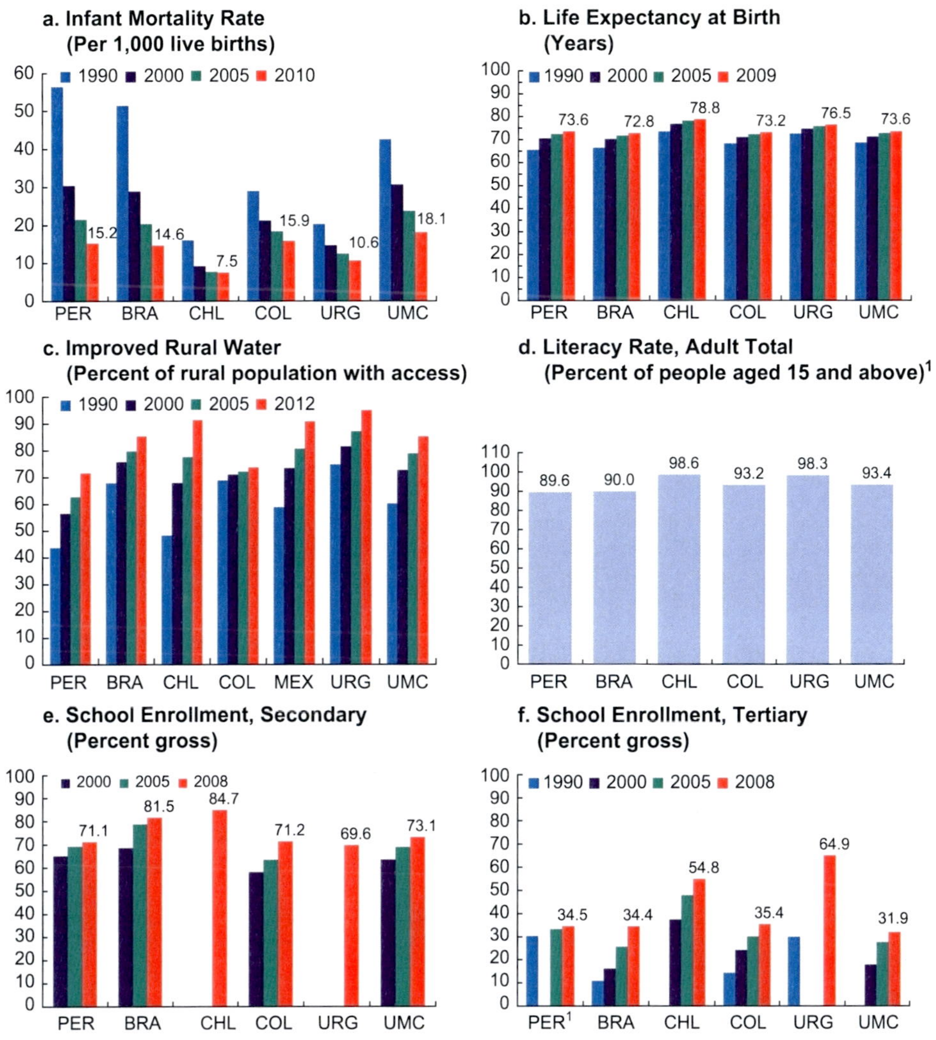


Source: World Bank, World Development Index database.

Note: Countries are divided among income groups according to 2010 gross national income per capita, calculated using the World Bank Atlas method: low income, $1,005 or less; lower middle income, $1,006–$3,975; upper middle income, $3,976–$12,275; and high income, $12,276 or more BRA = Brazil; CHL = Chile; COL = Colombia; MEX = Mexico; PER = Peru; URG = Uruguay; UMC = upper middle income countries.

[1] Latest data available are 2007 for Peru and 2008 for Brazil and Chile.

**Figure 23.6** Selected Social Indicators

extreme poverty (compared to 1 percent in urban areas). By geographical distribution, 47.2 percent of the poor are concentrated in the highlands (*Sierra*), followed by coastal areas (35.9 percent) and forest areas (*Selva*) (16.9 percent) in 2013.

While extreme poverty levels in rural areas are still high, they have declined significantly since 2001 (Figure 23.8). The national population living in extreme poverty dropped by close to 20 percentage points during 2001–13 to 4.7 percent. Extreme poverty in rural areas declined more rapidly, by 35 percentage points, from 51 percent in 2001 to 16 percent in 2013. The national population living below the poverty line declined by close to 31 percentage points from 2001 to 2013 (to 23.9 percent). A similar decline is seen in the share of the rural population living below the poverty line, which dropped from 78 percent of the rural population in 2001 to 48 percent in 2013.

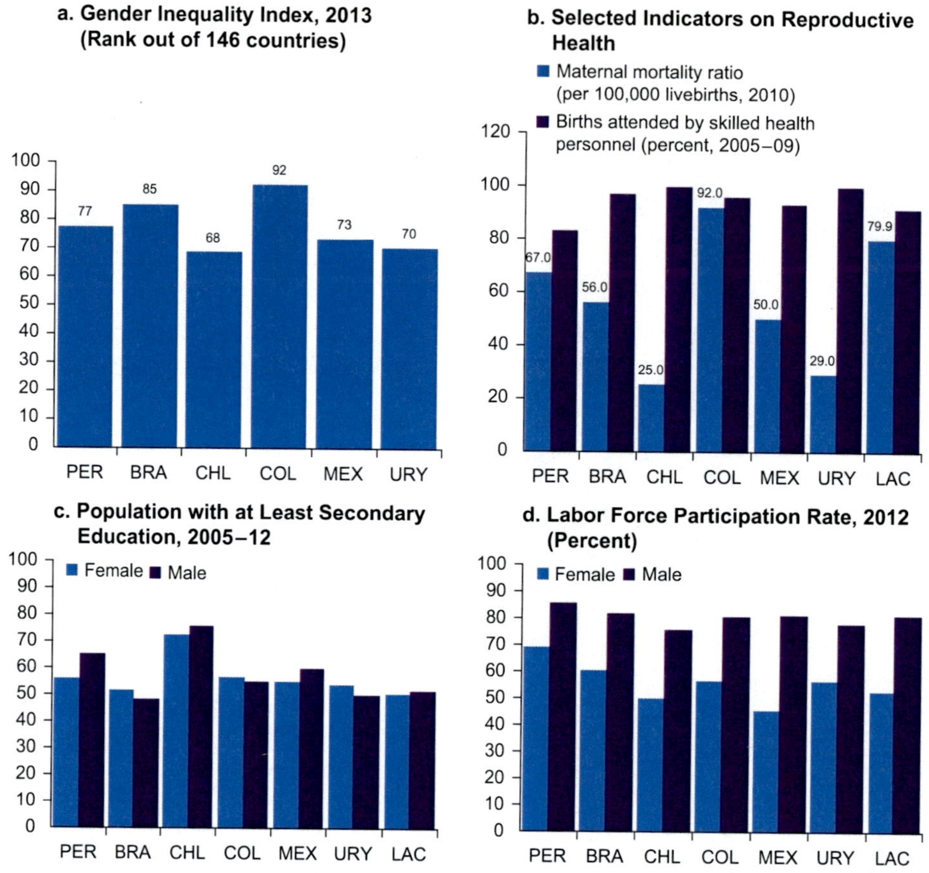


Source: United Nations Development Programme (2014).

Note: The Gender Inequality Index is a composite measure reflecting inequality in achievements between women and men in three dimensions: reproductive health, empowerment, and the labor market. LAC = Latin America and the Caribbean. See page vii for a list of three-letter country codes used in this volume.

**Figure 23.7** Selected Gender Inequality Indicators

**TABLE 23.1**

Distribution of Poor and Extreme Poor Population *(Percent)*

| | Poverty | | Extreme Poverty | |
|---|---|---|---|---|
| | 2010 | 2013 | 2010 | 2013 |
| Area of Residence | 100.0 | 100.0 | 100.0 | 100.0 |
| Urban | 47.9 | 50.7 | 17.9 | 16.7 |
| Rural | 52.1 | 49.3 | 82.1 | 83.3 |
| Geographical Region | 100.0 | 100.0 | 100.0 | 100.0 |
| Costa | 34.7 | 35.9 | 10.4 | 9.2 |
| Sierra | 48.5 | 47.2 | 68.3 | 71.9 |
| Selva | 16.8 | 16.9 | 21.3 | 18.9 |

Source: Instituto Nacional de Estadística e Informática (2011).

Poverty is particularly high among the indigenous population, the self-employed and primary sector workers, and populations with lower education attainment. The incidence of poverty in 2013 was 27 percent among those who classify themselves as indigenous (including Quechua, Aymara, and Amazonian origin), although this marked a decline from 30.2 percent in the previous year. By type of employment, 42.6 percent of the poor (47.1 percent of the extreme poor) were self-employed compared to 32 percent of the nonpoor in 2013. In addition, 54.3 percent of

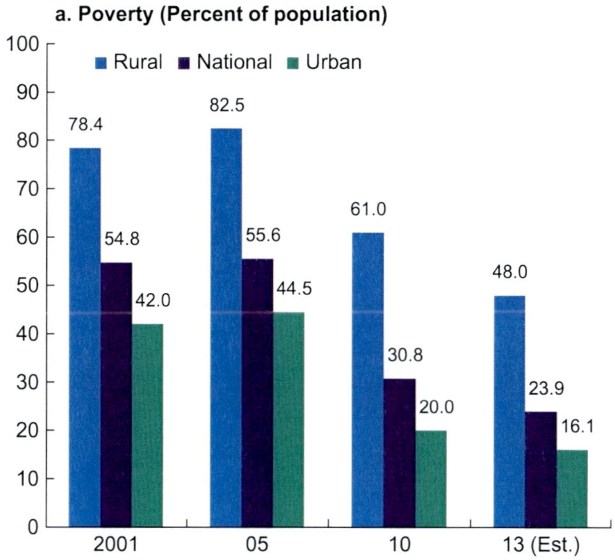


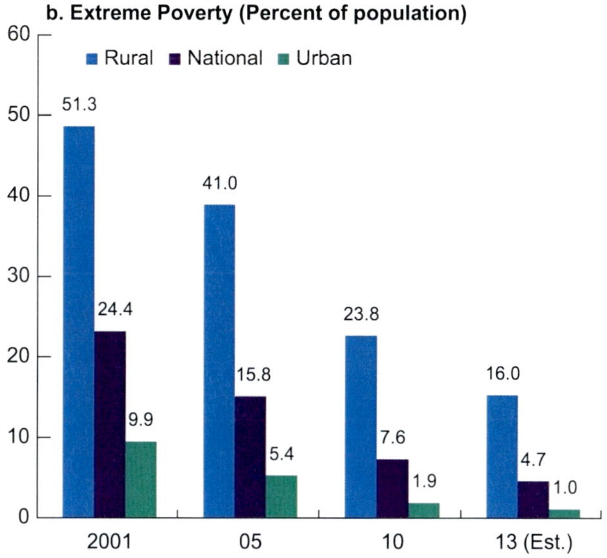


Source: Peru National Institute of Statistics and Information Technology.

**Figure 23.8** Poverty and Extreme Poverty in Peru, 2001, 2005, 2010, and 2013

the working-age poor (80.4 percent of the extreme poor) were working in the agriculture, fishery, and mining sector, whereas only 18.3 percent of the nonpoor were employed in these sectors. Low education attainment contributes directly to poverty incidence. An adult living in poverty averages 7.3 years of formal education and an adult living in extreme poverty averages 5.7 years. In contrast, an adult nonpoor person has an average of 10.5 years of education (Instituto Nacional de Estadística e Informática 2014).

Employment growth has been an important driver in reducing poverty. Household income has increased through higher employment and higher wages. For the period 2001–09, the employed economically active population grew by 24.4 percent, with even higher growth of

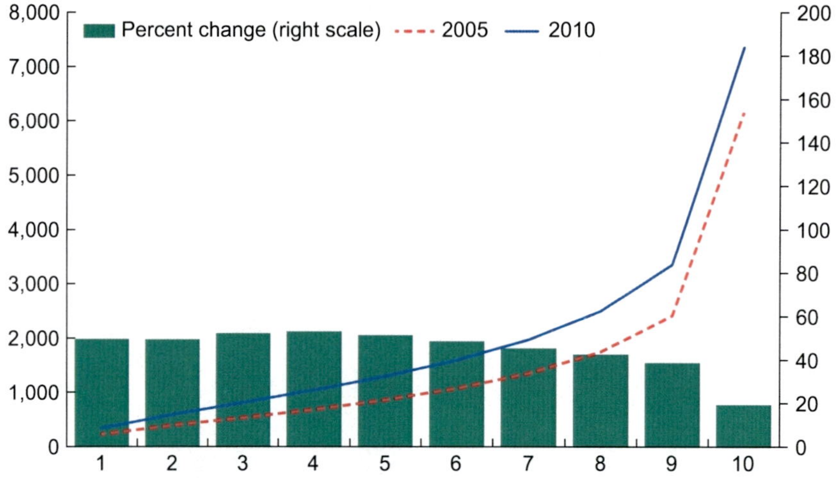


Source: Central Reserve Bank of Peru; and Instituto Nacional de Estadística e Informática (2010).
Note: Percent change in constant U.S. dollars, at prices in Metropolitan Lima, 2001.

**Figure 23.9** Average Real Income per Capita by Income Deciles

30.3 percent in Metropolitan Lima (Instituto Nacional de Estadística e Informática 2010). Real income per capita of the population in the lowest third, fourth, and fifth income deciles increased by more than 50 percent between 2005 and 2010 (Figure 23.9). Other studies such as Economic Commission for Latin America and the Caribbean (2010) have found that poverty reduction in Peru during 2002–09 was mainly due to the growth effect (78 percent), whereas the distribution effect (22 percent) was much smaller.

Peru's macroeconomic management success in recent years has helped reduce poverty and create jobs, and this will likely continue with sound macroeconomic policies. A large number of studies have examined the reasons why economic growth has not generated a faster reduction in poverty (World Bank 2005, 2011). Beside geographical and endowment differences, growth has been based on natural resource extraction industries—which are high in capital intensity but create few jobs. At the same time, rural agriculture and urban informal employment sectors are characterized by relatively lower productivity and low wage growth. Strengthening the linkage between growth and employment creation would require microeconomic reforms to achieve higher productivity levels and a more diversified economy, including more labor-intensive sectors. In addition, increasing the efficiency of public investments would reduce the regional gaps in physical and human capital and bring about greater redistribution over the medium term.

## PUBLIC SPENDING COMPARISON

Peru has lower public expenditures on education and health than other LA6 countries. Comparable data from the World Bank's World Development Indicators show that Peru's total public expenditures on education and health are below 6 percent of GDP, the lowest among the LA6, which average from 8–10 percent of GDP (Figure 23.10). This is in part due to the smaller size of Peru's government revenue, which is only about 20 percent of GDP (Figure 23.11). This suggests that mobilizing more government revenue would help provide the additional resources to increase social spending beyond current levels.

Fiscal policy has had a limited effect in lowering inequality in Peru to date. A study by the Organisation for Economic Co-operation and Development (2012) shows that cash transfer has been effective in reducing income inequalities in countries outside the region. However, in the

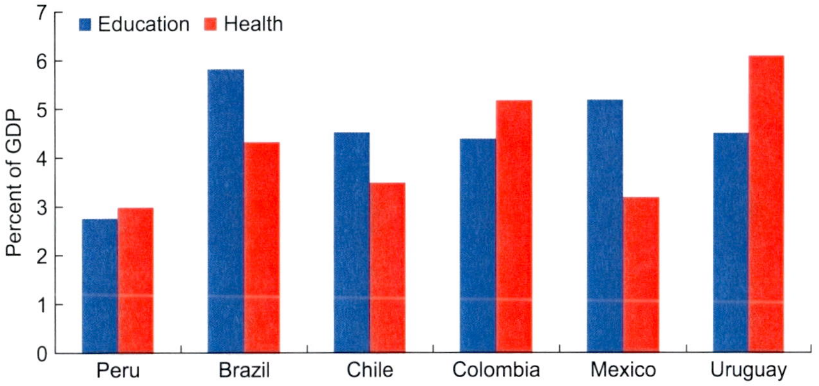


Source: World Bank, World Development Indicators database.
Note: For education expenditure, data are available for earlier years only for Brazil (2010), and Mexico and Uruguay (2011).

**Figure 23.10** Peru and Selected Latin American Countries: Public Expenditures in Education and Health, 2012

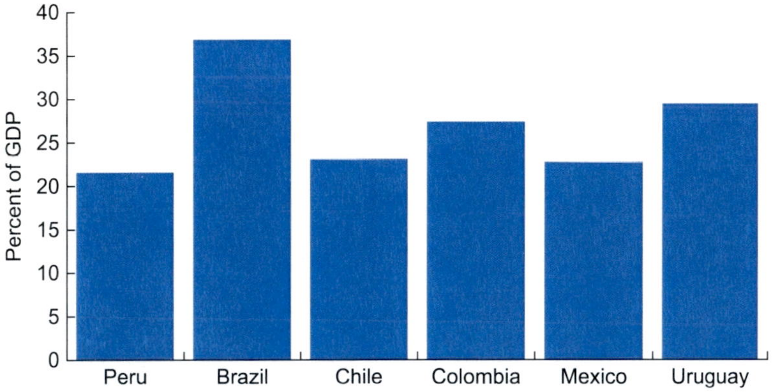


Source: IMF, World Economic Outlook database.

**Figure 23.11** Government Revenue in Peru and Selected Latin American Countries, 2009–14

case of Peru and other LA6 countries, such transfers appear to have only a limited impact on lowering income inequality (Figure 23.12).

Targeted social programs have attempted to alleviate poverty and promote development of low-income populations. In Peru, universal coverage of health and education accounts for about 40 percent of social spending. Targeted social programs for the purpose of mitigating extreme poverty showed the largest increase among the different categories of social spending, increasing by an average of 14.5 percent during 2005–10 (Table 23.2). They accounted for 1.7 percent of GDP or about 16 percent of total social expenditure in 2010. There are 22 social programs conducted by state agencies, including major programs such as the Juntos Cash Transfer Program, Comprehensive Nutrition Program, Integral Health Insurance Program (*Seguro Integral de Salud*), Glass of Milk Program, and the National Education Infrastructure Program. Results-based budgeting for these programs has been in place since the 2007 Budget Act.

The authorities have highlighted the need to further improve the quality and targeting of social expenditure. Social expenditure effectiveness is hindered by the presence of imperfect targeting—leakage (benefiting nontarget populations) surpasses 40 percent in four out of five

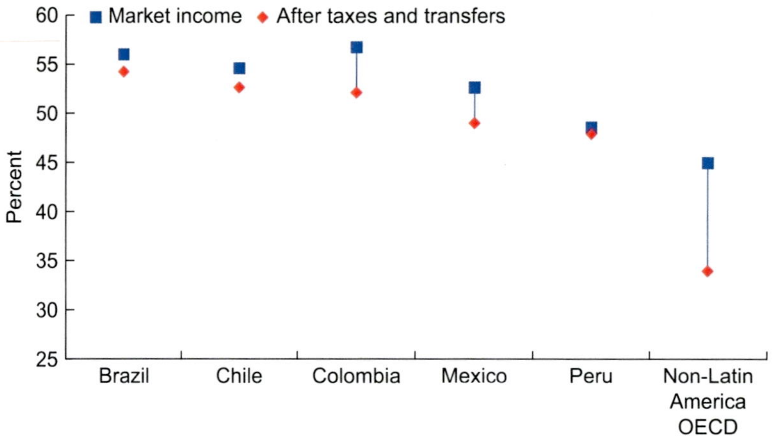


Source: OECD (2012).
Note: OECD = Organisation for Economic Co-operation and Development.

**Figure 23.12** Income Inequality in Select Latin America Countries Relative to Income Inequality in Countries outside the Region

major social programs, and undercoverage (not benefiting the target population) ranges from 46 percent in the program with the smallest rates of exclusion to 97 percent in the worst case. The cost of leakage in these five programs is estimated by the government to represent more than one-third of their total budget (Llanos and Rosas 2010, 4). In this context, better utilization of the Household Targeting System (*Sistema de Focalizacion de Hogares*) could help achieve greater delivery efficiency. For instance, the application of the National Identity Document for minors has allowed for identifying 11 million children who are the recipients of the bulk of social programs (Ministry of the Economy and Finance 2011).

## THE GOVERNMENT'S KEY PRIORITIES AND ACTION PLAN

The Peruvian authorities are committed to delivering more socially inclusive growth. Over the last few years, the approved budgets have allocated additional resources for strengthening human capital and social inclusion (Table 23.3). The government has also released a set of key quantitative social targets that include reducing the overall poverty ratio (national definition) to 20 percent, and reducing extreme poverty by half to 5 percent and rural poverty to 27 percent, respectively, by 2016 (Table 23.4). In addition, a new Ministry of Social Development and Inclusion was created in August 2011 to better coordinate social programs previously managed by the Ministry of Women's Affairs, the Ministry of Economy and Finance, and the Cabinet.[7]

Priorities include greater focus on the poorest districts and expanding the coverage of successful social programs. The authorities are focusing their programs on the 800 poorest districts through the household targeting system. Other key measures include expanding successful social programs, such as the *Juntos* cash transfer program, to additional districts, and increasing the coverage of targeted programs for persons over the age of 65 (S/. 250 every two months) living in extreme poverty and who have not received state benefits by way of the expanded coverage of *Pension 65*. The program initially aimed to expand coverage from 70,000 persons with

[7] See Chapter 26 on the establishment of the Ministry of Social Development and Inclusion.

**TABLE 23.2**

## Public Sector Social Expenditure

| | | | Share of GDP | | Average Increase | Share of General Government Expenditure | | Share in Total | |
|---|---|---|---|---|---|---|---|---|---|
| | 2005 | 2010 | 2005 | 2010 | 2005–10 | 2005 | 2010 | 2005 | 2010 |
| | (Millions of nuevos soles) | | | | | (Percent) | | | |
| **Total Social Expenditure and Pensions** | **28,607** | **46,367** | **10.9** | **10.7** | **10.1** | **57.8** | **52.3** | **100.0** | **100.0** |
| **Universal Coverage (Education and health)**[1] | **10,587** | **18,979** | **4.0** | **4.4** | **12.4** | **21.4** | **21.4** | **37.0** | **40.9** |
| Education | 7,527 | 11,292 | 2.9 | 2.6 | 8.4 | 15.2 | 12.7 | 26.3 | 24.4 |
| Health | 3,060 | 7,687 | 1.2 | 1.8 | 20.2 | 6.2 | 8.7 | 10.7 | 16.6 |
| **Targeted Programs (Extreme poverty)** | **3,711** | **7,300** | **1.4** | **1.7** | **14.5** | **7.5** | **8.2** | **13.0** | **15.7** |
| **Nontargeted Social Programs** | **12,951** | **16,215** | **4.9** | **3.7** | **4.6** | **26.2** | **18.3** | **45.3** | **35.0** |
| Social Health Insurance (ESSALUD) | 3,626 | 5,609 | 1.4 | 1.3 | 9.1 | 7.3 | 6.3 | 12.7 | 12.1 |
| Pensions | 9,324 | 10,605 | 3.6 | 2.4 | 2.6 | 18.8 | 12.0 | 32.6 | 22.9 |
| Housing Development Program (FONAVI) | 1 | 0 | 0.0 | 0.0 | ... | 0.0 | 0.0 | 0.0 | 0.0 |
| **Other Social Expenditure**[2] | **1,358** | **3,873** | **0.5** | **0.9** | **23.3** | **2.7** | **4.4** | **4.7** | **8.4** |

Source: Ministry of Economy and Finance.

[1] Net of spending on education and health already included in the extreme poverty programs. Includes social expenditure of the three levels of government: national, regional, and local.

[2] Includes other social expenditure of the local and regional government.

**TABLE 23.3**

**Key Policy Priorities on Growth with Social Inclusion**

1. Early childhood
   - Launch of More Cradle (*CUNA MAS*), comprehensive care for children up to three years focusing on nutrition and early education, and *SAMU*, a government-run mobile emergency care service
   - Expansion of the Coordinated Nutrition Program
   - Expansion of the Maternal and Newborn Health Program
2. Education for children and adolescents
   - More schools and teachers in rural areas
   - Instruction that takes into account the diversity, multilingualism, and multiculturalism of the country
   - Evaluating the learning achievements of student and teacher performance
   - Educational support
3. Providing young people with opportunities for advancement through scholarships in universities and technical colleges: *Beca 18*
4. Assisting poor families with minimum income: the expansion of the *Juntos* program
5. Assisting the elderly in extreme poverty without a retirement pension through *Pension 65*
6. Rural development
   - Coordinated infrastructure investment (e.g., rural roads, electrification, sanitation) tendered to bidder requesting the lowest subsidy.

Source: Ministry of the Economy and Finance.

**TABLE 23.4**

**Social Indicator Outcomes and Goals** *(Percent)*

| | 2010 | Goal 2016 |
|---|---|---|
| **Poverty** | | |
| Poverty Rate | 31 | 20 |
| Extreme Poverty | 10 | 5 |
| Rural Poverty | 54 | 27 |
| **Health** | | |
| Chronic Infant Malnutrition | 18 | 5 |
| Neonatal Mortality (per 1,000 population) | 9 | 5 |
| **Education** | | |
| Coverage of Initial Education | 70 | 95 |
| Rural Elementary Education[1] | 8 | 40 |
| **Social Services**[2] | | |
| Rural Electrification | 60 | 85 |
| Rural Water Supply | 39 | 57 |
| Rural Sanitation | 11 | 45 |

Sources: Macroconsult; and IMF staff estimates.
[1] Completion.
[2] Coverage of homes.

S/. 47 million in 2011, to 170,000 persons with S/. 241 million in 2012, and to 267,000 persons with S/. 400 million in 2013.

It is necessary to further enhance social spending programs and raise more resources to increase social expenditure. While the current expenditure envelope allows for initial increases in social spending, additional fiscal space needs to be created (when it is macroeconomically feasible) to accommodate higher spending in the medium term by increasing revenue mobilization. In this context, the modified mineral taxation regime introduced in 2011—consisting of profit margin–based royalties, a new special mining tax as revenue for the central government, and a special voluntary levy on profits targeting companies holding stability contracts—could generate an additional US$1 billion (about 0.5 percent of GDP) annually.

## CONCLUSIONS

Although Peru compares well with its regional peers in key social indicators despite low levels of social spending, there is much room for improvement in specific areas such as gender inequality. Importantly, large regional and rural-urban disparities persist and further reduction of rural poverty remains a key policy challenge. While economic growth and macroeconomic stability remain the prerequisites for poverty reduction, further enhancing the efficiency of social spending and raising more resources to increase social expenditure are needed. In addition, increasing the efficiency of public investments would reduce the regional gaps in physical and human capital and bring about greater redistribution over the medium term.

## REFERENCES

Economic Commission for Latin America and the Caribbean. 2010. *Social Panorama of Latin America 2010.* Santiago: ECLAC.

Instituto Nacional de Estadística e Informática. 2010. "Perú: Evolución de los Indicadores de Empleo e Ingresos por Departamentos, 2001–2009." Instituto Nacional de Estadística e Informática, Lima.

———. 2011. "Evolución de la Pobreza al 2010." Instituto Nacional de Estadística e Informática, Lima.

———. 2014. "Evolución de la Pobreza Monetaria 2009-2013." Instituto Nacional de Estadística e Informática, Lima.

Llanos, D., and N. Rosas. 2010. *Cry Over Spilled Milk: Improving Targeting Outcomes in Social Programs in Peru.* Cambridge, Massachusetts: Harvard Kennedy School of Government.

Ministry of the Economy and Finance. 2011. "Macro Macroeconómico Multiannual, 2012–14." Ministry of the Economy and Finance, Lima (May).

Organisation for Economic Co-operation and Development. 2012. *Latin American Economic Outlook 2012.* Paris: Organisation for Economic Co-operation and Development.

United Nations Development Programme. 2013. *Human Development Report 2013.* New York: United Nations Development Programme.

———. 2014. *Human Development Report 2014.* New York: United Nations Development Programme.

World Bank. 2005. "Peru Opportunities for All—Peru Poverty Assessment." World Bank, Washington, DC.

———. 2011. *Peru en el umbral de una nueva era.* Washington, DC: World Bank.

PART III

# Challenges Ahead

CHAPTER 24

# Some Thoughts on Fiscal Policy and the Unfinished Agenda

ALONSO SEGURA

*Peru has achieved a positive fiscal policy track record over the past 25 years thanks to an ongoing process of strengthening the macrofiscal framework. This first involved taking steps to correct existing distortions, such as the tendency to run fiscal deficits, the volatility of the main fiscal aggregates that reduced the predictability and credibility of fiscal management, and the haphazard approach to budgetary decision making, which lacked a clear, single objective. Once macroeconomic stability and credibility were restored, the authorities continued their efforts to consolidate the macrofiscal framework and institutionalize fiscal policy through binding rules governing the preparation of the budget. In an international setting that in coming years may pose challenges for the medium-term growth of economies such as Peru, there is room to consolidate the current macrofiscal framework and to maintain fiscal sustainability through action on three fronts: increasing permanent revenues through measures to broaden the tax base, seeking greater efficiency in public spending and prioritizing expenditures on the basis of an ex post evaluation of results, and reforming the system of intergovernmental transfers based on the principles of predictability in public spending, limitations on the capacity to absorb the resources transferred, and accountability.*

The prudent management of fiscal policy that has been consistently applied in recent decades in Peru is one of the pillars of the country's current economic success. This is reflected in the credibility of the Peruvian economy, as recognized through its solid credit ratings, as well as its fiscal indicators, which are even better than those of countries with the same or higher credit ratings. This confidence has translated into lower costs for investing and persistent high rates of growth, both in investment and in national output. Responsible management of fiscal policy, together with other reforms, has created a climate that encourages the private sector to take medium- and long-term decisions with greater confidence and thereby improve economic productivity, a vital ingredient for growth over the long term.

Thus, what Peru has achieved today is part of an ongoing strengthening process that began some 25 years ago. The process included correcting the glaring distortions at that time, such as the persistent tendency to run fiscal deficits and the marked volatility of the main fiscal aggregates—which reduced the predictability and credibility of fiscal management—as well as the haphazard approach to budgetary decision making, which lacked a clear, single objective. In fact, during the 1980s, fiscal policy was characterized by a steady series of large fiscal deficits and an economy that was unable to obtain financing except through monetary issuance, with the attendant high inflation. Subsequently, the 1990s saw the initial reforms that made it possible to stabilize the macroeconomy and earn credibility among economic agents. In the last 10 years, the policies pursued have allowed Peru to consolidate its fiscal policy with a focus on balanced management of public finances over the economic cycle, and the strengthening of fiscal institutions, so as to impart predictability and stability to the existing macrofiscal framework. The country must now be careful not to undo all that effort and must focus on building upon what has been achieved, keeping an eye on the goals that have been established and taking nothing for granted.

In particular, the international setting that is expected to prevail in coming years will pose challenges for the medium-term growth of economies such as Peru. With a view to boosting the growth potential in the next few years and responding to the looming international context, the government has recently proposed actions within a framework along three fronts geared to ensuring greater investment and gains in productivity and competitiveness: (1) strengthening human capital and reducing informality, (2) reducing the infrastructure gap, and (3) cutting red tape and reducing excess costs.

Peruvian fiscal policy is being conducted within a macrofiscal framework that will have to be maintained and consolidated in the coming years. Indeed, in the macroeconomic setting that the world is likely to witness over the next few years, the current macrofiscal framework can be supplemented so as to optimize the functioning of fiscal policy in terms of sustainability and its stance vis-à-vis the economic cycle.

Fiscal sustainability is an essential condition for promoting needed structural reforms which take years or even decades to achieve. The last 25 years of Peru's economic history are evidence of this, because without prudent management of fiscal policy it would never have been possible to construct the macrofiscal cushions for dealing with the 2008–09 global financial crisis or with the current external shock. Empirical evidence reveals countless examples of countries that abandoned their commitment to responsible fiscal policy, even if only temporarily, thereby losing credibility and consistency over time, and making fiscal imbalances a self-fulfilling prophecy. Peru must eschew this route, especially because the economy has a propensity toward sharp swings in its terms of trade and the country is prone to natural disasters.

The unfinished agenda that will allow Peru to cope more effectively with the new challenges in the years ahead could in fact be quite lengthy. This chapter, however, will focus on the following items that are a good point of departure for continuing with a fiscal reform process that was launched nearly 25 years ago, and that is still yielding good results: (1) boosting permanent tax revenues, which requires broadening the tax base and making further efforts to reduce informality, which is one of the main factors constraining economic growth; (2) significantly improving the efficiency of public spending and setting spending priorities in light of an ex post evaluation of results, together with mechanisms to minimize the time needed to design and implement a timely and time-bound fiscal response to mitigate the situation in a countercyclical manner; and (3) reforming the system of intergovernmental transfers for all types of financing sources on the basis of the principles of predictability in public spending, limitations on the capacity to absorb the transferred resources, accountability, and ex post evaluations.

Table 24.1 and Figure 24.1, as well as the sections that follow, outline the phases of fiscal policy in Peru since the 1980s.

## FIRST PHASE: FISCAL AUTARKY WITH HIGH RECURRING DEFICITS AND A CONSEQUENT LACK OF CREDIBILITY

During the 1970s and 1980s, the government believed that it could stimulate the economy through state-sponsored investment by making use of the international financial facilities that were available at the time. Yet this approach was both inefficient and failed to consider the vagaries of the international economy. Thus growth fell substantially when the international setting turned less favorable, with sharp drops in prices for the commodities that Peru was exporting, slow growth in the world economy, and rising international interest rates. This was accompanied by an approach to macroeconomic management that was uncertain and unpredictable, and also by idiosyncratic shocks such as the El Niño phenomenon of 1983. As a result, average growth in GDP per capita from 1980–89 fell to about 1.5 percent, hyperinflation reached 7,481 percent in 1990, the current account deficit averaged about 5.5 percent of GDP a year, net international

**TABLE 24.1**

## Phases of Fiscal Policy in Peru

| Phase 1: Fiscal Austerity, Recurrent Deficits, and Scant Credibility | Phase 2: Fiscal Stabilization and the Quest for Credibility | Phase 3: Institution Building and Fiscal Consolidation | Phase 4: Strengthening of Institutions |
|---|---|---|---|
| **1980s** | **1990s** | **2000s** | **2010 to date** |
| ***Setting*** | | | |
| 1980: End of the boom in export prices (1980)<br>1983: El Niño phenomenon | Crises: Asia (1997), Russia (1990), Brazil (1999)<br>1998: El Niño phenomenon | 2002: Boom in export prices | 2008–09: Global financial crisis<br>2011: End of the boom in export prices |
| ***Policy*** | | | |
| 1985–87: Reduction in the general sales tax; increase in the payroll at the expense of public investment | 1991: Tax reform; resumption of payment on the debt | 2003: Decentralization; administrative systems for the general sales tax | 2011: New mining regime |
| | 1993: New Constitution; creation of the "Cash Committee" | 2008: Results-based budgeting | 2013: Promulgation of the Law to Strengthen Fiscal Responsibility and Transparency |
| 1986–89: Distortionary taxes introduced; financing through monetary emission | 1999: Promulgation of the Fiscal Prudence and Transparency Act; creation of the Fiscal Stabilization Fund | | |

Source: Author's compilation.

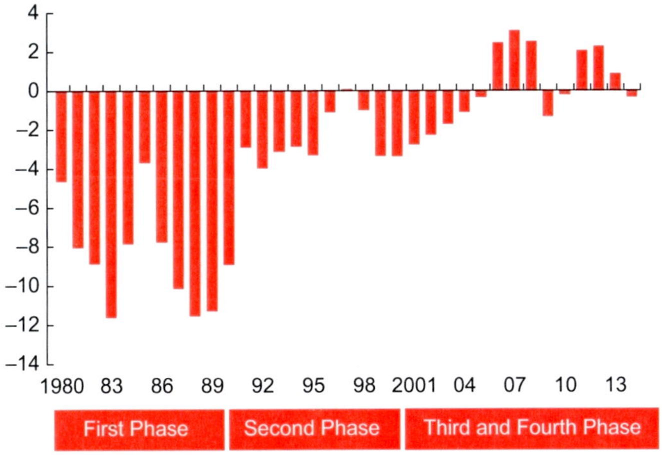


Source: Central Reserve Bank of Peru.

**Figure 24.1** Peru: Economic Outcome of the Nonfinancial Public Sector *(Percent of GDP)*

reserves turned negative, and there were recurrent and growing fiscal deficits that amounted to 9 percent of GDP, while payments on the public debt were suspended.

In this context, the country's productive system came to a virtual standstill, as reflected in public sector revenues. Moreover, the tax system had serious distortions (with the attendant economic costs for society), such as an excessive and growing number of taxes and tax rates, and a virtual loss of control and oversight by the authorities.

During this period there were six different general taxes (income tax, wealth tax, import duties, export duties, production taxes, and consumption taxes), and these in turn contained multiple subclassifications and different regimes. In addition, there were many taxes imposed on specific transactions, with the result that the effective number of taxes exceeded 100. This showed the weakness of a tax system that, in practice, was unworkable. The units responsible for the administration and supervision of taxes and customs duties were extremely weak, and there was no effective compliance with tax and customs obligations. In general terms, the tax system was complex, distortive, inefficient, and unfair, and did nothing to contribute to the sound management of fiscal policy.

As a result of this situation, it was difficult to collect greater revenues when the Peruvian economy fell victim to a major external shock and a prolonged period of slow growth. Thus, current revenues shrank from 20.5 percent of GDP in 1982 to 9 percent in 1989.

Despite the scant capacity to finance the public budget through tax revenues, public spending was the equivalent of 13.5 percent of GDP in 1989, and there was significant budgetary rigidity. This was reflected in wage and salary increases, pension outlays, and price controls that were introduced to alleviate the impact of hyperinflation on people's real incomes. Thus, for example, public payroll expenditures rose on average by 10.5 percent in real terms during 1985 and 1987. Prices were fixed during this period for such goods as gasoline, public services, and basic food items, including cooking oil, pasta, and sugar, in some cases entailing state subsidies. As a result, current expenditure (primarily on payrolls and pensions) represented more than 75 percent of nonfinancial public spending. Another characteristic that shows the rigidity and inefficiency of spending during the period was the many state-owned enterprises in most sectors of the economy. In 1980, there were at least 23 state-owned enterprises, operating in most economic sectors, including food (Epsa), tourism (Entur), commerce (Enci), and mining (MineroPerú).

By contrast, public investment served as the adjustment variable in spending policy during this period. Public investment declined by as much as 30 percent in some years until by the end of the 1980s it stood at about 3 percent of GDP. The low revenue collection capacity, combined with inefficient and rigid public spending, led to recurrent fiscal deficits that had to be financed. At the same time, however, external financing dried up in the wake of the decision by the authorities to declare a moratorium on payment of the public debt, a move that effectively cut Peru off from the international financial community. Consequently, the fiscal deficits were financed by internal borrowing, primarily in the form of monetary emissions by the central bank. For example, in 1987 financing provided by the central bank to the public treasury amounted to nearly 4 percentage points of GDP. This internal financing through the central bank merely increased the already high inflation rate and exacerbated macroeconomic imbalances. Moreover, the payments that were actually made lagged well behind those authorized, reflecting the financing problems facing the authorities.

By the end of the 1980s, the fiscal situation was dire and a series of reforms were needed to eliminate distortions, regain credibility in financial markets, and initiate a process of macroeconomic stabilization.

## SECOND PHASE: STABILIZATION AND THE QUEST FOR CREDIBILITY

At the beginning of the 1990s, in the midst of the crisis then gripping the Peruvian economy, an in-depth program of macroeconomic stabilization was launched to correct the macroeconomic imbalances, including the high and recurrent fiscal deficits, hyperinflation, shortage of foreign exchange, and other problems noted above. The program also aimed to liberalize the economy, restore the country's access to international financial markets, and lay the foundation for a domestic capital market.

On the fiscal front, an important reform was implemented on the revenue side based on the principles of efficiency, neutrality, simplicity, and fairness in the tax system. Accordingly, 41 tax exemptions were suspended and 64 taxes were eliminated at the beginning of the decade. At the same time, a system was introduced based on only four taxes—the income tax, value-added tax, excise tax, and customs duties—together with a special regime for small taxpayers designed to reduce tax informality. The strengthening of the tax system also included a move to modernize and reinforce the National Superintendency of Tax Administration and the Superintendency of Customs Administration, an initiative undertaken with the technical support of international agencies and drawing upon experience in developed economies. It should be noted that these two supervisory bodies were merged in 2003. This set of measures soon began to bear fruit: tax revenues rose from 9 percent of GDP in 1989 to nearly 16 percent in 1995.

Another set of reforms that served to make the economy more efficient and generate additional tax revenues involved the program to privatize money-losing public enterprises and free up external trade. A legal framework was established to effect the sale of state-owned enterprises, and agencies were created to handle both the regulatory and promotional aspects of privatizations and concessions. As a result of these moves, the government was able to sell enterprises that were showing losses, such as Peruana de Teléfonos, AeroPerú, and ElectroLima. In terms of liberalizing foreign trade, customs duties were simplified and reduced, with the result that the average tariff was brought down from 66 percent to 16 percent, and the enormous array of rates and provisions was cut to three simple rates in 1993.

The rationalization of the tax system had to be accompanied by strict control over public spending. Accordingly, the Ministry of the Economy and Finance (MEF) was reinforced as the central body for making decisions with budgetary impact, thus doing away with the scattering of responsibilities that had prevailed until then. A Cash Committee (*Comité de Caja*) was created to set expenditure ceilings based on the availability of public funds, as well as to make decisions on cash management and debt service. In addition, all tax legislation that included any type of tax exemption was to be accompanied by a report from the MEF, and emergency decrees could no longer be used to amend taxation provisions. These changes remain in place today.

Along with the internal corrections to the tax system and the budget process, a plan was launched to restore the Peruvian economy's access to the international financial market through an orderly process for refinancing payment of the external debt. This reintegration process was achieved with the assistance of a group of Latin American economies as well as advanced economies, led by Japan and the United States, accompanied by specific commitments with international agencies, which supplied the financing needed for the stabilization programs. Subsequently, amounts owed to the Paris Club were renegotiated in a way that would not exert pressure on the fiscal accounts.

This marked the launch of the process of macroeconomic stabilization. Thanks to that process the fiscal deficit, which stood at 8.9 percent of GDP during the 1980s, was reduced to an average of 1 percent in the 1990s (with primary surpluses). As a result, inflation fell sharply to less than 4 percent in 2000, and annual economic growth averaged 1.5 percent in per capita terms. This macroeconomic situation, together with the renegotiation of the public debt, succeeded in restoring Peru's credibility with economic agents. The next step was to consolidate these gains and make them sustainable and consistent over time.

## THIRD PHASE: INSTITUTION BUILDING AND FISCAL CONSOLIDATION

The macrofiscal framework was institutionalized in 1999 with promulgation of the Fiscal Prudence and Transparency Act (*Ley de Prudencia y Transparencia Fiscal* [LPTF]). The general principle underlying that law was "to establish a commitment to a balanced fiscal outcome over the cycle, building up fiscal surpluses in favorable periods and allowing only moderate and nonrecurrent fiscal deficits in times of slower growth." To make the law operational, macrofiscal rules were incorporated into the framework, with the objective of diminishing the room for discretion and more solidly institutionalizing macrofiscal policy.

In the same vein, escape clauses or rules of exception (Article 5) were included to allow for more flexible fiscal management in the event of a national emergency or an international crisis that might seriously affect the national economy (provisions that could be invoked only upon a request from the executive branch to the Congress) or when there was sufficient evidence of a fall in GDP in real terms (as confirmed in a report to the legislative branch from the MEF).

Finally, a countercyclical tool known as the Fiscal Stabilization Fund (*Fondo de Estabilización Fiscal* [FEF]) was included, making it possible for public funds saved during "good" years to be set aside for use in "bad" years through a temporary boost in public spending. It is important to note that specific clauses were established for the use of funds from the FEF.

The LPTF also included a mechanism to govern formulation of the public budget following a two-stage procedure. The first stage involved approval by the Council of Ministers of the Multiyear Macroeconomic Framework (*Marco Macroeconómico Multianual* [MMM]), a document containing the guidelines for fiscal policy and establishing limits on overall expenditure and borrowing consistent with the fiscal rules and the country's macroeconomic situation. In the second stage, the annual budget was to be approved, disaggregating expenditures for each category in each section to reflect the policy debate on government priorities, while respecting the fiscal rules and limits set out in the MMM.

In addition, the LPTF made provision for more transparent management of public finances in the form of a Statement of Fiscal Policy Principles spelling out in advance the guidelines and the medium-term objectives to be pursued in fiscal policy. This document was accompanied by monitoring and evaluation reports and an ex post statement on compliance with fiscal responsibility, with a view to verifying not only the observance of the fiscal rules but also the degree of any deviation from the macrofiscal targets spelled out in the MMM, thereby making for greater accountability. If there are any significant deviations between the projections in the MMM and the results observed in practice, they must be explained and corrective measures must be adopted.

In 2003, the LPTF was revised and renamed the Fiscal Responsibility and Transparency Act (*Ley de Responsabilidad y Transparencia Fiscal*). The principal amendments included a change in the coverage of the national fiscal rules, the introduction of rules for subnational levels of government, and an improved definition of the rules of exception. In 2003 and in subsequent years as well, the expenditure ceiling was increased to reflect the potential for growth in the economy, and the scope of the ceiling was confined to current spending by the central government.

This bolstering of the institutions for fiscal policy, together with a highly favorable international setting characterized by rising commodity prices, strong growth in trading partners, and lower financing costs, has contributed to the extraordinary performance of the Peruvian economy. Between 2000 and 2014, the economy averaged annual growth of 5.3 percent, sustained by private investment that rose from 13 percent of GDP in 2000 to 22 percent in 2014. In contrast to previous episodes, this rapid growth went hand in hand with macroeconomic stability, including annual inflation of 2.7 percent (within the target range of the central bank), fiscal accounts in balance, a public debt reduced to the equivalent of 20 percent of GDP, a slight deficit on the current account averaging 1.5 percent of GDP, the accumulation of net international reserves equivalent to 30 percent of GDP, and an improvement in the country's credit rating to investment grade (Figure 24.2). Taken together, these figures made Peru, together with Mexico, the second best-rated economy in the region, behind only Chile.

The decade was also marked by other reforms that complemented the improvement in the macrofiscal framework. In 2002, the government introduced a program of withholdings and a special system for tax collection with a view to combating evasion. The value-added tax (IGV) targeted the informal sectors and other sectors of the economy that are difficult to supervise and have high evasion levels. In the case of the corporate ("legal persons") income tax, the Temporary Tax on Net Assets (*Impuesto Temporal a los Activos Netos*) was introduced. It involved withholding ½ percent of the net assets of the firm, an amount that could be used as an offsetting credit against income tax due.

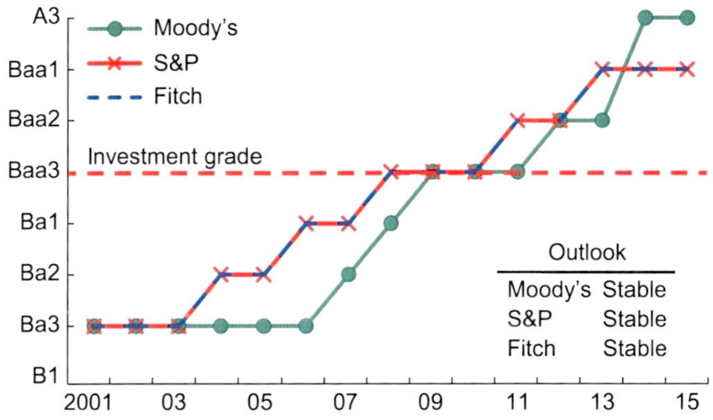


Sources: Fitch Ratings; Moody's Investors Service; and Standard & Poor's Financial Services.
Note: S&P = Standard & Poor's Financial Services.

**Figure 24.2** Peru: Credit Rating

Similarly, a tax reform in 2007 expanded the tax base by dismantling tax exemptions and benefits and reducing customs duties. With respect to the IGV, the reform was targeted at tax exemptions for specific geographic areas of the country (Amazonia), while in the case of the income tax it was targeted at exemptions applicable to interest and capital gains. As for customs duties, the rates were reduced gradually over the course of the decade with a view to promoting external trade and opening up the economy. Thus, the average tariff rate, which stood at 13.5 percent in 1998, fell to 3.2 percent by the end of 2013.

The process of strengthening the taxation framework continued in 2011 with the Law for Strengthening the National Superintendency of Customs and Tax Administration and a change in the mining tax regime to make it more progressive in order to ensure its neutrality and enhance competitiveness in the sector. As stated in the 2015–17 MMM (MEF 2015–17, p. 62):

> the reform strengthening the [Law for Strengthening the National Superintendency of Customs and Tax Administration] has given it greater operating, economic, financial, and budgetary autonomy in order to facilitate its task of combating tax evasion and avoidance, smuggling, and illicit trafficking in goods, stimulate foreign trade, and broaden the tax base. In the context of the legislative powers granted to the executive branch by means of Law 29884 to amend the tax rules with a view to enhancing the efficiency and effectiveness of the national taxation system, 19 legislative decrees were approved in July 2012, dealing with: (a) amendments to the tax code, (b) amendments to the Income Tax Act, (c) the Law on the General Sales Tax and the Selective Consumption Tax, (d) systems for paying the General Sales Tax, (e) improvements to the tax regulations intended to simplify taxpayers' compliance with their obligations, (f) reinforcement of the Tax Court, and (g) repeal of Law 29707, which allowed the cancellation of debts using means of payment.

On the public expenditure side, the reforms focused on improving the efficiency of spending and optimizing the use of public funds. Thus, in 2000 the National Public Investment System (SNIP) was created as a state administrative system that seeks, through a set of principles, methods, procedures, and standards, to improve the quality, efficiency, and sustainability of public spending and ensure the prompt and efficient delivery of goods and services to the population. In the context of public investment projects, the SNIP calls for identifying a given problem in society, analyzing the alternative solutions, and selecting the one that is most efficient and evaluating its implications.[1] Thus, public investment as a proportion of GDP has risen from 3.2 percent in 2001 to the present level of about 5.5 percent.

[1]This is done over what is called the "investment project lifecycle," as the SNIP provides for three differentiated phases in the preparation of a project: (1) preinvestment (where the profile and the feasibility of the project are evaluated), (2) investment (technical and execution report), and (3) postinvestment (maintenance, operation, and ex post evaluations).

In line with the objective indicated earlier, a performance-based budgeting system was introduced in 2008, with plans for its gradual implementation in all entities of public administration and at all levels of government across the country. As indicated in the 2015–17 MMM (MEF 2015–17, p. 63):

> the performance-based budgeting system constitutes a new approach to budget preparation, in which the interactions to be financed with public funds are designed, implemented and evaluated in light of the changes they promote in favor of the population, particularly the most vulnerable segments.

The system has produced some important achievements, including the Integrated National Program, which seeks to reduce chronic malnutrition among children under five years old, and the Neonatal Health Program, which aims to reduce maternal and neonatal mortality. Currently, 58 percent of the government budget, excluding pensions and debt service, is allocated under the principles of performance-based budgeting, and this proportion will continue to rise in coming years.

In terms of pension reform, the government has moved to eliminate certain unfair systems that were created on the basis of pension regimes that posed a significant risk to the sustainability of public finances. This is the case with the pension regimes under the regulatory framework of Decree Laws 19990 and 20530 (the latter known as the *Cédula viva*). Those systems were characterized by very low contributions by beneficiaries that bore no relation to the benefits they would receive upon retirement. In the case of the pension regime under Legislative Decree 20530, at retirement the beneficiary was entitled to a pension equal to the last salary earned. In addition, a reduced number of qualifying years of service was required to qualify for a pension, and there was no minimum age for retirement. It is estimated that the elimination of those schemes as part of the pension reform has produced fiscal savings in excess of US$5 billion in present-value terms.

A reform of the civil service was undertaken in 2012 with a view to providing better public services and enhancing the human capital of the public sector through an ongoing training program and ex post evaluation of performance. This is a key reform, as it took place in a context in which the responsibilities of public servants were increasing faster than their capacity to carry them out. Thus, between 2003 and 2011, while the funds administered in public investments grew by a factor of 4.4, payroll spending went up by only 1.8 times. With these reforms, it is expected that average payroll expenditure over the period 2016–18 will return to levels at the beginning of this century, but under a new regime of ongoing training and ex post performance evaluation.

Some important steps have also been taken to integrate the country into the international debt market and develop the domestic capital market, including that for public debt. Having concluded programs for restructuring the debt, which in aggregate terms ended with the Brady-type agreement of 1997 on commercial debt, Peru was in a position to pursue a more active public borrowing program. In 2002, the government successfully placed $500 million on the international market, and was thereafter able to float progressively larger issues at longer terms and under better conditions (including the issuance of a 50-year bond), as the market's perception of the country improved. In 2003, Peru began to issue bonds in local currency through the Market Makers Program (*Programa de Creadores de Mercado*), the objective of which was to develop a domestic market for public debt and strengthen the Peruvian capital market. The good reception accorded these issues could be attributed to the consolidation of domestic institutional investors, particularly private pension fund administrators, and the development of banks, which supported demand for these products, as well as to renewed confidence among both foreign and local investors. Thanks to an active and fiscally responsible approach to debt management, the profile of public debt has been improving: public debt in foreign currency fell from more than 80 percent in 2000 to 46.1 percent in March 2015, the average term to maturity of public debt has risen and today stands at 12.6 years, and the proportion of public debt at fixed rates is 84.3 percent. In addition, the liquidity of sovereign bonds has been gradually increasing, thereby generating a sovereign yield curve that serves as a benchmark for domestic currency issuances by private firms and institutions (Figure 24.3). At present, Peru has debt instruments outstanding with maturities

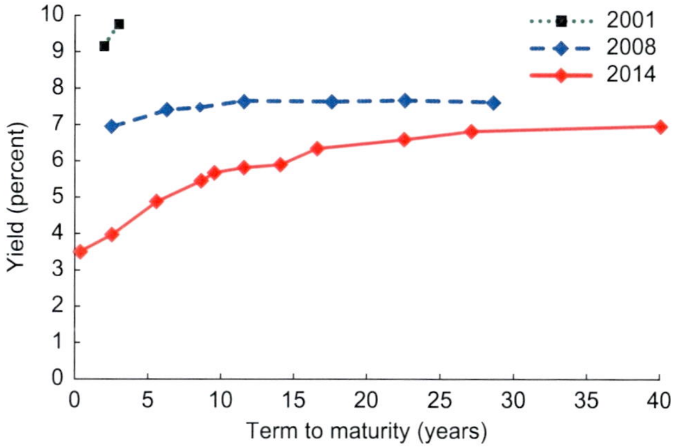


Source: Ministry of the Economy and Finance.

**Figure 24.3** Sovereign Yield Curve

extending as far out as 2050 for global bonds, and to 2042 for sovereign bonds, and the yield curve for comparable tranches is lower than that in 2008.

A crosscutting feature of fiscal policy as a whole in recent years has been the move to decentralize resources and responsibilities to the regions and municipalities. The objective is to have the regions set priorities for using the funds transferred so that they can meet the principal demand for goods and services in their area, which by definition will differ from one area to the next. The decentralization process was launched in 2002 using intergovernmental transfers as the main sources of funds. A portion of these transfers is made at the discretion of the government for the purpose of financing payroll expenses, goods and services, and public investment in line with local needs. However, there is also a predetermined or statutory component, which is significant in some localities. It is linked to the income tax collected on local extractive activities, and is to be used by the subnational authorities to finance public investment. As an illustration of the importance of these authorities, it may be noted that their share in total investment rose from 44 percent in 2004 to 63 percent in 2014.

## FOURTH PHASE: STRENGTHENING INSTITUTIONAL ARRANGEMENTS

Notwithstanding the success of Peru's macrofiscal framework, it must be borne in mind that the structural characteristics of the country's economy have changed since the start of the 2000s, thereby presenting the need to design a new macrofiscal framework consistent with those new features. Such considerations include:

- *Consolidation of public debt.* At the beginning of the past decade, public finances were in an early phase of stabilization, with public debt amounting to close to 50 percent of GDP (Figure 24.4) and little in the way of public assets. At present, public finances are in a consolidation phase, with public debt of about 20 percent of GDP and public assets representing about 16 percent of GDP. Thus, on a net basis, Peru's public debt is one of the lowest in the region (Figure 24.5).
- *Importance of public investment for economic growth over the medium term.* At the beginning of the past decade, the ratio of public investment to GDP was only 2.8 percent, while it currently stands at nearly 6 percent of GDP, above the levels in Uruguay (4 percent), Colombia (4 percent), Chile (3 percent), and Brazil (2 percent).

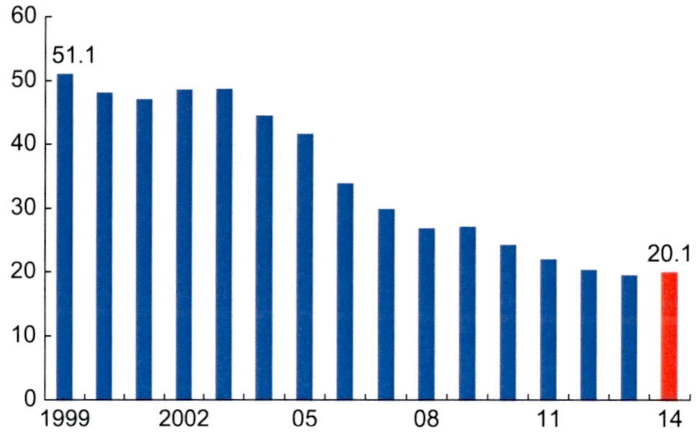


Source: Central Reserve Bank of Peru.

**Figure 24.4** Public Debt *(Percent of GDP)*

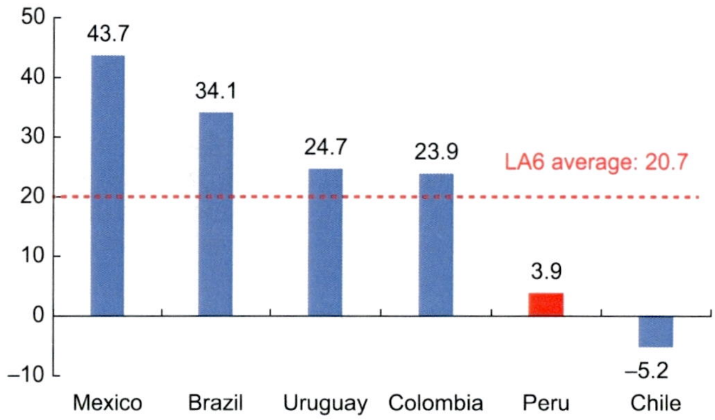


Sources: Central Reserve Bank of Peru; Ministries of Finance; and IMF staff estimates.
Note: Nonfinancial public sector for Peru. LA6 = Brazil, Chile, Colombia, Mexico, Peru, and Uruguay.

**Figure 24.5** LA6: Net Public Debt Balance of General Government, 2014 *(Percent of GDP)*

- *Higher levels of spending by regional and local governments.* At present, investment by those levels of government represents 67 percent of total public investment. A macrofiscal framework has been designed for these levels of government but, as indicated in the report of the Commission for Strengthening the Macro-Fiscal Framework (MEF 2014), "there are still shortcomings that must be corrected with respect to design, transparency, recording, monitoring and compliance."
- *Greater impact of the natural resource sectors on public finances.* At the beginning of the past decade, tax revenues derived from the natural resource sectors amounted to 2.4 percent of total tax revenues of the general government, while that proportion has now risen to 12.4 percent. As well, the volatility of tax revenues derived from the natural resource sectors over the same period was 1.5, more than double the rate for other tax revenues (0.6). Although raw material prices in the years to come will be lower than those in the recent past, a series of mining projects are expected to come on stream by 2017, with the result that copper production will double from its level in 2013.

- *A more open trading regime that is having an impact on the effectiveness of fiscal policy.* The degree of commercial openness, measured as the ratio of exports plus imports to GDP, was 34 percent at the beginning of the past decade and is now 50 percent.

Against this backdrop, the macrofiscal framework, based as it was on rigid numerical rules, was not sufficiently flexible to adapt to the economic and institutional shifts mentioned above. As a result, there have been continuous amendments to the Fiscal Responsibility and Transparency Act over the past decade, affecting its predictability, simplicity, and transparency.

On the other hand, the introduction of the macrofiscal framework spelled out in the Fiscal Responsibility and Transparency Act did not eliminate or even reduce the procyclical bias of fiscal policy. A fiscal deficit rule (procyclical, by definition), together with an expenditure rule with coverage confined solely to current spending, could not ensure a fiscal policy response that was neutral or countercyclical. On this point, the IMF noted in 2013 that while the macrofiscal framework contained some important countercyclical components (such as the FEF), it did not provide for a fully countercyclical response to shocks to output or to commodity prices.

In this context, Law 29854 was passed, creating a technical entity known as the Commission for Strengthening the Macro-Fiscal Framework, which was assigned responsibility for evaluating and preparing a proposal to improve the existing macrofiscal framework, in particular with respect to the mechanisms for responsibility and transparency, and for fiscal rules.

Acting on the recommendations of that commission, the MEF subsequently prepared a draft law governing the macrofiscal framework, the Law for Strengthening Responsibility and Fiscal Transparency, Law 30099, which was approved on October 31, 2013, and came into effect with the preparation of the government budget for fiscal year 2015.

This new fiscal framework represents a continuation of the process of institutional change that began at the beginning of the past decade with the Fiscal Responsibility and Transparency Act. The process of strengthening the macrofiscal framework was intended to serve the following objectives, which were to be achieved under a more flexible and predictable regime that would also reinforce the commitment to fiscal responsibility:

- To lend greater predictability to public spending by de-linking it from the most volatile source of public revenues, that is, revenues flowing from the natural resource sectors. As indicated in the Statement of Fiscal Policy Principles in the 2015–17 MMM (MEF 2015–17, p. 11), "public spending must not be volatile, as this generates costs in terms of sector policy efficiency and management capacity; consequently, the management of public finances must be insulated from the high volatility of revenues derived from the main commodities that we export." Historically, commodity prices have been volatile and erratic, and thus difficult to project.
- To ensure fiscal solvency by keeping public debt at a low level that makes it possible to cope with negative shocks such as severe natural disasters, contingencies, international financial crises, etc.
- To avoid macroeconomic crises through countercyclical measures that will be triggered in a timely manner and only in settings in which the economy deviates sharply from its medium-term trend. To the extent that the fiscal rule insulates public spending from the temporary effects of output, commodity prices, and other similar factors, the stance of fiscal policy is by definition cyclically neutral (acyclical).

However, the fiscal rule does provide for countercyclical responses in a discretionary manner, but only for events of low probability and high impact. The factors that limit fiscal policy to this context alone (and not to fine-tuning) are the following: (1) fiscal policy operates with significant lags; (2) it is impossible to exert full control over the entire range of fiscal stimulus (spending by regional and local governments financed with statutory resource revenue transfers, compensation funds, and tax revenues of local governments); (3) the current system of transfers to regional and local governments is procyclical and finances a significant percentage of spending, especially for public investment; (4) there is uncertainty as to the size of the fiscal multipliers; and (5) there is ex ante uncertainty as to the origin of the shock (supply or demand). Given the impossibility of controlling all these factors, fiscal policy may in the end have the unfortunate effect of increasing the volatility of output over the short term. Because of this, the Law for Strengthening Responsibility and Fiscal Transparency seeks to:

- Simplify the fiscal rules for regional and local governments. The main problems arise from the heterogeneity of these governments' public finances, their weak observance of fiscal rules, and the scarcity of corrective measures. This in turn reflects the absence of efficient measures for information, monitoring, and follow-up, as well as the lack of incentives.
- Strengthen the institutional framework of the FEF, providing it with a technical secretariat that, among other functions, would propose investment guidelines to the board for generating greater returns.
- Strengthen the institutional arrangements for fiscal policy by creating a Fiscal Council. The new macrofiscal framework does away with the old, rigid regime of fiscal rules, but this new degree of discretion must be restricted in the sense that there must be an independent entity to audit or validate it.

The objectives mentioned above will be achieved with the new macrofiscal rule covering the level of nonfinancial spending by the national government, which is based on an ex ante exercise of cyclical adjustment for the nonfinancial public sector. This fiscal rule limits the spending over which the national government has discretion, and it is more comprehensive in comparison with the previous spending rule.[2] Taking the figures for 2014, the new spending rule for the national government covers 85.9 percent of its nonfinancial spending, whereas the previous consumption rule covered only 47.8 percent. As well, it is important to note that the spending rule for the national government includes both current and capital spending, with the objective of achieving greater consistency between the increase in the stock of public capital and the amount spent on equipment and maintenance of that stock. On this point, the report of the Commission for Strengthening the Macro-Fiscal Framework (MEF 2014) declares that "it is important to note that the distinction between public investment and current spending in the public sector is weak and in part artificial, and consequently some public investments do not generate any substantial social return, while many components of current spending, such as maintenance of public infrastructure and expenditures on health and education, may produce a higher return."

A new element of this macrofiscal framework is the use of structural variables (public revenues and GDP) and the announcement of a structural balance indicative target, which is linked to budgetary programming and formulation through the expenditure limits imposed by the rules. Thus, in determining the binding expenditure rules for budgetary formulation, an incoming administration must first (within 90 days after taking office) define and announce its fiscal policy objectives (through a Macro-Fiscal Policy Statement) for the term of its mandate, and the impact of those objectives on the structural economic outcome of the nonfinancial public sector (structural balance indicative target). That indicative balance is in fact binding for the formulation of public budgets, but the ex post evaluation relates to the spending limit that flows from the structural balance target.

[2]The nonfinancial spending rule for the national government covers the sum of nonfinancial spending by the national government and transfers to entities of the nonfinancial public sector, with the exception of funds deriving from the *canon, sobrecanon* and royalties, the *Fondo de Compensación Municipal*, the *Fondo de Desarrollo Socioeconómico de Camisea*, and the share of regional and local governments in customs revenues.

With respect to the ex post analysis of fiscal rules, this requires corrective measures in case there are any deviations, something that strengthens the commitment in the macrofiscal framework to responsible management of public finances. Thus, Ter-Minassian (2010, p. 15) notes that "[t]o be effective, rules need also to be supported by appropriate enforcement mechanisms, including provisions for correction of past deviations that do not call for a permanent revision of the rule."

This new macrofiscal framework provides for two types of corrective measures. The first involves the creation of an account for compensation and correction of deviations (referred to in the economic literature as the "notional account"). In the case where accrued spending by the national government exceeds the limit established by the fiscal rule for a given year, this deviation will be added to that account. If the cumulative balance on the account is less than ½ percent of GDP, the nonfinancial spending limit of the national government will be reduced, at least proportionately, over the following two years, provided a negative gap exceeding 2 percent of potential GDP is not projected. On the other hand, if the cumulative balance on this account is ½ percent of GDP or greater, the nonfinancial spending limit of the national government will be immediately cut. In this way, the account for compensation and correction of deviations plays the role of an automatic enforcer in the case of breaches of the fiscal rules. In addition, to minimize the perverse incentive to postpone the task of correction to a future administration, there is a provision that the balance on the notional account must not exceed 0.3 percent of GDP at the end of the current administration's mandate.

The second corrective measure, in line with the objective of ensuring fiscal sustainability, requires that, if the debt of the public sector is found or expected to be greater than 30 percent of GDP in the following three years, the Macro-Fiscal Policy Statement and the structural balance target for the nonfinancial public sector must be amended, incorporating measures deemed appropriate to restrict expenditures or to boost revenues in order to return the debt to a level below that limit within a period of no more than seven years.

The objective of this latter measure is to correct the projected path both of expenditure and revenues in accordance with the structural balance target for the nonfinancial public sector in the case of a macrofiscal scenario that would put fiscal sustainability at risk. Economies are subject to unexpected shocks of low probability but high impact. For example, in 2007 the general government debt in Spain and Ireland stood at 36.3 percent and 20 percent of GDP, respectively. Those levels were considered low, as reflected in the solid scores granted by the credit rating agencies. Yet within five years (by 2012), those countries' debt levels had risen to 69.2 percent and 117.1 percent of GDP, respectively. In the context of a new, more flexible macrofiscal framework that can be adjusted to the medium-term potential of the economy, a low public debt level is proposed as a signal of the government's commitment to prudent management of public finances. A level of debt no higher than 30 percent will ensure sustainability, even under shock scenarios, and will make it possible to maintain an investment-grade sovereign credit rating that translates into lower financing costs for the public and private sectors alike.

On the other hand, because the proposed macrofiscal framework is supposed to be more flexible than the previous one, as it can be adjusted to the economy's medium-term potential and is based on the ex ante application of a cyclical adjustment methodology, it was deemed necessary to enhance transparency in the management of the public finances through the creation of a Fiscal Council. The purpose of this council is to conduct an independent technical analysis of macrofiscal policy and to issue opinions on the MMM, the short- and medium-term evolution of public finances, and proper application of the methodology for calculating the structural accounts and potential GDP. The reports issued by the Fiscal Council—which is comprised of at least three independent professionals with broad fiscal experience—are to be published and made known to the general public.

Lastly, when it comes to the management of assets, it is important to note that the new macrofiscal framework strengthens the institutional framework and the financial administration of the FEF,

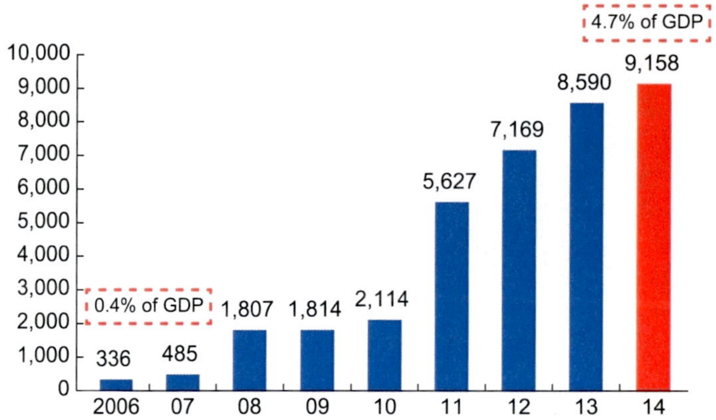


Sources: Central Reserve Bank of Peru; and the Ministry of the Economy and Finance.

**Figure 24.6** Cumulative Savings in the Fiscal Stabilization Fund *(Millions of U.S. dollars)*

in line with the Santiago Principles,[3] and provides it with a technical secretariat that, among other functions, will propose investment guidelines to the board designed to increase the return on the FEF, as part of the Global Strategy for Management of the Assets and Liabilities of the Public Treasury.

Thus, the present institutional framework for fiscal policy represents to some extent a continuation of current policy, but with improvements. Peruvian fiscal policy is in effect based on a system of fiscal rules governing the level of spending, determined by a cyclically adjusted fiscal balance exercise consistent with a structural balance target, and is designed to bring greater predictability and stability to public spending. In a complementary manner, the FEF serves as a countercyclical tool that allows savings to be built up during "good" years so as to provide a cushion that can be used in "bad" years in the form of a temporary fiscal stimulus (Figure 24.6). In this way, it follows the state of the art in countries with characteristics similar to those of Peru, such as an open trading system and a concentration on commodity exports.

The public budget, which is financed by a simple, transparent, and equitable tax system, is formulated in two stages. The first stage involves preparation of the MMM, which contains fiscal policy guidelines and sets limits on overall spending and indebtedness in observance of the existing fiscal rules and in a manner consistent with a projected macroeconomic scenario for the year of the budget and the two following years. In the second stage, the annual budget is approved. It reflects the government's priorities, and it complies with the fiscal rules set forth in the MMM. In addition to this detailed budgetary formulation, there are other tools, such as the SNIP and the results-based budgeting system, that are designed to maximize efficiency in the allocation and use of public funds.

## CHALLENGES AND THE UNFINISHED AGENDA

The international environment over the next few years will be characterized by slower growth in the advanced economies than that recorded in the years preceding the 2008–09 global financial crisis. There will also be higher financing costs and a permanent fall in commodity prices. All of this poses challenges over the medium term for the growth of economies such as Peru. For example, in its *World Economic Outlook* of April 2015, the IMF suggests that output growth in emerging countries will decline from around 7 percent from 2001–07 to 5.2 percent from 2015–20, with the prospect that this downward trend may continue in the absence of structural

[3] Santiago Principles are a set of 24 voluntary guidelines that assign best practices for the operations of sovereign wealth funds.

reforms. The IMF also points out that this reduction in the potential output of emerging economies can be explained in large part by a deterioration in productivity.

With a view to boosting the growth potential in the next few years and responding to the looming international context, the Peruvian government has over the last two years been proposing actions within a framework along three fronts geared to ensuring greater investment and gains in productivity and competitiveness: (1) strengthening human capital and reducing informality, (2) reducing the infrastructure gap, and (3) cutting red tape and reducing excess costs.

For its part, Peruvian fiscal policy is being conducted within a recent macrofiscal framework that must be maintained and consolidated in the coming years. And in the global macroeconomic setting that is likely to prevail for the next few years, the current macrofiscal framework can be supplemented in ways that will optimize the functioning of fiscal policy in terms of fiscal sustainability and the stance vis-à-vis the economic cycle.

Fiscal sustainability is a necessary condition for promoting any type of structural reform that may be needed. The last 25 years of Peru's economic history are evidence of this, for without responsible and prudent management of fiscal policy, it would not have been possible to build the macrofiscal cushions to cope with the 2008–09 global financial crisis or with the current external shock. During the 2008–09 crisis, Peru undertook a fiscal stimulus equal to 3.5 percent of GDP (MEF 2011–13), and between 2014 and 2015, it has been pursuing a further fiscal stimulus of 3.1 percent of GDP (MEF 2016–18), in contrast to other countries of the region that, despite a negative output gap, are still making budget cuts this year.

Similarly, the complex international environment can have a direct impact on the sustainability of countries' public finances in the form of higher financing costs, downward pressures on the exchange rate, falling tax revenues, and lower potential growth. It is essential, then, that Peruvian fiscal policy continue to distance itself from that of other emerging countries, as it has in recent years. Only in this way can the country maintain high credibility among economic agents and thereby attract capital, reduce financing costs for the public and private sectors alike, and achieve high and sustained economic growth. Empirical evidence reveals countless examples of countries that abandoned their commitment to responsible fiscal policy, even if only temporarily, and thereby lost credibility and consistency over time, making fiscal imbalances a self-fulfilling prophecy. Peru must eschew this route.

When it comes to the taxation system, as noted earlier, while it is in line with international principles, there is room to increase permanent revenues; strengthen the system in terms of its fairness, efficiency, and transparency; and broaden the tax base to reduce informality, which is one of the main problems constraining back growth. Measures must be geared to reducing tax evasion and avoidance, applying risk management systems in tax and customs supervision and enforcement, and taking further steps to automate the corresponding processes and procedures and allow them to be handled online.

Similarly, in the context of decentralization, Peru must establish incentives to boost municipal taxation, where there is still much room for improvement. According to De Cesare (2012), property taxes collected by subnational levels of government in Peru represent 0.17 percent of GDP, barely one-quarter of their level in Colombia, where the institutional structure is similar to that of Peru, and far below the level in Chile, which is the regional leader.

Peru also needs to step up efforts to rationalize and eliminate tax exemptions, and to review excise taxes in light of the negative externalities they generate. As part of Peru's efforts to join the Organisation for Economic Co-operation and Development, the country must bring its tax regulations into line with international standards and improve fiscal transparency so as to facilitate the sharing of information among tax administrations.

In a context of a permanent fall in tax revenues and a public budget that has seen a 140 percent cumulative increase in the last 10 years, the challenge is to make public spending more efficient and to set spending priorities based on an ex post evaluation of results. From an economic policy viewpoint, it is important not to overlook the need to "sell" these priority-setting policies to society, and to strengthen the institutional underpinnings of fiscal policy. The crisis of 2008–09 showed that, for the world in general, fiscal policy can play a more important stabilization role than had previously been recognized. Yet in the case of Peru, experience with the 2008–09 crisis and with the current shock shows that there are rigidities that impede implementation of a timely and time-bound discretionary, countercyclical fiscal response. Consequently, to minimize delays in the design and implementation of this fiscal response, Peru will need to evaluate various measures such as establishing a fund or bank for public or public-private investment projects that are outside the public budget and can be activated swiftly and executed over a short time.

Last, but of no less importance, is the process of decentralization, which Peru must continue to improve. While decentralization implies a broader institutional reform that embraces concepts of political reform and reform of the state, on the fiscal front it must surely be a priority to reform the intergovernmental transfer system for all types of financing sources, based on the principles of predictability in public spending, the capacity to absorb the transferred resources, accountability, and ex post evaluations.

In conclusion, the unfinished agenda toward a fiscal policy that will allow Peru to cope more effectively with the new global context in the coming years could in fact be quite lengthy. However, the elements mentioned here are a good point of departure for pursuing a process of gradual strengthening that began nearly 25 years ago and that is still producing good results today.

## REFERENCES

De Cesare, C. 2012. "Improving the Performance of the Property Tax in Latin America." Policy Focus Report, Lincoln Institute of Land Policy, Cambridge, Massachusetts.

International Monetary Fund. 2015. *World Economic Outlook: Uneven Growth—Short- and Long-Term Factors.* Washington, April.

Ministry of Economy and Finance. 2011–13. Marco Macroeconómico Multianual. 2011 -2013. Ministry of Economy and Finance, Lima, Peru.

———. 2014. Report of the Commission for Strengthening the Macro Fiscal Framework. Unpublished. Lima, Peru.

———. 2015–17. Marco Macroeconómico Multianual. Ministry of Economy and Finance, Lima, Peru.

———. 2016–18. Marco Macroeconómico Multianual. Ministry of Economy and Finance, Lima, Peru.

Ter-Minassian, Teresa. 2010. "Preconditions for a Successful Introduction of Structural Fiscal Balance Based Rules in Latin America and the Caribbean: A Framework Paper." Institutional Capacity and Finance Sector Discussion Paper No. IDB-DP-157, Inter-American Development Bank, Washington, DC.

# CHAPTER 25

# The Future of Monetary Policy

JULIO VELARDE

*The global financial crisis demonstrated the need to provide financial stability and stability in terms of inflation in order to preserve the transmission mechanism of monetary policy. The Central Reserve Bank of Peru (Banco Central de Reserva del Perú [BCRP]) has achieved these twin goals through the use of conventional and nonconventional instruments (e.g., reserve requirements and foreign exchange intervention). Looking ahead, monetary policy will need to properly calibrate nonconventional policy instruments to the financial cycle and ensure that financial intermediaries fully internalize financial risks. The Peruvian authorities will also need to adapt policies to developments in capital markets and as macroprudential measures are implemented. Also, the macroprudential framework may need to be strengthened.*

The way in which monetary policy is implemented in most countries has undergone a considerable transformation over the past 10 years. The consensus as to what central banks can and should do is moving rapidly from price stability as the sole objective of monetary policy toward a broader definition of macroeconomic stability in which central banks also address financial stability concerns. In addition, the use of multiple policy instruments besides the short-term interest rate is now more widely accepted as a necessary condition to effectively implement monetary policy, especially when financial markets become dysfunctional.

Are these changes in the monetary policy framework permanent? Or are they just transitory responses to a more volatile world where global financial markets tend to overreact more frequently than in normal times? Should the time horizon for monetary policy be extended in order to properly accommodate financial cycles within the monetary policy design?

This chapter addresses these questions by looking at Peru as an illustrative example of how monetary policy can achieve price stability and at the same time reduce financial vulnerabilities associated with financial dollarization. The Peruvian experience is interesting not only because it shows the perils of implementing monetary policy in a dollarized economy, where financial vulnerabilities are tightly linked to macroeconomic developments, but also because it illustrates how monetary policy instruments can be constantly adapted to maintain their effectiveness within different macroeconomic scenarios.

The chapter first examines the policy instruments that can be deployed within the inflation-targeting design adopted by the BCRP. It then looks at how these instruments have been adapted to address a more demanding external scenario. The chapter provides an overview of aspects that future monetary policy design might need to take into account to be able to provide both financial stability and stability in terms of inflation.

## THE CURRENT STATE OF PERUVIAN MONETARY POLICY

Inflation targeting started in Latin America after the 1997–99 financial crisis that spread across emerging market economies. Peru was relatively late in adopting inflation targeting,[1] although

[1] Brazil adopted inflation targeting in June 1999, while Colombia and Chile adopted the regime in September 1999.

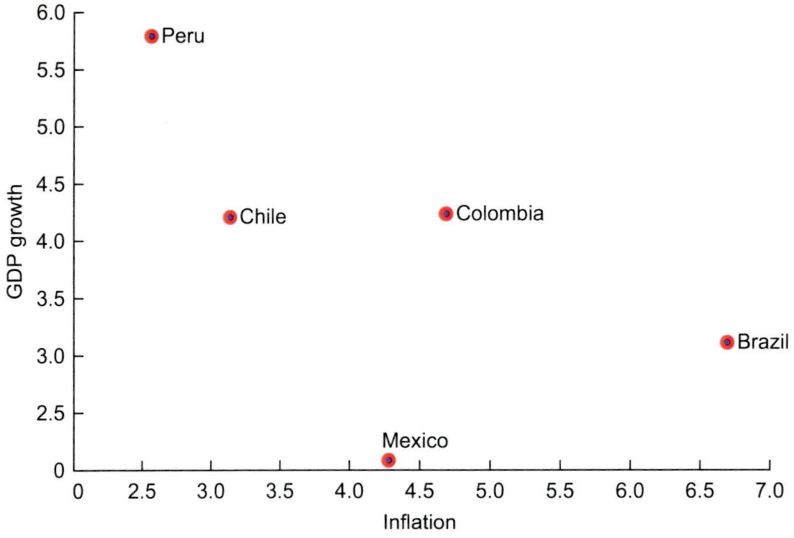


Source: IMF staff calculations.

**Figure 25.1** Inflation and GDP Growth in the Five Larger Inflation-Targeting Countries, 2001–14 *(Percent)*

it was the first highly dollarized economy to adopt the regime. By the time Peru implemented inflation targeting, its economy was in recession and facing mild deflation. In sharp contrast to other emerging economies that adopted inflation targeting, Peru needed to put in place an expansionary monetary policy to move inflation to a credible target. Inflation targeting was not intended for inflation convergence from above but to anchor a credible rate of inflation from below.

It was clear by then that inflation targeting had to be complemented by additional instruments to address financial risks in a broadly dollarized economy. This is related to widespread concerns about financial stability for monetary policy in developed economies as a result of the 2008–09 global financial crisis. Both the adoption of inflation targeting after the financial crisis that hit emerging economies (and Peru in particular) and the successful use of a managed floating exchange rate regime paved the way for the design of the inflation-targeting regime in Peru.

Also fundamental for implementation of the inflation-targeting regime in Peru were the reforms introduced during the early 1990s that granted independence to the central bank and assigned monetary stability as its single objective, as well as the establishment of the floating exchange rate regime.

Since 2001, average annual inflation in Peru has been 2.6 percent while the country's average annual growth rate has been 5.8 percent (Figure 25.1). In the group of the five largest Latin American inflation targeters[2]—which share somewhat similar economic structures and are subject to the same types of external shocks—Peru achieved the lowest inflation and the highest growth rate.

Theory suggests that full dollarization provides a strong inflation anchor. However, Table 25.1 suggests that inflation targeting in Peru has delivered lower and even more stable inflation compared with countries that have officially dollarized, such as Ecuador, El Salvador, and Panama.

[2]Brazil, Chile, Colombia, Mexico, and Peru.

**TABLE 25.1**

**Inflation in Peru and in Fully Dollarized Economies *(Percent)***

| Annual Inflation (2001–14)[1] | Average | Standard Deviation[2] |
|---|---|---|
| Ecuador | 5.7 | 3.4 |
| Panama | 2.6 | 2.5 |
| El Salvador | 3.0 | 2.4 |
| Peru | 2.6 | 1.6 |

Source: IMF staff calculations.
[1] Ecuador officially dollarized in 2000, and El Salvador officially dollarized in 2001. Figures for El Salvador figures correspond to 2002–04.
[2] Standard deviation of year-on-year inflation.

## Policy Rate

The outstanding results in delivering price stability have helped consolidate the BCRP's credibility as a successful implementer of inflation targeting. The keys to achieving these results were the active use of a short-term interest rate to anchor inflation expectations and the proper calibration of complementary instruments to preserve financial stability and the transmission of monetary policy. Indeed, the policy rate path can be rationalized within a Taylor-type rule that considers inflation expectations and GDP growth as its determinants:

$$i_t = \overline{i} + a_\pi\left(\pi_{t-1}^{e} - \pi_t^{target}\right) + a_y\left(\Delta y_{t-2} - \overline{\Delta y}\right), \tag{25.1}$$

where $\pi_{t-1}^{e}$ is defined as the inflation expectation for the next calendar year (a proxy for medium-term inflation expectations) taken in the month prior to the policy decision.[3] Likewise, $\Delta y_{t-2}$ refers to the year-over-year monthly growth of two lagged months of GDP.[4] In addition, $\overline{i}$ stands for the neutral interest rate, and $\pi_t^{target}$ is the target inflation rate that was set to 2.5 percent in 2002 and changed to 2 percent in 2007. Finally, $\overline{\Delta y}$ is the average rate of GDP growth during the inflation-targeting period.

The fact that this policy rule depends on the GDP growth rate and not on an estimated output gap is because of the imprecise nature of the gap (Orphanides and Van Norden 2002) and because the growth rate in the rule may be even better in terms of welfare than a gap-based rule (Sims 2013). Estimation of a simple equation such as equation (25.1) can help directly identify how, on average, the central bank changes its monetary policy stance in terms of relevant variables available in the information set at the moment of the decision. The estimated rule is depicted in equation (25.2):

$$\underset{(0.00)^*}{}\; i_t = 3.2 + 1.3(\pi_{t-1}^{e} - \pi_t^{target}) + 0.2(\Delta y_{t-2} - 6.1). \tag{25.2}$$

$$(0.00)^*(0.2)^* \qquad\qquad (0.05)^*$$

A key feature of this estimation[5] is that the policy rate always changes more than proportionally to changes in observed inflation expectations, a feature called the Taylor principle (Figure 25.2).

[3] Inflation expectation surveys are gathered and published by the BCRP at the end of each month, while policy decisions are made within the first two weeks of each month.

[4] GDP figures are published with a two-month lag around mid-month by the national statistical agency (*Instituto Nacional de Estadística e Informática*). Even if GDP publication dates sometimes fall after monetary policy decisions, the staff at the central bank provides close estimates of the $t - 2$ growth rate at the time of monetary policy meetings.

[5] The estimation uses the generalized method of moments to guarantee that the equation residuals are not correlated with information available at the time of decisions such as observed inflation and core inflation rates, credit growth, and past interest rate levels. In equation (25.1), standard errors are in parentheses and the asterisks denote significance at the 1 percent level.

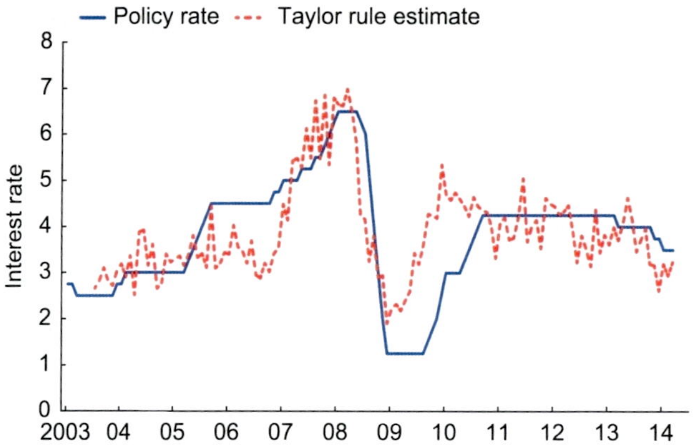


Sources: Central Reserve Bank of Peru; and author's calculations.

**Figure 25.2** Observed Reference Interest Rate and Interest Rate Implied by Estimated Taylor Rule (*Percent*)

Also, the rule conforms to a flexible inflation-targeting framework, as policy takes into account changes in economic activity.

A particular feature of inflation targeting in Peru is that it departs from textbook implementation and relies on a number of instruments in addition to the standard policy interest rate. These complementary instruments aim to reduce the vulnerabilities that financial dollarization generates and contribute to preserving the transmission mechanism of monetary policy during periods of financial stress associated with the global financial crisis in 2009, and after the implementation of policy responses in advanced economies. The additional instruments used by the BCRP, commonly known as unconventional policies,[6] come in two sets: (1) reserve requirement policies differentiated by currency, and (2) foreign exchange market intervention policies.

## Reserve Requirement Policies

The BCRP uses reserve requirements mainly for monetary control, the mitigation of dollarization risks, and the lengthening of the maturity of the banking system's external leverage. High reserve requirements in dollars help banks to internalize dollarization risks and, by increasing banks' liquidity in foreign currency, enhance the financial system's capacity to absorb shocks, particularly those associated with capital flow fluctuations.

In addition, since 2008 the BCRP has used reserve requirements in a more cyclical fashion by raising their average and marginal levels during periods of capital flow surges and cutting them during capital reversal episodes. By increasing reserve requirements in foreign currency during periods of intense capital inflows, the BCRP reduces banks' incentives to lend in dollars. At the same time, it creates a foreign currency buffer to reduce banks' vulnerability to capital reversals.

The 2008–09 global financial crisis put the inflation target cum financial risk control to the test. Inflation was running above target during the first half of 2008. High inflation called for higher domestic policy interest rates and the widening of the spread against foreign interest rates. In turn, higher interest rate spreads against the U.S. federal funds rate induced more carry trades and short-term capital inflows in the run-up to the crisis. The important bank liquidity levels originated by capital inflows hindered the conduct of monetary policy and intensified

[6]In fact, since the beginning of the 1990s, the BCRP has used these two sets of policies.

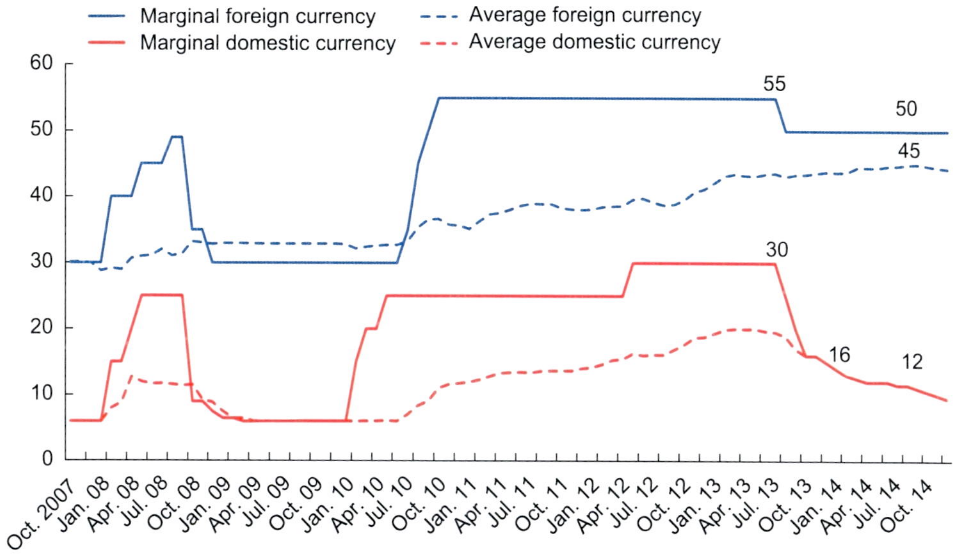


Source: Central Reserve Bank of Peru.

**Figure 25.3** Reserve Requirement in Domestic and Foreign Currency (*Percentage of total liabilities*)

appreciation pressures. In this context, in addition to raising the reference rate (from 4.5 percent in July 2007 to 6.5 percent in August 2008) in response to inflation pressures, the BCRP increased reserve requirements on domestic and foreign currency deposits to ensure an orderly expansion of liquidity and credit. The BCRP also accumulated a significant amount of international reserves, mainly by foreign exchange intervention sterilized with fiscal savings.

In September 2008, the BCRP responded immediately to the turbulence caused by the collapse of Lehman Brothers by injecting liquidity up to 9.3 percent of GDP through a wide range of instruments, including the reduction of reserve requirements to end-2007 levels, the use of foreign exchange sales of $6.8 billion during September 2008–February 2009, and the provision of liquidity trough repo operations and currency swaps.

These measures cushioned the domestic financial system from the impact of the crisis and facilitated a swift and sustained recovery of credit and growth starting in the second half of 2009. During the worst episode of the crisis (October 2008–March 2009), access to credit was preserved and nonperforming bank loans remained low.

The 2008–09 global financial crisis provided policymakers worldwide with an important lesson: monetary policy needs to and can take greater account of financial stability concerns. During the crisis, central banks in developed economies made innovative policy moves that included explicit guidance to steer expectations of future interest rates and quantitative easing. These policies spilled over into emerging market economies, which had to face unprecedented levels of capital inflows. Under these circumstances, monetary policy in Peru had to maneuver to sail against the wind and apply a sort of quantitative tightening (Armas, Castillo, and Vega 2014). This implied raising reserve requirements, as depicted in Figure 25.3. The surges in capital flows that followed the implementation of quantitative easing by the U.S. Federal Reserve had a significant impact on monetary and credit conditions in Peru, which required more active use of complementary policy instruments such as reserve requirements. As shown in Figure 25.3, the BCRP increased not only the marginal reserve requirement rate several times, but also the average rate, which has a stronger impact on banks' intermediation costs in foreign currency, limiting credit expansion in foreign currency.

By more rapidly increasing reserve requirements during this period, the BCRP tightened monetary conditions in foreign currency, reducing the need for further increases in the domestic interest rate to manage inflation. At the same time, higher reserve requirements reduced deposits rates and the incentives for short-term capital flows to the banking system. Additionally, higher reserve requirements in foreign currency generated a faster accumulation of international liquidity in the banking system, strengthening banks' liquidity buffers.

In 2013, with the U.S. recovery under way and the consequent tapering announcements, Peru sharply reversed the course of it reserve requirement policy. In sum, the cyclical use of reserve requirements by the BCRP illustrates how a policy instrument can be adapted to more effectively address a challenging external scenario.

An additional nonconventional tool used by the BCRP to limit dollarization risks is the accumulation of international reserves, which are used as a buffer to increase the BCRP's capability to inject liquidity in the presence of adverse external shocks (such as capital flow reversals and drastic falls in the terms of trade). In a world with incomplete international financial markets, the accumulation of international reserves is a self-insurance mechanism against negative balance of payments shocks, such as sudden reversals in capital flows or falls in the terms of trade. This is particularly relevant for emerging market economies, which have experienced these kinds of shocks more frequently. These shocks have caused large output losses and banking credit disruptions in several emerging market economies, as occurred during the Asian and Russian crises at the end of the 1990s. As a result, emerging market economies have developed a greater risk aversion to external shocks, which has prompted them to accumulate more international reserves. In the case of Peru, most economic crises experienced during the past century had their roots in balance of payments shocks.

## Foreign Exchange Market Intervention Policies

The main purpose of foreign exchange intervention in Peru is to reduce the volatility of the exchange rate and accumulate international reserves in order to prevent balance sheet effects on the partially dollarized financial position of the domestic private sector. There is no implied level, ceiling, or floor. No announcement regarding the amount of the interventions is made beforehand, because having to adjust this amount could have a high cost and because the volatile nature of foreign exchange flows requires a more discretionary approach to central bank intervention. Therefore, the exchange rate reacts to whatever shock hits its value, but extreme jumps are avoided.

As a result, daily percentage changes of the nuevo sol against the U.S. dollar correlate well with changes in other exchange rates, as shown in Figure 25.4, reflecting the fact that currencies in small open economies tend to move in the same directions when common shocks arise. Foreign exchange interventions do not preclude flexibility of exchange rates in the form of necessary adjustments, which are the fundamental mechanism in place to absorb external shocks such as capital flow reversals or lower terms of trade. The interventions aim only to avoid excessive volatility.

Excess exchange rate volatility emerges as a natural consequence of noisy information and imperfectly informed traders. The excess volatility of exchange rates, caused by the flow of private heterogeneous information, has real effects on the economy, particularly in a situation where agents are not hedged adequately. The reasons include the low state of development of the financial markets, the "original sin" documented by Eichengreen and Hausmann (1999), and the country's habits such as invoicing, holding assets, and transaction technologies in foreign currency. Thus, in a country like Peru, which has a relatively high degree of financial dollarization (currently around 40 percent), balance sheet effects are an important channel to consider in the monetary and foreign exchange intervention policy design.

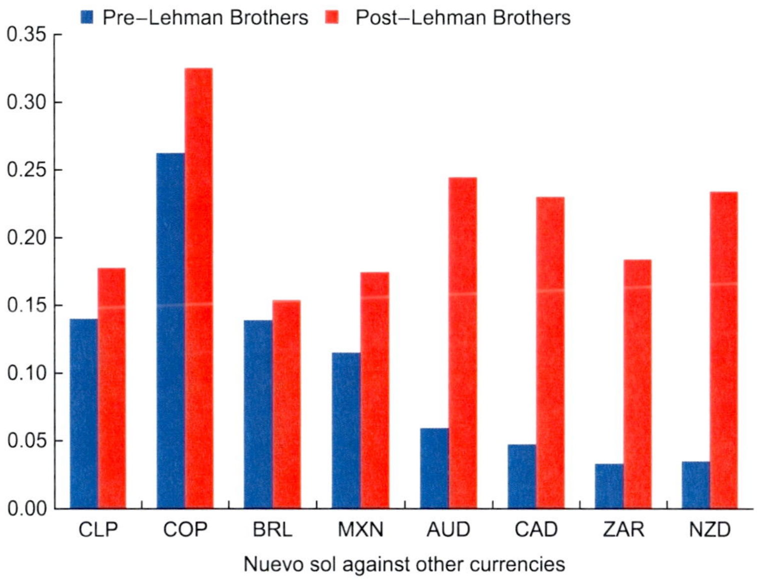


Sources: Quandl; and author's estimates.
Note: AUD = Australian dollar; BRL = Brazilian real; CAD = Canadian dollar; CLP = Chilean peso; COP = Colombian peso; MXN = Mexican peso; NZD = New Zealand dollar; ZAR = South African rand.

**Figure 25.4** Correlations of Peru's Exchange Rate with Other Countries

**TABLE 25.2**

Variance of Daily Nominal Exchange Rate Changes, 2000–14

| | CLP | PEN | MXN | COP | BRL |
|---|---|---|---|---|---|
| Total Variance | 0.50 | 0.28 | 0.43 | 0.47 | 0.66 |
| Precrisis | 0.49 | 0.23 | 0.41 | 0.45 | 0.70 |
| Postcrisis | 0.50 | 0.37 | 0.48 | 0.52 | 0.58 |

Sources: Quandl; and author's estimates.
Note: BRL = Brazilian real; CLP = Chilean peso; COP = Colombian peso; MXN = Mexican peso; PEN = Peruvian nuevo sol.

Interventions are implemented by purchases or sales of U.S. dollars in the spot market and by carrying out swaps with the issuance of certificates of deposits linked to the exchange rate. In 2014, the BCRP started using derivatives-based intervention instruments. Swaps are used mainly when there are pressures from the nondeliverable forward market that could force banks to transfer this pressure into the spot market. A swap operation with the central bank can provide temporary coverage against the risks involved in a nondeliverable forward market without affecting the availability of the bank's liquidity in domestic currency.

Indicators of relative volatility of the exchange rate among peer economies are a simple measure of the effectiveness of foreign exchange interventions. In Latin America, despite different levels of foreign exchange intervention, exchange rate trends are similar. However, in the case of Peru, volatility is lower.

Table 25.2 shows the variance of daily nominal exchange rate changes for five Latin American countries since 2000. The variance of the Peruvian exchange rate is lower than that of peer countries. After the global financial crisis, the variance of the Peruvian exchange rate increased in relation to the precrisis period.

In sum, Peru's inflation-targeting framework has considered conventional monetary policy instruments as well as nonconventional policies that have also played the role of macroprudential policies. Standard conventional monetary instruments work according to best practices in central

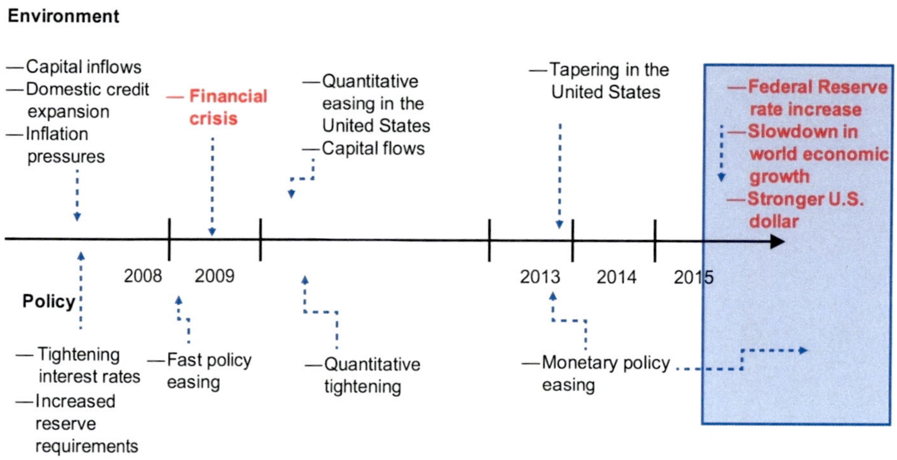


Source: Central Reserve Bank of Peru.

**Figure 25.5** Broad Timing of Monetary Policy Actions and the Environment

banking, while nonconventional policies use (1) discretionary foreign exchange interventions to support a managed floating exchange rate regime envisaged to reduce dollarization risks, and (2) reserve requirement policies to control undue credit expansion and differentiated reserve requirement policies according to the currency denomination of bank liabilities to fight credit-induced dollarization risks. All in all, the framework has delivered macroeconomic and financial stability.

## CHALLENGES FOR FUTURE MONETARY POLICY

One of the key lessons from the global financial crisis and from the Peruvian experience is that to deliver both price stability and an effective monetary policy transmission mechanism, central banks need to take into account the financial cycle in the design and implementation of the monetary framework. This poses several challenges for central banks. First, it requires lengthening the time horizon of monetary policy, particularly to properly calibrate nonconventional policy instruments. In contrast to typical business cycles that last between 8 and 32 quarters, financial cycles tend to last longer, which prompts the need to fine-tune the set of policy instruments to different time horizons.

In the case of Peru, most of the nonconventional policy instruments were tailored to accumulate international reserves and limit banks' exposure to the surge of capital flows generated by quantitative easing policies. In this way, the risks for the financial sector during the reversal of the Federal Reserve's expansionary policies were reduced (Figure 25.5).

Second, it is fundamental to maintain an appropriate balance in using different types of nonconventional instruments. These instruments can induce financial intermediaries to internalize ex ante financial risks, and if properly calibrated can also help reduce the probability of spreading the impact of shocks within the financial system. Consequently, the instruments can increase the capability of the central bank and the financial system to absorb this shock. However, if not properly calibrated, such instruments can also generate efficiency costs that can delay the development of financial markets.

The development of financial markets can also contribute to the resilience of the financial system to future external shocks, although it may also generate further challenges for implementing nonconventional policy instruments that may need to be adapted in the future to the way monetary policy is implemented.

Going forward, deeper integration of local financial markets with global financial markets will make the domestic market largely visible and open, a trend that may increase the size of foreign exchange markets relative to what the central bank can potentially intervene. This may in turn reduce the scope for an effective foreign exchange intervention. Under such circumstances, as Chinn (2014) notes, it may be hard for any central bank, let alone the BCRP, to perform sterilized foreign exchange interventions and remain in the center of the trilemma triangle as has been the case to date (Aizenman and Ito 2012).

More developed foreign exchange markets have to be accompanied by more developed financial markets that allow more economic agents to hedge risky positions. This would eliminate exchange rate movements as a source of shock and instead turn them into shock absorbers.

This particular feature of financial development is even more important for a financially dollarized economy like Peru. To foster dedollarization and minimize instances of credit riskiness due to dollar-denominated liabilities, the BCRP has introduced conditional reserve requirements for banks' dollar liabilities based on their performance in reducing outstanding dollar credits relative to starting values. In a healthy economy, only firms that generate income in dollars should resort to dollar credit and still hedge their positions to smooth their expected income profile.

Further development of capital markets would be welcome in Peru. However, several possible challenges loom. First, if more firms resort to bond issuance as a substitute for bank credit, reserve requirement policies would likely be weakened, while the conventional interest rate policy may still be effective.

Second, in terms of the issuance of bonds denominated in dollars, potential mismatches may cause problems for nonfinancial companies, as noted by Avdjiev, Chui, and Shin (2014). Although the current magnitude of this latter risk seems to be limited up until now in Peru, it serves as a warning in terms of possible future trends, and regulatory measures by the Superintendency of Security Markets may be desirable.

Third, the instruments and technological platforms of financial flows are becoming more sophisticated and change with the pace of technology. Transaction recording and official statistics rely on manuals that do not keep pace. The problem is that good financial information is necessary in the day-to-day management of monetary policy. In the foreseeable future, the fine-tuning of policy will likely have to be carried out with more noise. Investing heavily in technological improvements and platforms to gather information from the different available sources that can be quickly updated could be effective in reducing this potential information gap. The experiences of more advanced countries are valuable in this respect.

Fourth, the macroprudential framework may need to be strengthened. The BCRP's stance in terms of monetary and macroprudential measures ought to be in line with the microprudential regulation and macroprudential measures of other regulatory and financial service authorities. For example, reserve requirement policies need to go hand in hand with liquidity regulation proposed by Basel III and implemented by local financial service authorities.

Maintaining price stability will continue to be an important challenge for the region's central banks in the coming years, particularly in the case of a prolonged period of U.S. dollar adjustment. The recent experience in addressing the effects of the tapering episode illustrates that exchange rate pass-through might be nonlinear, particularly when the adjustment in the exchange rate is rapid and sizable. Indeed, Pérez-Forero and Vega (2015) show that exchange rate pass-through to prices may be twice as large in a depreciation phase than in an appreciation phase. In sharp contrast to the low inflation and even deflation levels observed in advanced economies, the current picture in the major Latin American economies is that of high inflation relative to the target, as shown in Table 25.3.

Price stability is essential for monetary policy not only because it fosters central bank credibility, which in turns strengthens the transmission mechanism of monetary policy, but also because it can improve the economy's ability to absorb external shocks. In the case of dollarized

**TABLE 25.3**

**Year-over-Year Inflation Rates in the Larger Latin American Inflation-Targeting Countries *(Percent)***

| Date | Brazil | Colombia | Chile | Mexico | Peru |
|---|---|---|---|---|---|
| July 2014 | 6.5 | 2.9 | 4.5 | 4.1 | 3.3 |
| August 2014 | 6.5 | 3.0 | 4.5 | 4.2 | 2.7 |
| September 2014 | 6.8 | 2.9 | 4.9 | 4.2 | 2.7 |
| October 2104 | 6.6 | 3.3 | 5.7 | 4.3 | 3.1 |
| November 2014 | 6.6 | 3.7 | 5.5 | 4.2 | 3.2 |
| December 2014 | 6.4 | 3.6 | 4.6 | 4.1 | 3.2 |
| January 2015 | 7.1 | 3.8 | 4.5 | 3.1 | 3.1 |
| February 2015 | 7.7 | 4.4 | 4.4 | 3.0 | 2.8 |
| March 2015 | 8.1 | 4.6 | 4.2 | 3.1 | 3.0 |

Source: Bloomberg, L.P.

economies, it can promote a decline in dollarization by increasing the confidence in the domestic currency.

The BCRP continues intervening in the foreign exchange market through outright sales of U.S. dollars in the spot market or other exchange rate intervention instruments to tame exchange rate depreciations. Foreign exchange intervention to avoid undue exchange rate depreciation is geared toward reducing financial vulnerabilities associated with highly dollarized and currency-mismatched liabilities. In turn, lower reserve requirements are meant to allow expansion of the domestic-currency credit supply.

Finally, potential GDP growth is slowing for emerging market economies. Diminishing potential growth rates may be a widespread trend in emerging economies as a whole, perhaps because of China's deceleration, the so-called secular stagnation hypothesis due to global demographic factors, or the hypothesized end of the commodity price supercycle. The potential slowdown can also be attributed to domestic bottlenecks in investment spending due to still-unsolved structural problems, which require speeding up structural reforms in order to increase potential GDP growth.

In the case of Peru, the potential output growth rate is now estimated to be about 5 percent. Monetary policy cannot do much to speed up growth above potential growth, and authorities need to remain vigilant in order to provide the appropriate amount of monetary stimulus. Other types of policies—particularly structural reforms in education, health services, and the provision of infrastructure—are urgently needed to prevent a further decline in the potential output growth rate.

## CONCLUSIONS

Since the early 1990s, monetary policy in Peru has emphasized the importance of containing inflation and maintaining financial stability. In turn, the stability of the financial system has allowed for safeguarding the transmission mechanism channels of monetary policy. Based on this experience, this chapter has provided an overview of the current monetary policy strategy of the Central Reserve Bank of Peru and highlighted possible challenges for the future of monetary policy.

The chapter has emphasized the policy instruments that the central bank can deploy within the inflation-targeting design. To limit system-wide credit risk induced by high dollarization, the conventional interest rate monetary policy operational target is complemented by additional unconventional instruments such as reserve requirements and foreign exchange market intervention policies. The chapter has also highlighted the importance of adapting these instruments to more challenging external scenarios.

## REFERENCES

Aizenman, Joshua, and Hiro Ito. 2012. "Trilemma Policy Convergence Patterns and Output Volatility." *The North American Journal of Economics and Finance* 23 (3): 269–85.

Armas, Adrián, Paul Castillo, and Marco Vega. 2014. "Inflation Targeting and Quantitative Tightening: Effects of Reserve Requirements in Peru." *Economía* 15 (1): 133–75.

Avdjiev, Stefan, Michael Chui, and Hyun Song Shin. 2014. "Non-financial Corporations from Emerging Market Economies and Capital Flows." *BIS Quarterly Review* (December), Bank for International Settlements, Basel.

Chinn, Menzie. 2014. "Central Banking: Perspectives from Emerging Economies." Working Paper 2014-006, La Follette School of Public Affairs, Madison, Wisconsin.

Eichengreen, Barry, and Ricardo Hausmann. 1999. "Exchange Rates and Financial Fragility." NBER Working Paper No. w7418, National Bureau of Economic Research, Cambridge, Massachusetts.

Orphanides, Athanasios, and Simon Van Norden. 2002. "The Unreliability of Output-Gap Estimates in Real Time." *Review of Economics and Statistics* 84 (4): 569–83.

Pérez-Forero, Fernando, and Marco Vega. 2015. "Asymmetric Exchange Rate Pass Through: Evidence from Peru." Central Bank of Peru, Lima.

Sims, Erick. 2013. "Growth or the Gap? Which Measure of Economic Activity Should Be Targeted in Interest Rate Rules?" Working Paper, University of Notre Dame, South Bend, Indiana.

# CHAPTER 26

# Making Growth Inclusive: Establishment of the Ministry of Social Development and Inclusion

CAROLINA TRIVELLI

*Peru has a long history of uncoordinated and not necessarily effective social policies. Only recently has the government recognized the need to adapt social policies to achieve inclusion objectives and coordinate policies within different time horizons. Against this backdrop, the government created the Ministry of Social Development and Inclusion (MIDIS) in 2011 with an ambitious agenda to accelerate poverty reduction and achieve inclusive growth. While progress has been uneven, preliminary evidence suggests that the government is on the right track to achieve objectives set for 2016. For the future, it will be important to redouble efforts to continue implementing the National Strategy for Social Development and Inclusion, which will reduce chronic child malnutrition, strengthen early childhood development, enhance programs for children of school age, promote innovative economic inclusion, and broaden protection for the elderly.*

At the start of President Ollanta Humala's administration in 2011, the government undertook a wide-ranging initiative to achieve social inclusion by targeting the most vulnerable segments of the Peruvian population. To that end, a decision was made to reform the entire set of government social initiatives and establish a unified strategy to ensure mutually reinforcing public sector efforts to reduce poverty, thereby boosting the impact of those initiatives and achieving a shared, fundamental, and broad-based social protection floor for all Peruvians.

The commitment to social inclusion is based not just on considerations of justice and fairness, but also reflects a conscious resolve to ensure that all Peruvians, male or female, can contribute to the development of their family and community and thereby to the growth of the country as a whole. The task is to make sure that the Peruvian State has the tools, strategies, and resources to ensure that all citizens—no matter where they reside, what language they speak, what their parents do, or what resources are at their disposal—can get ahead in life and achieve their goals, thus contributing to Peru and its development.

## STARTING POINT

Social policies, and especially policies targeting excluded segments of the population, have been around for a long time. In the specific case of Peru, one of the oldest social programs—the Drops of Milk (*Gotas de Leche*) Program dates to the administration of President Augusto B. Leguía in the early twentieth century.[1] Social policy has obviously changed significantly since then, to the

This chapter is based on a number of papers written in 2014 about the experience of establishing the Ministry of Social Development and Inclusion (Trivelli 2014a, 2014b; Trivelli and Vargas 2014; Vargas 2014). The author would like to thank Jhonatan Clausen for his support during the writing of this chapter.

[1] *Gotas de Leche* reflected the Leguía administration's concern with lowering the infant mortality rate and setting up health clinics, day nurseries, and so on. A reference to these governmental initiatives can be found in President Leguía's speech to the National Congress in October 1924. http://www4.congreso.gob.pe/museo/mensajes/Mensaje-1924-1.asp.

point where there are now coordinated programs to address specific segments of the population and specific needs.

During Peru's more recent history of social policy, the interest in improving coordination among programs can be traced to the government of Alejandro Toledo (2001–06), when initial efforts were undertaken to achieve some degree of coordination of social policies through the Inter-Ministerial Committee on Social Affairs (CIAS), headed by the Office of the President of the Council of Ministers. In 2003, the CIAS published the Guidelines for the National Strategy to Overcome Poverty,[2] followed a year later by adoption of the National Plan for Overcoming Poverty 2004–06.[3] The strategy encompassed the entire set of programs and interventions associated with poverty reduction and put forth overall objectives to achieve that reduction. It also proposed that each sector align its own plan for overcoming poverty with the national strategy. As often happens, each entity complied with its obligation to draw up a plan and at that point coordination of the strategy ceased, despite the emphasis in the strategy itself on dovetailing and coordinating efforts.

During the administration of Alan García (2006–11), CIAS devised the CRECER (Growth) National Strategy as a fresh attempt to foster coordinated actions to tackle the main problems associated with poverty. CRECER made headway in particular with efforts to combat child malnutrition. Chapter IV of the CRECER National Strategy's Work Plan (*Plan de Operaciones*) specifically established operational procedures for both horizontal and vertical functional coordination of the various public sector interventions targeting that problem.[4] Although the CRECER strategy set three objectives, coordination improved only with respect to the first (combating malnutrition). Specifically, consensus was achieved regarding a model for complementary sectoral interventions that together would work to reduce malnutrition. Regional processes for implementing the CRECER strategy proved to be especially valuable, particularly in areas where efforts were reinforced by social coalitions and local authorities, supported by joint interventions by international and donor agencies. Good examples were in Ayacucho, with CRECER Wari,[5] Puno (in Carabaya, in particular), and Huancavelica.

The start of President Humala's administration in July 2011 triggered a debate over the need to organize social policy, direct it to overcome the country's major social challenges, and coordinate it with other national policies. The objective was to ensure that universal social services (health, education, and civil identity) in fact reach all citizens. President Humala proposed mobilizing resources for social policies to promote inclusion and, at the same time, ensuring that that enhanced inclusion sustained the country's growth. To that end, the MIDIS was established in October 2011 to manage the principal targeted social policies in a coordinated manner and to serve as the social development and inclusion policymaking body. The president assigned the new ministry the dual challenge of ensuring universal access to public services and incorporating more Peruvians into the fabric of those services as a strategy for ensuring Peru's ongoing growth.

In addition, the MIDIS was assigned responsibility for coordinating policies targeting the population in situations of poverty and vulnerability and for directly executing five social programs, four of which already existed and one that was still being developed. The five programs

---

[2]The guidelines (*Las Bases para la Estrategia Nacional de Superación de la Pobreza*) were adopted through Supreme Decree No. 002-2003-PCM. http://www.congreso.gob.pe/comisiones/2002/discapacidad/ds/002-2003-pcm.htm.

[3]The plan (*Plan Nacional para la Superación de la Pobreza 2004–2006*) was adopted through Supreme Decree No. 064-2004-PCM. http://www.mesadeconcertacion.org.pe/documentos/legislacion/leg_00371.pdf.

[4]The work plan (*Plan de Operaciones de la Estrategia Nacional CRECER*) was adopted through Supreme Decree No. 080-2007-PCM. http://www.observatorioseguridadalimentaria.org/sites/default/files/politicas_publicas/archivos/PlanOperaciones_CRECER.pdf.

[5]Section 1.5.1 of the CRECER Strategy Work Plan for Wari establishes general guidelines for horizontal and vertical coordination of the strategy. http://goo.gl/TNgxc6.

are (1) *Juntos*, a conditional cash transfer program; (2) FONCODES, the remnant of what was once the social investment fund set up during the structural adjustment of the 1990s; (3) *Wawawasi*, a day care center program, which would expand its services and coverage and eventually become today's *Cuna Más* program; (4) PRONAA, the government food procurement/logistics body for distributing food to various vulnerable groups; and (5) *Pensión65*, the social program that was to start delivering noncontributory pensions (as of 2012) to persons over the age of 65 living in extreme poverty.

The MIDIS thus began with the challenge not only to expand, improve, and coordinate those five programs, but also to coordinate their activities among the programs themselves and with actions undertaken by other government entities.

## THE IDEA BEHIND THE MIDIS

The establishment of the MIDIS reflects the need for more effective and coordinated policies to address the challenges posed by still-high poverty rates, especially in rural areas. Although the poverty rate has declined significantly in Peru (from 58 percent in 2001 to 26 percent in 2012), the country still suffers from stark divides. Extreme poverty is virtually nonexistent in the big cities, while it exceeds 30 percent in the most remote rural areas. The child malnutrition rate in rural areas is more than double the national average.[6] For these reasons, the MIDIS has largely focused since its inception on closing gaps associated with poverty and marginalization.

The establishment of the MIDIS was opposed by some because there were concerns that it might become an instrument of government patronage or another government bureaucracy put in place just to meet electoral promises. Fortunately, in the three years since the ministry was established, neither of those problems has materialized. However, given those concerns, it is important to clarify the role of the MIDIS and the scope of its actions.

The MIDIS was shaped by a particular context that justified its establishment and proactively facilitated its implementation (Vargas 2014). First, Peru had been experiencing a period of sustained economic growth, associated with substantial increases in the government budget and in investment, along with a significant decline in poverty rates. However, those positive circumstances disguise the existence of gaps that are not being closed by higher economic growth, lower aggregate poverty, or greater investment. In other words, while the country as a whole is doing well, there are many Peruvians who not only fail to perceive improvements in their standard of living, they also feel disconnected from the activities bringing about the overall improvement. They are being left behind, or are falling further behind, and for that reason there is a need to target specific policies toward them so that they can catch up and, ideally, progress at the pace of the country as a whole, both for their own well-being and for the well-being of the nation.[7] The MIDIS was established to find new ways to meet that challenge, to build on existing efforts, and to ensure that the fruits of growth translate into enhanced capacity and opportunity for all.

One of the MIDIS's first tasks was to clarify the term "social inclusion," which it defined as "circumstances in which everyone can exercise his or her rights, use their skills and make the most of the opportunities available to them" (MIDIS 2013a).

---

[6]Section 1.3 of the National Social Development and Inclusion Strategy, "Making Growth Inclusive," emphasizes the need to narrow poverty gaps (whereby poverty is defined as multidimensional) between urban and rural areas. One of the criteria for defining the population encompassed by the social development and inclusion process precisely cites belonging to a rural household, defined as households located in settlements of 400 or fewer homes. The strategy is available at http://www.MIDIS.gob.pe/files/estrategianacionaldedesarrolloeinclusinsocialincluirparacrecer.pdf.

[7]Urban-rural divides and those between certain social groups highlight the groups that are lagging behind: the rural population, indigenous groups, poorly educated households, and, clearly, the poorest households. For example, the rural poverty rate is more than triple the urban rate, and chronic malnutrition in the most excluded group is more than double the national average.

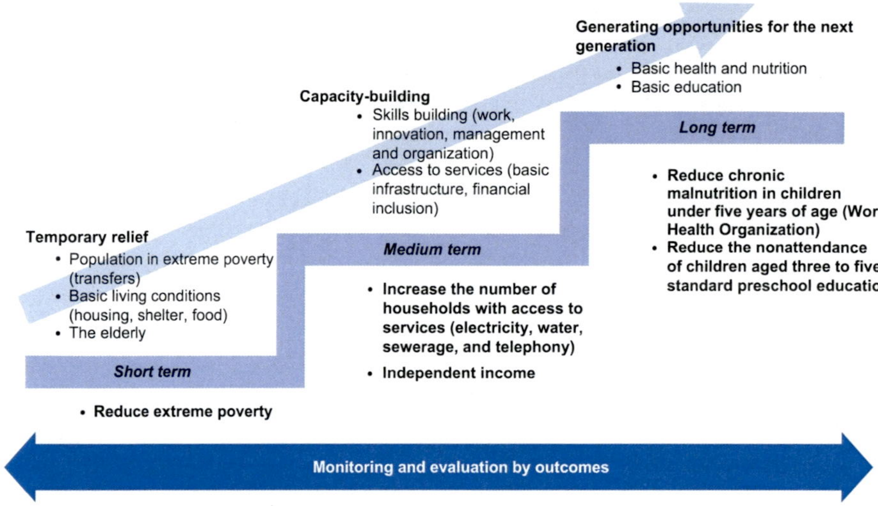


Source: Ministry of Social Development and Inclusion (2013a).

**Figure 26.1** Operational Approach of the Ministry of Social Development and Inclusion

Once a consensus was reached on the definition, the ministry had to be made operational. To that end, based on the human development approach, the MIDIS devised a model with three complementary time frames: short, medium, and long term (Figure 26.1).

- In the short term, through direct assistance programs, the focus is on providing temporary relief from conditions causing households to suffer exclusion and poverty. The idea is to enable families to overcome day-to-day challenges by providing them with the minimum resources needed to exercise their rights and access the public services to which they are entitled.
- In the medium term, the focus is on developing the capacity that will enable households to pursue, in a sustained and dignified manner, paths to overcome the conditions of poverty and exclusion that beset them. Thus the main thrust here is on broadening access to a basic services and infrastructure package and increasing autonomy with respect to the provision of sustainable livelihoods by generating better living conditions (healthy homes, food security, etc.) and incomes through higher productivity, financial inclusion processes, and so on.
- Longer-term efforts will focus on pursuing policies to generate next-generation opportunities, with particular emphasis on human capital factors: nutrition, health, and quality education. Here, the idea is to reduce the intergenerational transmission of poverty so that the children of families suffering poverty and exclusion today are not condemned to be poor and excluded as well, and to find paths to inclusion for them.

These three time frames should not be understood as consecutive stages; rather, the MIDIS is committed to simultaneously mobilizing resources for all three. The challenge for development and inclusion policy is to design and promote complementary interventions that address short-, medium-, and long-term needs at the same time.

However obvious as it may seem, not all sectors have a set of established indicators, much less clearly defined targets. Being a multisectoral ministry, the MIDIS set out to define indicators and targets, but at the same time it proposed that those indicators and targets reflect progress in social development and inclusion more broadly—that is to say, the entire set of intergovernmental and

**TABLE 26.1**

**Ministry of Social Development and Inclusion: Policy Indicators and Targets *(Percent)***

| | National | | Population Encompassed by the Social Development and Inclusion Process | |
|---|---|---|---|---|
| | Baseline 2010 | Target by 2016 | Baseline 2010 | Target by 2016 |
| Poverty Gap | 7.9 | 6.0 | 28.6 | 16.3 |
| Extreme Poverty | 8.3 | 5.0 | 38.2 | 20.0 |
| Extreme Poverty Based on Households' Independent Income | 11.0 | 7.0 | 50.5 | 26.7 |
| Households with an Integrated Services Package | 59.4 | 70.0 | 13.2 | 46.9 |
| Attendance of Children Aged Three to Five Years in Standard Preschool Education | 73.8 | 85.0 | 60.6 | 78.4 |
| Chronic Malnutrition in Children Under Five Years | 23.2 | 10.0 | 50.7 | 23.8 |

Source: Ministry of Social Development and Inclusion (2012b).

intersectoral interventions aimed at producing the prioritized outcomes. Along those same lines, it was agreed that it should be possible to calculate the indicators using national statistics, so as to ensure independence and transparency in their measurement.

Given that the MIDIS assigned priority to addressing social disparities, six indicators were proposed both for the national aggregate and the most excluded segment of the population (Table 26.1). To that end, the ministry began by defining this group, which was called the "population encompassed by the social development and inclusion process." The criteria used to define this population stemmed from a multidimensional approach to poverty that includes both monetary and nonmonetary criteria. Operationally, the population encompassed by the social development and inclusion process is comprised of households that have at least three of the four characteristics associated with the exclusion process, which are the following: rural households, that is, those located in settlements of 400 or fewer dwellings (2,000 people); households with a female head of household or spouse who never completed primary school; households with a head or spouse whose mother tongue is an indigenous language (Quechua, Aymara, or Amazonian); and households in the lowest quintile of national distribution of expenditure per capita.

As for the territorial distribution of the population encompassed by the social development and inclusion process, when the MIDIS was established the regions with the largest share of this population as a percentage of their total population were Huancavelica, Apurímac, Ayacucho, Huánuco, and Puno. The regions with the lowest share were Tumbes, Callao, Ica, and Lima, where this group accounts for 2 percent or less of the respective populations (MIDIS 2013b). In absolute terms, as shown in Figure 26.2, the population encompassed by the social development and inclusion process amounted to almost 5 million Peruvians, a little over 16 percent of Peru's total population.

The six indicators established by the MIDIS correspond to the short-, medium- and long-term time frames identified in the operational approach of the social development and inclusion policy. As shown in Table 26.1, the indicators are the poverty gap, extreme poverty, extreme poverty based on households' independent income, households with an integrated services package, attendance of children ages three to five years in standard preschool education, and chronic malnutrition in children under five years.

While establishing social sector targets and indicators might seem an obvious step, the fact is that in Peru's case it was far from self-evident. When a Ministry of the Economy is asked about its performance, everyone knows what indicators will be used (inflation, growth, the fiscal deficit,

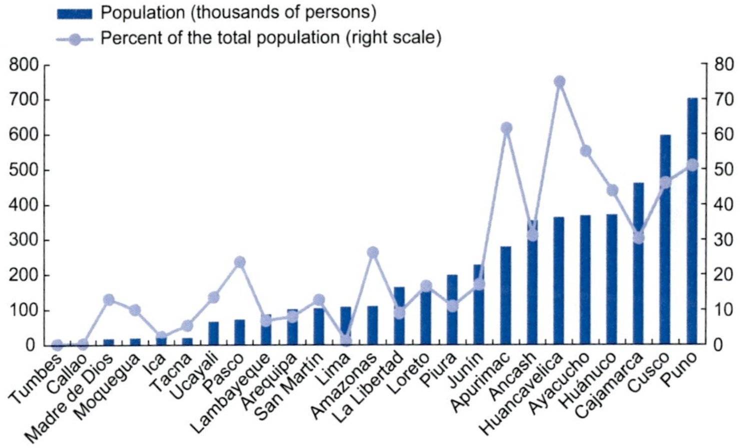


Source: Ministry of Social Development and Inclusion (2013b).

**Figure 26.2** Regional Distribution of the Population Encompassed by the Social Development and Inclusion Process

and so on), so it is the targets that are of most interest. In the social sectors, on the other hand, there is still not always agreement even on the indicators. Therefore, the MIDIS set out to establish both indicators and targets from the outset and to set the targets through to the end of President Humala's term in office (in 2016).

Outcomes to date show that the MIDIS has made headway toward the targets established. As discussed below, by the halfway point of the administration, indicators showed progress, but there were also some warning signs that have since enabled the MIDIS to redouble its efforts in certain areas. The warning signs demonstrate the importance of having a set of timely indicators that can help the ministry stay on track. The most notable outcome thus far is that the extreme poverty reduction target for 2016 (5 percent) was already achieved in 2013.

## ESTABLISHING A SECTOR STRATEGY: A KEY TOOL FOR MANAGEMENT, COORDINATION, AND INCLUSION

The key to achieving these outcomes is to have a clear road map, know what to do and how to do it, and know who the participants are. That is why, once the MIDIS was established, targets set, and all available instruments assessed,[8] it was essential for the ministry to generate a feasible and workable strategy to guide its actions and coordinate efforts with other government entities and agencies.

The National Strategy for Social Development and Inclusion (ENDIS) was thus adopted in May 2013. Based on person-centered and coordinated interaction throughout the life cycle, the strategy makes it possible to address the principal disadvantages faced by poor families and at the same time provide them with the new services and tools they need to make progress in life.

[8] As discussed earlier in the chapter, after the MIDIS was established, it was assigned five social programs in January 2012. A decision was made to adopt a plan to evaluate each program and prepare adjustment measures for each one. That process was complicated and had to be done quickly, but it did help bring order to the programs, clarify their modus operandi, and set a clear road map for each program. The main findings of the program evaluations can be found at http://goo.gl/0XB9Wz.

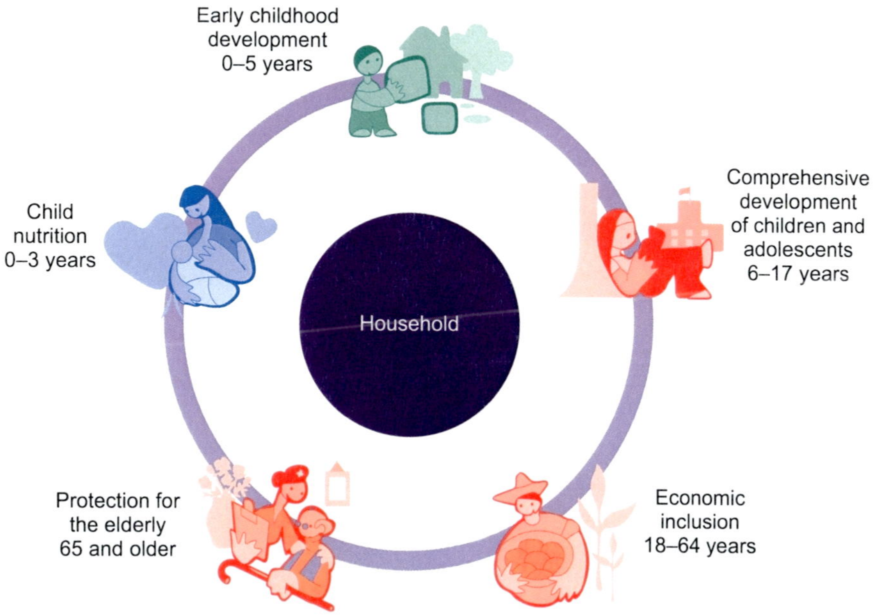


Source: Ministry of Social Development and Inclusion (2013a).

**Figure 26.3** The Five Pillars of the National Strategy for Social Development and Inclusion

Figure 26.3 presents the five pillars of the strategy. In some areas, the strategy builds on what is already in place by incorporating previous advances, such as the decision to make fighting malnutrition a pillar of the strategy. In other areas, it posits new types of action and new objectives, as in the economic inclusion pillar, where it is not just a question of helping families with isolated public interventions, but rather of providing them with a whole package of measures that increases their resource base of public and private assets, their productivity, and the return on their assets. This economic inclusion pillar probably represents the area in which social protection efforts have dovetailed most effectively with attempts to foster independent development for the poorest families.

The ENDIS also serves as a two-pronged instrument for the MIDIS. On the one hand, it sets the agenda for coordination with other sectors and levels of government in each of the five pillars. On the other, it establishes the road maps for the five programs executed by the MIDIS in order to ensure that each program performs a function in the pillars in which the program intervenes. These programs play a vital part in ensuring that the recipients (mainly women) gain access to and use basic public services. For many, access and use of these services represents an acknowledgment of full citizenship.

## PRINCIPLES AND STRATEGIES COMPLEMENTING THE ENDIS

Ever since the MIDIS was established, the idea has been to attain a highly professional, results-oriented social sector that makes efficient use of the public resources allocated to it. To that end, a number of principles and strategies were adopted to complement the ENDIS and ensure transparent, efficient, and person-centered management geared toward bringing about substantive changes in the living conditions and opportunities of the population living in poverty and vulnerability.

Some of the principles and strategies adopted were very simple, but had direct implications for management. Five are worth noting here:

- First, the goal is not so much to dream up solutions, but rather to build on experience. Hence, the objectives of the ENDIS include achieving progress through a cumulative process, joining forces with other sectors, building on previous experiences, and pooling efforts with other levels of government. The aim is to forge collective and coordinated efforts and build on progress already made.
- Second, actions need to be results oriented, which is why it is important that the five MIDIS programs are now governed by results-based program budgets. More than 90 percent of the ministry's budget is now performance-based.[9] What is more, this principle forced all the programs to clarify what they expected to achieve through their actions and thereby rationalize their efforts.
- Third, policy formulation and evaluation had to be evidence based. The only way to make progress toward effective and efficient interventions is to evaluate what is done, propose and promote improvements, and then reevaluate what is achieved. Evaluation of impacts, results, and processes is also vital to determine what initiatives need to be discontinued because they are not producing the desired results. Thanks to this principle, the MIDIS in 2012 closed a social program—for the first time ever in Peru—that was failing to deliver results (the PRONAA).
- Fourth, it was clearly established that effective and inclusive policies require a thorough understanding of the beneficiaries, communities, families, and markets involved. The establishment of the MIDIS revealed how little information there was about which programs were underway across Peru, the populations groups served by them, and the challenges that needed to be overcome. Moreover, gaining knowledge to achieve inclusiveness introduced transparency with respect to the rules under which programs operate and in their territorial distribution (for instance, through InfoMIDIS, on the ministry's website). At the same time, that information has shed light on the living conditions of beneficiaries of MIDIS programs and on the coordinated actions undertaken within each pillar of the ENDIS.
- Fifth, achieving results means moving away from business as usual in the operation of social programs, so it is critical that the MIDIS remain receptive to social innovation. Inclusiveness through innovation is a must if the government wants to promote services and programs more swiftly and effectively identify better ways of touching the lives of beneficiaries. This approach has enabled the MIDIS to venture into areas such as the financial inclusion of beneficiaries of MIDIS transfer programs. It has also tested the creativity of both businesspersons and public administration officials in seeking ways to reach more than 3 million children with school meals based on decentralized purchases.

## HAS PROGRESS BEEN MADE SINCE THE MIDIS WAS ESTABLISHED?

As mentioned above, the MIDIS has made progress both at the institutional level and in terms of the prominence of social inclusion issues on the policy agenda. It is now widely recognized that the government cannot abdicate its responsibility to protect and include all citizens. There is also

[9]When the MIDIS was assigned the five social programs in January 2012, only one of them operated with a results-based budget.

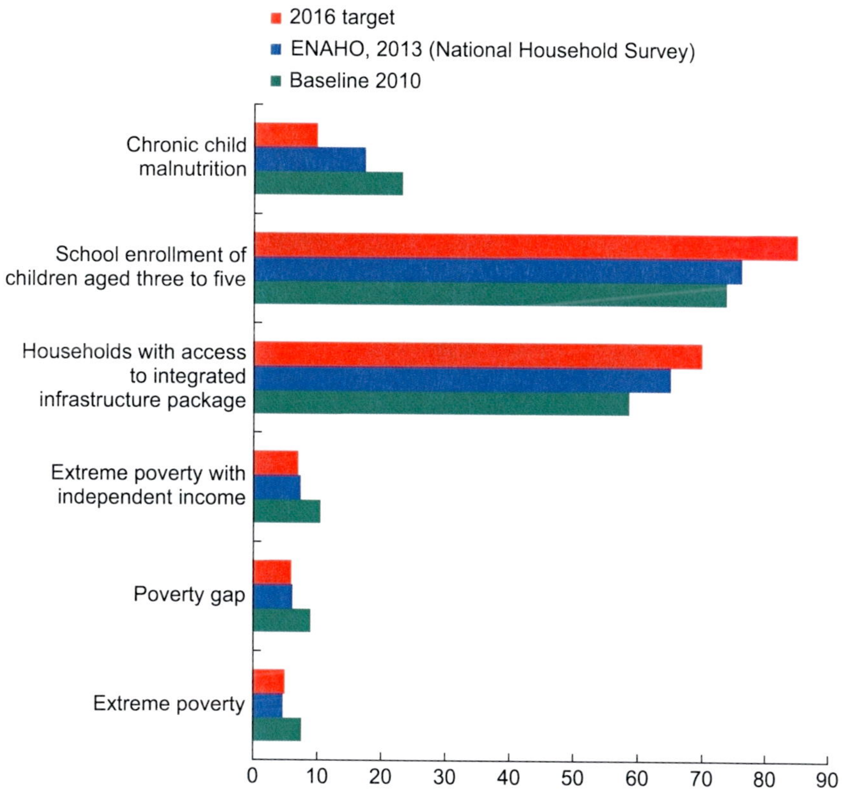


Sources: Household and Health Survey (ENAHO), 2013; Ministry of Social Development and Inclusion (2012a); and author's calculations.

**Figure 26.4** Ministry of Social Development and Inclusion Indicators at the National Level (*Percent*)

clear progress in the indicators that the MIDIS developed: halfway through the current presidential term, the government is well on track to meet targets set by the MIDIS for 2016. The findings are based on official statistics from the national household and health survey known as ENAHO. Some indicators are advancing slowly, but as a result of early warning signs, steps are being taken to create new policy instruments (such as the Performance Incentive Fund) and undertake new social policy actions. As was to be expected, more progress is being made at the aggregate level than with respect to the population encompassed by the social development and inclusion process, which is where the major challenges lie and where, despite some progress, meeting targets will prove more elusive.

Predictably, the first targets met (or that are close to being met) are those related to short-term actions to relieve the plight of the poor and vulnerable. This is due to the expansion in coverage (and resources) of the principal relief programs. The extreme poverty rate in 2013 was 4.7 percent and the poverty gap ratio was slightly over 6 percent (Figure 26.4).[10] There has been major progress with respect to the medium-term indicators, where the goal is to boost people's autonomy and capacity to access opportunities to get ahead. Likewise, as a result of efforts coordinated with

[10] Peru's social sector budget remains one of the lowest in Latin America, although the budget has increased considerably under the Humala administration. The MIDIS budget (essentially concentrated in its five programs) increased significantly between 2012 (the first year in which the ministry operated) and 2014 (the amended budget for 2014 was almost 46 percent larger than in 2012). See the User-Friendly Consultation on the Economic Transparency site of the Ministry of the Economy and Finance at http://apps5.mineco.gob.pe/transparencia/Navegador/default.aspx?y=2012&ap=ActProy.

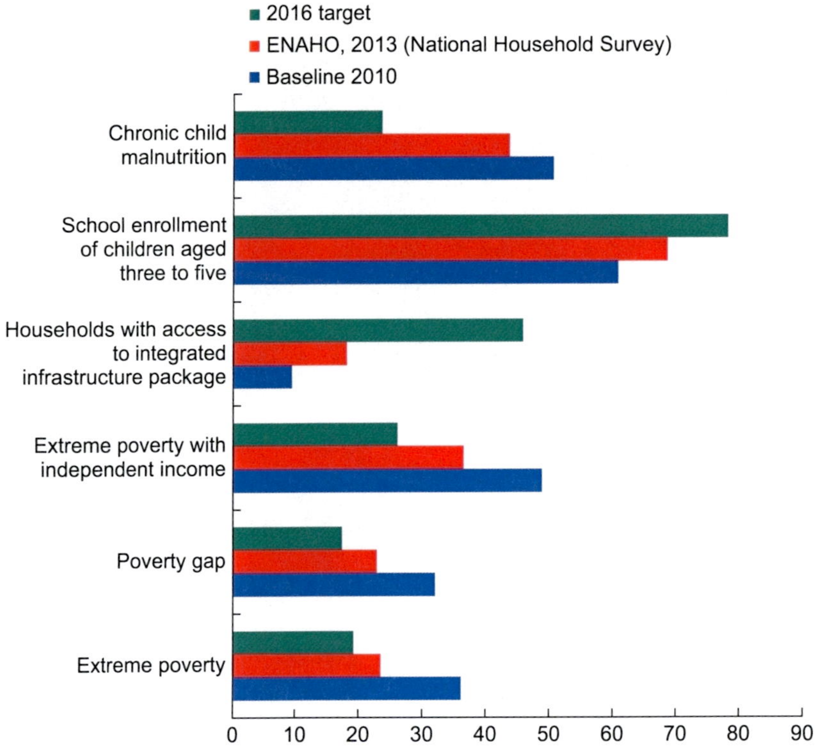


Sources: Household and Health Survey (ENAHO), 2013; Ministry of Social Development and Inclusion (2012a); and author's calculations.

**Figure 26.5** Ministry of Social Development and Inclusion Indicators for the Population Encompassed by the Social Development and Inclusion Process (*Percent*)

the health, education, and housing sectors and with local and regional governments, significant progress is being made with respect to a key long-term indicator: the reduction in chronic child malnutrition. Peru has met the Millennium Development Goal target in that area and is close to achieving the goal of reducing chronic child malnutrition to 10 percent or less (in 2010 it stood at 23.1 percent) (Figure 26.5).

It is vital that the indicators and targets put in place by MIDIS for measuring social progress continue, and the hope is to add additional indicators going forward. Ideally, all national, regional, and local government entities should identify the indicators and targets by which their progress can be evaluated. Such a step would mark a milestone in the way that public administration and policymaking are conducted and perceived.

## THE CHALLENGE: PRESERVE AND BUILD ON THE RESULTS ACHIEVED

Progress on the five pillars of the ENDIS has been uneven. The starting points differed and only limited tools were available for implementing policies and programs under several pillars. The ENDIS can be used to pinpoint where efforts need to focus going forward in order to consolidate social policies such that they transition to becoming full-fledged public policies.

For the first pillar, the administration set an ambitious target of reducing chronic child malnutrition to 10 percent by 2016 from 23.1 percent in 2010. By mid-2014, chronic child malnutrition was at 14 percent. That signaled substantial progress, but much remains to be done because it is not just a question of reducing the problem at the national level, but also of lowering it in the regions where it is most prevalent. What the progress has shown is that a method and set of tools have been identified to effectively tackle chronic child malnutrition. Two factors explain that progress. First, a decision was taken to continue programs inherited from the previous government under the CRECER strategy such as *Juntos* and investments in safe water and infrastructure. Second, a clear diagnostic assessment was carried out to identify what was not working properly and which mechanisms were needed to resolve those issues. Those mechanisms included improving local investments to install safe water connections, encouraging regional governments to allocate budgetary resources to such projects, and generating useful information for timely decision making. The Peruvian government needs to commit to consolidating processes, keeping the package of policies and instruments up and running, and maintaining regional monitoring indicators as the basis for ongoing efforts.

Under the second pillar, early childhood development, a multisectoral comprehensive strategy is about to be adopted, which is essential to ensure that work continue in this area. The expansion of Comprehensive Health Insurance (*Seguro Integral de Salud*), to which every Peruvian child under three years of age is now entitled, is a major step forward for this pillar. From the standpoint of the MIDIS, external evaluation of programs such as *Cuna Más*, and above all its new services serving rural communities, will yield information as to how to best proceed in those areas. Clearly, however, the immediate priority is to prepare and implement the pending strategy.

The third pillar, regarding children of school age, is breaking new ground because of the coordination of MIDIS activities with the Ministries of Education and Health in public schools. Today, children attending public preschools and primary schools have health insurance and a health evaluation and screening plan, and receive food supplements to enhance their concentration. In addition, children from poorer households that receive conditional cash transfers under the *Juntos* program are required to maintain certain school attendance levels. This coordinated plan, known as Healthy Learning (*Aprende Saludable*), is a pilot program whose achievements need to be expanded to consolidate institutional coordination mechanisms among the three sectors, as well as among the national, regional, and local governments. The role of the different sectors and governmental levels in developing this new way of working with public schools needs to be formalized.

The MIDIS also needs to continue its efforts to consolidate the *Qali Warma* school food program to ensure that it remains on a sound footing and that parents, school directors, and teachers know how to keep it running. It is worth noting that this program serves twice as many children as the previous program (PRONAA) and does so on twice the number of days.[11]

The fourth pillar, economic inclusion, is the most innovative area for a socially oriented ministry such as the MIDIS. It requires that those involved continually identify practices and interventions that generate economic opportunities for the poorest families. The MIDIS has two such initiatives that need to be consolidated: FONCODES' *Haku Wiñay* program, which serves more than 60,000 families by providing them with assets and resources for technical assistance, investment, and training; and *Haku Wiñay*, which coordinates with *Juntos* and encourages rural families to improve their living standards, dwellings, food security, and opportunities to earn incomes autonomously. Initial (independent) evaluations of *Haku Wiñay* show that it is proceeding well but is still in its early stages of achieving its objectives.

Within that same pillar, MIDIS' efforts to advance financial inclusion reflect the emergence of a number of successful initiatives. Today, more than 1.2 million recipients of social programs have a savings account under their own name where they receive government transfers via the

[11] In 2014, *Qali Warma* served over 3 million pupils in the public preschool and primary education system, reaching over 57,000 schools.

MIDIS. More than 400,000 recipients of *Juntos* already have a debit card that they can use at automatic teller machines accessible through an extensive network of points of sale at banks, stores, and pharmacies. A financial inclusion strategy is in place, methodologies and materials have been developed to provide financial education, and the MIDIS has entered into partnerships with public and private stakeholders to consolidate this process and provide more economic opportunities for the beneficiaries of social programs. These innovations need to be further developed, scaled up, and consolidated.

The fifth pillar, protection for the elderly, is an area in which Peru is just beginning to develop policies. The pillar revolves around *Pensión65*. Today, more than 400,000 older persons receive a cash transfer and have a national identity card, savings account, and health insurance. In more than 80 districts, they can take part in the Productive Knowledge (*Saberes Productivos*) Program. However, much remains to be done to ensure that the final years of life are always dignified and secure, regardless of where one lives or how much money one has. Clearly, the challenge is to combine the effort to achieve good outcomes with the discussion about pensions, protection, and retirement. However, perhaps the most appropriate approach would be for the MIDIS to focus on expanding services that complement the transfers and leave the rest to the other entities involved, notably the Ministry of the Economy and Finance and the Superintendency of Banks, Insurance and Pensions.

## CONCLUSIONS

Social program coverage has increased in Peru as a result of the establishment of the Ministry of Social Development and Inclusion and the formulation of a clear results-oriented policy. That policy is based partly on a bold approach to partnerships with other sectors, levels of government, and other institutions (for example, the *Banco de la Nación*), but also on much more substantial funding. *Juntos* has so far almost doubled its coverage under the current administration. *Pensión65* and *Haku Wiñay* did not exist in 2010. *Cuna Más* has maintained its services and developed new services for rural areas, while *Qali Warma* has quadrupled the size of the school food program.

Despite these advances, the challenges still facing Peru in terms of social inclusion are enormous. As a country, Peru needs to set the goal of guaranteeing that any Peruvian eligible for a social program can access it, which means eliminating undercoverage in targeted social programs. Today, this is only true of *Pensión65*.

As has been shown in this chapter, there are different challenges for each pillar of the ENDIS. To those challenges three additional key tasks need to be added:

- *Consolidating the transition from ad hoc initiatives to policies that are coordinated and guaranteed by the state.* The government stills needs to reach all those who need (and qualify for) social programs, not just with programs here and there, but with the basic package of services to which every Peruvian is entitled purely by virtue of having been born in Peru.
- *Innovating, testing, and evaluating new (smart) mechanisms for intersectoral and intergovernmental coordination to achieve agreed-upon social objectives.* The government must continue to search for the best ways to achieve a well-coordinated and consistent presence of the State throughout Peru, with a useful and comprehensive set of policies for citizens, especially the poorest and most vulnerable.
- *Ensuring that all Peruvians are aware that these social policies are investments in the sustainability of the country's development process, and that they represent Peru's commitment to recognizing itself as a country of equals where growth is inclusive.*

## REFERENCES


Ministry of Social Development and Inclusion. 2012a. "Cien días de gestión." Ministry of Social Development and Inclusion, Lima.

———. 2012b. "Evaluación y reorganización de los programas sociales." Ministry of Social Development and Inclusion, Lima. http://goo.gl/I2g921.

———. 2013a. "Estrategia Nacional de Desarrollo e Inclusión Social 'Incluir para Carecer.'" Ministry of Social Development and Inclusion, Lima. http://www.midis.gob.pe/files/estrategianacionaldedesarrolloeinclusin socialincluirparacrecer.pdf.

———. 2013b. "Mapa de la Población en Proceso de Desarrollo e Inclusión Social." Ministry of Social Development and Inclusion, Lima.

Trivelli, C. 2014a. "Consolidar políticas sociales de inclusión social para que sean políticas de Estado." *IDEELE* 246 (December). http://revistaideele.com/ideele/content/consolidar-pol%C3%ADticas-de-inclusión-social-para -que-sean-pol%C3%ADticas-de-estado.

———. 2014b. "A mitad de camino" *Poder* (August).

———, and S. Vargas. 2014. "Entre el Discurso y la Acción, Desafíos, decisiones y dilemas en el marco de la creación del Ministerio de Desarrollo e Inclusión Social." IEP Working Paper No. 208, Instituto de Estudios Peruanos. http://www.iep.org.pe/biblioteca_virtual.html.

Vargas, S. 2014. "Política de desarrollo e inclusión social: balance y lecciones al primer año de creación del Ministerio de Desarrollo e Inclusión Social." In *Inclusión social: enfoques, políticas y gestión pública,* edited by Ismael Muñoz, Ismael. Lima: Fondo Editorial PUCP.